Lecture Notes in Computer Science 14217

The series Lecture Notes in Computer Science (LNCS), including its subseries Lecture Notes in Artificial Intelligence (LNAI) and Lecture Notes in Bioinformatics (LNBI), has established itself as a medium for the publication of new developments in computer science and information technology research, teaching, and education.

LNCS enjoys close cooperation with the computer science R & D community, the series counts many renowned academics among its volume editors and paper authors, and collaborates with prestigious societies. Its mission is to serve this international community by providing an invaluable service, mainly focused on the publication of conference and workshop proceedings and postproceedings. LNCS commenced publication in 1973.

Mingwu Zhang · Man Ho Au · Yudi Zhang
Editors

Provable and Practical Security

17th International Conference, ProvSec 2023
Wuhan, China, October 20–22, 2023
Proceedings

Springer

Editors
Mingwu Zhang
Hubei University of Technology
Wuhan, China

Man Ho Au
Hong Kong Polytechnic University
Kowloon, Hong Kong

Yudi Zhang
University of Wollongong
Wollongong, NSW, Australia

ISSN 0302-9743 ISSN 1611-3349 (electronic)
Lecture Notes in Computer Science
ISBN 978-3-031-45512-4 ISBN 978-3-031-45513-1 (eBook)
https://doi.org/10.1007/978-3-031-45513-1

This Springer imprint is published by the registered company Springer Nature Switzerland AG
The registered company address is: Gewerbestrasse 11, 6330 Cham, Switzerland

Preface

The 17th International Conference on Provable and Practical Security (ProvSec 2023) was held in Wuhan during 20–22 October 2023. The conference was hosted by Hubei University of Technology and co-organized by Talent Base for Discipline of Intelligent Science and Technology of Hubei Province of China. ProvSec is an international conference on provable security in cryptography and practical security for information systems. ProvSec is designed to be a forum for theoreticians, system and application designers, protocol developers, and practitioners to discuss and express their views on the current trends, challenges, and state-of-the-art solutions related to various issues in provable and practical security. Topics of interest include but are not limited to provable security for asymmetric cryptography, provable security for symmetric cryptography, provable security for physical attacks, privacy and anonymity technologies, secure cryptographic protocols and applications, security notions, approaches, and paradigms, leakage resilient cryptography, lattice-based cryptography and post-quantum cryptography, blockchain and cryptocurrency, IoT security, cloud security, and access control.

The conference received 72 submissions. Each submission was reviewed by at least three Program Committee members or external reviewers. The Program Committee members accepted 20 full papers and three short papers to be included in the conference program.

We thank the Program Committee members and the external reviewers for their hard work reviewing the submissions. We thank the Organizing Committee and all volunteers for their time and effort dedicated to arranging the conference.

July 2023

Mingwu Zhang
Man Ho Au

Organization

Program Chairs

Mingwu Zhang	Hubei University of Technology, China
Man Ho Au	Hong Kong Polytechnic University, China

General Chairs

Xiaochun Song	Hubei University of Technology, China
Willy Susilo	University of Wollongong, Australia
Zhiwei Ye	Hubei University of Technology, China

Publication Chairs

Yudi Zhang	University of Wollongong, Australia
Hua Shen	Hubei University of Technology, China
Fagen Li	UESTC, China

Program Committee

Amin Sakzad	Monash University, Australia
Atsushi Takayasu	University of Tokyo, Japan
Baodong Qin	Xi'an University of Posts and Telecommunications, China
Cheng-Kang Chu	Huawei, Singapore
Chunhua Su	University of Aizu, Japan
Daniel Slamanig	AIT Austrian Institute of Technology, Austria
Elena Andreeva	TU Wien, Austria
Fagen Li	University of Electronic Science and Technology of China, China
Fangguo Zhang	Sun Yat-sen University, China
Federico Pintore	University of Oxford, UK
Fei Gao	Beijing University of Posts and Telecommunications, China
Haiyang Xue	Hong Kong Polytechnic University, China

Jiang Zhang	Institute of Software, Chinese Academy of Sciences, China
Jie Chen	East China Normal University, China
Joonsang Baek	University of Wollongong, Australia
Joseph Liu	Monash University, Australia
Junqing Gong	East China Normal University, China
Kaitai Liang	TU Delft, The Netherlands
Katsuyuki Takashima	Mitsubishi Electric, Japan
Keita Emura	NICT, Japan
Keita Xagawa	TII, UAE
Khoa Nguyen	University of Wollongong, Australia
Kirill Morozov	University of North Texas, USA
Lei Wang	Shanghai Jiao Tong University, China
Lei Zhang	East China Normal University, China
Liangfeng Zhang	ShanghaiTech University, China
Mingwu Zhang	Hubei University of Technology, China
Man Ho Au	Hong Kong Polytechnic University, China
Olivier Sanders	Orange Labs, France
Peng Xu	Huazhong University of Science and Technology, China
Rupeng Yang	University of Wollongong, Australia
Sabyasachi Karati	Indian Statistical Institute, India
Shengli Liu	Shanghai Jiao Tong University, China
Shi Bai	Florida Atlantic University, USA
Shi-Feng Sun	Shanghai Jiao Tong University, China
Somindu C. Ramanna	IIT Kharagpur, India
Tetsu Iwata	Nagoya University, Japan
Tsuyoshi Takagi	University of Tokyo, Japan
Weiqiang Wen	Univ Rennes, CNRS, IRISA, France
Willy Susilo	University of Wollongong, Australia
Xingye Lu	Hong Kong Polytechnic University, China
Xinyi Huang	Hong Kong University of Science and Technology, China
Xiong Fan	Rutgers University, USA
Yang Li	University of Electro-Communications, Japan
Yanhong Xu	University of Calgary, Canada
Yi Deng	Institute of Information Engineering, Chinese Academy of Sciences, China
Yong Yu	Shaanxi Normal University, China
Yuntao Wang	Osaka University, Japan
Zhe Xia	Wuhan University of Technology, China
Zhen Liu	Shanghai Jiao Tong University, China

Zheng Gong	South China Normal University, China
Zuoxia Yu	University of Wollongong, Australia

Workshops Co-chairs

Yuntao Wang	Osaka University, Japan
Debiao He	Wuhan University, China
Zhe Xia	Wuhan University of Technology, China
Jiageng Chen	Central China Normal University, China
Hanping Hu	Huazhong University of Science and Technology, China

Organizing Committee Co-chairs

Ou Yuan	Hubei University of Technology, China
Bingbing Li	Hubei University of Technology, China
Yuanyuan Zhang	Hubei University of Technology, China
Yuzhu Wang	GUET, China

Contents

Fundamentals and Cryptographic Primitives

Efficient Zero-Knowledge Arguments for Matrix Relations over Rings and Non-malleable Enhancement

Yuan Tian(✉), Xinke Tian, and Yongda Pang

Software School, Dalian University of Technology, Dalian, Liao Ning, People's Republic of China
tianyuan_ca@dlut.edu.cn

Abstract. Various matrix relations widely appeared in data-intensive private computations, as a result their efficient zero-knowledge proofs/ arguments are indispensable in such applications. In the first part of this paper, we concretely establish efficient zero-knowledge arguments for linear matrix relation $\mathbf{AU} = \mathbf{B}$ over the residue ring Z_m with logarithmic message complexity. We take a direct, matrix-oriented (rather than vector-oriented in usual) approach to such establishments on basis of the elegant commitment scheme over finite ring recently established by Attema et al. (2022). The commit-and-proof protocol is public-coin and in c.r.s paradigm (c.r.s used only as the public-key of the commitment scheme), suitable for matrices in any size and significantly outperforms the protocols constructed in usual approach with smaller-sized c.r.s.(e.g., decreased by a factor of d where d is the extension degree of Galois ring and n is the order of the witness square), fewer rounds (decreased by a fraction $> \log d/2\log n$) and lower message complexity (e.g., number of ring elements decreased by a fraction $> \log d/\log n$) for large-size squares. The on-line computational complexities are almost the same in both approaches. In the second part, on basis of the simulation-sound tag-based trapdoor commitment scheme we establish a general compiler to transform any public coin proof/argument protocol into the one which is concurrently non-malleable with unchanged number of rounds, slightly increased message and computational complexity. Such enhanced protocols, e.g., the version compiled from the construction in the first part of this work, can run in parallel environment while keeping all their security properties, particularly resisting man-in-the-middle attacks.

Keywords: Zero-Knowledge · Linear Matrix Equation · $\mathbf{\Sigma}$−Protocol · Concurrent Non-malleability · Galois Ring

1 Introduction

1.1 Basic Problems and Related Works

Efficient zero-knowledge proofs for various relations are crucial techniques to support multiparty private computing tasks [1,2], secure distributed ledger systems [3–5] and many other cryptographic applications. In data-intensive private

M. Zhang et al. (Eds.): ProvSec 2023, LNCS 14217, pp. 3–26, 2023.
https://doi.org/10.1007/978-3-031-45513-1_1

computation, lots of data relations appear in the form of high dimensional vector or large-size matrix quations [6,12] and efficient zero-knowledge proof/argument protocols (ZKP/ZKA) with low message complexity are highly valuable to support these applications in complicated network environment.

Recently, some innovative techniques have been developed in [6,7] to construct highly efficient ZKAs for linear vector relation $\boldsymbol{a}^{\mathrm{T}}\boldsymbol{u} = b$ and inner product relation $\boldsymbol{u}^{\mathrm{T}}\boldsymbol{v} = w$ over finite field. The constructed ZKAs have message complexity of only $\mathrm{O}(\log n)$ where n is the dimension of witness space, significantly improving previous works in performance. This approach was further developed in [8] to construct ZKA for vectors' quadratic relation $\boldsymbol{u}^{\mathrm{T}}\mathbf{A}\boldsymbol{u}+\boldsymbol{b}^{\mathrm{T}}\boldsymbol{u} = c$ over finite field with logarithmic message complexity and lots of other improvements in performance. This approach was also applied to constructing ZKAs with logarithmic message complexity for bilinear relations on groups with pairing structure [9,10] and partial-knowledge proof [11].

After succeeding in developing efficient ZKAs for linear vector relations over finite field, it is natural to establish efficient ZKAs for nonlinear relations over finite field and other arithmetic systems, e.g., finite rings Z_M or integer ring Z.

In the first direction, bilinear relation is the simplest non-linear relation which efficient ZKA construction was partially solved, e.g., [6–8] has established the protocols with logarithmic message complexity in some special cases. More specifically, the protocols constructed in [6,7] are only for inner-product relation, and the protocols in [8] are only for quadratic relation with 1-rank coefficient matrix. So far with the author's knowledge there is no direct work on bilinear relation $\boldsymbol{u}^{\mathrm{T}}\mathbf{Q}\boldsymbol{v} = y$ with general $\mathbf{Q}$ or with witnesses not only $\boldsymbol{u}$ and $\boldsymbol{v}$ but also $\mathbf{Q}$ and y. These relations naturally appear in contemporary cryptographic applications. For non-linear relations, so far the most common and effective approach is linearization [12]. In this approach, any relation over the finite field can be equivalently transformed into a (maybe very high dimensional) linear relation through secrete sharing techniques. On the other hand, as indicated in [9], the compilation from nonlinear to linear relation comes at the price of losing conceptual simplicity and modularity in protocol design. Therefore, developing direct approach for specific non-linear relation is still useful in cryptography theory and applications. [9–11] are heuristic examples in this direction.

In the second direction, recently a ZKA with polynomial-logarithmic message complexity was constructed in [13] where the centric relation is a linear relation over the integer ring Z. [16] established a family of general and elegant commitment schemes for vectors over Galois ring, and the ZKA with logarithmic message complexity is constructed, by generalizing techniques in [12], for linear relations over the ring. The ZKA for any nonlinear relation over Galois ring can be also constructed via the linearization approach and related techniques developed in multiparty private computation over the ring. However, a straightforward generalization of ZKA-construction from the finite field to finite ring does not sufficiently make use of all flexibilities provided by this scheme. There are new and interesting problems for applying this new commitment scheme in ZKA-construction, even for linear relations.

Contributions. Our contributions in this paper have two parts. In the first part (Sect. 3) we concretely establish an efficient zero-knowledge argument (ZKA) protocols for linear matrix relation $\mathbf{AU} = \mathbf{B}$ over the residue ring Z_m with logarithmic message complexity(the more technically-involved ZKA for bilinear matrix relation $\mathbf{U}^{\mathbf{T}}\mathbf{QV} = \mathbf{Y}$ can be also constructed in a similar way and is presented in the full version paper). In private computing applications various data relations can be represented by or reduced to some matrix relation, e.g., the (private) isomorphic relation between two lattices or graphs; multiplicative, inverse or similarity relations between two private matrices, etc. In addition, Z_m is one of the most widely used arithmetic systems in practice. One of the main challenges in constructing ZKA protocols for relations over a ring(rather than a field) is how to ensure sufficient number of challenges to fulfill the necessary soundness requirements. This is achieved in [16] by committing over the extended ring S, which elements are polynomials of some finite degree d over Z_m. As a direct result, a Z_m-vector is regarded as a special S-vector and the ZKA protocol for a relation over Z_m is simply constructed as a ZKA protocol for a relation over S, by generalizing techniques (e.g., amortization, compression, etc.) from Galois fields to Galois rings. However, in private computing applications, what is actually needed is to prove relations over, e.g., Z_m, rather than over its extension S, so when establishing the ZKA protocol for a matrix relation this vector-oriented approach(dealing with a matrix as a collection of vectors) is not as efficient as desired.

We take a matrix-oriented approach on basis of an observation that a n-dimensional vector over the Galois ring S can be effectively related with a Z_m-matrix. For example, by re-arranging a large-size, n-by-td Z_m-matrix $\mathbf{U}$ to be a nt-by-d matrix $\mathbf{U}^*$, it can be equivalently regarded as a nt-dimensional S-vector $\boldsymbol{u}^*$ so its commitment can be always valued in G^d, i.e., its commitment size can be independent of its total size and only determined by the targeted knowledge-error in ZKA.

Our matrix-oriented approach to ZKA for matrix relation is able to deal with Z_m-matrix in any size. The construction has almost the same on-line computational complexity as those constructions in vector-oriented approach. It outperforms the vector-oriented approach in all other important performances when number of columns > log(number of rows) with smaller c.r.s, shorter commitments, fewer rounds and lower message complexity. For example, for linear relation with the witness of n-by-n Z_m-matrix, number of rounds can be reduced from $4 \log n$ to $4 \log n - 2 \log d$ and message complexity can be reduced from $4d \log n$ to $4d \log n - 2d \log d$ (for number of group elements) and from $6d \log n$ to $6d \log n - 3d \log d$ (for number of ring elements). In addition, the number of group elements in c.r.s can be reduced by a factor of d. Such advantages are not only valuable for interactive but also for noninteractive argument.

All constructed protocols in this paper are public-coin and in c.r.s paradigm, where the c.r.s is only used as the commitment scheme's public key.

In the second part (Sect. 4), on basis of the general and formal public-coin protocol structure, we establish a general compiler to transform any multi-round proof/argument protocol into the protocol which is *concurrently non-malleable* with unchanged number of rounds, properly increased message and computational complexity (by nearly constant times). The innovative approach developed in [20–22] for only 3-round protocols is generalized to multi-round public-coin protocols via some recent analysis and results in [13]. The basic tool is the simulation-sound trap-door commitment scheme introduced in [20–22]. Such enhanced protocols, e.g., all the enhanced versions of protocols in Sects. 3 and 4, can run in parallel environment while keeping all its security properties, particularly resisting man-in-the-middle attacks.

Some Notes on Terminologies. In second part of our work, we simply inherit the terminology *non-malleability* from [22] but it is strictly weaker than the "*non-malleability*" in [20,21] which is actually equivalent to *universal composability.* In addition, "*tag-based*" and "*simulation soundness*" for the trapdoor commitment scheme are terminologies inherited from [20] which are similar (but not exactly the same) as the properties proposed in [22] in different names.

2 Preliminaries

Notations and Conventions. λ usually represents the security parameter,poly (λ) represents a polynomial in λ. A function $\varepsilon(\lambda)$ is called *asymptotically negligible* or simply negligible if $\lim_{\lambda\to\infty} \text{poly}(\lambda)\varepsilon(\lambda) = 0$.

P.P.T. means Probabilistic Polynomial Time.

$u \overset{\text{R}}{\leftarrow} J$ means a random variable u is sampled on a set J under uniform distribution.

2.1 Zero-Knowledge Proofs/Arguments

A binary relation R is NP-class if there exists a polynomial-time algorithm A to decide whether (x, w) is in R.$\text{L}_\text{R} \equiv \{x : \text{there exists } (x, w) \in \text{R}\}$.

In an interactive proof system (P, V) where P and V are P.P.T prover and verifier, σ represents the common reference string(c.r.s.), x represents the public information for P and V,w represents the private information only for P, i.e., the witness, $< \text{P}(w); \underline{\text{V}} >_\sigma (x)$ represents the output of V valued in $\{0, 1\}$ after the interaction with P on input x and c.r.s. σ,Tr $< \text{P}, \text{V} >_\sigma (x)$ the trace during the interaction between P and V. These notations have the same meaning for any interactive algorithms A and B.

Definition 1 (Zero-Knowledge Proof). For a relation R and some given function $\kappa(\lambda)$, an interactive proof system (P,V) is defined as a *zero-knowledge proof of knowledge* for R, **ZKPoK** hereafter, if it has all the following properties:

(1) **Complete.** For any $(x, w) \in \mathrm{R}$ there holds $\mathrm{P}\left[< \mathrm{P}(w); \underline{\mathrm{V}} >_\sigma (x) = 1\right] = 1$.
(2) **Knowledge-Sound with Knowledge-Error.** $\kappa(\lambda)$ There exists a polynomial q(.) and an algorithm Ext (called *extractor*) with expected polynomial time complexity, such that for any (maybe dishonest) prover P^* which can be rewound by Ext there holds
$\mathrm{P}\left[w^* \leftarrow \mathrm{Ext}^{\mathrm{P}^*}(\sigma, x, \mathrm{Tr} < \mathrm{P}^*,\ \mathrm{V} >_\sigma (x)) : (x, w^*) \in \mathrm{R}\right] \geq (\mu(x) - \kappa(|x|))$
$/\mathrm{q}(|x|)$ where $\mu(x) \equiv \mathrm{P}\left[< \mathrm{P}^*; \underline{\mathrm{V}} >>_\sigma (x) = 1\right] \geq \kappa(|x|)$.
(3) **Zero-Knowledge.** There exists a P.P.T. algorithm S, called *simulator*, such that for any (maybe dishonest) verifier V^*, the output of $\mathrm{S}(\sigma, x)$ and $\mathrm{Tr} < \mathrm{P}, \mathrm{V}^* >_\sigma (x)$ are statistically indistinguishable for any $x \in \mathrm{L_R}$.

For knowledge soundness, there is an equivalent definition ([18] Sect. 4.7) that on input of x and $\mathrm{Tr} < \mathrm{P}^*,\ \mathrm{V} >_\sigma (x)$ with $< \mathrm{P}^*, \underline{\mathrm{V}} >_\sigma (x) = 1$ and Ext can rewind P^*, Ext outputs a witness $w^* : (x, w^*) \in \mathrm{R}$ with the expected time at most $\mathrm{q}(|x|)/(\mu(x) - \kappa(|x|))$.

If knowledge soundness only holds for P.P.T. prover P^*, the proof system is called *knowledge argument*, notated by **ZKAoK** hereafter.

Definition 2 ($\boldsymbol{\Sigma}$−Protocol and Generalized $\boldsymbol{\Sigma}$−Protocol). An interactive proof system (P,V) for relation R is called a $\boldsymbol{\Sigma}$−Protocol, if it has 3 rounds with the first message from P to V and the second message just being a random coin from V to P independent of the session context.

An interactive proof system (P,V) for relation R is called a *generalized* $\boldsymbol{\Sigma}$−Protocol, if it has $2k + 1$ rounds with the first message from P to V and any messages from V to P just being random coins independent of each other and session context.

A generalized $\boldsymbol{\Sigma}$−Protocol for relation R is called *special honest verifier zero-knowledge*(**SHVZK**) if there exists a P.P.T. algorithm S such that for any verifier V^*, the real trace $\mathrm{Tr} < \mathrm{P}, \mathrm{V}^* >_\sigma (x)$ and the output of S on input $(\sigma, x; e_1, \ldots, e_k)$ have the same distribution for any $x \in \mathrm{L_R}$ and independent random coins $e_1, \ldots, e_k$.

Definition 3 ($(\mu_1, \ldots, \mu_k)$-Special Soundness and Session-Tree for a Generalized $\boldsymbol{\Sigma}$−Protocol). A $(\mu_1, \ldots, \mu_k)$-*session-tree*, denoted by $\mathrm{T}_\sigma(x)$, for the proof system of relation R with c.r.s. σ is a tree in which:

(1) Each node is associated with a message instance form P to V in the interaction between P and V with public information x, in particular the root is with the first message in the interaction.
(2) Each edge is a random coin from V to P.
(3) At level-i (the root being at level-1) each node α has μ_i edges and the random coin instances $e_{\alpha/1}, \ldots,\quad e_{\alpha/\mu_i}$ associated with these edges are distinct. The downstream node of each edge is associated with the message instance of P in response to the random coin.
Each integer μ_i is called the *soundness factor* of the i-th round.

Obviously, each path from the root to a leaf in the tree $\mathrm{T}_\sigma(x)$ is a complete session instance, i.e., a trace. The number of paths in a tree $\mathrm{T}_\sigma(x)$ is $(\mu_1, \ldots, \mu_k)$. If the verifier V outputs 1 on all these paths, the tree $\mathrm{T}_\sigma(x)$ is called ***accepting***.

A generalized **Σ**−Protocol is called $(\mu_1, \ldots, \mu_k)$-*special sound*, if there exists a P.P.T. algorithm (*extractor*) which with overwhelming probability outputs a witness $w^* : (x, w^*) \in \mathrm{R}$ on input of σ, x and the accepting tree $\mathrm{T}_\sigma(x)$.

Recently [13] proved a fundamental fact that $(\mu_1, \ldots, \mu_k)$-soundness implies knowledge soundness, a general fact without imposing any restrictions on the challenge set where the random coins are sampled.

2.2 Commitment Scheme

Definition 4 (Commitment Scheme). A Commitment scheme CS ≡ (CGen, Cmt, Cvf) is composed of three P.P.T. algorithms with the following properties:

(1) **Complete.** For any message x there holds

$$\mathrm{P}[pk \leftarrow \mathrm{CGen}(\lambda); (c, d) \leftarrow \mathrm{Cmt}(pk, x) : \mathrm{Cvf}(pk, c, x, d) = 1] = 1$$

(2) **Binding.** There exists a negligible function $\varepsilon(\lambda)$ s.t. for any P.P.T. algorithm A:

$$\begin{aligned}\mathrm{P}\,[pk \leftarrow \mathrm{CGen}(\lambda); (c, x_1, x_2, d_1, d_2) \leftarrow \mathrm{A}(pk) : \mathrm{Cvf}\,(pk, c, x_1, d_1)\\ = 1 \wedge \mathrm{Cvf}\,(pk, c, x_2, d_2) = 1 \wedge x_1 \neq x_2] \leq \varepsilon(\lambda)\end{aligned}$$

(3) **Hiding.** For any pk generated by CGen and messages $x1$, $x2$ in the same size, variables $c_1 : (c_1, d_1) \leftarrow \mathrm{Cmt}\,(pk, x_1)$ and $c_2 : (c_2, d_2) \leftarrow \mathrm{Cmt}\,(pk, x_2)$ has the same distribution.

2.3 Basic Facts About Galois Ring

Formally, a Galois ring is a finite ring with multiplicative unit 1 such that all of zero divisors (including 0) forms a principal ideal $(p1)$ for some prime number p.

One of the most important examples for Galois ring is the residue ring Z_m where $m = p^s$ and p is a prime number. Another important example is $\mathrm{Z}_m[X]/(f(X))$ where Z_m is as before and $f(X)$ is a monic irreducible polynomial of degree d over Z_m. This ring is the extended ring of Z_m of degree d, notated as $\mathrm{GR}(m, d)$ hereafter.

The most important facts about Galois ring useful in this paper are stated here. All details and proofs can be seen, e.g., in Chap. 14 of [17], particularly its theorem 14.1, 14.6, 14.8 and lemma 14.20 and 14.29.

Fact 1. Let S be a Galois ring of characteristic p^s (i.e., $p^s 1 = 0$ and $N1 \neq 0$ for any integer $N \neq 0 \bmod p^s$) and cardinality p^{sd} where p is a prime, s and d are positive integers. Then S is isomorphic to the ring $\mathrm{GR}(m, d) \equiv \mathrm{Z}_m[X]/(f(X))$ for $m = p^s$ and any irreducible polynomial $f(X)$ of degree d over Z_m.

Fact 2. In Galois ring $\mathrm{GR}(m,d) \equiv \mathrm{Z}_m[X]/(f(X))$ with $m = p^s$:

(1) There exists an element ξ of order $p^d - 1$ such that $f(\xi) = 0$ and $f(X)$ is the unique monic polynomial of degree $\leq d$ over Z_m with ξ as its root.
(2) $X^{p^{d-1}} - 1 = 0 \bmod f(X)$ and $X^N - 1 \neq 0 \bmod f(X)$ for $0 < N < p^d - 1$.
(3) $\mathrm{GR}(m,d) = \mathrm{Z}_m[\xi] \equiv \{a_0 + a_1\xi + a_2\xi^2 + \ldots + a_{d-1}\xi^{\xi d-1} : a_0, a_1, a_2, \ldots, a_{d-1} \text{ in } \mathrm{Z}_m\}$
(4) Let $\mathrm{E}_{GR(m,d)} \equiv \{\xi^i : i = 0, 1, 2, \ldots, p^d - 2\}$ then any u in $\mathrm{GR}(m,d)$ has a unique p-adic representation as

$$u = A_0 + A_1 p + A_2 p^2 + \ldots + A_{s-1} p^{s-1}$$

with each A_i in $\mathrm{E}_{GR(m,d)} \cup \{0\}$. Furthermore, u is invertible in $\mathrm{GR}(m,d)$ iff $A_0 \neq 0$.
(5) $\mathrm{E}_{\mathrm{GR}(m,d)}$ is called the exceptional set of Galois ring $\mathrm{G}(m,d)$.$\mathrm{E}_{\mathrm{GR}(m,d)}$ is a cyclic multiplicative group of order $p^d - 1$ and is isomorphic to the multiplicative subgroup of finite field F_{p^d}.$\xi^i - \xi^j$ is in $\mathrm{E}_{\mathrm{GR}(m,d)}$ for any $i \neq j$, i.e., $\xi^i - \xi^j$ is always invertible in $\mathrm{GR}(m,d)$.
(6) $f(X)$ has roots $\xi, \xi^p, \xi^{p^2}, \ldots, \xi^{p^{d-1}}$.

Fact 3. Let S be $\mathrm{GR}(m,d)$ and $l < p^d - 1$, then any non-identically zero polynomial $\varphi(X) \in \mathrm{S}[X]$ of degree $\leq l$ cannot have more than l roots in the exceptional set E_S.

2.4 Vector Commitments over Galois Ring

Attema T., et al. in [16] established a family of general and elegant commitment schemes for vectors over any finite ring. Let S be $\mathrm{GR}(m,d) \equiv \mathrm{Z}_m[X]/(f(X))$ and $\boldsymbol{u}$ be a n-dimensional S-vector, i.e.,

$$\boldsymbol{u} = \begin{bmatrix} u_1(X) \\ \cdot \\ \cdot \\ u_n(X) \end{bmatrix} \in S^n \tag{2.1}$$

with $u_k(X) = u_1(k) + u_2(k)X + u_3(k)X^2 + \ldots + u_d(k)X^{d-1} \in \mathrm{S}$ for each $k = 1, \ldots, n$. Let R be the set on which to select the random element for hiding, then the commitment to $\boldsymbol{u}$ is an element in product group G^d where G is the commitment-friendly group [16], e.g., $\mathrm{G} = \mathrm{Z}_N^*$ (for m odd) or $\mathrm{J}^+(N)$ (for m even) with some strong RSA module N, which is computed by:

$$\mathrm{Cmt}(\sigma \mid \boldsymbol{u}; \boldsymbol{r}) = \begin{bmatrix} \mathrm{cmt}_\sigma\left(u_1(1), \ldots, u_1(n); r_1\right) \\ \vdots \\ \mathrm{cmt}_\sigma\left(u_d(1), \ldots, u_d(n); r_d\right) \end{bmatrix} \in G^d : \mathrm{S}^n \times \mathrm{R}^d \to \mathrm{G}^d \tag{2.2}$$

where $\mathrm{cmt}_\sigma(\boldsymbol{w}; r) : \mathrm{Z}_m^n \times \mathrm{R} \to \mathrm{G}$ is a basic commitment scheme for any n-dimensional Z_m-vector $\boldsymbol{w}$. A general method is provided to construct the basic scheme $\mathrm{cmt}_\sigma(.;.)$ in [22] to ensure the properties of unconditional completeness, perfect hiding and computational binding. Specifically, given the commitment key $\sigma \equiv [G, \boldsymbol{g}, m]$ with $\boldsymbol{g} \equiv (g_1, \ldots, g_n)$ being group elements[1], for $\boldsymbol{w} = [w_1, \ldots, w_n] \in \mathrm{Z}_m^n$ with m odd then:

$$\mathrm{cmt}_\sigma(\boldsymbol{w}; r) = r^m \boldsymbol{g}[\boldsymbol{w}] \equiv r^m g_1^{w_1} \ldots g_n^{w_n} \text{ where } r \in \mathrm{R} \tag{2.3}$$

For m even:

$$\mathrm{cmt}_\sigma(\boldsymbol{w}; r) = r^m(-1)^b \boldsymbol{g}[\boldsymbol{w}] \equiv r^m(-1)^b g_1^{w_1} \ldots g_n^{w_n} \text{ where } (b, r) \in \{0, 1\} \times \mathrm{R} \tag{2.4}$$

Note that we denote $g_1^{w_1} \ldots g_n^{w_n}$ as $\boldsymbol{g}[\boldsymbol{w}]$, $g_1^e \ldots g_n^e$ as $\boldsymbol{g}[e]$ for simplification.

Besides security properties, homomorphism is also crucial for these commitment scheme's applications. It is straightforward to show that (2.3) and (2.4) have the usual homomorphism properties required for a commitment. Furthermore, scheme $\mathrm{Cmt}(\sigma \mid .;.) : \mathrm{S}^n \times \mathrm{R}^d \to \mathrm{G}^d$ has a algebraic property useful in protocol construction.

Lemma 1. Let e be in Galois ring $\mathrm{S} = \mathrm{GR}(m, d) \equiv \mathrm{Z}_m[X]/(f(X))$ and $\mathrm{M}_e \in \mathrm{Z}_m^{d \times d}$ be its associated matrix, i.e., for any

$$u = u_1 + u_2 X + u_3 X^2 + \ldots + u_d X^{d-1} \in \mathrm{S}$$

there holds

$$eu = \sum_{i=1}^{d} \left(\sum_{j=1}^{d} M_e(i, j) u_j \right) X^{i-1} \bmod f(X) \tag{2.5}$$

Also let

$$\mathrm{Cmt}(\sigma \mid \boldsymbol{u}; \boldsymbol{r}) = \begin{bmatrix} C_1 \\ \cdot \\ \dot{C}_d \end{bmatrix} \in S^d$$

and $\boldsymbol{u}$ be the S-vector in (2.1), then

$$\mathrm{Cmt}(\sigma \mid e\boldsymbol{u}; \boldsymbol{s}) = \begin{bmatrix} \prod_{j=1}^{d} C_j^{M_e(1,j)} \\ \cdot \\ \cdot \\ \prod_{j=1}^{d} C_j^{M_e(d,j)} \end{bmatrix} \tag{2.6}$$

where $\boldsymbol{s}$ can be efficiently computed from $\boldsymbol{u}, \boldsymbol{r}, e$[2] and is uniformly distributed if $\boldsymbol{r}$ or e are uniformly distributed. Equality (2.6) is denoted as $\mathrm{Cmt}(\sigma \mid e\boldsymbol{u}; \boldsymbol{s}) = \mathrm{Cmt}(\sigma \mid \boldsymbol{u}; \boldsymbol{s})^e$.

[1] Each g_i is the m-th power of some element in G, as a result the commitment to any message is always in G^m (except for a random factor -1 in case of even m) [22].

[2] For simplicity, here and in the following arguments we always omit the long expressions for random objects which can be easily derived from basic formulas in Sect. 3.1 in [22].

Remark 1. This result was basically established in [16] and Lemma 2.1 presents it in a more explicit formulism (2.6). Furthermore, when the commitment (2.2) to a S-vector $\boldsymbol{u}$ in (2.1) is equivalently regarded as a commitment to a Z_m-matrix

$$\mathbf{U} = \begin{bmatrix} u_1(1) & \cdots & u_d(1) \\ \vdots & \ddots & \vdots \\ u_1(n) & \cdots & u_d(n) \end{bmatrix} \in \mathrm{Z}_m^{n\times d}$$

and denoted by $\mathrm{Cmt}(\sigma \mid \mathbf{U})$, then (2.6) implies

$$\mathrm{Cmt}\left(\sigma \mid \mathbf{U}\mathbf{M}_e^{\mathrm{T}}\right) = \mathrm{Cmt}(\sigma \mid \mathbf{U})^e \tag{2.7}$$

This view of equalizing S-vectors and Z_m-matrices is useful in the following work.

3 Efficient ZKA Protocol for Matrix Relation AU = B

Consider the matrix equation $\mathbf{AU} = \mathbf{B}$ in residue ring Z_m where matrices $\mathbf{U} \in \mathrm{Z}_m^{n\times h}$, $\mathbf{A} \in \mathrm{Z}_m^{l\times n}$ and $\mathbf{B} \in \mathrm{Z}_m^{l\times h}$. Both n and h are sufficiently large and $h = td$ for some integer t. The extension degree of Galois ring S over Z_m is d and determined by $p^{-d} \log n <$ the target knowledge error. Matrix $\mathbf{U}$ is the witness while $\mathbf{A}$ and $\mathbf{B}$ are public.

3.1 Basics

To present the main idea explicitly, let's consider the case $t = 1$ at first, i.e., $\mathbf{AU} = \mathbf{B}$ in residue ring Z_m where matrices $\mathbf{U} \in \mathrm{Z}_m^{n\times d}$, $\mathbf{A} \in \mathrm{Z}_m^{l\times n}$ and $\mathbf{B} \in \mathrm{Z}_m^{l\times d}$. There is no performance advantage in this case in comparison with the standard, vector-oriented approach. The objective of this section is to present the main ideas and techniques in our matrix-oriented approach.

In order to construct an efficient proof protocol with commitment to Z_m-matrix $\mathbf{U}$, the first step is to find some relation over S which is equivalent to the original linear matrix relation over Z_m.

For $\mathrm{S} \equiv \mathrm{Z}_m[X]/(f(X)) = \mathrm{GR}(m, d)$ with degree-d irreducible monic polynomial $f(X)$ and matrix $\mathbf{A} \in \mathrm{Z}_m^{l\times n}$, define a S-linear operator:

$$\mathrm{L}_\mathrm{A} : \mathrm{S}^n \to \mathrm{S}^l : \mathrm{L}_\mathrm{A}(\boldsymbol{u})_i \equiv \sum_{k=1}^{n} a_{ik} u_k(X) \bmod f(X), i = 1, \ldots, l \tag{3.1}$$

where $u_k(X) \in \mathrm{S}$ is the k-th component of vector $\boldsymbol{u}$ in S^n.

For the Z_m-matrices

$$\mathbf{U} = \begin{bmatrix} u_1(1) & \cdots & u_d(1) \\ \vdots & \ddots & \vdots \\ u_1(n) & \cdots & u_d(n) \end{bmatrix}, \quad \mathbf{B} = \begin{bmatrix} b_1(1) & \cdots & b_d(1) \\ \vdots & \ddots & \vdots \\ b_1(l) & \cdots & b_d(l) \end{bmatrix} \tag{3.2}$$

and each $i = 1, \ldots, l, k = 1, \ldots, n$, let:

$$b_i(X) \equiv \sum\nolimits_{j=1}^{d} b_j(i) X^{j-1} = b_1(i) + b_2(i)X + \cdots + b_d(i)X^{d-1}$$
$$u_k(X) \equiv u_1(k) + u_2(k)X + \cdots + u_d(k)X^{d-1}$$

Regard **U** and **B** as vectors with components $u_k(X)$'s and $b_i(X)$'s in S, the corresponding S-vectors are:

$$\boldsymbol{u} = \begin{bmatrix} u_1(X) \\ \cdot \\ \cdot \\ u_n(X) \end{bmatrix} \in S^n, \quad \boldsymbol{b} = \begin{bmatrix} b_1(X) \\ \cdot \\ \cdot \\ b_l(X) \end{bmatrix} \in S^l \tag{3.3}$$

This correspondence is very useful and can be transformed by:

$$\boldsymbol{u} = \mathbf{U} \begin{bmatrix} 1 \\ X \\ X^2 \\ \dot{X}^{d-1} \end{bmatrix}, \boldsymbol{b} = \mathbf{B} \begin{bmatrix} 1 \\ X \\ X^2 \\ \dot{X}^{d-1} \end{bmatrix} \tag{3.4}$$

Then for the S-vector $\boldsymbol{u}$ corresponding to matrix **U** in (3.2) one has, for each i :

$$\mathrm{L_A}(\boldsymbol{u})_i = \sum\nolimits_{k=1}^{n} a_{ik} u_k(X) = \sum\nolimits_{j=1}^{d} \left(\sum\nolimits_{k=1}^{n} a_{ik} u_j(k) \right) X^{j-1} \bmod f(X)$$

As a result, it's easy to show the fact that:

$$\mathbf{L_A}(\boldsymbol{u}) = \boldsymbol{b} \text{ over S}$$

$$\text{if and only if} \sum_{k=1}^{n} a_{ik} u_j(k) = b_j(i) \text{ for all } i, j, \text{ i.e., } \mathbf{AU} = \mathbf{B} \text{ over } \mathrm{Z_m} \tag{3.5}$$

Based on the fact (3.5), the problem of constructing a ZKA protocol for a linear matrix relation over Z_m can be transformed into a problem of constructing a ZKA protocol for a linear relation over Galois ring S. For this purpose, we define a formal linear relation over S.

Let Galois ring $\mathrm{S} \equiv \mathrm{GR}(m, d)$, let σ be the public key of the S-vector commitment scheme and be used as c.r.s. of the proof protocol. The commitment is valued in product group G^d where G is commitment-friendly. The linear relation **SLR** on space S^n is defined as(all variables in the frame stand for witnesses):

$$\begin{aligned} &\mathrm{SLR}(\sigma \mid U, \boldsymbol{b}, \mathbf{A}; \boxed{\boldsymbol{r}, \boldsymbol{u}}) : \\ &U = \mathrm{Cmt}(\sigma \mid \boldsymbol{u}; \boldsymbol{r}) \wedge \mathbf{L_A}(\boldsymbol{u}) = \boldsymbol{b} \end{aligned} \tag{3.6}$$

where $\mathbf{L_A}$ is defined in (3.1) with $\mathbf{A} \in \mathrm{Z}_m^{l \times n}, \boldsymbol{b} \in S^l$; witnesses $\boldsymbol{u}$ is a n-dimensional Svector, $\boldsymbol{r}$ is a d-dimensional random vector with components in set R.

In the above formulation, the commitment to S-vector $\boldsymbol{u}$

$$U = \mathrm{Cmt}(\sigma \mid \boldsymbol{u}; \boldsymbol{r}) = \mathrm{Cmt}\left(\sigma \mid \begin{bmatrix} u_1(1) & \cdots & u_d(1) \\ \vdots & \ddots & \vdots \\ u_1(n) & \cdots & u_d(n) \end{bmatrix}, \begin{bmatrix} r_1 \\ \cdot \\ \cdot \\ r_d \end{bmatrix}\right)$$

$$= \begin{bmatrix} \mathrm{cmt}_\sigma\,(u_1(1), \ldots, u_1(n); r_1) \\ \cdot \\ \cdot \\ \mathrm{cmt}_\sigma\,(u_d(1), \ldots, u_d(n); r_d) \end{bmatrix}$$

can be reasonably regarded as the commitment to Z_m-matrix $\mathbf{U}$, so also notated as $\mathrm{Cmt}(\sigma \mid \mathbf{U}; \boldsymbol{r})$. All these basics are summarized in Theorem 1 which is the starting point to construct ZKA protocol for linear matrix relation in Z_m.

Theorem 1. The linear matrix relation over Z_m :

$$\mathbf{MLR}(\sigma \mid U, \mathbf{B}, \mathbf{A}; \boxed{\boldsymbol{r}, \mathbf{U}}):$$

$$U = \mathrm{Cmt}(\sigma \mid \mathbf{U}; \boldsymbol{r}) \wedge \mathbf{AU} = \mathbf{B} \tag{3.7}$$

with $\mathbf{U} \in \mathrm{Z}_m^{n\times d}$ (witness), $\mathbf{A} \in \mathrm{Z}_m^{l\times n}$, $\mathbf{B} \in \mathrm{Z}_m^{l\times d}$ is equivalent to the linear relation over Galois ring $\mathrm{S} = \mathrm{GR}(m, d) = \mathrm{Z}_m[X]/(f(X))$:

$$\mathbf{SLR}\left(\sigma \mid V, \boldsymbol{b}, \mathbf{L}_\mathrm{A}; \boxed{\boldsymbol{r}, \boldsymbol{u}}\right):$$

$$V = \mathrm{Cmt}(\sigma \mid \boldsymbol{u}; \boldsymbol{r}) \wedge \mathbf{L}_\mathrm{A}(\boldsymbol{u}) = \boldsymbol{b} \tag{3.8}$$

where $\boldsymbol{u} \in \mathrm{S}^n$ (witness), $\mathbf{L}_\mathrm{A}$ is the linear operator defined in (3.1), $b_i = \sum_{j=1}^{d} b_j(i) X^{j-1}$ and $V = U$. These two relations' witnesses have the simple correspondence

$$\mathbf{U} \cong \boldsymbol{u}$$

where $\cong$ means that n-dimensional S-vectors $\boldsymbol{u}$ is equivalently regarded as a n-by-d matrix in Z_m (see (3.2) and (3.4)).

3.2 Compressed Protocol with Logarithmic Message Complexity

S-linear relation SLR in (3.8) is the starting point to construct the efficient proof protocol for linear Z_m-matrix relation MLR in (3.7). However, $\mathbf{L}_\mathrm{A}(\boldsymbol{u}) = \boldsymbol{b}$ in (3.8) is actually a system of l linear equations in S. For the sake of efficiency, this equation system can be further reduced to just one linear equation via standard probabilistic equivalence reduction techniques.

Define a polynomial $\varphi(T)$ as

$$\varphi(T) \equiv \sum_{\mathrm{i}=1}^{l} (\,\mathrm{L}_\mathrm{A}(\boldsymbol{u})_i - b_i)\, T^{i-1} \in \mathrm{S}[T] \tag{3.9}$$

Let ρ be randomly sampled from the exceptional set $\mathrm{E_S}$ in ring S. If there exists a $\boldsymbol{u} \in \mathrm{S}^n$ such that $\mathbf{L}_\mathrm{A}(\boldsymbol{u}) = \boldsymbol{b}$, i.e., $\mathrm{L}_\mathrm{A}(\boldsymbol{u})_i = b_i$ for each $i = 1, \ldots, l$, then

$$\sum\nolimits_{\mathrm{i}=1}^{l} (\, \mathrm{L_A}(\boldsymbol{u})_{\mathrm{i}} - b_{\mathrm{i}})\, \rho^{\mathrm{i}-1} = \varphi(\rho) = 0$$

On the other hand, if $\varphi(\rho) = 0$ for φ defined in (3.9) and ρ in $\mathrm{E_S}$, then ρ is a zero of $\varphi(T)$ in $\mathrm{E_S}$. Since $\varphi(T)$ has at most $l-1$ zeroes in $\mathrm{E_S}$, for $\mathrm{S} \equiv \mathrm{GR}(m, d), m = p^s$ and $l < p^d$ one has the conclusion that $\varphi(T) \equiv 0$ with probability $> 1 - lp^{-d}$. Since $\varphi(T) \equiv 0$ implies $\mathbf{L_A}(\boldsymbol{u}) = \boldsymbol{b}$, we have obtained the following result:

Theorem 2. Linear relation $\mathbf{SLR}\left(\sigma \mid V, \boldsymbol{b}, \mathbf{L}_{\mathrm{A}}; \boxed{\boldsymbol{r}, \boldsymbol{u}}\right)$ in (3.8) is probabilistically equivalent to the linear relation (3.10) with soundness factor l :

$$\mathrm{sl}-\mathrm{R}\left(\sigma \mid V, \boldsymbol{b}, l_{\mathrm{A},\rho}; \boxed{\boldsymbol{r}, \boldsymbol{u}}\right):$$

$$V = \mathrm{Cmt}(\sigma \mid \boldsymbol{u}; \boldsymbol{r}) \wedge l_{\mathrm{A},\rho}(\boldsymbol{u}) = b_\rho \tag{3.10}$$

where $b_\rho \equiv \sum_{i=1}^{l} b_{\mathrm{i}}\rho^{i-1} \in \mathrm{S}$ and the S-linear functional $l_{\mathrm{A},\rho}$ is defined as

$$l_{\mathrm{A},\rho}(\boldsymbol{w}) \equiv \sum\nolimits_{i=1}^{l} \sum\nolimits_{k=1}^{n} a_{ik} w_k \rho^{i-1} : \mathrm{S}^n \to \mathrm{S}$$

The efficient protocol for linear Z_m-matrix relation (3.7) can now be constructed equivalently for the simple S-linear relation (3.10), via compressed techniques [6,7,12]. In fact, [16] has presented such a protocol framework with $\mathrm{O}(\log n)$ message complexity and provided detailed analysis about its completeness, zero-knowledge and knowledge soundness properties so we don't repeat it here.

3.3 Vector-Oriented Approach and Comparisons

According to the basic result in [16], for $n = 2^k$ the compressed protocol for matrix relation $\mathbf{AU} = \mathbf{B}$ in Z_m is $2k + 1$ round, complete, $(2, 3, \ldots, 3)$-special sound henceforth knowledge sound with knowledge error $\leq kp^{-d}$ and total message complexity $\mathrm{O}(dk)$.

A standard, vector-oriented approach to constructing the efficient protocol for $\mathbf{AU} = \mathbf{B}$ is the amortization method. Let $\mathbf{U} = [\boldsymbol{u}_1, \ldots, \boldsymbol{u}_d]$ and $\mathrm{B} = [\boldsymbol{b}_1, \ldots, \boldsymbol{b}_d]$ where columns $\boldsymbol{u}_i \in \mathrm{Z}_m^n, \boldsymbol{b}_i \in \mathrm{Z}_m^l$, then $\mathbf{AU} = \mathbf{B}$ is a system of d linear equations $\mathbf{A}\boldsymbol{u}_i = \boldsymbol{b}_i$. For any randomness ρ in $\mathrm{E_S}$, it is equivalently reduced to a single vector equation:

$$\mathbf{A}\boldsymbol{u}_\rho = \boldsymbol{b}_\rho \text{ where } \boldsymbol{u}_\rho = \sum\nolimits_{i=1}^{d} \boldsymbol{u}_i \rho^{i-1} \in S^n, \boldsymbol{b}_\rho = \sum\nolimits_{i=1}^{d} \boldsymbol{b}_i \rho^{i-1} \in S^l$$

and furthermore, by left-multiplying the row-vector $\left(1, \delta, \delta^2, \ldots, \delta^{l-1}\right)$ for an independent randomness δ in $\mathrm{E_S}$ on both sides, the above equality is equivalent to a scalar equation in S :

$$\boldsymbol{a}(\delta)^{\mathrm{T}} \boldsymbol{u}_\rho = b_{\rho,\delta} \tag{3.11}$$

where $\boldsymbol{a}(\delta)^{\mathrm{T}} = \left(1, \delta, \delta^2, \ldots, \delta^{l-1}\right) \mathbf{A}$ and $b_{\rho,\delta} = \left(1, \delta, \delta^2, \ldots, \delta^{l-1}\right) \boldsymbol{b}_\rho$. In this way the linear matrix relation $\mathbf{AU} = \mathbf{B}$ in Z_m is (probabilistically) equivalent to the relation (3.11) with witness $\boldsymbol{u}_\rho$. If all Z_m-vectors $\boldsymbol{u}_i^{'}s$ have been individually committed to, then the commitment to $\boldsymbol{u}_\rho$ can be computed by (see (2.6)):

$$\mathrm{Cmt}\left(\sigma \mid \boldsymbol{u}_\rho\right) = \prod_{i=1}^{d} \mathrm{Cmt}\left(\sigma \mid \boldsymbol{u}_i\right)^{\rho^{i-1}} \tag{3.12}$$

It's easy to see that in this case these two approaches also have the same message complexity and the same on-line computational complexity. In summary, there are no significant differences in performance for $t = 1$.

However, when $t > 1$ the standard approach either (by regarding matrix $\mathbf{U}$ as a collection of tdn-dimensional Z_m-vectors and committing to these vectors individually) needs totally td G-elements and n G-elements in c.r.s., or (by regarding $\mathbf{U}$ as a ntd-dimensional Z_m-vector) needs 1 G-elements for commitments and ntd G-elements in c.r.s. On the other hand, by carefully making use of the commitment scheme, the matrix-oriented approach can implement the protocol with proper number of G-elements in both commitments and c.r.s while improving the performance.

3.4 Matrix-Oriented Construction

Consider $t = 2$, i.e., the equation $\mathbf{AU} = \mathbf{B}$ with $\mathbf{A} \in \mathrm{Z}_m^{l\times n}, \mathrm{Z}_m^{n\times 2d} \ni \mathbf{U} \equiv [\mathbf{U}_1, \mathbf{U}_2]$ with each $\mathbf{U}_i \in \mathrm{Z}_m^{n\times d}$; $\mathrm{Z}_m^{l\times 2d} \ni \mathbf{B} \equiv [\mathbf{B}_1, \mathbf{B}_2]$ with each $\mathbf{B}_i \in \mathrm{Z}_m^{l\times d}$ and:

$$\mathbf{U}_1 = \begin{bmatrix} u_1(1) & \cdots & u_d(1) \\ \vdots & \ddots & \vdots \\ u_1(n) & \cdots & u_d(n) \end{bmatrix}, \quad \mathbf{U}_2 = \begin{bmatrix} v_1(1) & \cdots & v_d(1) \\ \vdots & \ddots & \vdots \\ v_1(n) & \cdots & v_d(n) \end{bmatrix}$$

In this case we take $\boldsymbol{g}$ of $2n$ elements in G for committing to $\mathbf{U}$, i.e., let $\sigma \equiv [G, \boldsymbol{g},\ m\ ]$ with $\boldsymbol{g} \equiv (g_1, \ldots, g_{2n})$ (see (2.3) or (2.4)). Since the equation $\mathbf{A}[\mathbf{U}_1, \mathbf{U}_2] = [\mathbf{B}_1, \mathbf{B}_2]$ is equivalent to $\mathbf{AU}_i = \mathbf{B}_i, i = 1, 2$, i.e.,

$$\begin{bmatrix} \boldsymbol{A} & \boldsymbol{O} \\ \boldsymbol{O} & \boldsymbol{A} \end{bmatrix} \begin{bmatrix} \boldsymbol{U}_1 \\ \boldsymbol{U}_2 \end{bmatrix} = \begin{bmatrix} \boldsymbol{B}_1 \\ \boldsymbol{B}_2 \end{bmatrix} \text{ i.e., } \mathbf{A}^*\mathbf{U}^* = \mathbf{B}^* \tag{3.13}$$

where $\mathbf{A}^* \epsilon \mathrm{Z}_m^{2l\times 2n}$ and $\mathbf{U}^* \epsilon \mathrm{Z}_m^{2n\times d}$ are the matrices on the left side and $\mathbf{B}^*$ is the matrix on the right side. If committing to $\mathbf{U}^*$ (i.e., our definition of "the commitment to matrix $\mathbf{U}$") then with public key σ we have 1 commitment in G^d with its j-th component as ($\boldsymbol{u}_j$ and $\boldsymbol{v}_j$ are the j-th column in $\mathbf{U}_1$ and $\mathbf{U}_2$):

$$\mathrm{Cmt}\left(\sigma \mid \mathbf{U}^*\right)_j = \mathrm{cmt}_\sigma\left(\left[\boldsymbol{u}_j^{\mathrm{T}}, \boldsymbol{v}_j^{\mathrm{T}}\right]\right) \in \mathrm{G}, j = 1, \ldots, d \tag{3.14}$$

Now the ZKA protocol construction in Sects. 3.1 and 3.2 can be applied to equation (3.13) which (by Theorems 1 and 2) corresponding linear relation is on S^{2n} with commitments (3.14). More generally, for any $t > 1 : \mathrm{Z}_m^{n\times td} \ni \mathbf{U} \equiv [\mathbf{U}_1, \ldots, \mathbf{U}_t]$ and $\mathbf{AU} = \mathbf{B}$ we can apply the efficient ZKA protocol construction to the equivalent linear relation

$$\begin{bmatrix} \mathbf{A} \,..\, \boldsymbol{O} \\ ..\ ..\ .. \\ \boldsymbol{O} \,..\, \boldsymbol{A} \end{bmatrix} \begin{bmatrix} \boldsymbol{U}_1 \\ \cdots \\ \boldsymbol{U}_t \end{bmatrix} = \begin{bmatrix} \boldsymbol{B}_1 \\ \cdots \\ \boldsymbol{B}_t \end{bmatrix}, \mathbf{U}^* \equiv \begin{bmatrix} \boldsymbol{U}_1 \\ \cdots \\ \boldsymbol{U}_t \end{bmatrix} \in \mathrm{Z}_m^{\mathrm{tn}\times\mathrm{d}} \tag{3.15}$$

with nt group elements in c.r.s. σ and the commitments

$$\mathrm{Cmt}\left(\sigma \mid \mathbf{U}^{*}\right)_{j}=\mathrm{cmt}_{\sigma}\left(\left[\boldsymbol{u}_{j}^{(1)\mathrm{T}},\ldots,\boldsymbol{u}_{j}^{(t)\mathrm{T}}\right]\right)\in \mathrm{G}, j=1,\ldots,d \tag{3.16}$$

where each $\boldsymbol{u}_j^{(k)}$ is the j-th column Z_m-vector in $\mathbf{U}_k$. The corresponding S-linear relation of (3.15) is on space S^{nt}(see (3.8) in Theorem 1). As indicated in Sect. 3.2, [16] has presented a O(log$n$) message complexity protocol for such S-linear relation with security analysis which we don't repeat it here.

Table 1(a) summaries the performance comparisons for different approaches (on basis of Sect. 4.4 in [16]). Note that when $\mathbf{U} \in \mathrm{Z}_m^{n\times td}$ is regarded as a ntd-

Table 1. Performance of different approaches to ZKA for linear matrix relation

(a)witness $\mathrm{U} \in \mathrm{Z}_m^{n\times td}$

	Vector-oriented (e.g., [12, 16])	Matrix-oriented (ours)
	Both with targeted knowledge error $\leq p^{-d}\log n$ and $\mathbf{U} \in \mathrm{Z}_m^{n\times td}$	
number of G-elements in c.r.s.	①ntd or ②n	nt
number of G-elements for commitment.	①:1 ②:td	d
number of rounds	①:$2\log n+2\log t+2\log d-1$ ②:$2\log t+2\log d-1$	$2\log n+2\log t-1$
message complexity	①:$(2\log(ntd)-3)d$G-element $1+2\log(ntd)$ S-elements $\log(ntd)-1$ $\mathrm{E_S}$-element ②: $(2\log n-3)d$ G-element $1+2\log n$ S-elements $\log n-1$ $\mathrm{E_S}$-element	$(2\log(nt)-3)d$ G-element. $1+2\log(nt)$ S-elements $\log(nt)-1$ $\mathrm{E_S}$−element

(b)witness $\mathrm{U} \in \mathrm{Z}_m^{n\times n}$

	Vector-oriented (e.g., [12, 16])	Matrix-oriented (ours)
	Both with targeted knowledge error $\leq p^{-d}\log n$ and $\mathbf{U} \in \mathrm{Z}_m^{n\times n}$	
number of G-elements in c.r.s.	①n^2 or ②n	n^2/d
number of G-elements for commitment.	①:1 ②:n	d
number of rounds	①:$4\log n-1$ ②:$2\log n-1$	$4\log n-2\log d-1$
message complexity	①:$(4\log n-3)d$ G-element $1+4\log n$ S-elements $2\log n-1\mathrm{E_S}$-element ②: $(2\log n-3)d$ G-element $1+2\log n$ S-elements $\log n-1\mathrm{E_S}$-element	$(4\log n-2\log d-3)d$ G-element; $1+4\log n-2\log d$ S-elements; $2\log n-\log d-1$ $\mathrm{E_S}$-element

dimensional vector then ntd G-elements are needed in c.r.s. while when regarded as a collection of td n-dimensional vectors then n G-elements needed in c.r.s. Table 1(b) provides the special case for square $\mathbf{U} : td = n$.

Note that in the second sub-case in vector-oriented approach (regarding matrix $\mathbf{U}$ as a collection of tdn-dimensional Z_m-vectors so that each column is committed individually) there may be too many (totally td) commitments needed, showing that this sub-approach becomes inefficient when $td > \log n$. In particular, for square $\mathbf{U}(td = n)$ the matrix-oriented approach is greatly superior to the vector-oriented one. For example, the number of rounds is reduced from $4 \log n$ to $4 \log n - 2 \log d$ and message complexity is reduced from $4d \log n$ to $4d \log n - 2d \log d$ (for number of group elements) and from $6d \log n$ to $6d \log n - 3d \log d$ (for number of ring elements). In addition, the number of group elements in c.r.s is reduced by a factor of d (see Table 1).

4 Concurrently Non-malleable Enhancement

In various private computing applications, zero-knowledge proof protocols need to be composed in complicated running environment. However, the protocols established in Sect. 3 (and similar works by other authors) can only ensure security in sequential composition. The concurrent nonmalleable ZKA protocol [22] has such a property that even a dishonest prover playing man-in-the-middle role by concurrently interacting with multiple honest provers, it still cannot efficiently generate a new statement and convince the verifier without knowing its witness. Such property enhances zero-knowledge proof protocol's security in concurrent environment. [20–22] developed a general approach to compile any $\mathbf{\Sigma}-$protocol into a non-malleable one. In this section, we extend this method to compile any $2k+1$-round argument protocol into a non-malleable one with the same number of rounds and properly increased message and computational complexity.

4.1 Basic Tools

One of the crucial tools needed is the tag-based simulation-sound trapdoor commitment scheme. This is a trapdoor commitment scheme with input (x, t) where x is plaintext and t is a tag variable(usually some identity). Intuitively, its security ensures that an adversary cannot efficiently destroy the binding property even after collecting arbitrary number of commitments and related plaintexts, so its security is stronger than ordinary commitment schemes.

Definition 5 (Tag-Based Commitment Scheme [20]). CS ≡ (CGen,Cmt, Cvf) is called a *Tag-based Commitment Scheme* if CGen, Cmt, Chf are all P.P.T algorithms and have the following properties:

(1) **Complete.** For any (x, t) there holds

$$\mathrm{P}[pk \leftarrow \mathrm{CGen}(\lambda); (y, d) \leftarrow \mathrm{Cmt}(pk, x, t) : \mathrm{Cvf}(pk, y, x, t, d) = 1] = 1$$

(2) **Binding.** There exists a negligible function $\varepsilon(\lambda)$ s.t. for any P.P.T algorithm A:

$$\mathrm{P}\left[pk \leftarrow \mathrm{CGen}(\lambda); (y, t, x_1, x_2, d_1, d_2) \leftarrow \mathrm{A}(pk) : \mathrm{Cvf}\left(pk, y, x_1, t, d_1\right) = 1 \wedge \mathrm{Cvf}\left(pk, y, x_2, t, d_2\right) = 1 \wedge x_1 \neq x_2\right] \leq \varepsilon(\lambda)$$

(3) **Hiding.** For any pk generated by CGen, any x_1, x_2 in the same bit-size and any tag t, the output $c_1 : (c_1, d_1) \leftarrow \mathrm{Cmt}\left(pk, x_1, t\right)$ and $c_2 : (c_2, d_2) \longleftarrow \mathrm{Cmt}\left(pk, x_2, t\right)$ are computationally indistinguishable.

In the following definition, the algorithm TCGen outputs public and private keypair, i.e., $(pk, sk) \leftarrow \mathrm{CGen}(\lambda)$. The symbol TCGen_{pk} notates such a algorithm the same as TCGen but only outputs pk.

Definition 6 (Tag-Based Trapdoor Commitment Scheme [20]). TC $\equiv$ (TCGen, TCmt, TCvf, TCFakeCmt, TCFakeDmt) is a *tag-based trapdoor commitment scheme*, if all the five algorithms are P.P.T with (TCGen_{pk}, TCmt, TCvf) satisfying properties (1) $\sim$ (3) in Definition 5. In addition, for any (x, t) the two outputs

$$(pk, x, t, y^*, d^*) : (pk, sk) \leftarrow \mathrm{TCGen}(\lambda); (y^*, \delta) \leftarrow \mathrm{TCFakeCmt}(pk, sk, t); \quad d^* \leftarrow \mathrm{TCFakeDmt}\left(\delta, y^*, x, t\right);$$

and (pk, x, t, y, d) :$(pk, sk) \leftarrow \mathrm{TCGen}(\lambda); (y, d) \leftarrow \mathrm{TCmt}(pk, x, t)$; are computationally indistinguishable.

Definition 7 (Simulation Soundness of Tag-Based Trapdoor Commitment Scheme [20]). The scheme in Definition 6 is called *simulation sound* if there exists a negligible function $\varepsilon(\lambda)$ such that for any P.P.T. algorithm A:

$$\mathrm{Adv}_{TC}^{SS}(\lambda) \equiv \mathrm{P}\left[(pk, sk) \longleftarrow \mathrm{TCGen}(\lambda); (y, t, x_1, x_2, d_1, d_2) \longleftarrow \mathrm{A}^{\mathrm{O}(.|sk)}(pk) : \mathrm{TCvf}\left(pk, y, x_1, t, d_1\right) = 1 \wedge \mathrm{TCvf}\left(pk, y, x_2, t, d_2\right) = 1 \wedge x_1 \neq x_2 \wedge t \notin \mathrm{Q}\right] \leq \varepsilon(\lambda)$$

where the oracle $\mathrm{O}(. \mid sk)$ with the private key sk works in the following way:

(1) Initialize Q to be empty.
(2) For each query ["commit", t]:
$\mathrm{O}(. \mid sk)$ computes $(y^*, \delta) = \mathrm{TCFakeCmt}(pk, sk, t)$; Store (y^*, t, δ); $\mathrm{Q} = \mathrm{Q}\cup\{t\}$; Output y^*.
(3) For each query ["decommit", y^*, x]:
IF some (y^*, t, δ) exists in current storage
THEN $d^* = \mathrm{TCF\ akeDmt}\left(\delta, y^*, x, t\right)$; output d^*;

For efficient constructions of simulation sound trapdoor commitment(SSTC hereafter) scheme, see [1,15,16].

Another tool required for constructing the compiler is the strongly unforgeable one-time signature scheme, which constructions can be seen in [19,23].

4.2 Concurrently Non-malleable ZKA Protocol

For a given interactive algorithm M, let $\boxed{\mathrm{M}}$ be a set of multiple instances of M running in any concurrent way. $\boxed{\mathrm{M}}$ receives two classes of input instructions:

Instruction [START, id, x, w] : start a new instance of M, assign identifier id and input (σ, x, w) to it, where σ is the c.r.s.

Instruction [MSG, id, m]: send message m to the instance M(id) and return the output of this instance.

Given three interactive algorithms $\mathrm{S}, \mathrm{A} \equiv (\mathrm{A}_1, \mathrm{A}_2)$ and B, let $< (\mathrm{S}, \mathrm{A}_1 \mid \mathrm{A}_2, \mathrm{B}) >$ denote the interactions of A_1 with S and A_2 with B where $(\mathrm{A}_1, \mathrm{A}_2)$ are coordinated, any information obtained by A_1 can be used by A_2 to generate the message sent to B and vice versa.

In any interaction, a trace is defined as a sequence of messages $Tr = [+m_1-m_2 + m_3 - m_4 \ldots]$ where $+$ and $-$ represent the opposite message transmission directions. Two traces Tr_1 and Tr_2 are called matched if they have the same message terms but in opposite directions, e.g., $Tr_1 = [+m_1 - m_2 + m_3 - m_4 \ldots]$ and $Tr_2 = [-m_1 + m_2 - m_3 + m_4 \ldots]$.

Definition 8 (Concurrent Non-malleability of Zero Knowledge Proof/Argument [16]**).** (D,P,V,(S_1, S_2)) is called a concurrently non-malleable zero knowledge argument protocol for a relation R if all algorithms $\mathrm{D}, \mathrm{P}, \mathrm{V}, \mathrm{S}_1$, S_2 are P.P.T. and have the following properties:

(1) **Completeness.** For $\sigma \longleftarrow \mathrm{D}(\lambda)$ and $(x, w) \in \mathrm{R}$ there holds $\mathrm{P}\left[\langle \mathrm{P}(w); \underline{\mathrm{V}} >_\sigma (x) = 1\right] = 1$.

(2) **Witness Extraction.** For P.P.T algorithm $\mathrm{P}^* \equiv ({\mathrm{P}_1}^*, {\mathrm{P}_2}^*)$ consider the game $\mathrm{Exp}^{\mathrm{P}^*}(\lambda)$:

$(\sigma, \tau) \leftarrow \mathrm{S}_1(\lambda)$;

$(x^*, Tr^*, b^*) \leftarrow \left\langle \boxed{\mathrm{S}^*(\tau)}, \mathrm{P}_1^* \middle| \mathrm{P}_2^*, \mathrm{V} \right. >_\sigma$;

$\mathrm{Q} \longleftarrow \boxed{\mathrm{S}^*(\tau)}$'s traces during the interactions;

IF $b^* = 1 \Lambda_{Tr \in Q}$ Tr^* is unmatched with any Tr

THEN output 1 ;

ELSE output 0 ;

(Tr is the trace between interactions of ${\mathrm{P}_1}^*$ and $\boxed{\mathrm{S}^*}$; b^* is the output of V on trace Tr^*; *unmatched* means Tr^* cannot be a copy of any trace appeared in the interactions between ${\mathrm{P}_1}^*$ and $\boxed{\mathrm{S}^*}$.)

On each input (x, w), $\boxed{\mathrm{S}^*(\tau)}$ decides whether $\mathrm{R}(x, w) = 1$: if true then it starts an instance $\mathrm{S}_2(\tau, \sigma, x)$ otherwise does nothing. Let

$$\pi\left(\mathrm{P}^* \mid \lambda\right) \equiv \mathrm{P}\left[\mathrm{Exp}^{\mathrm{P}^*}(\lambda) = 1\right]$$

There exists an expected polynomial time algorithm Ext, a positive valued function κ and a negligible function ε such that, if $\pi\left(\mathrm{P}^* \mid \lambda\right) > \kappa(\lambda)$ then Ext with rewind access to P^* can compute a w^* such that $(x^*, w^*) \in \mathrm{R}$ with probability $\geq \pi\left(\mathrm{P}^* \mid \lambda\right) - \kappa(\lambda) - \varepsilon(\lambda)$ where x^* is the output of P^* in $\mathrm{Exp}^{\mathrm{P}^*}$.

(3) **Zero-Knowledge.** For any P.P.T. algorithm V* there has the computational indistinguishability

$$\text{Tr} < \boxed{\text{P}}, \text{V}^* >_\sigma (x) \overset{C}{\leftrightarrow} \text{Tr} < \boxed{\text{S}^{**}(\tau)}, \text{V}^* >_\sigma (x)$$

where σ on the left side is generated by $\text{D} : \sigma \leftarrow \text{D}(\lambda)$ and σ on the right side is generated by $\text{S}_1 : (\sigma, \tau) \leftarrow \text{S}_1(\lambda)$. On each input $(x, w), \text{S}^{**}$ decides whether $\text{R}(x, w) = 1$: if true then it starts an instance $\text{S}_2(\tau, \sigma, x)$ otherwise does nothing. Note that S_2 always has the input $x \in \text{L}_R$ but not w.

4.3 Concurrently Non-malleable ZKA Protocol's Construction

Let $\text{R}(\sigma \mid x, w)$ be the relation with c.r.s. σ, public input x and witness w; ZKAoK/R be the public-coin argument protocol for R with logarithmic message complexity and $2k + 1$ rounds; A, A_i, B_i and ψ be polynomial-time algorithms in the protocol.

Protocol **ZKAoK/R**

$\text{P} \rightarrow \text{V}$: P computes $(x_1, \xi_1) = A(\sigma, x, w)$ and sends x_1 to V;
//The 1st session
$\text{P} \leftarrow \text{V}$: V samples e_1 at random and sends it to P;
V computes $(b_2, \eta_2) = B_1(\sigma, x_1, e_1)$;
$\text{P} \rightarrow \text{V}$: P computes $(x_2, \xi_2) = A_1(\xi_1, e_1)$ and sends x_2 to V;
//2nd session
$\text{P} \leftarrow \text{V}$: V samples e_2 at random and sends it to P;
V computes $(b_3, \eta_3) = B_2(\eta_2, x_2, e_2)$;
$\text{P} \rightarrow \text{V}$: P computes $(x_3, \xi_3) = A_2(\xi_2, e_2)$ and sends x_3 to V;
....
/ /The i-th session
$\text{P} \leftarrow \text{V}$: V samples e_i at random and sends it to P;
V computes $(b_{i+1}, \eta_{i+1}) = B_i(\eta_i, x_i, e_i)$;
$\text{P} \rightarrow \text{V}$: P computes $(x_{i+1}, \xi_{i+1}) = A_i(\xi_i, e_i)$ and sends x_{i+1} to V;
....
//The last session
$\text{P} \leftarrow \text{V}$: V samples e_k at random and sends it to P;
V computes $(b_{k+1}, \eta_{k+1}) = B_k(\eta_k, x_k, e_k)$;
$\text{P} \rightarrow \text{V}$: P computes $x_{k+1} = A_k(\xi_k, e_k)$ and sends x_{k+1} to V;
V : V verifies $\psi(\sigma, b_{k+1}, x_{k+1}, x) = 1$.

Let SSTC $\equiv$ (TCGen, TCmt,TCvf, TCFakeCmt, TCFakeDmt) be the simulationsound tag-based trapdoor commitment scheme defined in Sect. 5.1; SG $\equiv$ (KG, Sgn, Vf) be the strongly unforgeable one-time signature scheme with key generator KG, signing algorithm Sgn and verification algorithm Vf; H be a collision-resistant hash function. With these basic cryptographic schemes, a new argument protocol sfor relation R is compiled from protocol ZKAoK/R with new c.r.s. $\sigma^* \equiv [\sigma, pk]$ where σ is the original protocol's c.r.s. and pk is the public key of scheme SSTC.

Protocol CNM-ZKAoK/R

P → V : P computes: $(s\_vk, s\_sk) = \mathrm{KG}(\lambda)$;
$(x_1, \xi_1) = A(\sigma, x, w)$;
$(y_1, d_1) \leftarrow \mathrm{TCmt}\left(pk, x_1, \mathrm{H}\left(s\_vk\|1\right)\right)$;
//Here x_1 in the original protocol is committed to with $\mathrm{H}\left(s\_vk||1\right)$ used as a tag. P sends message $[s\_vk, y_1]$ to V;

//The 1st session

P ← V : V samples e_1 at random and sends it to P;

P → V : P computes $(x_2, \xi_2) = A_1\left(\xi_1, e_1\right); (y_2, d_2) \leftarrow \mathrm{TCmt}\left(pk, x_2, \mathrm{H}\left(s\_vk\|2\right)\right)$;
P sends y_2 to V;

//2nd session

P ← V : V samples e_2 at random and sends it to P;

P → V : P computes $(x_3, \xi_3) = A_2\left(\xi_2, e_2\right); (y_3, d_3) \leftarrow \mathrm{TCmt}\left(pk, x_3, \mathrm{H}\left(s\_vk\|3\right)\right)$;
P sends y_3 to V;

//i-th session

P ← V : V samples e_i at random and sends it to P;

P → V : P computes $(x_{i+1}, \xi_{i+1}) = A_i\left(\xi_i, e_i\right); (y_{i+1}, d_{i+1}) \leftarrow \mathrm{TCmt}\left(pk, x_{i+1}, \mathrm{H}\left(s\_vk||i+1\right)\right)$;
P sends y_{i+1} to V;

//The last session

P ← V : V samples e_k at random and sends it to P;

P → V : P computes $x_{k+1} = A_k\left(\xi_k, e_k\right); z = \left(x_1, d_1, \ldots, x_k, d_k, x_{k+1}\right)$;
$\boldsymbol{u} = \left(y_1, e_1, \ldots, y_k, e_k\right); s = \mathrm{Sgn}\left(s\_sk, s\_vk\|\boldsymbol{u}\|\boldsymbol{z}\right)$;
//operator ÃćâĆňÅŞ||ÃćâĆňÂÏ means joining the string
P sends $[\boldsymbol{z}, s]$ to V;

V : On receiving the last message $\boldsymbol{z}$ from P, V computes:

$$(b_2, \eta_2) = B_1\left(\sigma, x_1, e_1\right); (b_{i+1}, \eta_{i+1}) = B_i\left(\eta_i, x_i, e_i\right), i = 2, \ldots, k$$

then verifies

$$\psi\left(\sigma, b_{k+1}, x_{k+1}, x\right) = 1 \wedge \mathrm{Vf}\left(s\_vk, s\_vk \,\|(y_1, e_1, \ldots, y_k, e_k)\|\, \boldsymbol{z}, s\right) = 1$$

$$\bigwedge_{i=1}^{k} \mathrm{TCvf}\left(pk, y_i, x_i, \mathrm{H}\left(s\_vk||i\right), d_i\right) = 1$$

About the new protocol's properties, we have the following conclusions.

Lemma 2 If ZKAoK/R has SHVZK property, then CNM – ZKAoK/R is zero-knowledge in the sense of Definition 8(3).

Proof. Straightforward (also seen in the full version paper [24])

Lemma 3. Suppose the protocol ZKAoK/R is $(\mu_1, \ldots, \mu_k)$-special sound, then there exists an extractor Ext for protocol CNM-ZKAoK/R as specified in Definition 8. Let the event EXT be "Ext outputs a w^* s.t. $(x^*, w^*) \in \mathrm{R}$ for an accepting statement x^*", |E| be the cardinality of the space for the verifier to sample challenges, then:

$$\mathrm{P[EXT]} > \pi\left(\mathrm{P}^* \mid \lambda\right) - \sum_{i=1}^{k} \mu_i/|\mathrm{E}| - \mathrm{Adv}_{TC}^{SS}(\lambda) \prod_{i=1}^{k} \mu_i + \mathrm{poly}(\lambda)\, \mathrm{Adv}_{SG}^{UF(1)}(\lambda)$$

(Adv $^{SS}_{TC}$ specified in Definition 7, $\pi\left(\mathrm{P}^* \mid \lambda\right)$ in Definition 8) and Ext's running time is poly(λ).

Proof. In Appendix A.

In Conclusion, one obtains the general result:

Theorem 3. If ZKAoK/R is an argument protocol for relation R with special soundness and SHVZK property (in terms of Definitions 2 and 3), then CNM-ZKAoK/R is a concurrently non-malleable zero knowledge argument protocol for R in terms of Definition 8.

5 Summaries and Future Works

Since various important relations can be represented in or reduced to matrix formalisms, a direct approach to constructing efficient ZKA protocols for such relations are valuable in private computing applications. In this paper efficient ZKA protocols for some typical linear and bilinear matrix relations over the ring Z_m are established, with greatly improved efficiency in communication and computational complexity, size of c.r.s while keeping the size of commitments fixed (only determined by the targeted knowledge-error) compared with other approaches. Our matrix-oriented approach is suitable to Z_m-matrix in any size. How to deal with nonlinear matrix relations more complicated than the bilinear relation, matrix polynomial relation, some tensor-product relation, etc., in this approach is worthwhile to investigate in the future.

In other aspect, a general compiler is constructed in the second part of this work to enhance any multi-round ZKA protocol to a concurrently non-malleable ZKA protocol with the same message complexity but able to resist man-in-the-middle attacks in parallel running environments. However, how to further enhance such protocols to higher security level, e.g., universal composability, is an open problem.

Appendix A. Proof of Lemma 3

Let $\mathrm{P}^* \equiv (\mathrm{P}_1{}^*, \mathrm{P}_2{}^*)$ be a P.P.T. algorithm which convinces the verifier with a statement x^* in the game $\mathrm{Exp}^{\mathrm{P}^*}$ in Definition 8 , i.e.:

$$(x^*, \mathrm{Tr}^*, b^*) = \left\langle \boxed{\mathrm{S}^*(\tau)}, \mathrm{P}_1{}^* \,\middle|\, \mathrm{P}_2{}^*,\ \mathrm{V} \right\rangle_\sigma$$
$$\text{with } b^* = 1 \bigwedge\nolimits_{\mathrm{Tr}\in\mathrm{Q}} \mathrm{Tr}^* \text{ is unmatched with any Tr.}$$

where $\mathrm{Tr}^* \equiv [s\_vk^*, y_1{}^*, \ldots, y_k{}^*, (x_1{}^*, d_1{}^*, \ldots, x_k{}^*, d_k{}^*, x_{k+1}{}^*), s^*], \mathrm{S} \equiv (\mathrm{S}_1, \mathrm{S}_2)$ be the simulator constructed in Lemma 3's proof. For presentational simplicity, let $\mu_1 = \ldots = \mu_k \equiv \mu$, otherwise for $\mu \equiv \max \mu_i$ the following argument is still valid.

We construct a P.P.T. extractor **Ext** which calls P * and interacts with it both in the role of prover (via its component algorithm Ext::P) and the role of verifier (via the component algorithm Ext:V). Since Ext can rewind P^* (mainly $\mathrm{P}_2{}^*$ in the following) to any state, for presentational simplicity we take an equivalent view in concurrent environment that Ext can *fork* P^* instance at any state. The forked instance inherits its parent state and proceeds as specified in the protocol from that state on.

Ext executes the interactions with P^* in the follow way:

In the role of prover, Ext::P calls the simulator S to interact with $\mathrm{P}_1{}^*$. Note that S_1 calls SSTC's key-generator TCGen to generate and output the public/secret key pair (pk, sk) so Ext can obtain this key pair from S.

In the role of verifier, each time right before Ext::V sends the first challenge e_1 to $\mathrm{P}_2{}^*$, Ext forks it into μ $\mathrm{P}_2{}^*$-instances and sends randomly independent and pairwise distinct challenges $e_i^{(1)}, i = 1, \ldots, \mu$ to each $\mathrm{P}_2{}^*$-instance.

Every time right before Ext::V sends the second challenge e_2 to some $\mathrm{P}_2{}^*$-instance, Ext forks it into μ $\mathrm{P}_2{}^*$-instances, sends independent and pairwise distinct challenges $e_1{}^{(2)}, \ldots, e_\mu{}^{(2)}$ to each instance.

Every instance inherits its parent's state and proceeds after receiving its challenge. Such operations proceed until all rounds are finished in protocol CNMZKAoK/R.

Let $\mathrm{T}(x^*)$ be a tree constructed as stated in Definition 3 for the above interactions, with $[s\_vk^*, y_1^*]$ as its root. According to the above operation, $\mathrm{T}(x^*)$ is a session tree and each path γ in the tree is a trace $\mathrm{Tr} < \mathrm{P}_2{}^*,\ \mathrm{V} > (x^*)$.

Since the verifier generates k challenges in CNM-ZKAoK/R, i.e., each path in $\mathrm{T}(x^*)$ has k edges along it, so in the tree:

$$\begin{aligned} &\text{Total number of edges } \mathrm{N} = \mu + \mu^2 + \ldots + \mu^k < \mu^{k+1} \\ &\text{Total number of nodes } \mathrm{M} = 1 + \mu + \mu^2 + \ldots + \mu^{k-1} < \mu^k \\ &\mathrm{K} = \text{ total number of leaves } = \mu^k \end{aligned} \tag{A.1}$$

Define a event $\boxed{\text{Succ}}$ as:

Tree $\mathrm{T}(x^*)$ is accepting, i.e., $b^*(\gamma) = 1$ for every path γ in the tree.

Consider two subevents $\mathrm{P}\left[\text{Succ} \wedge \mathrm{T}^0(x^*)\right]$ and $\mathrm{P}\left[\text{Succ} \wedge \sim \mathrm{T}^0(x^*)\right]$.

In the event of $\boxed{\text{Succ} \wedge \mathrm{T}^0(x^*)}$, Succ occurs and all session variables x_i associated with nodes $y_i(\gamma)$ ($y_i(\gamma)$ stands for a node on path γ and at level i) in the accepting tree $\mathrm{T}(x^*)$ are in consistency with each other, i.e., $x_i(\gamma) = x_i(\beta)$ for any path γ and β bifurcating at node $y_i(\gamma)$ (so $y_i(\gamma) = y_i(\beta) \equiv y_i, i \geq 1$), so after replacing each node y_i with x_i one can obtain an accepting session tree of protocol ZKAoK/R., denoted as $\mathrm{T}^0(x^*)$.

Since ZKAoK/R is $(\mu_1, \ldots, \mu_k)$-special sound, its P.P.T. extractor Ext^0 can be called by Ext to output a w^* s.t. $(x^*, w^*) \in \mathrm{R}$. In particular:

$$\mathrm{P}\left[\mathrm{Succ} \wedge \mathrm{T}^0\left(x^*\right)\right] \leq \mathrm{P}\left[\text{ Ext outputs a } w^* \text{ s.t. } \left(x^*, w^*\right) \in \mathrm{R}\right] \tag{A.2}$$

and note that the event on the right side is just $\boxed{\mathrm{EXT}}$.

For arguments on the complimentary event $\boxed{\mathrm{Succ} \wedge \sim \mathrm{T}^0\left(x^*\right)}$, i.e., no session tree for protocol ZKAoK/R can be successfully derived from $\mathrm{T}\left(x^*\right)$ in the abovementioned way, we consider two further subcases.

Case I : *s_vk^* Does Not Appear in Any Message Output from* S_2

We construct a P.P.T. algorithm **A** on basis of P^* to destroy SSTC's simulation soundness in this case. **A** has SSTC's public key pk as one of its input, has access to oracle-$\mathrm{O}(. \mid sk)$ and controls interactions of S (in role of prover) and V with P^* similarly as Ext does. During the interactions, whenever S_2 needs to generate the message Y_i or D_i in the protocol(see (A.1) and (A.2)), **A** queries its oracle-$\mathrm{O}(. \mid sk)$ with ["commit", t_i] or ["decommit", Y_i, X_i] and returns the oracle's response to S_2.

In the event of $\mathrm{Succ} \wedge \sim \mathrm{T}^0\left(x^*\right)$, there exist at least two paths γ^* and β^* in $\mathrm{T}\left(x^*\right)$ which bifurcate at some node $y_i\left(\gamma^*\right) = y_i\left(\beta^*\right) \equiv y_i^* (i \geq 1)$ with the associated session variables unequal: $x_i\left(\gamma^*\right) \neq x_i\left(\beta^*\right)$. On the other hand, $b\left(\gamma^*\right) = b\left(\beta^*\right) = 1$ so

$$\mathrm{TCvf}\left(pk, y_i^*, x_i\left(\gamma^*\right), t_i, d_i\left(\gamma^*\right)\right) = 1 \wedge \mathrm{TCvf}\left(pk, y_i^*, x_i\left(\beta^*\right), t_i, d_i\left(\beta^*\right)\right) = 1$$

where $t_i = \mathrm{H}\left(s\_vk^* || i\right)$ is independent with any path.

In case I s_vk^* does not appear in any message output from S_2 and H is collision-resistant, no t_i can be in the set of tags once received by oracle-$\mathrm{O}(. \mid sk)$. As a result, the algorithm **A** generates a output destroying scheme SSTC's simulation soundness with the probability

$$p_{\mathrm{I}} \equiv \mathrm{P}\left[\mathrm{Succ} \wedge \sim \mathrm{T}^0\left(x^*\right) \wedge \text{ Case I}\right] \leq \mathrm{MAdv}_{TC}^{SS}(\lambda) < \mu^k\, \mathrm{Adv}_{TC}^{SS}(\lambda) \tag{A.3}$$

Case II : *s_vk^* Does Appear in Some Message Output from* S_2

On basis of P^*, we construct a P.P.T. algorithm **B** to destroy strong unforgeabililty of the one-time signature scheme SG in this case. **B** has the signature verification key s_vk^* as one of its input and has access to the signing oracle-$\mathrm{OSgn}(. \mid s\_sk^*)$ at most one-time.

Let T be total number of message sequences output from S_2 during interactions with P^*. B selects a $m \in \{1, 2, \ldots, T\}$ uniformly, inserts s_vk^* into the m-th message sequence during the interactions between S_2 and P_1^*, and generates the signature of this trace required by CNM-ZKAoK/R via accessing oracle-$\mathrm{OSgn}(. \mid s\_sk^*)$.

If the m-th sequence Tr_m is the one where s_vk^* appeared, then B makes P^* succeed in generating an accepting trace $\mathrm{Tr}^* \neq \mathrm{Tr}_m$. The fact that Tr^* contains a signature s^* satisfying $\mathrm{Vf}\left(s\_vk^*, \mathrm{Tr}^*, s^*\right) = 1$ implies B's success in destroying SG's onetime unforgeability. Obviously:

$$p_{\mathrm{II}} \equiv \mathrm{P}\left[\mathrm{Succ} \wedge \sim \mathrm{T}^{0}\left(x^{*}\right) \wedge \text{ Case II }\right] \leq \mathrm{TAdv}_{SG}^{UF(1)}(\lambda) \tag{A.4}$$

Since Case I and II are complementary, from (A.3) and (A.4) one obtains

$$\mathrm{P}\left[\mathrm{Succ} \wedge \sim \mathrm{T}^{0}\left(x^{*}\right)\right] = p_{\mathrm{I}} + p_{\mathrm{II}} \leq \mu^{k}\, \mathrm{Adv}_{TC}^{SS}(\lambda) + \mathrm{TAdv}_{SG}^{UF(1)}(\lambda) \tag{A.5}$$

Combining (A.2) and (A.5) one has:

$$\begin{aligned} &\mathrm{P}[\text{ Succ }] = \mathrm{P}\left[\mathrm{Succ} \wedge \mathrm{T}^{0}\left(x^{*}\right)\right] + \mathrm{P}\left[\mathrm{Succ} \wedge \sim \mathrm{T}^{0}\left(x^{*}\right)\right] \\ &\leq \mathrm{P}[\mathrm{EXT}] + \mu^{k}\, \mathrm{Adv}_{TC}^{SS}(\lambda) + \mathrm{TAdv}_{SG}^{UF(1)}(\lambda) \end{aligned} \tag{A.6}$$

On the other hand, one can apply an analysis similar as that in Sect. 3 in [13] (see Lemma 5 there) to obtain a lower-bound of P[Succ] as:

$$\mathrm{P}[\mathrm{Succ}] > \pi\left(\mathrm{P}^{*} \mid \lambda\right) - k\mu/|\mathrm{E}| \tag{A.7}$$

So

$$\mathrm{P}[\mathrm{EXT}] > \pi\left(\mathrm{P}^{*} \mid \lambda\right) - k\mu/|\mathrm{E}| - \mu^{k}\, \mathrm{Adv}_{TC}^{SS}(\lambda) + \mathrm{TAdv}_{SG}^{UF(1)}(\lambda) \tag{A.8}$$

Note that n, $\mathrm{T} = \mathrm{poly}(\lambda), \mu = \mathrm{O}(1)$ and $k = \mathrm{O}(\log n)$ so the third and fourth terms in (A.8) are both negligible in λ. According to Ext's construction, its running time is $\mu^{k}\,\mathrm{poly}(n) = \mathrm{O}(\mathrm{poly}(n)) = \mathrm{O}(\mathrm{poly}(\lambda))$. This completes the proof.

References

1. Damagard, I., Cramer, R., Nielsen, J.B.: Secure Multiparty Computation and Secret Sharing. Cambridge University Press, Cambridge (2015)
2. Furukawa, J., Lindell, Y.: Two-thirds honest-majority MPC for malicious adversaries at Almost the Cost of Semi-Honest. In: 26th ACM CCS, pp. 1557–1571 (2019)
3. Kosba, A., Papamanthou, C., Shi, E.: xJsnark: a framework for efficient verifiable computation. IEEE Symposium on Privacy and Security, pp. 128–149 (2018)
4. Cecchetti, E., Zhang, F., Ji, Y., Kosba, A., Juels, A., Shi, E.: Solidus: Confidential Distributed Ledger Transactions via PVORM, pp. 701–718. ACM Computer and Communication Security, Dalas (2017)
5. Bünz, B., Fisch, B., Szepieniec, A.: Transparent SNARKs from DARK compilers. In: Canteaut, A., Ishai, Y. (eds.) EUROCRYPT 2020. LNCS, vol. 12105, pp. 677–706. Springer, Cham (2020). https://doi.org/10.1007/978-3-030-45721-1_24
6. Bootle, J., Cerulli, A., Chaidos, P., Groth, J., Petit, C.: Efficient zero-knowledge arguments for arithmetic circuits in the discrete log setting. In: Fischlin, M., Coron, J.-S. (eds.) EUROCRYPT 2016. LNCS, vol. 9666, pp. 327–357. Springer, Heidelberg (2016). https://doi.org/10.1007/978-3-662-49896-5_12
7. Bünz, B., Bootle, J., Boneh, D., Poelstra, A., Wuille, P., Maxwell, G.: Bulletproofs: short proofs for confidential transactions and more. In: IEEE Symposium on Security and Privacy, pp. 315–334. IEEE Computer Society Press (2018)

8. Hoffmann, M., Klooß, M., Rupp, A.: Efficient zero-knowledge arguments in discrete log setting, revisited. In: ACM Conference on Computer and Communication Security (2019)
9. Attema, T., Cramer, R., Rambaud, M.: Compressed Σ-protocols for bilinear group arithmetic circuits and application to logarithmic transparent threshold signatures. In: Tibouchi, M., Wang, H. (eds.) ASIACRYPT 2021. LNCS, vol. 13093, pp. 526–556. Springer, Cham (2021). https://doi.org/10.1007/978-3-030-92068-5_18
10. Russell, W., Lai, F., Malavolta, G., Ronge, V.: Succinct arguments for bilinear group arithmetic: practical structure -preserving cryptography. ACM Conference on Computer and Communications Security, pp. 2057–2074 (2019)
11. Attema, T., Cramer, R., Fehr, S.: Compressing proofs of k-out-of-n partial knowledge. In: Malkin, T., Peikert, C. (eds.) CRYPTO 2021. LNCS, vol. 12828, pp. 65–91. Springer, Cham (2021). https://doi.org/10.1007/978-3-030-84259-8_3
12. Attema, T., Cramer, M.: Compressed Σ-protocol theory and practical application to plug and play secure algorithms. In: CRYPTO, LNCS, pp. 513–543. Springer, Heidelberg (2020). Full-version available at IACR ePrint 2020/152
13. Attema, T., Cramer, R., Kohl, L.: A compressed Σ-protocol theory for lattices. In: Malkin, T., Peikert, C. (eds.) CRYPTO 2021. LNCS, vol. 12826, pp. 549–579. Springer, Cham (2021). https://doi.org/10.1007/978-3-030-84245-1_19
14. Couteau, G., Peters, T., Pointcheval, D.: Removing the Strong RSA Assumption from Arguments over the Integers. In: Coron, J.-S., Nielsen, J.B. (eds.) EUROCRYPT 2017. LNCS, vol. 10211, pp. 321–350. Springer, Cham (2017). https://doi.org/10.1007/978-3-319-56614-6_11
15. Damgård, I., Fujisaki, E.: A statistically-hiding integer commitment scheme based on groups with hidden order. In: Zheng, Y. (ed.) ASIACRYPT 2002. LNCS, vol. 2501, pp. 125–142. Springer, Heidelberg (2002). https://doi.org/10.1007/3-540-36178-2_8
16. Attema, T., Cascudo, I., Cramer, R., Damgard, I., Escudero, D.: Vector commitments over rings and compressed Sigma-protocols. In: Theory of Cryptography Conference, pp. 173–202 (2022)
17. Wan, Z.: Lectures on Finite Fields and Galois Rings. Academy of Sciences Press, Beijing (2006)
18. Goldreich, O.: Foundations of Cryptography. Basic Techniques, vol. 1. Cambridge University Press, Cambridge (2005)
19. Katz, J., Lindell, Y.: Modern Cryptography. Chapman Hall/CRC Press (2020)
20. MacKenzie, P., Yang, K.: On simulation-sound trapdoor commitments. In: Cachin, C., Camenisch, J.L. (eds.) EUROCRYPT 2004. LNCS, vol. 3027, pp. 382–400. Springer, Heidelberg (2004). https://doi.org/10.1007/978-3-540-24676-3_23
21. Garay, J.A., MacKenzie, P., Yang, K.: Strengthening zero-knowledge protocols using signatures. J. Cryptol. **19**(2), 169–209 (2006). https://doi.org/10.1007/s00145-005-0307-3
22. Gennaro, R.: Multi-trapdoor commitments and their applications to proofs of knowledge secure under concurrent man-in-the-middle attacks. In: Franklin, M. (ed.) CRYPTO 2004. LNCS, vol. 3152, pp. 220–236. Springer, Heidelberg (2004). https://doi.org/10.1007/978-3-540-28628-8_14
23. Bleichenbacher, D., Maurer, U.: On the efficiency of one-time digital signatures. In: Kim, K., Matsumoto, T. (eds.) ASIACRYPT 1996. LNCS, vol. 1163, pp. 145–158. Springer, Heidelberg (1996). https://doi.org/10.1007/BFb0034843
24. Yuan, T.: Efficient zero-knowledge arguments for some matrix relations over rings and non-malleable enhancement. IACR eprint.iacr.org 2022/1689

Reversible Data Hiding in Encrypted Images Based on Block Classification Coding of Sparse Representation

Fuhu Wu, Lin Wang, Shun Zhang(✉), Jie Cui, and Hong Zhong

School of Computer Science and Technology, Anhui University, Hefei 230601, China
szhang@ahu.edu.cn

Abstract. Reversible data hiding has attracted great attention, especially in the field of encrypted images. Due to the strong similarity among neighboring pixels in the local area of images, the pixels can be compressed for embedding more secret data. However, the embedding room is usually vacated by fixed length coding of sparse coefficients, then the embedding capacity may be negative when the error is too large. To address this issue, this paper proposes a reversible data hiding scheme in encrypted images via block classification coding of sparse representation called RDHEI-BCCSR, which is achieved by the difference of sparse coefficients. Two embedding methods are adopted for different blocks by setting adaptive threshold. A series of experiments are conducted on public datasets, whose results demonstrate that the RDHEI-BCCSR scheme is superior to the related schemes.

Keywords: Reversible data hiding · Encrypted image · Sparse coefficient · Adaptive threshold

1 Introduction

In recent years, with the great divergence of geopolitical landscape, data security has risen from the traditional protection of personal privacy to the maintenance of national security. The complexity of data security issues has made the governance of global data security encounter multiple realistic challenges in its infancy. From the perspective of development trend, global data security issues show remarkable characteristics, which pose new challenges in terms of building consensus on international cooperation, promoting the construction of global data security system and enhancing national governance capacity. Data hiding (DH) [1–3] as a solution in the field of data security is also attracting more and more attention from scholars and experts. Reversible data hiding (RDH) [4–8] ensures that digital media is not distorted during information transmission. There are various multimedia that can be used for data hiding, such as image, video [9,10], audio [11], text [12,13], etc. The schemes mainly fall into the following categories: lossless compression [14,15], difference expansion [16,17], and

M. Zhang et al. (Eds.): ProvSec 2023, LNCS 14217, pp. 27–43, 2023.
https://doi.org/10.1007/978-3-031-45513-1_2

histogram shifting [18–20]. In order to protect the original image, reversible data hiding in encrypted image (RDHEI) appeared. According to the time of making redundant room, the reversible data hiding schemes in encrypted images can be divided into vacating room after encryption (VRAE) and reserving room before encryption (RRBE).

In 2011, Zhang [21] first proposed a RDHEI scheme based on VRAE. The scheme embedded secret data into non-overlapping blocks. Flipping three LSBs (Least Significant Bit) of half the pixels in the blocks and extracting the embedded data through spatial correlation. In 2018, Tang et al. [22] proposed a RDHEI scheme based on differential compression, which used XOR to encrypt the original image. The difference between pixels is small, so fewer bits can be used to store the difference. In 2021, Qiu et al. [23] designed an efficient ERGA method which can generate an embedding space after image encryption, and used pixel prediction as well as entropy coding to achieve embedding of secret data.

In 2013, the RDHEI scheme based on RRBE was proposed by Ma et al. [24]. The image was divided into rough area and smooth area. Rough area embedding secret data, smooth area embedding the LSBs of rough area. In 2014, Zhang et al. [25] proposed a scheme based pixel prediction. The data can be embedded by shifting the histogram of prediction error. In 2016, Cao et al. [26] introduced patch-level sparse representation into the RDH scheme. The scheme compressed the entire block as a whole, represented the block with sparse coding, and conducted fixed length coding for sparse coefficients to make room. The range of sparse coefficients was limited to [-1024,1023], and all of them were represented by integers. The more coefficients that were repeatedly expressed, the more room was be wasted. The scheme also did not take into account some blocks with poor dictionary representation, for which there may be negative embedding capacity.

In this paper, we classify the blocks based on the threshold of error coding length. For blocks that can be well represented by the dictionary, the proposed block structure coding method based on the difference of sparse coefficients is adopted. For blocks that cannot be well represented, the block classification coding method is adopted.

The main contributions of our work are as follows:

- A new scheme named RDHEI-BCCSR is proposed based on block classification coding of sparse representation. By adaptively setting the threshold of error coding length, image blocks are divided into two types for adopting different coding.
- By applying sparse representation to encrypted images, a block structure coding based on the difference of sparse coefficients is proposed to improve the efficiency of sparse coefficients coding.
- Through a series of comparative experiments on the datasets, the results show that the RDHEI-BCCSR scheme has better embedding performance than the previous RDHEI schemes.

The rest of this paper is organized as follows. The Sect. 2 describes the details of the RDHEI-BCCSR scheme. Section 3 analyzes the experimental results and compares it with the related schemes. Finally, we conclude in Sect. 4.

2 Proposed Scheme

In this section, the details of the RDHEI-BCCSR scheme will be introduced as the following steps: (1) image encryption (2) data hiding in encrypted images (3) data extraction and image recovery. Figure 1 shows the scheme in detail.

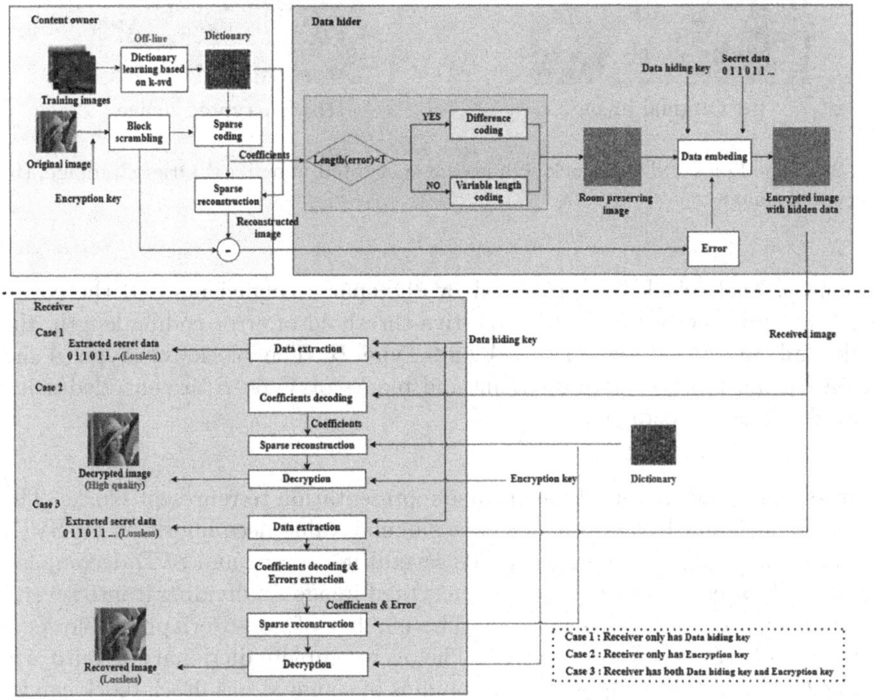

Fig. 1. Framework of the RDHEI-BCCSR scheme.

2.1 Image Encryption

In the process of image encryption, the original image I with size $N_1 \times N_2$ is divided into several non-overlapping blocks of size $n \times n$. Using the encryption key k_e to scramble the positions of blocks to make them pseudo-random and disordered to obtain the encrypted image I_e. Figure 2 shows the image Lena and the block scrambling encrypted image. The encryption is operated between blocks, which not only ensures the security of the original image, but also preserves the correlation between pixels in the blocks for the training of the dictionary.

2.2 Data Hiding in Encrypted Images

In the process of data hiding, three parts: 1) sparse representation; 2) adaptive threshold; 3) partition embedding. For the image I_e, it is divided into blocks. The sparse coefficients of each block are obtained according to the over-complete

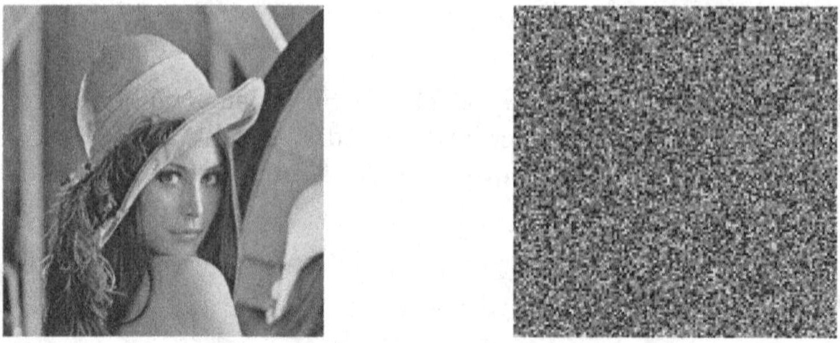

(a) Original image (b) Encrypted image

Fig. 2. Image Lena and the block scrambling encrypted image. (a) Original image, (b) Encrypted image.

dictionary. Each block is represented by the sparse coefficients and the corresponding error. According to the adaptive threshold of error coding length, the blocks fall into two types, Type A and Type B. The blocks of Type A are encoded using block structure coding and blocks of Type B are encoded using block classification coding.

Sparse Representation. Using sparse representation to represent blocks. The dictionary is trained based on K-means singular value decomposition (K-SVD) [27,28] algorithm. The algorithm needs several iterations, and SVD decomposition is used for each iteration. For an encrypted image I_e, dividing it into several non-overlapping blocks of size $n \times n$. The number of non-overlapping blocks is represented by S, $S = (N_1 \times N_2)/n^2$. The over-complete dictionary $\mathbf{D}$ with size of $n^2 \times K(K > n^2)$ is composed of K columns of signal atoms. Each block can be represented as a sparse combination of these columns. Each block is represented by a sparse vector $\mathbf{x_i}(i = 1, 2, ..., S)$, which contains two non-zero coefficients.

Since the dictionary and sparse coefficients are non-integer, the result obtained is non-integer that approximates the actual pixel. $\widetilde{\mathbf{x}}_i = \lfloor \mathbf{x}_i \rfloor$ is the rounding operation to facilitate subsequent coding operations. The pixel vector $\mathbf{y}_i$ of the original block can be expressed as follows.

$$\mathbf{y_i} = \lfloor \mathbf{D}\widetilde{\mathbf{x}}_i \rfloor + \mathbf{e}_i \tag{1}$$

where $i = 1, 2, ..., S$, $\widetilde{\mathbf{x}}_i \in \mathbb{Z}^{K \times 1}$, $\mathbf{e}_i \in \mathbb{Z}^{n^2 \times 1}$, $\mathbf{y}_i \in \mathbb{Z}^{n^2 \times 1}$, $\mathbf{e}_i$ is considered as the error. Most sparse coefficients have a range of [-1024,1023]. Once the coefficients are out of range, the excess is added to the error.

Adaptive Threshold. The error of each block is not equal, and the encoding length of the error is also different. With one coding length as the threshold T, the blocks will fall into two types. Different embedding methods will be used respectively. When the coding length is less than the threshold T, the block structure coding based on the difference of sparse coefficients is used. On the contrary, block classification coding is used. The threshold is chosen to combine the two embedding methods in the most effective way. Different thresholds T will affect the embedding rate. By fitting the minimum error coding length l_{min} and maximum error coding length l_{max} with the corresponding threshold of the image in the dataset, the correlation between the threshold and the length can be obtained as shown in Eq. (2). Based on the correlation, the threshold can be obtained. α, β, γ are the specific parameters.

$$T = \lfloor \alpha * l_{min} - \beta * l_{max} + \gamma \rfloor \tag{2}$$

Partition Embedding. Blocks are divided into two types according to the threshold T, Type A and Type B. When the error coding length is less than the threshold, the block is classified into Type A; otherwise, Type B. The block structure coding based the difference of sparse coefficients is adopted for Type A, while the block classification coding proposed by Qin et al. [29] is adopted for Type B.

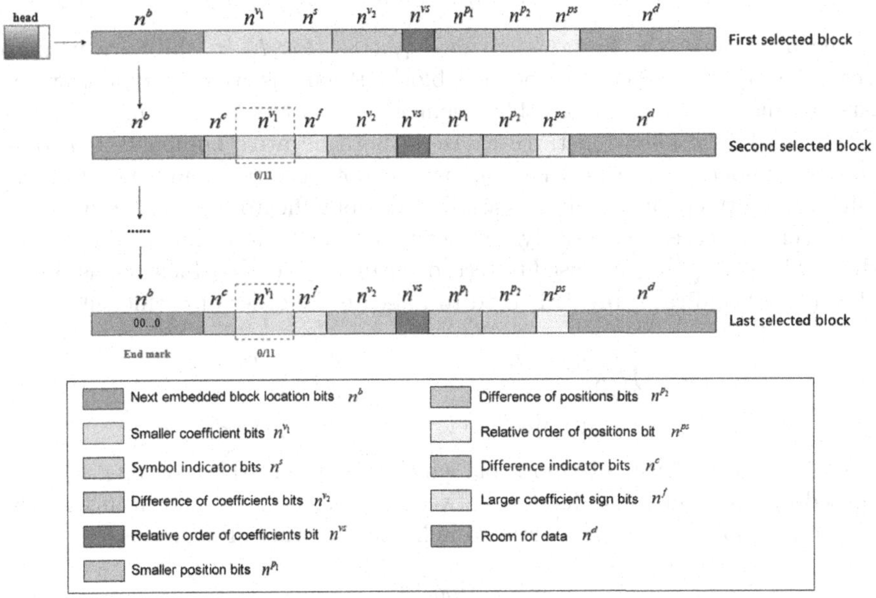

Fig. 3. Block structure coding of Type A.

Assume that there are C blocks in Type A, they are sorted according to the sparse coefficients. v_1 and v_2 are the coefficients of the block, the smaller coefficient v_1 is selected as the basis for the arrangement. Due to the ordering of the coefficients, the coefficients v_1 in consecutive blocks are very close even equal. In order to avoid the coefficients v_1 being coded repeatedly and to reduce the information needed to record coefficients v_2, the difference of sparse coefficients is used to represent coefficients, as shown in Fig. 3.

Table 1. Symbol indicator bits s of sparse coefficients.

Smaller coefficient v_1	Larger coefficient v_2	Symbol indicator bits s
$-$	$-$	"0"
$-$	$+$	"10"
$+$	$+$	"11"

In each block $A_i (i = 1, 2, ..., C)$ after sorting in Type A, the position (p_x, p_y) of the next embedded block A_{i+1}, the sparse coefficients v_1 and v_2, as well as the corresponding positions p_1 and p_2 in the sparse vector need to be recorded. The position (p_x, p_y) is calculated as follows, where p_k represents the index of blocks scanned in the image.

$$p_x = \begin{cases} \lfloor p_k/(N_2/n) \rfloor, & mod(p_k, (N_2/n)) = 0 \\ \lfloor p_k/(N_2/n) \rfloor + 1, & mod(p_k, (N_2/n)) \neq 0 \end{cases} \tag{3}$$

$$p_y = \begin{cases} \lfloor N_2/n \rfloor, & mod(p_k, (N_2/n)) = 0 \\ mod(p_k, (N_2/n)), & mod(p_k, (N_2/n)) \neq 0 \end{cases} \tag{4}$$

For the first block, the first $n_i^b = \lceil log_2 N_1/n \rceil + \lceil log_2 N_2/n \rceil$ bits are used to record the position of next embedded block. Binary is used to represent the sparse coefficient v_1, $n_i^{v_1} = 11$. The coefficient v_1 is less than v_2 in the block, there are only the following three cases: 1) both negative numbers; 2) v_1 is a negative number, v_2 is a positive number; 3) both positive numbers. Huffman coding is performed for the three cases, the symbol indicator bits s is used n_i^s bits to represent the cases respectively. As shown in Table 1. According to the symbol indicator bits s, $n_i^{v_2}$ bits are used to record the difference of coefficients, as shown in Eq. (5). An indicator bit vs is used to indicate the order of coefficients.

$$n_i^{v_2} = \begin{cases} \lceil log_2 |v_1| \rceil, & v_1 < 0, v_2 < 0 \\ 10, & v_1 < 0, v_2 \geqslant 0 \\ \lceil log_2(1023 - v_1 + 1) \rceil, & v_1 \geqslant 0, v_2 \geqslant 0 \end{cases} \tag{5}$$

Assume that p_1 is the smaller position, which is represented by $n_i^{p_1}$ bits. $n_i^{p_2}$ bits are used to represent the difference between the positions, as shown in Eqs. (6) and (7). An indicator bit ps is used to indicate the order of positions.

$$n_i^{p_1} = \lceil log_2 |K| \rceil \tag{6}$$

$$n_i^{p_2} = \lceil log_2(K - p_1 + 1) \rceil \tag{7}$$

For the non-first blocks, the embedding method is different from the first block. The position of the next embedded block is recorded at the front n_i^b bits. The difference dif between the coefficients v_1 of consecutive blocks is represented by difference indicator bits c used n_i^c bits. There are three cases of difference dif: 1) the difference is 0 with the indicator bit "0"; 2) the difference is 1 with the indicator bits "10"; 3) the difference is greater than 1 with the indicator bits "11". As shown in Table 2, the coefficient v_1 can be represented with fewer bits

Table 2. Difference indicator bits c of the sparse coefficient v_1.

Difference dif	Difference indicator bits c
dif=0	"0"
dif=1	"10"
dif>1	"11"

by the difference dif. When the difference dif is greater than 1, 11 bits are used to record the coefficient v_1 completely, $n_i^{v_1} = 11$. When the difference dif is 0 or 1, the coefficient v_1 does not need to be recorded, $n_i^{v_1} = 0$. An indicator bit f is used to indicate the symbol of the coefficient v_2, and $n_i^{v_2}$ bits are used to represent the difference between v_1 and v_2. The subsequent processing is the same as the first block. For the last block, there is no next embedded block, the first n_i^b bits are all set to 0. In each block, the sparse coefficients and the corresponding positions occupy n_i^v, n_i^p bits respectively, n_i^d bits are room for data, as expressed in the following equations.

$$n_i^v = \begin{cases} 11 + n_i^s + n_i^{v_2} + 1, & i = 1 \\ n_i^c + n_i^{v_1} + n_i^{v_2} + 2, & i \neq 1 \end{cases} \tag{8}$$

$$n_i^p = n_i^{p_1} + n_i^{p_2} + 1 \tag{9}$$

$$n_i^d = 8n^2 - n_i^b - n_i^v - n_i^p \tag{10}$$

M bits are vacated in Type A, the calculation is shown in Eq. (11). Note that after the data is embedded, the LSBs in the first row are replaced by the first embedded block position of Type A, the replaced LSBs are embedded as additional information.

$$M = \sum_{i=1}^{C} n_i^d \tag{11}$$

Figure 4 gives an example comparing the coding method proposed by Cao et al. [26] with the block structure coding. Here, the block size is 4. The sparse coefficients and corresponding positions in a block are given, (701,64) and (−54, 52). Cao et al. [26] converted all coefficients and positions directly into binary, coefficients 701 and −54 accounted for 22 bits, positions 64 and 52 accounted for 12 bits, and 14 bits were used to represent the position of the next embedded block. Each block can free up $n^d = 128 - 2(11 + 6) - 14 = 80$ bits. In the block structure coding, the first 14 bits are used to represent the position of the next embedded block. Here, the difference between the coefficient −54 and the coefficient v_1 of the previous block is 0, the first code "0" means that the coefficients v_1 are equal. The second code "0" means the coefficient 701 is positive, and "01010111101" is used to represent the coefficient 701. Recording whether the order of the embedding coefficients is correct, the code "0" indicates the reverse embedding order. Using "110011" to represent the smaller position 52,

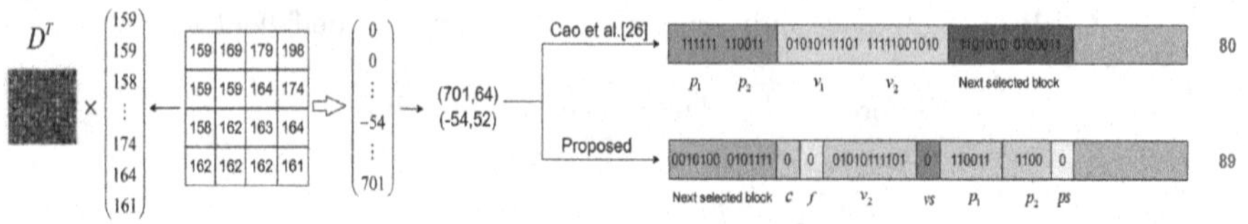

Fig. 4. Comparison between the coding method of Cao et al. [26] and proposed block structure coding method.

"1100" to represent the difference 12 between the positions, the code "0" indicates the reverse embedding order of positions.

In the example, the proposed method can free up 89 bits, 9 more than the method of Cao et al. [26]. If the difference of the coefficients or positions is smaller, the more room of the method will free up.

For the blocks in Type B, the error coding length is greater than the threshold T, the image I_B with size $N_{B_1} \times N_{B_2}$ is reconstructed. The block classification coding proposed by Qin et al. [29] is adopted. The size of the image I_B is as follows.

$$\begin{cases} N_{B_1} = n \times \lfloor (S - C)/(N_2/n) \rfloor \\ N_{B_2} = N_2 \end{cases} \tag{12}$$

The data hider embeds all the data in the room vacated by Type A and B. The additional information msg such as error and dictionary, and the secret data are embedded through different embedding methods into the two types of blocks. When the room M is larger than the additional information, Type A is embedded with additional information msg and part of secret data, Type B is embedded with the remaining secret data. On the contrary, Type A is embedded with part of additional information, Type B is embedded with the remaining additional information and secret data. Data embedding in both cases is shown in the Fig. 5.

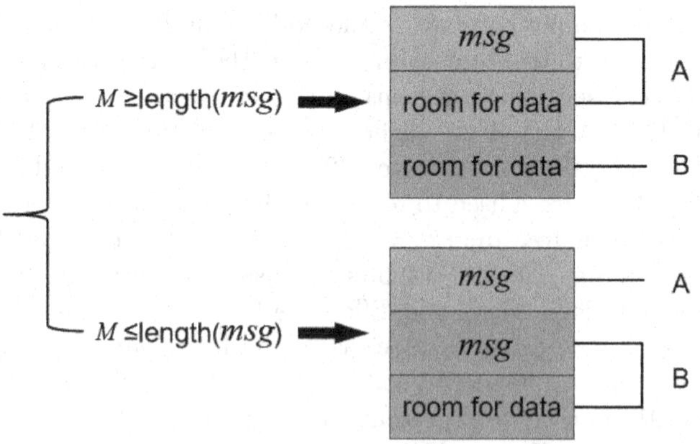

Fig. 5. Two cases of data embedding.

2.3 Data Extraction and Image Recovery

According to the different possession of the keys, there will exist three situations for the receiver: 1) Only possessing the data hiding key k_d; 2) Only possessing the encryption key k_e; 3) Possessing data hiding key k_d and encryption key k_e.

Only Possessing the Data Hiding Key k_d. If the receiver only has the data hiding key k_d, the position of the first block in Type A is extracted firstly. The data embedded in the blocks of Type A is extracted by the block structure coding based on the difference of sparse coefficients. For the blocks in Type B, the data embedded in Type B is extracted by the method of block classification coding. Using the data hiding key k_d to recover the data. The extracted data is lossless, and the content of images is not accessed during the entire extraction process.

Only Possessing the Encryption Ky k_e. If the receiver only has the encryption key k_e, different methods are adopted to recover the encrypted image blocks according to the type where the block belongs. For Type A, the sparse coefficients are extracted and combined with the dictionary to form blocks. For Type B, the blocks are recovered according to the block classification coding. The complete encrypted image is obtained by combining the blocks of Type A and Type B. The encrypted image is decrypted using the encryption key k_e to obtain the original image.

Possessing Data Hiding Key k_d and Encryption Key k_e. If the receiver has both the data hiding key k_d and the encryption key k_e, the data hiding key k_d is used to recover the data extracted from Type A and Type B, and the encryption key k_e is used to decrypt the encrypted image to get the original image. In the process, the extracted data and the recovered image are lossless.

3 Experimental Results and Analysis

In this section, a series of experiments are performed to evaluate the performance of the RDHEI-BCCSR scheme. Eight classic images are used, as shown in Fig. 6. In order to reduce the impact of selecting test images at random, the scheme also tested on the three datasets: BOSSbase, BOWS-2 and ImageNet-dog, where ImageNet-dog is the dataset about dog in ImageNet [30]. To verify the performance of the scheme, through the embedding ratio (ER), the peak signal-to-noise ratio (PSNR) and the structural similarity index measurement (SSIM) between the original image and the recovered image to prove the superiority of the scheme.

3.1 Analysis of Adaptive Threshold

For different images, the embedding rate obtained by using different thresholds is different. If the blocks can be well represented by the dictionary, the efficiency of the RDHEI-BCCSR scheme is higher than the scheme proposed by Cao et al. [26]; conversely, it is lower. With the change of the threshold from small to large,

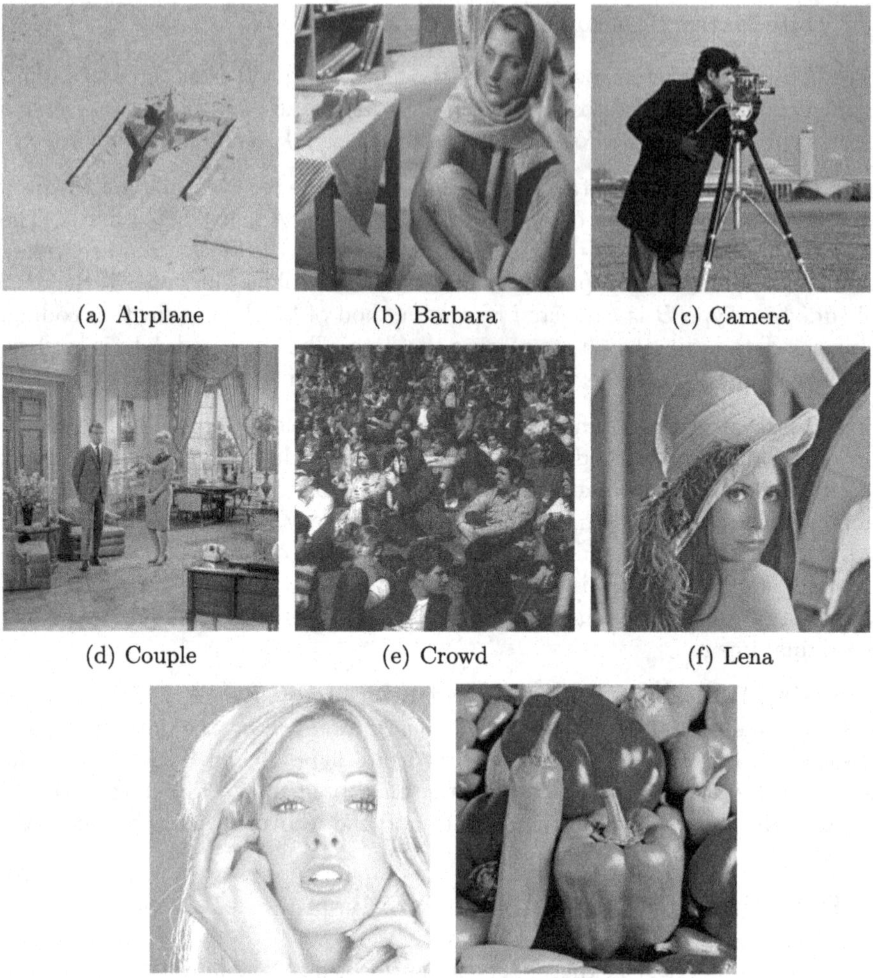

(a) Airplane (b) Barbara (c) Camera

(d) Couple (e) Crowd (f) Lena

(g) Tiffany (h) Peppers

Fig. 6. Eight test images. (a) Airplane, (b) Barbara, (c) Camera, (d) Couple, (e) Crowd, (f) Lena, (g) Tiffany, (h) Peppers.

the embedding rate also changes. As shown in Fig. 7, it is clear that regardless of the magnitude of the change in the embedding rate, there will be a change of first rising and then decreasing.

Table 3 shows the relationship between the embedding rate and threshold of eight images. The peak in each image is similar, almost all in the interval [60,70]. Data fitting is performed on the thresholds of 20580 images to find the relationship among the optimal threshold, the maximum and minimum of error coding length. The specific relationship is shown in Eq. (13).

$$T = \lfloor 0.4 * l_{min} - 0.1 * l_{max} + 81.3 \rfloor \tag{13}$$

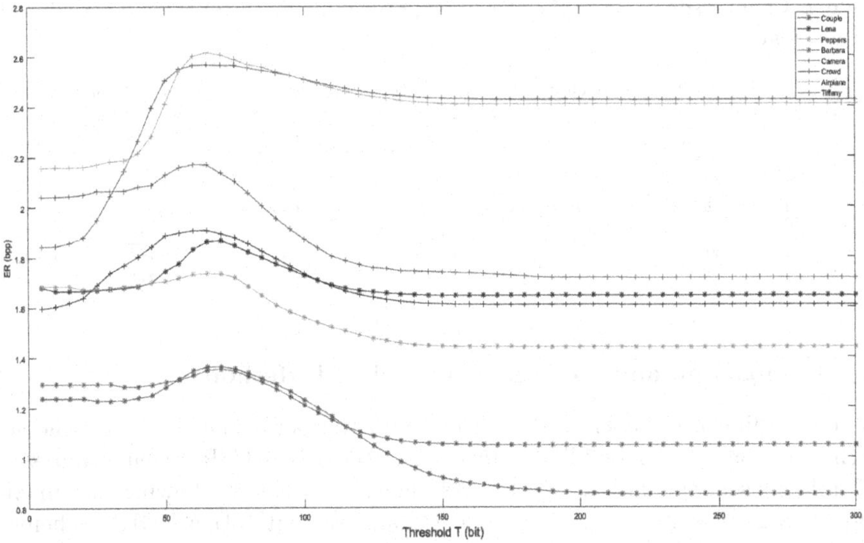

Fig. 7. Embedding rate corresponding to the threshold of error coding length on eight images.

Table 3. Relation between threshold T and embedding rate (bpp) of eight images.

Images	Threshold T									
	T=10	T=20	T=30	T=40	T=50	T=60	T=70	T=80	T=90	T=100
Airplane	2.1594	2.1607	2.1838	2.2144	2.4114	2.6030	2.6086	2.5696	2.5406	2.5090
Barbara	1.2382	1.2382	1.2296	1.2411	1.2832	1.3488	1.3658	1.3385	1.2933	1.2323
Camera	1.8459	1.8789	2.0448	2.2632	2.5050	2.5670	2.5667	2.5557	2.5370	2.5109
Couple	1.2954	1.2954	1.2954	1.2859	1.3043	1.3306	1.3558	1.3258	1.2755	1.2116
Crowd	1.6038	1.6388	1.7385	1.8029	1.8868	1.9083	1.8953	1.8559	1.7956	1.7337
Lena	1.6655	1.6655	1.6731	1.6841	1.7456	1.8340	1.8666	1.8229	1.7750	1.7278
Tiffany	2.0426	2.0502	2.0647	2.0811	2.1282	2.1707	2.1362	2.0566	1.9557	1.8732
Peppers	1.6848	1.6717	1.6771	1.6862	1.7040	1.7325	1.7351	1.6854	1.6107	1.5608

Table 4 shows the comparison between the embedding rate of fitting threshold and actual embedding rate of eight images. The optimal threshold is obtained through the maximum and minimum error coding length. It can be seen that the fitting threshold is very close to the optimal threshold, the error of corresponding embedding rate is also very small, about 0.01 bpp. The fitting threshold can be considered as the optimal threshold of the image. Different images have different maximum and minimum error coding lengths, so each image has a different threshold, the threshold changes adaptively.

Table 4. Comparison between the embedding rate of fitting threshold and actual peak on eight images.

Images	l_{min} (bit)	l_{max} (bit)	Fitting threshold (bit)	Fitting ER (bpp)	Actual threshold (bit)	Actual ER (bpp)	Error (bpp)
Airplane	4	215	61	2.6127	67	2.6185	0.0058
Barbara	22	217	68	1.3644	70	1.3658	0.0014
Camera	1	201	61	2.5682	66	2.5697	0.0015
Couple	33	191	76	1.3463	70	1.3558	0.0095
Crowd	1	167	64	1.9063	63	1.9116	0.0053
Lena	6	166	67	1.8615	69	1.8688	0.0073
Tiffany	1	215	59	2.1778	62	2.1804	0.0026
Peppers	19	177	71	1.7328	67	1.7441	0.0113

3.2 Comparison and Analysis with Related Methods

The embedding rate (ER) is used to evaluate the performance of the scheme. In this section, the embedding rate of the RDHEI-BCCSR scheme and several related schemes are compared. As shown in Table 5, showing the maximum embedding rates of eight test images compared with other RDHEI schemes [26,31–35].

As can be seen from Table 5, the RDHEI-BCCSR scheme has a higher embedding rate than other schemes. Compared with the scheme of Cao et al. [26], the embedding rate of image Tiffany has been improved by about 1 bpp, reaching 2.1804 bpp. The image Peppers has improved by about 0.8 bpp. It shows that the RDHEI-BCCSR scheme fully utilizes the room wasted by repeatedly expressing sparse coefficients. Compared with the other five schemes, the embedding rate of the RDHEI-BCCSR scheme has also been improved to a certain extent.

Table 5. Comparison of embedding rate between the RDHEI-BCCSR scheme and other schemes on eight images.

Images	Cao et al. [26]	Liu et al. [31]	Fu et al. [32]	Chen [33]	Wang et al. [34]	Li et al. [35]	RDHEI-BCCSR
Airplane	2.3000	2.0259	2.5154	2.5771	0.8470	0.6779	2.6185
Barbara	1.3000	1.1973	1.3546	0.8625	0.2515	0.9008	1.3658
Camera	2.2000	1.7374	2.3504	2.0338	0.5922	0.7147	2.5697
Couple	1.1000	1.2370	1.2861	1.0368	0.4350	0.9306	1.3558
Crowd	1.6000	1.4643	1.6845	1.5392	0.6735	0.7937	1.9116
Lena	1.7000	1.5833	1.8183	1.4177	0.7003	0.8657	1.8688
Tiffany	1.1000	1.9175	2.0406	1.7000	0.1890	0.8348	2.1804
Peppers	0.9000	1.5858	1.5769	1.3586	0.1666	0.8980	1.7441

In addition, in order to reduce the influence caused by random selection of test images, the detailed embedding rates of the proposed scheme in the three datasets are shown in Table 6. In the best case, the embedding rates of the RDHTI-BCCSR scheme were 5.3887 bpp, 4.5322 bpp and 4.8694 bpp, respectively. If the original image can be represented by the dictionary optimally, the error is smaller, the embedding rate can reach about 5 bpp in the best case. If

Table 6. The embedding rate of the RDHEI-BCCSR scheme on the three datasets.

Datasets	Indicators	Best case	Worst case	Average
BOSSbase	ER(bpp)	5.3887	0.0529	2.5367
	PSNR(dB)	$+\infty$	$+\infty$	$+\infty$
	SSIM	1	1	1
BOWS-2	ER(bpp)	4.5322	0.0235	2.3845
	PSNR(dB)	$+\infty$	$+\infty$	$+\infty$
	SSIM	1	1	1
ImageNet-dog	ER(bpp)	4.8694	0.1306	2.1149
	PSNR(dB)	$+\infty$	$+\infty$	$+\infty$
	SSIM	1	1	1

the original image is poorly represented by the dictionary, the error is larger, the embedding rate less than 0.1 bpp in the worst case. In summary, the average embedding rate of the RDHEI-BCCSR scheme can still reach more than 2.3 bpp on the three datasets. Moreover, PSNR is $+\infty$ and SSIM is 1, the scheme is reversible and can recover the image lossless.

Figure 8 shows the results of the RDHEI-BCCSR scheme on the image Camera, the embedding rate can reach 2.5697 bpp. Figure 8(b) is the encrypted image, which is obtained by block scrambling. The secret data is embedded in the encrypted image to obtain the marked image. Figure 8(d) shows the decrypted image, it is visually similar with original image due to lower distortion. When the receiver has the encryption key and the data hiding key at the same time, the image can be fully recovered, the recovered image Fig. 8(e) is obtained.

Figure 9 compares the average embedding rate of the RDHEI-BCCSR scheme with the related schemes in the three datasets. Li et al. [35] used the prediction model of bilinear regression for a single bit plane to predict the five pixels around a pixel, so the embedding rate was lower than 1 bpp. Wang et al. [34] took advantage of the strong correlation between pixels in the block. Some blocks exist that were not embeddable, and the auxiliary information occupied too much room, the embedding rate was not too high. Liu et al. [31] used the block classification, and Chen [33] performed Huffman coding for the error of pixels. Fu et al. [32] took advantage of the correlation in blocks and adopted adaptive block coding, which greatly improved the embedding rate. Cao et al. [26] adopted fixed length coding of sparse coefficients, many coefficients were repeatedly expressed, resulting in a certain waste of room. The RDHEI-BCCSR scheme solves the problem. As can be seen from Fig. 9, the average embedding rate of the scheme proposed by Cao et al. [26] in the three datasets is about 1.8 bpp, while the RDHEI-BCCSR scheme reaches above 2.3 bpp. In the BOSSbase, the average embedding rate even reaches 2.5 bpp, significantly improving the embedding rate. Based on the above analysis, the proposed RDHEI-BCCSR scheme has better performance.

(a) Original image (b) Encrypted image (c) Marked image

(d) Decrypted image (e) Recovered image

Fig. 8. Experimental results of the RDHEI-BCCSR scheme on the image Camera. (a) Original image, (b) Encrypted image, (c) Marked image, (d) Decrypted image, (e) Recovered image.

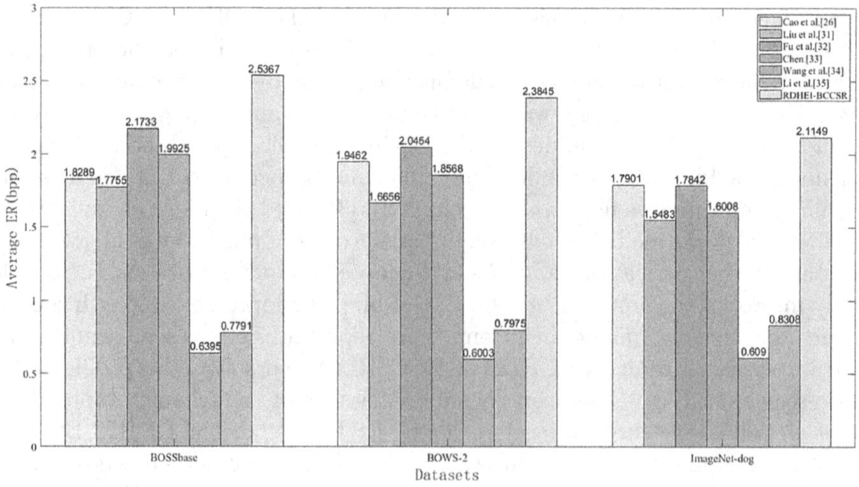

Fig. 9. Comparison of embedding rate between the RDHEI-BCCSR method and other methods on the three datasets.

4 Conclusion

In this paper, we propose a scheme based on block classification coding of sparse representation (RDHEI-BCCSR). Through adaptive threshold of error coding length, the blocks are divided into two types. And different embedding methods are used for blocks of different types. The embedding ability of the scheme is significantly improved compared with several related RDHEI schemes. For the receiver, data extraction and image recovery are separable and lossless, which is conducive to the flexible application of the scheme. In the future, we will study more effective schemes based on sparse coefficients to further improve the embedding ability.

Acknowledgements. The work was supported in part by the National Natural Science Foundation of China under Grant 62272002 and Grant U1936220, the University Synergy Innovation Program of Anhui Province under Grant GXXT-2022-049, and Anhui Provincial Natural Science Foundation (Grant No. 2008085MF187). The authors are very grateful to the anonymous referees for their detailed comments and suggestions regarding this paper.

References

1. Su, W., Ni, J., Hu, X., Fridrich, J.J.: Image steganography with symmetric embedding using Gaussian Markov random field model. IEEE Trans. Circuits Syst. Video Technol. **31**, 1001–1015 (2021)
2. Sarmah, D.K., Kulkarni, A.J.: JPEG based steganography methods using cohort intelligence with cognitive computing and modified multi random start local search optimization algorithms. Inf. Sci. **430**, 378–396 (2018)
3. Yuan, H.: Secret sharing with multi-cover adaptive steganography. Inf. Sci. **254**, 197–212 (2014)
4. Wu, F., Zhou, X., Chen, Z., Yang, B.: A reversible data hiding scheme for encrypted images with pixel difference encoding. Knowl. Based Syst. **234**, 107583 (2021)
5. Du, Y., Yin, Z.: New framework for code-mapping-based reversible data hiding in JPEG images. Inf. Sci. **609**, 319–338 (2020)
6. Li, F., Zhang, L., Qin, C., Wu, K.: Reversible data hiding for JPEG images with minimum additive distortion. Inf. Sci. **595**, 142–158 (2022)
7. Xiong, X., Chen, Y., Fan, M., Zhong, S.: Adaptive reversible data hiding algorithm for interpolated images using sorting and coding. J. Inf. Secur. Appl. **66**, 103137 (2022)
8. Chang, Q., Li, X., Zhao, Y., Ni, R.: Adaptive pairwise prediction-error expansion and multiple histograms modification for reversible data hiding. IEEE Trans. Circuits Syst. Video Technol. **31**, 4850–4863 (2021)
9. Shanableh, T.: Data hiding in MPEG video files using multivariate regression and flexible macroblock ordering. IEEE Trans. Inf. Forensics Secur. **7**(2), 455–464 (2012)
10. Bhaskar, T., Oruganti, M.: Reversible data hiding scheme for video. Int. J. Inf. Secur. Priv. **13**, 1–13 (2019)
11. Mat Kiah, M.L., Bahaa, B., Zaidan, A., Ahmed, M., Al-Bakri, S.: A review of audio based steganography and digital watermarking. Int. J. Phys. Sci. **6**(16), 3837–3850 (2011)

12. Zhong, S., Cheng, X., Chen, T.: Data hiding in a kind of PDF texts for secret communication. Int. J. Netw. Secur. **4**, 17–26 (2007)
13. Satir, E., Isik, H.: A compression-based text steganography method. Multim. Tools Appl. **85**(10), 2385–2394 (2012)
14. Rahman, M., Hamada, M.: A prediction-based lossless image compression procedure using dimension reduction and Huffman coding. Multim. Tools Appl. **82**, 4081–4105 (2022)
15. Wei, Z., Niu, B., Xiao, H., He, Y.: Isolated points prediction via deep neural network on point cloud lossless geometry compression. IEEE Trans. Circuits Syst. Video Technol. **33**, 407–420 (2023)
16. Ding, W., Zhang, H., Reulke, R., Wang, Y.: Reversible image data hiding based on scalable difference expansion. Pattern Recogn. Lett. **159**, 116–124 (2022)
17. Mandal, P.C., Mukherjee, I., Chatterji, B.N.: High capacity reversible and secured data hiding in images using interpolation and difference expansion technique. Multim. Tools Appl. **80**, 3623–3644 (2020)
18. Li, Q., Wang, X., Pei, Q.: A robust reversible watermarking scheme overcomes the misalignment problem of generalized histogram shifting. Multim. Tools Appl. **82**, 7207–7227 (2022)
19. Xie, X.Z., Chang, C., Hu, Y.C.: An adaptive reversible data hiding scheme based on prediction error histogram shifting by exploiting signed-digit representation. Multim. Tools Appl. **79**, 24329–24346 (2020)
20. Jia, Y., Yin, Z., Zhang, X., Luo, Y.: Reversible data hiding based on reducing invalid shifting of pixels in histogram shifting. Signal Process. **163**, 238–246 (2019)
21. Zhang, X.: Reversible data hiding in encrypted image. IEEE Signal Process. Lett. **18**(4), 255–258 (2011)
22. Tang, Z., Xu, S., Yao, H., Qin, C., Zhang, X.: Reversible data hiding with differential compression in encrypted image. Multim. Tools Appl. **78**, 9691–9715 (2018)
23. Qiu, Y., Ying, Q., Yang, Y., Zeng, H., Li, S., Qian, Z.: High-capacity framework for reversible data hiding in encrypted image using pixel prediction and entropy encoding. IEEE Trans. Circuits Syst. Video Technol. **32**(9), 5874–5887 (2022)
24. Ma, K., Zhang, W., Zhao, X., Yu, N., Li, F.: Reversible data hiding in encrypted images by reserving room before encryption. IEEE Trans. Inf. Forensics Secur. **8**(3), 553–562 (2013)
25. Zhang, W., Ma, K., Yu, N.: Reversibility improved data hiding in encrypted images. Signal Process. **94**, 118–127 (2014)
26. Cao, X., Du, L., Wei, X., Meng, D., Guo, X.: High capacity reversible data hiding in encrypted images by patch-level sparse representation. IEEE Trans. Cybernet. **46**(5), 1132–1143 (2016)
27. Aharon, M., Elad, M., Bruckstein, A.: K-SVD: An algorithm for designing overcomplete dictionaries for sparse representation. IEEE Trans. Signal Process. **54**(11), 4311–4322 (2006)
28. Rubinstein, R., Peleg, T., Elad, M.: Analysis K-SVD: a dictionary-learning algorithm for the analysis sparse model. IEEE Trans. Signal Process. **61**(3), 661–677 (2013)
29. Qin, C., Qian, X., Hong, W., Zhang, X.: An efficient coding scheme for reversible data hiding in encrypted image with redundancy transfer. Inf. Sci. **487**, 176–192 (2019)
30. Deng, J., Dong, W., Socher, R., Li, L.J., Li, K., Li, F.F.: Imagenet: a large-scale hierarchical image database. In: 2009 IEEE Conference on Computer Vision and Pattern Recognition, pp. 248–255 (2009)

31. Liu, Z.L., Pun, C.M.: Reversible data-hiding in encrypted images by redundant space transfer. Inf. Sci. **433**, 188–203 (2018)
32. Fu, Y., Kong, P., Yao, H., Tang, Z., Qin, C.: Effective reversible data hiding in encrypted image with adaptive encoding strategy. Inf. Sci. **494**, 21–36 (2019)
33. Chen, K.M.: High capacity reversible data hiding based on the compression of pixel differences. Mathematics **8**, 1435 (2020)
34. Wang, Y., Cai, Z., He, W.: High capacity reversible data hiding in encrypted image based on intra-block lossless compression. IEEE Trans. Multim. **23**, 1466–1473 (2021)
35. Li, F., Zhu, H., Yu, J., Qin, C.: Double linear regression prediction based reversible data hiding in encrypted images. Multim. Tools Appl. **80**(2), 2141–2159 (2021)

Signcryption-Based Encrypted Traffic Detection Scheme for Fast Establishing Secure Connections

Hao Zhu[1], Fagen Li[2], Lihui Liu[3], Yong Zeng[1], Xiaoli Li[1](✉), and Jianfeng Ma[1]

[1] School of Cyber Engineering, Xidian University, Xi'an 710071, China
yzeng@mail.xidian.edu.cn, lixl_aurora@163.com

[2] School of Computer Science and Engineering, University of Electronic Science and Technology, Chengdu 611731, China
fagenli@uestc.edu.cn

[3] WuHan Marine Communication Research Institute, Wuhan 430000, China

Abstract. The popularity of Internet traffic encryption has made encrypted traffic detection becoming a hot topic in the present academic community. Due to its fine-grained detection strategy that avoids the influence of traffic shaping, the encrypted payload detection method based on deep packet inspection (DPI) can obtain better detection results when compared to machine learning detection methods based on traffic features. Yet, existing DPI-based methods will cause non-negligible delays due to encryption in real-time scenarios. Signcryption can improve the delay in DPI-based detection scenarios. However, existing signcryption schemes fail to resolve the conflict between the correctness of detection results and message confidentiality. This paper proposes an encrypted traffic detection scheme based on signcryption that can effectively reduce latency. Furthermore, in the high concurrency scenario, the gateway is introduced to replace the client to complete the preprocessing protocol with the middle agent, avoiding the execution of preprocessing protocols between each client and the middle agent, thus reducing the latency caused by excessive calculation. In this paper, the algorithms of rule signcryption, preprocessing protocol, client processing packet, and traffic detection are designed for this scheme. The confidentiality and unforgeability of the scheme are analyzed by the random oracle model. Finally, through simulation experiments, our scheme significantly improves the delay problem in the preprocessing phase compared with the state-of-the-art methods.

Keywords: Signcryption · Encrypted traffic inspection · Middlebox privacy

1 Introduction

With the rapid development of the Internet, computer applications have become widespread in our daily life. However, to provide better convenience to users,

M. Zhang et al. (Eds.): ProvSec 2023, LNCS 14217, pp. 44–63, 2023.
https://doi.org/10.1007/978-3-031-45513-1_3

these applications often collect users' private information, making them susceptible to criminal attacks. Therefore, encrypted traffic is increasingly being used for network security defense. Encrypted transmission protocols like HTTPS, TLS, and VPN can protect messages from eavesdropping and man-in-the-middle (MitM) attacks [5,15,26]. Nevertheless, malicious traffic also leverages encryption to conceal its activities, such as malicious payload or command-and-control delivery, and data leakage [20,24]. According to the literature [2], more than 60% of network traffic is currently encrypted with TLS/SSL, of which malicious traffic accounts for more than 10%. Encryption blurs the distinction between normal and malicious traffic and poses serious threats to network security. With the rise of the sixth-generation mobile communication technology (6G), a multi-heterogeneous network architecture working together and a diversified network with unlimited connections of massive heterogeneous terminals make the boundary between normal traffic and abnormal traffic more unclear [11]. As a result, one of the hottest research in the field of cyberspace security is the detection of encrypted traffic.

At present, there are two main methods for detecting encrypted traffic: methods based on traffic behavior features and methods based on deep packet inspection (DPI) of encrypted traffic payloads. Behavioral feature-based detection schemes rely on features such as IP, port, entropy distribution, and other communication characteristics to identify traffic [1,25]. However, the advent of traffic shaping [8,14] has reduced the accuracy of this approach, especially for those based on machine learning. On the other hand, DPI-based traffic detection schemes incorporate third-party detection in the communication network and use transparent agents to identify encrypted traffic, which can avoid the impact of traffic shaping. Therefore, DPI-based traffic inspection schemes have gained more and more attention. The initial approach was to read the content of user data by decrypting the message, as demonstrated by Radivilova *et al.* [19], who used this approach to detect malicious behavior transmitted over the SSL/TLS protocol. However, the decryption-then-detection is not suitable for all scenarios, while decryption changes the original purpose of encryption to protect data privacy.

Sherry *et al.* [21] have proposed BlindBox, which directly detects the ciphertext payload without being aware of the data packets' behavior characteristics. By using keyword search to find malicious information and avoiding the problem of the decrease in detection accuracy caused by the changed traffic behavior characteristics, it protects sensitive information. As shown in Fig. 1, the client first establishes a normal TLS connection to the server using the obfuscated circuit and roblivious transfer randomly encrypt rules, and then performs deep packet inspection on the encrypted token generated by the traffic. Due to the obfuscation circuit, the time for BlindBox to compute rule encryption is proportional to the number of attack rules. Therefore, it is appropriate for setups that use long or persistent connections rather than actual short, independent streams. Inspired by the literature [21], researchers have designed several improved ciphertext matching detection methods, such as PrivDPI [17], Pine [16], P2DPI [13], and so on. Ning *et al.* [17] proposed a deep packet inspection method based on

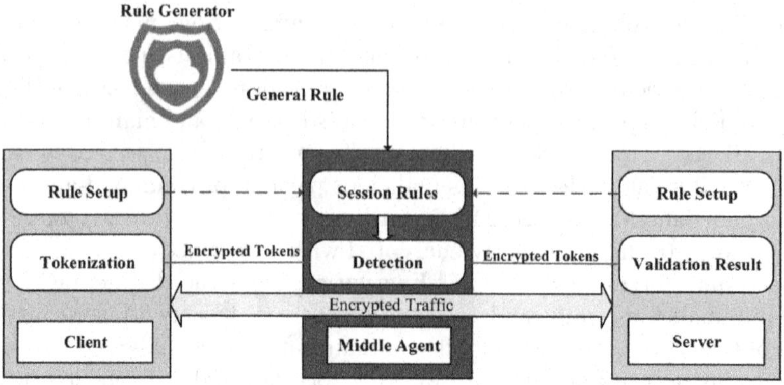

Fig. 1. DPI-based encrypted traffic detection model

reusable fuzzy rules called PrivDPI, which optimizes BlindBox and uses multi-party secure computation to re-encrypt the rules with session keys. The time it takes for the system to initialize rules can be reduce by reusing the created obfuscation rules in subsequent sessions. However, experiments in [17] show that PrivDPI generates ciphertext tokens 6 times slower than BlindBox, resulting in slightly higher communication overhead during system initialization than the obfuscated circuit approach [21]. Nevertheless, for smaller rule domains, the PrivDPI is susceptible to brute force attacks [16]. In the literature [13], homomorphic properties were used to increase the effectiveness of session rule preparation. By using homomorphism, the signature of this technique can also be further implemented, increasing the total effectiveness of both encryption and signatures [7]. These schemes are based on traditional public key encryption. Specifically, the message is first encrypted and then digitally signed and transmitted over a public network. However, this encryption method has the disadvantage of being inefficient and computationally intensive because it requires encryption-then-signature.

In order to solve the delay problem caused by encryption-then-signature, this paper introduces signcryption to improve the computational overhead and increase the efficiency of DPI system, as illustrated in Fig. 1. Because signcryption [27] combines encryption and signature in a single logical step, it can significantly lower computation costs, corresponding research findings have emerged in the fields of the Internet of Things, cloud computing, blockchain [4,6,12], and so on. But it is worth noting that detection rules are usually encrypted with the public key of rule generators to protect the security and privacy of the rules in Fig. 1. Therefore, the existing signcryption approach is unsuitable for DPI-based encrypted traffic detection scenarios for the following two reasons. To begin, if the sender uses the server's public key to signcrypt the message, the third party (Middle Agent) cannot guarantee the correctness of the equality detection for encrypted traffic because the detection rules and traffic are signcrypted with separate keys. Second, if the sender uses the third party's public key to signcrypt the message, the third party can decrypt the ciphertext, hence this approach does not satisfy the confidentiality requirements. As a result, this paper designs a suitable signcryption scheme according to the deep packet inspection scenario. Additionally, with the development of high concurrency scenarios, PriDPI and P2DPI methods require a considerable amount of encryption and signature computation. The computation latency grows exponentially with the number of users. A gateway similar to the literature [16] is added in this paper to further improve the HTTPS connection. The gateway is used to connect with the middle agent, which avoids the interaction between each client and the middle agent and decreases the computational consumption.

The delay issue with DPI-based encrypted traffic detection is addressed in this paper by the proposal of a signcryption-based encrypted traffic detection scheme for fast establishing secure connections (STDS). The main contributions are as follows:

- To address the delay problem of existing DPI-based traffic detection schemes, this paper adopts signcryption to design the encryption and signature scheme instead of the traditional encryption-then-signature, which can complete the encryption and signature of messages faster.
- In high concurrency scenarios, this paper uses a new gateway instead of the client to execute TLS connections with the middle agent. It improves the initial connection and reduces session latency while maintaining rules and data privacy.
- Under the random oracle model, this paper proves that the scheme is confidentiality and unforgeability through security analysis, and verifies that the scheme can successfully reduce the delay in the initial stage of the client through simulation.

2 System Overview

2.1 System Model

The system model of this scheme is shown in Fig. 2, which mainly includes five entities: rule generator, client, gateway, server, and middle agent. The client (C) and the external server (S) are normal endpoints for sending and receiving TLS-protected network traffic. The rule generators (RG) are typically implemented by organizations such as Symantec [23], which generates attack rule tuples for middle agents. Each attack rule describes an attack, which contains one or more keywords to be matched in network traffic. The middle agent (MA) can use the attack rule tuples to detect attack behaviors in network traffic, which is a network device that inspects and filters network traffic using attack rule tuples published by a rule generator. The new gateway (G) in the communication network is a device located between a group of clients and servers, which connects the clients with external servers.

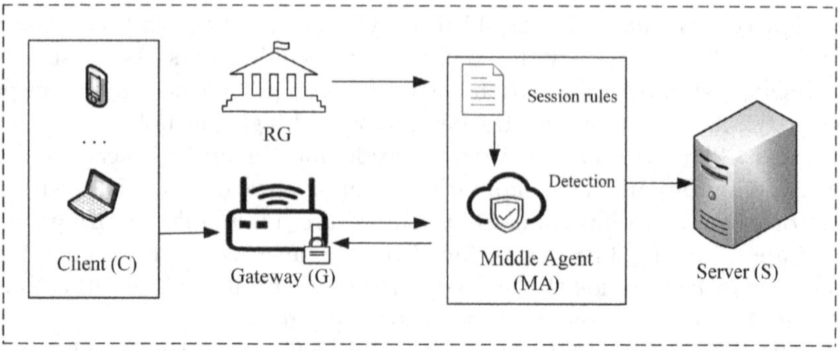

Fig. 2. Framework of encrypted traffic detection system for fast establishing secure connections

2.2 Threat Model

There are three types of threat models considered in this scheme: malicious client or server (known as endpoint), the attacker at the middle agent and the attacker at the gateway. We assume that one of the endpoints is honest because two malicious endpoints can negotiate a session key to communicate using a well-established encryption scheme, which is not practical.

The attacker at the gateway: The gateway setup is similar to other conventional computer network setups. In this paper, we make the assumption that the gateway serves as the sole point of contact between the internal network and external servers. Specifically, it is a semi-honest model in which the gateway honestly follows the protocol negotiated for communication delivery, but it tries to learn the plaintext of the traffic and infers detection rules.

The attacker at the middle agent: As in literature [17], this paper considers the middle agent as a semi-honest model. It strictly performs traffic detection, but tries to obtain user private information and infer detection rules based on sensitive information in encrypted traffic. Furthermore, because it is deployed in an untrusted environment, there is a risk of hacking and eavesdropping. The goal of the system is for middle agents to perform DPI without obtaining the message. It may recover the partial or complete content or rule after the middle agent is aware of any rule or token. Therefore, we need to protect encryption rules and data privacy from leaking.

Malicious communication endpoint: Assume that either the client or the server is a malicious endpoint. Its ultimate purpose is to conceal malicious behavior and evade detection, for example, by generating encrypted tokens that do not match actual traffic. And even a normal client might try to get the detection rules out of curiosity. In this model, the communication user and the middle agent are independent of each other, and the middle agent cannot cooperate with the user to output malicious behavior.

3 The Proposed System

According to the communication process, the construction of this scheme includes rule preparation, preprocessing protocol, client processing message, token detection, and token verification. The parameter symbols involved in the scheme are shown in Table 1:

Table 1. Notation

Symbol	Description
p	p is a large prime number
q	q is a large prime factor of $p-1$
Z_q^*	Z_q^* is a non-zero multiplicative group of q
g	g is a generator of the group $\mathbb{G}$
H	A one-way *hash* function
H_i	A one-way *hash* function with key i
k	k is a security parameter, $k \in Z_p$
y	y is the session key in the TLS handshake
r_i	Detecion rules generated by RG, $i \in$ [N]
I_i	Fuzzy rules on the middle agent, $i \in$ [N]
R_i	Session rule, $i \in$ [N]
g^u	g^u is a key of G, $u \in Z_q^*$
w/g^w	Private/public key of RG, $w \in Z_p$
c/g^c	Client's private/public key, $c \in Z_q^*$
s/g^s	Server's private/public key, $s \in Z_q^*$
$E_k()/D_k()$	Symmetric encryption/decryption algorithm, k is the key

3.1 Rule Signcryption Algorithm

Before communication, the gateway (G) chooses a key g^u, where $u \in Z_q^*$. It subscribes the encrypted traffic detection service from the rule generator (RG) and sends u to RG. After receiving the subscription from G, RG generates two encrypted random number w and k, where w, $k \in Z_p$. The rule preparation algorithm uses the key provided by G and the random number selected by RG to generate the rule signcryption key pair K_{r_1}, K_{r_2}, then RG signcrypt the rule $r_i(r_i \in R, i \in [\text{N}])$ in the rule domain R, and sends the encrypted rule tuple (C_r, v_r, s_r, k) to the middle agent (MA). The details of the algorithm are shown in Algorithm 1. In processing rules, the one-way *hash* function can hide the rule information, and the plaintext of the rules cannot be obtained by reverse decryption. And since MA cannot know g^u, it cannot brute force the content of the rule by selecting keywords.

Algorithm 1. Rule Signcryption Algorithm

Input: RG input u, and selects random number $w, k \in Z_p$
Output: Signcryption tuple (C_r, v_r, s_r, k)
1: Compute: $U = g^u$
2: $K_{r_1} = hash\,(g^{uw})$
3: $K_{r_2} = g^w$
4: $C_r = (g^{H_{K_{r_1}}(r_i)})^k$
5: $v_r = H_{K_{r_2}}(C_r)$
6: $s_r = w/(v_r + u) \bmod q$
7: **return** (C_r, v_r, s_r, k)

3.2 Preprocessing Protocol

In the traditional deep packet inspection system of encrypted traffic, the preprocessing protocol is completed by the client (or server) and the middle agent. Similar to the Pine [16], this paper introduces an entity to quickly establish a connection in order to speed up the TLS connection between the client and the server. The main idea is to make the gateway act as a client representative in the enterprise intranet, and the gateway only needs to perform a preprocessing protocol with the middle agent in advance. After that, the client and the gateway share the necessary parameters need for the connection, and the connection is established quickly, which greatly reduces the calculation and communication overhead of the connection between the client and the server.

The gateway and the middle agent can generate an intermediate reusable mixed rule through the preprocessing protocol. The operation of the protocol is shown in Fig. 3, in which the two sides respectively perform an obfuscation calculation on the rule. The first is that the gateway confuses the rules and performs signature verification on the received encrypted tuple (C_r, v_r, s_r). After the gateway's signature verification is successful, the gateway uses a randomly selected x as the random key to encrypt and obfuscate the rules, and obtain the first obfuscated reusable rule I_1. It is worth noting that the encryption and signature methods are signcryption, so the gateway needs to calculate the relevant security parameters for signature authentication according to its own knowledge. It not only ensures the privacy of the rules but also checks the signature of the rules. For the second obfuscation rule, the middle agent uses the security parameter k provided by RG to calculate $I_2 = I_1/g^k = g^{H_{K_{r1}}(r_i)(k-1)x}$, thus completing the second obfuscation of the detection rule. In order to ensure that the gateway has not tampered with the rules, the middle agent uses the random number g^x of G and the encryption rule C_r of RG to calculate whether the equation $e(g, I_1) = e(g^k, g^{H_{K_{r1}}(r_i)k})$ is true, that is, bilinear pairing is used to check whether the gateway is abnormal.

3.3 Session Rule Generation Algorithm

The client and server negotiate the session key y with the TLS handshake before this phase, and the gateway sends the necessary initial parameters (g^w, g^x, u) to

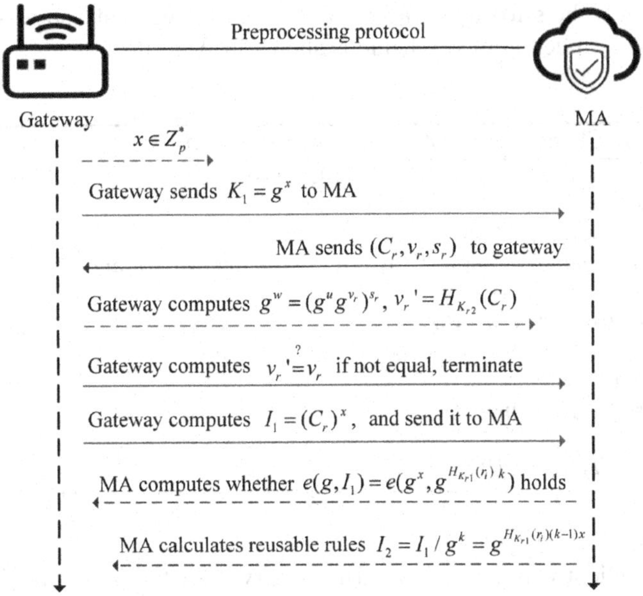

Fig. 3. Preprocessing protocol for middle agent and gateway

the client. The session detection rules are generated according to the reusable rules and session key after two obfuscations in the preprocessing protocol, so they are applicable to this session. The protocol is mainly executed between the client (C), the server (S), and the middle agent (MA). The details of the protocol are shown in Algorithm 2, and only simple calculations are required for each session.

Algorithm 2. Session Rule Generation Algorithm

Input: The client (server) inputs y, and the middle agent inputs I_2
1: C: C computes $K_2 = g^y$, and sends K_2 to MA
2: S: S sends $K_3 = y$ to MA
3: MA: MA checks whether K_2 and g^{K_3} are equal, if so, it calculates the session rule $R_i = (I_2)^{K_3}$

3.4 Client Signcryption Message Algorithm

The client uses signcryption to encrypt and sign messages and tokens. The client first needs to calculate the signcrypted key pair Kc_1, Kc_2 and the parameter $W = g^{xy}$ required for token encryption. Message encryption in this scheme uses AES with the calculated signcryption key Kc_1. For each token $t_i (t_i \in m)$, this scheme uses the **sliding window** algorithm to segment the message, then encrypted them. The detailed scheme is shown in Algorithm 3.

Algorithm 3. Client Signcrypts Message Algorithm

Input: Client inputs g^w, g^x, u, $a(a \in Z_q)$, message m, client private key c, server public key g^s
Output: (C_c, T_i, v_c, s_c, P)
1: Compute key pair $Kc_1 = (g^s)^{ay} \bmod p$, $Kc_2 = hash(g^{wu})$, and $P = g^a$, $W = g^{yu}$
2: Compute $C_c = E_{kc_1}(m)$
3: **for** each toke $t_i(t_i \in m)$ **do**
4: $T_i = (g^{xy})^{H_{kc_2}(t_i)}$
5: $v_c = H(T_i||W)$
6: $s_c = uy/(v_c + c) \bmod q$
7: **end for**
8: **return** (C_c, T_i, v_c, s_c, P)

When the client communicates with the server for the first time, it needs to select a *salt* ($salt \in Z_p$) and send it to the MA along with the first session. Initialize a record table HashTable, let $Cou_t = 0$ to count updated tokens, to prevent frequency analysis attacks caused by multiple identical tokens using deterministic encryption. For the t_i corresponding to each T_i calculated in Algorithm 3, if the token does not exist in the HashTable, calculate $Enc_t = H\ (salt,\ T_i)$, and insert the record (t_i, T_i, Cou_t) in the HashTable; If t_i exists in the HashTable, update the counter $Cou_t = Cou_t + 1$ and calculate the corresponding value $Enc_t = H\ (salt + Cou_t,\ T_i)$.

3.5 Token Detection

When detecting on the middle agent, the main principle is to achieve the matching of ciphertext, so the same counter is also executed for the session rules. The algorithm description of traffic detection is shown in Algorithm 4, and then a search tree is generated using encryption rules. The token is used to search in the search tree. If a rule matching the token is found, the middle agent takes corresponding actions, such as recording but not forwarding this traffic, and then updates the corresponding encrypted rules in the search tree.

3.6 Token Validation

The server can use the corresponding security parameters and its own private key to calculate the signcryption key pair. After decrypting the message, the token is generated and compared with the received one in the same way. This step is similar to the traditional way of verifying the signature. Malicious clients may try to avoid detection by creating encrypted tokens that do not represent actual traffic. This paper assumes that at least one of the client and server is honest.

Algorithm 4. Preparation Algorithm for Detection Rules

The r_i corresponding to each session rule R_i:
  Initialization:
    let $Cou_r = 0$, MA initializes the count table RuleTable
    compute $Enc_r = H\ (salt,\ R_i)$
    insert Enc_r into RuleTable
  Detection:
    if the token matches the rule, $Cou_r = Cou_r + 1$
    update Enc_r, $Enc_r = H\ (salt + Cou_r,\ R_i)$

Therefore, the scheme in this paper can be used to protect honest web servers from malicious clients, or protect honest clients from malicious web servers.

4 Scheme Analysis

4.1 Formal Security Model

In this scheme, if the signcryption algorithm STDS meets the condition of confidentiality, then the adversary in CCA2 (Adaptive Chosen Ciphertext Attack) will satisfy the ciphertext indistinguishability. If the signcryption algorithm STDS is to achieve the security condition of unforgeability, the adversary satisfies the unforgeability under CMA (Chosen Message Attack). The corresponding security models are given as follows.

The general signcryption scheme [6,27] usually consists of the following three algorithms:

- **Setup:** Enter the security parameter 1^λ, then generate and output the sender's and receiver's key pairs $(sk_s,\ pk_s)$ and $(sk_r,\ pk_r)$.
- **Signcryption:** the sender inputs the message m, the receiver's public key pk_r and the sender's private key sk_s, encrypts the signature, and outputs the signed tuple σ of the ciphertext C.
- **Unsigncryption:** After the receiver receives the signed tuple σ, it uses the private key sk_r, the sender's public key pk_s and related parameters to calculate the signed key pair, and then performs signature verification and decryption to obtain the plaintext m.

Definition 1 (Confidentiality). *In the next game, when the algorithm is attacked and there is no adversary $\mathcal{A}$ that can win the game with a non-negligible probability in the polynomial bounded running time, the STDS is IND-CCA2. We define the game as follows.*

Initial: The challenger $\mathcal{C}$ performs the **setup** algorithm with security parameter k, generates system parameters $params$, and sends it to the adversary $\mathcal{A}$.

Phase 1: The adversary $\mathcal{A}$ adaptively executes a finite series of polynomial-in-time queries, where each query relies on the results of responses to previous queries.

Signcryption query: The $\mathcal{A}$ inquiries signcryption oracle with the signcryptor's public key g^c, the receiver's public key g^s and the message m. $\mathcal{C}$ calculates and sends $\sigma = signcrypt(c, r_1, s_1)$ to $\mathcal{A}$.

Unsigncryption query: The $\mathcal{A}$ inquiries unsigncryption oracle with signcrypted tuple σ. If the tuple σ is legal, $\mathcal{C}$ calculates and sends the message m to $\mathcal{A}$, otherwise return $\perp$.

Challenge: $\mathcal{A}$ outputs two messages m_0, m_1 of the same length and send them to the challenger $\mathcal{C}$ for challenge. The $\mathcal{C}$ randomly chooses $b \in \{0,1\}$, computes $\sigma = signcrypt(m_b, r_1, s_1)$ and returns the result σ to $\mathcal{A}$.

Phase 2: The adversary $\mathcal{A}$ can query the signcryption and unsigncryption oracles as query stage but is prohibited from submitting σ to unsigncryption oracle.

Guess: After the adversary $\mathcal{A}$ adaptively asks a polynomial bounded number of queries again, outputs a bit b'. If b'=b, $\mathcal{A}$ wins the game with the advantage $Adv(\mathcal{A}) = |Pr[b' = b] - 1/2|$.

Definition 2 (Unforgeability). *In the next game, when the algorithm is attacked and there is no adversary $\mathcal{A}$ that can win the game with a non-negligible probability in the polynomial bounded running time, the STDS is EUF-CMA.*

Initial: The challenger $\mathcal{C}$ performs the **setup** algorithm with security parameter k, generates system parameters *params*, and sends it to the adversary $\mathcal{A}$.

Attack: $\mathcal{A}$ makes a polynomially bounded number of signcryption and unsigncryption oracle queries, the signcryption/unsigncryption query here is the same as that of the IND-CCA2 game.

Forgery: $\mathcal{A}$ randomly select a message m^* to send to the challenger. $\mathcal{C}$ calculates ciphertext message $\sigma^* = signcrypt(m^*, r_1, s_1)$. (Let M denote the set of messages asked by the adversary $\mathcal{A}$).

Guess: If the adversary outputs a signcrypted message pair (m, σ) and after unsigncrypting σ, $m \notin M$. Then the adversary $\mathcal{A}$ wins the challenge.

4.2 Correctness Analysis

Theorem 1. *The unsigncryption algorithm of STDS scheme is correct.*

Proof. After receiving the signcrypted ciphertext, S calculates $Ks_1 = P^{sy} \bmod p = g^{asy} \bmod p$ and $m = D_{Ks_1}(C_c)$ according to its own public key g^s, private key s, and system parameters *params*. If the ciphertext is not attacked or any error occurs during the communication process, S can decrypt the message plaintext m normally.

Theorem 2. *The token verifies that the message integrity algorithm is correct.*

Proof. According to the plaintext m obtained by unsigncryption and the sender's public key g^c, it can calculate W:

$$\begin{aligned} W &= (g^{v_c} g^c)^{s_c} \\ &= g^{(v_c+c)uy/(v_c+c)} \\ &= g^{uy} \end{aligned} \tag{1}$$

For each token $t_i(t_i \in m)$, it computes $T_i{}' = (g^{xy})^{H_{kc_2}(t_i)}$ and then obtains $v_c{}' = H(T_i{}'||W)$, so when $v_c{}'$ equal to v_c, the token can verify the integrity of the message.

4.3 Security Analysis

Theorem 3. *In the random oracle model, if an IND-CCA2 adversary $\mathcal{A}$ can win the game of Definition 1 with probability ε within time T, and at most q_0 queries hash oracle, q_1 queries H_{Kc_2} oracle, q_2 queries H_W oracle, q_p public key queries, q_s signcryption queries and q_u unsigncryption queries, then there is an algorithm $\mathcal{C}$ that can solve the difficult DLP (Discrete Logarithm Problem) problem under the advantages of $\varepsilon/(q_0 q_1 q_2)$.*

Proof. Assuming that an adversary $\mathcal{A}$ can win the game with a non-negligible probability in a polynomial bounded time, the challenger $\mathcal{C}$ sets $\mathcal{A}$ as a subroutine in the IND-CCA2 game to solve the DLP difficulty problem. The purpose is to find $g^x = z$, given the $z \in \mathbb{Z}_p^*$, the generator g of the cyclic subgroup $\mathbb{G}$.

Setup: The challenger $\mathcal{C}$ chooses $hash$,H_{Kc_2},H_W as the oracle. Then $\mathcal{C}$ sends the public parameters $params = (hash, H_{Kc_2}, H_W)$ and system parameters (n, g) to $\mathcal{A}$, where is known $n = pq$. In addition, $\mathcal{C}$ maintains the following four lists $L_i(i = 0, 1, 2)$ and L_p, which record the query information of $hash$, H_{Kc_2}, H_W and public key respectively.

Phase 1: In this stage, the adversary $\mathcal{A}$ will perform a bounded polynomial query. It is worth noting that the result of any signcryption query is not used to unsigncryption query, and the signcryptor's public key is different from the recipient's public key.

1. $hash$ oracle query: $\mathcal{A}$ inquiries $hash(g^{wu})$ oracle, if there has a record (g^{wu}, Kc_2) in list L_0, $\mathcal{C}$ returns the previous definition Kc_2 to $\mathcal{A}$. Otherwise, $\mathcal{C}$ randomly chooses $x \in \mathbb{Z}_p$ and computes $Kc_2 = hash(g^{uw})$, then it adds (g^{wu}, Kc_2) to list L_0 and Kc_2 send to $\mathcal{A}$.
2. H_{Kc_2} oracle query: $\mathcal{A}$ inquires $H_{Kc_2}(t_i)$ oracle and gets token T_i. If there has record (Kc_2, t_i, g^x, y, T_i) in L_1, $\mathcal{C}$ sends the defined T_i to $\mathcal{A}$. Otherwise, $\mathcal{C}$ randomly chooses $x, y \in \mathbb{Z}_p$, computes T_i, then it adds (Kc_2, t_i, g^x, y, T_i) to list L_1, and sends T_i to $\mathcal{A}$.
3. H_W oracle query: $\mathcal{A}$ inquiries $H_W(T_i)$ oracle. If there has record (T_i, g^{uy}, v_2) in list L_2, then $\mathcal{C}$ sends the defined v_2 to $\mathcal{A}$. Otherwise, $\mathcal{C}$ randomly chooses $u, y \in \mathbb{Z}_p$, computes v_2, then adds (T_i, g^{uy}, v_2) to list L_2, and sends v_2 to $\mathcal{A}$.
4. Signcryption query: Given the signcryptor's public key g^c, the receiver's public key g^s and the message m. Then $\mathcal{C}$ perform the following steps.
   a. $\mathcal{C}$ randomly choose y, v_c, a, $Kc_2 \in \mathbb{Z}_p^*$.
   b. $\mathcal{C}$ compute $T_i{}' = g^{xyH_{Kc_2}(t_i)}$, $t_i \in m$, if there has tuple (Kc_2, t_i, g^{xy}, T_i) in list L_1, $\mathcal{C}$ stop it and repeat step a. Otherwise, $\mathcal{C}$ adds the record (Kc_2, t_i, g^{xy}, T_i) to list L_1.
   c. If there is a record (T_i, g^{uy}, v_2) in list L_2, $\mathcal{C}$ stop it and repeat step a-b. Otherwise, $\mathcal{C}$ computes $Kc_1 = y_s{}^{ay} \bmod p$, $c' = E_{Kc_1}(m)$, then $\mathcal{C}$ adds

the record (T_i, g^{uy}, v_2) to list L_2, and sends the result of the signcryption $\sigma = (c', T_i', v_c, g^a)$ to $\mathcal{A}$.

5. Unsigncryption query: $\mathcal{A}$ queries the unsigncryption oracle by giving the signcryptor's public key g^c, the receiver's public key g^s and the ciphertext tuple (c', T_i', v_c). Then, $\mathcal{C}$ searches record (Kc_2, t_i, g^{xy}, T_i) in list L_1 and record (T_i, g^{uy}, v_2) in list L_2. If they all exist, $\mathcal{C}$ sends $m = D_{Kc_1}(c)$, otherwise the query ends.

Challenge: $\mathcal{A}$ chooses two messages of equal length m_0, m_1 to challenge. $\mathcal{C}$ randomly chooses $b \in \{0,1\}$ and signcrypts m_b as follow. $\mathcal{C}$ randomly selects $y \in \mathbb{Z}_p$, lets $r_2 = z$, $\mathcal{C}$ computes $c = E_{Kc_1}(m_b)$, $T_i = g^{xyH_{Kc_2}(t_i)}$, $W = g^{uy}$, $v_c = H(T_i||W)$, and output the ciphertext $\sigma = (c, T_i, v_c)$ of m_b.

Phase 2: The adversary $\mathcal{A}$ again adaptively asks a polynomially bounded number of queries, as in Phase 1, but $\mathcal{A}$ never sends ciphertext σ to $\mathcal{C}$ for unsigncryption oracle queries. $\mathcal{A}$ gives a guess b' for b after the queries is over. If $\mathcal{A}$ has a non-negligible advantage ε to distinguish b, it must satisfy $H(g^{xyH_{Kc_2}(t_i)}||W) = v_c$, so there is

$$\left.\begin{array}{r} W = g^{uy} \\ hash(T_i||W) = hash(g^{xyH_{Kc_2}(t_i)}||g^{uy}) \\ hash(T_i||W) = v_c \\ v_c = hash(z) \end{array}\right\} \Rightarrow hash(g^{xyH_{Kc_2}(t_i)}||g^{uy}) = hash(z) \tag{2}$$

In other words, it chooses $xyH_{Kc_2}(t_i)$ as x in the DLP hard problem, *i.e.* the hard problem is solved.

In the case that the probability of $\mathcal{A}$ query $hash(g^{uw})$ oracle will not be greater than $1/q_0$. The probability of $H_{Kc_2}(t_i)$ oracle query will not be greater than $1/q_1$. The probability of $H_W(T_i)$ oracle query will not be greater than $1/q_2$, $\mathcal{A}$ performs any query outside the above three cases, and the simulation will fail. Therefore, the probability of $\mathcal{C}$ solving the DLP problem is at least $\varepsilon/(q_0q_1q_2)$.

Theorem 4. *This scheme has unforgeability under CMA. If the adversary $\mathcal{A}$ has a non-negligible advantage ε over EUF-CMA within the time T, and performs $q_i (i = 0, 1, 2)$ queries to the hash, H_{Kc_2}, H_W oracle, q_p public key queries, q_s signcryption queries, and q_u unsigncryption query, there is an algorithm $\mathcal{C}$ to solve the DLP (Discrete Logarithm Problem) with probability $\varepsilon/(q_0q_1q_2)$.*

Proof. Suppose $\mathcal{C}$ is the challenger, $\mathcal{A}$ is an adversary, and set $\mathcal{A}$ as a subroutine in the EUF-CMA game. Without loss of generality, suppose that the generator of the group $\mathbb{G}$ is g, where $g^x, g^y, g^z \in \mathbb{G}$. The goal of $\mathcal{C}$ is to find g^z, where $z = xy$.

Setup: $\mathcal{C}$ select three hash functions $hash$, H_{Kc_2}, H_W as oracles to perform at most q_i $(i = 0, 1, 2)$, and then send $params = (g, hash, H_{Kc_2}, H_W)$ to $\mathcal{A}$. At the same time, $\mathcal{C}$ keeps three lists L_i $(i = 0, 1, 2)$ for recording queries to oracles $hash$, H_{Kc_2}, H_W.

Query Phase: The simulation of H_{Kc_2}, H_W oracle query, signcryption query and unsigncryption query is the same as Theorem 3.

hash oracle query: $\mathcal{A}$ query $hash(Ti, W)$, if there has record (T_i, W, v_c) in list L_0, $\mathcal{C}$ sends the defined v_c to $\mathcal{A}$. Otherwise, $\mathcal{C}$ randomly chooses $x \in \mathbb{Z}_p$ and computes $v_c = hash(T_i||W)$, then adds (T_i, W, v_c) in list L_0 and sends v_c to $\mathcal{A}$.

Forgery: After the query phase, the $\mathcal{A}$ forges the signcryption $\sigma^* = (c, T_i, v_c, s_c, g^a)$ of m^* with a non-negligible probability, and there is no query related to m^* in the query set. $\mathcal{C}$ can construct another valid signcryption $\sigma^{*\prime} = (c', T_i', v_c', s_c', g^{a\prime})$ of m^*. By the bifurcation lemma in Pointcheval [18] with non-negligible advantage ε', m^* has two signcryption $\sigma^* = (c, T_i, v_c, s_c, g^a)$ and $\sigma^{*\prime} = (c', T_i', v_c', s_c', g^{a\prime})$, and $hash(T_i, W) \neq hash(T_i, W')$, $S_c = uy/(v_c + c) \bmod q$, $S_c' = uy/(v_c' + c) \bmod q$, so have

$$c = uys_c^{-1} - v_c \bmod q \tag{3}$$

$$s_c' = uy/(v_c' + uys_c^{-1} - v_c) \tag{4}$$

Since $W = (g^c g^{v_c})^{S_c}$, $W' = (g^c g^{v_c'})^{S_c'}$, let $W' = g^{(c+v_c')uy/(v_c'+uys_c^{-1}-v_c)}$, chooses $e = uy/(v_c' + uys_c^{-1} - v_c)$, that is, $\mathcal{C}$ can solve the DLP problem.

In the case that the probability of $\mathcal{A}$ query $hash(Ti, W)$ oracle will not be greater than $1/q_0$, the probability of $H_{Kc_2}(t_i)$ oracle query will not be greater than that $1/q_1$, the probability of $H_W(T_i, r_2, y)$ oracle query will not be greater than that $1/q_2$, $\mathcal{A}$ performs any query outside the above three cases, the query will fail. Therefore, the advantage of $\mathcal{C}$ solving the discrete logarithm problem is at least $\varepsilon/(q_0 q_1 q_2)$.

Theorem 5. *Tokens in this scheme can provide public verifiability.*

Proof. The token can be publicly verified in the STDS. When the signcryptor submits (g,g^c,s_c,T_i,v_c) to a third-party verifier, the third-party computes $W = (g^c g^{v_c})^{s_c}$ and then verifies whether the equation $v_c = hash(T_i||W) \bmod p$ holds. This process does not require the recipient's private key s and plaintext m, so the scheme is publicly verifiable.

5 Efficiency Analysis

In the scheme of using DPI to detect encrypted traffic, delay has always been a problem to be solved, and scholars have put forward many excellent schemes. Each scheme can effectively improve the delay problem in appropriate scenarios. This paper summarizes the applicable scenarios of the scheme, as shown in Table 2. Some are suitable for scenarios with small a number of users and long connections, while others are suitable for high concurrency scenarios.

To improve the delay in high concurrency scenarios, this paper proposes a signcryption-based encrypted traffic detection scheme to quickly establish TLS. It can be divided into two stages according to the user joining time: one is the preprocessing stage between the gateway and the middle agent, and the other is the rapid establishment of session rules and communication after the client TLS connection. In this paper, gateways and middle agent are added to pre-authenticate identities and generate intermediate obfuscation rules to reduce the

Table 2. Summary of application scenarios of different schemes

Scheme	Few users	High concurrency
PrivDPI [17]	✓	✗
Pine [16]	✗	✓
P2DPI [13]	✓	✗
STDS	✗	✓

computational consumption in the initial stage of new users joining. Therefore, according to the computational cost required by different number of users, we simulated and compared the Pine scheme and its related scheme PrivDPI, and proved that for high concurrency scenarios, the signcryption with gateway can enable users to quickly establish TLS connections and reduce the delay in the initial stage.

5.1 Theoretical Efficiency Analysis

This section mainly analyzes the computational communication consumption of this scheme from the performance. The results comparing the STDS detection scheme with PrivDPI and Pine show that this scheme is more effective than other schemes in DPI detection systems with used signcryption and added gateways.

In Table 3, the time complexity conversion of each operation unit to modular multiplication is given [9,10]. Taking modular multiplication as the unit, modular exponentiation, hashing, and pairing are converted into multiples of modular multiplication. For example, computing a pair takes 87 times as long as the modular multiplication.

Table 3. Definition and conversion of operating units [9,10]

Definition	Notation	Conversion
Time for computing a modular multiplication	Mul	-
Time for computing a modular exponentiation	Exp	$1T_{Exp} = 240T_{Mul}$
Time for computing a bilinear pairing	P	$1T_P = 87T_{Mul}$
Time for computing a point multiplication	Pm	$1T_{Pm} = 29T_{Mul}$
Time for computing a hash function	H	$1T_H \approx 29T_{Mul}$

In Table 4, it is shown that our scheme and Pine use modular multiplication, modular exponentiation, point multiplication, hash operation and bilinear number of pairs in the preprocessing stage of gateway and middle agent preparation detection rules before communication, although in this stage the preprocessing stage of this scheme uses bilinear pair calculation, but the calculation consumption of this scheme is still slightly lower than that of the Pine scheme. Corresponding to the relevant data in Table 3, the relevant calculation consumption of pine can be obtained as

$$\begin{aligned} &T_{Mul} + 2T_{Pm} + 10T_{Exp} + T_H \\ &= T_{Mul} + 2 \times 29T_{Mul} + 10 \times 240T_{Mul} + 29T_{Mul} \\ &= 2,488T_{Mul} \end{aligned} \tag{5}$$

The computational cost of this scheme is

$$\begin{aligned} &T_{Mul} + 2T_{Pm} + 9T_{Exp} + 3T_H + 2T_P \\ &= T_{Mul} + 2 \times 29T_{Mul} + 9 \times 240T_{Mul} + 3 \times 29T_{Mul} + 2 \times 87T_{Mul} \\ &= 2,480T_{Mul} \end{aligned} \tag{6}$$

Since the gateway and the middle agent have pre-established intermediate obfuscation rules, when the client communicates with the server, the session key can be obtained by simply processing the identities of both parties. As shown in Table 5, we calculate the computational overheads required by PrivDPI, Pine, and STDS from session key establishment to traffic detection stage respectively. Since each client of PrivDPI participates in the preprocessing protocol, when n sessions are established, it need 3,120n modular multiplication. However, Pine and STDS both use gateways and middle agent to communicate confusion rules in advance, so the overhead is smaller than PrivDPI, which is 2,222n and 1,770n modular multiplication.

Table 4. Comparison of initial communication calculation consumption of different schemes

Scheme	T_{Mul}	T_{Pm}	T_{Exp}	T_h	T_P
Pine	1 T_{Mul}	2 T_{Pm}	10 T_{Exp}	1 T_h	-
STDS	1 T_{Mul}	2 T_{Pm}	9 T_{Exp}	3 T_h	2 T_P

Table 5. Comparison of consumption required for communication of different schemes

Scheme	Consumption
PrivDPI	$12nT_{Exp} + 8nT_{Mul} + 2nT_H + 2nT_P = 3,120nT_{Mul}$
Pine	$9nT_{Exp} + 4nT_{Mul} + nT_{Pm} + nT_H = 2,222nT_{Mul}$
STDS	$7nT_{Exp} + 3nT_{Mul} + 3nT_H = 1,770nT_{Mul}$

5.2 Experiment Analysis

Experiment Environment: We execute the client (C), server (S), RG and MA on Windows 10 computer system with Intel(R) Core (TM) i5-10210U CPU @ 1.60 GHz 2.11 Hz, 8.0 GB RAM. Due to the limitations of the software and hardware of the experimental equipment, the results only compare the performance of each scheme in this environment. This paper uses Snort (a general lightweight intrusion detection rule set) [22] as the ruleset in this paper. This scheme is implemented on IntelliJ IDEA software with Java 8 programming language, and introduces the JPBC library [3], which is a prototype cryptosystem. And we realize the scheme with the help of the convenient JPBC library and IDEA development platform.

To compare the time consumption of different clients joining the initial phase, we choose the token and rule as 500. In this paper, we consider the time required to generate session rules and the user's initial connection and encrypt the message and token when the number of users is 1, 100, 500, 1,000 and 1,500.

Analysis of Experiment Results: Both Pine and STDS add gateways for scenarios involving a large number of users. Therefore, we compare the session rule computation overhead for similar scenarios with 1, 100, 500, 1000, and 1500 users. As shown in Fig. 4, we compare the generation time of session rules under different numbers of users between Pine and STDS schemes. The results show that our scheme requires less time in scenarios with different numbers of users, and has time advantages.

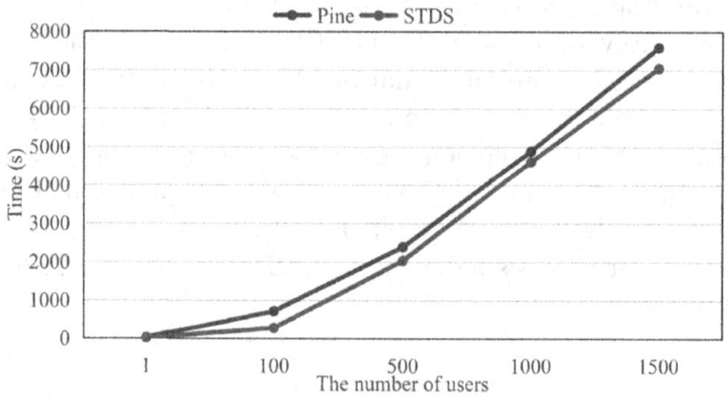

Fig. 4. Session rule generation time for different number of users

In Fig. 5, we compare the PrivDPI scheme, Pine scheme, and STDS scheme for the initial establishment of TLS connection, the time to generate session rules and encrypted messages and tokens. When the number of tokens and rules is 500, the larger the number of users, the more obvious the role of the gateway, that is, the less time required for pre-processing. As the number of users increases, the time required for the PrivDPI scheme doubles. It takes nearly 31 min for 100 users, because each client needs to participate in the preprocessing protocol when establishing communication. The second is the Pine scheme, which introduces gateway improvements based on the PrivDPI scheme, it takes 19.4 min when the number of users is 100. The STDS scheme uses signcryption to improve the traditional encrypted signature, so when the number of users is 100, it only takes 12.4 min. Therefore, this scheme is very beneficial for high concurrency scenarios. Compared with similar schemes, it is proved that signcryption can effectively reduce the computational cost of encrypted signature. Therefore, the experimental results are consistent with the theoretical analysis results.

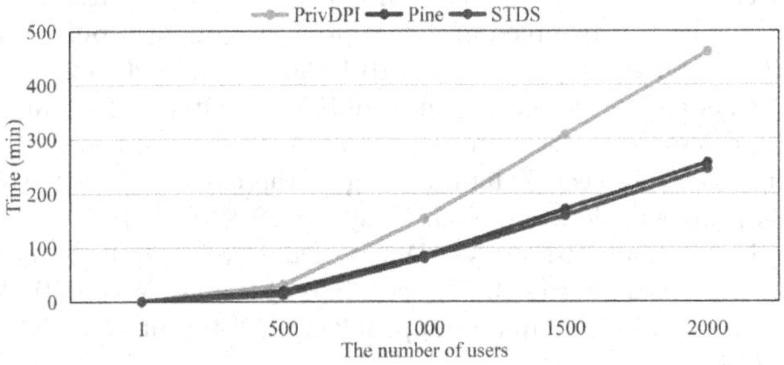

Fig. 5. First communication time for different number of users

6 Conclusion

This paper proposes an encrypted traffic detection scheme based on signcryption. The scheme adopts signcryption and establishes intermediate rules in advance, which can quickly establish TLS connections. Meanwhile, it improves the traditional method of encryption-then-signature, using signcryption to improve the encryption calculation time of traffic and tokens, and using gateways and middle agents to execute obfuscation rules in advance, saving more computing overhead for the client. Therefore, the time for the client and the middle agent to generate the session rules is reduced, and the delay problem in the preprocessing stage is effectively improved. In addition, the security analysis of the scheme is executed under the provable security theory, and it is proved that the scheme satisfies confidentiality, unforgeability and public verifiability through reduction. Compared with the PrivDPI scheme and the Pine scheme, our scheme is more efficient in high concurrency scenarios.

Acknowledgments. This work was supported by the Foundation for Innovative Research Groups of the National Natural Science Foundation of China (Grant No. 62121001)

References

1. Anderson, B., Paul, S., McGrew, D.: Deciphering malware's use of TLS (without decryption). J. Comput. Virol. Hacking Techniques **14**, 195–211 (2018). https://doi.org/10.1007/s11416-017-0306-6
2. Cisco: 2018 Annual Cybersecurity Report: The evolution of malware and rise of artificial intelligence, https://www.cisco.com/c/en/us/products/security/security-reports.html. Accessed 22 Jul 2019
3. De Caro, A., Iovino, V.: jPBC: Java pairing based cryptography. In: 2011 IEEE Symposium On Computers And Communications (ISCC), pp. 850–855. IEEE (2011). https://doi.org/10.1109/ISCC.2011.5983948
4. Deng, N., Deng, S., Hu, C., Lei, K.: An efficient revocable attribute-based signcryption scheme with outsourced unsigncryption in cloud computing. IEEE Access **8**, 42805–42815 (2019). https://doi.org/10.1109/ACCESS.2019.2963233
5. Durumeric, Z., et al.: The security impact of HTTPS interception. In: NDSS (2017)
6. Eltayieb, N., Elhabob, R., Hassan, A., Li, F.: A blockchain-based attribute-based signcryption scheme to secure data sharing in the cloud. J. Syst. Architect. **102**, 101653 (2020). https://doi.org/10.1016/j.sysarc.2019.101653
7. Gorbunov, S., Vaikuntanathan, V., Wichs, D.: Leveled fully homomorphic signatures from standard lattices. In: Proceedings of the Forty-seventh Annual ACM symposium on Theory of Computing, pp. 469–477 (2015). https://doi.org/10.1145/2746539.2746576
8. Grubbs, P., et al.: Pancake: Frequency smoothing for encrypted data stores. In: Usenix Security (2020)
9. Islam, S.H., Biswas, G.: A pairing-free identity-based authenticated group key agreement protocol for imbalanced mobile networks. Annals of télécommunications-annales des telecommunications **67**, 547–558 (2012). https://doi.org/10.1007/s12243-012-0296-9
10. Islam, S.H., Khan, M.K., Al-Khouri, A.M.: Anonymous and provably secure certificateless multireceiver encryption without bilinear pairing. Security Commun. Netw. **8**(13), 2214–2231 (2015). https://doi.org/10.1002/sec.1165
11. Jianjin, Z., Qi, L., Shengli, L., Yanqing, Y., Yueping, H.: Towards traffic supervision in 6g: a graph neural network-based encrypted malicious traffic detection method. SCIENTIA SINICA Inform. **52**, 270–286 (2022). https://doi.org/10.1360/SSI-2021-0280
12. Karati, A., Fan, C.I., Hsu, R.H.: Provably secure and generalized signcryption with public verifiability for secure data transmission between resource-constrained iot devices. IEEE Internet Things J. **6**(6), 10431–10440 (2019). https://doi.org/10.1109/JIOT.2019.2939204
13. Kim, J., Camtepe, S., Baek, J., Susilo, W., Pieprzyk, J., Nepal, S.: P2DPI: practical and privacy-preserving deep packet inspection. In: Proceedings of the 2021 ACM Asia Conference on Computer and Communications Security, pp. 135–146 (2021). https://doi.org/10.1145/3433210.3437525
14. Lacharité, M.S., Paterson, K.G.: Frequency-smoothing encryption: preventing snapshot attacks on deterministically encrypted data. Cryptology ePrint Archive (2017)
15. Naylor, D., Finamore, A., Leontiadis, I., Grunenberger, Y., Mellia, M., Munafò, M.: The cost of the "s" in https. In: Proceedings of the 10th ACM International on Conference on Emerging Networking Experiments and Technologies, pp. 133–140 (2014). https://doi.org/10.1145/2674005.2674991

16. Ning, J., et al.: Pine: enabling privacy-preserving deep packet inspection on TLS with rule-hiding and fast connection establishment. In: Chen, L., Li, N., Liang, K., Schneider, S. (eds.) Computer Security – ESORICS 2020: 25th European Symposium on Research in Computer Security, ESORICS 2020, Guildford, UK, September 14–18, 2020, Proceedings, Part I, pp. 3–22. Springer, Cham (2020). https://doi.org/10.1007/978-3-030-58951-6_1
17. Ning, J., Poh, G.S., Loh, J.C., Chia, J., Chang, E.C.: Privdpi: Privacy-preserving encrypted traffic inspection with reusable obfuscated rules. In: Proceedings of the 2019 ACM SIGSAC Conference on Computer and Communications Security, pp. 1657–1670 (2019). https://doi.org/10.1145/3319535.3354204
18. Pointcheval, D., Stern, J.: Security proofs for signature schemes. In: Maurer, U. (ed.) EUROCRYPT 1996. LNCS, vol. 1070, pp. 387–398. Springer, Heidelberg (1996). https://doi.org/10.1007/3-540-68339-9_33
19. Radivilova, T., Kirichenko, L., Ageyev, D., Tawalbeh, M., Bulakh, V.: Decrypting SSL/TLS traffic for hidden threats detection. In: 2018 IEEE 9th International Conference on Dependable Systems, Services and Technologies (DESSERT), pp. 143–146. IEEE (2018). https://doi.org/10.1109/DESSERT.2018.8409116
20. Roccia, T.: Malware packers use tricks to avoid analysis, detection. McAfee Blogs (2017)
21. Sherry, J., Lan, C., Popa, R.A., Ratnasamy, S.: Blindbox: Deep packet inspection over encrypted traffic. In: Proceedings of the 2015 ACM Conference on Special Interest Group on Data Communication, pp. 213–226 (2015). https://doi.org/10.1145/2785956.2787502
22. Snort: Snort rules. https://www.snort.org/ Accessed 12 Mar (2022)
23. Symantec: Four pillars of integrated cyber defense. https://www.broadcom.com/products/cyber-security Accessed 11 Apr 2021
24. Yaacoubi, O.: The rise of encrypted malware. Netw. Secur. **2019**(5), 6–9 (2019). https://doi.org/10.1016/S1353-4858(19)30059-5
25. Zhang, H., Papadopoulos, C., Massey, D.: Detecting encrypted botnet traffic. In: 2013 Proceedings IEEE INFOCOM, pp. 3453–1358. IEEE (2013). https://doi.org/10.1109/INFCOM.2013.6567180
26. Zhang, Z., Kang, C., Xiong, G., Li, Z.: Deep forest with LRRS feature for fine-grained website fingerprinting with encrypted SSL/TLS. In: Proceedings of the 28th ACM International Conference on Information and Knowledge Management, pp. 851–860 (2019). https://doi.org/10.1145/3357384.3357993
27. Zheng, Y.: Digital signcryption or how to achieve cost (signature & encryption) $\ll$ cost (signature) + cost (encryption). In: Advances in Cryptology-CRYPTO'97: 17th Annual International Cryptology Conference Santa Barbara, California, USA August 17–21, 1997 Proceedings 17, pp. 165–179. Springer (1997). https://doi.org/10.1007/bfb0052234

Cryptanalysis

Improved Key-Recovery Attacks Under Imperfect SCA Oracle for Lattice-Based KEMs

Wenhao Shi[1(✉)], Jiang Han[2], Haodong Jiang[1(✉)], and Zhi Ma[1(✉)]

[1] Henan Key Laboratory of Network Cryptography Technology, Zhengzhou, China
swh3006@163.com, hdjiang13@gmail.com, ma.zhi@meac-skl.cn

[2] TCA of State Key Laboratory of Computer Science, Institute of Software, Chinese Academy of Sciences, Beijing, China

Abstract. Plaintext-checking (PC) oracle-based side-channel-attacks (SCAs) is a major class of key recovery chosen-ciphertext SCAs on lattice-based key encapsulation mechanisms (KEMs). In practice, the PC oracle derived in SCAs is usually imperfect. In this paper, we propose an improved SCA for lattice-based KEMs with lower sample complexity (i.e. the required number of traces) when the PC oracle is imperfect. The basic idea of our method is to roughly recover the secret key and detect the erroneous position in the secret key, later correct the problematic entries with various known attacks for LWE (e.g., primal attack).

We experimentally verified our method on Kyber512, and the reduction of sample complexity is significant. For example, it can reduce the sample complexity by 54.06% when the accuracy is 0.890, for higher accuracy 0.950, the reduction of sample complexity is 35.81%. We also estimate the concrete security of Kyber512 after the side-channel-attack for different accuracy levels, including the primal attack, dual attack, decoding approach and the hybrid attack.

Keywords: Lattice algorithms · G6K · Side-channel-attacks · Kyber

1 Introduction

With the development of the quantum computation, NIST's PQC selection process started in 2016 and has attracted attention from all over the world. There are 4 finalists and 5 alternative candidates for Public Key Encryption (PKE) or Key Encapsulation Mechanism (KEM) in the third-round list. Lattice-based KEMs are the majority. Recently, Kyber [1] has been selected as the main KEM algorithm for final standardization [2]. Kyber is an IND-CCA2-secure key-encapsulation mechanism, and the security of Kyber is based on the hardness of solving the learning-with-errors problem in module lattices (MLWE).

Side-channel-attacks (SCAs) were first introduced by Kocher in [3]. The implemented cryptographic algorithms may leak information about the secret

M. Zhang et al. (Eds.): ProvSec 2023, LNCS 14217, pp. 67–82, 2023.
https://doi.org/10.1007/978-3-031-45513-1_4

key or message in some ways, such as measurements from timing, power consumption. Key recovery SCAs against lattice-based KEMs which recovers the long-term secret key is an important research topic and can be classified into two main types. The first type is the reaction-type side-channel-attacks [4,5], which will build an oracle to check whether the decryption is successful. This kind of side-channel-attacks can be extended to code-based KEMs [4,6,7]. The second type side-channel-attacks will recover the entries of the long-term secret key by choosing some certain message and achieves key recovery through a message-recovery approach. And this kind of attacks is called as message-recovery-type SCAs. The initial message-recovery-type SCAs introduced by [8] is also named as plaintext-checking (PC) oracle-based SCA. At the beginning of this class of SCAs, they can only obtain at most 1 bit of the secret from one call of the decryption function. Some advanced attacks are discovered later, such as [9,10], these attacks can recover more information about the secret key or message simultaneously. However, these attacks usually require strong leakage from the implements. R. Ueno et al. [6] presented a side-channel-attack on key encapsulation mechanism. This attack will exploit side-channel leakage during execution of a pseudorandom function or pseudorandom number generator in the re-encryption of KEM decapsulation. They show that the side-channel leakage of re-encryption can be generally exploited to break the CCA security, and present a generic power/EM SCA methodology for KEMs based on FO transformation and its variants. Moreover, they present a deep-learning-based distinguisher for implementing the plaintext-checking oracle, which helps to build the PC oracle to attack the lattice-based KEMs even when there're SCA counter-measurements.

Due to reasons like environmental noises, measurement limitations such as the inaccuracy of the distinguisher, the oracle will become inaccurate. In order to successfully recover the secret key under the imperfect SCA oracle, works are discovered to improve the oracle accuracy, such as the majority-voting technique. However, this kind of technique will also result in a much higher sample complexity. Take Kyber512 as an example, when the oracle is perfect without inaccuracy, the total traces needed for key recovery is 2560, however, it increases rapidly to 7680 when the majority-voting technique is applied under an imperfect oracle [11]. Recently, in [12], M. Shen et al. investigate the message-recovery-type SCA against Kyber to improve the sample complexity when the oracle is imperfect. Instead of amplifying the accuracy of the oracle, their method will find the problematic entries in the roughly recovered key and correct them with a "recollection step". The major advantage of their key recovery strategy is that they make best use of the current information of the roughly recovered key, since although the oracle is imperfect and inaccurate, there are only a small amount of entries are problematic, so they just find them and perform recollection for the suspicious entries. In order to realize their method, they designed a fast checking method to find the error positions in the roughly recovered secret key, and further corrected with some additional traces. This method improve the sample complexity significantly, take Kyber512 as an example, their method can reduce the sample complexity for about 46.1% when the accuracy is 0.900 and even

58.2% for accuracy 0.995. However, we find that even if the accuracy is high, for example, accuracy 0.990, the recollection step which aims to correct the error entries step still make up a large proportion of the sample complexity, namely 22.44% and increases to $\geq 50\%$ when the accuracy level $\alpha < 0.910$. To sum up, the recollection which aims to correct the error entries is costly to some degree. Therefore, can we find a more efficient way to recover the secret key with the roughly recovered key?

Contributions. We combine the side-channel-attack framework introduced by M. Shen et al. in [12] with various known attacks for LWE (e.g., primal attack), aiming to improve the sample complexity when the oracle is imperfect. The basic idea is to use lattice attacks such as primal attack to recover the secret key from the roughly recovered key, since we find that after the roughly key recovery step, the corresponding dimension of the LWE instance is small, so we can solve it directly within a reasonable time. Thus we can replace the costly "recollection" step which aims to correct the problematic entries by lattice attacks. These lattice attacks for LWE usually transform the LWE problem into hard problems in lattice, such as shortest vector problem (SVP) and closest vector problem (CVP), and solve them by lattice algorithms such as lattice reduction or sieving.

The reduction of sample complexity is significant, take Kyber512 as an example, when the accuracy of the imperfect oracle is 0.890, we can recover the secret key s with 3856.252 traces on average, which reduces the total traces for 54.06%, the primal attack will cost 9946.28 s. However, when the accuracy is higher, the cost of primal attack will decrease rapidly. For example, when the accuracy $\alpha = 0.900$, our method can reduce the sample complexity for about 52.07% with the primal attack costs 1697.79 s, and when $\alpha = 0.950$, the reduction in sample complexity is 35.81% and the primal attack costs only 0.92 s (Table 1). All the experiments are perform on a laptop, and the reduction in sample complexity is significant. Moreover, we also estimate the concrete security of Kyber512 after the side-channel-attack under various known attacks for LWE for different accuracy levels, including the primal attack and dual attack, the decoding approach and the hybrid attack which combines the Meet-in-the-Middle (MitM) attack with dual attack.

2 Preliminaries

2.1 Lattices

A lattice Λ is a discrete subgroup in $\mathbb{R}^m$. Such a lattice is generated by a lattice basis of linearly independent vectors, denoted as $B = (b_0, b_1, \cdots, b_{m-1}) \subset \mathbb{Z}^m$. The lattice $\Lambda(B)$ can be presented as $\Lambda(B) = \mathrm{B} \cdot \mathbb{Z}^m = \{B \cdot x : x \in \mathbb{Z}\}$. The volume of a lattice Λ can be defined as $Vol(\Lambda) = \sqrt{B \cdot B^T}$, where B^T stands for the transpose of matrix B. Here B is an arbitrary basis of Λ, volume is a lattice invariant since it is independent of the lattice basis used. We use

$\pi_i : \mathbb{R}^m \mapsto span(b_0, b_1, \cdots, b_{i-1})^\perp, i = 0, 1, \cdots, m-1$ to present the orthogonal projections. Particularly, $\pi_0(\cdot)$ stands for the identity. The Gram-Schmidt orthogonalization (GSO) of B is denoted as $B^* = (b_0^*, b_1^*, \cdots, b_{m-1}^*)$, where $b_i^* = \pi_i(b_i), i = 0, 1, \cdots, m-1$. We use $\lambda_i(\Lambda)$ to denote the $i-th$ successive minimum in lattice Λ, which means the smallest r such that $\Lambda \cap \mathcal{B}(0, r)$ has i linearly independent vectors, where $\mathcal{B}(0, r)$ stands for the ball of radius r centered at zero. Particularly, $\lambda_1(\Lambda)$ is the norm of the shortest non-zero vector in a lattice Λ.

Let $\mathcal{S} \subset \mathbb{R}^d$ be a measurable subset with finite volume, then we can use the Gaussian Heuristic to predicate the number of lattice points in $\mathcal{S}$:

$$|\mathcal{S} \cap \Lambda| \approx \frac{Vol(\mathcal{S})}{Vol(\Lambda)} \tag{1}$$

when $\mathcal{S}$ becomes a closed hyber ball of dimension d, which leads to the predication of the length of a non-zero shortest vector in Λ. We denote the expectation of the norm of the non-zero shortest vector in Λ as $GH(\Lambda)$, then $GH(\Lambda)$ is given by:

$$GH(\Lambda) = \frac{\Gamma(1 + d/2)^{1/d}}{\sqrt{\pi}} \cdot Vol(\Lambda)^{1/d} \approx \sqrt{\frac{d}{2\pi e}} \cdot Vol(\Lambda)^{1/d} \tag{2}$$

where $\Gamma(\cdot)$ is the Gamma function, which is related to the factorial by $\Gamma(n) = (n-1)!$. Thus the norm of the non-zero vector in a lattice Λ is usually estimated by $\lambda_1(\Lambda) = GH(\Lambda) = \sqrt{\frac{d}{2\pi e}} \cdot Vol(\Lambda)^{1/d}$.

2.2 Lattice Algorithms

Sieving [13–17] takes a list of points as input, denoted as $L \in \Lambda$, and searches for linear combinations of the points that are short. If the initial list is large enough, then it is believed that SVP can be solved by this process recursively. Each point in the list is sampled in polynomial time in d.

Assuming that the distribution of the angles of the lattice points in L is the same as the distribution of angles sampled randomly from the unit sphere, Phong Q. Nguyen and Thomas Vidick proposed a heuristic sieving algorithm with time complexity of $2^{0.415d+o(d)}$ and memory complexity of $2^{0.2075d+o(d)}$ [16]. Later, Thijs Larrhoven and Benne de Weger sped it up it with Locality Sensitive Hashing, achieving a time complexity of $2^{0.3366d+o(d)}$ and memory complexity of $2^{0.415d+o(d)}$ [17]. The asymptotically fastest sieve achieves a time complexity of $2^{0.292d+o(d)}$ and a memory complexity of $2^{0.415d+o(d)}$, which is sped up by using the Locality Sensitive Filter [14].

If the linear combination takes k points at the same time, it is called k-sieve. For example, 2-sieve searches for integer combinations of lattice vectors $u, v \in L$ for $u \neq \pm v$. In high dimensions, we may use the 3-sieve since it requires less memory compared with 2-sieve, but more time consumption.

The LLL Algorithm was developed by A. K. Lenstra, H. W. Lenstra, Jr and L. Lovasz in 1982, which can solve the approximate SVP by achieving an approximation factor of $(\frac{2}{\sqrt{3}})^n$. Given a parameter $\frac{1}{4} < \delta \leq 1$, a lattice basis $B = (b_0, b_1, \cdots, b_{d-1})$ is LLL reduced if the Gram–Schmidt orthogonalization of B satisfies $\mu_{i,j} \leq \frac{1}{2}$ for $i > j$, and $(\delta - \mu_{i+1,i}^2) \cdot ||b_i^{*2}|| \leq ||b_{i+1}^{*2}||$ (Lovasz conditions). Let $\alpha = 1/(\delta - 1/4)$, then the first vector of a LLL reduced basis satisfies $||b_0|| \leq \alpha^{(n-1)/2} \cdot \lambda_1(\Lambda)$. For $\frac{1}{4} < \delta < 1$, the LLL algorithm can be computed in polynomial time in the dimension.

The BKZ Algorithm was proposed by Schnorr in 1987 [18,19] and can be seen as a generalization variant of the LLL algorithm. It obtains higher quality of the output lattice basis, however, with a running time in exponential in the dimension d. The BKZ algorithm uses an oracle that solves SVP in the β dimension "block", and inserts the short vector to the lattice basis recursively. It first finds the shortest vector in the first block $\pi_1(b_1)$ and the shortest in $\pi_1(b_1)$ will be inserted to the basis. It then proceeds to the next "block" until it reaches the last "block" $\pi_{d-2}(b_{d-1})$, which is called a BKZ-tour. After a BKZ-tour, the algorithm will go to the first block and continue this process until the lattice basis remains unchanged. A small, constant number of BKZ-tour is enough for many applications.

The SVP oracle can be instantiated by enumeration or sieving. When it is instantiated by enumeration, it achieves a running time of $1.02^{\beta^2+O(\beta)}$ and a polynomial memory cost in β. As for sieving, the asymptotic time complexity becomes $2^{0.292\beta+o(\beta)}$ and the memory complexity is $2^{0.2075\beta+o(\beta)}$.

Root Hermite factor δ is a numerical value to evaluate quality of reduced basis. It is defined as follows:

Definition 1 (Root Hermite Factor). The root-Hermite-factor of a basis B is defined as:

$$\delta(B) = (||b_1||/vol(\mathcal{L})^{1/n})^{1/n} \tag{3}$$

The root-Hermite-factor is bigger than 1, and for larger block size β, δ gets closer to 1. The speed of approaching 1 is increasing slower as the root-Hermite-factor gets closer to 1. The relationship between δ and β is given by [20,21]: $\delta(\beta) = ((\pi\beta)^{1/\beta} \cdot \beta/(2\pi e))^{1/2(\beta-1)}$.

2.3 The Learning with Errors (LWE) Problem

The Learning with Errors (LWE) problem is first introduced by Regev in [22], and is defined as follows.

Definition 2 (LWE). Let $n, m, q \in \mathbb{N}$, and χ_e, χ_s be distributions over $\mathbb{Z}_q$. Denote by $LWE_{m,n,q,\chi_s,\chi_e}$ the probability distribution on $\mathbb{Z}_q^{m\times n} \times \mathbb{Z}_q^m$ obtained by sampling the coordinates of the matrix $A \in \mathbb{Z}_q^{m\times n}$ independently and uniformly over $\mathbb{Z}_q$, sampling the coordinates of $s \in \mathbb{Z}_q^n$ and $e \in \mathbb{Z}_q^m$ independently from the distributions χ_s and χ_e respectively, and outputting $(A, As + e)$.

We define two problems:

- *Decision-LWE.* Distinguish the uniform distribution over $\mathbb{Z}_q^{m\times n} \times \mathbb{Z}_q^m$ from $LWE_{m,n,q,\chi_s,\chi_e}$.
- *Search-LWE.* Given a sample from LWE_{n,q,χ_s,χ_e}, recover s.

2.4 Kyber

Kyber is an IND-CCA2-secure key-encapsulation mechanism (KEM) and the security of Kyber is based on the hardness of solving the learning-with-errors problem in module lattices (M-LWE). In a M-LWE problem, the secret vector s and the rows of A are sampled in a module, which makes kyber more efficient.

In Kyber, the polynomial is defined over $\mathcal{R}_q = \mathbb{Z}_q[x]/(x^n+1)$, where $q = 3329$ and $n = 256$, $\mathbb{Z}_q$ is the ring with all elements are integers modulo q. All the additions and multiplications are operated modulo the polynomial $x^n + 1$. Noise in Kyber is sampled from a centered binomial distribution B_η with $\eta = 2$ or $\eta = 3$. B_η is defined as follows:

$$\begin{array}{ll} Sample\ (a_1, \cdots, a_\eta, b_1, \cdots, b_\eta) \leftarrow 0, 1^{2\eta} \\ Output \qquad\qquad \sum_{i=1}^{n}(a_i - b_i) \end{array} \tag{4}$$

the vectors s, e is sampled from B_η^n.

3 Previous PC-Based Side-Channel-Attack Against Kyber and Our Main Strategy

3.1 Previous PC-Based Side-Channel-Attack Against Kyber

Key recovery Side-Channel-Attacks against lattice-based KWEs can be classified into two types. The first type will construct an oracle and check the response to decide whether the decryption is success. The second type will construct some certain messages to achieve key recovery through a message-recovery approach. There are much work on PC-oracle, however, due to the inaccuracy, people needs more effects to recovery the key. Some work aim to improve the accuracy of the oracle, such as improving it by major-voting. However, compared with perfect oracle, this will cost more traces to recover the key. For example, [6] will vote 3 times to improve the accuracy, thus the number of traces under an imperfect oracle is 3 times compared with a perfect oracle.

In [12], M.Shen et al. propose an efficient way to mount a recovery under an imperfect oracle. They investigate the message-recovery-type SCA against Kyber and aim at improving the sample complexity under the imperfect oracle. They proposed a new method to efficiently find the problematic entries in the recovered key and correct them with some additional traces. Compared with previous methods, their method reduces the sample complexity significantly, for example, for Kyber512, it can reduce the sample complexity by $58.2\%, 57.8\%, 46.1\%$ for accuracy $\alpha = 0.995, 0.950, 0.900$, respectively.

Instead of amplifying the accuracy of the oracle, they will detect error position of the recovered key and then correct the errors. Let s denotes the secret key, their method can be divided into 3 steps:

- Step 1: Perform the RoughKeyRecovery Algorithm to get a s_0 with some problematic entries.
- Step 2: Perform the fast checking method to find the problematic positions.
- Step 3: Perform the targeted recollection to correct the error entries.

The first step will output a vector s_0 which has some problematic entries, then the error positions will be found by the second step and finally be corrected by the last step.

Algorithm 1. PC oracle $\mathcal{O}_{SCA}$ enacted by SCA [12]

Input: Ciphertext *ct*, profiled waveforms W_{m_0}, W_{m_1}
Output: 0 or 1

Query the device with *ct* and collect waveform $W_m^{'}$
if $Dist(W_m^{'}, W_{m_1}) < Dist(W_m^{'}, W_{m_0})$ **then**
    Return 1
else
    Return 0
end if

Algorithm 2. RoughKeyRecovery [12]

Input: An imperfect PC oracle $\mathcal{O}_{SCA}$
Output: Secret Key s
  Return KeyRecovery($\mathcal{O}_{SCA}$)

The main idea of Step 2 introduced in [12] is to treat it as a coding problem. They will divide the secret vector s into blocks where each block may have 1 or more entries. In order to check the block successfully, they need to generate proper ciphertexts to encode the block to some special codewords. For example, assume that the secret vector s has been divided into 5 blocks and we want to check the last block, they will expect that a chipertext will encode it into a special codeword c_{succ}, while other blocks should be encoded into different codewords. For each block, if the responses is not equal to c_{succ}, then there are errors in this block.

3.2 Our Main Strategy

After the first two steps, we will have a LWE instance with roughly recovered secret key s_0, i.e., the correct $s = s_0 + s_1$ for some unknown s_1. Since we have found the error positions in Step 2, we can reduce the dimension of the LWE instance: without loss of generality, assume that the error positions are the first k entries, thus $s_1 = (s_{11}, s_{12}, \cdots, s_{1k}, 0, \cdots, 0)$, so we have $b - As_0 = As_1 + e \bmod q$, the dimension of this LWE instance is actually k since the last components of s_1 is zero. The parameter k is related to the accuracy level α, the lower the accuracy is, the higher the dimension becomes.

In [12], M. Shen et al. will correct the roughly recovered secret key by a recollection step (Step 3), it will add some additional traces, take Kyber512 as an example, on average, it will add 4041.573 traces when $\alpha = 0.900$, approximated 52.07% the proportion of the total traces (7761.448). However, solving the LWE instance directly is not hard for almost all accuracy levels, since the corresponding LWE after the first two step only has a low dimension, i.e., 120.13 on average for Kyber512 when $\alpha = 0.900$, and only 62.92 when $\alpha = 0.950$, which can be solved directly within 1 s on a laptop (see more details in Table 1), thus we can reduce the sample complexity for 35.81% for $\alpha = 0.950$. For higher accuracy, such as $\alpha = 0.990$, the dimension of the LWE instance is 13.01 on average, just a toy example and can be solved within 0.1 s, but reduce the total sample complexity significantly for 22.44% on average.

Thus, we will follow the first two steps introduced by [12] but replace the last step by various known attacks for LWE (e.g., primal attack) to solve the LWE directly, that is:

- Step 1: Perform the RoughKeyRecovery Algorithm to get a candidate vector s_0 with some problematic entries, i.e., the correct secret key $s = s_0 + s_1$ for some unknown s_1.
- Step 2: Perform the fast checking method to find the problematic positions.
- Step 3: Perform lattice attack (e.g.,primal attack) to solve the LWE instance to find s_1, then $s = s_0 + s_1$.

We experimentally verified our method and solved LWE for different accuracy levels within a reasonable time. What's more, we estimate the concrete security of the Learning with Errors instances under various algorithms for different accuracy levels (Table 2).

4 Analysis with Respect to Known Attacks

M-LWE as LWE. Since the best known attacks against the M-LWE problem in Kyber do not take advantage of the structure in the lattice, we analyze the hardness of M-LWE problem as an LWE problem.

4.1 Primal Attack

The primal attack will construct a unique-SVP instance from the LWE problem and solving it via lattice algorithms, usually by BKZ. Given the LWE instance $(A, b = As + e)$, the attacker will construct the lattice $\Lambda = \{x \in \mathbb{Z}^{m+kn+1} : (A, I_m, -b) \cdot x = 0 \bmod q\}$ of dimension $d = m + kn + 1$, volume q^m. The solution of the unique-SVP in Λ is $v = (s, e, 1)$ of norm $\lambda_1 \approx \varsigma\sqrt{kn + m}$, where ς is the standard deviation of the individual secret / noise coefficients. For Kyber, the number of samples m can be choose between 0 and $(k + 1)n$.

When BKZ reduction is applied to solve the unique-SVP, we should estimate how large the block size β is required to find the solution. With the geometric series assumption (GSA), the BKZ reduction algorithm will find a basis whose Gram-Schmidt norms are given by $||b_i^*|| = \delta^{d-2i-1} \cdot Vol(\Lambda)^{1/d}$, where $\delta(\beta) = ((\pi\beta)^{1/\beta} \cdot \beta/(2\pi e))^{1/2(\beta-1)}$. The short vector $v = (s, e, 1)$ will be found if the projection of v onto the vector space spanned by the last β Gram-Schmidt vectors is shorter than $b_{d-\beta}^*$. The projection norm is expected to be $\varsigma\sqrt{\beta}$, thus the success condition is:

$$\varsigma\sqrt{\beta} \leq \delta^{2\beta-d-1} \cdot q^{m/d} \tag{5}$$

4.2 Dual Attack

Given the LWE instance $(A, b = As + e)$, the attacker construct the dual lattice $\Lambda' = \{(x, y) \in \mathbb{Z}^m \times \mathbb{Z}^{kn} : A^t x = y \bmod q\}$. Assume that we have found a vector $v = (x, y)$ of length l, then the attacker computes $z = v^t \cdot b = v^t As + v^t e = w^t s + v^t e \bmod q$, which is distributed as a Gaussian of standard deviation $l\varsigma$ if (A, b) is an LWE instance. This distribution has maximal variation distance from uniform distribution bounded by $\epsilon = 4exp(-2\pi^2\tau^2)$, where $\tau = l\varsigma/q$. The attacker should amplify the success probability by building about $1/\epsilon^2$ many short vectors. Since lattice sieving algorithms can provide $2^{0.2075\beta}$ short vectors, thus the sieving algorithm should be repeated R times where $R = \max(1, 1/(2^{0.2075\beta}\epsilon^2))$. This is a conservative estimation since it assumes that the vectors provided by sieving algorithm are as short as the shortest one. The time complexity of dual attack is $T_{dual} = R \cdot T_{BKZ_{\beta,d}}$, where $T_{BKZ_{\beta,d}}$ is the time of performing BKZ reduction with a block size β in a lattice of dimension d.

4.3 Meet in the Middle Attack

The Meet-in-the-Middle (MitM) attack is a classical combinatorial attack for LWE, for key space size $\mathcal{S}$ runs in time $\mathcal{S}^{0.5}$. This attack is first introduced by Odlyzko in 1996 [23], originally designed for binary vectors, but the generalization to small max-norm vectors is straight-forward. Here we take ternary LWE as an example.

Locality-sensitive hashing (LSH) function introduced by Indyk and Motwani [24] plays an important role in the MitM attack. Locality-sensitive hashing will map vectors w to sketches $h(w)$, such that vectors nearby have a high probability of having the same sketch and vectors far away will be mapped to the same sketch with low probability. For Odlyzko's MitM attack, they proposed a simple locality-sensitive hashing function ℓ as follows:

$$\ell : \mathbb{Z}_q^n \to 0, 1^n : \begin{cases} 0 & 0 \leq x_i < \lfloor q/2 \rfloor - 1 \\ 1 & \lfloor q/2 \rfloor - 1 \leq x_i < q - 1 \end{cases} \tag{6}$$

Actually, $\ell(\cdot)$ can be interpreted as the most significant bits of vectors. Here are two border values $\lfloor q/2 \rfloor - 1$ and $q - 1$ where the ternary error e may results in a flip of the hash value, so they assign for these two border values both 0 and

1. For example, let $q = 1024$, then $x = (1, 511, 2, 1023)$ will be mapped to 4 sketches: $\ell(x) = (0,0,0,0), (0,1,0,0), (0,0,0,1), (0,1,0,1)$, since the second and the last position in x are border values.

For ternary LWE, let $\mathcal{T}^n(w/2) = \{s \in \mathcal{T}^n | s \textit{ has } w/2 \; 1-\textit{entries and } w/2 \; -1-\textit{entries}\}$. Given the ternary LWE instance $(A, b = As + e)$, Odlyzko split $s = (s_1, s_2) \in \mathcal{T}^{n/2}(w/4) \times \mathcal{T}^{n/2}(w/4)$. Accordingly, the matrix A will be split into $A = (A_1, A_2)$. Since $b = As + e \bmod q$, we have:

$$A_1 s_1 = b - A_2 s_2 + e \bmod q \textit{ where } e \in \{-1, 0, 1\}^n \tag{7}$$

which means $A_1 s_1$ is close to $b - A_2 s_2$ for correct $s = (s_1, s_2)$. Thus the algorithm will enumerate s_1, s_2 and use the locality sensitive hash function $\ell(\cdot)$ to check whether the corresponding values $\ell(A_1 s_1)$ and $\ell(b - A_2 s_2)$ are the same.

Algorithm 3. Odlyzko's Meet-in-the-Middle attack.

Input: LWE key (A, b), the hamming weight ω of s.
Output: $s \in \mathcal{T}^n(w/2)$ such that $e = b - As \bmod q \in \mathcal{T}^n$

for all $s_1 \in \mathcal{T}^{n/2}(w/4)$ **do**
  Compute $\ell(A_1 s_1)$ and store $(s_1, \ell(A_1 s_1))$ in list L_1
end for
for all $s_2 \in \mathcal{T}^{n/2}(w/4)$ **do**
  Compute $(s_2, \ell(b - A_2 s_2))$
  for all $(s_1, \cdot)$ which matches $(s_2, \ell(b - A_2 s_2))$ in the second component **do**
    if $s = (s_1, s_2)$ satisfies $b - As \bmod q \in \mathcal{T}^n$ **then**
      return $s = (s_1, s_2)$
    end if
  end for
end for

Correctness. On the one hand, for the correct secret vector $s = (s_1, s_2)$, $A_1 s_1 = b - A_2 s_2 + e \bmod q$ for some $e \in \{-1, 0, 1\}^n$, thus leads to colliding sketches $\ell(A_1 s_1) = \ell(b - A_2 s_2)$.

On the other hand, with the randomness of A, the probability of $s = (s_1, s_2)$ satisfies $\ell(A_1 s_1) = \ell(b - A_2 s_2)$ but not satisifies $b - As \bmod q \in \mathcal{T}^n$ is roughly only 2^{-n}.

Runtime. Clearly, the runtime of Odlyzko's MitM algorithm is dominated by the size of $|L_1|$ and $|L_2|$. Let $\mathcal{S} = |\mathcal{T}^n(w/2)|$ to denote the size of the secret vector s, Odlyzko's MitM runs in time $\mathcal{O}(\mathcal{S}^{0.5})$.

4.4 Decoding Approach

This approach solves LWE by solving the corresponding BDD problem. BDD problem can be solved by various method, here we mainly focus on the method introduced by Liu and Nguyen in [25], since we use it to estimate the security of the LWE instance for different accuracy levels. We will introduce the Nearest Plane algorithm [26] first. Given a lattice basis B and a target vector t, the Babai's Nearest Plane algorithm will output a vector v such that $v - t \in \mathcal{P}_{1/2}(B^*)$. This algorithm solves BDD instance with probability $\prod_{i=0}^{m-1} erf(\frac{||b_i^*||\sqrt{\pi}}{2\alpha q})$, where $erf(x) = \int_0^x e^{-y^2} dy$.

Lindner and Peikert amplify the probability of e falling into the fundamental parallelepiped by widen it in the direction of b_i^* by a factor of some integer $d_i \in \mathbb{Z}_{>0}$. Thus the corresponding probability becomes to $\prod_{i=0}^{m-1} erf(\frac{d_i||b_i^*||\sqrt{\pi}}{2\alpha q})$.

Liu and Nguyen apply the pruned enumeration to solve BDD, as well as randomising the input basis. Here they use linear pruning which means the radius $R_k = \sqrt{k/m}R_m$.

4.5 Hybrid Dual Attack

The Meet-in-the-Middle attack can be combined with the lattice methods to mount the hybrid attack. Usually it can be combined with the dual attack as well as the primal attack, here we mainly discuss the hybrid of dual and MitM attack introduced by [27], since we use it to estimate the security of LWE instances in Sect. 6.

In this algorithm, the dual attack will reduce the original LWE instances by dimension but increase the infinite norm of the error e, which is called as "dimension-error tradeoff". After the tradeoff, the $||e||_\infty$ is large, so it's hard for the original Meet-in-the-Middle attack to solve this kind of instances. The authors solve it by generalizing the locality-sensitive hashing function by adding more border values, thus result in a new MitM attack which can solve LWE with large errors. Briefly speaking, the hybrid of dual and MitM attack consists of two steps: first it mounts the "dimension-error tradeoff" by dual attack and then solving the corresponding LWE instances by their generalized Meet-in-the-Middle attack.

The runtime of this hybrid attack algorithm consists of two parts: the lattice reduction phase and the Meet-in-the-Middle phase. For the lattce reduction phase, it costs $T_{lat} \approx T_{BKZ_{d,\beta}}$, where $T_{BKZ_{d,\beta}}$ stands for the time cost for performing a BKZ reduction with block size β in a lattice of dimension d. The cost of MitM can be divided into T_{pre} for preprocessing step and T_{search} for the searching step. Let $N_\tau = \sum_{i=1}^{h_1} \binom{n}{i} \cdot 2^i$, $N_q = \sum_{i=1}^{h_2} \binom{n}{i} \cdot 2^i$, then $T_{pre} = N_\tau \cdot (k^2 + \tau)$ and $T_{search} = \mathcal{O}(N_q \cdot 2^{4\tau B/q})$. Here the h_1, h_2 are the hamming weight for the secrect vector s_1 and s_2 respectively, τ is the number of samples for MitM step and k is the dimension of the LWE instance after the "dimension-error tradeoff". B is a parameter which bounds the norm of the error, can be estimated in polynomial time.

5 Solving LWE for Different Accuracy Levels

After the two steps introduced in Sect. 3, we have recovered a large proportion of the secret key s, only a small number of components of s needs to be recovered.

Since we know the error positions in s, we can reduce the dimension of the LWE instance: given a LWE instance $(A, b = As + e)$, we can write $s = s_0 + s_1$, where s_0 is the key recovered by the first two steps and s_1 is the unknown part. Without loss of generality, we assume the error positions in s are the first k components, thus $s_1 = (s_{11}, s_{12}, \cdots, s_{1k}, 0, \cdots, 0)$, so we have the following equations:

$$As + e = b \bmod q \tag{8}$$

$$As_0 + As_1 + e = b \bmod q \tag{9}$$

$$As_1 + e = b - As_0 \bmod q \tag{10}$$

since s_0 is known and the last $n - k$ components of s_1 is 0, we have a new LWE instance with dimension of k. We solve the LWE instances by primal attack implemented in G6K [28].

The accuracy α will affect the dimension of the corresponding LWE, the lower the accuracy is, the harder the LWE becomes, in [12], they also need more traces for the recollection step. We have solved all LWE instances for $\alpha \geq 0.890$ in a reasonable time, and list the results in Table 1.

Table 1. Resources required for our method

α	ErrCof	Time	Ours	Orig Step1 [12]	Orig Step2,3 [12]	Orig total [12]	Comparison
0.890	131.15	9946.28 s	3856.252	1293.642	7101.352	8394.994	−54.06%
0.895	125.76	2007.77 s	3787.200	1294.017	6786.617	8080.634	−53.13%
0.900	120.13	1697.79 s	3719.875	1294.670	6466.778	7761.448	−52.07%
0.910	109.24	1241.82 s	3604.785	1295.684	5893.267	7188.951	−49.86%
0.920	97.97	445.61 s	3503.019	1295.880	5342.351	6638.231	−47.23%
0.930	86.50	121.68 s	3416.592	1298.191	4815.423	6113.614	−44.12%
0.940	74.79	24.16 s	3341.834	1299.881	4316.310	5616.191	−40.50%
0.950	62.92	0.92 s	2487.187	1301.763	2572.711	3874.474	−35.81%
0.960	50.79	0.68 s	2387.396	1303.536	2121.361	3424.897	−30.29%
0.990	13.01	0.10 s	1565.932	1309.749	709.318	2019.067	−22.44%

Here α is the accuracy level of the oracle, for all the accuracy levels, we run the experiments with 10,000 randomly generated secret key for Kyber512 to get the parameters "ErrCof", "Ours" and "Orig Step1,2,3 and total". ErrCof stands for the corresponding dimension of the LWE instance, Time is the runtime for solving LWE, Ours is the total number of traces needed for our method, Orig Step1 stands for the average number of RoughKeyRecovery step in [12], which is the first step to roughly obtain a key, and Orig Step2,3 stands for the sum of average number of samples for the FastCheck step and Recollection step in [12] which will find the problematic entries and correct them. Orig total stands for the sum of Orig Step1 and Orig Step2,3, which is the number of traces needed for [12], Comparison is the reduction in the number of traces on average. All the experiments are performed on a laptop with Intel(R) Core(TM) i7-8750H CPU @2.20 GHZ.

6 Estimating the Security for Different Accuracy Levels

We estimate the concrete security of the Learning with Errors instances corresponding to different accuracy α, since for the low accuracy α, such as $\alpha < 0.890$, the corresponding error coefficient is large, thus solving the corresponding LWE directly will become expensive. The estimation is done by the LWE-estimator [20].

For Kyber512, given the oracle accuracy α, the number of errors can be estimated as $N \approx (1-\alpha)Q_{RR}$, where $Q_{RR} = 1312$ for Kyber512. Thus we can estimate the concrete security of Kyber512 after the first two steps by estimating the dimension of the LWE instance under certain accuracy levels. The parameter "ErrCof" in Table 2 is obtained by running the experiments with 10,000 randomly generated secret key and taking an average.

Table 2. The concrete security of Kyber512 after the first two step SCAs.

α	ErrCof	Primal				BDD			Dual				Hybrid		
		rop	β	d	δ	rop	β	d	rop	m	β	d	rop	β	d
0.700	300.94	$2^{87.9}$	206	601	1.006169	$2^{85.0}$	192	600	$2^{90.8}$	336	213	637	$2^{88.5}$	204	614
0.800	219.56	$2^{67.3}$	132	465	1.008011	$2^{64.8}$	120	456	$2^{69.4}$	257	136	477	$2^{68.0}$	131	460
0.850	172.28	$2^{55.6}$	91	355	1.009686	$2^{53.2}$	79	363	$2^{57.3}$	211	93	384	$2^{56.5}$	89	368
0.885	137.36	$2^{46.3}$	58	288	1.011578	$2^{43.5}$	44	295	$2^{48.0}$	176	60	313	$2^{47.7}$	59	303
0.890	131.15	$2^{44.8}$	53	279	1.011887	$2^{41.9}$	41	287	$2^{46.6}$	171	55	303	$2^{46.4}$	55	294
0.895	125.76	$2^{42.8}$	46	274	1.012285	$2^{41.3}$	40	262	$2^{44.8}$	166	49	292	$2^{44.7}$	49	281
0.900	120.13	$2^{41.2}$	41	252	1.012505	$2^{40.9}$	40	239	$2^{43.2}$	162	44	283	$2^{43.5}$	40	255

In Table 2, α is the accuracy level, and ErrCof is the average dimension of the LWE instance, "Primal" is the primal attack, rop stands for the number of operations, which is approximately equal to CPU cycles, β is the block size used in BKZ reduction and d is the lattice dimension, δ is the root-Hermite factor, the success condition for primal attack is the same as mentioned in Sect. 4. "BDD" is the decoding approach introduced by Liu and Nguyen in [25]. "Dual" stands for the dual attack and m is the number of samples needed. "Hybrid" is the dual hybrid attack mentioned in [29], for this attack, if the optimization of MitM is "True", then it becomes the hybrid attack mentioned in Subsect. 4.5. Here we don't list the security results for $\alpha > 0.90$ since the corresponding LWE instances are easy to solve, for example, we can solve it within 1 s when $\alpha \geq 0.950$. When the accuracy level is low, the LWE instance becomes unsolvable, for example, when $\alpha = 0.700$, the average dimension of the LWE instance is larger than 300, and the complexity of solving it is $> 2^{85}$.

7 Conclusions

We have presented a method which combines SCAs with lattice attacks (e.g., primal attack) to reduce the sample complexity for NIST lattice-based KEMs.

We use the side-channel-attack framework proposed in [12] to roughly recover the secret key and correct it by various known attacks for LWE, such as primal attack. Extensive experiments have been performed to verify our method for different accuracy levels, and it shows that the improvement in sample complexity is significant: it can be larger than 52% when the accuracy is lower than 0.900.

Since the relationship between accuracy levels and the dimension of the corresponding LWE instance is clear, we also estimate the concrete hardness of Kyber512 after the first two steps side-channel-attack under different attacks for various accuracy levels by the LWE-estimator [20]. We choose several different algorithms to estimate the concrete security and exclude algorithms irrelevant for our parameter set. The attacks we use for estimation are the primal/dual attack, decoding approach and the hybrid attack.

Acknowledgement. We thank the reviewers' valuable comments. Haodong Jiang was funded by the National Key R&D Program of China (No. 2021YFB3100100) and the National Natural Science Foundation of China (No. 62002385). Zhi Ma was funded by the National Natural Science Foundation of China (No. 61972413).

References

1. Avanzi, R., et al.: Crystals-kyber algorithm specifications and supporting documentation. NIST PQC Round **2**(4), 1–43 (2017)
2. Alagic, G., et al.: Status report on the third round of the NIST post-quantum cryptography standardization process. US Department of Commerce, NIST (2022)
3. Kocher, P.C.: Timing attacks on implementations of Diffie-Hellman, RSA, DSS, and other systems. In: Koblitz, N. (ed.) CRYPTO 1996. LNCS, vol. 1109, pp. 104–113. Springer, Heidelberg (1996). https://doi.org/10.1007/3-540-68697-5_9
4. Guo, Q., Johansson, T., Nilsson, A.: A key-recovery timing attack on post-quantum primitives using the Fujisaki-Okamoto transformation and its application on FrodoKEM. In: Micciancio, D., Ristenpart, T. (eds.) CRYPTO 2020. LNCS, vol. 12171, pp. 359–386. Springer, Cham (2020). https://doi.org/10.1007/978-3-030-56880-1_13
5. Bhasin, S., D'anvers, J.P., Heinz, D., Pöppelmann, T., Van Beirendonck, M.: Attacking and defending masked polynomial comparison for lattice-based cryptography. In: IACR Transactions on Cryptographic Hardware and Embedded Systems, pp. 334–359, 2021. https://eprint.iacr.org/2021/104
6. Ueno, R., Xagawa, K., Tanaka, Y., Ito, A., Takahashi, J., Homma, N.: Curse of re-encryption: A generic power/EM analysis on post-quantum KEMs. In: IACR Transactions on Cryptographic Hardware and Embedded Systems, pp. 296–322, 2022 (2021)
7. Guo, Q., Hlauschek, C., Johansson, T., Lahr, N., Nilsson, A., Schröder, R.L.: Don't reject this: Key-recovery timing attacks due to rejection-sampling in HQC and bike. In: IACR Transactions on Cryptographic Hardware and Embedded Systems, **2022**(3), 223–263 (2022)
8. D'Anvers, J.P., Tiepelt, M., Vercauteren, F., Verbauwhede, I.: Timing attacks on error correcting codes in post-quantum schemes. In: Proceedings of ACM Workshop on Theory of Implementation Security Workshop, pp. 2–9 (2019)

9. Xu, Z., Pemberton, O., Roy, S.S., Oswald, D., Yao, W., Zheng, Z.: Magnifying side-channel leakage of lattice-based cryptosystems with chosen ciphertexts: The case study of kyber. IEEE Transactions on Computers (Early Access) (2021)
10. Ravi, P., Ezerman, M.F., Bhasin, S., Chattopadhyay, A., Roy, S.S.: Will you cross the threshold for me? - generic side-channel assisted chosen-ciphertext attacks on ntru-based kems. IACR Trans. Cryptograph. Hardware Embedded Syst. pp. 722–761 (2022)
11. Ravi, P., Roy, S.S., Chattopadhyay, A., Bhasin, S.: Generic side-channel attacks on CCA-secure lattice-based PKE and KEM schemes. IACR Trans. Cryptogr. Hardw. Embed. Syst., **2020**(3), 307–335 (2020)
12. Shen, M., Cheng, C., Zhang, X., Guo, Q., Jiang, T.: Find the bad apples:an efficient method for perfectkey recovery under imperfect SCA oracles- a case study of kyber. IACR Trans. Cryptograph. Hardware Embedded Syst. (TCHES) **2023**(1), 89–112 (2023)
13. Ajtai, M., Kumar, R., Sivakumar, D.: A sieve algorithm for the shortest lattice vector problem. In: Symposium on the Theory of Computing (2001)
14. Becker, A., Ducas, L., Gama, N., Laarhoven, T.: New directions in nearest neighbor searching with applications to lattice sieving. In: Proceedings of the Twenty-Seventh Annual ACM-SIAM Symposium on Discrete Algorithms, SODA '16, pp. 10–24, USA (2016). Society for Industrial and Applied Mathematics
15. Becker, A., Gama, N., Joux, A.: Speeding-up lattice sieving without increasing the memory, using sub-quadratic nearest neighbor search. IACR Cryptol. ePrint Arch. **2015**, 522 (2015)
16. Nguyen, P.Q., Vidick, T.: Sieve algorithms for the shortest vector problem are practical. J. Math. Cryptol. **2**(2), 181–207 (2008)
17. Laarhoven, T.: Sieving for shortest vectors in lattices using angular locality-sensitive hashing. In: Gennaro, R., Robshaw, M. (eds.) CRYPTO 2015. LNCS, vol. 9215, pp. 3–22. Springer, Heidelberg (2015). https://doi.org/10.1007/978-3-662-47989-6_1
18. Schnorr, C.P., Euchner, M.: Lattice basis reduction: Improved practical algorithms and solving subset sum problems. In: Budach, L., (ed), Fundamentals of Computation Theory, pages 68–85, Springer Berlin, Heidelberg (1991)
19. Schnorr, C.P.: A hierarchy of polynomial time lattice basis reduction algorithms. Theoret. Comput. Sci. **53**(2), 201–224 (1987)
20. Albrecht, M.R., Player, R., Scott, S.: On the concrete hardness of learning with errors. J. Math. Cryptol. **9**, 169–203 (2015)
21. Chen, Y.: Lattice reduction and concrete security of fully homomorphic encryption. PhD thesis, l'Université Paris Diderot, (2013). http://www.di.ens.fr/~ychen/research/these.pdf
22. Regev, O.: On lattices, learning with errors, random linear codes, and cryptography. In: Proceedings of the Annual ACM Symposium on Theory of Computing, pp. 84–93, 2005. 13th Color Imaging Conference: Color Science, Systems, Technologies, and Applications; Conference date: 07–11-2005 Through 11–11-2005
23. Hoffstein, J., Pipher, J., Silverman, J.H.: NTRU: a ring-based public key cryptosystem. In: Buhler, J.P. (ed.) ANTS 1998. LNCS, vol. 1423, pp. 267–288. Springer, Heidelberg (1998). https://doi.org/10.1007/BFb0054868
24. Har-Peled, S., Indyk, P., Motwani, R.: Approximate nearest neighbors: towards removing the curse of dimensionality. In: Symposium on the Theory of Computing (1998)

25. Liu, M., Nguyen, P.Q.: Solving BDD by enumeration: an update. In: Dawson, E. (ed.) CT-RSA 2013. LNCS, vol. 7779, pp. 293–309. Springer, Heidelberg (2013). https://doi.org/10.1007/978-3-642-36095-4_19
26. Babai, L.: On Lovász' lattice reduction and the nearest lattice point problem. Combinatorica **6**, 1–13 (1986)
27. heon, J.H., Hhan, M., Hong, S., Son, Y.: A hybrid of dual and meet-in-the-middle attack on sparse and ternary secret LWE. IEEE Access **7** 89497–89506 (2019)
28. Albrecht, M.R., Ducas, L., Herold, G., Kirshanova, E., Postlethwaite, E.W., Stevens, M.: The general sieve kernel and new records in lattice reduction. In: Ishai, Y., Rijmen, V. (eds.) EUROCRYPT 2019. LNCS, vol. 11477, pp. 717–746. Springer, Cham (2019). https://doi.org/10.1007/978-3-030-17656-3_25
29. Espitau, T., Joux, A., Kharchenko, N.: On a dual/hybrid approach to small secret LWE. In: Bhargavan, K., Oswald, E., Prabhakaran, M. (eds.) INDOCRYPT 2020. LNCS, vol. 12578, pp. 440–462. Springer, Cham (2020). https://doi.org/10.1007/978-3-030-65277-7_20

Linear Cryptanalysis of Lightweight Block Cipher WARP

Hong Xu(✉), Chunyu Hao, Zhichao Xu, and Wenfeng Qi

Information Engineering University, Zhengzhou, China
xuhong0504@163.com

Abstract. WARP is 128-bit lightweight block cipher proposed by Banik et al. in SAC 2020, which is currently the smallest 128-bit block cipher in terms of hardware. In this paper, we evaluate the security of WARP against linear cryptanalysis with SAT method. Using the SAT-based automatic search algorithms, the lower bound on the number of minimal linearly active S-boxes and the maximal linear correlation for WARP up to 30 rounds are presented, and a 23-round linear cryptanalysis of WARP is presented with a 19-round linear hull with correlation $2^{-58.16}$ by extending two rounds forward and backward the distinguisher.

Keywords: WARP · lightweight block cipher · linear cryptanalysis · SAT-based automatic search

1 Introduction

Linear cryptanalysis [1] is an effective cryptanalysis method proposed by Matsui at Eurocrypt 1993. Linear cryptanalysis is a kind of known-plaintext attack, which is used to distinguish block ciphers from random permutations or even recover the corresponding subkey bits by finding linear approximations with high correlation between the plaintext and the ciphertext.

How to search the linear approximations with high correlation efficiently is the focus of linear cryptanalysis. In recent years, many automatic tools have been widely used in the field of cryptanalysis such as MILP (Mixed Integer Linear Programming) [2,3], SAT (Boolean Satisfiability Problem) [4–7], and Constrained Programming(CP) [8], and many better distinguishers have been found for block ciphers using these methods.

WARP is a lightweight block cipher proposed by Banik *et al.* [9] at SAC 2020 with a variant of the 32-nibble Type-2 Generalised Feistel Network (GFN). In [9], Banik *et al.* evaluated the security of WARP against linear and differential attacks by providing the lower bound for the number of differentially and linearly active S-boxes up to 19 rounds with a MILP-aided automatic search method. Teh and Biryukov [10] searched the differential trails for up to 20 rounds of WARP using SMT method, and presented a 23-round differential attack on WARP based on an 18-round differential distinguisher. Lallemand *et al.* [11] presented a 26-round rectangle attack on WARP with a 23-round boomerang distinguisher, and Sun *et al.* [12] presented a 33-round multiple zero-correlation linear attack on WARP with a 21-round distinguisher.

M. Zhang et al. (Eds.): ProvSec 2023, LNCS 14217, pp. 83–90, 2023.
https://doi.org/10.1007/978-3-031-45513-1_5

In this paper, we further evaluate the security of WARP against linear cryptanalysis with SAT method, and present two algorithms to search for the lower bound on the number of linearly active S-boxes and the maximal linear correlation. With these algorithms, the lower bound on the number of minimal linearly active S-boxes and the maximal linear correlation for WARP up to 30 rounds are presented. With a 19-round linear hull with high correlation, we present a 23-round linear cryptanalysis by extending two rounds forward and backward the distinguisher.

2 A Brief Review of WARP

WARP is a lightweight block cipher proposed by Banik *et al.* [9] at SAC 2020 with 128-bit key and 128-bit block. WARP is energy-efficient, and smallest in hardware among known 128-bit block ciphers, which can be used as a lightweight replacement of AES-128 without changing the mode of operation.

The general structure of WARP is a variant of the 32-nibble Type-2 Generalised Feistel Network (GFN). The round function of WARP is shown in Fig. 1, the number of rounds of WARP is 41, and the details for the S-box and the nibble permutation are shown in Table 1 and Table 2. The 128-bit key K of WARP is expressed as two 64-bit keys $K^0 = (K^0_0, K^0_1, \ldots, K^0_{15})$ and $K^1 = (K^1_0, K^1_1, \ldots, K^1_{15})$. K^0 and K^1 are used alternately, and the i-th round key RK^r is expressed as $RK^r = K^{(r-1) \bmod 2}, r = 1, \ldots, 41$.

Table 1. S-box of WARP

x	0	1	2	3	4	5	6	7	8	9	a	b	c	d	e	f
$S(x)$	c	a	d	3	e	b	f	7	8	9	1	5	0	2	4	6

Table 2. Nibble permutation of WARP

i	0	1	2	3	4	5	6	7	8	9	10	11	12	13	14	15
$\pi(i)$	31	6	29	14	1	12	21	8	27	2	3	0	25	4	23	10
i	16	17	18	19	20	21	22	23	24	25	26	27	28	29	30	31
$\pi(i)$	15	22	13	30	17	28	5	24	11	18	19	16	9	20	7	26

3 SAT-Based Automatic Search Algorithms for WARP

Denote by $\Gamma_{in} \in F_2^4$ and $\Gamma_{out} \in F_2^4$ the input mask and output mask of the S-box, respectively. For every pair of the masks $(\Gamma_{in}, \Gamma_{out})$, calculate the number of $x \in F_2^4$ such that $\Gamma_{in} \cdot x = \Gamma_{out} \cdot S(x)$ holds. Denote

$$N_s(\Gamma_{in}, \Gamma_{out}) = \#\{x \in F_2^4 : \Gamma_{in} \cdot x = \Gamma_{out} \cdot S(x)\},$$

then $C(\Gamma_{in}, \Gamma_{out}) = |N_s(\Gamma_{in}, \Gamma_{out}) - 8|/16$ is the correlation such the linear approximation $\Gamma_{in} \cdot x = \Gamma_{out} \cdot S(x)$ holds, where $\Gamma_{in} \in F_2^4$ and $\Gamma_{out} \in F_2^4$ are the input mask and output mask of the S-box, respectively. When $\Gamma_{in}, \Gamma_{out}$ traverse all 4-bit nibbles over F_2^4, we can obtain the Linear Approximation Table (LAT) of the S-box of WARP as shown in Table 3.

Using the same method as in [6,7], we can establish the SAT model for search of lower bound on the number of minimal linearly active S-boxes and the maximal correlation for the linear trail of WARP.

Table 3. Linear approximation table for S-box

Γ_{in}	Γ_{out}															
	0	1	2	3	4	5	6	7	8	9	A	B	C	D	E	F
0	16	8	8	8	8	8	8	8	8	8	8	8	8	8	8	8
1	8	10	12	10	6	8	10	8	6	8	10	8	12	6	8	6
2	8	12	8	8	12	8	8	8	4	8	8	8	8	12	8	8
3	8	10	8	10	6	8	10	12	10	4	6	8	8	10	8	10
4	8	6	12	6	10	8	6	8	6	4	6	8	8	6	8	10
5	8	8	8	8	8	8	8	8	8	8	4	4	8	8	12	4
6	8	10	8	10	6	8	10	4	6	8	6	8	4	6	8	10
7	8	8	8	12	8	8	4	8	8	8	8	4	8	8	4	8
8	8	6	4	10	6	8	6	8	4	6	8	10	10	8	10	8
9	8	8	8	4	4	8	8	8	6	10	6	6	10	10	6	10
A	8	10	8	6	6	4	6	8	8	6	12	6	6	8	10	8
B	8	8	8	8	8	4	8	4	10	6	6	10	10	10	6	6
C	8	12	8	8	8	8	4	8	10	10	6	10	10	6	10	10
D	8	6	12	10	6	8	6	8	8	10	8	10	6	12	10	8
E	8	8	8	8	8	12	8	4	10	6	10	6	10	10	10	10
F	8	6	8	10	10	4	10	8	8	10	8	6	10	8	10	12

Algorithm 1 and Algorithm 2 illustrates the process to search for linear trails with prescribed bound on the correlation or the number of linearly active S-boxes. By adjusting the value of w_{min} or N_{min} continuously, the linear trail

Algorithm 1. Automatic search of linear trails of WARP with prescribed bound on the correlation

Input: number of rounds n, bound w_{min} on the weight of the correlation
Output: linear trails with prescribed bound on the correlation
for $1 \leq r \leq n$ **do**
    Set the SAT model for the linear operations of WARP;
    Set the SAT model for S-box with correlation of WARP;
end for
Set the SAT model for the constraint that at least one bit of the input or output mask are non-zero;
Set the SAT model for the constraints on w_{min} using sequence encoding method;
Call the SAT solver to solve the SAT model;
if the solver returns the solution **then**
    Output linear trail
else
    There exists no linear trail with correlation c such that $-\log_2(c) \leq w_{min}$.
end if

with maximal correlation or minimal number of linearly active S-boxes can be obtained.

Algorithm 2. Automatic search of linear trails of WARP with prescribed bound on the number of linearly active S-boxes

Input: number of rounds n, bound N_{min} on the number of the linearly active S-boxes
Output: linear trails with prescribed bound on the number of active S-boxes
for $1 \leq r \leq n$ **do**
  Set the SAT model for the linear operations of WARP;
  Set the SAT model for S-box without correlation of WARP;
end for
Set the SAT model for the constraint that at least one bit of the input or output mask are non-zero;
Set the SAT model for the constraints on N_{min} using sequence encoding method;
Call the SAT solver to solve the SAT model;
if the solver returns the solution **then**
  Output linear trail
else
  There exists no linear trail with N linearly active S-boxes such that $N \leq N_{min}$.
end if

Using the SAT-based automatic search algorithm presented above, we compute the lower bound on the number of minimal linearly active S-boxes and the maximal linear correlations of WARP, and the detailed value is shown in Table 4. It can be seen that the linear correlation for 19-round WARP is at least 2^{-66}, thus there exists no efficient linear attack with individual 19-round linear trail.

Table 4. Bounds on the number of minimal active S-boxes and maximal linear correlation of WARP

Round	#Active S-boxes	Maximal correlation	Round	#Active S-boxes	Maximal correlation
1	0	2^{-0}	16	52	2^{-52}
2	1	2^{-1}	17	57	2^{-57}
3	2	2^{-2}	18	61	2^{-61}
4	3	2^{-3}	19	66	2^{-66}
5	4	2^{-4}	20	70	2^{-70}
6	6	2^{-6}	21	75	2^{-75}
7	8	2^{-8}	22	79	2^{-79}
8	11	2^{-11}	23	82	2^{-82}
9	14	2^{-14}	24	85	2^{-85}
10	17	2^{-17}	25	89	2^{-89}
11	22	2^{-22}	26	93	2^{-93}
12	28	2^{-28}	27	97	2^{-97}
13	34	2^{-34}	28	101	2^{-101}
14	40	2^{-40}	29	106	2^{-106}
15	47	2^{-47}	30	109	2^{-109}

Besides, we also observed strong linear hull effect for WARP form 13 to 21 rounds when the input and output masks are randomly selected. Particularly, we find a 19-round linear hulls of WARP with correlation $2^{-58.16}$ as $(00000000a00000a5f00000a500a0005a, 0000000a005000f00000000a00000505)$.

4 Linear Cryptanalysis on 23-Round WARP

Using the above 19-round linear hull with correlation $2^{-58.16}$, we can present a linear attack on 23-round WARP as shown in Fig. 2 by extending two rounds before and after the distinguisher.

Let $X^i = (X_0^i, \ldots, X_{31}^i)$ the input of the i-round of WARP, where X_j^i is the j-th nibble of X^i. Denote by $X_{j,k}^i = X_j^i || X_k^i$ the cascade of the j-th and k-th nibbles of X^i. Let $K^i = (K_0^i, \ldots, K_{31}^i)$ be the 64-bit subkey of the i-round of WARP, where K_j^i is the j-th nibble of K^i. Denote by $K_j^i[s]$ the s-th bit of K_j^i, and $K_j^i[s,t] = K_j^i[s] || K_j^i[t]$ the cascade of the s-th and t-th bits of K_j^i.

To present a 23-round linear attack with the above 19-round linear hull, we need to choose N pairs of plaintexts and ciphertexts, partially encrypt and decrypt the cipher by guessing the corresponding subkey bits, and calculate the number of pairs of plaintexts and ciphertexts such that the following linear approximation holds.

$$\begin{aligned} &(1010) \cdot X_8^3 \oplus (1010) \cdot X_{14}^3 \oplus (0101) \cdot X_{15}^3 \oplus (1111) \cdot X_{16}^3 \oplus (1010) \cdot X_{22}^3 \oplus \\ &(0101) \cdot X_{23}^3 \oplus (1010) \cdot X_{26}^3 \oplus (0101) \cdot X_{30}^3 \oplus (1010) \cdot X_{31}^3 \\ &\quad = (1010) \cdot X_7^{22} \oplus (0101) \cdot X_{10}^{22} \oplus (1111) \cdot X_{14}^3 \oplus \\ &\quad\quad (1010) \cdot X_{23}^3 \oplus (0101) \cdot X_{29}^3 \oplus (0101) \cdot X_{31}^3 \end{aligned} \tag{1}$$

If the number is larger than the threshold, then accept the corresponding subkeys as the right subkeys. When N is large enough, the right subkey can be determined successfully.

The calculation of the above linear approximation (1) is related to 17 nibbles of plaintexts $X^1_{0,1,2,3,8,9,10,11,18,19,20,24,25,26,27,30,31}$ and 14 nibbles of ciphertexts $X^{24}_{1,2,5,8,11,12,14,17,19,21,24,27,28,29}$, which corresponds to 62-bit plaintext and 50-bit ciphertext with nonzero mask bits. There are totally 64-bit subkeys involved in the calculation, where 42-bit subkeys are used in the partial encryption of the first two rounds, 30-bit subkeys are used in the partial decryption of the last two rounds, and 8-bit subkeys are used twice.

Since a linear distinguisher with correlation $2^{-58.16}$ is used in the attack, at least $2^{116.32}$ known plaintexts is needed. To further reduce the time complexity, we use the techniques of partial-sum and partial subkey guessing, where the subkey nibbles are guessed one by one. To efficiently reduce the size of remained state, the order for the guessing is adjusted accordingly. Table 5 presents the details for the guessed subkeys and the time complexity of each step, where the time complexity is evaluated as the number of S-boxes involved in the calculation.

Complexity Analysis. According to the complexity analysis method of linear analysis presented in [16], if $N = 2^{119.62}$ plaintext-ciphertext pairs are used in

Table 5. Time complexity of key recover process of 23-round WARP

Step	Guess key	Remained state (bit number involved)	Time complexity
0		$X^1_{0,1,2,3,8,9,10,11,18,19,20,24,25,26,27,30,31}, Y^{23}_{2,3,4,5,6,7,8,9,20,21,22,23,24,26}(112)$	$2^2 \cdot 2^{112} = 2^{114}$
1	$K^0_1[1,3]$	$X^1_{0,1,8,9,10,11,18,19,20,24,25,26,27,30,31}, X^3_{23}, X^{22}_{10}, Y^{23}_{4,5,6,7,8,9,20,21,22,23,24,26}(116)$	$2^2 \cdot 2^{112} = 2^{114}$
2	$K^0_9[0\text{–}3]$	$X^1_{0,1,8,9,10,11,20,24,25,26,27,30,31}, X^2_{30}, X^3_{23}, X^{22}_{10}, Y^{23}_{24,26}, Y^{23}_{4,5,6,7,8,9,20,21,22,23}(112)$	$2^6 \cdot 2^{116} = 2^{122}$
3	$K^0_{12}[0\text{–}3]$	$X^1_{0,1,8,9,10,11,20,26,27,30,31}, X^2_{18}, X^2_{30}, X^3_{23}, X^{22}_{10}, Y^{22}_{23,31}, Y^{23}_{4,5,6,7,8,9,20,21,22,23}(108)$	$2^{10} \cdot 2^{112} = 2^{122}$
4	$K^0_2[0\text{–}3]$	$X^1_{0,1,8,9,10,11,20,26,27,30,31}, X^2_{18,30}, X^3_{23}, X^{22}_{10}, Y^{22}_{23,31}, X^{23}_5, Y^{23}_{6,7,8,9,20,21,22,23}(104)$	$2^{14} \cdot 2^{108} = 2^{122}$
5	$K^1_{11}[0,2]$	$X^1_{0,1,8,9,10,11,20,26,27,30,31}, X^2_{18,30}, X^3_{23}, X^{22}_{23}, X^{22}_{10}, Y^{22}_{31}, Y^{23}_{6,7,8,9,20,21,22,23}(100)$	$2^{16} \cdot 2^{104} = 2^{122}$
6	$K^0_3[0\text{–}3]$	$X^1_{0,1,8,9,10,11,20,26,27,30,31}, X^2_{18,30}, X^3_{23}, X^{22}_{10,23}, X^{23}_7, Y^{22}_{31}, Y^{23}_{8,9,20,21,22,23}(96)$	$2^{20} \cdot 2^{100} = 2^{120}$
7	$K^0_{11}[0\text{–}3]$	$X^1_{0,1,8,9,10,11,20,26,27,30,31}, X^2_{18,30}, X^3_{23}, X^{22}_{10,23}, X^{22}_{14}, Y^{22}_{30,31}, Y^{23}_{8,9,20,21}(92)$	$2^{24} \cdot 2^{96} = 2^{120}$
8	$K^0_4[0\text{–}3]$	$X^1_{0,1,10,11,20,26,27,30,31}, X^2_{27,2}, X^2_{18,30}, X^3_{23}, X^{22}_{10,14,23}, Y^{22}_{7,28}, Y^{22}_{30,31}, Y^{23}_{20,21}(92)$	$2^{28} \cdot 2^{92} = 2^{120}$
9	$K^1_{15}[1,3]$	$X^1_{0,1,10,11,20,26,27,30,31}, X^2_{2,18,27,30}, X^3_{23}, X^{22}_{10,14,23}, X^{22}_{31}, Y^{22}_{7,28}, Y^{23}_{20,21}(88)$	$2^{30} \cdot 2^{92} = 2^{122}$
10	$K^0_0[0\text{–}3]$	$X^1_{2,10,11,20,26,27,30,31}, X^2_{31,6}, X^2_{2,18,27,30}, X^3_{23}, X^{22}_{10,14,23,31}, Y^{22}_{7,28}, Y^{23}_{20,21}(88)$	$2^{34} \cdot 2^{88} = 2^{122}$
11	$K^1_{15}[0,2]$	$X^1_{10,11,20,26,27,30,31}, X^3_{26}, X^2_{2,6,18,27}, X^3_{23}, X^{22}_{10,14,23,31}, Y^{22}_{7,28}, Y^{23}_{20,21}(84)$	$2^{36} \cdot 2^{88} = 2^{124}$
12	$K^0_5[0,2]$	$X^1_{20,26,27,30,31}, X^2_3, X^3_{31}, X^2_{2,6,18,27}, X^3_{23,26}, X^{22}_{10,14,23,31}, Y^{22}_{7,28}, Y^{23}_{20,21}(84)$	$2^{38} \cdot 2^{84} = 2^{122}$
13	$K^1_1[0,2]$	$X^1_{20,26,27,30,31}, X^3_{14}, X^2_{6,18,27}, X^3_{23,26,31}, X^{22}_{10,14,23,31}, Y^{22}_{7,28}, Y^{23}_{20,21}(80)$	$2^{40} \cdot 2^{84} = 2^{124}$
14	$K^0_{13}[0\text{–}3]$	$X^1_{20,30,31}, X^2_{19,16}, X^2_{6,18,27}, X^3_{14,23,26,31}, X^{22}_{10,14,23,31}, Y^{22}_{7,28}, Y^{23}_{20,21}(80)$	$2^{44} \cdot 2^{80} = 2^{124}$
15	$K^1_9[1,3]$	$X^1_{20,30,31}, X^2_{6,16,27}, X^3_{30}, X^3_{14,23,26,31}, X^{22}_{10,14,23,31}, Y^{22}_{7,28}, Y^{23}_{20,21}(76)$	$2^{46} \cdot 2^{80} = 2^{126}$
16	$K^0_{15}[0\text{–}3]$	$X^1_{20}, X^2_{7,26}, X^2_{6,16,27}, X^3_{14,23,26,30,31}, X^2_{14,23,31}2, Y^{22}_{7,10,28}, Y^{23}_{20,21}(76)$	$2^{50} \cdot 2^{76} = 2^{126}$
17	$K^1_3[0,2]$	$X^1_{20}, X^2_{16,26,27}, X^3_8, X^3_{14,23,26,30,31}, X^{22}_{10,14,23,31}, Y^{22}_{7,28}, Y^{23}_{20,21}(72)$	$2^{52} \cdot 2^{76} = 2^{128}$
18	$K^1_{13}[0\text{–}3]$	$X^1_{20}, X^2_{16}, X^3_{16}, X^3_{8,14,23,26,30,31}, X^{22}_{10,14,23,31}, Y^{22}_{7,28}, Y^{23}_{20,21}(68)$	$2^{56} \cdot 2^{72} = 2^{128}$
19	$K^0_{10}[0\text{–}3]$	$X^1_{20}, X^2_{16}, X^3_{8,14,16,23,26,30,31}, X^{22}_{10,14,23,31}, Y^{22}_{29,6}, Y^{22}_{7,28}(68)$	$2^{60} \cdot 2^{68} = 2^{128}$
20	$K^1_3[0,2]$*	$X^1_{20}, X^2_{16}, X^3_{8,14,16,23,26,30,31}, X^{22}_{10,14,23,31}, X^{22}_7, Y^{22}_{28,29}(64)$	$2^{60} \cdot 2^{68} = 2^{128}$
21	$K^1_{14}[1,3]$	$X^2_{17}, X^2_{16}, X^3_{8,14,16,23,26,30,31}, X^{22}_{7,10,14,23,31}, X^{22}_{29}(60)$	$2^{62} \cdot 2^{64} = 2^{126}$
22	$K^1_8[0,2]$	$X^3_{15,22}, X^3_{8,14,16,23,26,30,31}, X^{22}_{7,10,14,23,29,31}(60)$	$2^{64} \cdot 2^{60} = 2^{124}$

the attack with $a = 4$-bit advantage, then the probability of success of the attack will be about $P_s = \Phi(2 \cdot \sqrt{N} \cdot \varepsilon - \Phi^{-1}(1 - 2^{-(a+1)})) \approx 90\%$, where $\varepsilon = 2^{-59.16}$ is the bias of the linear hull.

From Table 5 we know that the total time complexity of the key recovery process is approximately $(2^{114}+3\cdot 2^{120}+7\cdot 2^{122}+4\cdot 2^{124}+3\cdot 2^{126}+4\cdot 2^{128})/(16\cdot 22) \approx 2^{121.88}$ 23-round encryptions of WARP, where 64-bit key can be recovered in the attack. Since the maximal size for the remained state is 116-bit, the memory complexity is about 2^{126} blocks.

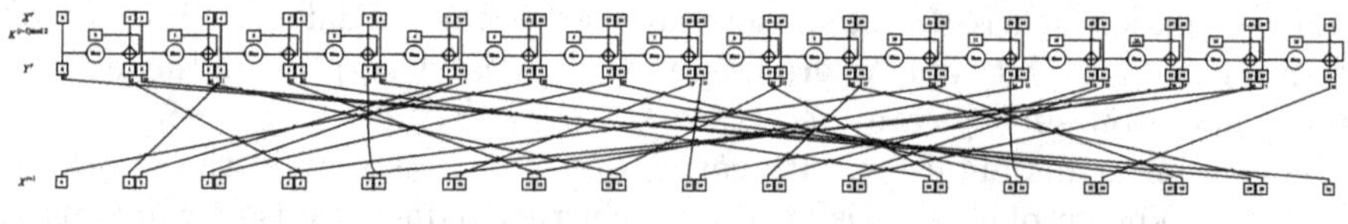

Fig. 1. Round function of WARP

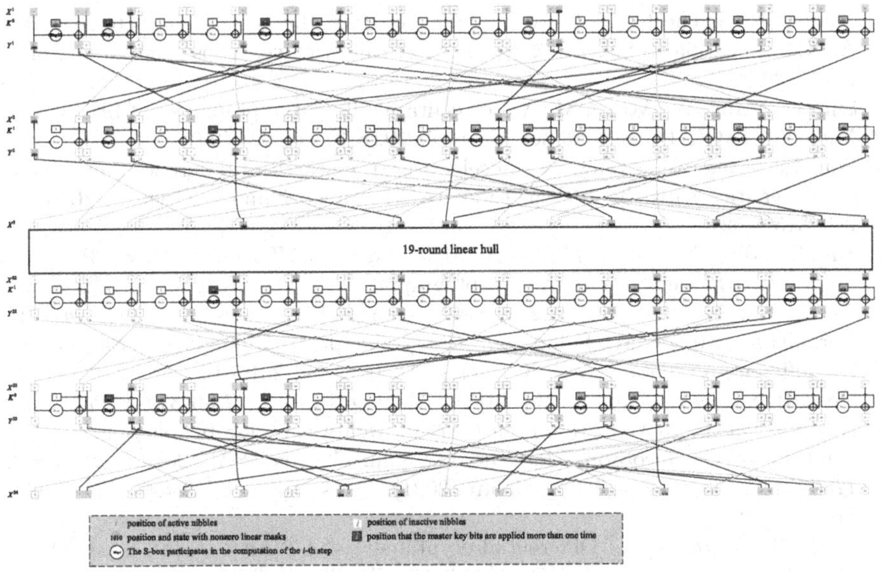

Fig. 2. Key-recovery Attack on 23-round WARP

5 Conclusion

In this paper, the security of WARP against linear cryptanalysis is evaluated based on SAT method, and two automatic search algorithms are presented to search for linear trails of WARP. With these algorithms, the lower bound on the number of linearly active S-boxes and the maximal linear correlation of WARP up to 30 rounds is presented, and strong linear hull effect is observed for WARP from 12 to 21 rounds. Using a 19-round linear hull of WARP with correlation $2^{-58.16}$, a linear attack on 23-round WARP is presented by extending two rounds forward and backward the distinguisher.

References

1. Matsui, M.: Linear cryptanalysis method for DES cipher. In: Helleseth, T. (ed.) EUROCRYPT 1993. LNCS, vol. 765, pp. 386–397. Springer, Heidelberg (1994). https://doi.org/10.1007/3-540-48285-7_33
2. Mouha, N., Wang, Q., Gu, D., Bart, P.: Differential and linear cryptanalysis using mixed-integer linear programming. In: Wu, C.-K., Yung, M., Lin, D. (eds.) Inscrypt 2011. LNCS, vol. 7537, pp. 57–76. Springer, Heidelberg (2012). https://doi.org/10.1007/978-3-642-34704-7_5
3. Sun, S., Hu, L., Wang, P., Qiao, K., Ma, X., Song, L.: Automatic security evaluation and (related-key) differential characteristic search: application to SIMON, PRESENT, LBlock, DES(L) and other bit-oriented block ciphers. In: Sarkar, P., Iwata, T. (eds.) ASIACRYPT 2014. LNCS, vol. 8873, pp. 158–178. Springer, Heidelberg (2014). https://doi.org/10.1007/978-3-662-45611-8_9

4. Mouha, N., Preneel, B.: Towards finding optimal differential characteristics for ARX: application to Salsa20. Cryptology ePrint Archive, https://eprint.iacr.org/2013/328
5. Sun, L., Wang, W., Wang, M.: More accurate differential properties of LED64 and Midori64. IACR Trans. Symmet. Cryptol. **2018**(3), 93–123 (2018)
6. Sun, L., Wang, W., Wang, M.: Accelerating the search of differential and linear characteristics with the SAT method. IACR Trans. Symmet. Cryptol. **2021**(1), 269–315 (2021)
7. Sun, L., Wang, W., Wang, M.: Improved attacks on GIFT-64. In: AlTawy, R., Hülsing, A. (eds.) Selected Areas in Cryptography. SAC 2021. LNCS, vol. 13203, pp. 246–265. Springer, Cham (2022) https://doi.org/10.1007/978-3-030-99277-4_12
8. Gerault, D., Minier, M., Solnon, C.: Constraint programming models for chosen key differential cryptanalysis. In: Rueher, M. (ed.) CP 2016. LNCS, vol. 9892, pp. 584–601. Springer, Cham (2016). https://doi.org/10.1007/978-3-319-44953-1_37
9. Banik, S., et al.: WARP: revisiting GFN for lightweight 128-bit block cipher. In: Dunkelman, O., Jacobson, M.J., Jr., O'Flynn, C. (eds.) SAC 2020. LNCS, vol. 12804, pp. 535–564. Springer, Cham (2021). https://doi.org/10.1007/978-3-030-81652-0_21
10. Teh, J.S., Biryukov, A.: Differential cryptanalysis of WARP. J. Inf. Secur. Appl. **70**, 103316 (2022). https://doi.org/10.1016/j.jisa.2022.103316
11. Lallemand, V., Minier, M., Rouquette, L.: Automatic search of rectangle attacks on feistel ciphers: application to WARP. IACR Trans. Symmet. Cryptol. **2022**(2), 113–140 (2022)
12. Sun, L., Wang, W., Wang, M.: Key-Recovery Attacks on CRAFT and WARP. Cryptology ePrint Archive. https://eprint.iacr.org/2022/997 to appear in SAC 2022
13. Rickmann, S.: Logic friday (version 1.1. 3) [computer software] (2011)
14. Sinz, C.: Towards an optimal CNF encoding of boolean cardinality constraints. In: van Beek, P. (ed.) CP 2005. LNCS, vol. 3709, pp. 827–831. Springer, Heidelberg (2005). https://doi.org/10.1007/11564751_73
15. Blondeau, C., Nyberg, K.: Joint data and key distribution of simple, multiple, and multidimensional linear cryptanalysis test statistic and its impact to data complexity. Des. Codes Crypt. **82**(1), 319–349 (2017)
16. Selçuk, A.A.: On probability of success in linear and differential cryptanalysis. J. Cryptol. **21**(1), 131–147 (2008)

Linicrypt in the Ideal Cipher Model

Zahra Javar(✉) and Bruce M. Kapron(✉)

University of Victoria, Victoria, BC, Canada
{zahrajavar,bmkapron}@uvic.ca

Abstract. We extend the Linicrypt framework for characterizing hash function security as proposed by McQuoid, Swope, and Rosulek (TCC 2018) to support constructions in the ideal cipher model. In this setting, we give a characterization of collision- and second-preimage-resistance in terms of a linear-algebraic condition on Linicrypt programs, and present an efficient algorithm for determining whether a program satisfies the condition. As an application, we consider the case of the block cipher-based hash functions proposed by Preneel, Govaerts, and Vandewall (Crypto 1993), and show that the semantic analysis of PGV given by Black et. al. (J. Crypto. 2010) can be captured as a special case of our characterization.

Keywords: Collision-resistant hash function · Compression function · Ideal cipher model · Linicrypt

1 Introduction

Two fundamental properties of cryptographic hash functions which are the basis for their cryptographic application are *collision resistance* and *2nd-preimage resistance*. Applications of cryptographic hash functions include message authentication code [2] and hash-based signatures [6,12,13,15]. One basic approach to build hash functions is by the iteration of a fixed-length *compression function*.

In this work, we extend the approach of [14] to characterize collision-resistance properties of compression functions constructed in the ideal cipher model, and demonstrate that such an approach is amenable to automated validation and generation.

In [14] the *Linicrypt* formalism [8] is applied to give a characterization of collision- and 2nd-preimage resistance of hash functions constructed via straight-line algebraic programs with access to a random oracle. In this paper, as suggested by [14], we extend the characterization given in that paper to the ideal cipher model. As the ideal cipher model is a standard setting for the construction of cryptographic hash functions, in particular modeling block-cipher-based construction of compression functions, this is a natural and relevant extension of the previous work.

Work supported in part by NSERC Discovery Grant RGPIN-2021-02481.

M. Zhang et al. (Eds.): ProvSec 2023, LNCS 14217, pp. 91–111, 2023.
https://doi.org/10.1007/978-3-031-45513-1_6

A well-studied group of block-cipher-based compression functions was proposed by Preneel, Govaerts, and Vandewalle (PGV) [16]. They proposed a systematic way to construct *rate-1* block-cipher-based compression functions which make a single call to the ideal cipher, using only simple algebraic operations.

In a generalization of [16], Black, Rogaway, and Shrimpton [4] introduced 64 rate-1 compression functions $h : \{0,1\}^l \times \{0,1\}^l \rightarrow \{0,1\}^l$ utilizing a single call to a block-cipher $E : \{0,1\}^l \times \{0,1\}^l \rightarrow \{0,1\}^l$ of the form $h^E(h,m) = E_a(b) \oplus c$ where $a, b, c \in \{h, m, h \oplus m, v\}$, and v is a fixed constant, which they term *PGV compression functions.* They then prove that of the 64 PGV compression functions, 12 of them, referred to as *group-1*, are collision-resistant and preimage resistant up to the birthday bound, and 8 of them, which are called *group-2* are only collision resistant after some iteration. The proofs in [4] are given on a per-function basis, with canonical examples and an indication of how these could be generalized to any function in the corresponding group. In subsequent work, [5] characterized group-1 and group-2 PGV compression functions via a more general approach which considers fundamental combinatorial properties of the definitions, based on *pre-* and *post-processing functions.* A related work by Stam [18] presents these properties in an algebraic setting, partly anticipating the approach presented in the current paper. In Sect. 4, we model the PGV compression functions in Linicrypt and show the properties proposed in [5] may in fact be obtained as a special case of our general characterization.

Contributions. Our main contributions are summarized as follows:

1. A formulation in the ideal cipher model of the notion of *collision structure*, introduced in [14] for the random oracle model (Definition 4).
2. A characterization showing a Linicrypt program is collision resistant (and 2nd-preimage resistant) if and only if it does not have a collision structure (Theorem 1).
3. An efficient algorithm for finding collision structures (Algorithm 1).
4. In the rate-1 setting, giving an alternate proof the collision-resistance of *group-1* PGV compression functions as originally established in [4] using our characterization (Theorem 2.)

While our approach largely follows that of [14], the extension to the ideal cipher model is non-trivial, and the application to the PGV functions presents an interesting case where the Linicrypt approach sheds new light on existing approaches to hash function security.

2 Preliminaries

In our presentation, we largely follow the approach of [14]. Programs are defined over a finite field $\mathbb{F}$, elements of which are denoted by lower-case non-bold letters[1], vectors over $\mathbb{F}$ by lowercase bold letters and matrices over $\mathbb{F}$ by uppercase

[1] We usually use Roman letters, but may also use Greek or script letters depending on the setting.

bold letters. We write $\boldsymbol{a} \cdot \boldsymbol{b}$ or $\boldsymbol{ab}$ for the inner product and $\boldsymbol{M} \times \boldsymbol{a}$ or $\boldsymbol{Ma}$ for the matrix-vector product. Note that we will sometimes think of matrices as a column vector of row vectors (so we may write $\boldsymbol{M} = (\boldsymbol{m}_1, \ldots, \boldsymbol{m}_k)^\top$.)

2.1 Ideal Cipher Model

It is often challenging to design cryptographic primitives which provably provide a needed security property, even in the presence of computational assumptions. One approach to deal with this problem is to assume the existence of an ideal primitive, such as an ideal block cipher or a random oracle which may be used to prove the security of new primitives. The new primitive is then implemented using a real-world instantiation of the ideal primitive. While this approach is not sound in general — there are primitives that can be proven secure when using a truly random oracle but not when using a non-ideal hash function [7] — it is widely used in practice and is considered to provide some formal assurance of security.

The idea of modeling a block cipher as a random permutation appears as early as the work of Shannon [17]. In the *ideal cipher model*, the adversary has access to oracles E and E^{-1}, where E is a random block cipher $E : \{0,1\}^k \times \{0,1\}^n$ and E^{-1} is its inverse. Thus each key $k \in \{0,1\}^n$ determines a uniformly selected permutation $E_k = E(k, \cdot)$ on $\{0,1\}^n$, and the adversary is given oracles for E and E^{-1}. The latter, on input (k, y), returns the x such that $E_k(x) = y$. As is standard in this setting (see, e.g., [3],) programs used to construct hash functions are given access to E.

2.2 Linicrypt

The Linicrypt framework [8] was introduced by Carmer and Rosulek to formally model cryptographic algorithms with access to a random oracle, and using linear operations. In that work, they give an algebraic condition to efficiently decide if two Linicrypt programs induce computationally indistinguishable distributions. As mentioned above, in [14] the framework is applied to characterize collision-resistance properties of hash functions.

A Linicrypt program is a straight-line program over a fixed vector $(v_1, \ldots, v_m)$ of *program variables*, where the first k are designated as *inputs*. A program is a sequence of lines specifying assignments to (non-input) program variables where the right-hand side of each assignment is either[2]

1. A call to the random oracle on a previously assigned variable or input
2. A $\mathbb{F}$-linear combination of previously assigned variables and inputs

This defines a function $\mathcal{P}^H : \mathbb{F}^k \to \mathbb{F}^r$ for some k, r which on input vector $\boldsymbol{x} = (x_1, \cdots, x_k)$ returns output vector $\boldsymbol{\ell} = (l_1, \ldots, l_r)$. The field is parameterized by a *security parameter* λ. In particular $\mathbb{F} = \mathbb{F}_{p^\lambda}$ for some prime p. In this work, we

[2] The Linicrypt model, introduced in [8], also allows the assignment of a random field element to a variable. Here, as in [14], we consider only deterministic programs.

assume a *uniform* model in which there is a single program $\mathcal{P}$ (with constants from $\mathbb{F}_p$.) As discussed in [8], it is also possible to consider families of programs depending on λ.

As described in [8,14], Linicrypt programs can be given a purely *algebraic* representation. We will give a slightly modified (but equivalent) version of this as presented in [14]. We first note that in the straight-line program representation, if there are no assignments of random field elements to variables, then all assignments of the second form may be eliminated, via successive in-lining. In this case, a program $\mathcal{P}$ over a field $\mathbb{F}$ is given by a set of *base variables* $\boldsymbol{v}_{base} = (v_1, \ldots, v_{k+n})^\top$, where $v_i \in \mathbb{F}$ and the first k variables are $\mathcal{P}$'s input and the last n variables correspond to the results of oracle queries. This means that, algebraically, for each program variable v_i we can write $v_i = \mathbf{e}_i \boldsymbol{v}_{base}$ where $\mathbf{e}_i$ denotes the ith canonical basis vector over $\mathbb{F}^{k+n}$. Similarly, the output may be given as a vector of $\mathbb{F}$-linear combinations of program base variables, and this may be specified by the *output matrix* $\boldsymbol{M} = (\boldsymbol{m}_1, \ldots, \boldsymbol{m}_r)^\top$, where $\boldsymbol{m}_i \in \mathbb{F}^{k+n}$ and $\boldsymbol{M}\boldsymbol{v}_{base} = (l_1, \cdots, l_r)$ is the vector of program outputs. Finally, each oracle call $v_i = H(t, v_{i_1}, \cdots, v_{i_m})$ where t is a *nonce* and $v_i \in \mathbb{F}$, is represented by an *oracle constraint* $c = (t, \boldsymbol{Q}, \boldsymbol{a})$, indicating that when H is called on input $(t, \boldsymbol{Q} \times \boldsymbol{v}_{base}) = (t, v_{i_1}, \cdots, v_{i_m})$, the returned value is $\boldsymbol{a} \cdot \boldsymbol{v}_{base} = v_i$.

This representation allows us to abstract away from the straight-line syntax, and reason about programs in a purely algebraic fashion. In particular, as noted in [8,14], if we let $\mathcal{C}$ denote the set of oracle constraints, then the behavior of a program $\mathcal{P}$ is completely specified by its *algebraic representation* $(\boldsymbol{M}, \mathcal{C})$. In particular, the characterization of collision-resistance properties is completely determined by algebraic properties of $(\boldsymbol{M}, \mathcal{C})$.

The following is an example of a two-input Linicrypt program with random oracle H

$$\begin{aligned}
&\underline{\mathcal{P}^H(v_1, v_2):}\\
&\quad v_3 := H(t_1, v_1)\\
&\quad v_4 := H(t_2, v_2)\\
&\quad v_5 := v_3 + v_4\\
&\quad \mathit{return}\ v_5
\end{aligned}$$

In the algebraic presentation, the program is specified by:

$$\boldsymbol{v}_{base} = (v_1, v_2, v_3, v_4)^\top$$
$$\boldsymbol{M} = \begin{bmatrix} 0\,0\,1\,1 \end{bmatrix}$$
$$\mathcal{C} = \langle (t_1, \boldsymbol{q}_1, \boldsymbol{a}_1), (t_2, \boldsymbol{q}_2, \boldsymbol{a}_2) \rangle$$

where

$$\boldsymbol{q}_1 = (1,0,0,0) \quad \boldsymbol{q}_2 = (0,1,0,0)$$
$$\boldsymbol{a}_1 = (0,0,1,0) \quad \boldsymbol{a}_2 = (0,0,0,1)$$

In moving to programs in the ideal cipher model, for assignments of the first type, we now have calls to an ideal cipher $E(.,.)$ on a pair of values which are either program inputs or previously assigned variables. These inputs to E correspond to the key and input of an encryption query. Thus, supposing $\mathcal{P}$ has n oracle calls, for $i \in [n]$, each call is of the form $\boldsymbol{a}_i \cdot \boldsymbol{v}_{base} = E(\boldsymbol{q}_{K_i} \cdot \boldsymbol{v}_{base}, \boldsymbol{q}_{X_i} \cdot \boldsymbol{v}_{base})$ and can be represented by an *oracle constraint* $c = (\boldsymbol{q}_K, \boldsymbol{q}_X, \boldsymbol{a})$ where $\boldsymbol{q}_K, \boldsymbol{q}_X, \boldsymbol{a} \in \mathbb{F}^{k+n}$. To simplify the presentation we define $K_i := \boldsymbol{q}_{K_i} \cdot \boldsymbol{v}_{base}$, $X_i := \boldsymbol{q}_{X_i} \cdot \boldsymbol{v}_{base}$ and $Y_i := \boldsymbol{a}_i \cdot \boldsymbol{v}_{base}$. Letting $\mathcal{C}$ denote the set of oracle constraints and $\boldsymbol{M}$ the output matrix, we again have an algebraic representation $(\boldsymbol{M}, \mathcal{C})$. The following is a simple example of such a program:

$$\begin{aligned} &\underline{\mathcal{P}^E(v_1, v_2):} \\ &\quad v_4 := E(v_1, v_2) \\ &\quad \mathit{return}\ v_4 + v_2 \end{aligned}$$

$$\boldsymbol{M} = (0,1,0,1),\ \mathcal{C} = (\boldsymbol{q}_K, \boldsymbol{q}_X, \boldsymbol{a}),\ \boldsymbol{v}_{base} = (v_1, v_2, v_4)^\top$$
$$\boldsymbol{q}_K = (1,0,0,0) \quad \boldsymbol{q}_X = (0,1,0,0) \quad \boldsymbol{a} = (0,0,1,0)$$

Further examples are given in the Appendices. We also refer the reader to [8,14] for a more detailed introduction to Linicrypt.

Constant Values. In practice, the definition of a hash function may depend on the use of a constant value from the underlying field or domain, typically referred to as an *initialization vector (IV)*. Such definitions involve affine expressions and so, strictly speaking, are beyond the model provided by Linicrypt. One approach to deal with this problem is to utilize some underlying algebraic property of operations involving constant values. This is the approach taken in the algebraic analysis of [18], where it is noted that translation by a constant preserves bijectivity. We take a more general approach, treating constants *parametrically*. Namely, a constant c used in a program $\mathcal{P}$ is treated as an additional input and also as an output of the program, making it a fixed parameter. In particular, $\mathcal{P}$ has base variables $v_1, \ldots, v_{k+n}$ and inputs $v_1, \ldots, v_k$ the modified program with a constant c has base variables $v_1, \ldots, v_{k+n+1}$ where $v_{k+1} := c$ and $\boldsymbol{M}$ and $\mathcal{C}$ are updated appropriately. Finally, the single row $\mathbf{e}_{k+1}$ is appended to $\boldsymbol{M}$ (indicating that c is an output.) By following this convention, we can analyze the security properties of hash functions defined by Linicrypt programs using constants without making any modifications to our definitions and proofs. Moreover, any property which does not depend on a particular property (e.g., the bit-level representation) of a constant value used in a program will be preserved by this convention. While this does not capture implementation-level details, it provides a level of analysis consistent with works such as [5].

Security Definitions. We assume the number of oracle queries the adversary makes to E is q_E and to E^{-1} is q_D.

Definition 1 ([14] **Definition 2**). *Program $\mathcal{P}$ is* (q, ϵ)-collision resistant *if any oracle adversary $\mathcal{A}$ making at most $q = q_E + q_D$ queries has probability of success at most ϵ in the following game:*

$$(\boldsymbol{x}, \boldsymbol{x}') \leftarrow \mathcal{A}^{E,E^{-1}}(\lambda);\ \textit{return}\ (\boldsymbol{x} \neq \boldsymbol{x}')\ \textit{and}\ \mathcal{P}^E(\boldsymbol{x}) = \mathcal{P}^E(\boldsymbol{x}') \quad (1)$$

Definition 2 ([14] **Definition 3**). *Program $\mathcal{P}$ is* (q, ϵ)-2nd-preimage resistant *if any oracle adversary $\mathcal{A}$ making at most $q = q_E + q_D$ queries has probability of success at most ϵ in the following game:*

$$\boldsymbol{x} \leftarrow \mathbb{F}^k; \boldsymbol{x}' \leftarrow \mathcal{A}^{E,E^{-1}}(\boldsymbol{x}, \lambda);\ \textit{return}\ (\boldsymbol{x} \neq \boldsymbol{x}')\ \textit{and}\ \mathcal{P}^E(\boldsymbol{x}) = \mathcal{P}^E(\boldsymbol{x}') \quad (2)$$

3 Characterizing Collision Resistance

In this section, we give an algebraic condition to characterize collision resistance and 2nd-preimage resistance for Linicrypt programs in the ideal cipher model (Definition 4). Before giving the definition we note some programs fail trivially to be collision-resistant because two different inputs produce exactly the same queries to the oracle. This is formalized in the following:

Definition 3. *Program $\mathcal{P} = (M, \mathcal{C})$ is* degenerate *if*

$$\mathsf{span}(\{\mathbf{e}_1, \ldots, \mathbf{e}_{k+n}\}) \not\subseteq \mathsf{span}(\{\boldsymbol{q}_K \mid (\boldsymbol{q}_K, \boldsymbol{q}_X, \boldsymbol{a}) \in \mathcal{C}\} \cup \{\boldsymbol{q}_X \mid (\boldsymbol{q}_K, \boldsymbol{q}_X, \boldsymbol{a}) \in \mathcal{C}\} \cup \{\boldsymbol{a} \mid (\boldsymbol{q}_K, \boldsymbol{q}_X, \boldsymbol{a}) \in \mathcal{C}\} \cup \mathsf{rows}(\boldsymbol{M}))$$

Lemma 1. *If $\mathcal{P}$ is degenerate then 2nd-preimages can be found with probability 1.*

Proof. Assume the adversary $\mathcal{A}$ is given a preimage $\boldsymbol{x}$, and it determines the base vector $\boldsymbol{v}_{base}$ in the execution of $\mathcal{P}(\boldsymbol{x})$. We define the matrix $\boldsymbol{P} = \begin{bmatrix} \boldsymbol{Q}_K \\ \hdashline \boldsymbol{Q}_X \\ \hdashline \boldsymbol{A} \\ \hdashline \boldsymbol{M} \end{bmatrix}$ where $\boldsymbol{Q}_K, \boldsymbol{Q}_X, \boldsymbol{A}$ are matrices whose rows correspond to the components of the elements of $\mathcal{C}$ (ordered arbitrarily.) If the adversary can determine a 2nd-preimage $\boldsymbol{x}' \neq \boldsymbol{x}$ where $\boldsymbol{P}\boldsymbol{v}_{base} = \boldsymbol{P}\boldsymbol{v}'_{base}$ where $\boldsymbol{v}'_{base}$ is the base vector in the calculation of $\mathcal{P}(\boldsymbol{x}')$ then $\mathcal{P}(\boldsymbol{x}) = \mathcal{P}(\boldsymbol{x}')$ and $\mathcal{A}$ wins. Since program $\mathcal{P}$ is degenerate, the rows of $\boldsymbol{P}$ cannot span all $k + n$ basis vectors which means $\text{rank}(\boldsymbol{P}) < k + n$, and thus, for some $\boldsymbol{v} \neq \boldsymbol{0}$, $\boldsymbol{P}\boldsymbol{v} = \boldsymbol{0}$. The adversary can solve for this $\boldsymbol{v}$ and set $\boldsymbol{v}'_{base} = \boldsymbol{v}_{base} + \boldsymbol{v}$. Then $\boldsymbol{P}(\boldsymbol{v}'_{base} - \boldsymbol{v}_{base}) = \boldsymbol{0}$, so $\boldsymbol{v}'_{base} \neq \boldsymbol{v}_{base}$ and $\boldsymbol{P}\boldsymbol{v}'_{base} = \boldsymbol{P}\boldsymbol{v}_{base}$. In particular, this allows $\mathcal{A}$ to compute $\boldsymbol{x}' \neq \boldsymbol{x}$ such that $\mathcal{P}(\boldsymbol{x}') = \mathcal{P}(\boldsymbol{x})$. □

The following definition gives a syntactic condition on programs that will be used to characterize collision resistance. Intuitively, for a program to have a collision $\boldsymbol{x} \neq \boldsymbol{x}'$, there must first be a query for which the adversary can pick an arbitrary input. This means at least two of K, X, Y need to be independent of all other fixed values. Secondly, to get the same output value on this different input $\boldsymbol{x}'$, the results of the remaining queries must be independent of other fixed values which implies one of Y or X must be independent of the previous queries and output values. This leads to the following definition:

Definition 4. *Let $\mathcal{P} = (\boldsymbol{M}, \mathcal{C})$ be a Linicrypt program. A collision structure for $\mathcal{P}$ is a tuple $(i^*, c_1, \ldots, c_n)$ where $c_1, \cdots, c_n$ is an ordering of $\mathcal{C}$ and $i^* \in [1, n]$, such that for $i = i^*$ at least two of the following conditions are true, and for all $i > i^*$ at least one of (C2) or (C3) is true.*

(C1) $\boldsymbol{q}_{K_i} \notin \mathsf{span}(\{\boldsymbol{q}_{K_1}, \ldots, \boldsymbol{q}_{K_{i-1}}\}, \{\boldsymbol{q}_{X_1}, \cdots \boldsymbol{q}_{X_{i-1}}\}, \{\boldsymbol{a}_1, \ldots, \boldsymbol{a}_{i-1}\}, \mathsf{rows}(\boldsymbol{M}))$
(C2) $\boldsymbol{q}_{X_i} \notin \mathsf{span}(\{\boldsymbol{q}_{K_1}, \ldots, \boldsymbol{q}_{K_i}\}, \{\boldsymbol{q}_{X_1}, \cdots \boldsymbol{q}_{X_{i-1}}\}, \{\boldsymbol{a}_1, \ldots, \boldsymbol{a}_i\}, \mathsf{rows}(\boldsymbol{M}))$
(C3) $\boldsymbol{a}_i \notin \mathsf{span}(\{\boldsymbol{q}_{K_1}, \ldots, \boldsymbol{q}_{K_i}\}, \{\boldsymbol{q}_{X_1}, \cdots \boldsymbol{q}_{X_i}\}, \{\boldsymbol{a}_1, \ldots, \boldsymbol{a}_{i-1}\}, \mathsf{rows}(\boldsymbol{M}))$

Lemma 2. *If a Linicrypt program $\mathcal{P}$ with n constraints has a collision structure $(i^*, c_1, \ldots, c_n)$ then there exists a collision adversary $\mathcal{A}$ with access to E and E^{-1} which given an input $\boldsymbol{x}$ makes at most $2n$ queries and returns $\boldsymbol{x}' \neq \boldsymbol{x}$ such that $\mathcal{P}^E(\boldsymbol{x}') = \mathcal{P}^E(\boldsymbol{x})$, and so has success probability of 1 in Game 2.*

Proof. The adversary $\mathcal{A}$ first determines a setting of the base variables $\boldsymbol{v}$ by running $\mathcal{P}^E(\boldsymbol{x})$, and creates linear constraints on unknowns $\boldsymbol{v}'$ as follows:

- add constraint $\boldsymbol{M}\boldsymbol{v}' = \boldsymbol{M}\boldsymbol{v}$
- for $i < i^*$, add constraints $\boldsymbol{q}_{K_i} \cdot \boldsymbol{v}' = \boldsymbol{q}_{K_i} \cdot \boldsymbol{v}$, $\boldsymbol{q}_{X_i} \cdot \boldsymbol{v}' = \boldsymbol{q}_{X_i} \cdot \boldsymbol{v}$ and $\boldsymbol{a}_i \cdot \boldsymbol{v}' = \boldsymbol{a}_i \cdot \boldsymbol{v}$
- For $i \geq i^*$,
  - if (C1) holds, choose $K_i' \in \mathbb{F}$ so that $K_i' \neq \boldsymbol{q}_{K_i} \cdot \boldsymbol{v}$ and add the constraint $\boldsymbol{q}_{K_i} \cdot \boldsymbol{v}' = K_i'$
  - if (C2) holds, set $X_i' := E^{-1}(\boldsymbol{q}_{K_i} \cdot \boldsymbol{v}', \boldsymbol{a}_i \cdot \boldsymbol{v}')$ and add the constraint $\boldsymbol{q}_{X_i} \cdot \boldsymbol{v}' = X_i'$
  - if (C3) holds, set $Y_i' := E(\boldsymbol{q}_{K_i} \cdot \boldsymbol{v}', \boldsymbol{q}_{X_i} \cdot \boldsymbol{v}')$ and add the constraint $\boldsymbol{a}_i \cdot \boldsymbol{v}' = Y_i'$
  - if (C2) and (C3) both hold, choose $X_i' \in \mathbb{F}$ such that $X_i' \neq \boldsymbol{q}_{X_i} \cdot \boldsymbol{v}$, set $Y_i := E(\boldsymbol{q}_{K_i} \cdot \boldsymbol{v}', X_i')$ and add the constraints $\boldsymbol{q}_{X_i} \cdot \boldsymbol{v}' = X_i'$ and $\boldsymbol{a}_i \cdot \boldsymbol{v}' = Y_i'$

We claim that the constraints have a unique solution $\boldsymbol{v}' \neq \boldsymbol{v}$ such that if $x_i' = \mathbf{e}_i \cdot \boldsymbol{v}'$, $1 \leq i \leq k$, then $\boldsymbol{x}' \neq \boldsymbol{x}$ and $\mathcal{P}^E(\boldsymbol{x}') = \mathcal{P}^E(\boldsymbol{x})$.

To see that $\boldsymbol{v}' \neq \boldsymbol{v}$, note that for $i = i^*$, either (C1) holds, or both (C2) and (C3) hold. The choice of K_{i^*}' in the first case and X_{i^*}' in the second, ensure $\boldsymbol{v}' \neq \boldsymbol{v}$.

The constraints that are added for the output matrix and for $i < i^*$ are consistent, as they already have a solution, namely $\boldsymbol{v}$. For $i \geq i^*$, a new constraint is added only in the case that the corresponding $\boldsymbol{q}_{K_i}, \boldsymbol{q}_{X_i}$ or $\boldsymbol{a}_i$ is independent of the vectors added in previous constraints, and so consistency is maintained as constraints are added. Once all constraints are added, nondegeneracy ensures that $\boldsymbol{v}'$ is unique.

Finally, $\boldsymbol{v}'$ is consistent with the values returned by E and E^{-1}. This means that $\boldsymbol{v}'$ corresponds to the setting of base variables resulting from evaluating $\mathcal{P}^E(\boldsymbol{x}')$, so from $\boldsymbol{v}' \neq \boldsymbol{v}$ we conclude $\boldsymbol{x}' \neq \boldsymbol{x}$, and from the $\boldsymbol{M}$ constraint, $\mathcal{P}^E(\boldsymbol{x}') = \mathcal{P}^E(\boldsymbol{x})$. □

Lemma 3. *Let $\mathcal{P}$ be a Linicrypt program with n constraints. If there is an adversary $\mathcal{A}$ for $\mathcal{P}$ making at most N oracle queries with success probability $> N^{2n}/|\mathbb{F}|$ in the collision-resistance game (Game 1) or success probability $> N^n/|\mathbb{F}|$ in the 2nd-preimage game (Game 2) then the $\mathcal{P}$ is either degenerate or has a collision structure $(i^*, c_1, \ldots, c_n)$.*

Proof. We may assume the following without loss of generality:

1. $\mathcal{A}$ does not repeat a query or make the inverse of a query it has already made. This can be achieved by recording queries as they are made.
2. For queries made in the execution of $\mathcal{P}(\boldsymbol{x})$ and $\mathcal{P}(\boldsymbol{x}')$, $\mathcal{A}$ makes either the query or its corresponding inverse query before returning. For Game 1, this is achieved by having $\mathcal{A}$ run $\mathcal{P}(\boldsymbol{x})$ and $\mathcal{P}(\boldsymbol{x}')$ before returning and making the corresponding queries subject to restriction (1). For Game 2 this is achieved by having $\mathcal{A}$ initially make all the queries that result from running $\mathcal{P}(\boldsymbol{x})$ and also running $\mathcal{P}(\boldsymbol{x}')$ before returning, and making any corresponding query, subject to restriction (1), before returning.
3. $\mathcal{A}$ actually returns $\boldsymbol{v}, \boldsymbol{v}'$ which are the settings of base variables determined by the execution of $\mathcal{P}(\boldsymbol{x})$ and $\mathcal{P}(\boldsymbol{x}')$, respectively.

The assumptions imply that for an oracle constraint $c = (\boldsymbol{q}_K, \boldsymbol{q}_X, \boldsymbol{a})$ occurring in $\mathcal{P}$, $\mathcal{A}$ determines the value of triples $(\boldsymbol{q}_K \cdot \boldsymbol{v}, \boldsymbol{q}_X \cdot \boldsymbol{v}, \boldsymbol{a} \cdot \boldsymbol{v})$ through exactly one of its N queries, which is either a E-query or E^{-1}-query. Based on this fact, we define two mappings $T, T' : \mathcal{C} \to [N]$ where $\mathcal{C}$ is the set of constraints in $\mathcal{P}$ and the $T(c_i)$th and $T'(c_i)$th adversary queries correspond to constraint c_i in the computation of $\mathcal{P}(\boldsymbol{x})$ and $\mathcal{P}(\boldsymbol{x}')$, and determine the triple $(\boldsymbol{q}_K \cdot \boldsymbol{v}, \boldsymbol{q}_X \cdot \boldsymbol{v}, \boldsymbol{a} \cdot \boldsymbol{v})$ and $(\boldsymbol{q}_K \cdot \boldsymbol{v}', \boldsymbol{q}_X \cdot \boldsymbol{v}', \boldsymbol{a} \cdot \boldsymbol{v}')$ respectively. In Game 1, $T(c_i)$ and $T'(c_i)$ are each mapped to one of N queries made by $\mathcal{A}$, so the number of possible mappings (T, T') is N^{2n}. In Game 2, Assumption 2 implies that T is fixed, so the number of possible mappings (T, T') is N^n. Using the pigeonhole principle and $\mathcal{A}$'s assumed advantage in each game, there is a specific mapping (T, T') for which $\mathcal{A}$'s advantage when using this mapping is at least $1/|\mathbb{F}|$. We will assume that the adversary is using this mapping — for any other mapping, it returns $\perp$ as its last action.

Using the same terminology as [14], a query $c \in \mathcal{C}$ is *convergent* if $T(c) = T'(c)$, and *divergent* otherwise. Because $\boldsymbol{x} \neq \boldsymbol{x}'$ is a collision and $\mathcal{P}$ is nondegenerate there is at least one divergent constraint. Define $\texttt{finish}(c) = \max\{T(c), T'(c)\}$. Note in contrast to [14], here we do not have unique nonces, so two different constraints can be mapped to the same adversary query, thus `finish` is not an injective function. However, we will show that there is an ordering of $\mathcal{C}$ as $(c_1, \ldots, c_n)$ where the convergent constraints come first, in any order, followed by divergent constraints in some non-decreasing order, and letting i^* denote the index of the first divergent constraint, we claim that $(i^*, c_1, \ldots, c_n)$ is a collision structure for $\mathcal{P}$.

For $i < i^*$, since each c_i is convergent we have $\boldsymbol{q}_{K_i} \cdot \boldsymbol{v}' = \boldsymbol{q}_{K_i} \cdot \boldsymbol{v}$, $\boldsymbol{q}_{X_i} \cdot \boldsymbol{v}' = \boldsymbol{q}_{X_i} \cdot \boldsymbol{v}$ and $\boldsymbol{a}_i \cdot \boldsymbol{v}' = \boldsymbol{a}_i \cdot \boldsymbol{v}$ and because $\mathcal{P}(\boldsymbol{x}) = \mathcal{P}(\boldsymbol{x}')$ we have $\boldsymbol{M}\boldsymbol{v}' = \boldsymbol{M}\boldsymbol{v}$.

For $i = i^*$ the query c_i is divergent thus at least one of the following inequalities holds $\boldsymbol{q}_{K_i} \cdot \boldsymbol{v}' \neq \boldsymbol{q}_{K_i} \cdot \boldsymbol{v}$, $\boldsymbol{q}_{X_i} \cdot \boldsymbol{v}' \neq \boldsymbol{q}_{X_i} \cdot \boldsymbol{v}$ or $\boldsymbol{a}_i \cdot \boldsymbol{v}' \neq \boldsymbol{a}_i \cdot \boldsymbol{v}$. If $\boldsymbol{a}_i \cdot \boldsymbol{v}' \neq \boldsymbol{a}_i \cdot \boldsymbol{v}$ or $\boldsymbol{q}_{X_i} \cdot \boldsymbol{v}' \neq \boldsymbol{q}_{X_i} \cdot \boldsymbol{v}$ then at least one of the other inequalities hold since the ideal cipher is a permutation when the key is fixed.

This gives five possible cases. Without loss of generality, in all cases, we assume that $T(c_i) < T'(c_i)$.

1. $K_i = K_i'$ and $X_i \neq X_i'$ and $Y_i \neq Y_i'$.

   In this case, we prove both conditions (C2) and (C3) hold. By way of contradiction assume (C3) does not hold, say

$$\boldsymbol{a}_i = \sum_{j \leq i} \alpha_j \boldsymbol{q}_{K_j} + \sum_{j \leq i} \beta_j \boldsymbol{q}_{X_j} + \sum_{j < i} \gamma_j \boldsymbol{a}_j + \boldsymbol{\delta M}, \tag{3}$$

   for some $\boldsymbol{\alpha}, \boldsymbol{\beta}, \boldsymbol{\gamma}, \boldsymbol{\delta}$. After multiplying both side of the equation by $(\boldsymbol{v}' - \boldsymbol{v})$ and considering that all the queries before i^* are convergent, $\boldsymbol{M}(\boldsymbol{v}' - \boldsymbol{v}) = 0$, and $K_i = K_i'$ we have

$$\boldsymbol{a}_i \cdot \boldsymbol{v}' = \boldsymbol{a}_i \cdot \boldsymbol{v} + \beta_i \boldsymbol{q}_{X_i} \cdot (\boldsymbol{v}' - \boldsymbol{v})$$

   Also because $Y_i \neq Y_i'$ and $X_i \neq X_i'$ we know $\beta_i \neq 0$. If $T'(c_i)$ is an encryption query then the right-hand side of the equation is a fixed value but the left-hand side is a query result, so the advantage of the adversary is $\leq 1/|\mathbb{F}|$ contrary to assumption. If $T'(c_i)$ is a decryption query then isolating $\boldsymbol{q}_{X_i} \cdot \boldsymbol{v}'$ gives us

$$\boldsymbol{q}_{X_i} \cdot \boldsymbol{v}' = \boldsymbol{q}_{X_i} \cdot \boldsymbol{v} + \frac{1}{\beta_i} \boldsymbol{a}_i \cdot (\boldsymbol{v}' - \boldsymbol{v})$$

   and again the right-hand side of the equation is determined while the left-hand side is a random value, again giving a contradiction. The proof for condition (C2) is similar.

2. $K_i \neq K_i'$ and $X_i = X_i'$ and $Y_i \neq Y_i'$.

   Because $K_i \neq K_i'$, condition (C1) holds. We want to show $T'(c_i)$ is an encryption query and (C3) holds. If $T'(c_i)$ is not an encryption then X_i is fixed and X_i' random so $X_i = X_i'$ holds with probability $\leq 1/|\mathbb{F}|$. If condition (C3) does not hold then 3 holds. Multiplying the equation to $(\boldsymbol{v}' - \boldsymbol{v})$ and applying $X_i = X_i'$ and $\boldsymbol{M}(\boldsymbol{v} - \boldsymbol{v}') = 0$ gives

$$\boldsymbol{a}_i \cdot \boldsymbol{v}' = \boldsymbol{a}_i \cdot \boldsymbol{v} + \alpha_i \boldsymbol{q}_{K_i} \cdot (\boldsymbol{v}' - \boldsymbol{v})$$

   The left-hand side of the above equation is a random value and the right-hand side is a fixed value, so the adversary advantage again is $\leq 1/|\mathbb{F}|$.

3. $K_i \neq K_i'$ and $X_i \neq X_i'$ and $Y_i = Y_i'$.

   This is similar to the preceding case. See Appendix A for details.

4. $K_i \neq K'_i$ and $X_i \neq X'_i$ and $Y_i \neq Y'_i$.

   Because $K_i \neq K'_i$, condition (C1) holds. We show if $T'(c_i)$ is an encryption query then (C3) holds and if it is a decryption query then (C2) holds. In the first case, assume for contradiction that (C3) does not hold, implying Eq. 3. Applying the assumption $\boldsymbol{M}(\boldsymbol{v}-\boldsymbol{v}')=0$ and canceling all the queries before i^* gives,

$$\boldsymbol{a}_i \cdot \boldsymbol{v}' = \boldsymbol{a}_i \cdot \boldsymbol{v} + \alpha_i \boldsymbol{q}_{K_i} \cdot (\boldsymbol{v}'-\boldsymbol{v}) + \beta_i \boldsymbol{q}_{X_i} \cdot (\boldsymbol{v}'-\boldsymbol{v})$$

   Here when the adversary is making query $T'(c_i)$, all the values on the right-hand side of the equation are fixed and so the adversary's advantage is $\leq 1/|\mathbb{F}|$, contrary to assumption. The case that $T'(c_i)$ is a decryption query and (C2) holds is similar.

5. $K_i \neq K'_i$ and $X_i = X'_i$ and $Y_i = Y'_i$.

   The probability of this case occurring is $\leq 1/|\mathbb{F}|$.

For $i > i^*$ by way of contradiction, assume (C2) and (C3) both fail:

$$\boldsymbol{q}_{X_i} = \sum_{j \leq i} \pi_j \cdot \boldsymbol{q}_{K_j} + \sum_{j<i} \rho_j \cdot \boldsymbol{q}_{X_j} + \sum_{j \leq i} \varsigma_j \cdot \boldsymbol{a}_j + \boldsymbol{\tau M}$$

$$\boldsymbol{a}_i = \sum_{j \leq i} \alpha_j \cdot \boldsymbol{q}_{K_j} + \sum_{j \leq i} \beta_j \cdot \boldsymbol{q}_{X_j} + \sum_{j<i} \gamma_j \cdot \boldsymbol{a}_j + \boldsymbol{\delta M}$$

Multiplying both sides by $(\boldsymbol{v}'-\boldsymbol{v})$ and canceling the terms having index less than i^* and noting $\boldsymbol{M}(\boldsymbol{v}-\boldsymbol{v}')=0$ we get,

$$\boldsymbol{q}_{X_i} \cdot \boldsymbol{v}' = \boldsymbol{q}_{X_i} \cdot \boldsymbol{v} + \sum_{i^* \leq j \leq i} \pi_j \boldsymbol{q}_{K_j} \cdot (\boldsymbol{v}'-\boldsymbol{v}) + \sum_{i^* \leq j < i} \rho_j \boldsymbol{q}_{X_j} \cdot (\boldsymbol{v}'-\boldsymbol{v}) + \sum_{i^* \leq j \leq i} \varsigma_j \boldsymbol{a}_j \cdot (\boldsymbol{v}'-\boldsymbol{v}) \tag{4}$$

$$\boldsymbol{a}_i \cdot \boldsymbol{v}' = \boldsymbol{a}_i \cdot \boldsymbol{v} + \sum_{i^* \leq j \leq i} \alpha_j \boldsymbol{q}_{K_j} \cdot (\boldsymbol{v}'-\boldsymbol{v}) + \sum_{i^* \leq j \leq i} \beta_j \boldsymbol{q}_{X_j} \cdot (\boldsymbol{v}'-\boldsymbol{v}) + \sum_{i^* \leq j < i} \gamma_j \boldsymbol{a}_j \cdot (\boldsymbol{v}'-\boldsymbol{v}) \tag{5}$$

Now, if the adversary is making query $T'(c_i)$ as an encryption query then in Eq. 5 all the values on the right-hand side of the equation are fixed and the left-hand side is random so the adversary advantage is at most $1/|\mathbb{F}|$, and if it is a decryption query, Eq. 4 will give the same contradiction. So at least one of the conditions (C2) or (C3) has to hold.

If there are multiple constraints with the same finish, say $\texttt{finish}(c_{i-k}) = \cdots = \texttt{finish}(c_i)$, we want to show at least one ordering of these constraints is a collision structure. Without loss of the generality suppose for these k constraints $\texttt{finish}(c_j) = T'(c_j)$ and this query is an encryption query. Consider the ordering $(i^*, c_1, \ldots, c_{i-k}, \ldots, c_i, \ldots, c_n)$. If this is not a collision structure then there is a constraint c_s where $i - k \leq s \leq i$ satisfies Eq. 5. If we call all the fixed terms on the right-hand side of this equation f then we can rewrite the equation as

$$\boldsymbol{a}_s \cdot \boldsymbol{v}' = f + \sum_{i-k \leq j \leq s-1} \gamma_j \boldsymbol{a}_j \cdot \boldsymbol{v}'$$

Applying the fact that all $\boldsymbol{a}_j \cdot v'$ in the above equation are equal to $\boldsymbol{a}_s \cdot v'$ we get

$$(1 - \sum_{i-k \leq j \leq s-1} \gamma_j) \boldsymbol{a}_s \cdot \boldsymbol{v}' = f$$

Now in the above equation, all the terms on the right-hand side are fixed and the left-side value is random, so the advantage of the adversary is at most $1/|\mathbb{F}|$. □

Combining the Lemmas of this section, we obtain:

Theorem 1. *(Main Theorem) Suppose $\mathcal{P}$ is a nondegenerate Linicrypt program in the ideal cipher model over $\mathbb{F}_\lambda$, with n constraints. For sufficiently large λ the following are equivalent*

- *$\mathcal{P}$ is $(N, N^{2n}/|\mathbb{F}|)$-collision resistant*
- *$\mathcal{P}$ is $(N, N^n/|\mathbb{F}|)$-2nd preimage resistant*
- *$\mathcal{P}$ is $(2n, 1)$-2nd preimage resistant*
- *$\mathcal{P}$ does not have a collision structure*

3.1 Efficiently Finding Collision Structures

An immediate benefit of the characterization given in the proceeding section is provided by Algorithm 1, which gives an efficient procedure for deciding whether a program has a collision structure. The algorithm splits the constraints into two stacks using two loops. In the beginning, all the constraints $\mathcal{C}$ are in the LEFT stack and the first loop runs until all the constraints that satisfy at least one of (C2) or, (C3) are assigned to the RIGHT stack. In the second loop, those constraints that don't satisfy at least two of (C1), (C2), or (C3) will be pushed back to the LEFT stack.

Each loop makes at most n iterations, where each iteration involves several span computations. This gives a total running time of $O(n^{\omega+1})$, where ω is the exponent in the complexity of matrix multiplication.

Lemma 4. *Algorithm **FindColStruct** $\mathcal{P}$ returns a collision structure for $\mathcal{P}$ iff one exists.*

Proof. First, we prove if the algorithm returns $(i^*, c_1, \ldots, c_n)$, this is a collision structure. Note that after the second loop ends,

$$V = \{\boldsymbol{q}_{K_1}, \ldots, \boldsymbol{q}_{K_{i^*-1}}\} \cup \{\boldsymbol{q}_{X_1}, \ldots, \boldsymbol{q}_{X_{i^*-1}}\} \cup \{\boldsymbol{a}_1, \ldots, \boldsymbol{a}_{i^*-1}\} \cup \mathsf{rows}(\boldsymbol{M}).$$

Also, the query c_{i^*} is still in RIGHT, so at least two of the conditions from Definition 4 hold, otherwise c_{i^*} would be sent back to LEFT.

For $i > i^*$, immediately before moving c_i from LEFT to RIGHT in the first loop, sLEFT still included $\{c_1, \ldots, c_{i-1}\}$ which means

$$V = \{\boldsymbol{q}_{K_1}, \ldots, \boldsymbol{q}_{K_i}\} \cup \{\boldsymbol{q}_{X_1}, \ldots, \boldsymbol{q}_{X_i}\} \cup \{\boldsymbol{a}_1, \ldots, \boldsymbol{a}_i\} \cup \mathsf{rows}(\boldsymbol{M}),$$

and $\boldsymbol{q}_X \notin \mathsf{span}(V \setminus \{\boldsymbol{q}_X\})$ or $\boldsymbol{a} \notin \mathsf{span}(V \setminus \{\boldsymbol{a}\})$. Hence,

Algorithm 1. FindColStruct $\mathcal{P}(\boldsymbol{M}, \mathcal{C})$

LEFT $:= \mathcal{C}$
RIGHT := empty stack
$V := \{\boldsymbol{q}_K | (\boldsymbol{q}_K, \boldsymbol{q}_X, \boldsymbol{a}) \in \mathcal{C}\} \cup \{\boldsymbol{q}_X | (\boldsymbol{q}_K, \boldsymbol{q}_X, \boldsymbol{a}) \in \mathcal{C}\} \cup \{\boldsymbol{a} | (\boldsymbol{q}_K, \boldsymbol{q}_X, \boldsymbol{a}) \in \mathcal{C}\} \cup \mathsf{rows}(M)$

while $\exists (\boldsymbol{q}_K, \boldsymbol{q}_X, \boldsymbol{a}) \in$ LEFT where $\boldsymbol{q}_X \notin \mathsf{span}(V \setminus \{\boldsymbol{q}_X\})$ or $\boldsymbol{a} \notin \mathsf{span}(V \setminus \{\boldsymbol{a}\})$ **do**
  remove $(\boldsymbol{q}_K, \boldsymbol{q}_X, \boldsymbol{a})$ from LEFT
  push $(\boldsymbol{q}_K, \boldsymbol{q}_X, \boldsymbol{a})$ to RIGHT
  reduce multiplicity of $\boldsymbol{q}_K, \boldsymbol{q}_X$ and $\boldsymbol{a}$ in V by 1
end while

while $\exists (\boldsymbol{q}_K, \boldsymbol{q}_X, \boldsymbol{a}) \in$ RIGHT where
 $(\boldsymbol{q}_K \in \mathsf{span}(V) \wedge \boldsymbol{q}_X \in \mathsf{span}(V \cup \boldsymbol{q}_K \cup \boldsymbol{a}))$ or
 $(\boldsymbol{q}_K \in \mathsf{span}(V) \wedge \boldsymbol{a} \in \mathsf{span}(V \cup \boldsymbol{q}_K \cup \boldsymbol{q}_X))$ or
 $(\boldsymbol{q}_X \in \mathsf{span}(V \cup \boldsymbol{q}_K \cup \boldsymbol{a}) \wedge \boldsymbol{a} \in \mathsf{span}(V \cup \boldsymbol{q}_K \cup \boldsymbol{q}_X))$ **do**
  remove $(\boldsymbol{q}_K, \boldsymbol{q}_X, \boldsymbol{a})$ from RIGHT
  add $(\boldsymbol{q}_K, \boldsymbol{q}_X, \boldsymbol{a})$ to LEFT
  increase multiplicity of $\boldsymbol{q}_K, \boldsymbol{q}_X$ and $\boldsymbol{a}$ in V by 1
end while

if RIGHT is nonempty **then**
  $i^* := |\mathsf{LEFT}| + 1$
  let LEFT $= (c_1, \ldots, c_{i^*-1})$ where order doesn't matter
  let RIGHT $= (c_{i^*}, \ldots, c_n)$ in reverse order of insertion
  return $(i^*, c_1, \ldots, c_n)$
else return $\perp$
end if

$$\boldsymbol{q}_{X_i} \notin \mathsf{span}(\{\boldsymbol{q}_{K_1}, \ldots, \boldsymbol{q}_{K_i}\} \cup \{\boldsymbol{q}_{X_1}, \ldots, \boldsymbol{q}_{X_{i-1}}\} \cup \{\boldsymbol{a}_1, \ldots, \boldsymbol{a}_i\} \cup \mathsf{rows}(\boldsymbol{M}))$$

or

$$\boldsymbol{a}_i \notin \mathsf{span}(\{\boldsymbol{q}_{K_1}, \ldots, \boldsymbol{q}_{K_i}\} \cup \{\boldsymbol{q}_{X_1}, \ldots, \boldsymbol{q}_{X_i}\} \cup \{\boldsymbol{a}_1, \ldots, \boldsymbol{a}_{i-1}\} \cup \mathsf{rows}(\boldsymbol{M}))$$

satisfying one the conditions (C2), (C3) from Definition 4.

To prove the other direction, we prove if there is a collision structure for $\mathcal{P}$ then the second phase c_{i^*} is not sent back from RIGHT to LEFT, and so RIGHT $\neq \perp$. By contradiction suppose the algorithm adds c_{i^*} to LEFT. Denote by S the set of indices of constraints in LEFT immediately before c_{i^*} is added.

Then, for c_{i^*} to be sent back, at least 2 of the following conditions must hold

$$\boldsymbol{q}_{K_i^*} = \sum_{j\in S} \kappa_j \boldsymbol{q}_{K_j} + \sum_{j\in S} \lambda_j \boldsymbol{q}_{X_j} + \sum_{j\in S} \mu_j \boldsymbol{a}_j + \boldsymbol{\nu M} \tag{6}$$

$$\boldsymbol{q}_{X_i^*} = \sum_{j\in S\cup\{i^*\}} \pi_j \boldsymbol{q}_{K_j} + \sum_{j\in S} \rho_j \boldsymbol{q}_{X_j} + \sum_{j\in S\cup\{i^*\}} \varsigma_j \boldsymbol{a}_j + \boldsymbol{\tau M} \tag{7}$$

$$\boldsymbol{a}_{i^*} = \sum_{j\in S\cup\{i^*\}} \alpha_j \boldsymbol{q}_{K_j} + \sum_{j\in S\cup\{i^*\}} \beta_j \boldsymbol{q}_{X_j} + \sum_{j\in S} \gamma_j \boldsymbol{a}_j + \boldsymbol{\delta M} \tag{8}$$

Since, after the first loop $\{c_{i^*},\ldots,c_n\} \subseteq$ RIGHT, and if any c_j for $j > i^*$ is sent back to LEFT it means at least 2 of $\{\boldsymbol{q}_{K_j}, \boldsymbol{q}_{X_j}, \boldsymbol{a}_j\}$ were already in the right-hand side of the above equations which is the span of vectors in LEFT and rows($\boldsymbol{M}$), so we can rewrite Eqs. 6, 7 and 8 as follows where the $S_1 \cup S_2 \cup S_3 = \{i^*,\ldots,n\}$ and each index appears at least 2 times in the unions of these three sets.

$$\boldsymbol{q}_{K_i^*} = \sum_{j\in S\setminus S_1} \kappa'_j \boldsymbol{q}_{K_j} + \sum_{j\in S\setminus S_2} \lambda'_j \boldsymbol{q}_{X_j} + \sum_{j\in S\setminus S_3} \mu'_j \boldsymbol{a}_j + \boldsymbol{\nu' M} \tag{9}$$

$$\boldsymbol{q}_{X_i^*} = \sum_{j\in S\setminus S_1} \pi'_j \boldsymbol{q}_{K_j} + \sum_{j\in S\setminus S_2} \rho'_j \boldsymbol{q}_{X_j} + \sum_{j\in S\cup\{i^*\}\setminus S_3} \varsigma'_j \boldsymbol{a}_j + \boldsymbol{\rho' M} \tag{10}$$

$$\boldsymbol{a}_{i^*} = \sum_{j\in S\setminus S_1} \alpha'_j \boldsymbol{q}_{K_j} + \sum_{j\in S\cup\{i^*\}\setminus S_2} \beta'_j \boldsymbol{q}_{X_j} + \sum_{j\in S\setminus S_3} \gamma'_j \boldsymbol{a}_j + \boldsymbol{\delta' M} \tag{11}$$

Assume 2 of these equations hold. If in these equations j_1, j_2, and j_3 be the maximum indices in $S \setminus S_1$, $S \setminus S_2$ and $S \setminus S_3$ then there are 2 cases,

If $j_1, j_2, j_3 \le i^*$ then all the indices on the right-hand side are less than i^* and because at least two of the Eqs. 9, 10 and 11 are true, this contradicts with the condition for i^* in Definition 4.

If j_3, j_2, and j_1 are more than i^* then the coefficients with these indices in the above equations are nonzero. If the $\max\{j_1, j_2, j_3\} = j_1$ it means $\boldsymbol{q}_{K_{j_1}}$ was not in the span of V but both $\boldsymbol{q}_{X_{j_1}}$ and $\boldsymbol{a}_{j_1}$ where in the span of constraints with smaller indices and rows($\boldsymbol{M}$) which is a contradiction otherwise they would not be in the RIGHT after the first loop. Thus, the $\max\{j_1, j_2, j_3\}$ is either j_2 or j_3. If j_3 is the max then $\boldsymbol{a}_{j_3}$ was not in the span of LEFT and rows($\boldsymbol{M}$) so the other two vectors $\boldsymbol{q}_{K_{j_3}}$ and $\boldsymbol{q}_{X_{j_3}}$ had to be in the span of LEFT and rows($\boldsymbol{M}$) and all the vectors in LEFT have smaller index than j_3 thus for c_{j_3} to be sent to RIGHT in the first loop, $\boldsymbol{a}_{j_3}$ had to be independent of previous constraints and the output (condition (C3)), but we can rewrite Eq. 9 as follow,

$$\boldsymbol{a}_{j_3} = -\frac{1}{\gamma_{j_3}}\Big(\sum_{j\in S\setminus S_1} \alpha'_j \boldsymbol{q}_{K_j} - \boldsymbol{q}_{K_{i^*}} + \sum_{j\in S\setminus S_2} \beta'_j \boldsymbol{q}_{X_j} + \sum_{j\in S\setminus\{S_3\cup j_3\}} \gamma'_j \boldsymbol{a}_j + \boldsymbol{\delta' M}\Big), \tag{12}$$

contradicting condition (C3) of Definition 4. The case for j_2 is similar. □

4 Rate-1 Compression Functions

A compression function is *rate-1* if it uses one call to an underlying primitive, such as a random oracle or ideal cipher. In the latter case, we assume (without loss of generality) that there is one call to the ideal encryption function. The systematic study of such compression functions has a long history. Building on the initial work of [4,16] gives a definition of 64 possible rate-1 compression functions mapping $D \times D \rightarrow D$, where $D = \mathbb{GF}(2^\lambda)$, that is definable using $\oplus$ and a constant value from D. Typically, these functions are referred to as *PGV compression functions*. Among its results, [4] identifies a subset of these functions, the *group-1* functions, and proves that these are exactly the PGV compression functions that are collision-resistant.

Our goal in this section is to give a characterization of the group-1 functions in Linicrypt. In particular, we will show that a PGV compression function is group-1 iff it does not have a collision structure. Thus the characterization of [4] may be viewed as a special case of our general characterization.

The results of [4] are revisited in [5], and proven via a more unified approach, building on the approach of [18]. This is based on the factorization of a compression function f into two component functions f' and f''. In particular, for a *message* m and *chaining value* h, $f(h, m) = f''(h, m, y)$, where $y = E_k(x)$ and $(k, x) = f'(h, m)$. In the case that f' is bijective, the function f^* is defined by $f^*(k, x, y) = f''(h, m, y)$ where $(h, m) = f^{-1}(k, x)$. Using f', f'', and f^*, the following properties of f are defined:

P1 f' is bijective.
P2 $f''(h, m, \cdot)$ is bijective for all (h, m).
P3 $f^*(k, \cdot, y)$ is bijective for all (k, y).

In [4,5], a stronger notion of collision-resistance for compression functions is used:

Definition 5 ([5] Definition 3). *Program $\mathcal{P}$ is (q, ϵ)-*collision resistant *if for any $h_0 \in \mathbb{F}$, any oracle adversary $\mathcal{A}$ making at most $q = q_E + q_D$ queries has probability of success at most ϵ in the following game:*

$$(\boldsymbol{x}, \boldsymbol{x}') \leftarrow \mathcal{A}^{E,E^{-1}}(\lambda);\ \textit{return}\ (\boldsymbol{x} \neq \boldsymbol{x}')\ \textit{and}\ \mathcal{P}^E(\boldsymbol{x}) = \mathcal{P}^E(\boldsymbol{x}')\ \textit{or}\ \mathcal{P}^E(\boldsymbol{x}) = h_0 \tag{13}$$

Letting T1 denote the conjunction of P1, P2, and P3, we have

Lemma 5 ([5] Lemma 3). *Suppose $f : \mathbb{GF}(2^\lambda) \times \mathbb{GF}(2^\lambda) \rightarrow \mathbb{GF}(2^\lambda)$ is a PGV compression function satisfying T1. Then for any $h_0 \in \mathbb{GF}(2^\lambda)$ the advantage of any adversary $\mathcal{A}$ making q queries in Game 13 is at most $q(q + 1)/2^\lambda$.*

Remark 1. The compression functions satisfying T1 are exactly the *group 1* functions defined in [4].

In the Linicrypt framework, a PGV compression function f is specified via

- An output matrix $\boldsymbol{M} = \begin{bmatrix} \boldsymbol{m}_1 \\ \boldsymbol{m}_2 \end{bmatrix}$, where $\boldsymbol{m}_2$ is always $(0,0,1,0)$ (corresponding to the fixed value c, as described below,) while $\boldsymbol{m}_1$ is one of $(1,0,0,1)$, $(0,1,0,1)$, $(1,1,0,1)$ or $(0,0,1,1)$.
- A single query constraint $\left(\begin{bmatrix} \boldsymbol{q}_K \\ \boldsymbol{q}_X \end{bmatrix}, \boldsymbol{a}\right)$, where each $\boldsymbol{q}_i$, $i \in \{K, X\}$, is one of $(1,0,0,0)$, $(0,1,0,0)$, $(1,1,0,0)$ or $(0,0,1,0)$, and $\boldsymbol{a}$ is $(0,0,0,1)$.

Here use $\boldsymbol{m}_2$ to capture the use of a constant value in the Linicrypt setting, as described in Sect. 2.2. Up to our convention regarding the constant value c, f'' corresponds to $\boldsymbol{m}_1$ while f' corresponds to $\begin{bmatrix} \boldsymbol{q}_K \\ \boldsymbol{q}_X \end{bmatrix}$. In particular, writing $\boldsymbol{q}_i = (q_i^1, q_i^2, q_i^3, q_i^4)$, $i \in \{K, X\}$, we have $f'(h,m) = \begin{bmatrix} \boldsymbol{q}'_K \\ \boldsymbol{q}'_X \end{bmatrix} \times (h, m, c)$, where $\boldsymbol{q}'_i = (q_i^1, q_i^2, q_i^3)$, $i \in \{K, X\}$. We also have $f''(h,m,y) = \boldsymbol{m}_1 \cdot (h, m, c, y)$.

We will use the following simple fact in several proofs below:

Proposition 1. *Over any field $\mathbb{F}$, a function of the form $g(x) = rx + s$, where $r, s \in \mathbb{F}$, is bijective iff $r \neq 0$.*

In the following, let f denote a compression function defined by $\boldsymbol{m}_1$,$\boldsymbol{m}_2$,$\boldsymbol{q}_K$,$\boldsymbol{q}_X$,$\boldsymbol{a}$, as described above, with respect to a fixed constant c. Define the following matrices

$$\boldsymbol{R} = \begin{bmatrix} \boldsymbol{q}_K \\ \boldsymbol{q}_X \\ \boldsymbol{m}_2 \\ \boldsymbol{a} \end{bmatrix} \qquad \boldsymbol{S} = \begin{bmatrix} \boldsymbol{q}_K \\ \boldsymbol{m}_1 \\ \boldsymbol{m}_2 \\ \boldsymbol{a} \end{bmatrix}$$

Lemma 6. *Writing $\boldsymbol{m}_1 = (m_1^1, m_1^2, m_1^3, m_1^4)$, f satisfies P2 iff $m_1^4 \neq 0$.*

Proof. For fixed h, m, $f'(h,m,y) = \boldsymbol{m}_1 \cdot (h,m,c,y) = m_1^4 y \oplus s$, where s is fixed. □

We note that every PGV compression function satisfies $m_1^4 \neq 0$ and hence P2.

Lemma 7. *f satisfies P1 iff $\boldsymbol{R}$ is nonsingular.*

Proof. Let $\boldsymbol{R}' = \boldsymbol{R}[1\text{-}3; 1\text{-}3]$ be the 3×3 principle submatrix of $\boldsymbol{R}$. Given the possible values of $\boldsymbol{q}_K$ and $\boldsymbol{q}_X$, $\boldsymbol{R}$ is nonsingular iff $\boldsymbol{R}'$ is nonsingular. For any h, m, $f'(h,m) = \boldsymbol{R}' \times (h, m, c)$, which is a bijection iff $\boldsymbol{R}'$ is nonsingular. □

Lemma 8. *Assume $\boldsymbol{R}$ is nonsingular. Then f satisfies P3 iff $\boldsymbol{S}$ is nonsingular.*

Proof. First note that $f^*(k,x,y) = \boldsymbol{m}_1 \cdot (h,m,c,y) = \boldsymbol{m}_1 \cdot (\boldsymbol{R}^{-1} \times (k,x,c,y)) = (\boldsymbol{m}_1 \boldsymbol{R}^{-1}) \times (k,x,c,y)$. Let $\boldsymbol{u} = (u_1, u_2, u_3, u_4) = \boldsymbol{m}_1 \boldsymbol{R}^{-1}$. Then for fixed k, y, $f^*(k,x,y) = u_2 x \oplus s$, where s is fixed. Thus, it is enough to show $\boldsymbol{S}$ is nonsingular iff $u_2 \neq 0$. Since $\boldsymbol{R}$ is nonsingular, $\boldsymbol{S}$ is nonsingular iff $\boldsymbol{S}\boldsymbol{R}^{-1}$ is nonsingular. But $\boldsymbol{S}\boldsymbol{R}^{-1} = (\boldsymbol{e}_1, \boldsymbol{u}, \boldsymbol{e}_3, \boldsymbol{e}_4)$, which is nonsingular iff $u_2 \neq 0$. □

Together, the preceding Lemmas give the following

Lemma 9. *A PGV function f satisfies T1 iff $\boldsymbol{R}$ and $\boldsymbol{S}$ are nonsingular.*

In the rate-1 setting conditions (C1), (C2), (C3) become

(C1) $\boldsymbol{q}_K \notin \mathsf{span}(\{\boldsymbol{m}_1, \boldsymbol{m}_2\})$
(C2) $\boldsymbol{q}_X \notin \mathsf{span}(\{\boldsymbol{q}_K, \boldsymbol{a}, \boldsymbol{m}_1, \boldsymbol{m}_2\})$
(C3) $\boldsymbol{a} \notin \mathsf{span}(\{\boldsymbol{q}_K, \boldsymbol{q}_X, \boldsymbol{m}_1, \boldsymbol{m}_2\})$

Given the possible values of $\boldsymbol{q}_K, \boldsymbol{m}_1$ and $\boldsymbol{m}_2$, (C1) may be further simplified to

(C1) $\boldsymbol{q}_K \neq \boldsymbol{m}_2$

Lemma 10. *Suppose f is a PGV compression function specified by $\boldsymbol{q}_K$, $\boldsymbol{q}_X$, $\boldsymbol{m}_1$, $\boldsymbol{m}_2$, $\boldsymbol{a}$. If both $\boldsymbol{R}$ and $\boldsymbol{S}$ are nonsingular, then two of the conditions (C1), (C2), (C3) must fail.*

Proof. If (C1) fails, then S is necessarily singular, so we must show that under the assumption, both (C2) and (C3) fail. Clearly, if $\boldsymbol{S}$ is nonsingular,

$$\boldsymbol{q}_X \in \mathsf{span}(\mathsf{rows}(\boldsymbol{S})) = \mathsf{span}(\{\boldsymbol{q}_K, \boldsymbol{m}_1, \boldsymbol{m}_2, \boldsymbol{a}\}) \qquad (*)$$

so (C2) fails. Now since $\boldsymbol{R}$ is nonsingular $\boldsymbol{q}_X \notin \mathsf{span}(\{\boldsymbol{q}_K, \boldsymbol{m}_2, \boldsymbol{a}\})$, which in combination with (*) means that $\boldsymbol{m}_1 \in \mathsf{span}(\{\boldsymbol{q}_K, \boldsymbol{q}_X, \boldsymbol{m}_2, \boldsymbol{a}\})$ (**). Noting that the last component of $\boldsymbol{m}_1$ is always nonzero, we have $\boldsymbol{m}_1 \notin \mathsf{span}(\{\boldsymbol{q}_K, \boldsymbol{q}_X, \boldsymbol{m}_2\})$. Combining this last fact with (**), we conclude

$$\boldsymbol{a} \in \mathsf{span}(\{\boldsymbol{q}_K, \boldsymbol{q}_X, \boldsymbol{m}_1, \boldsymbol{m}_2\}),$$

so that (C3) also fails. □

Lemma 11. *Suppose f is a nondegenerate PGV compression function specified by $\boldsymbol{q}_K$, $\boldsymbol{q}_X$, $\boldsymbol{m}_1$, $\boldsymbol{m}_2$, $\boldsymbol{a}$. If one of $\boldsymbol{R}, \boldsymbol{S}$ is singular, then two of the conditions (C1), (C2), (C3) must hold.*

Proof. First, suppose (C2) fails, so $\boldsymbol{q}_X \in \mathsf{span}(\{\boldsymbol{q}_K, \boldsymbol{m}_1, \boldsymbol{m}_2, \boldsymbol{a}\})$. Then, if $\boldsymbol{S}$ is singular,

$$\mathsf{span}(\{\boldsymbol{q}_K, \boldsymbol{q}_X, \boldsymbol{m}_1, \boldsymbol{m}_2, \boldsymbol{a}\}) = \mathsf{span}(\mathsf{rows}(S)) \not\supseteq \{\mathrm{e}_1, \mathrm{e}_2, \mathrm{e}_3, \mathrm{e}_4\},$$

which means f is degenerate. Thus $\boldsymbol{S}$ is nonsingular. As in the proof of Lemma 10, this means $\boldsymbol{q}_K \neq \boldsymbol{m}_2$. Also if $\boldsymbol{S}$ in nonsingular then by the assumption, $\boldsymbol{R}$ is singular, so we must have $\boldsymbol{q}_K = \boldsymbol{q}_X$ or $\boldsymbol{q}_X = \boldsymbol{m}_2$. If the former holds, $\boldsymbol{a} \in \mathsf{span}(\{\boldsymbol{q}_K, \boldsymbol{q}_X, \boldsymbol{m}_1, \boldsymbol{m}_2\})$ implies $\boldsymbol{q}_K = \boldsymbol{q}_X = \boldsymbol{a} \oplus \boldsymbol{m}_1$, and so

$$\mathsf{span}(\{\boldsymbol{q}_K, \boldsymbol{q}_X, \boldsymbol{m}_1, \boldsymbol{m}_2, \boldsymbol{a}\}) = \mathsf{span}(\{\boldsymbol{m}_1, \boldsymbol{m}_2, \boldsymbol{a}\}) \not\supseteq \{\mathrm{e}_1, \mathrm{e}_2, \mathrm{e}_3, \mathrm{e}_4\},$$

If the latter holds then $\boldsymbol{a} \in \mathsf{span}(\{\boldsymbol{q}_K, \boldsymbol{q}_X, \boldsymbol{m}_1, \boldsymbol{m}_2\})$ implies

$$\mathsf{span}(\{\boldsymbol{q}_K, \boldsymbol{q}_X, \boldsymbol{m}_1, \boldsymbol{m}_2, \boldsymbol{a}\}) = \mathsf{span}(\{\boldsymbol{q}_K, \boldsymbol{m}_1, \boldsymbol{m}_2\}) \not\supseteq \{\mathrm{e}_1, \mathrm{e}_2, \mathrm{e}_3, \mathrm{e}_4\},$$

So in both cases, by nondegeneracy $\boldsymbol{a} \notin \mathsf{span}(\{\boldsymbol{q}_K, \boldsymbol{q}_X, \boldsymbol{m}_1, \boldsymbol{m}_2\})$, and we have that if (C2) fails, both (C1) and (C3) must hold.

Now suppose (C2) holds and (C1) fails. Then

$$\mathsf{span}(\{\boldsymbol{q}_K, \boldsymbol{q}_X, \boldsymbol{m}_1, \boldsymbol{m}_2\}) = \mathsf{span}(\{\boldsymbol{q}_X, \boldsymbol{m}_1, \boldsymbol{m}_2\}),$$

and so, if $\boldsymbol{a} \in \mathsf{span}(\{\boldsymbol{q}_K, \boldsymbol{q}_X, \boldsymbol{m}_1, \boldsymbol{m}_2\})$,

$$\begin{aligned}\mathsf{span}(\{\boldsymbol{q}_K, \boldsymbol{q}_X, \boldsymbol{m}_1, \boldsymbol{m}_2, \boldsymbol{a}\}) &= \mathsf{span}(\{\boldsymbol{q}_K, \boldsymbol{q}_X, \boldsymbol{m}_1, \boldsymbol{m}_2\}) \\ &= \mathsf{span}(\{\boldsymbol{q}_X, \boldsymbol{m}_1, \boldsymbol{m}_2\}) \not\supseteq \{\mathbf{e}_1, \mathbf{e}_2, \mathbf{e}_3, \mathbf{e}_4\}.\end{aligned}$$

In conclusion, if (C2) holds, then one of (C1) or (C3) must hold. □

Combining Lemmas 9,10, and 11, we obtain

Theorem 2. *A PGV compression function is group-1 iff it does not have a collision structure.*

Discussion. Beyond validating the correspondence between our characterization of collision resistance for rate-1 compression functions and the well-known notion of group-1 for PGV, Theorem 2 situates our understanding of the group-1 functions as part of a general framework for collision resistance using Linicrypt. As an immediate application of Theorem 2 and Algorithm 1, we can automatically generate all group 1 PGV compression functions.[3] In particular, this provides a purely *syntactic* characterization using algebraic properties of the defining program $\mathcal{P}$, including the possibility of automated identification using **FindColStruct**. However, we note that [4,5] provide a finer analysis of the PGV compression functions, also identifying the *group-2* functions which, although not collision-resistant as compression functions, are still suitable for constructing collision-resistant hash functions and analyzing the preimage resistance of group-1 and -2 PGV functions. We leave an extended analysis of this sort in the Linicrypt setting to future work. We give some examples of definitions of PGV compression functions from [4] and their analysis on the same GitHub page.

5 Discussion

We note that the significance of our results is somewhat limited by the fact that a characterization of collision-resistance for rate-1 (which is the most significant from a practical perspective) was already provided by [4]. However, our more general setting does provide some advantages. Our characterization is uniform and based solely on the syntax of programs (expressed algebraically). We have noted that the approach of [4] is ad-hoc, while that of [5] depends on semantic properties (i.e. bijectiveness) of the component functions. One benefit of our

[3] A sample implementation in Octave is available at https://github.com/zahrajavar/PGVCollisionResistantCompressionFunctions.git.

approach is that it immediately gives an efficient automated enumeration technique. We also note that in order to obtain security properties beyond collision resistance (see below) we may need to consider programs that make more than one call to the ideal cipher. The general characterization for collision resistance may be viewed as a step towards characterizations of other properties. Finally, our results demonstrate that the utility of the Linicrypt framework is not limited to the random oracle model.

6 Conclusion and Future Work

We have demonstrated the utility of the Linicrypt framework beyond the random oracle model by giving characterizations of collision-resistance properties for Linicrypt programs in the ideal cipher model. We also show that in the case of the PGV compression function our characterization is equivalent to the notion of group-1 for the PGV functions.

There are a number of ways in which this work might be extended. First of all, in the rate-1 setting, we have not addressed the finer analysis provided by [4,5] which also characterizes group-2 functions and compares the pre-image resistance of group-1 and group-2 functions. Can we give a general notion of group-2 for arbitrary Linicrypt programs which generalizes the corresponding notion for rate-1 functions? We note that it is possible to give a characterization of *pre-image awareness*, a stronger notion of hash function security introduced by [10], for Linicrypt programs with random oracles, and it should be possible to extend this characterization to the ideal cipher model. It would also be interesting to consider even stronger properties for hash functions, such as *indifferentiability* [9]. A more ambitious goal would be to extend the analysis provided by Linicrypt beyond purely algebraic constructions. In particular, it would be very useful to consider using bit-string operations, especially truncation, and concatenation, which are used in many constructions such as the sponge construction which is the basis of Keccak/SHA-3. Here it might be useful to revisit [1], which considers equivalence properties of algebraic programs over $\mathbb{GF}(2^\lambda)$ which include bit-string operations but do not have access to random oracles, ideal ciphers or (as in the case of Keccak) random permutations.

A Missing Proofs

Lemma 2 *Case 3:* Because $K_i \neq K_i'$, condition (C1) holds. We want to show $T'(c_i)$ has to be a decryption query and (C2) holds. If it is not a decryption query then the probability of a random value Y_i' being equal to the fixed value Y_i would be $1/|\mathbb{F}|$, which contradicts the assumption, so we assume $T'(c_i)$ is a decryption query. If condition (C2) does not hold then we have

$$\boldsymbol{q}_{X_i} = \sum_{j \leq i} \pi_j \cdot \boldsymbol{q}_{K_j} + \sum_{j<i} \rho_j \cdot \boldsymbol{q}_{X_j} + \sum_{j \leq i} \varsigma_j \cdot \boldsymbol{a}_j + \boldsymbol{\tau M}$$

Multiplying the equation to $(\boldsymbol{v}' - \boldsymbol{v})$ and applying $Y_i = Y_i'$ and $\boldsymbol{M}(\boldsymbol{v} - \boldsymbol{v}') = 0$ and canceling convergent queries, gives

$$\boldsymbol{q}_{X_i} \cdot \boldsymbol{v}' = \boldsymbol{q}_{X_i} \cdot \boldsymbol{v} + \pi_i \boldsymbol{q}_{K_i} \cdot (\boldsymbol{v}' - \boldsymbol{v})$$

The left-hand side of the above equation is a random value and the right-hand side is a fixed value, so the adversary advantage again is at most $1/|\mathbb{F}|$ which is a contradiction.

B Motivating Example

The following example gives the idea of characterizing collision structure for Linicrypt programs and how a collision attack can be applied to a program. A more formal and precise algorithm to find a collision is given in the proof of Lemma 2.

$$\begin{aligned} &\underline{\mathcal{P}^E(v_1, v_2):} \\ &\quad v_3 := E(v_1, v_2) \\ &\quad v_4 = E(v_1, v_3) \\ &\quad \mathit{return}\ v_4 + v_1 \end{aligned}$$

$$\begin{aligned} \boldsymbol{q}_{K_1} &= (1,0,0,0) \quad \boldsymbol{q}_{X_1} = (0,1,0,0) \quad \boldsymbol{a}_1 = (0,0,1,0) \\ \boldsymbol{q}_{K_2} &= (1,0,0,0) \quad \boldsymbol{q}_{X_2} = (0,0,1,0) \quad \boldsymbol{a}_2 = (0,0,0,1) \\ &\qquad\qquad \boldsymbol{m} = (1,0,0,1) \end{aligned}$$

This program is not collision resistant and the adversary can find a collision as follow

- The adversary $\mathcal{A}$ picks an arbitrary input $\boldsymbol{x} = (x_1, x_2) \in \mathbb{F}^2$ and runs the program on $\boldsymbol{x}$ and gets the output l.
- $\mathcal{A}$ picks arbitrary $x_1' \neq x_1 \in \mathbb{F}$ and makes the query $v_3' = E^{-1}(x_1', l + x_1')$.
- $\mathcal{A}$ makes the query $x_2' = E^{-1}(x_1', v_3')$ to find x_2'.
- $\mathcal{A}$ returns $\boldsymbol{x}' = (x_1', x_2')$.

This attack was possible because of the following,

- x_1' was independent of the output in other words $\boldsymbol{q}_{K_1} \neq \boldsymbol{m}$.
- In step two after fixing x_1' and the output l the value of v_3' was not fixed which in algebraic representation means $\boldsymbol{q}_{X_1} \notin \mathsf{span}(\boldsymbol{q}_{K_1}, \boldsymbol{m})$ so the adversary could determine this value by making a decryption query.
- In the third step because $\boldsymbol{q}_{X_2} \notin \mathsf{span}(\boldsymbol{q}_{K_1}, \boldsymbol{q}_{K_2}, \boldsymbol{q}_{X_1}, \boldsymbol{a}_1, \boldsymbol{a}_2, \boldsymbol{m})$ the value of x_2' is not fixed so via a decryption query the adversary finds a compatible value for x_2'.

References

1. Barthe, G., Daubignard, M., Kapron, B., Lakhnech, Y., Laporte, V.: On the equality of probabilistic terms. In: Clarke, E.M., Voronkov, A. (eds.) LPAR 2010. LNCS (LNAI), vol. 6355, pp. 46–63. Springer, Heidelberg (2010). https://doi.org/10.1007/978-3-642-17511-4_4
2. Bellare, M., Canetti, R., Krawczyk, H.: Keying hash functions for message authentication. In: Koblitz, N. (ed.) CRYPTO 1996. LNCS, vol. 1109, pp. 1–15. Springer, Heidelberg (1996). https://doi.org/10.1007/3-540-68697-5_1
3. Black, J.: The ideal-cipher model, revisited: an uninstantiable blockcipher-based hash function. In: Robshaw, M. (ed.) FSE 2006. LNCS, vol. 4047, pp. 328–340. Springer, Heidelberg (2006). https://doi.org/10.1007/11799313_21
4. Black, J., Rogaway, P., Shrimpton, T.: Black-box analysis of the block-cipher-based hash-function constructions from PGV. In: Yung, M. (ed.) CRYPTO 2002. LNCS, vol. 2442, pp. 320–335. Springer, Heidelberg (2002). https://doi.org/10.1007/3-540-45708-9_21
5. Black, J., Rogaway, P., Shrimpton, T., Stam, M.: An analysis of the Blockcipher-based hash functions from PGV. J. Cryptol. **23**(4), 519–545 (2010)
6. Bos, J.N.E., Chaum, D.: Provably unforgeable signatures. In: Brickell, E.F. (ed.) CRYPTO 1992. LNCS, vol. 740, pp. 1–14. Springer, Heidelberg (1993). https://doi.org/10.1007/3-540-48071-4_1
7. Canetti, R., Goldreich, O., Halevi, S.: The random oracle methodology, revisited. J. ACM **51**(4), 557–594 (2004)
8. Carmer, B., Rosulek, M.: Linicrypt: a model for practical cryptography. In: Robshaw, M., Katz, J. (eds.) CRYPTO 2016. LNCS, vol. 9816, pp. 416–445. Springer, Heidelberg (2016). https://doi.org/10.1007/978-3-662-53015-3_15
9. Coron, J.-S., Dodis, Y., Malinaud, C., Puniya, P.: Merkle-Damgård revisited: how to construct a hash function. In: Shoup, V. (ed.) CRYPTO 2005. LNCS, vol. 3621, pp. 430–448. Springer, Heidelberg (2005). https://doi.org/10.1007/11535218_26
10. Dodis, Y., Ristenpart, T., Shrimpton, T.: Salvaging Merkle-Damgard for practical applications. In: IACR Cryptol. ePrint Arch., p. 177 (2009) Full version of [11].
11. Dodis, Y., Ristenpart, T., Shrimpton, T.: Salvaging Merkle-Damgård for Practical Applications. In: Joux, A., et al. (eds.) Advances in Cryptology - EUROCRYPT 2009, pp. 371–388. Springer Berlin Heidelberg, Berlin, Heidelberg (2009). https://doi.org/10.1007/978-3-642-01001-9_22
12. Even, S., Goldreich, O., Micali, S.: On-line/off-line digital signatures. J. Cryptol. **9**(1), 35–67 (1996). https://doi.org/10.1007/BF02254791
13. Lamport, L.: Constructing digital signatures from a one-way function. Technical Report CSL 98, SRI International (1979)
14. McQuoid, I., Swope, T., Rosulek, M.: Characterizing collision and second-preimage resistance in Linicrypt. In: Hofheinz, D., Rosen, A. (eds.) TCC 2019. LNCS, vol. 11891, pp. 451–470. Springer, Cham (2019). https://doi.org/10.1007/978-3-030-36030-6_18
15. Merkle, R.C.: A digital signature based on a conventional encryption function. In: Pomerance, C. (ed.) CRYPTO 1987. LNCS, vol. 293, pp. 369–378. Springer, Heidelberg (1988). https://doi.org/10.1007/3-540-48184-2_32
16. Preneel, B., Govaerts, R., Vandewalle, J.: Hash functions based on block ciphers: a synthetic approach. In: Stinson, D.R. (ed.) CRYPTO 1993. LNCS, vol. 773, pp. 368–378. Springer, Heidelberg (1994). https://doi.org/10.1007/3-540-48329-2_31

17. Shannon, C.E.: Communication theory of secrecy systems. Bell Syst. Tech. J. **28**(4), 656–715 (1949)
18. Stam, M.: Blockcipher-Based Hashing Revisited. In: Dunkelman, O. (ed.) FSE 2009. LNCS, vol. 5665, pp. 67–83. Springer, Heidelberg (2009). https://doi.org/10.1007/978-3-642-03317-9_5

Signature

SMHSDVS: A Secure and Mutual Heterogeneous Strong Designated Signature Between PKI and IBC

Yibing Wang[1], Xiaoxiao Wang[1], Chin-tser Huang[2], Dejun Wang[1], Binhao Ma[1], and Bo Meng[1(✉)]

[1] South -Central Minzu University, Wuhan, China
mengscuec@gmail.com
[2] University of South Carolina, South Carolina, USA

Abstract. The homogeneous strong designated verifier signature scheme cannot meet the requirements of heterogeneous cryptography communication. With the idea of Heterogeneous Signcryption and strong designated verifier signature, we present a securely and mutually heterogeneous strong designated verifier signature (SMHSDVS) scheme between Public Key Infrastructure and Identity-based Cryptography, which has correctness, non-transferability, unforgeability, strongness, source hiding and non-delegatability. In addition, we use the Computational Diffie-Hellman model in oracle to analyze unforgeability and use mechanized tool CryptoVerif to analyze non-transferability. Finally, we evaluate the performance of heterogeneous digital signature scheme by compared with related schemes, and the results show that the proposed scheme is secure and efficient.

Keywords: Heterogeneous · Public Key Infrastructure · Identity-based Cryptography · Unforgeability · Non-transferability

1 Introduction

The heterogeneous cryptography means supporting the establishment of secure communication between communication parties of different cryptosystem. Conversely, the homogeneous cryptography means same cryptosystem between communication parties. As the network application environment becomes more and more complex, different application may use different security techniques even if the same kind of network is used, so the communicating parties need support different cryptographic systems and achieve a safety certification. Thus, the heterogeneous cryptography communication mechanism in which the communicating parties support different cryptographic systems becomes a hot issue. Public Key Infrastructure (PKI) and Identity-based Cryptography (IBC) have already been widely applied in the area of network. Hence, to achieve secure heterogeneous cryptograhy communication between PKI and IBC is vital.

M. Zhang et al. (Eds.): ProvSec 2023, LNCS 14217, pp. 115–130, 2023.
https://doi.org/10.1007/978-3-031-45513-1_7

The heterogeneous signcryption (HS) [2–10] means a digital signature algorithm for heterogeneous cryptography communication. Designated verifier signature (DVS) is a digital signature scheme whose signature is verified by a designated verifier. The homogeneous strong designated verifier signature (SDVS) [1] in homogeneous cryptography communication is presented and widely used in tender and electronic voting. The signer Alice sent a signature to the receiver Bob who is the designated verifier. Only Bob can verify the validity of the signature with his secret key. The strong designated verifier signature not only can ensure the correction of signature, but also can protect the signer's privacy. Until now, a lot of homogeneous SDVS have been introduced by researchers, but do not satisfy the requirements of heterogeneous cryptography communication. Therefore, it is crucial to propose a heterogeneous SDVS scheme to provide a digital signature with security and privacy.

Therefore, with the idea of HS and SDVS, based on the Bilinear Diffie-Hellman problem (BDHP) and Computational Diffie-Hellman problem (CDHP), this paper designs a secure and mutual heterogeneous strong designated verifier signature (SMHSDVS) scheme between PKI and IBC. The main works are presented as follows:

1) Learning the idea of HS and SDVS, we propose an SMHSDVS scheme between PKI and IBC which is based on the BDHP and CDHP.
2) We define and formulate the security model and general requirements for the proposed SMHSDVS scheme between PKI and IBC. We analyze the proposed scheme, and the results show that it supports correctness, non-transferability, unforgeability, strongness, source hiding and non-delegatability.
3) Compared to the related signature schemes, the proposed SMHSDVS scheme between PKI and IBC has superiority in terms of computation cost.

The rest of the paper is organized as follows. Section 2 discusses the related work of HS and SDVS. Section 3 presents the SMHSDVS scheme between PKI and IBC. Section 4 defines a security model of unforgeability and gives proofs about security requirements. Section 5 makes comparisons of performance. Finally, Sect. 6 concludes the paper and discusses future work.

2 Related Work

A heterogeneous SDVS is closely related to HS and DVS. HS is widely used in heterogeneous cryptography communication systems to provide digital signature [11–14] and encryption. DVS [1] can only be verified by the designated verifier, but can not be verified by any third party. In SDVS, Alice, the signer, has sent a signature to Bob, the designated verifier. Only Bob can verify the validity of the signature by using his secret key. However, Bob cannot convince a third party that Alice has created the signature, because Bob can simulate a signature that is indistinguishable from Alice's signature.

HS schemes [2–10] are based on the bilinear pairing besides scheme [7,10]. In 2010, Sun and Li [2] introduced the first HS scheme between PKI and IBC.

However, it only resists outside attacks, and does not support non-repudiation. In 2016, Zhang et al. [3] proposed an efficient HS scheme between Certificateless Public Key Cryptography and Traditional PKI to protect user's privacy. It has ciphertext anonymity. In 2017, Wang et al. [5] proposed an IBC-to-PKI HS scheme in the standard model; Zhang et al. [6] presented a concrete HS scheme between IBC and Certificateless Cryptography (CLC). In 2018, Liu et al. [8] proposed two signcryption schemes without the bilinear pairing between PKI and CLC, which provides mutual heterogeneous communications for 5G network slicings. In 2019, Cao et al. [9] put forward the improvement of PKI-to-IBC scheme and IBC-to-PKI scheme and proved the security in the standard model. In 2020, Xiong et al. [10] proposed a signcryption scheme using proxy resignature to achieve heterogeneous communication between ID-based and CLC.

In 2003, Saeednia et al. [15] proposed a DVS scheme based on the Schnorr signature and the Zheng signcryption schemes, which has a low communication rate and low computational cost. In 2015, Sarde and Banarjee [16] proposed an efficient SDVS scheme based on the DLP, which has higher efficiency performance than [15]. In 2016, based on bilinear pairing, Xu et al. [17] presented a new SDVS scheme based on identity, which is unforgeable under adaptive selective message and selective identity attack; Du et al. [18] proposed multi signature based on a certificateless SDVS, which is efficient in execution.

In 2017, Masoumeh et al. [19] proposed the SDVS scheme which is unforgeable under a chosen message attack in Random Oracle Model; Ge et al. [21] proposed two HSDVS schemes which ensure that the signer's privacy is not compromised. We found that the proof of correctness and non-transferability in [21] is incorrect and it does not meet non-delegatability and low efficiency in computation. In 2018, Zheng et al. [22] proposed a SDVS scheme based on the identity, which is safe and efficient and suitable for intelligent distribution network cloud storage. In 2019, Han et al. [23] proposed a certificateless verifiable SDVS, which satisfies the requirements of verifiability, unforgeability, non-delegability, non-transferability and signer ambiguity. In 2020, Nayak et al. [24] proposed a new SDVS scheme based on hybrid problems: factorization and discrete logarithm, which provides a higher security level compared with the previous SDVS schemes. In 2021, Lin et al. [25] combined the concept of SDVS and multi-recipients to propose an efficient Strong Designated Multi-Verifier Signature (SDMVS) scheme to promote e-commerce applications for privacy protection groups.

In 2019, Parvin et al. [26] proposeed the first non-delegatable universal designated verifier scheme (UDVS), and proved its non-delegatability in the standard model. In 2020, Zhang et al. [27] proposed secure and efficient quantum DVS, which is information-theoretically secure. In 2022, Xin et al. [28] proposed a quantum public-key DVS, which astisfies source non-traceability, non-transferability and unforgeability.

The difficult problems used in the schemes proposed in [1,16,22] are based on DLP. When we analyze the security requirements, only [23,26] meet non-delegatability, [17,23,28] satisfy unforgeability, and [24] has undeniability.

3 The SMHDVS Scheme

Based on the HS and SDVS, we propose an SMHSDVS scheme between PKI and IBC, which has the properties of correctness, non-transferability, unforgeability, strongness, source hiding, and non-delegatability. The proposed SMHSDVS scheme between PKI and IBC consists of PKI→IBC heterogeneous SDVS scheme (PKI→IBC HSDVSS) and IBC→PKI heterogeneous SDVS scheme (IBC →PKI HSDVSS). The symbol âĂIJ→âĂİ means that the signer generates heterogeneous strong designated verifier signature and sends to the designated verifier to verify the validity of the signature.

The proposed SMHSDVS scheme between PKI and IBC is composed of five algorithms: Setup, KeyGen, SDVS Signature, SDVS Verification, and Transcript Simulation. The Setup algorithm accepts a security parameter as the input and produces system parameter, master public key, and master private key. Apart from that, it publishes the system public parameters. The KeyGen algorithm generates the public key and private key for the communicating parties who are in the PKI and IBC cryptosystems, respectively. The SDVS Signature algorithm generates a signature for the designated verifier. The SDVS Verification algorithm verifies the signature. The Transcript Simulation algorithm generates signature simulation. In the following subsections, we introduce each algorithm in more details.

3.1 Setup and KeyGen Algorithm

PKI→IBC HSDVSS and IBC→PKI HSDVSS have the similar Setup and KeyGen algorithms.

(1) Setup Algorithm

The Setup algorithm is a probabilistic algorithm running by a trusted third party PKG(Private Key Generation). Input security parameter k, PKG chooses a cyclic additive group G_1 of a large prime order $q.P$ is a generator of G_1. Define a Bilinear Pairing $e : G_1 \times G_1 \rightarrow G_2$.

Define two collisionless hash functions: $H_1 : \{0,1\}^* \rightarrow Z_q^*, H_2 : G_2 \times \{0,1\}^{\mathrm{n}} \rightarrow Z_q^*$. Among them, the role of H_1 is to mapping the user's identity information to the integer group Z_q^*,$\{0,1\}^*$ indicates the length of the collection for binary sequence combination of bits,Z_q^* denotes finite domain $Z_q^* = \{1, 2, 3, \cdots, q-1\}$ except integer element 0, and H_2 means a group of a collisionless hash function, that is, the order of prime and the cycle of multiplicative group mapped to integer group Z_q^*,$\{0,1\}^{\mathrm{n}}$ denotes the length of as collections of bits of binary sequences.

PKG selects a master secret key $s \in Z_q^*$ randomly and sets the master public key $Ppub = sP$. Then, PKG publishes system parameters and keeps the master secret key s as secret.

The output of Setup algorithm as follows: PKG publishes system parameters: param $= \{k, G_1, G_2, P, e, H_1, H_2, P_{pub}\}$, and keeps the master secret key s as secret.

(2) KeyGen Algorithm

A user in PKI cryptosystem submits his/her identity ID_A to Certificate Authority (CA). CA binds certificate with identity. A user belonging to PKI cryptosystem selects $x \in Z_q^*$ randomly, sets $SK_A = x$ as private key SK_A, and computes $SK_A = xP$ as public key PK_A. For user in PKI cryptosystem, his/her public key is PK_A, private key is SK_A, and the key pair is (PK_A, SK_A).

A user in IBC cryptosystem submits his/her identity ID_B to PKG. PKG computes $SK_B = \frac{1}{s+x_B}P = \frac{1}{s+H_1(ID_B)}P$ as private key as SK_B, sends private key SK_B to user. User computes $PK_B = (s + x_B)P = (s + H_1(ID_B))P$ as public key PK_B,$H_1()$ is a hash function,s is master secret key. For user in IBC cryptosystem, his/her public key is PK_B, private key is SK_B, his/her key pair is (PK_B, SK_B).

The output of KeyGen algorithm as follows: User in PKI cryptosystem, his/her private key is SK_A, $SK_A = x$,x is a random number and $x \in Z_q^*$, his/her public key is PK_A,$PK_A = xP$, his/her key pair is (PK_A, SK_A).User in IBC cryptosystem, his/her public key is PK_B,$PK_B = (s + x_B)P = (s + H_1(ID_B))P$, his/her private key is SK_B,$SK_B = \frac{1}{s+x_B} = \frac{1}{s+H_1(ID_B)}$,$H_1()$ is a hash function, his/her key pair is (PK_B, SK_B).

3.2 PKI→IBC HSDVSS

PKI→IBC HSDVSS includes five algorithms: Setup, KeyGen, SDVS Signature, SDVS Verification and Transcript Simulation. We assume that the signer supports the PKI cryptosystem and the designated verifier belongs to the IBC cryptosystem. The signer in the PKI cryptosystem is to generate a heterogeneous strong designated verifier signature (HSDVS). The designated verifier in the IBC cryptosystem is to verify and simulate an HSDVS. The signer performs SDVS Signature algorithm to generate a signature. The designated verifier verifies the validity of the signature. The designated verifier makes Transcript Simulation. The Setup algorithm and KeyGen algorithm have been introduced. Next, we introduce the SDVS Signature, SDVS Verification, Transcript Simulation algorithms.

(1) SDVS Signature algorithm

The signer's key pair is (PK_A, SK_A), the designated verifier's public key is PK_B. The signer selects $r_1, r_2 \in Z_q^*$ randomly.

Compute $R_1 = r_1 SK_A PK_B, R_2 = r_2 PK_B$

Compute $W_1 = e(r_2 P, P), h_1 = H_2(W_1, m)$

Compute $S = (r_1 h_1 SK_A + r_2)P$.

The signature is $\sigma = (R_1, R_2, S)$, the signer sends $\delta = (\sigma, m)$ to the designated verifier.

(2) SDVS Verification algorithm

The designated verifier's key pair is (PK_B, SK_B). The designated verifier receives $\delta = (\sigma, m)$, then verifies it.

Compute $W_2 = e(R_2, SK_B)$

Compute $h_2 = H_2(W_2, m)$

Verify $e(S, P) = W_2^{h_2} e(R_1, SK_B)$ equation, accept $\delta = (\sigma, m)$ if and only if the equation is satisfied, otherwise return 0.

(3) Transcript Simulation algorithm

The designated verifier's key pair is (PK_B, SK_B). The designated verifier selects $r_1', r_2' \in Z_q$ randomly.

Compute $R_1' = r_2' P, R_2' = r_1' P$.

Compute $W_2' = e(R_2', SK_B), h_2' = H_2(W_2', m)$.

Compute $S' = (r_1' h_2' + r_2') SK_B$.

The SDVS simulation is $\sigma' = (R_1', R_2', S')$.

Generated SDVS $\delta' = (\sigma', m)$ satisfies the equation $e(S, P) = W_2^{h_2} e(R_1, SK_B)$.

The SDVS simulation $\sigma' = (R_1', R_2', S')$ generated by the designated verifier is as valid as the signature generated by the signer, two signatures make the equation $e(S, P) = W_2^{h_2} e(R_1, SK_B)$ satisfied. For SDVS simulation $\sigma' = (R_1', R_2', S')$, that is, the equation $e(S', P) = W_2^{h_2} e(R_1', SK_B)$ is met.

3.3 IBC→PKI HSDVSS

IBC→PKI HSDVSS includes five algorithms: Setup, KeyGen, SDVS Signature, SDVS Verification, Transcript Simulation as shown. We assume that the signer supports the PKI cryptosystem and the designated verifier belongs to the IBC cryptosystem. The signer in the IBC cryptosystem is to generate a HSDVS. The designated verifier in the PKI cryptosystem is to verify and simulate an HSDVS. The signer performs the SDVS Signature algorithm to generate a signature. The designated verifier verifies the validity of the signature. The designated verifier makes Transcript Simulation. We have introduced the Setup and KeyGen algorithms. In this subsection, we introduce the SDVS Signature, SDVS Verification, Transcript Simulation algorithms.

(1) SDVS Signature algorithm

The signer's key pair is (PK_B, SK_B),the designated verifier's public key is PK_A. The signer selects $r_1, r_2 \in Z_q^*$ randomly.

Compute $R_1 = r_2 PK_A, R_2 = r_1 SK_B$

Compute $W_1 = e(r_2 PK_B, SK_B) = e(r_2 P, P)$, hash value $h_1 = H_2(W_1, m)$

Compute $S = r_1 h_1 SK_B + r_2 PK_A$.

The signature is $\sigma = (R_1, R_2, S)$, the signer sends $\delta = (\sigma, m)$ to the designated verifier.

(2) SDVS Verification algorithm

The designated verifier's key pair is (PK_A, SK_A).The designated verifier receives $\delta = (\sigma, m)$, then verifies it.

Compute $W_2 = e(R_1, SK_A^{-1}P)$.

Compute $h_2 = H_2(W_2, m)$.

Verify $e(S, P) = W_2^{SK_A} e(R_2, P)^{h_2}$ equation, accept $\delta = (\sigma, m)$ if and only if the equation is satisfied, otherwise return 0.

(3) Transcript Simulation algorithm

The designated verifier's key pair is (PK_A, SK_A) . The designated verifier selects $r_1', r_2' \in Z_q^*$ randomly.

Compute $R_1' = r_2'PK_A, R_2' = r_1'SK_APK_B$.

Compute $W_2' = e\left(r_1'PK_A, SK_A^{-1}P\right) = e\left(r_1'P, P\right), h_2' = H_2\left(W_2', m\right)$.

Compute $S' = r_1'h_2'SK_APK_B + r_2'PK_A$

The SDVS simulation is $\sigma' = (R_1', R_2', S')$

Generated SDVS $\delta' = (\sigma', m)$ satisfies the equation $e(S, P) = W_2^{SK_A}$ $e\left(R_2, P\right)^{h_2}$.

The SDVS simulation $\sigma' = (R_1', R_2', S')$ generated by the designated verifier is as valid as the signature generated by the signer, two signatures make the equation $e(S, P) = W_2^{SK_A} e\left(R_2, P\right)^{h_2}$ satisfied. For SDVS simulation $\sigma' = (R_1', R_2', S')$, that is, the equation $e\left(S', P\right) = W_2{}^{SK_A} e\left(R_2', P\right)^{h_2}$ is met.

4 Security

In this section, we will provide security analysis of the new scheme. In detail, we prove the properties of correctness, non-transferability, unforgeability, strongness, source hiding, non-delegatability in the proposed SMHSDVS scheme between PKI and IBC. And we provide the security model of unforgeability and discuss it.

4.1 Correctness

We first give the definition of correctness, and then, prove the correctness of PKI→IBC HSDVSS and IBC→PKI HSDVSS, which includes two parts: correctness of HSDVS $\delta = (\sigma, m)$, and correctness of HSDVS simulation $\delta' = (\sigma', m)$

Definition 1. Correctness: A valid HSDVS scheme can be verified successfully by the SDVS Verification algorithm if the HSDVS is created by the SDVS Signature algorithm or the Transcript Simulation algorithm.

Correctness of PKI→IBC HSDVSS **Proof. Correctness of HSDVS** $\delta = (\sigma, m)$ **in PKI→IBC HSDVSS**.

In order to prove the correctness of HSDVS $\delta = (\sigma, m)$ in PKI→IBC HSDVSS, we must show that the generated HSDVS $\delta = (\sigma, m)$ meets the equation $e(S, P) = W_2^{h_2} e(R_1, SK_B)$. The detailed proof is as below:

$$e(S,P) = e\left(\left(r_1 h_1 SK_A + r_2\right) P, P\right)$$
$$= e\left(r_1 h_1 PK_A + r_2 P, P\right)$$
$$W_2^{h_2} e\left(R_1, SK_B\right) = e\left(r_1 SK_A PK_B, SK_B\right)^{h_2} e\left(r_2 PK_B, SK_B\right)) =$$
$$e\left(\left(r_1 h_2 SK_A + r_2\right) PK_B, SK_B\right)$$
$$=e\left(\left(r_1 h_2 SK_A + r_2\right) P, P\right)$$
$$= e\left(r_1 h_2 PK_A + r_2 P, P\right)$$
$$= e\left(r_1 h_2 PK_A, P\right) e\left(r_2 P, P\right)$$
$$h_1 = H_2\left(W_1, m\right)$$
$$h_2 = H_2\left(W_2, m\right)$$
$$\because W_1 = W_2$$
$$\therefore h_1 = h_2$$
$$\because e(S,P) = W_2^{h_2} e\left(R_1, SK_B\right) = e\left(r_1 h_2 PK_A, P\right) e\left(r_2 P, P\right)$$
$$\therefore e(S,P) = W_2^{h_2} e\left(R_1, SK_B\right)$$

Therefore, the correctness of PKI→IBC HSDVSS is proved.

Proof. Correctness of HSDVS simulation $\delta' = (\sigma', m)$ in PKI→IBC HSDVSS.

In order to prove the correctness of HSDVS simulation $\delta' = (\sigma', m)$ in PKI→IBC HSDVSS, we must show that the generated signature HSDVS simulation $\delta' = (\sigma', m)$ satisfies the equation $e(S,P) = W_2^{h_2} e\left(R_1, SK_B\right)$. The detailed proof is as below:

$$e\left(S', P\right) = e\left(\left(r_1' h_2' + r_2'\right) SK_B, P\right)$$
$$= e\left(r_1' h_2' P, SK_B\right) e\left(r_2' P, SK_B\right)$$
$$W_2^{h_2} e\left(R_1', SK_B\right) = e\left(R_2', SK_B\right)^{h_2} e\left(R_1', SK_B\right)$$
$$= e\left(r_1' h_2' P, SK_B\right) e\left(r_2' P, SK_B\right)$$
$$\therefore e\left(S', P\right) = W_2^{h_2} e\left(R_1', SK_B\right)$$

The result shows that, the equation $e\left(S', P\right) = (W_2')^{h_2'} e\left(R_1', SK_B\right)$ is satisfied. Therefore, the correctness of HSDVS simulation $\delta' = (\sigma', m)$ in PKI→IBC HSDVSS is proved.

Correctness of IBC→PKI HSDVSS **Proof. Correctness of HSDVS $\delta = (\sigma, m)$ in IBC→PKI HSDVSS.**

In order to prove the correctness of HSDVS $\delta = (\sigma, m)$ in IBC→PKI HSDVSS, we must show that the generated SDVS signature $\delta = (\sigma, m)$ meets the equation $e(S,P) = W_2^{SK_A} e\left(R_2, P\right)^{h_2}$. The detailed proof is similar to PKI→IBC HSDVSS.

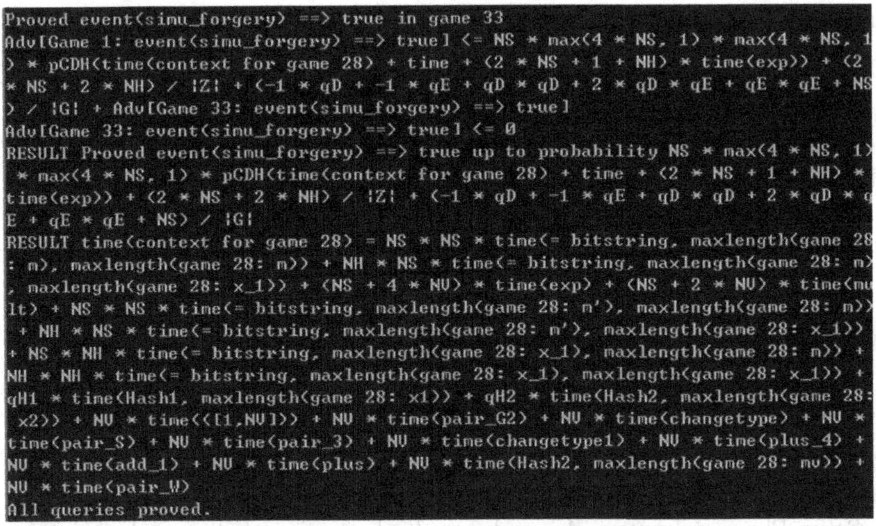

```
Proved event(simu_forgery) ==> true in game 33
Adv[Game 1: event(simu_forgery) ==> true] <= NS * max(4 * NS, 1) * max(4 * NS, 1
) * pCDH(time(context for game 28) + time + (2 * NS + 1 + NH) * time(exp)) + (2
* NS + 2 * NH) / |Z| + (-1 * qD + -1 * qE + qD * qD + 2 * qD * qE + qE * qE + NS
) / |G| + Adv[Game 33: event(simu_forgery) ==> true]
Adv[Game 33: event(simu_forgery) ==> true] <= 0
RESULT Proved event(simu_forgery) ==> true up to probability NS * max(4 * NS, 1)
 * max(4 * NS, 1) * pCDH(time(context for game 28) + time + (2 * NS + 1 + NH) *
time(exp)) + (2 * NS + 2 * NH) / |Z| + (-1 * qD + -1 * qE + qD * qD + 2 * qD * q
E + qE * qE + NS) / |G|
RESULT time(context for game 28) = NS * NS * time(= bitstring, maxlength(game 28
: m), maxlength(game 28: m)) + NH * NS * time(= bitstring, maxlength(game 28: m)
, maxlength(game 28: x_1)) + (NS + 4 * NU) * time(exp) + (NS + 2 * NU) * time(mu
lt) + NS * NS * time(= bitstring, maxlength(game 28: m'), maxlength(game 28: m))
 + NH * NS * time(= bitstring, maxlength(game 28: m'), maxlength(game 28: x_1))
+ NS * NH * time(= bitstring, maxlength(game 28: x_1), maxlength(game 28: m)) +
NH * NH * time(= bitstring, maxlength(game 28: x_1), maxlength(game 28: x_1)) +
qH1 * time(Hash1, maxlength(game 28: x1)) + qH2 * time(Hash2, maxlength(game 28:
 x2)) + NU * time(([1,NU])) + NU * time(pair_G2) + NU * time(changetype) + NU *
time(pair_S) + NU * time(pair_3) + NU * time(changetype1) + NU * time(plus_4) +
NU * time(add_1) + NU * time(plus) + NU * time(Hash2, maxlength(game 28: mv)) +
NU * time(pair_W)
All queries proved.
```

Fig. 1. The result of non-transferability in PKI→IBC MHSDVSS in CryptoVerif.

4.2 Non-Transferability

Definition 2. Non-Transferability: The designated verifier generates a signature simulation σ' with his own private key, and simulation signature's validity is the same as the signer's signature so that the third party can't distinguish the two signatures σ and σ'.

Non-Transferability is modeled with event by using CryptoVerif. The mechanized prover CryptoVerif can directly prove the security properties of cryptographic protocols in the computational model in which the cryptographic primitives are functions on bitstrings and the adversary is a polynomial-time Turing machine. The output of the system is essentially the same.

Non-Transferability of PKI→IBC HSDVSS Non-Transferability of PKI→IBC HSDVSS is proved in Random Oracle model. We use the form of oracles front-end as the input of CryptoVerif. PKI→IBC HSDVSS is translated the HSDVSS into the syntax of CryptoVerif, corresponding CryptoVerif inputs can be generated in the form of oracles front-end. The analysis was performed by CryptoVerif after 33 games of transformation and succeeded. The result is shown in Fig 1, and then the non-transferability of PKI→IBC HSDVSS is proved.

Non-Transferability of IBC→PKI HSDVSS The proof of non-transferability in IBC→PKI HSDVSS is similar to non-transferability of PKI→IBC HSDVSS. And the non-transferability of IBC→PKI HSDVSS can be proved by the CryptoVerif.

4.3 The Security Model of Unforgeability

Definition 3. Unforgeability: It's impossible for a third party to generate a valid SDVS unless you have the designated verifier's private key. That is, although public key and public system parameters is known publicly, it is insufficient to make the verification equation valid. For modern digital signature schemes the essential property is existential unforgeability under chosen message attacks. This property basically requires that an adversary cannot construct a signature for a message that the key owner did not sign previously. In detail, a signature scheme is considered secure against existential unforgeability under an adaptive chosen-message attack (EUF-CMA) [30], if the adversary attacking the scheme could not create a new valid message-signature pair with non-negligible probability without knowing the corresponding signing key.

The security model of unforgeability consists of three phases: Setup Phase, Queries Phase, and Forgery Queries Phase, and uses the Forking Lemma [29] to prove the unforgeability is contradictory to CDHP and BDHP. After the Setup Phase finishes, adversary A_{II} performs multiple queries in the Queries Phase, including H_1 Queries, Key Extract Queries, SDVS Signature Queries, SDVS Verification Queries, and challenger F gives corresponding responses. More details about the three phases are below.

Setup Phase: Adversary A_{II} makes multiple queries, challenger F maintains lists $l_1 - l_3$ that are empty initially.

Initialization: Challenger F runs the Initialization algorithm. Input system security param k, challenger F generates system master private key $t \in Z_q^*$, master public key $P_{pub} = tP$ and system public param $param = \{k, q, G_1, G_2, P, e, H_1, H_2, P_{pub}\}$, and sends them to adversary A_{II}. Set $a, b \in Z_q^*$,$PK_A = aP$,$PK_B = bP$.

Queries Phase: Adversary A_{II} performs the following queries, and challenger F responds correspondingly.

H_1 Queries: When adversary A_{II} presents query on ID_j, challenger F maintains a hash list $H_1 - list$ that is initially empty including two-tuples (ID_j, Q_j). Challenger$F$ checks whether record exists in a hash list $H_1 - list$. If so, challenger returns corresponding record, else challenger makes the following responses:

$$Q_j = \begin{cases} \alpha_j P, ID_j \neq ID_B \\ H_1(ID_j), ID_j = ID_B \end{cases}$$

Key Extract Queries: Adversary A_{II} asks query on the public and private keys of the users in PKI and IBC cryptosystem, ID_i represents the identity of the user in PKI cryptosystem, and ID_j represents the identity of the user in IBC cryptosystem, and stores the corresponding results into the list.

SDVS Signature Queries: Challenger F outputs signature $\delta = (\sigma, m) = (R_1, R_2, S, m)$ to adversary A_{II}.

Challenger F outputs signature $\delta' = (\sigma', m), \sigma' = (R_1', R_2', S')$ to adversary A_{II}. If the signer is the real signer and the designated verifier is the real designated verifier, challenger F aborts.

SDVS Verification Queries: Adversary asks for verification of the signature, and if $ID_A = ID_i, ID_B = ID_j$, stops query. Otherwise, the challenger F calculates the private key of the signer or the designated verifier, and puts it into the equation in SDVS verification algorithm to verify the validity of the signature. If the equation is true, it accepts the signature and outputs 1. Otherwise, outputs 0.

Forgery Queries Phase: Adversary A_{II} outputs a valid signature $\delta = (\sigma, m) = (R_1, R_2, S)$ on message m, among them, i denotes the signer, j denotes the designated verifier, ID_i expressed as the signer's identity, ID_j expressed as the designated verifier's identity. Adversary A_{II} forges signature $\delta'' = (\sigma'', m), \sigma'' = (R_1'', R_2'', S'')$ successfully; otherwise, the challenge fails.

When adversary A_{II} forges the two same commitment signatures $\delta = (\sigma, m) = (R_1, R_2, S)$ and $\delta'' = (\sigma'', m), \sigma'' = (R_1'', R_2'', S'')$, in order to solve CDH and BDH problem, an algorithm L is constructed as following:

According to the Forking lemma, challenger F performs SDVS signature algorithm of SDVS signature query, and obtains two signatures S and S'', where S'' is a simulation of S. Challenger F outputs a value as a solution to CDH, which is contradictory to the CDHP.

According to the Forking lemma, adversary A_{II} forges a signature $\delta'' = (\sigma'', m), \sigma'' = (R_1'', R_2'', S'')$. However, when adversary A_{II} asks query on h_1 and W_1, challenger F sets $h_1 = H_2(W_1, m)$. Adversary A_{II} forges a signature $\delta'' = (\sigma'', m), \sigma'' = (R_1'', R_2'', S'')$. Challenger F searches corresponding value from $H_2 - list$, and then, the BDHP can be solved.

According to $SK_B = cP, SK_B = bP$, finally, obtain an equation $W_1 = e(P, P)^{abc}$. Obviously, this is contradictory to the BDHP. Therefore, PKI→IBC HSDVSS has un-forgeability.

4.4 Strongness

Next, we provide the proof of strongness in the two schemes, PKI→IBC HSDVSS and IBC→PKI HSDVSS.

Definition 4. Strongness: Without the designated verifier's private key or only derivatives of the signer or the designated verifier's private key, the signature cannot be verified to be true and valid. The private key is a necessary parameter in verifying the validity of the signature.

Proof. Strongness of PKI→IBC HSDVSS. In PKI→IBC HSDVSS, as long as the equation $e(S, P) = W_2^{h_2} e(R_1, SK_B)$ is true, then, the validity of SDVS is verified. While verifying the equation, the designated verifier's private key SK_B is required. Therefore, PKI→IBC HSDVSS satisfies strongness.

Proof. Strongness of IBC→PKI HSDVSS. In IBC→PKI HSDVSS, as long as the equation $e(S, P) = W_2^{SK_A} e(R_2, P)^{h_2}$ is true, then, the validity of SDVS is verified. While verifying the equation, the designated verifier's private key SK_A is required. Therefore, IBC→PKI HSDVSS satisfies strongness.

4.5 Source-Hiding

In this section, we provide the proof of source hiding in the two schemes, PKI→IBC HSDVSS and IBC→PKI HSDVSS.

Definition 5. Source hiding: Given an SDVS signature on a given message, it is infeasible to determine whether distinguish the signer or the designated verifier creates even though a third party knows all private key.

Proof. Source hiding of PKI→IBC HSDVSS. In PKI→IBC HSDVSS, according to the proof of correctness of HSDVS simulation $\delta' = (\sigma', m)$ in PKI→IBC HSDVSS in Sect. 4.1, the signature generated by the signer and the designated verifier are indistinguishable, and two signatures are valid. Because the two SDVS signatures can be verified successfully. Even though the third party knows the signer's and the designated verifier's private key, it can't determine which one is generated by the signer or the designated verifier. In other words, the source of signature is uncertain. Therefore, PKI→IBC HSDVSS satisfies source hiding.

Proof. Source hiding of IBC→PKI HSDVSS. In IBC→PKI HSDVSS, according to the proof of correctness of HSDVS simulation $\delta' = (\sigma', m)$ in PKI→IBC HSDVSS in Sect. 4.1, the signature generated by the signer and the designated verifier are indistinguishable, and both of them are valid. Because the two SDVS signatures can be verified successfully. Even though the third party knows the signer's and the designated verifier's private key, it cannot determine which one is generated by the signer or the designated verifier, that is, the signature source is uncertain. Therefore, IBC→PKI HSDVSS satisfies source hiding.

4.6 Non-delegatability

In this section, we provide the proof of non-delegatability in the two schemes, PKI→IBC HSDVSS and IBC→PKI HSDVSS.

Definition 6. Non-delegatability: Any third party who gets a derivation about the signer's private key or the designated verifier's private key cannot generate a true and valid signature. It is difficult to get the signer's private key.

Non-delegatability means that the legal signature of the designated verifier should contain the knowledge proof of the signer or the designated verifier. Furthermore, the private key of the signer and the designated verifier is a necessary parameter in generating a signature. According to the definition of non-delegatability, there is a black-box knowledge extractor, where F represents an algorithm, and F generates a valid signature on the message. On the basis of the analysis of unforgeability, it is difficult to obtain private key, which indicates that the scheme has the non-delegatability.

Proof. Non-delegatability of PKI→IBC HSDVSS. A_{II} stands for the adversary. F denotes the challenger.

Adversary A_{II} outputs a valid signature $\delta = (\sigma, m)$,$\sigma = (R_1, R_2, S)$ on given message m, i means the signer, j means the designated verifier,ID_i denotes the signer's identity, and ID_j denotes the designated verifier's identity. If $ID_i = ID_A$ and $ID_j = ID_B$, then adversary A_{II} forges $\delta'' = (\sigma'', m), \sigma'' = (R_1'', R_2'', S'')$ successfully, otherwise challenge fails.

When adversary A_{II} forges two signatures $\delta = (\sigma, m) = (R_1, R_2, S)$ and $\delta'' = (\sigma'', m), \sigma'' = (R_1'', R_2'', S'')$ successfully, in order to solve the problem, an algorithm L is constructed, challenger F executes SDVS Signature algorithm, and obtains two signatures $\delta = (\sigma, m) = (R_1, R_2, S)$ and $\delta'' = (\sigma'', m), \sigma'' = (R_1'', R_2'', S'')$. Among them, $S = (r_1 h_1 SK_A + r_2) P, S'' = (r_1 h_1'' SK_A + r_2) P, h_1 \neq h_1''$.

We can derive $S - S'' = r_1 SK_A (h_1 - h_1'') P$, and then $SK_A = \frac{S-S''}{r_1(h_1-h_1'')P} = abP.r_1$ is a limitation for adversary A_{II}, which is contradictory to CDH. It is hard to get the signer's private key SK_A. Therefore, PKI→IBC HSDVSS satisfies non-delegatability.

Proof. Non-delegatability of IBC→PKI HSDVSS. Adversary A_{II} outputs a valid signature $\delta = (\sigma, m) = (R_1, R_2, S)$ on given message m, i means the signer, j means the designated verifier, ID_i denotes the signer's identity, ID_j denotes the designated verifier's identity. If $ID_i = ID_A$ and $ID_j = ID_B$, then adversary A_{II} forges $\delta'' = (\sigma'', m), \sigma'' = (R_1'', R_2'', S'')$ successfully, otherwise challenge fails.

When adversary A_{II} forges two signatures $\delta = (\sigma, m) = (R_1, R_2, S)$ and $\delta'' = (\sigma'', m), \sigma'' = (R_1'', R_2'', S'')$ successfully, in order to solve the problem, an algorithm L is constructed, challenger F executes SDVS Signature algorithm, and obtains two signatures $\delta = (\sigma, m) = (R_1, R_2, S)$ and $\delta'' = (\sigma'', m), \sigma'' = (R_1'', R_2'', S'')$. Among them,$S = r_1 h_1 SK_j + r_2 PK_A, S'' = r_1 h_1'' SK_j + r_2 PK_A, h_1 \neq h_1''$. We can derive $S - S'' = r_1 SK_B (h_1 - h_1'')$, and then $SK_B = \frac{S-S''}{r_1(h_1-h_1'')} = abP.r_1$ is a limitation for adversary A_{II}, which is contradictory to CDH. It is hard to get the signer's private keySK_B. Therefore, IBC→PKI HSDVSS satisfies non-delegatability.

Table 1. Performance Comparison.

Scheme	Signature computation	Verification computation	Transcript Simulation computation	Total computation
DVS [14]	4mod+1hash+4exp	1hash+6exp	6mod+6exp	10mod+ 2hash+16exp
SDVS [15]	2mod+1hash +2exp	1mod+1hash +3exp	4mod+1hash +5exp	3mod+3hash +10exp
SDVS [16]	1xor+2mod+2pair+2hash+2exp	1xor+1mod+2pair+2hash	1xor+2mod+2pair+2hash+1exp	3xor+5mod+6pair+6hash+3exp
CLSDVS [19]	1pair+2hash	1pair+2hash	1pair+2hash	3pair+6hash
UDVS [26]	5exp	2pair+2exp	2pair+4exp	4pair+11exp
HSDVS1 [21]	1pair+3hash	3pair+1hash+1exp	1pair+1hash	5pair+5hash+1exp
HSDVS2 [21]	1pair+1hash	3pair+2hash+1exp	1pair+3hash+1exp	5pair+6hash+1exp
PKI→IBC HSDVSS	1pair+1hash	3pair+1hash+1exp	1pair+1hash	5pair+3hash+1exp
IBC→PKI HSDVSS	1pair+1hash	3pair+1hash+2exp	1pair+1hash	5pair+3hash+2exp

5 Performance

We analyze the proposed SMHSDVS scheme between PKI and IBC from computations including Sign computation, Verification computation, Transcript Simulation computation, Total computation. Since there is a similar HSDVS scheme proposed in [21], we will compare our schemes with it. Moreover, the schemes in DVS [14], SDVS [15,16,19], UDVS [26] are compared with our proposed schemes. The results are shown in Table 1. Among these computations, mod denotes modulo division operation, pair expressed as bilinear pairing operation, exp indicated as exponentiation operation, hash means hash operation, and xor means exclusive-OR operation.

In our proposed PKI→IBC HSDVSS, Signature computation is 1pair+1hash, Verification computation is 3pair+1hash+ 1exp, Transcript Simulation is 1pair+ 1hash, Total computation is 5pair+3hash+1exp. In IBC→PKI HSDVSS, Signature computation is 1pair+1hash, Verification computation is 3pair+1hash+ 2exp, Transcript Simulation computation is 1pair+1hash, total computation is 5pair+3hash+2exp. Obviously, there is no mod or xor computation. Exp computation is the least in our schemes.

6 Conclusion

In order to ensure the correction of signature and protect the privacy of signer in heterogeneous cryptography communication, we presented a secure and mutual heterogeneous strong designated verifier signature scheme between PKI and IBC based on BDHP and CDHP. On the basis of correctness, the unforgeability is proved in a random oracle model. Our schemes satisfy many important security requirements, including correctness, non-transferability, unforgeability, strongness, source hiding, and non-delegatability. Compared with existing schemes such as DVS, SDVS, UDVS, our schemes have no mod computation, XOR computation and exp computation keeping the least by making performance analysis.

In our scheme, the cost of bilinear pairing computation is not efficient. Therefore, the next step is to construct an efficient scheme by reducing bilinear pairing computation.

Funding Information. This work was supported in part by the National key R&D Program of China No. 2020YFC1522900; the Fundamental Research Funds for the Central Universities No.CZZ21001 and No. QSZ17007; and natural science foundation of Hubei Province under the grants No. 2018ADC150.

References

1. Jakobsson, M., Sako, K., Impagliazzo, R.: Designated verifier proofs and their applications. In: Maurer, U. (ed.) EUROCRYPT 1996. LNCS, vol. 1070, pp. 143–154. Springer, Heidelberg (1996). https://doi.org/10.1007/3-540-68339-9_13
2. Sun, Y.X., Li, H.: Efficient signcryption between TPKC and IDPKC and its multi-receiver construction. Sci. China Inform. Sci. **53**(3), 557–566 (2010). https://doi.org/10.1007/s11432-010-0061-5
3. Li, F., Zhang, H., Takagi, T.: Efficient signcryption for heterogeneous systems. IEEE Syst. J. **7**(3), 420–429 (2013)
4. Zhang, Y., Zhang, L., Zhang, Y., Wang, H., Wang, C.: CLPKC to TPKI heterogeneous signature scheme with Anonymity. Acta Electron. Sin. **44**(10), 2432–2439 (2016)
5. Wang, C., Li, Y., Zhang, Y., Niu, S.: Efficient Signcryption scheme under the Standard Model. J. Electron. Inf. Technol. **39**(4), 881–886 (2017)

6. Zhang, Y., Zhang, L., Wang, C., Ma, Y., Zhang, Y.: Provable secure IDPKC-to-CLPKC hetero-geneous signcryption scheme. Electron. Inf. Technol **39**(9), 2127–2133 (2017)
7. Wang, C., Liu, C., Li, Y., Niu, S., Zhang, Y.: Bidirectional anonymous heterogeneous signature scheme based on PKI and IBC. J. Commun. **38**(10), 10–17(2017). https://doi.org/10.11959/J.issn.1000-436x.2017194
8. Liu, J., Zhang, L., Sun, R., Du, X., Guizani, M.: Mutual Heterogeneous Signcryption Schemes for 5G Network Slicings. IEEE Access **1–1**(6), 7854–7863 (2018). https://doi.org/10.1109/Access.2018.2797102
9. Cao, S., Lang, X., Liu, X., Wang, C., Zhang, Y.: Improvement of a Verifiable and secure bidirec-tional anonymous heterogeneous signature scheme for PKI and IBC. J. Electron. Inf. Technol. **41**(8), 1787–1792 (2019)
10. Xiong, H., Wu, Y., Jin, C., et al.: Efficient and privacy-preserving authentication protocol for heterogeneous systems in IIoT. IEEE Internet Things J. **7**(12), 11713–11724 (2020)
11. Yang, X., Zhang, Y., Deng, Z.: Research on trusted Two-Dimensional Code Technology based on PKI. Sci. Technol. Innov. Appl. **33**, 89–90 (2015)
12. Sun, S.: A random individual digital signature authentication scheme. Inform. Security Technol. **6**(7), 29–30+37 (2015)
13. Zhen, P., Zhao, G., Min, L., Li, X.: A forward secure digital Signature scheme based on identity. Comput. Appl. Softw. **32**(11), 295–298 (2015)
14. Zhang, J., Xiao, H., Wang, J.: Efficient identity based on RSA multiple digital signature. J. Chin. Comput. Syst. **9**, 1978–1981 (2018)
15. Saeednia, S., Kremer, S., Markowitch, O.: An efficient strong designated verifier signature scheme. In: Lim, J.-I., Lee, D.-H. (eds.) Information Security and Cryptology - ICISC 2003, pp. 40–54. Springer, Berlin, Heidelberg (2004). https://doi.org/10.1007/978-3-540-24691-6_4
16. Pankaj, S., Amitabh, B.: Strong designated verifier signature scheme based on discrete logarithm problem. J. Discr. Math. Sci. Crypt. **18**(6), 877–885 (2015)
17. Xu, D., Yu, B.: A secure identity-based strongly specified verifier signature scheme. Comput. Sci. **43**(4), 50–52+57 (2016)
18. Du, H., Wen, Q.: Multi signature based on Certificateless strong designated verifier. J. Commun. **37**(6), 20–28 (2016)
19. Shooshtari, M.K., Ahmadian-Attari, M., Aref, M.R.: Provably secure strong designated verifier signature scheme based on coding theory. Int. J. Commun. Syst. **30**(7), e3162 (2017)
20. Yue, F.: Research on efficient signature system of designated verifier and its application. University of Electronic Science and Technology (2016)
21. Ge, L.: Study on Strong Designated Verifier signature scheme. Xihua Universit (2017)
22. Yu, Z., Feng, H., Xu, H.: Strong designated verifier signature scheme based on identity in cloud storage of smart distribution network. Comput. Digital Eng. **46**(10), 2042–2046+2088 (2018)
23. Han, S., Xie, M., Yang, B., et al.: A certificateless verifiable strong designated verifier signature scheme. IEEE Access **7**, 126391–126408 (2019)
24. Nayak, B.: Elliptic curve cryptography-based signcryption scheme with a strong designated verifier for the internet. Mach. Learn. Inform. Process.: Proc. ICMLIP **2020**(1101), 485 (2019)
25. Lin, H.Y., Tsai, T.T., Ting, P.Y., et al.: An efficient strong designated multi-verifier signature scheme with shared verification[J]. Int. J. Technol. Eng. Stud. **7**(1), 10–16 (2021)

26. Parvin, R., Mehdi, B., Mohammad, D., Willy, S.: Universal designated verifier signature scheme with non-delegatability in the standard model. Inf. Sci. **479**, 321–334 (2019)
27. Zhang, Y., Xin, X., Li, F.: Secure and efficient quantum designated verifier signature scheme. Modern Phys. Lett. A, **35**(18), 2050148 (2020). https://doi.org/10.1142/S0217732320501485
28. Xin, X., Ding, L., Li, C., et al.: Quantum public-key designated verifier signature. Quantum Inf. Process. **21**(1), 1–16 (2022)
29. Bellare, M., Neven, G.: Multi-signatures in the plain public-key model and a general forking lemma. In: Proceedings of the 13th ACM Conference on Computer and Communications Security, pp. 390–399 (2006)
30. Goldwasser, S., Micali, S., Rivest, R.L.: A digital signature scheme secure against adaptive chosen-message attacks. SIAM J. Comput. **17**(2), 281–308 (1988). https://doi.org/10.1137/0217017

Key-Range Attribute-Based Signatures for Range of Inner Product and Its Applications

Masahito Ishizaka(✉)

KDDI Research, Inc., Saitama, Japan
xma-ishizaka@kddi.com

Abstract. In attribute-based signatures (ABS) for range of inner product (ARIP), recently proposed by Ishizaka and Fukushima at ICISC 2022, a secret-key labeled with an n-dimensional vector $\mathbf{x} \in \mathbb{Z}_p^n$ for a prime p can be used to sign a message under an n-dimensional vector $\mathbf{y} \in \mathbb{Z}_p^n$ and a range $[L, R] = \{L, L+1, \cdots, R-1, R\}$ with $L, R \in \mathbb{Z}_p$ iff their inner product is within the range, i.e., $\langle \mathbf{x}, \mathbf{y} \rangle \in [L, R] \pmod p$. We consider its key-range version, named key-range ARIP (KARIP), where the range $[L, R]$ is associated with a secret-key but not with a signature. We propose three generic KARIP constructions based on linearly homomorphic signatures and non-interactive witness-indistinguishable proof, which lead to concrete KARIP instantiations secure under standard assumptions with different features in terms of efficiency. We also show that KARIP has various applications, e.g., key-range ABS for range evaluation of polynomials/weighted averages/Hamming distance/Euclidean distance, key-range time-specific signatures, and key-range ABS for hyperellipsoid predicates.

Keywords: Key-Range attribute-based signatures for range of inner product · Adaptive unforgeablity · Signer-privacy · Key-delegatability

1 Introduction

Attribute-Based Encryption (ABE) for Inner Products. In ABE for inner products [12], n-dimensional vector $\mathbf{x} \in \mathbb{Z}_p^n$ (resp. $\mathbf{y} \in \mathbb{Z}_p^n$) for a prime p is associated with secret-key (resp. ciphertext). The decryption succeeds iff $\langle \mathbf{x}, \mathbf{y} \rangle = 0 \pmod p$. It can be generically transformed into various ABE primitives, e.g., (anonymous) identity-based encryption (IBE), hidden-vector encryption (HVE) [6], the dual variant of HVE (= wildcarded IBE [1]), ABE for evaluation of polynomials/weighted averages, ABE for conjunctive/disjunctive normal form (CNF/DNF) formulas, and ABE for exact thresholds.

Attribute-Based Signatures for Range of Inner Product (ARIP) [10]. ARIP is a generalization of attribute-based signatures (ABS) for inner products which

M. Zhang et al. (Eds.): ProvSec 2023, LNCS 14217, pp. 131–156, 2023.
https://doi.org/10.1007/978-3-031-45513-1_8

is the digital signature version of the above ABE for inner products. A secret-key associated with an n-dimensional vector $\mathbf{x} \in \mathbb{Z}_p^n$ is used to sign a message M under an n-dimensional vector $\mathbf{y} \in \mathbb{Z}_p^n$ and a range $[L, R]$ with $L, R \in \mathbb{Z}_p$. The signing succeeds iff $\langle \mathbf{x}, \mathbf{y} \rangle \in [L, R] \pmod p$. Two security requirements are defined, unforgeability and signer-privacy. The latter means that any signature leaks no more information about $\mathbf{x}$ than the fact that its inner product with $\mathbf{y}$ is in the range $[L, R]$. ARIP has various applications. An ARIP scheme can be transformed into any of the following ABS primitives, ABS for range evaluation (RE) of polynomials (AREP), ABS for RE of weighted averages (AREWA), fuzzy identity-based signatures (FIBS), time-specific signatures (TSS) [11,14], ABS for RE of Hamming distance (AREHD), ABS for RE of Euclidean distance (AREED) and ABS for hyperellipsoid predicates (AHEP).

In this paper, we consider its key-range version, named key-range ARIP (KARIP). The range $[L, R]$ is associated with a secret-key but not with a signature. The ABS scheme by Sakai et al. [15] supporting any circuit as signer-predicate can be a KARIP scheme by properly configuring the circuit. Both a vector $\mathbf{x} \in \mathbb{Z}_p^n$ and a range $[L, R]$ are transformed into a binary attribute $x \in \{0,1\}^{(n+2)\cdot\lambda}$. In their ABS scheme, at signature generation, a signer generates a commitment of the non-interactive witness indistinguishable proof (NIWI) system by Groth and Sahai (GS) [8] for each bit $x[i] \in \{0,1\}$ of x. Thus, at least, its signature length linearly increases with $n\lambda$.

1.1 Contribution

In this work, we propose three generic constructions of KARIP, which lead to three concrete KARIP schemes with distinct features in terms of efficiency and key-delegatability. We show that KARIP has various applications.

1st Construction. It is generically constructed by NIWI, linearly homomorphic signatures (LHS)[1] [5] and append-only signatures (AOS)[2] [13]. In key-generation for $(\mathbf{x}, L, R)$, we choose an LHS tag τ, then define $n+2$ vectors $\boldsymbol{v}_1, \cdots, \boldsymbol{v}_{n+2} \in \mathbb{Z}_p^{n+3}$ as $\boldsymbol{v}_i := (x_i, \underbrace{0, \cdots, 0}_{i-1}, 1, \underbrace{0, \cdots, 0}_{n-i}, 0, 0, 0)$ for each $i \in [1, n]$, $\boldsymbol{v}_{n+1} := (0, \cdots, 0, 1, 0)$ and $\boldsymbol{v}_{n+2} := (0, \cdots, 0, 0, 1)$. We generate an LHS signature σ_i on each vector $\boldsymbol{v}_i$ under the common tag τ. In signing for $(\mathbf{y}, M)$, they are used to derive an LHS signature σ' with the same tag τ on $\boldsymbol{v}' := (\langle \mathbf{x}, \mathbf{y} \rangle, y_1, \cdots, y_n, M)$. In key-generation, we also generate AOS signatures. We consider a complete binary tree with p leaf nodes. C denotes the set of intermediate nodes covering all of the leaf nodes associated with from $[L]_2$ to $[R]_2$, where $[a]_2$ is the binary value of a. For each $c \in C$, parsed as $c[1] \| \cdots \| c[h_c]$ with $c[i] \in \{0,1\}$ and length $h_c \in [1, \lambda]$, we generate an AOS signature θ_c on $(\tau, c[1], \cdots, c[h_c]) \in (\{0,1\}^N)^{h_c+1}$. In signing,

[1] In LHS, l signatures $\{\sigma_i\}_{i=1}^l$ on vectors $\{\boldsymbol{v}_i\}_{i=1}^l$ associated with the common tag τ make us derive a signature on any linear summation $\sum_{i=1}^l \beta_i \cdot \boldsymbol{v}_i$ with same tag τ.

[2] In AOS, each message has a hierarchical structure. Any signature on a message M makes us derive a new signature on any descendant message M'.

one of the AOS signatures is used to generate an AOS signature θ' on $(\tau, \langle \mathbf{x}, \mathbf{y}\rangle[1], \cdots, \langle \mathbf{x}, \mathbf{y}\rangle[\lambda]) \in (\{0,1\}^N)^{\lambda+1}$. If $\langle \mathbf{x}, \mathbf{y}\rangle \in [L, R]$, there exists a node $c \in C$ s.t. c is whether identical to or an ancestor of $\langle \mathbf{x}, \mathbf{y}\rangle$. An AOS signature θ_c for such a node c derives θ'. Finally, we generate an NIWI proof that both of the LHS and AOS signatures σ', θ' are correct under the witness $(\langle \mathbf{x}, \mathbf{y}\rangle, \tau, \sigma', \theta')$. Clearly, our 1st construction is key-delegatable because of the message-appendability of the underlying AOS.

To instantiate it, we use the simplified ALP LHS scheme [10] and the GS proof [8]. As AOS, we search for a candidate satisfying both of the following conditions, namely (1) *Based on symmetric bilinear paring with prime order* and (2) *Its verification algorithm consists of only PPEs.* We refer to an hierarchical identity-based signatures scheme in by Chatterjee and Sarkar [7] to construct an original AOS scheme satisfying the conditions and rigorously prove its security, i.e., unforgeability, under the CDH assumption. To evaluate efficiency of the instantiated scheme, we rigorously calculate its secret-key and signature sizes. They are $N + (n + \lambda^2)|g|$ [bit] and $(27N + 27\lambda + 40)|g|$ [bit], where $|g|$ denotes bit length of an element in the bilinear group $\mathbb{G}$.

2nd Construction. It is generically constructed by LHS and NIWI. This construction is similar to the 1st ARIP scheme in [10]. In key-generation for $(\mathbf{x}, L, R)$, we define $n+2$ vectors $\boldsymbol{v}_1, \cdots, \boldsymbol{v}_{n+2} \in \mathbb{Z}_p^{n+5}$ as $\boldsymbol{v}_i := (x_i, \underbrace{0, \cdots, 0}_{i-1}, 1, \underbrace{0, \cdots, 0}_{n-i}, 0, 0, 0, 0)$ for each $i \in [1, n]$, $\boldsymbol{v}_{n+1} := (0, \cdots, 0, L, R, 0, 1)$ and $\boldsymbol{v}_{n+2} := (0, \cdots, 0, 0, 0, 1, 0)$. For each vector $\boldsymbol{v}_i$, we generate an LHS signature σ_i with the common tag τ. In signing for $(\mathbf{y}, M)$, an LHS signature σ' with the tag τ on $\boldsymbol{v}' := (\langle \mathbf{x}, \mathbf{y}\rangle, y_1, \cdots, y_n, L, R, M, 1)$ is derived. Then, we generate an NIWI proof that σ' is a correct signature on $\boldsymbol{v}'$ and $\langle \mathbf{x}, \mathbf{y}\rangle \in [L, R]$.

We instantiate it by the simplified ALP LHS scheme [10] and the GS proof [8] to obtain a KARIP scheme secure under the DLIN, CDH and FlexCDH assumptions. To efficiently prove $\langle \mathbf{x}, \mathbf{y}\rangle \geq L$, we use the following fact. If $\langle \mathbf{x}, \mathbf{y}\rangle \geq L$, $\langle \mathbf{x}, \mathbf{y}\rangle = L$ or there exists a single index $t \in [1, \lambda]$ s.t. the leftmost $t-1$ bits of $\langle \mathbf{x}, \mathbf{y}\rangle$ and L are identical and the t-th bits of $\langle \mathbf{x}, \mathbf{y}\rangle$ and L are 1 and 0, respectively. More formally, $\exists t \in [1, \lambda+1]$ s.t. $\bigwedge_{i=1}^{t-1} \langle \mathbf{x}, \mathbf{y}\rangle[i] = L[i] \bigwedge \langle \mathbf{x}, \mathbf{y}\rangle[t] = 1 \bigwedge L[t] = 0$. To prove $\langle \mathbf{x}, \mathbf{y}\rangle \leq R$, we also use the same fact. We rigorously prove that its secret-key and signature sizes are $N+4(n+2)|g|$ and $(18N+132\lambda+39)|g|$.

3rd Construction. It is generically constructed by LHS, NIWI and collision-resistant hash function (HF). It is similar to the 2nd ARIP scheme in [10]. In key-generation, we define only two vectors $\boldsymbol{v}_1 := (x_1, x_2, \cdots, x_n, L, R, 0, 1), \boldsymbol{v}_2 := (0, \cdots, 0, 1, 0) \in \mathbb{Z}_p^{n+4}$, then generate an LHS signature σ_i with the common tag τ on each vector $\boldsymbol{v}_i$. In signing, an LHS signature σ' on $\boldsymbol{v}' := (x_1, \cdots, x_n, L, R, h, 1)$, where h is the hash value of $(\mathbf{y}, M)$. Then, we generate an NIWI proof that σ' is a correct signature on $\boldsymbol{v}'$, $\langle \mathbf{x}, \mathbf{y}\rangle \in [L, R]$, and the inner product value is correctly calculated, i.e., $\langle \mathbf{x}, \mathbf{y}\rangle = \sum_{i=1}^{n} x_i \cdot y_i \pmod{p}$.

To instantiate it, we use the same building blocks as our 2nd construction. We rigorously prove that its secret-key and signature sizes are $N + 8|g|$ and $(9n + 18N + 132\lambda + 42)|g|$.

Applications. As formally shown in [10], an ARIP scheme can be transformed into any of the following ABS primitives, namely AREP, AREWA, FIBS, TSS [11,14], AREHD, AREED and AHEP. The same transformation techniques also work for KARIP. A KARIP scheme can be transformed into their key-range versions. We emphasize that if the underlying KARIP scheme has key-delegatablity, the property is directly inherited after the transformation.

Paper Organization. In Sect. 2, we explain some notations, and define some computational assumptions, NIWI, LHS and AOS. In Sect. 3, we formally define KARIP. In Sect. 4 (resp. 5, 6), we propose our 1st (resp. 2nd, 3rd) generic KARIP construction, prove its security, and introduce its instantiation. In Sect. 7, we introduce the applications of KARIP.

2 Preliminaries

Notations. For $\lambda \in \mathbb{N}$, 1^λ denotes a security parameter. A function $f : \mathbb{N} \to \mathbb{R}$ is negligible if for every $c \in \mathbb{N}$, there exists $x_0 \in \mathbb{N}$ s.t. for every $x \geq x_0$, $f(x) \leq x^{-c}$. Given a binary string $x \in \{0,1\}^L$, for every $i \in [1, L]$, let $x[i] \in \{0,1\}$ denote its i-th bit. PPTA means probabilistic polynomial time algorithm. For a set A, $a \xleftarrow{U} A$ means that an element a is chosen uniformly at random from A. For an integer $a \in \mathbb{N}$, $[a]_2$ denotes its binary value.

Symmetric Bilinear Pairing on Groups with Prime Order. $\mathcal{G}$ takes a security parameter 1^λ with $\lambda \in \mathbb{N}$ and outputs a group description $(p, \mathbb{G}, \mathbb{G}_T, e, g)$. p is a prime with bit length λ. $\mathbb{G}$ and $\mathbb{G}_T$ are multiplicative groups with order p. g is a generator of $\mathbb{G}$. $e : \mathbb{G} \times \mathbb{G} \to \mathbb{G}_T$ is an efficiently computable function which satisfies the following two conditions, (1) **Bilinearity:** For any $a, b \in \mathbb{Z}_p$, $e(g^a, g^b) = e(g, g)^{ab}$, (2) **Non-degeneracy:** $e(g, g) \neq 1_{\mathbb{G}_T}$, where $1_{\mathbb{G}_T}$ denotes the unit element of $\mathbb{G}_T$. In this work, $|g|$ denotes bit length of an element in the bilinear group $\mathbb{G}$.

Assumptions. We define the three computational hardness assumptions.

Definition 1. *The computational Diffie-Hellman (CDH) assumption holds on the group* $\mathbb{G}$ *if for every PPT* $\mathcal{A}$, $\mathit{Adv}^{\mathit{CDH}}_{\mathcal{A},\mathbb{G}}(\lambda) := \Pr[g^{ab} \leftarrow \mathcal{A}(g, g^a, g^b)]$ *with* $a, b \xleftarrow{U} \mathbb{Z}_p$, *is negligible.*

Definition 2. *The flexible CDH (FlexCDH) assumption [4] holds on the group* $\mathbb{G}$ *if for every PPT* $\mathcal{A}$, $\mathit{Adv}^{\mathit{FlexCDH}}_{\mathcal{A},\mathbb{G}}(\lambda) := \Pr[(g^\mu, g^{a\cdot\mu}, g^{ab\cdot\mu}) \leftarrow \mathcal{A}(g, g^a, g^b)]$ *with* $a, b \xleftarrow{U} \mathbb{Z}_p$ *and* $\mu \neq 0$, *is negligible.*

Definition 3. *The decisional linear (DLIN) assumption holds on the group* $\mathbb{G}$ *if for every PPT* $\mathcal{A}$, $\mathit{Adv}^{\mathit{DLIN}}_{\mathcal{A},\mathbb{G}}(\lambda) := |\Pr[1 \leftarrow \mathcal{A}(g^a, g^b, g^{ab}, g^{bd}, g^{c+d})]| - \Pr[1 \leftarrow \mathcal{A}(g^a, g^b, g^{ab}, g^{bd}, g^z)]$ *with* $a, b, c, d, z \xleftarrow{U} \mathbb{Z}_p$, *is negligible.*

2.1 Non-Interactive Witness Indistinguishable Proof (NIWI)

An NIWI system for the NP relation $R : \{0,1\}^* \times \{0,1\}^* \rightarrow 1/0$ consists of the following 3 polynomial-time algorithms. Note that $\mathtt{Ver}$ is deterministic and the others are probabilistic. Setup algorithm $\mathtt{Setup}$ takes a security parameter 1^λ for $\lambda \in \mathbb{N}$, then outputs a common reference string (CRS) crs. Proving algorithm $\mathtt{Pro}$ takes the CRS crs, a statement $x \in \{0,1\}^*$ and a witness $w \in \{0,1\}^*$, then outputs a proof π. Verification $\mathtt{Ver}$ takes the CRS crs, a statement $x \in \{0,1\}^*$ and a proof π, then outputs a verification result 1/0. We require every NIWI system to be correct. An NIWI system is correct if for every $\lambda \in \mathbb{N}$, every $crs \leftarrow \mathtt{Setup}(1^\lambda)$, every $x \in \{0,1\}^*$, every $w \in \{0,1\}^*$ s.t. $1 \leftarrow R(x,w)$, and every $\pi \leftarrow \mathtt{Pro}(crs, x, w)$, it holds that $1 \leftarrow \mathtt{Ver}(crs, x, \pi)$.

We define two security requirements, namely perfect witness-indistinguishability ($\mathtt{WI}$) and perfect witness-extractability ($\mathtt{WE}$).

Definition 4. *An NIWI system is perfectly witness-indistinguishable ($\mathtt{WI}$), if for every $\lambda \in \mathbb{N}$, every $crs \leftarrow \mathtt{Setup}(1^\lambda)$, every $x \in \{0,1\}^*$, and every $w_0, w_1 \in \{0,1\}^*$ s.t. $1 \leftarrow R(x, w_b)$ for each $b \in \{0,1\}$, $\mathtt{Pro}(crs, x, w_0)$ distributes identically to $\mathtt{Pro}(crs, x, w_1)$.*

Definition 5. *An NIWI system is perfectly witness-extractable ($\mathtt{WE}$), if for every $\lambda \in \mathbb{N}$, there exist two algorithms $\mathtt{SimSetup}$ and $\mathtt{Extract}$ that satisfy both of the following two conditions.*

1. *For every PPT algorithm $\mathcal{A}$, $Adv^{\mathtt{WE}}_{\Sigma_{\mathrm{NIWI}},\mathcal{A}}(\lambda) := |\Pr[1 \leftarrow \mathcal{A}(crs) \mid crs \leftarrow \mathtt{Setup}(1^\lambda)] - \Pr[1 \leftarrow \mathcal{A}(crs) \mid (crs, ek) \leftarrow \mathtt{SimSetup}(1^\lambda)]|$ is negligible.*
2. *For every probabilistic algorithm $\mathcal{A}$,*

$$\Pr\left[\begin{array}{c}(crs, ek) \leftarrow \mathtt{SimSetup}(1^\lambda); (x, \pi) \leftarrow \mathcal{A}(crs); \\ w \leftarrow \mathtt{Extract}(crs, ek, x, \pi) : 1 \leftarrow \mathtt{Ver}(crs, x, \pi) \wedge 0 \leftarrow R(x, w)\end{array}\right] = 0.$$

2.2 Linearly Homomorphic Signatures (LHS) [4,5]

An LHS scheme consists of the following 4 polynomial-time algorithms. Note that $\mathtt{Setup}$ and $\mathtt{Sig}$ are probabilistic, $\mathtt{Ver}$ is deterministic and $\mathtt{Derive}$ is (possibly) probabilistic.

Key-Generation $\mathtt{KGen}$: It takes a security parameter 1^λ for $\lambda \in \mathbb{N}$ and an integer $n \in \mathbb{N}$ that indicates the dimension of a vector to be signed, then outputs a key-pair (pk, sk). $(pk, sk) \leftarrow \mathtt{KGen}(1^\lambda, n)$

Signing $\mathtt{Sig}$: It takes the secret-key sk, a tag $\tau \in \{0,1\}^*$ and a vector $\boldsymbol{v} \in \mathbb{Z}_p^n$ to be signed, then outputs a signature σ. $\sigma \leftarrow \mathtt{Sig}(sk, \tau, \boldsymbol{v})$

Derivation $\mathtt{Derive}$: It takes the public-key pk, a tag $\tau \in \{0,1\}^*$ and l triples $\{\boldsymbol{v}_i, \sigma_i, \beta_i\}_{i=1}^l$, consisting of a vector $\boldsymbol{v}_i \in \mathbb{Z}_p^n$, a signature σ_i and a weight β_i, then outputs a signature $\overline{\sigma}$ on the weighted vector $\overline{\boldsymbol{v}} := \sum_{i=1}^l \beta_i \cdot \boldsymbol{v}_i \in \mathbb{Z}_p^n$. $\overline{\sigma} \leftarrow \mathtt{Derive}(pk, \tau, \{\boldsymbol{v}_i, \sigma_i, \beta_i\}_{i=1}^l)$

Verification Ver: It takes the public-key pk, a tag $\tau \in \{0,1\}^*$, a vector $\boldsymbol{v} \in \mathbb{Z}_p^n$ and a signature σ, then outputs 1 or 0. $1/0 \leftarrow \texttt{Ver}(pk, \tau, \boldsymbol{v}, \sigma)$

We require every LHS scheme to be correct. An LHS scheme is correct if for any $\lambda \in \mathbb{N}$, any $n \in \mathbb{N}$ and any $(pk, sk) \leftarrow \texttt{KGen}(1^\lambda, n)$, the following two conditions hold, namely (1) $1 \leftarrow \texttt{Ver}(pk, \tau, \boldsymbol{v}, \texttt{Sig}(sk, \tau, \boldsymbol{v}))$ *for any tag* $\tau \in \{0,1\}^*$ *and any* $\boldsymbol{v} \in \mathbb{Z}_p^n$, and (2) $1 \leftarrow \texttt{Ver}(pk, \tau, \sum_{i=1}^{l} \beta_i \boldsymbol{v}_i, \texttt{Derive}(pk, \tau, \{\boldsymbol{v}_i, \sigma_i, \beta_i\}_{i=1}^{l}))$ *for any tag* $\tau \in \{0,1\}^*$, *any integer* $l \in \mathbb{N}$ *and any* l *triples* $\{\boldsymbol{v}_i \in \mathbb{Z}_p^n, \sigma_i, \beta_i \in \mathbb{Z}_p\}_{i=1}^{l}$ *s.t.* $1 \leftarrow \texttt{Ver}(pk, \tau, \boldsymbol{v}_i, \sigma_i)$ *for each* $i \in [1, l]$.

As security notions for P-homomorphic signatures [2], a generalization of LHS and AOS, unforgeability and unlinkability-related strong context-hiding (SCH) and complete context-hiding (CCH) [3] have been defined. Since these notions are not needed for our KARIP constructions, we define only *weak* unforgeability weaker than the original notion of unforgeablity [2]. We consider the following experiment, where a PPT algorithm $\mathcal{A}$ adaptively accesses a signing oracle to get a signature on an arbitrarily chosen vector $\boldsymbol{v}$, then outputs a forged signature.

$\boldsymbol{Expt}_{\Sigma_{\mathrm{LHS}},\mathcal{A}}^{\mathtt{wUNF}}(1^\lambda, n)$:

1. $(pk, sk) \leftarrow \texttt{Setup}(1^\lambda, n)$. $(\tau^* \in \{0,1\}^*, \boldsymbol{v}^* \in \mathbb{Z}_p^n, \sigma^*) \leftarrow \mathcal{A}^{\mathfrak{Sign}}(pk)$.

- -

- $\mathfrak{Sign}(\tau \in \{0,1\}^*, \boldsymbol{v} \in \mathbb{Z}_p^n)$: $Q := Q \cup \{(\tau, \boldsymbol{v})\}$. **Rtrn** $\sigma \leftarrow \texttt{Sig}(sk, \tau, \boldsymbol{v})$.

- -

2. **Rtrn** 1 if (1) $1 \leftarrow \texttt{Ver}(pk, \tau^*, \boldsymbol{v}^*, \sigma^*)$ and (2) one of the following conditions is satisfied.
   (a) $\tau^* \neq \tau_i$ for any entry $(\tau_i, \cdot) \in Q$ and $\boldsymbol{v}^* \neq \boldsymbol{0}$.
   (b) $\tau^* = \tau_i$ for $k > 0$ entries $(\tau_i, \boldsymbol{v}_i)$ in Q and $\boldsymbol{v}^* \notin \mathbf{span}\{\boldsymbol{v}_1, \cdots, \boldsymbol{v}_k\}$.

Definition 6. *An LHS scheme* Σ_{LHS} *is wUNF if for every* $\lambda \in \mathbb{N}$, *every* $n \in \texttt{poly}(\lambda)$ *and every PPT* $\mathcal{A}$, $\mathcal{A}$*'s advantage defined as* $\boldsymbol{Adv}_{\Sigma_{\mathrm{LHS}},\mathcal{A}}^{\mathit{wUNF}}(\lambda) := \Pr[1 \leftarrow \boldsymbol{Expt}_{\Sigma_{\mathrm{LHS}},\mathcal{A}}^{\mathit{wUNF}}(1^\lambda, n)]$ *is negligible.*

2.3 Append-Only Signatures (AOS) [13]

An AOS scheme consists of the following 4 polynomial-time algorithms. Note that `Setup` and `Sig` are probabilistic, `Ver` is deterministic and `Derive` is (possibly) probabilistic.

Key-Generation KGen: It takes a security parameter 1^λ, the maximum depth of message $H \in \mathbb{N}$ and bit length of a sub-message $L \in \mathbb{N}$, then outputs a key-pair (pk, sk). $(pk, sk) \leftarrow \texttt{KGen}(1^\lambda, H, L)$

Signing Sig: It takes the secret-key sk and a message $M \in (\{0,1\}^L)^{h \le H}$, then outputs a signature σ. $\sigma \leftarrow \texttt{Sig}(sk, M)$

Derivation Derive: It takes the public-key pk, a message $M \in (\{0,1\}^L)^{h \le H}$, a signature σ and a message $M' \in (\{0,1\}^L)^{h' \le H}$, then outputs a signature σ'. $\sigma' \leftarrow \texttt{Derive}(pk, M, \sigma, M')$

Verification Ver: It takes the public-key pk, a message $M \in (\{0,1\}^L)^{h \le H}$ and a signature σ, then outputs 1 or 0. $1/0 \leftarrow \mathtt{Ver}(pk, M, \sigma)$

We require every AOS scheme to be correct. An AOS scheme is correct if for any $\lambda \in \mathbb{N}$, any $H, L \in \mathbb{N}$ and any $(pk, sk) \leftarrow \mathtt{KGen}(1^\lambda, H, L)$, both of the following conditions hold, (1) $1 \leftarrow \mathtt{Ver}(pk, M, \mathtt{Sig}(sk, M))$ *for any* $M \in (\{0,1\}^L)^{h \le H}$, and (2) $1 \leftarrow \mathtt{Ver}(pk, M', \mathtt{Derive}(pk, M, \sigma, M'))$ *for any* $M \in (\{0,1\}^L)^{h \le H}$, $M' \in (\{0,1\}^L)^{h' \le H}$ *s.t.* $h \le h' \bigwedge_{i=1}^{h} M_i = M'_i$ *and any* σ *s.t.* $1 \leftarrow \mathtt{Ver}(pk, M, \sigma)$.

As LHS, we define only weak unforgeablity (wUNF) for AOS.

$\boldsymbol{Expt}^{\mathtt{UNF}}_{\Sigma_{\mathrm{AOS}},\mathcal{A}}(1^\lambda, H, L)$:

1. $(pk, sk) \leftarrow \mathtt{Setup}(1^\lambda, H, L)$. $(M^* \in (\{0,1\}^L)^{h^*}, \sigma^*) \leftarrow \mathcal{A}^{\mathfrak{Sign}}(pk)$.

- $\mathfrak{Sign}(M \in (\{0,1\}^L)^h)$: $Q := Q \cup \{M\}$. **Rtrn** $\sigma \leftarrow \mathtt{Sig}(sk, M)$.

2. **Rtrn** 1 if (1) $1 \leftarrow \mathtt{Ver}(pk, M^*, \sigma^*)$, and (2) $h > h^* \vee \exists i \in [1, h]$ *s.t.* $m_i \neq m_i^*$ *for any* $M \in Q$, *where* $M \in (\{0,1\}^L)^h$ *for some* $h \le H$.
3. **Rtrn** 0.

Definition 7. *An AOS scheme* Σ_{AOS} *is wUNF if for every* $\lambda \in \mathbb{N}$, *every* $H, L \in \mathbb{N}$ *and every PPT* $\mathcal{A}$, $\boldsymbol{Adv}^{wUNF}_{\Sigma_{\mathrm{AOS}},\mathcal{A}}(\lambda) := \Pr[1 \leftarrow \boldsymbol{Expt}^{wUNF}_{\Sigma_{\mathrm{AOS}},\mathcal{A}}(1^\lambda, H, L)]$ *is negligible.*

3 Key-Range ABS for Range of Inner-Product (KARIP)

A KARIP consists of the following four polynomial-time algorithms. Ver is deterministic and the others are probabilistic.

Setup Setup: It takes a security parameter 1^λ for $\lambda \in \mathbb{N}$ and a number of dimensions $n \in \mathbb{N}$, then outputs a public parameter pp and master-key mk. Assume that a prime p with bit length λ is chosen and included in pp. The other algorithms implicitly take pp as input. $(pp, mk) \leftarrow \mathtt{Setup}(1^\lambda, n)$

Key-Generation KGen: It takes mk and an n-dimensional vector $\mathbf{x} \in \mathbb{Z}_p^n$ and a range $[L, R] = \{L, L+1, \cdots, R-1, R\}$ with $L, R \in \mathbb{Z}_p$, then outputs a secret-key sk. $sk \leftarrow \mathtt{KGen}(mk, \mathbf{x}, L, R)$

Signing Sig: It takes a secret-key sk, a message $M \in \mathcal{M}$ and an n-dimensional vector $\mathbf{y} \in \mathbb{Z}_p^n$, then outputs a signature σ. $\sigma \leftarrow \mathtt{Sig}(sk, M, \mathbf{y})$

Verification Ver: It takes a signature σ, a message $M \in \mathcal{M}$ and an n-dimensional vector $\mathbf{y} \in \mathbb{Z}_p^n$, then outputs 1 or 0. $1/0 \leftarrow \mathtt{Ver}(\sigma, M, \mathbf{y})$

Every KARIP scheme must be correct. A KARIP scheme is correct if $\forall \lambda \in \mathbb{N}$, $\forall n \in \mathbb{N}$, $\forall (pp, mk) \leftarrow \mathtt{Setup}(1^\lambda, n)$, $\forall \mathbf{x} \in \mathbb{Z}_p^n$, $\forall L, R \in \mathbb{Z}_p$, $\forall sk \leftarrow \mathtt{KGen}(mk, \mathbf{x}, L, R)$, $\forall M \in \mathcal{M}$, $\forall \mathbf{y} \in \mathbb{Z}_p^n$ s.t. $\langle \mathbf{x}, \mathbf{y} \rangle \in [L, R] \pmod{p}$, $\forall \sigma \leftarrow \mathtt{Sig}(sk, M, \mathbf{y})$, $1 \leftarrow \mathtt{Ver}(\sigma, M, \mathbf{y})$ holds.

As security for KARIP, we require unforgeability and signer-privacy. As a notion of unforgeability, we define unforgeability against adaptively chosen predicate attack (UNF). For a PPT algorithm $\mathcal{A}$, we consider the following experiment.

$\boldsymbol{Expt}^{\mathtt{UNF}}_{\Sigma_{\mathrm{KARIP}},\mathcal{A}}(1^\lambda)$:

1. $(pp, mk) \leftarrow \mathtt{Setup}(1^\lambda)$. $(\sigma^*, M^* \in \mathcal{M}, \mathbf{y}^* \in \mathbb{Z}_p^n) \leftarrow \mathcal{A}^{\mathfrak{Reveal},\mathfrak{Sign}}(pp)$.

- -

- $\mathfrak{Reveal}(\mathbf{x} \in \mathbb{Z}_p^n, L, R \in \mathbb{Z}_p)$: $sk \leftarrow \mathtt{KGen}(mk, \mathbf{x})$. $Q := Q \cup \{(\mathbf{x}, L, R)\}$. **Rtrn** sk.
- $\mathfrak{Sign}(\mathbf{x} \in \mathbb{Z}_p^n, L, R \in \mathbb{Z}_p, M \in \mathcal{M}, \mathbf{y} \in \mathbb{Z}_p^n)$:
  $sk \leftarrow \mathtt{KGen}(mk, \mathbf{x}, L, R)$. $\sigma \leftarrow \mathtt{Sig}(sk, M, \mathbf{y})$.
  $Q' := Q' \cup \{(M, \mathbf{y}, \sigma)\}$. **Rtrn** σ.

- -

2. **Rtrn** 1 if (1) $1 \leftarrow \mathtt{Ver}(\sigma^*, M^*, \mathbf{y}^*)$, (2) $\forall(\mathbf{x}, L, R) \in Q$, $\langle \mathbf{x}, \mathbf{y}^* \rangle \notin [L, R]$ and (3) $(M^*, \mathbf{y}^*, \cdot) \notin Q'$.
3. **Rtrn** 0.

Definition 8. *A KARIP scheme Σ_{KARIP} is UNF if for every PPT $\mathcal{A}$, its advantage $\boldsymbol{Adv}^{\mathit{UNF}}_{\Sigma_{\mathrm{KARIP}},\mathcal{A}}(\lambda) := \Pr[1 \leftarrow \boldsymbol{Expt}^{\mathit{UNF}}_{\Sigma_{\mathrm{KARIP}},\mathcal{A}}(1^\lambda, n)]$ is negligible.*

As a notion of signer-privacy, we define perfect signer-privacy (PRV). For a probabilistic algorithm $\mathcal{A}$, we consider the following two experiments.

$\boldsymbol{Expt}^{\mathtt{PRV}}_{\Sigma_{\mathrm{KARIP}},\mathcal{A},0}(1^\lambda)$: // $\boldsymbol{Expt}^{\mathtt{PRV}}_{\Sigma_{\mathrm{KARIP}},\mathcal{A},1}$

$(pp, mk) \leftarrow \mathtt{Setup}(1^\lambda)$. $(pp, mk, \mu) \leftarrow \mathtt{SimSetup}(1^\lambda)$. **Rtrn** $b' \leftarrow \mathcal{A}^{\mathfrak{Reveal},\mathfrak{Sign}}(pp, mk)$.

- -

- $\mathfrak{Reveal}(\mathbf{x} \in \mathbb{Z}_p^n, L, R \in \mathbb{Z}_p)$:
  $sk \leftarrow \mathtt{KGen}(mk, \mathbf{x}, L, R)$. $sk \leftarrow \mathtt{SimKGen}(mk, \mu, \mathbf{x}, L, R)$.
  $Q := Q \cup \{(\mathbf{x}, L, R, sk)\}$. **Rtrn** sk.
- $\mathfrak{Sign}(\mathbf{x} \in \mathbb{Z}_p^n, L, R \in \mathbb{Z}_p, sk, M \in \mathcal{M}, \mathbf{y} \in \mathbb{Z}_p^n)$:
  Rtrn $\perp$ if $(\mathbf{x}, L, R, sk) \notin Q \vee \langle \mathbf{x}, \mathbf{y} \rangle \notin [L, R] \pmod p$.
  $\sigma \leftarrow \mathtt{Sig}(sk, M, \mathbf{y})$. $\sigma \leftarrow \mathtt{SimSig}(mk, \mu, M, \mathbf{y})$. **Rtrn** σ.

The latter is associated with 3 polynomial-time algorithms $\{\mathtt{SimSetup}, \mathtt{SimKGen}, \mathtt{SimSig}\}$. The grey parts are considered in the latter, but ignored in the former.

Definition 9. *A KARIP scheme Σ_{KARIP} is perfectly signer-private (PRV) if for every probabilistic algorithm $\mathcal{A}$, there exist polynomial-time algorithms $\{\mathtt{SimSetup}, \mathtt{SimKGen}, \mathtt{SimSig}\}$ such that $\mathcal{A}$'s advantage $\boldsymbol{Adv}^{\mathit{PRV}}_{\Sigma_{\mathrm{KARIP}},\mathcal{A}}(\lambda) := |\sum_{b=0}^{1}(-1)^b \Pr[1 \leftarrow \boldsymbol{Expt}^{\mathit{PRV}}_{\Sigma_{\mathrm{KARIP}},\mathcal{A},b}(1^\lambda)]|$ becomes 0.*

Key-Delegatability. We say that a KARIP scheme is key-delegatable if for any vector $\mathbf{x} \in \mathbb{Z}_p^n$, any range $[L, R] \subseteq \mathbb{Z}_p$ and any subrange $[l, r] \subseteq \mathbb{Z}_p$ s.t. $L \leq l \leq r \leq R$, any secret-key for $(\mathbf{x}, L, R)$ can generate a secret-key for $(\mathbf{x}, l, r)$.

4 Our 1st Generic Construction of KARIP

4.1 Construction

We use an algorithm `Cover` called covering. Consider a complete binary tree with 2^λ leaf nodes. The leftmost (resp. rightmost) leaf node is associated with 0^λ (resp. 1^λ). Since p is of bit length λ, for every integer $i \in \mathbb{Z}_p$, $[i]_2 \in \{0,1\}^\lambda$ is corresponded to a leaf node one-to-one. `Cover` takes a range $[L, R] \subseteq \mathbb{Z}_p$, then outputs a set C with the minimal cardinality, composed of intermediate nodes which *covers* all of the leaf nodes from $[L]_2$ to $[R]_2$. For every $i \in [L, R]$, there is a single $c \in C$ s.t. c is either identical to or an ancestor of $[i]_2$. Such a set can be efficiently and easily derived. Refer to Subsect. Appendix 1 for the definition of Cover.

Our generic KARIP construction is built by an LHS scheme $\{\mathsf{L.KGen}, \mathsf{L.Sig}, \mathsf{L.Derive}, \mathsf{L.Ver}\}$, an AOS scheme $\{\mathsf{A.KGen}, \mathsf{A.Sig}, \mathsf{A.Derive}, \mathsf{A.Ver}\}$ and an NIWI proof system $\{\mathsf{N.Setup}, \mathsf{N.Pro}, \mathsf{N.Ver}\}$.

$\mathtt{Setup}(1^\lambda, L)$: Generate $crs \leftarrow \mathsf{N.Setup}(1^\lambda)$, $(pk_\mathsf{L}, sk_\mathsf{L}) \leftarrow \mathsf{L.KGen}(1^\lambda, n+3)$ with tags whose bit length is $N \in \mathtt{poly}(\lambda)$ and $(pk_\mathsf{A}, sk_\mathsf{A}) \leftarrow \mathsf{A.KGen}(1^\lambda, N+\lambda, 1)$. Output $pp := (crs, pk_\mathsf{L}, pk_\mathsf{A})$ and $mk := (sk_\mathsf{L}, sk_\mathsf{A})$.

$\mathtt{KGen}(mk, \mathbf{x}, L, R)$: Choose a tag $\tau \xleftarrow{\text{U}} \{0,1\}^N$. Conduct the following two steps.

1. For each $i \in [1, n]$, let $\boldsymbol{v}_i := (x_i, \underbrace{0, \cdots, 0}_{i-1}, 1, \underbrace{0, \cdots, 0}_{n-i}, 0, 0) \in \mathbb{Z}_p^{n+3}$. Let $\boldsymbol{v}_{n+1} := (0, \cdots, 0, 1, 0) \in \mathbb{Z}_p^{n+3}$ and $\boldsymbol{v}_{n+2} := (0, \cdots, 0, 0, 1) \in \mathbb{Z}_p^{n+3}$. For each $\boldsymbol{v}_i$, generate an LHS signature with tag τ by $\sigma_i \leftarrow \mathsf{L.Sig}(sk_\mathsf{L}, \tau, \boldsymbol{v}_i)$.
2. For each $c \in C$, generate an AOS signature on $(\tau, c[1], \cdots, c[h_c])$, i.e., $\theta_c \leftarrow \mathsf{A.Sig}(sk_\mathsf{A}, (\tau, c[1], \cdots, c[h_c]))$, where c is parsed as $c[1] \| \cdots \| c[h_c]$ for some $h_c \in [1, \lambda]$. Note that this construction is key-delegatable. Consider a subrange $[l, r] \subseteq [L, R]$, and let $C' \leftarrow \mathtt{Cover}(l, r)$. For any $c' \in C'$, there must exist a single $c \in C$ s.t. c is either identical to or an ancestor of c'.

Output $sk := (\tau, \{\sigma_i\}_{i=1}^{n+2}, \{\theta_c\}_{c \in C})$.

$\mathtt{Sig}(sk, M, \mathbf{y})$: Parse sk as above. Let $d := \langle \mathbf{x}, \mathbf{y} \rangle \pmod p$. Assume that $d \in [L, R]$. Conduct the following three steps.

1. Generate an LHS signature on $\boldsymbol{v}' := (d, y_1, \cdots, y_n, M, 1)$ by $\sigma' \leftarrow \mathsf{L.Derive}(pk_\mathsf{L}, \tau, \{\boldsymbol{v}_i, \sigma_i, \beta_i\}_{i=1}^{n+2})$, where $\beta_{n+1} := M$, $\beta_{n+2} := 1$ and $\beta_i := y_i$ for each $i \in [1, n]$.
2. $d \in [L, R]$ implies that there is $c \in C$ s.t. c is whether identical to or an ancestor of $[d]_2$. Derive an AOS signature on $(\tau, d[1], \cdots, d[\lambda])$ from θ_c, i.e., $\theta' \leftarrow \mathsf{A.Derive}(pk_\mathsf{A}, (\tau, c[1], \cdots, c[h_c]), \theta_c, (\tau, d[1], \cdots, d[\lambda]))$, where $[d]_2$ is parsed as $d[1] \| \cdots \| d[\lambda]$.
3. Define the NIWI relation $\mathcal{R}_\mathsf{N}$ as follows.
   - A statement $x = (\hat{\mathbf{y}}, \hat{M})$ consists of a vector $\hat{\mathbf{y}} = (\hat{y}_1, \cdots, \hat{y}_n) \in \mathbb{Z}_p^n$ and a message $\hat{M} \in \mathbb{Z}_p$. A witness $w = (\hat{d}, \hat{\tau}, \hat{\sigma}, \hat{\theta})$ consists of an inner product value $\hat{d} \in \mathbb{Z}_p$, an LHS tag $\hat{\tau} \in \{0,1\}^L$, an LHS signature $\hat{\sigma}$ and an AOS signature $\hat{\theta}$. $\mathcal{R}_\mathsf{N}$ takes a statement x and witness w then outputs 1 if both of the following conditions are satisfied.
     1. $1 \leftarrow \mathsf{L.Ver}(pk_\mathsf{L}, \hat{\tau}, \hat{\boldsymbol{v}}, \hat{\sigma})$, where $\hat{\boldsymbol{v}} := (\hat{d}, \hat{y}_1, \cdots, \hat{y}_n, \hat{M}, 1)$.
     2. $1 \leftarrow \mathsf{A.Ver}(pk_\mathsf{A}, (\hat{\tau}, \hat{d}[1], \cdots, \hat{d}[\lambda]), \hat{\theta})$.

   If we set $x := (\mathbf{y}, M)$ and $w := (d, \tau, \sigma, \theta)$, it obviously holds that $1 \leftarrow \mathcal{R}_\mathsf{N}(x, w)$. Output $\sigma \leftarrow \mathsf{N.Pro}(crs, x, w)$.

$\mathtt{Ver}(\sigma, M, \mathbf{y})$: Set $x := (\mathbf{y}, M)$ and output $1/0 \leftarrow \mathsf{N.Ver}(crs, x, \sigma)$.

As explained in the key-generation algorithm, this construction is key-delegatable. For its privacy and unforgeability, we give the following two theorems.

Theorem 1. *Our 1st KARIP scheme is* PRV *if the NIWI scheme is* WI.

Proof. The signer-privacy experiments w.r.t. our 1st KARIP scheme are simply denoted by $\boldsymbol{Expt}_0$ and $\boldsymbol{Expt}_1$. For the three simulation algorithms associated with $\boldsymbol{Expt}_1$, SimSetup and SimKGen are identical to the original ones[3]. SimSig is defined as follows.

SimSig$(mk, M, \mathbf{y})$: Arbitrarily choose $\mathbf{x} \in \mathbb{Z}_p^n$ and $L, R \in \mathbb{Z}_p$ s.t. $d(:= \langle \mathbf{x}, \mathbf{y} \rangle) \in [L, R] \pmod p$. Choose $\tau \xleftarrow{U} \{0,1\}^N$. Generate an LHS signature on $\boldsymbol{v}' := (d, y_1, \cdots, y_n, M, 1)$ by $\sigma' \leftarrow \mathsf{L.Sig}(sk_{\mathsf{L}}, \tau, \boldsymbol{v}')$. Generate an AOS signature on $(\tau, d[1], \cdots, d[\lambda])$ by $\theta'_c \leftarrow \mathsf{A.Sig}(sk_{\mathsf{A}}, (\tau, d[1], \cdots, d[\lambda]))$. Generate an NIWI proof $\pi \leftarrow \mathsf{N.Pro}(crs, x, w)$, where $x := (\mathbf{y}, M)$ and $w := (d, \tau, \sigma', \theta')$, then return π.

It holds that $1 \leftarrow \mathcal{R}_{\mathsf{N}}(x, w)$. Hence, if the NIWI scheme is WI, the simulated signature π distributes identically to the real one in $\boldsymbol{Expt}_0$. □

Theorem 2. *Our 1st KARIP scheme is* UNF *if the LHS scheme is* wUNF*, the AOS scheme is* wUNF*, and the NIWI system is* WI *and* WE.

Proof. We define six experiments as follows.

$\boldsymbol{Expt}_0$: The standard UNF experiment w.r.t. the KARIP scheme.

$\boldsymbol{Expt}_1$: The same as $\boldsymbol{Expt}_0$ except that it aborts when we choose a tag on the key-revelation or signing oracle, the tag matches a tag previously chosen.

$\boldsymbol{Expt}_2$: The same as $\boldsymbol{Expt}_1$ except for the signature generation on the signing oracle. In $\boldsymbol{Expt}_2$, we directly generate both of an LHS signature σ' on $\boldsymbol{v}' := (\langle \mathbf{x}, \mathbf{y} \rangle, y_1, \cdots, y_n, M, 1)$ and an AOS signature θ' on $(\tau, \langle \mathbf{x}, \mathbf{y} \rangle[1], \cdots, \langle \mathbf{x}, \mathbf{y} \rangle[\lambda])$ by using the LHS and AOS secret-keys, respectively.

$\boldsymbol{Expt}_3$: The same as $\boldsymbol{Expt}_2$ except for the CRS generation. In $\boldsymbol{Expt}_3$, the CRS crs is generated by $(crs, ek) \leftarrow \mathtt{SimSetup}(1^\lambda)$.

$\boldsymbol{Expt}_4$: Basically the same as $\boldsymbol{Expt}_3$. In $\boldsymbol{Expt}_4$, we extract the NIWI witness w^* for the NIWI proof σ^* by using the extraction key ek. Formally, extract $w^* \leftarrow \mathtt{Extract}(crs, ek, x^*, \sigma^*)$, where $x^* := (\mathbf{y}^*, M^*)$. The witness is parsed as $(d^* \in \mathbb{Z}_p, \tau^* \in \{0,1\}^N, \sigma^*, \theta^*)$. $\boldsymbol{Expt}_4$ aborts if w^* is not the correct witness for the statement x^*, i.e., $0 \leftarrow \mathcal{R}_{\mathsf{N}}(x^*, w^*)$.

$\boldsymbol{Expt}_5$: The same as $\boldsymbol{Expt}_4$ except that it aborts if one of the following three events occurs.

- **E1:** The extracted tag τ^* is identical to no tag previously chosen.
- **E2:** The tag τ^* has been already chosen on the signing oracle.
- **E3:** The tag τ^* has been already chosen on the key-revelation oracle and it holds that $d^* \neq \langle \hat{\mathbf{x}}, \mathbf{y}^* \rangle \pmod p$, where $d^* \in \mathbb{Z}_p$ is the extracted inner product value and $\hat{\mathbf{x}} \in \mathbb{Z}_p^n$ is the n-dimensional key-vector queried by $\mathcal{A}$.

[3] The auxiliary variable μ outputted by SimSetup is null.

For each $i \in [0, 5]$, let W_i denote the event that the experiment $\boldsymbol{Expt}_i$ outputs 1. We obtain $\mathtt{Adv}^{\mathtt{UNF}}_{\Sigma_{\mathrm{KARIP}},\mathcal{A},n}(\lambda) = \Pr[W_0] \leq \sum_{i=1}^{5} |\Pr[W_{i-1}] - \Pr[W_i]| + \Pr[W_5] \leq q(q-1)/2^{N+1} + \mathtt{Adv}^{\mathtt{WI}}_{\Sigma_{\mathrm{NIWI}},\mathcal{B}_3}(\lambda) + \mathtt{Adv}^{\mathtt{wUNF}}_{\Sigma_{\mathrm{LHS}},\mathcal{B}_5}(\lambda) + \mathtt{Adv}^{\mathtt{wUNF}}_{\Sigma_{\mathrm{AOS}},\mathcal{B}_6}(\lambda)$ for some PPT adversary $\mathcal{B}_3, \mathcal{B}_5, \mathcal{B}_6$. The last inequality is obtained because of the following six lemmas. Lemma 1 is the same as Lemma 1 in [10] and can be proven in the same manner. Lemma 3 is true because the CRSs in $\boldsymbol{Expt}_2$ and $\boldsymbol{Expt}_3$ are indistinguishable if the NIWI system is WE. The other lemmas are proven below. For each $i \in \{1, 4, 5\}$, abort_i denotes the abort event firstly introduced in the experiment $\boldsymbol{Expt}_i$. □

Lemma 1. $\Pr[W_0] - \Pr[W_1] \leq q(q-1)/2^{N+1}$, *where* $q \in \mathtt{poly}(\lambda)$ *is the total number of times that* $\mathcal{A}$ *uses the key-revelation and signing oracles.*

Lemma 2. $|\Pr[W_1] - \Pr[W_2]| = 0$ *if the NIWI system is* WI.

Proof. In $\boldsymbol{Expt}_2$, on the signing oracle, we directly generate both of an LHS signature σ' and an AOS signature θ' by the LHS and AOS secret-keys, then generate a signature $\sigma (:= \pi)$ as $\pi \leftarrow \mathsf{N.Pro}(crs, x, w)$, where $x := (\mathbf{y}, M)$ and $w := (d, \tau, \sigma', \theta')$. Since it holds that $1 \leftarrow \mathcal{R}_{\mathsf{N}}(x, w)$, the NIWI proof π distributes identically to the one in $\boldsymbol{Expt}_1$ if the NIWI system is WI. □

Lemma 3. $\Pr[W_2] - \Pr[W_3]$ *is negligible if the NIWI system is* WE. *Formally, there exists a PPT algorithm* $\mathcal{B}_3$ *s.t.* $\Pr[W_2] - \Pr[W_3] \leq \mathit{Adv}^{\mathit{WE}}_{\Sigma_{\mathrm{NIWI}},\mathcal{B}_3}(\lambda)$.

Lemma 4. $\Pr[W_3] - \Pr[W_4] = 0$ *if the NIWI system is* WE.

Proof. Obviously, $\Pr[W_4] = \Pr[W_3 \wedge \neg\mathsf{abort}_4]$. By a basic mathematical theorem, $\Pr[W_3] = \Pr[W_3 \wedge \mathsf{abort}_4] + \Pr[W_3 \wedge \neg\mathsf{abort}_4]$, which implies $\Pr[W_3] - \Pr[W_4] = \Pr[W_3 \wedge \mathsf{abort}_4]$. Assume that the case where $W_3 \wedge \mathsf{abort}_4$ occurs. Because of the event W_3, $1 \leftarrow \mathsf{N.Ver}(crs, x^*, \sigma^*)$. Because of the event abort_4, $0 \leftarrow \mathcal{R}_{\mathsf{N}}(x^*, w^*)$. That contradicts to the WE. Hence, $\Pr[W_3] - \Pr[W_4] = 0$. □

Lemma 5. $\Pr[W_4] - \Pr[W_5]$ *is negligible if the LHS scheme is* wUNF. *Formally, there exists a PPT algorithm* $\mathcal{B}_5$ *s.t.* $\Pr[W_4] - \Pr[W_5] \leq \mathit{Adv}^{\mathit{wUNF}}_{\Sigma_{\mathrm{LHS}},\mathcal{B}_5}(\lambda)$.

Proof. As the proof of Lemma 4, $\Pr[W_4] - \Pr[W_5] = \Pr[W_4 \wedge \mathsf{abort}_5]$ holds. Assume that $\mathcal{A}$ is a PPT algorithm which makes the event $W_4 \wedge \mathsf{abort}_5$ occur with a non-negligible probability. By using $\mathcal{A}$, a PPT simulator $\mathcal{B}_5$ attempts to win the wUNF experiment w.r.t. the LHS scheme.

$\mathcal{B}_5$ receives an honestly-generated public-key pk_{L}. $\mathcal{B}_5$ can access to the signing oracle $\mathfrak{Sign}_{\mathsf{L}}$. $\mathcal{B}_5$ honestly generates crs, ek, pk_{A} and sk_{A}. $\mathcal{B}_5$ sends $pp := (crs, pk_{\mathsf{L}}, pk_{\mathsf{A}})$ to $\mathcal{A}$ and run it. When $\mathcal{A}$ makes a query to the key-revelation or signing oracle, $\mathcal{B}_5$ behaves as follows.

$\mathfrak{Reveal}(\mathbf{x}, L, R)$: Choose a tag $\tau \xleftarrow{\mathrm{U}} \{0,1\}^N$. Honestly generate the $n+2$ vectors $\boldsymbol{v}_1, \cdots, \boldsymbol{v}_{n+2} \in \mathbb{Z}_p^{n+3}$. For each vector $\boldsymbol{v}_i$, generate an LHS signature by $\sigma_i \leftarrow \mathfrak{Sign}_{\mathsf{L}}(\tau, \boldsymbol{v}_i)$. Let $C := \mathtt{Cover}(L, R)$. For each $c \in C$, generate $\theta_c \leftarrow \mathsf{A.Sig}(sk_{\mathsf{A}}, (\tau, c[1], \cdots, c[h_c]))$. Return $sk := (\tau, \{\sigma_i\}_{i=1}^{n+2}, \{\theta_c\}_{c \in C})$.

$\mathfrak{Sign}(\mathbf{x}, L, R, \mathbf{y}, M)$: Choose $\tau \xleftarrow{U} \{0,1\}^N$. Let $d := \langle \mathbf{x}, \mathbf{y} \rangle \pmod{p}$. Generate an LHS signature on a vector $\boldsymbol{v}' := (d, y_1, \cdots, y_n, M, 1)$ by $\sigma' \leftarrow \mathfrak{Sign}_{\mathsf{L}}(\tau, \boldsymbol{v}')$. Honestly generate an AOS signature on $(\tau, d[1], \cdots, d[\lambda])$, i.e., $\theta' \leftarrow \mathsf{A.Sig}(sk_{\mathsf{A}}, (\tau, d[1], \cdots, d[\lambda]))$. Generate an NIWI proof $\pi \leftarrow \mathsf{N.Pro}(crs, x, w)$, where $x := (\mathbf{y}, M)$ and $w := (d, \tau, \sigma', \theta')$, then return it.

Given a forged KARIP signature π^*, $\mathcal{B}_6$ extracts the witness behind the NIWI proof π^* by $w^* \leftarrow \mathtt{Extract}(crs, ek, x^*, \pi)$, where $x^* := (\mathbf{y}^*, M^*)$, and parse it as $(d^*, \tau^*, \sigma^*, \theta^*)$. $\mathcal{B}_5$ outputs a forged LHS signature σ^* with tag τ^* on vector $\boldsymbol{v}^* := (d^*, y_1^*, \cdots, y_n^*, M^*, 1)$.

The above is how $\mathcal{B}_5$ behaves. Because we have assumed that $\mathcal{A}$ makes the event $W_4 \wedge \mathsf{abort}_5$ occur, one of the three events **E1**, **E2** and **E3** must occur. Any of the events leads $\mathcal{B}_5$ to win the wUNF experiment.

E1: Every tag queried to $\mathfrak{Sign}_{\mathsf{L}}$ is not identical to τ^*. $W_4 \wedge \mathsf{abort}_5$ implies $\neg\mathsf{abort}_4$, which implies that σ^* is a valid LHS signature on the non-zero vector $\boldsymbol{v}^*$.

E2: W_4 implies $\neg\mathsf{abort}_1$, which implies that the extracted tag τ^* is identical to a single tag chosen on the signing oracle. Among multiple vectors whom $\mathcal{B}_5$ queried to $\mathfrak{Sign}_{\mathsf{L}}$, $\hat{\boldsymbol{v}} := (\langle \hat{\mathbf{x}}, \hat{\mathbf{y}} \rangle, \hat{y}_1, \cdots, \hat{y}_n, \hat{M}, 1)$ is the only vector tagged by τ^*, where $\hat{\mathbf{x}}, \hat{L}, \hat{R}, \hat{\mathbf{y}}$ and $\hat{M}$ denote variables queried to the signing oracle when the tag τ^* was chosen. W_4 implies that $(\mathbf{y}^*, M^*) \neq (\hat{\mathbf{y}}, \hat{M})$. Obviously, $\boldsymbol{v}^*$ is linearly independent of $\hat{\boldsymbol{v}}$.

E3: W_4 implies $\neg\mathsf{abort}_1$, which implies that the extracted tag τ^* is identical to a single tag chosen on the key-revelation oracle and it holds that $d^* \neq \langle \hat{\mathbf{x}}, \mathbf{y}^* \rangle \pmod{p}$. Among multiple vectors whom $\mathcal{B}_5$ queried to $\mathfrak{Sign}_{\mathsf{L}}$, there are $n+2$ vectors $\hat{\boldsymbol{v}}_1, \cdots, \hat{\boldsymbol{v}}_{n+2}$ tagged by τ^*. The vectors are expressed as follows. For each $i \in [1, n]$, $\hat{\boldsymbol{v}}_i = (\hat{x}_i, \underbrace{0, \cdots, 0}_{i-1}, 1, \underbrace{0, \cdots, 0}_{n-i}, 0, 0)$. The others are $\hat{\boldsymbol{v}}_{n+1} = (0, \cdots, 0, 1, 0)$ and $\hat{\boldsymbol{v}}_{n+2} = (0, \cdots, 0, 0, 1)$. Since $d^* \neq \langle \hat{\mathbf{x}}, \mathbf{y}^* \rangle \pmod{p}$, $\boldsymbol{v}^* = (d^*, y_1^*, \cdots, y_n^*, M^*, 1)$ is not in $\mathbf{span}(\{\hat{\boldsymbol{v}}_1, \cdots, \hat{\boldsymbol{v}}_{n+2}\})$.

Therefore, $\Pr[W_4] - \Pr[W_5] \leq \mathsf{Adv}^{\mathtt{wUNF}}_{\Sigma_{\mathrm{LHS}}, \mathcal{B}_5}(\lambda)$. □

Lemma 6. $\Pr[W_5]$ *is negligible if the AOS scheme is wUNF. Formally, there exists a PPT algorithm* $\mathcal{B}_6$ *s.t.* $\Pr[W_5] \leq \boldsymbol{Adv}^{\mathit{wUNF}}_{\Sigma_{\mathrm{AOS}}, \mathcal{B}_6}(\lambda)$.

Proof. Assume that $\mathcal{A}$ is a PPT algorithm which makes $\boldsymbol{Expt}_5$ outputs 1 with a non-negligible probability. By using $\mathcal{A}$, a PPT simulator $\mathcal{B}_6$ attempts to win the weak unforgeability experiment w.r.t. the underlying AOS scheme.

$\mathcal{B}_6$ receives a public-key pk_{A}, which has been honestly generated. $\mathcal{B}_6$ can access to the signing oracle $\mathfrak{Sign}_{\mathsf{A}}$. $\mathcal{B}_6$ honestly generates crs, ek, pk_{L} and sk_{L}. $\mathcal{B}_6$ sends $pp := (crs, pk_{\mathsf{L}}, pk_{\mathsf{A}})$ to $\mathcal{A}$ and run it.

$\mathfrak{Reveal}(\mathbf{x}, L, R)$: Choose a tag $\tau \xleftarrow{U} \{0,1\}^N$. Honestly generate the $n+2$ vectors $\boldsymbol{v}_1, \cdots, \boldsymbol{v}_{n+2} \in \mathbb{Z}_p^{n+3}$. For each vector $\boldsymbol{v}_i$, generate $\sigma_i \leftarrow \mathsf{L.Sig}(sk_{\mathsf{L}}, \tau, \boldsymbol{v}_i)$. Let $C := \mathtt{Cover}(L, R)$. For each $c \in C$, generate $\theta_c \leftarrow \mathtt{Sig}_{\mathsf{A}}((\tau, c[1], \cdots, c[h_c]))$. Return $sk := (\mathbf{x}, L, R, \tau, \{\sigma_i\}_{i=1}^{n+2}, \{\theta_c\}_{c \in C})$.

$\mathfrak{Sign}(\mathbf{x}, L, R, \mathbf{y}, M)$: Choose $\tau \xleftarrow{U} \{0,1\}^N$. Let $d := \langle \mathbf{x}, \mathbf{y} \rangle \pmod{p}$. Generate an LHS signature on the vector $\boldsymbol{v}' := (d, y_1, \cdots, y_n, M, 1)$, i.e., $\sigma' \leftarrow \mathsf{L.Sig}(sk_{\mathsf{L}}, \tau, \boldsymbol{v}')$. Generate an AOS signature $\theta' \leftarrow \mathfrak{Sign}_{\mathsf{A}}((\tau, d[1], \cdots, d[\lambda]))$. Generate an NIWI proof $\pi \leftarrow \mathsf{N.Pro}(crs, x, w)$, where $x := (\mathbf{y}, M)$ and $w := (d, \tau, \sigma', \theta')$, then return it.

$\mathcal{A}$ outputs a forged KARIP signature π^* on M^* under $\mathbf{y}^*$. We extract the witness for the NIWI proof π^* by $w^* \leftarrow \mathtt{Extract}(crs, ek, x^*, \pi)$, where $x^* := (\mathbf{y}^*, M^*)$, and parse it as $(d^*, \tau^*, \sigma^*, \theta^*)$. $\mathcal{B}_6$ outputs a forged AOS signature θ^* on $(\tau^*, d^*[1], \cdots, d^*[\lambda])$.

The above is the behavior of $\mathcal{B}_6$. We prove that $\mathcal{B}_6$ wins the experiment.

The assumption that W_5 occurs implies that neither abort_1 nor abort_5 occurs. Thus, the forged tag τ^* is identical to a single tag which was chosen on the key-revelation oracle and it holds that $d^* = \langle \hat{\mathbf{x}}, \mathbf{y}^* \rangle \pmod{p}$. When the tag τ^* was chosen, $\mathcal{B}_6$ makes the signing oracle reveal signatures on $(\tau^*, c[1], \cdots, c[\hat{h}_c])$ for all $c = c[1] \parallel \cdots \parallel c[\hat{h}_c] \in \mathtt{Cover}(\hat{L}, \hat{R})$. W_5 implies that $\langle \hat{\mathbf{x}}, \mathbf{y}^* \rangle \notin [\hat{L}, \hat{R}] \pmod{p}$, which implies that no $c \in \mathtt{Cover}(\hat{L}, \hat{R})$ is neither $[d^*]_2$ nor its ancestor. Thus, $\mathcal{B}_6$ wins. Hence, $\Pr[W_5] \leq \mathtt{Adv}^{\mathtt{wUNF}}_{\Sigma_{\mathrm{AOS}}, \mathcal{B}_6}(\lambda)$. □

4.2 Our AOS Scheme

We instantiate our generic construction in Subsect. 4.3. We use an NIWI proof by Groth and Sahai (GS) [8] secure under the decisional linear (DLIN) assumption. Its CRS consists of 3 vectors $\vec{f}_1, \vec{f}_2, \vec{f}_3 \in \mathbb{G}^3$, where $\vec{f}_1 = (f_1, 1, g)$, $\vec{f}_2 = (1, f_2, g)$ and $f_1, f_2 \in \mathbb{G}$. A commitment $\vec{C}$ to a group element $\mathcal{X} \in \mathbb{G}$ is given as $\vec{C} := (1, 1, \mathcal{X}) \cdot \vec{f}_1^{\,r} \cdot \vec{f}_2^{\,s} \cdot \vec{f}_3^{\,t}$, where $r, s, t \xleftarrow{U} \mathbb{Z}_p$. In the GS NIWI system, the prover can efficiently prove that committed variables satisfy a paring-product equation (PPE) in the form of $\prod_{i=1}^{m} e(\mathcal{A}_i, \mathcal{X}_i) \cdot \prod_{i=1}^{m} \prod_{j=1}^{m} e(\mathcal{X}_i, \mathcal{X}_j)^{a_{ij}} = t_T$ for variables $\mathcal{X}_i \in \mathbb{G}$ and constants $\mathcal{A}_i \in \mathbb{G}$, $a_{ij} \in \mathbb{Z}_p$ and $t_T \in \mathbb{G}_T$.

Attrapadung, Libert and Peters (ALP) [4] proposed an LHS scheme unforgeable and CCH-secure under the flexible CDH (FlexCDH) assumption. Ishizaka et al. [10] simplified it to obtain another one weakly unforgeable under the same assumption. The LHS scheme is used for the instantiation. Its verification algorithm consists of only PPEs. Its full construction is described in the original paper [10] and the full paper of this paper [9].

We searched for an AOS scheme used for the instantiation satisfying both of the two conditions, (1) *Based on symmetric, i.e., type-1, bilinear pairing with prime order* and (2) *Its verification algorithm consists of only PPEs.* We modified a hierarchical identity-based signatures (HIBS) scheme named HIBS-1 in [7] based on asymmetric type-3 bilinear paring with prime order, then obtained the following AOS scheme.

$\mathtt{KGen}(1^\lambda, H, L)$: $(\mathbb{G}, \mathbb{G}_T, e)$ denote the bilinear group description. g is a generator of $\mathbb{G}$. Choose $\beta \xleftarrow{U} \mathbb{Z}_p$ and $g', U_1, \cdots, U_H, V_1, \cdots, V_L \xleftarrow{U} \mathbb{G}$. Output (pk, sk), where $pk := (g, g^\beta, g', \{U_i\}_{i=1}^{H}, \{V_i\}_{i=1}^{L})$ and $sk := \beta$.

$\mathtt{Sig}(sk, M)$: Parse $M \in (\{0,1\}^L)^{h \leq H}$ as $(m_1, \cdots, m_h)$. For each $i \in [1, h]$, choose $r_i \xleftarrow{U} \mathbb{Z}_p$ and calculate $B_i := g^{r_i}$. Calculate $A := (g')^\beta \prod_{i=1}^{h} (U_i \prod_{j=1}^{L} V_j^{m_i[j]})^{r_i}$, where m_i is parsed as $m_i[1] \| \cdots \| m_i[L]$. Output $\sigma := (A, B_1, \cdots, B_h)$.

$\mathtt{Derive}(pk, M, \sigma, M')$: Parse $M' \in (\{0,1\}^L)^{h' \leq H}$ as $(m'_1, \cdots, m_h, \cdots, m'_{h'})$. For each $i \in [1, h']$, choose $r'_i \xleftarrow{U} \mathbb{Z}_p$ and calculate $B'_i := B_i \cdot g^{r'_i}$ if $i \in [1, h]$ or $B'_i := g^{r'_i}$ otherwise. Then calculate $A' := A \cdot \prod_{i=1}^{h'} (U_i \prod_{j=1}^{L} V_j^{m'_i[j]})^{r'_i}$. Output $\sigma' := (A', B'_1, \cdots, B'_{h'})$.

$\mathtt{Ver}(pk, M, \sigma)$: Output 1 iff $e(A, g) = g(g^\beta, g') \prod_{i=1}^{h} e(B_i, U_i \prod_{j=1}^{L} V_j^{m_i[j]})$.

Theorem 3. *Our AOS scheme is wUNF under the CDH assumption w.r.t.* $\mathbb{G}$.

Proof. We assume that a PPT adversary $\mathcal{A}$ wins the wUNF experiment with a non-negligibility. A PPT simulator $\mathcal{B}$ solves the CDH problem by using $\mathcal{A}$. $\mathcal{B}$ receives a CDH problem instance (g, g^a, g^b), then behaves as follows.

Let $g^\beta := g^a$ and $g' := g^b$. Let $k := 2q$, where $q \in \mathtt{poly}(\lambda)$ denotes the maximal number of times that the signing oracle can be used. We assume that $k(L+1) < p$. For each $i \in [1, H]$, compute $U_i := (g^\beta)^{p-k \cdot s_i + x_i} \cdot g^{x'_i}$, where $s_i \xleftarrow{U} [0, L]$, $x_i \xleftarrow{U} \mathbb{Z}_k$ and $x'_i \xleftarrow{U} \mathbb{Z}_p$. For each $j \in [1, L]$, compute $V_j := (g^\beta)^{y_j} \cdot g^{y'_j}$, where $y_j \xleftarrow{U} \mathbb{Z}_k$ and $y'_j \xleftarrow{U} \mathbb{Z}_p$. For an index $i \in [1, H]$ and a sub-message $m \in \{0,1\}^L$, define the following three functions.

$$J_i(m) := x'_i + \sum_{j=1}^{L} y'_j \cdot m[j], \quad L_i(m) := x_i + \sum_{j=1}^{L} y_j \cdot m[j]$$

$$F_i(m) := p - k \cdot s_i + x_i + \sum_{j=1}^{L} y_j \cdot m[j] \quad (= p - k \cdot s_i + L_i(m))$$

Note that it holds that $U_i \prod_{j=1}^{L} V_j^{m[j]} = (g^\beta)^{F_i(m)} \cdot g^{J_i(m)}$. We often use the following theorem, which is proven in the full paper [9].

Theorem 4. *For any* $i \in [1, H]$ *and any* $m \in \{0,1\}^L$, *if* $F_i(m) = 0 \pmod p$ *then* $L_i(m) = 0 \pmod k$.

If $\mathcal{A}$ queries a message $M \in (\{0,1\}^L)^{h \leq H}$ to the signing oracle, the simulator $\mathcal{B}$ generates a signature σ as follows. Consider the following two cases, **(S1)** $\nexists i \in [1, h]$ s.t. $L_i(m_i) \neq 0 \pmod k$ and **(S2)** Otherwise.

S1: Abort the simulation.

S2: It holds that $\exists i \in [1, h]$ s.t. $L_i(m_i) \neq 0 \pmod k$. Let t denote such an index i. Contraposition of Theorem 4 guarantees that $F_t(m_t) \neq 0 \pmod p$. For each $i \in [1, h]$, choose $r_i \xleftarrow{U} \mathbb{Z}_p$ and compute $B_i := g^{r_i}$ if $i \neq t$ or

$B_i := (g')^{-1/F_t(m_t)} \cdot g^{r_t}$ otherwise. Compute

$$\Delta := (g')^{\frac{J_t(m_t)}{F_t(m_t)}} \cdot (g^{\beta})^{r_t \cdot F_t(m_t)} \cdot g^{r_t \cdot J_t(m_t)}$$
$$= (g')^{\beta} \cdot (g')^{-\frac{\beta \cdot F_t(m_t)}{F_t(m_t)}} \cdot (g')^{-\frac{J_t(m_t)}{F_t(m_t)}} \cdot (g^{\beta})^{r_t \cdot F_t(m_t)} \cdot g^{r_t \cdot J_t(m_t)}$$
$$= (g')^{\beta} \cdot g^{(r_t - \frac{b}{F_t(m_t)})(\beta \cdot F_t(m_t) + J_t(m_t))} = (g')^{\beta} \cdot (U_t \prod_{j=1}^{L} V_j^{m_t[j]})^{r_t - \frac{b}{F_t(m_t)}}$$

and $A := \Delta \cdot \prod_{i \in [1,h] \setminus \{t\}} U_i \prod_{j=1}^{L} V_j^{m_i[j]}$. Finalize $\sigma := (A, B_1, \cdots, B_h)$.

If $\mathcal{A}$ outputs a forged signature $\sigma^* = (A^*, B_1^*, \cdots, B_{h^*}^*)$ on a message $M^* = (m_1^*, \cdots, m_{h^*}^*)$ with depth $h^* \in [1, H]$, $\mathcal{B}$ considers the following two cases, **(F1)** $\exists i \in [1, h^*]$ s.t. $F_i(m_i^*) \neq 0 \pmod p$, and **(F2)** otherwise.

F1: Abort the simulation.

F2: It holds that $\forall i \in [1, h^*]$, $F_i(m_i^*) = 0 \pmod p$. We have assumed that $\mathcal{A}$ successfully forges a signature. There exist integers $r_1^*, \cdots, r_{h^*}^* \in \mathbb{Z}_p$ s.t. $A^* = (g')^{\beta} \prod_{i=1}^{h^*} (U_i \prod_{j=1}^{L} V_j^{m_i^*[j]})^{r_i^*}$ and $B_i^* = g^{r_i^*}$ for all $i \in [1, h^*]$. $\mathcal{B}$ outputs $A^* \cdot \{\prod_{i=1}^{h^*} (B_i^*)^{J_i(m_i^*)}\}^{-1} = (g')^{\beta} = g^{ab}$ as an answer to the CDH problem.

Let abort denote the event that $\mathcal{B}$ aborts the simulation. When abort does not occur, $\mathcal{B}$ perfectly simulates the weak unforgeability experiment to $\mathcal{A}$. Moreover, when abort does not occur and $\mathcal{A}$ wins, $\mathcal{B}$ solves the CDH problem. Thus, $\mathsf{Adv}^{\mathsf{wUNF}}_{\Sigma_{\mathrm{AOS}},\mathcal{A}}(\lambda) \leq \frac{1}{\Pr[\neg \mathsf{abort}]} \cdot \mathsf{Adv}^{\mathsf{CDH}}_{\mathbb{G},\mathcal{B}}(\lambda)$. As proven in [7], $\frac{1}{\Pr[\neg \mathsf{abort}]}$ is upper bounded by $2 \cdot \{2q(L+1)\}^H$. Its rigorous proof is given in the full paper [9]. □

4.3 Instantiation

For any $X \in \mathbb{G}$, $\iota_{\mathbb{G}}(X)$ denotes $(1_{\mathbb{G}}, 1_{\mathbb{G}}, X) \in \mathbb{G}^3$. For any $X \in \mathbb{G}_T$, $\iota_{\mathbb{G}_T}(X)$ denotes $(1_{\mathbb{G}_T}, 1_{\mathbb{G}_T}, X) \in \mathbb{G}_T^3$. Given $X \in \mathbb{G}_T$, $\Gamma_{\mathbb{G}_T}(X)$ denotes the 3×3 matrix which has X as the $(3,3)$-th element and $1_{\mathbb{G}_T}$ as any of the other elements. Given $h, g_1, g_2, g_3 \in \mathbb{G}$, $E(h, (g_1, g_2, g_3))$ denotes $(e(h, g_1), e(h, g_2), e(h, g_3)) \in \mathbb{G}_T^3$. For any $\vec{X} = (X_1, X_2, X_3) \in \mathbb{G}^3$ and $\vec{Y} = (Y_1, Y_2, Y_3) \in \mathbb{G}^3$, $F(\vec{X}, \vec{Y}) := \tilde{F}(\vec{X}, \vec{Y})^{1/2} \cdot \tilde{F}(\vec{Y}, \vec{X})^{1/2} \in \mathbb{G}_T^{3\times 3}$, where $\tilde{F}(\vec{X}, \vec{Y}) \in \mathbb{G}_T^{3\times 3}$ contains $e(X_i, Y_j)$ as the (i,j)-th element for all $i, j \in \{1, 2, 3\}$.

$\mathtt{Setup}(1^{\lambda}, L)$: Choose bilinear groups $(\mathbb{G}, \mathbb{G}_T)$ whose order is a prime p with bit length λ. Conduct the following three steps.

1. Generate a key-pair of the simplified ALP LHS scheme. Choose $\alpha \xleftarrow{U} \mathbb{Z}_p$. Choose $g, h, g_1, \cdots, g_{n+3} \xleftarrow{U} \mathbb{G}$. Choose $u', u_1, \cdots, u_N \xleftarrow{U} \mathbb{G}$ for $N \in \mathbb{N}$. $H_{\mathbb{G}} : \{0,1\}^N \to \mathbb{Z}_p$ is a function which takes $\tau = \tau[1] \| \cdots \| \tau[N] \in \{0,1\}^N$ and outputs $u' \prod_{i=1}^{N} u_i^{\tau[i]} \in \mathbb{G}$.
2. Generate a key-pair of our AOS scheme in Subsect. 4.2. Choose $\beta \xleftarrow{U} \mathbb{Z}_p$ and $H, U_1, \cdots, U_{\lambda+1}, V_1, \cdots, V_N \xleftarrow{U} \mathbb{G}$. Note that $H \in \mathbb{G}$ was originally $g' \in \mathbb{G}$.

3. Generate a GS CRS $\boldsymbol{f} = (\vec{f}_1, \vec{f}_2, \vec{f}_3)$ as $\vec{f}_1 := (f_1, 1, g)$, $\vec{f}_2 := (1, f_2, g)$ and $\vec{f}_3 := \vec{f}_1^{\xi_1} \cdot \vec{f}_2^{\xi_2} \cdot (1,1,g)^{-1}$, where $f_1, f_2 \xleftarrow{U} \mathbb{G}, \xi_1, \xi_2 \xleftarrow{U} \mathbb{Z}_p$.

Output (pp, mk), where $pp := (\mathbb{G}, \mathbb{G}_T, e, g, g^\alpha, h, \{g_i\}_{i=1}^{n+3}, u', \{u_i\}_{i=1}^{N}, g^\beta, H, \{U_i\}_{i=1}^{\lambda+1}, \{V_i\}_{i=1}^{N}, \boldsymbol{f})$ and $mk := (\alpha, \beta)$.

KGen$(mk, \mathbf{x}, L, R)$: Choose an LHS tag $\tau \xleftarrow{U} \{0,1\}^N$. Conduct the following two steps.

1. For each $i \in [1, n]$, let $\boldsymbol{v}_i := (x_i, \underbrace{0, \cdots, 0}_{i-1}, 1, \underbrace{0, \cdots, 0}_{n-i}, 0, 0) \in \mathbb{Z}_p^{n+3}$. Let $\boldsymbol{v}_{n+1} := (0, \cdots, 0, 1, 0) \in \mathbb{Z}_p^{n+3}$ and $\boldsymbol{v}_{n+2} := (0, \cdots, 0, 0, 1) \in \mathbb{Z}_p^{n+3}$. For $i \in [1, n+2]$, generate a signature of the ALP LHS scheme on $\boldsymbol{v}_i$ as $\sigma_i := (\sigma_{i,1}, \sigma_{i,2}, \sigma_{i,3}, \sigma_{i,4}) := (\{(\prod_{j=1}^{n+3} g_i^{v_{ij}}) \cdot h^{s_i}\}^\alpha H_{\mathbb{G}}(\tau)^{r_i}, g^{r_i}, g^{s_i}, g^{\alpha \cdot s_i})$, where $r_i, s_i \xleftarrow{U} \mathbb{Z}_p$.
2. Calculate $C \leftarrow$ Cover(L, R). Each $c \in C$ is parsed as $c[1] \parallel \cdots \parallel c[h_c]$ with length $h_c \in [1, \lambda]$. For each $c \in C$, generate a signature of our AOS scheme on $(\tau, c[1], \cdots, c[h_c])$ as $\theta_c := (A_c, B_{c,1}, \cdots, B_{h_c+1}) := (H^\beta \cdot (U_1 \prod_{i=1}^{N} V_i^{\tau[i]})^{t_1} \cdot \prod_{i=1}^{h_c} (U_{i+1} \cdot V_1^{c[i]})^{t_{i+1}}, g^{t_1}, \cdots, g^{t_{h_c+1}})$, where $t_1, \cdots, t_{h_c+1} \xleftarrow{U} \mathbb{Z}_p$.

Output $sk := (\tau, \{\sigma_i\}_{i=1}^{n+2}, \{\theta_c\}_{c \in C})$.

Sig$(sk, M, \mathbf{y})$: Parse sk as above. Let $d := \langle \mathbf{x}, \mathbf{y} \rangle \pmod p$. Assume that $d \in [L, R]$. Conduct the following four steps.

1. Derive an LHS signature on $\boldsymbol{v}' := (d, y_1, \cdots, y_n, M, 1)$. Let $\beta_{n+1} := M$, $\beta_{n+2} := 1$ and $\beta_i := y_i$ for each $i \in [1, n]$. Choose $r' \xleftarrow{U} \mathbb{Z}_p$. Compute $\sigma' := (\sigma_1', \sigma_2', \sigma_3', \sigma_4') := (\prod_{i=1}^{n+2} \sigma_{i,1}^{\beta_i} \cdot H_{\mathbb{G}}(\tau)^{r'}, \prod_{i=1}^{n+2} \sigma_{i,2}^{\beta_i} \cdot g^{r'}, \prod_{i=1}^{n+2} \sigma_{i,3}^{\beta_i}, \prod_{i=1}^{n+2} \sigma_{i,4}^{\beta_i})$.
2. $d \in [L, R]$ implies that there exists $c \in C$ s.t. c is either identical to or an ancestor of $[d]_2$. Parse c as $(c[1], \cdots, c[h_c])$. Parse θ_c as $(A, B_1, \cdots, B_{h_c+1})$. Compute $\theta' := (A', B_1', \cdots, B_{\lambda+1}') := (A \cdot (U_1 \prod_{i=1}^{N} V_i)^{t_1'} \prod_{i=1}^{\lambda} (U_{i+1} \cdot V_1^{d[i]})^{t_{i+1}'}, B_1 \cdot g^{t_1'}, \cdots, B_{h_c+1} \cdot g^{t_{h_c+1}'}, g^{t_{h_c+2}'}, \cdots, g^{t_{\lambda+1}'})$, where $t_1', \cdots, t_{\lambda+1}' \xleftarrow{U} \mathbb{Z}_p$.
3. Generate GS commitments for all of the following group elements.
   (a) $g^{\tau[i]}$, $g^{1-\tau[i]}$ and $V_i^{\tau[i]}$ (for all $i \in [1, N]$)
   (b) $H_{\mathbb{G}}(\tau)$
   (c) $g_1^{d[i]}$, $g_1^{1-d[i]}$ and $V_1^{d[i]}$ (for all $i \in [1, \lambda]$)
   (d) g_1^d
   (e) σ_1', σ_3' and σ_4'
   (f) A'

   They are denoted by $\vec{C}_{\tau[i]}$, $\vec{C}_{1-\tau[i]}$, $\vec{C}'_{\tau[i]}$, $\vec{C}_{H_{\mathbb{G}}(\tau)}$, $\vec{C}_{d[i]}$, $\vec{C}_{1-d[i]}$, $\vec{C}'_{d[i]}$, $\vec{C}_d$, $\vec{C}_{\sigma_1}$, $\vec{C}_{\sigma_3}$, $\vec{C}_{\sigma_4}$ and $\vec{C}_A$. A commitment $\vec{C}$ to an element $X \in \mathbb{G}$ is computed as $\iota_{\mathbb{G}}(X) \cdot \vec{f}_1^{r_X} \cdot \vec{f}_2^{s_X} \cdot \vec{f}_3^{t_X}$, where $r_X, s_X, t_X \xleftarrow{U} \mathbb{Z}_p$.
4. Generate GS proofs for all of the following PPEs.
   [a] $e(g^{\tau[i]}, g^{1-\tau[i]}) = 1_{\mathbb{G}_T}$, $e(g^{\tau[i]}, g) \cdot e(g^{1-\tau[i]}, g) = e(g, g)$ and $e(g^{\tau[i]}, V_i) = e(g, V_i^{\tau[i]})$ (for all $i \in [1, N]$)

[b] $e(H_{\mathbb{G}}(\tau), g) = e(u', g) \prod_{i=1}^{N} e(u_i, g^{\tau[i]})$

[c] $e(g_1^{d[i]}, g_1^{1-d[i]}) = 1_{\mathbb{G}_T}$, $e(g_1^{d[i]}, g_1) \cdot e(g_1^{1-d[i]}, g_1) = e(g_1, g_1)$ and $e(g^{d[i]}, V_1) = e(g, V_1^{d[i]})$ (for all $i \in [1, \lambda]$)

[d] $e(g_1^d, g) = \prod_{i=1}^{\lambda} e(g_1^{d[i]}, g^{2^{i-1}})$

[e] $e(\sigma_1', g) = e(g_1^d, g^\alpha) \cdot e(\prod_{i=1}^{n} g_{i+1}^{y_i} \cdot g_{n+2}^{M} \cdot g_{n+3}^{1}, g^\alpha) \cdot e(h, \sigma_4') \cdot e(H_{\mathbb{G}}(\tau), \sigma_2')$

[f] $e(\sigma_3', g^\alpha) = e(g, \sigma_4')$

[g] $e(A', g) = e(g^\beta, H) \cdot e(U_1, B_1') \prod_{i=1}^{\lambda} e(U_{i+1}, B_{i+1}') \prod_{i=1}^{N} e(V_i^{\tau[i]}, B_1') \prod_{i=1}^{\lambda} e(V_1^{d[i]}, B_{i+1}')$

All PPEs surrounded by a grey rectangle are quadratic. The others are linear. The generated proofs are denoted by $\vec{\pi}_{\tau[i],mul}$, $\vec{\pi}_{\tau[i],sum}$, $\vec{\pi}_{\tau[i]}$, $\vec{\pi}_{H_{\mathbb{G}}(\tau)}$, $\vec{\pi}_{d[i],mul}$, $\vec{\pi}_{d[i],sum}$, $\vec{\pi}_{d[i]}$, $\vec{\pi}_{d}$, $\vec{\pi}_{\sigma_1}$, $\vec{\pi}_{\sigma_3}$ and $\vec{\pi}_A$. A GS proof $\vec{\pi}$ for a linear (resp. quadratic) PPE consists of 3 (resp. 9) group elements.

Output a signature σ which is set to

$$\begin{pmatrix} \{\vec{C}_{\tau[i]}, \vec{C}_{1-\tau[i]}, \vec{C}'_{\tau[i]}, \vec{\pi}_{\tau[i],mul}, \vec{\pi}_{\tau[i],sum}, \vec{\pi}_{\tau[i]}\}_{i=1}^{N}, \\ \{\vec{C}_{d[i]}, \vec{C}_{1-d[i]}, \vec{C}'_{d[i]}, \vec{\pi}_{d[i],mul}, \vec{\pi}_{d[i],sum}, \vec{\pi}_{d[i]}\}_{i=1}^{\lambda}, \\ \vec{C}_{H_{\mathbb{G}}(\tau)}, \vec{\pi}_{H_{\mathbb{G}}(\tau)}, \vec{C}_d, \vec{\pi}_d, \vec{C}_{\sigma_1}, \sigma_2', \vec{C}_{\sigma_3}, \vec{C}_{\sigma_4}, \vec{\pi}_{\sigma_1}, \vec{\pi}_{\sigma_3}, \vec{C}_A, \{B_i'\}_{i=1}^{\lambda+1}, \vec{\pi}_A \end{pmatrix}. \quad (1)$$

$\texttt{Ver}(\sigma, M, \mathbf{y})$: Each GS proof $\vec{\pi} \in \mathbb{G}^3$ (resp. $\vec{\pi} \in \mathbb{G}^9$) is parsed as (π_1, π_2, π_3) (resp. $(\vec{\pi}_1, \vec{\pi}_2, \vec{\pi}_3)$ with $\vec{\pi}_i \in \mathbb{G}^3$). Output 1 iff all of the 11 equations hold.

1. $F(\vec{C}_{\tau[i]}, \vec{C}_{1-\tau[i]}) = \prod_{k=1}^{3} F(\vec{\pi}_{\tau[i],mul,k}, \vec{f}_k)$ (for all $i \in [1, N]$)
2. $E(g, \vec{C}_{\tau[i]}) \cdot E(g, \vec{C}_{1-\tau[i]}) = \iota_{\mathbb{G}_T}(e(g, g)) \prod_{k=1}^{3} E(\pi_{\tau[i],sum,k}, \vec{f}_k)$ (for all $i \in [1, N]$)
3. $E(g, \vec{C}_{H_{\mathbb{G}}(\tau)}) = \iota_{\mathbb{G}_T}(e(u', g)) \prod_{i=1}^{N} E(u_i, \vec{C}_{\tau[i]}) \prod_{k=1}^{3} E(\pi_{\tau[i],k}, \vec{f}_k)$
4. $E(V_i, \vec{C}_{\tau[i]}) = E(g, \vec{C}'_{\tau[i]}) \prod_{k=1}^{3} E(\pi_{\tau[i],k}, \vec{f}_k)$ (for all $i \in [1, N]$)
5. $F(\vec{C}_{d[i]}, \vec{C}_{1-d[i]}) = \prod_{k=1}^{3} F(\vec{\pi}_{d[i],mul,k}, \vec{f}_k)$ (for all $i \in [1, \lambda]$)
6. $E(g, \vec{C}_{d[i]}) \cdot E(g, \vec{C}_{1-d[i]}) = \iota_{\mathbb{G}_T}(e(g, g)) \prod_{k=1}^{3} E(\pi_{d[i],sum,k}, \vec{f}_k)$ (for all $i \in [1, \lambda]$)
7. $E(g, \vec{C}_d) = \prod_{i=1}^{\lambda} E(g^{2^{i-1}}, \vec{C}_{d[i]}) \prod_{k=1}^{3} E(\pi_{d,k}, \vec{f}_k)$
8. $E(V_1, \vec{C}_{d[i]}) = E(g, \vec{C}'_{d[i]}) \prod_{k=1}^{3} E(\pi_{d[i],k}, \vec{f}_k)$ (for all $i \in [1, \lambda]$)
9. $E(g, \vec{C}_{\sigma_1}) = E(g^\alpha, \vec{C}_d) \cdot \iota_{\mathbb{G}_T}(e(\prod_{i=1}^{n} g_{1+i}^{y_i} \cdot g_{n+2}^{M} \cdot g_{n+3}, g^\alpha)) \cdot E(h, \vec{C}_{\sigma_4}) \cdot E(\sigma_2', \vec{C}_{H_{\mathbb{G}}(\tau)}) \prod_{k=1}^{3} E(\pi_{\sigma_1,k}, \vec{f}_k)$
10. $E(g^\alpha, \vec{C}_{\sigma_3}) = E(g, \vec{C}_{\sigma_4}) \prod_{k=1}^{3} E(\pi_{\sigma_3,k}, \vec{f}_k)$
11. $E(g, \vec{C}_A) = \iota_{\mathbb{G}_T}(e(g^\beta, H) \cdot e(U_1, B_1') \prod_{i=1}^{\lambda} e(U_{i+1}, B_{i+1}')) \prod_{i=1}^{N} E(B_1', \vec{C}'_{\tau[i]}) \prod_{i=1}^{\lambda} E(B_{i+1}', \vec{C}'_{d[i]}) \prod_{k=1}^{3} E(\pi_{A,k}, \vec{f}_k)$

Corollary 1. *Our 1st KARIP scheme is* **UNF** *if the DLIN, CDH and FlexCDH assumptions hold in the group* $\mathbb{G}$*. The scheme is* **PRV** *unconditionally.*

Efficiency Analysis. Every signature is expressed as (1). It consists of $(27N + 27\lambda + 40)$ elements in $\mathbb{G}$. Thus, $|\sigma| = (27N + 27\lambda + 40)|g|$ [bit]. Each secret-key consists of $(\tau, \{\sigma_i\}_{i=1}^{n+2}, \{\theta_c\}_{c \in C})$. τ and $\{\sigma_i\}_{i=1}^{n+2}$ are of N [bit] and $4(n +$

$2)|g|$ [bit], respectively. Size of $\{\theta_c\}_{c\in C}$ is calculated as $|\{\theta_c\}_{c\in C}| = |\{(A_c, B_{c,1}, \cdots, B_{c,h_c+1})\}_{c\in C}| = \sum_{c\in C}(2+h_c)|g| = (2|C| + \sum_{c\in C} h_c)|g| \le (\lambda^2 + 5\lambda - 10)|g|$ [bit]. The last upper bound is because of the fact that both $|C|$ (= *the cardinality of the set* C) and $\sum_{c\in C} h_c$ are maximized when $[L, R] = [1, p-2]$ and their maximal values are $2\lambda - 2$ and $\lambda^2 + \lambda - 2$, respectively[4]. Thus, $|sk| = N + \mathcal{O}(n + \lambda^2)|g|$ [bit]. As explained in Subsect. 4.1, the KARIP scheme is key-delegatable. The analysis result is added as the first entry in Table 1.

Table 1. Comparison of our KARIP schemes w.r.t. efficiency and key-delegatability.

Schemes	$\|sk\|$ **[bit]**	$\|\sigma\|$ **[bit]**	**KD**
Ours 1	$N + \mathcal{O}(n + \lambda^2)\|g\|$	$(27N + 27\lambda + 40)\|g\|$	✓
2	$N + 4(n+2)\|g\|$	$(18N + 132\lambda + 39)\|g\|$	-
3	$N + 8\|g\|$	$(9n + 18N + 132\lambda + 42)\|g\|$	-

5 Our 2nd Construction of KARIP

5.1 Construction

Our generic KARIP construction is built by an LHS scheme $\{\texttt{L.KGen}, \texttt{L.Sig}, \texttt{L.Derive}, \texttt{L.Ver}\}$ and an NIWI proof system $\{\texttt{N.Setup}, \texttt{N.Pro}, \texttt{N.Ver}\}$.

$\texttt{Setup}(1^\lambda, L)$: $crs \leftarrow \texttt{N.Setup}(1^\lambda)$ and $(pk_{\mathsf{L}}, sk_{\mathsf{L}}) \leftarrow \texttt{L.KGen}(1^\lambda, n+5)$ with tags whose bit length is $N \in \texttt{poly}(\lambda)$. Output $pp := (crs, pk_{\mathsf{L}})$ and $mk := sk_{\mathsf{L}}$.

$\texttt{KGen}(mk, \mathbf{x}, L, R)$: Choose a tag $\tau \xleftarrow{U} \{0,1\}^N$. For each $i \in [1, n]$, let $\boldsymbol{v}_i := (x_i, \underbrace{0, \cdots, 0}_{i-1}, 1, \underbrace{0, \cdots, 0}_{n-i}, \underbrace{0, 0, 0, 0}_{4}) \in \mathbb{Z}_p^{n+5}$. Let $\boldsymbol{v}_{n+1} := (0, \cdots, 0, L, R, 0, 1) \in \mathbb{Z}_p^{n+5}$ and $\boldsymbol{v}_{n+2} := (0, \cdots, 0, 0, 0, 1, 0) \in \mathbb{Z}_p^{n+5}$. For each $\boldsymbol{v}_i$, generate an LHS signature with tag τ by $\sigma_i \leftarrow \texttt{L.Sig}(sk_{\mathsf{L}}, \tau, \boldsymbol{v}_i)$. Output $sk := (\tau, \{\sigma_i\}_{i=1}^{n+2})$.

$\texttt{Sig}(sk, M, \mathbf{y})$: Parse sk as above. Let $d := \langle \mathbf{x}, \mathbf{y} \rangle \pmod p$. Assume that $d \in [L, R]$. Conduct the following two steps.

1. Generate an LHS signature on $\boldsymbol{v}' := (d, y_1, \cdots, y_n, L, R, M, 1)$ by $\sigma' \leftarrow \texttt{L.Derive}(pk_{\mathsf{L}}, \tau, \{\boldsymbol{v}_i, \sigma_i, \beta_i\}_{i=1}^{n+2})$, where $\beta_{n+1} := 1$, $\beta_{n+2} := M$ and $\beta_i := y_i$ for each $i \in [1, n]$.
2. Define the NIWI relation $\mathcal{R}_{\mathsf{N}}$ as follows.
   - A statement $x = (\hat{\mathbf{y}}, \hat{M})$ consists of a vector $\hat{\mathbf{y}} = (\hat{y}_1, \cdots, \hat{y}_n) \in \mathbb{Z}_p^n$ and a message $\hat{M} \in \mathbb{Z}_p$. A witness $w = (\hat{L}, \hat{R}, \hat{d}, \hat{\tau}, \hat{\sigma})$ consists of integers $\hat{L}, \hat{R} \in \mathbb{Z}_p$, an inner product value $\hat{d} \in \mathbb{Z}_p$, an LHS tag $\hat{\tau} \in \{0,1\}^L$ and an LHS signature $\hat{\sigma}$. $\mathcal{R}_{\mathsf{N}}$ takes a statement x and witness w then outputs 1 if both of the two conditions are satisfied.

[4] The latter value is obtained by $2 \times (2 + 3 + \cdots + \lambda) = \lambda^2 + \lambda - 2$.

1. $1 \leftarrow \mathsf{L.Ver}(pk_{\mathsf{L}}, \hat{\tau}, \hat{\boldsymbol{v}}, \hat{\sigma})$, where $\hat{\boldsymbol{v}} := (\hat{d}, \hat{y}_1, \cdots, \hat{y}_n, \hat{L}, \hat{R}, \hat{M}, 1)$.
2. $\hat{d} \in [\hat{L}, \hat{R}] \pmod{p}$.

If we set $x := (\mathbf{y}, M)$ and $w := (L, R, d, \tau, \sigma)$, it obviously holds that $1 \leftarrow \mathcal{R}_{\mathsf{N}}(x, w)$. Output $\sigma \leftarrow \mathsf{N.Pro}(crs, x, w)$.

$\mathtt{Ver}(\sigma, M, \mathbf{y})$: Set $x := (\mathbf{y}, M)$ and output $1/0 \leftarrow \mathsf{N.Ver}(crs, x, \sigma)$.

Because of the page restriction, we omit the proof of the following theorem. It is given in the full paper [9] and basically the same as the proofs of the security theorems of our 1st KARIP construction.

Theorem 5. *The construction is* UNF *if the LHS scheme is wUNF, and the NIWI system is* WI *and* WE. *It is* PRV *if the NIWI system is* WI.

5.2 Instantiation

We use the simplified ALP LHS scheme [10] and the GS NIWI proof [8].

$\mathtt{Setup}(1^\lambda, L)$: Choose bilinear groups $(\mathbb{G}, \mathbb{G}_T)$ whose order is a prime p. Conduct the following two steps.

1. Generate a key-pair of the simplified ALP LHS scheme [4]. Choose $\alpha \xleftarrow{U} \mathbb{Z}_p$. Choose $g, h, g_1, \cdots, g_{n+5} \xleftarrow{U} \mathbb{G}$. Choose $u', u_1, \cdots, u_N \xleftarrow{U} \mathbb{G}$ for $N \in \mathbb{N}$. $H_{\mathbb{G}} : \{0,1\}^N \to \mathbb{Z}_p$ is a function which takes $\tau = \tau[1] \parallel \cdots \parallel \tau[N] \in \{0,1\}^N$ and outputs $u' \prod_{i=1}^{N} u_i^{\tau[i]} \in \mathbb{G}$.
2. Generate a GS CRS $\boldsymbol{f} = (\vec{f}_1, \vec{f}_2, \vec{f}_3)$.

Output $(pp, mk) := ((\mathbb{G}, \mathbb{G}_T, e, g, g^\alpha, h, \{g_i\}_{i=1}^{n+5}, u', \{u_i\}_{i=1}^{N}, \boldsymbol{f}), \alpha)$.

$\mathtt{KGen}(mk, \mathbf{x}, L, R)$: Choose an LHS tag $\tau \xleftarrow{U} \{0,1\}^N$. For each $i \in [1, n]$, let $\boldsymbol{v}_i := (x_i, \underbrace{0, \cdots, 0}_{i-1}, 1, \underbrace{0, \cdots, 0}_{n-i}, \underbrace{0, 0, 0, 0}_{4}) \in \mathbb{Z}_p^{n+5}$. Let $\boldsymbol{v}_{n+1} := (0, \cdots, 0, L, R, 0, 1) \in \mathbb{Z}_p^{n+5}$ and $\boldsymbol{v}_{n+2} := (0, \cdots, 0, 0, 0, 1, 0) \in \mathbb{Z}_p^{n+5}$. For $i \in [1, n+2]$, generate a signature of the ALP LHS scheme on $\boldsymbol{v}_i$ as $\sigma_i := (\sigma_{i,1}, \sigma_{i,2}, \sigma_{i,3}, \sigma_{i,4}) := (\{(\prod_{j=1}^{n+5} g_i^{v_{ij}}) \cdot h^{s_i}\}^\alpha H_{\mathbb{G}}(\tau)^{r_i}, g^{r_i}, g^{s_i}, g^{\alpha \cdot s_i})$, where $r_i, s_i \xleftarrow{U} \mathbb{Z}_p$. Output $sk := (\tau, \{\sigma_i\}_{i=1}^{n+2})$.

$\mathtt{Sig}(sk, M, \mathbf{y})$: Parse sk as above. Let $d := \langle \mathbf{x}, \mathbf{y} \rangle \pmod{p}$. Assume that $d \in [L, R]$. Firstly, conduct the following three steps.

1. Derive an LHS signature on $\boldsymbol{v}' := (d, y_1, \cdots, y_n, L, R, M, 1)$. Let $\beta_{n+1} := 1$, $\beta_{n+2} := M$ and $\beta_i := y_i$ for any $i \in [1, n]$. Compute $\sigma' := (\prod_{i=1}^{n+2} \sigma_{i,1}^{\beta_i} \cdot H_{\mathbb{G}}(\tau)^{r'}, \prod_{i=1}^{n+2} \sigma_{i,2}^{\beta_i} \cdot g^{r'}, \prod_{i=1}^{n+2} \sigma_{i,3}^{\beta_i}, \prod_{i=1}^{n+2} \sigma_{i,4}^{\beta_i})$, where $r' \xleftarrow{U} \mathbb{Z}_p$.
2. Generate GS commitments for all of the following group elements.
   (a) $g^{\tau[i]}$ and $g^{1-\tau[i]}$ (for all $i \in [1, N]$)
   (b) $H_{\mathbb{G}}(\tau)$
   (c) $g_1^{d[i]}, g_1^{1-d[i]}, g_{n+2}^{L[i]}, g_{n+2}^{1-L[i]}, g_{n+3}^{R[i]}$ and $g_{n+3}^{1-R[i]}$ (for all $i \in [1, \lambda]$)
   (d) g_1^d, g_{n+2}^L and g_{n+3}^R
   (e) σ_1', σ_3' and σ_4'

   They are denoted by $\vec{C}_{\tau[i]}, \vec{C}_{1-\tau[i]}, \vec{C}_{H_{\mathbb{G}}(\tau)}, \vec{C}_{d[i]}, \vec{C}_{1-d[i]}, \vec{C}_{L[i]}, \vec{C}_{1-L[i]}, \vec{C}_{R[i]}, \vec{C}_{1-R[i]}, \vec{C}_d, \vec{C}_L, \vec{C}_R, \vec{C}_{\sigma_1}, \vec{C}_{\sigma_3}$ and $\vec{C}_{\sigma_4}$.

3. Generate GS proofs for all of the following PPEs.
   [a] $e(g^{\tau[i]}, g^{1-\tau[i]}) = 1_{\mathbb{G}_T}$ and $e(g^{\tau[i]}, g) \cdot e(g^{1-\tau[i]}, g) = e(g, g)$ (for all $i \in [1, N]$)
   [b] $e(H_{\mathbb{G}}(\tau), g) = e(u', g) \prod_{i=1}^{N} e(u_i, g^{\tau[i]})$
   [c] $e(g_1^{d[i]}, g_1^{1-d[i]}) = 1_{\mathbb{G}_T}$, $e(g_1^{d[i]}, g_1) \cdot e(g_1^{1-d[i]}, g_1) = e(g_1, g_1)$, $e(g_{n+2}^{L[i]}, g_{n+2}^{1-L[i]}) = 1_{\mathbb{G}_T}$, $e(g_{n+2}^{L[i]}, g) \cdot e(g_{n+2}^{1-L[i]}, g) = e(g_{n+2}, g)$, $e(g_{n+3}^{R[i]}, g_{n+3}^{1-R[i]}) = 1_{\mathbb{G}_T}$ and $e(g_{n+3}^{R[i]}, g) \cdot e(g_{n+3}^{1-R[i]}, g) = e(g_{n+3}, g)$ (for all $i \in [1, \lambda]$)
   [d] $e(g_1^d, g) = \prod_{i=1}^{\lambda} e(g_1^{d[i]}, g^{2^{i-1}})$, $e(g_{n+2}^L, g) = \prod_{i=1}^{\lambda} e(g_{n+2}^{L[i]}, g^{2^{i-1}})$ and $e(g_{n+3}^R, g) = \prod_{i=1}^{\lambda} e(g_{n+3}^{R[i]}, g^{2^{i-1}})$
   [e] $e(\sigma_1', g) = e(g_1^d, g^\alpha) \cdot e(\prod_{i=1}^{n} g_{i+1}^{y_i} \cdot g_{n+4}^M \cdot g_{n+5}^1, g^\alpha) \cdot e(g_{n+2}^L, g^\alpha) \cdot e(g_{n+3}^R, g^\alpha) \cdot e(h, \sigma_4') \cdot e(H_{\mathbb{G}}(\tau), \sigma_2')$
   [f] $e(\sigma_3', g^\alpha) = e(g, \sigma_4')$

   They are denoted by $\vec{\pi}_{\tau[i],mul}$, $\vec{\pi}_{\tau[i],sum}$, $\vec{\pi}_{H_{\mathbb{G}}(\tau)}$, $\vec{\pi}_{d[i],mul}$, $\vec{\pi}_{d[i],sum}$, $\vec{\pi}_{L[i],mul}$, $\vec{\pi}_{L[i],sum}$, $\vec{\pi}_{R[i],mul}$, $\vec{\pi}_{R[i],sum}$, $\vec{\pi}_d$, $\vec{\pi}_L$, $\vec{\pi}_R$, $\vec{\pi}_{\sigma_1}$ and $\vec{\pi}_{\sigma_3}$.

What remains is proving $d \in [L, R] \pmod p$.
Firstly, we prove $d \geq L$. If $d \geq L$, there is only one index $i \in [1, \lambda + 1]$ s.t.

$$d[i] = 1 \bigwedge L[i] = 0 \bigwedge_{j=1}^{i-1} d[i] = L[i]. \tag{2}$$

For each $i \in [1, \lambda+1]$, a Boolean variable $A_i \in \{0, 1\}$ is defined to be 1 (resp. 0) if the condition (2) holds (resp. otherwise). It is obviously true that A_i is 1 iff $d \geq L$. Additionally, for each $i \in [1, \lambda]$, define three Boolean variables $B_i, C_i, D_i \in \{0, 1\}$. B_i is 1 iff $\bigwedge_{j=1}^{i} d[j] = L[j]$. C_i is 1 iff $d[i] = 1 \bigwedge L[i] = 0$. D_i is 1 iff $d[i] = L[i]$.
Conduct the following two steps.

1. Generate GS commitments for all of the following group elements.
   (f) $g_1^{B_i}$, $g_1^{C_i}$ and $g_1^{D_i}$ (for all $i \in [1, \lambda]$)
   They are denoted by $\vec{C}_{B_i}$, $\vec{C}_{C_i}$ and $\vec{C}_{D_i}$.
2. Generate GS proofs for all of the following PPEs.
   [g] $e(g_1^{C_i}, g_{n+2}) = e(g_1^{d[i]}, g_{n+2}^{1-L[i]})$ (for all $i \in [1, \lambda]$)
   [h] $e(g_1^{D_i}, g_{n+2}) = e(g_1^{d[i]}, g_{n+2}^{L[i]}) \cdot e(g_1^{1-d[i]}, g_{n+2}^{1-L[i]})$ (for all $i \in [1, \lambda]$)
   [i] $e(g_1^{B_1}, g_1) = e(g_1, g_1^{D_1})$
   [j] $e(g_1^{B_i}, g_1) = e(g_1^{B_{i-1}}, g_1^{D_i})$ (for all $i \in [2, \lambda]$)
   [k] $e(g_1, g_1^{C_1}) \prod_{i=1}^{\lambda} e(g_1^{B_{i-1}}, g_1^{C_i}) \cdot e(g_1^{B_\lambda}, g_1) = e(g_1, g_1)$

   For the equation [k], the term $e(g_1, g_1^{C_1})$ (resp. $e(g_1^{B_{i-1}}, g_1^{C_i})$, $e(g_1^{B_\lambda}, g_1)$) is equivalent to $e(g_1, g_1)^{A_1}$ (resp. $e(g_1, g_1)^{A_i}$, $e(g_1, g_1)^{A_{\lambda+1}}$). Thus, the left side of the equation [k] is equivalent to $e(g_1, g_1)^{\sum_{i=1}^{\lambda+1} A_i}$. The generated proofs are denoted by $\vec{\pi}_{C_i}$, $\vec{\pi}_{D_i}$, $\vec{\pi}_{B_1}$, $\vec{\pi}_{B_i}$ and $\vec{\pi}_A$, respectively.

Next, we prove $d \leq R$. If $d \leq R$, there is only one index $i \in [1, \lambda + 1]$ s.t.

$$d[i] = 0 \bigwedge R[i] = 1 \bigwedge_{j=1}^{i-1} d[i] = R[i]. \tag{3}$$

For each $i \in [1, \lambda+1]$, a Boolean variable $A'_i \in \{0,1\}$ is defined to be 1 (resp. 0) if the condition (3) holds (resp. otherwise). It is obviously true that A'_i is 1 iff $d \leq R$. Additionally, for each $i \in [1, \lambda]$, define three Boolean variables $E_i, F_i, G_i \in \{0,1\}$. E_i is 1 iff $\bigwedge_{j=1}^{i} d[j] = R[j]$. F_i is 1 iff $d[i] = 1 \bigwedge R[i] = 0$. G_i is 1 iff $d[i] = R[i]$.
Conduct the following two steps.

1. Generate GS commitments for all of the following group elements.
   (g) $g_1^{E_i}$, $g_1^{F_i}$ and $g_1^{G_i}$ (for all $i \in [1, \lambda]$)
   They are denoted by $\vec{C}_{E_i}$, $\vec{C}_{F_i}$ and $\vec{C}_{G_i}$.
2. Generate GS proofs for all of the following PPEs.
   [l] $e(g_1^{F_i}, g_{n+3}) = e(g_1^{1-d[i]}, g_{n+3}^{R[i]})$ (for all $i \in [1, \lambda]$)
   [m] $e(g_1^{G_i}, g_{n+3}) = e(g_1^{d[i]}, g_{n+3}^{R[i]}) \cdot e(g_1^{1-d[i]}, g_{n+3}^{1-R[i]})$ (for all $i \in [1, \lambda]$)
   [n] $e(g_1^{E_1}, g_1) = e(g_1, g_1^{G_1})$
   [o] $e(g_1^{E_i}, g_1) = e(g_1^{E_{i-1}}, g_1^{G_i})$ (for all $i \in [2, \lambda]$)
   [p] $e(g_1, g_1^{F_1}) \prod_{i=1}^{\lambda} e(g_1^{E_{i-1}}, g_1^{F_i}) \cdot e(g_1^{E_\lambda}, g_1) = e(g_1, g_1)$
   They are denoted by $\vec{\pi}_{F_i}$, $\vec{\pi}_{G_i}$, $\vec{\pi}_{E_1}$, $\vec{\pi}_{E_i}$ and $\vec{\pi}_{A'}$.

Output a signature σ which is set to

$$\left(\begin{array}{c} \{\vec{C}_{\tau[i]}, \vec{C}_{1-\tau[i]}, \vec{\pi}_{\tau[i],mul}, \vec{\pi}_{\tau[i],sum}\}_{i=1}^{N}, \\ \{\{\vec{C}_{x[i]}, \vec{C}_{1-x[i]}, \vec{\pi}_{x[i],mul}, \vec{\pi}_{x[i],sum}\}_{i=1}^{\lambda}, \vec{C}_x, \vec{\pi}_x\}_{x\in\{d,L,R\}}, \\ \vec{C}_{H_{\mathbb{G}}(\tau)}, \vec{\pi}_{H_{\mathbb{G}}(\tau)}, \vec{C}_{\sigma_1}, \sigma'_2, \vec{C}_{\sigma_3}, \vec{C}_{\sigma_4}, \vec{\pi}_{\sigma_1}, \vec{\pi}_{\sigma_3}, \vec{\pi}_A, \vec{\pi}_{A'}, \\ \{\vec{C}_{B_i}, \vec{C}_{C_i}, \vec{C}_{D_i}, \vec{\pi}_{B_i}, \vec{\pi}_{C_i}, \vec{\pi}_{D_i}, \vec{C}_{E_i}, \vec{C}_{F_i}, \vec{C}_{G_i}, \vec{\pi}_{E_i}, \vec{\pi}_{F_i}, \vec{\pi}_{G_i}\}_{i=1}^{\lambda} \end{array} \right). \quad (4)$$

$\texttt{Ver}(\sigma, M, \mathbf{y})$: Each GS proof $\vec{\pi} \in \mathbb{G}^3$ (resp. $\vec{\pi} \in \mathbb{G}^9$), composed of 3 (resp. 9) elements in $\mathbb{G}$, is parsed as (π_1, π_2, π_3) (resp. $(\vec{\pi}_1, \vec{\pi}_2, \vec{\pi}_3)$ with $\vec{\pi}_i \in \mathbb{G}^3$). Output 1 iff all of the following equations hold.

1. $F(\vec{C}_{\tau[i]}, \vec{C}_{1-\tau[i]}) = \prod_{k=1}^{3} F(\vec{\pi}_{\tau[i],mul,k}, \vec{f}_k)$ (for all $i \in [1, N]$)
2. $E(g, \vec{C}_{\tau[i]}) \cdot E(g, \vec{C}_{1-\tau[i]}) = \iota_{\mathbb{G}_T}(e(g,g)) \prod_{k=1}^{3} E(\pi_{\tau[i],sum,k}, \vec{f}_k)$ (for all $i \in [1, N]$)
3. $E(g, \vec{C}_{H_{\mathbb{G}}(\tau)}) = \iota_{\mathbb{G}_T}(e(u', g)) \prod_{i=1}^{N} E(u_i, \vec{C}_{\tau[i]}) \prod_{k=1}^{3} E(\pi_{\tau[i],k}, \vec{f}_k)$
4. $F(\vec{C}_{d[i]}, \vec{C}_{1-d[i]}) = \prod_{k=1}^{3} F(\vec{\pi}_{d[i],mul,k}, \vec{f}_k)$ (for all $i \in [1, \lambda]$)
5. $E(g, \vec{C}_{d[i]}) \cdot E(g, \vec{C}_{1-d[i]}) = \iota_{\mathbb{G}_T}(e(g,g)) \prod_{k=1}^{3} E(\pi_{d[i],sum,k}, \vec{f}_k)$ (for all $i \in [1, \lambda]$)
6. $E(g, \vec{C}_d) = \prod_{i=1}^{\lambda} E(g^{2^{i-1}}, \vec{C}_{d[i]}) \prod_{k=1}^{3} E(\pi_{d,k}, \vec{f}_k)$
7. $E(g, \vec{C}_{\sigma_1}) = E(g^\alpha, \vec{C}_d) \cdot \iota_{\mathbb{G}_T}(e(\prod_{i=1}^{n} g_{1+i}^{y_i} \cdot g_{n+4}^{M} \cdot g_{n+5}, g^\alpha)) \cdot E(g^\alpha, \vec{C}_L) \cdot E(g^\alpha, \vec{C}_R) \cdot E(h, \vec{C}_{\sigma_4}) \cdot E(\sigma'_2, \vec{C}_{H_{\mathbb{G}}(\tau)}) \prod_{k=1}^{3} E(\pi_{\sigma_1,k}, \vec{f}_k)$
8. $E(g^\alpha, \vec{C}_{\sigma_3}) = E(g, \vec{C}_{\sigma_4}) \prod_{k=1}^{3} E(\pi_{\sigma_3,k}, \vec{f}_k)$
9. $F(\vec{C}_{L[i]}, \vec{C}_{1-L[i]}) = \prod_{k=1}^{3} F(\vec{\pi}_{L[i],mul,k}, \vec{f}_k)$ (for all $i \in [1, \lambda]$)
10. $E(g_{n+2}, \vec{C}_{L[i]}) \cdot E(g_{n+2}, \vec{C}_{1-L[i]}) = \iota_{\mathbb{G}_T}(e(g_{n+2}, g)) \prod_{k=1}^{3} E(\pi_{L[i],sum,k}, \vec{f}_k)$ (for all $i \in [1, \lambda]$)
11. $E(g, \vec{C}_L) = \prod_{i=1}^{\lambda} E(g^{2^{i-1}}, \vec{C}_{L[i]}) \prod_{k=1}^{3} E(\pi_{L,k}, \vec{f}_k)$

12. $F(\vec{C}_{R[i]}, \vec{C}_{1-R[i]}) = \prod_{k=1}^{3} F(\vec{\pi}_{R[i],mul,k}, \vec{f}_k)$ (for all $i \in [1, \lambda]$)
13. $E(g_{n+3}, \vec{C}_{R[i]}) \cdot E(g_{n+3}, \vec{C}_{1-R[i]}) = \iota_{\mathbb{G}_T}(e(g_{n+3}, g)) \prod_{k=1}^{3} E(\pi_{R[i],sum,k}, \vec{f}_k)$ (for all $i \in [1, \lambda]$)
14. $E(g, \vec{C}_R) = \prod_{i=1}^{\lambda} E(g^{2^{i-1}}, \vec{C}_{R[i]}) \prod_{k=1}^{3} E(\pi_{R,k}, \vec{f}_k)$
15. $F(\iota_{\mathbb{G}}(g_{n+2}), \vec{C}_{C_i}) = F(\vec{C}_{d[i]}, \vec{C}_{1-L[i]}) \prod_{k=1}^{3} F(\vec{\pi}_{C_i,k}, \vec{f}_k)$ (for all $i \in [1, \lambda]$)
16. $F(\iota_{\mathbb{G}}(g_{n+2}), \vec{C}_{D_i}) = F(\vec{C}_{d[i]}, \vec{C}_{L[i]}) \cdot F(\vec{C}_{1-d[i]}, \vec{C}_{1-L[i]}) \prod_{k=1}^{3} F(\vec{\pi}_{D_i,k}, \vec{f}_k)$ (for all $i \in [1, \lambda]$)
17. $E(g_1, \vec{C}_{B_1}) = E(g_1, \vec{C}_{D_1}) \prod_{k=1}^{3} E(\pi_{B_1,k}, \vec{f}_k)$
18. $F(\iota_{\mathbb{G}}(g_1), \vec{C}_{B_i}) = F(\vec{C}_{B_{i-1}}, \vec{C}_{D_i}) \prod_{k=1}^{3} F(\vec{\pi}_{B_i,k}, \vec{f}_k)$ (for all $i \in [2, \lambda]$)
19. $F(\iota_{\mathbb{G}}(g_1), \vec{C}_{C_1}) \prod_{i=1}^{\lambda} \cdot F(\vec{C}_{B_{i-1}}, \vec{C}_{C_i}) \cdot F(\iota_{\mathbb{G}}(g_1), \vec{C}_{B_\lambda}) = \Gamma_{\mathbb{G}_T}(e(g_1, g_1)) \prod_{k=1}^{3} F(\vec{\pi}_{A,k}, \vec{f}_k)$
20. $F(\iota_{\mathbb{G}}(g_{n+3}), \vec{C}_{F_i}) = F(\vec{C}_{1-d[i]}, \vec{C}_{R[i]}) \prod_{k=1}^{3} F(\vec{\pi}_{F_i,k}, \vec{f}_k)$ (for all $i \in [1, \lambda]$)
21. $F(\iota_{\mathbb{G}}(g_{n+3}), \vec{C}_{G_i}) = F(\vec{C}_{d[i]}, \vec{C}_{R[i]}) \cdot F(\vec{C}_{1-d[i]}, \vec{C}_{1-R[i]}) \prod_{k=1}^{3} F(\vec{\pi}_{G_i,k}, \vec{f}_k)$ (for all $i \in [1, \lambda]$)
22. $E(g_1, \vec{C}_{E_1}) = E(g_1, \vec{C}_{G_1}) \prod_{k=1}^{3} E(\pi_{E_1,k}, \vec{f}_k)$
23. $F(\iota_{\mathbb{G}}(g_1), \vec{C}_{E_i}) = F(\vec{C}_{E_{i-1}}, \vec{C}_{G_i}) \prod_{k=1}^{3} F(\vec{\pi}_{E_i,k}, \vec{f}_k)$ (for all $i \in [2, \lambda]$)
24. $F(\iota_{\mathbb{G}}(g_1), \vec{C}_{F_1}) \prod_{i=1}^{\lambda} \cdot F(\vec{C}_{E_{i-1}}, \vec{C}_{F_i}) \cdot F(\iota_{\mathbb{G}}(g_1), \vec{C}_{E_\lambda}) = \Gamma_{\mathbb{G}_T}(e(g_1, g_1)) \prod_{k=1}^{3} F(\vec{\pi}_{A',k}, \vec{f}_k)$

Corollary 2. *Our 2nd KARIP scheme is* UNF *if the DLIN, CDH and FlexCDH assumptions hold in the group* $\mathbb{G}$. *The scheme is* PRV *unconditionally.*

Efficiency Analysis. Every secret-key sk consists of a tag $\tau \in \{0,1\}^N$ and $4(n+2)$ group elements, i.e., $|sk| = N + 4(n+2)|g|$ [bit]. Every signature σ is expressed as (4). Its size is calculated by summing up all of the elements' size, i.e., $|\sigma| = (18N + 126\lambda + 58)|g|$ [bit]. Refer to Table 1.

6 Our 3rd Construction of KARIP

6.1 Construction

Hash Function. A hash function consists of the following two algorithms. Key-generation `KGen` is a probabilistic polynomial-time algorithm which takes a security parameter 1^λ with $\lambda \in \mathbb{N}$, then outputs a hash key hk. Evaluation `Eval` takes the hash key hk and a message M, then outputs a hash value $h \in \{0,1\}^l$ with $l \in \mathtt{poly}(\lambda)$. Its security is collision-resistance. A hash function is collision-resistant if for any $\lambda \in \mathbb{N}$ and any PPT algorithm $\mathcal{A}$, the probability that $\mathcal{A}$ receives a hash key $hk \leftarrow \mathtt{KGen}(1^\lambda)$, then finds two messages M, M' s.t. $M \neq M' \wedge \mathtt{Eval}(hk, M) = \mathtt{Eval}(hk, M')$ is negligible.

Construction. Our generic KARIP construction is built by an LHS scheme $\{\mathsf{L.KGen}, \mathsf{L.Sig}, \mathsf{L.Derive}, \mathsf{L.Ver}\}$, an NIWI proof system $\{\mathsf{N.Setup}, \mathsf{N.Pro}, \mathsf{N.Ver}\}$ and a collision-resistant hash function $\{\mathsf{H.KGen}, \mathsf{H.Eval}\}$.

$\mathtt{Setup}(1^\lambda, L)$: Generate $crs \leftarrow \mathsf{N.Setup}(1^\lambda)$, $(pk_\mathsf{L}, sk_\mathsf{L}) \leftarrow \mathsf{L.KGen}(1^\lambda, n+4)$ whose bit length of each tag is $N \in \mathtt{poly}(\lambda)$ and $hk \leftarrow \mathsf{H.KGen}(1^\lambda)$. Output $pp := (crs, pk_\mathsf{L}, hk)$ and $mk := sk_\mathsf{L}$.

$\mathtt{KGen}(mk, \mathbf{x}, L, R)$: Choose a tag $\tau \xleftarrow{\text{U}} \{0,1\}^N$. Let $\boldsymbol{v}_1 := (x_1, x_2, \cdots, x_n, L, R, 0, 1) \in \mathbb{Z}_p^{n+4}$ and $\boldsymbol{v}_2 := (0, \cdots, 0, 1, 0) \in \mathbb{Z}_p^{n+4}$. For each $i \in \{1, 2\}$, generate an LHS signature with tag τ by $\sigma_i \leftarrow \mathsf{L.Sig}(sk_\mathsf{L}, \tau, \boldsymbol{v}_i)$. Output $sk := (\tau, \{\sigma_i\}_{i=1}^2)$.

$\mathtt{Sig}(sk, M, \mathbf{y})$: Parse sk as above. Let $d := \langle \mathbf{x}, \mathbf{y} \rangle \pmod p$. Assume that $d \in [L, R]$. Conduct the following three steps.

1. Let $h \leftarrow \mathsf{H.Eval}(hk, (\mathbf{y}, M))$. Generate an LHS signature on $\boldsymbol{v}' := (x_1, \cdots, x_n, L, R, h, 1)$ by $\sigma' \leftarrow \mathsf{L.Derive}(pk_\mathsf{L}, \tau, \{\boldsymbol{v}_i, \sigma_i, \beta_i\}_{i=1}^{n+4})$, where $\beta_1 := 1$ and $\beta_2 := h$.
2. Define the NIWI relation $\mathcal{R}_\mathsf{N}$ as follows.
   - A statement $x = (\hat{\mathbf{y}}, \hat{M})$ consists of a signature-vector $\hat{\mathbf{y}} = (\hat{y}_1, \cdots, \hat{y}_n) \in \mathbb{Z}_p^n$ and a message $M \in \mathbb{Z}_p$. A witness $w = (\hat{\mathbf{x}}, \hat{L}, \hat{R}, \hat{d}, \hat{\tau}, \hat{\sigma})$ consists of a key-vector $\hat{\mathbf{x}} \in \mathbb{Z}_p^n$, integer $\hat{L}, \hat{R} \in \mathbb{Z}_p$, an inner product value $\hat{d} \in \mathbb{Z}_p$, an LHS tag $\hat{\tau} \in \{0,1\}^L$, and an LHS signature $\hat{\sigma}$. $\mathcal{R}_\mathsf{N}$ takes a statement x and witness w then outputs 1 if all the following three conditions are satisfied.
     1. $1 \leftarrow \mathsf{L.Ver}(pk_\mathsf{L}, \hat{\tau}, \hat{\boldsymbol{v}}, \hat{\sigma})$, where $\hat{\boldsymbol{v}} := (\hat{x}_1, \cdots, \hat{x}_n, \hat{L}, \hat{R}, \hat{h}, 1)$ and $\hat{h} = \mathsf{H.Eval}(hk, (\hat{\mathbf{y}}, \hat{M}))$.
     2. $\hat{d} = \langle \hat{\mathbf{x}}, \hat{\mathbf{y}} \rangle \pmod p$.
     3. $\hat{d} \in [\hat{L}, \hat{R}]$.

   If we set $x := (\mathbf{y}, M)$ and $w := (\mathbf{x}, L, R, d, \tau, \sigma)$, it obviously holds that $1 \leftarrow \mathcal{R}_\mathsf{N}(x, w)$. Output $\sigma \leftarrow \mathsf{N.Pro}(crs, x, w)$.

$\mathtt{Ver}(\sigma, M, \mathbf{y})$: Set $x := (\mathbf{y}, M)$ and output $1/0 \leftarrow \mathsf{N.Ver}(crs, x, \sigma)$.

Proof of the following theorem is given in the full paper [9].

Theorem 6. *Our 3rd KARIP scheme is* UNF *if the LHS scheme is* wUNF*, and the NIWI system is* WI *and* WE*, and the hash function is* CR*. The scheme is* PRV *if the NIWI system is* WI*.*

6.2 Instantiation

As our 1st and 2nd instantiations, we use the simplified ALP LHS scheme [10] and the GS NIWI proof [8]. We describe the full construction in the full paper [9]. In key-generation, for the two vectors $\boldsymbol{v}_1, \boldsymbol{v}_2$, we generate a signature σ_i of the simplified ALP LHS. Every secret-key sk consists of a tag τ and only 8 group elements, i.e., $|sk| = N + 8|g|$ [bit]. Signing algorithm is almost the same as the one of our 2nd instantiation in Subsect. 5.2. Since the vector $\boldsymbol{v}'$ of the

LHS signature σ' has a form of $\boldsymbol{v}' = (x_1, \cdots, x_n, L, R, h, 1)$, the signer needs to additionally generate (1) GS commitments $\vec{C}_{x_i}, \vec{C}_{x_i} \in \mathbb{G}^3$ to $g^{x_i} \in \mathbb{G}$ and $g_i^{x_i} \in \mathbb{G}$ for each $i \in [1, n]$ and (2) GS proofs $\vec{\pi}_{x_i}, \vec{\pi}_{d,ip}$ for the PPEs $e(g_i^{x_i}, g) = e(g_i, g^{x_i})$ and $e(g^d, g) = \prod_{i=1}^{n} e(g^{x_i}, g^{y_i})$. Signature size is derived by simply adding bit length of newly generated GS commitments and proofs to signature size of our 2nd instantiated scheme, i.e., $|\sigma| = (6n + 18N + 126\lambda + 65)|g|$ [bit].

The 3rd instantiated scheme is the only one whose secret-key size is independent of n, and simultaneously the only one whose signature size is dependent on n. In comparison between the 1st and 2nd ones, the former has a disadvantage that its secret-key increases linearly with λ^2, but has an advantage that signature size is approximately one fifth of the size of the latter (if we ignore their constants and N-terms). Remind that only the 1st one is key-delegatable.

7 Applications of KARIP

[10] showed that an ARIP scheme is transformed into any of the following 7 ABS primitives, (1) ABS for range evaluation (RE) of polynomials (AREP), (2) ABS for RE of weighted averages (AREWA), (3) fuzzy identity-based signatures (FIBS), (4) time-specific signatures (TSS) [11,14], (5) ABS for RE of Hamming distance (AREHD), (6) ABS for RE of Euclidean distance (AREED) and (7) ABS for hyperellipsoid predicates (AHEP). The same transformations work for KARIP. A KARIP scheme is transformed into any of *key-range* versions of the 7 ABS primitives. We emphasize that key-delegatability is inherited. If we use a key-delegatable KARIP scheme such as our 1st instantiated scheme, we obtain a key-delegatable key-range ABS scheme.

Appendix 1 Formal Definition of the Covering Algorithm `Cover`

Assume that L and R are of bit length λ and $L \leq R$. An integer $a \in \mathbb{Z}_p$ with bit length λ is parsed as $a[1] \parallel \cdots \parallel a[\lambda]$ with $a[i] \in \{0, 1\}$. The algorithm `Cover` is defined as follows.

`Cover`(L, R): Let $l := L$. A set C is initially empty, i.e., $C := \emptyset$. While $l \leq R$, repeat the following steps.
- Derive the minimal integer $t \in [1, \lambda]$ satisfying both of the following conditions,
  1. $l[t] = \cdots = l[\lambda] = 0$
  2. $[\underbrace{l[1] \parallel \cdots \parallel l[t-1]}_{t-1} \parallel \underbrace{1^{\lambda+1-t}}_{\lambda+1-t}]_{10} \leq R$

  For a binary value a, $[a]_{10}$ means its decimal value. If such an integer t does not exist, $t := \lambda + 1$. Obviously, the node associated with $l[1] \parallel \cdots \parallel l[t-1] \in \{0, 1\}^{t-1}$ covers all of the leaf nodes associated with from $[l]_2$ to $[l + 2^{\lambda+1-t} - 1]_2$. Let $C := C \cup \{l[1] \parallel \cdots \parallel l[t-1]\}$ and $l := l + 2^{\lambda+1-t}$.

Return C.

For instance, in a complete binary tree with 8 leaf nodes depicted in Fig. 1, $\mathtt{Cover}(1,6) = \{001, 01, 10, 110\}$, $\mathtt{Cover}(0,4) = \{0, 100\}$, $\mathtt{Cover}(7,7) = \{111\}$, and $\mathtt{Cover}(0,7) = \emptyset$.

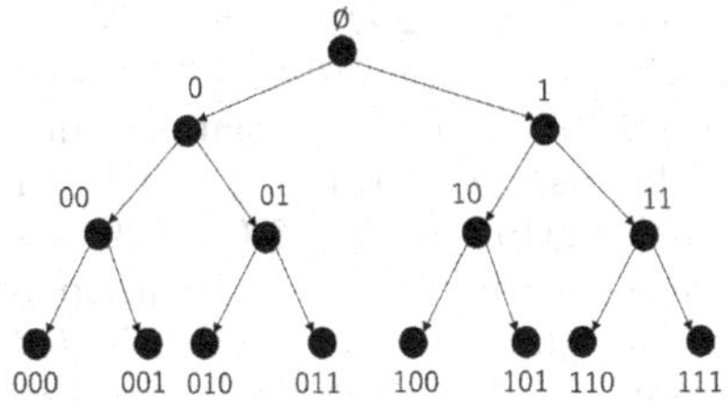

Fig. 1. A complete binary tree with depth 3

References

1. Abdalla, M., et al.: Wildcarded identity-based encryption. J. Cryptol. **24**(1), 42–82 (2011)
2. Ahn, J.H., Boneh, D., Camenisch, J., Hohenberger, S., Shelat, A., Waters, B.: Computing on authenticated data. In: Cramer, R. (ed.) TCC 2012. LNCS, vol. 7194, pp. 1–20. Springer, Heidelberg (2012). https://doi.org/10.1007/978-3-642-28914-9_1
3. Attrapadung, N., Libert, B., Peters, T.: Computing on authenticated data: new privacy definitions and constructions. In: Wang, X., Sako, K. (eds.) ASIACRYPT 2012. LNCS, vol. 7658, pp. 367–385. Springer, Heidelberg (2012). https://doi.org/10.1007/978-3-642-34961-4_23
4. Attrapadung, N., Libert, B., Peters, T.: Efficient completely context-hiding quotable and linearly homomorphic signatures. In: Kurosawa, K., Hanaoka, G. (eds.) Public-Key Cryptography – PKC 2013: 16th International Conference on Practice and Theory in Public-Key Cryptography, Nara, Japan, February 26 – March 1, 2013. Proceedings, pp. 386–404. Springer, Berlin, Heidelberg (2013). https://doi.org/10.1007/978-3-642-36362-7_24
5. Boneh, D., Freeman, D., Katz, J., Waters, B.: Signing a linear subspace: signature schemes for network coding. In: Jarecki, S., Tsudik, G. (eds.) Public Key Cryptography – PKC 2009: 12th International Conference on Practice and Theory in Public Key Cryptography, Irvine, CA, USA, March 18-20, 2009. Proceedings, pp. 68–87. Springer, Berlin, Heidelberg (2009). https://doi.org/10.1007/978-3-642-00468-1_5
6. Boneh, D., Waters, B.: Conjunctive, subset, and range queries on encrypted data. In: Vadhan, S.P. (ed.) TCC 2007. LNCS, vol. 4392, pp. 535–554. Springer, Heidelberg (2007). https://doi.org/10.1007/978-3-540-70936-7_29
7. Chatterjee, S., Sarkar, P.: Practical hybrid (hierarchical) identity-based encryption schemes based on the decisional bilinear Diffie-Hellman assumption. Int. J. Appl. Cryptograph. (IJACT) **3**(1), 47–83 (2013)
8. Groth, J., Sahai, A.: Efficient non-interactive proof systems for bilinear groups. In: Smart, N. (ed.) EUROCRYPT 2008. LNCS, vol. 4965, pp. 415–432. Springer, Heidelberg (2008). https://doi.org/10.1007/978-3-540-78967-3_24

9. Ishizaka, M.: Key-range attribute-based signatures for range of inner product and its applications. Cryptology ePrint Archive: Report 2023/747 (2023)
10. Ishizaka, M., Fukushima, K.: Attribute-based signatures for range of inner product and its applications. In: Seo, S.-H., Seo, H. (eds.) Information Security and Cryptology – ICISC 2022: 25th International Conference, ICISC 2022, Seoul, South Korea, November 30 – December 2, 2022, Revised Selected Papers, pp. 382–407. Springer, Cham (2023). https://doi.org/10.1007/978-3-031-29371-9_19
11. Ishizaka, M., Kiyomoto, S.: Time-specific signatures. In: Susilo, W., Deng, R.H., Guo, F., Li, Y., Intan, R. (eds.) ISC 2020. LNCS, vol. 12472, pp. 20–38. Springer, Cham (2020). https://doi.org/10.1007/978-3-030-62974-8_2
12. Katz, J., Sahai, A., Waters, B.: Predicate encryption supporting disjunctions, polynomial equations, and inner products. In: Smart, N. (ed.) EUROCRYPT 2008. LNCS, vol. 4965, pp. 146–162. Springer, Heidelberg (2008). https://doi.org/10.1007/978-3-540-78967-3_9
13. Kiltz, E., Mityagin, A., Panjwani, S., Raghavan, B.: Append-only signatures. In: Caires, L., Italiano, G.F., Monteiro, L., Palamidessi, C., Yung, M. (eds.) ICALP 2005. LNCS, vol. 3580, pp. 434–445. Springer, Heidelberg (2005). https://doi.org/10.1007/11523468_36
14. Paterson, K.G., Quaglia, E.A.: Time-specific encryption. In: Garay, J.A., De Prisco, R. (eds.) SCN 2010. LNCS, vol. 6280, pp. 1–16. Springer, Heidelberg (2010). https://doi.org/10.1007/978-3-642-15317-4_1
15. Sakai, Y., Attrapadung, N., Hanaoka, G.: Attribute-based signatures for circuits from bilinear map. In: Cheng, C.-M., Chung, K.-M., Persiano, G., Yang, B.-Y. (eds.) Public-Key Cryptography – PKC 2016: 19th IACR International Conference on Practice and Theory in Public-Key Cryptography, Taipei, Taiwan, March 6-9, 2016, Proceedings, Part I, pp. 283–300. Springer, Berlin, Heidelberg (2016). https://doi.org/10.1007/978-3-662-49384-7_11

A Certificateless Aggregate Signature Scheme with Better Security

Ran Xu, Yanwei Zhou(✉), Yu Han, and Bo Yang

School of Computer Science, Shaanxi Normal University, Xi'an, China
zyw@snnu.edu.cn

Abstract. In recent years, the Internet of Things (IOT) has been developing rapidly and popularizing the world. Smart home is one of its important applications, the devices and household appliances are connected together through the network to provide intelligent services. However, malicious attacks often occur during the transmission of data information, resulting in data leakage or data changes. Therefore, it is necessary to ensure the integrity and availability of data. Based on this, we propose a new pairing-free certificateless aggregate signature (CLAS) scheme, which achieves efficient authentication of multiple messages and improves the verification rate. In addition, we demonstrate its security based on the hardness of discrete logarithm problem in the random oracle model. Comparison with other CLAS schemes proves that our scheme has better security and higher efficiency through performance analysis.

Keywords: Certificateless Cryptography · Certificateless Aggregate Signature · Provable Security

1 Introduction

Certificateless signature (CLS) not only solves the certificate management problem of traditional public key encryption, but also eliminates the key escrow problem of identity based public key cryptography because the public and private keys are generated jointly by the user and the key generation center (KGC). Based on this, a series of CLS schemes have been proposed since Al Riyami *et al.* [1] proposed it firstly. In the actual application, a large number of messages need to be transmitted, so the costs of signature verification and communication costs are gradually increasing. A certificateless aggregate signature (CLAS) scheme aggregates multiple messages into one for verification, which effectively reduces computing costs. The notion of aggregate signature is described by Boneh *et al.* in [2]. That is, n signatures on n different messages for n different users are aggregated into a single signature. Gong *et al.* [3] proposed a CLAS scheme for the first time by combining certificateless cryptography with aggregate signature. However, Zhang *et al.* [4] showed thier scheme existed security issues, introduced a novel CLAS scheme with bilinear mapping and proved it security. Kumar et

M. Zhang et al. (Eds.): ProvSec 2023, LNCS 14217, pp. 157–165, 2023.
https://doi.org/10.1007/978-3-031-45513-1_9

al. [5] introduced a CLAS scheme with bilinear pairing, however it is found time-consuming, because bilinear pairing operation has large computation cost. Later, a pairing-free CLAS scheme for healthcare wireless medical sensor networks is shown by Kumar *et al.* [6]. However, Wu *et al.* [7] pointed out this scheme can not resist the attack of Type II adversary and proposed an improved scheme. Kamil and Ogundoyin [8] presented a CLAS scheme for vehicular ad hoc networks and showed their security proof in a random oracle model. Unfortunately, Zhao *et al.* [9] showed the above scheme [8] has not achieved the previous claimed security, their scheme is flimsy for signature forgery attack. Gayathri *et al.* [10] constructed a CLAS scheme for healthcare wireless medical sensor networks, they do not use paring to cut down the computational complexity. Liu *et al.* [11] analysed this scheme and showed it's signature is easily to be forged. Recently, Gong *et al.* [12] indicated the Liu *et al.*'s scheme [11] is insecure because the scheme is susceptible to signature forgery attacks. They proposed a new CLAS scheme without bilinear pairing, utilised pseudonym mechanism to protect the privacy, and showed their lower costs. However, we found that their scheme is still unable to resist the public key replacement attack of the Type-I adversary. Very recently, Yang *et al.* [13] pointed out that the existing CLAS scheme created in [14] is insecure, also, an improved CLAS scheme is proposed in [13]. In this scheme, in order to further reduce the length of the aggregation signature and improve the computational efficiency of the verification, the aggregator carries out some advance calculation. However, we find that any normal adversary can forge the aggregation signature, where the normal adversary is one who does not have the ability to replace the public key of any user and cannot obtain the user's private information, but only has the corresponding public information. For Yang *et al.*'s CLAS scheme [13], we believe that the aggregator's prediction undermines the security of the underlying CLS scheme. Therefore, even if their CLS scheme is secure, the upper CLAS scheme does not have unforgerability.

In this paper, we propose a novel pairing-free CLAS scheme realizing efficient verification of multiple messages for smart home applications. Through proving the security of our proposal by the hardness of discrete logarithm (DL) problem, we point out that it can resist attacks from Type-I and Type-II adversaries, showing that our scheme has better security.

2 Certificateless Aggregate Signature Scheme

2.1 Formal Definition

A CLAS scheme has the following algorithms.

Setup. KGC runs this algorithm with inputting κ as the security parameter to produce system public parameter $Params$ and master key msk. We express it as $(Params, msk) \leftarrow \mathsf{Setup}(1^{\kappa})$.

Partial Private Key. KGC runs this algorithm with inputting identity ID_i, system public parameter $Params$, and master key msk. Then KGC outputs partial private key d to user. We express it as $d \leftarrow \mathsf{PPKey}(Params, msk, ID_i)$.

Secret value. With getting system public parameter $Params$ and identity ID_i, user runs this algorithm to generate x as the secret value. We express it as $x \leftarrow \mathsf{SecretValue}(Params, ID_i)$.

Public/Private Key. With getting system public parameter $Prams$, identity ID_i, partial private key d and secret value x, user runs this algorithm to generate public key PK_i and private key SK_i. We express it as $(PK_i, SK_i) \leftarrow \mathsf{KeyGen}(Params, ID_i, d, x)$.

Sign. The signer runs this algorithm with inputting system public parameter $Params$, identity ID_i, message m_i and private key SK to generate the signature δ_i for the message m_i. We express it as $d \leftarrow \mathsf{Sign}(Params, ID_i, SK_i, m_i)$.

Verify. The verifier runs this algorithm with inputting system public parameter $Params$, identity ID_i, message m_i and signature δ_i. Then, the verifier accepts it if δ is valid; Otherwise, rejects it. We express it as $1/0 \leftarrow \mathsf{Verify}(Params, ID_i, m_i, \delta_i)$.

Aggregate. With getting ID_i, message m_i, PK_i and δ_i, for i from 1 to n, aggregator runs this algorithm to output the aggregate signature δ. We express it as $\delta \leftarrow \mathsf{Aggregate}\big(\{PK_i, ID_i, m_i, \delta_i\}_{i=1,\cdots,n}\big)$.

Aggregate Verification. With getting identity ID_i, message m_i, public key PK_i and aggregate signature δ, for i from 1 to n, aggregate verifier verifies the signature. if δ is valid, then the verifier outputs "1"; Otherwise, the verifier outputs "0". We express it as $1/0 \leftarrow \mathsf{AggSigVerify}\big(\{PK_i, ID_i, m_i\}_{i=1,\cdots,n}, \delta\big)$.

2.2 Security Model

In the CLAS scheme, there are two kinds of adversaries Type I adversary $\mathcal{A}_1$ and Type II adversary $\mathcal{A}_2$. Specially, $\mathcal{A}_1$ is a malicious user who initiates an external attack, it can replace the public key (public key replacement attack), but it can not get the system's master secret key. $\mathcal{A}_2$ is a malicious KGC who initiates an internal attack, it can get the master secret key (master secret key attack), but it can not replace the public key. The CLAS scheme should have unforgeability under adaptive choose message attacks.

Game 1: The game operation process is as below:

Initialization. $\mathcal{C}$ runs Setup to generate master secret key msk and system public parameter $Params$. $\mathcal{C}$ keeps msk secretly, and outputs $Params$ to $\mathcal{A}_1$.

Queries. $\mathcal{A}_1$ issues the following queries in this stage.

- *Creation User*: When $\mathcal{C}$ receives the creation user query from $\mathcal{A}_1$ with inputting identity ID_i, $\mathcal{C}$ executes PPKey algorithm to generate d, executes $\mathsf{SecretValue}$ to generate x, executes KeyGen to create (PK_i, SK_i), then outputs PK_i to $\mathcal{A}_1$.
- *Reveal Partial Private Key*: When $\mathcal{C}$ receives the query from $\mathcal{A}_1$ with inputting identity ID_i, $\mathcal{C}$ executes PPKey to generate d for $\mathcal{A}_1$.

- *Reveal Secret Value*: When $\mathcal{C}$ receives the query from $\mathcal{A}_1$ with inputting identity ID_i, $\mathcal{C}$ executes SecretValue to generate x for $\mathcal{A}_1$.
- *Reveal Private Key*: When $\mathcal{C}$ receives the query from $\mathcal{A}_1$ with inputting identity ID_i, $\mathcal{C}$ executes PPKey to generate d, SecVal to generate x, and KeyGen to create (PK_i, SK_i). Finally $\mathcal{C}$ outputs SK_i to $\mathcal{A}_1$.
- *Replace Public Key* :When $\mathcal{C}$ receives the query from $\mathcal{A}_1$ with tuple (ID_i, PK_i^*) as input, $\mathcal{C}$ replaces public key PK_i with PK_i^*.
- *Sign*: When $\mathcal{C}$ receives the query from $\mathcal{A}_1$ with tuple (ID_i, m_i) as input, $\mathcal{C}$ executes Sign algorithm to generating δ_i for $\mathcal{A}_1$.

Forgery. For (ID_i^*, m_i^*), $\mathcal{A}_1$ forges a signature δ_i^*. If the following conditions are true, then $\mathcal{A}_1$ wins the game, (1) $\mathcal{A}_1$ never submits *Reveal Partial Private Key* and *Reveal Private Key* queries for the challenge identity ID_i^* in any stage. (2) If the public key of identity ID_i has been replaced, $\mathcal{A}_1$ can never execute *Reveal Partial Private Key* query for this identity. (3) $\mathcal{A}_1$ never executes *Sign* query for (ID_i^*, m_i^*).

Therefore, the advantage that $\mathcal{A}_1$ wins this game is $\mathsf{Adv}_{\mathcal{A}_1}(\kappa) = \Pr[\mathcal{A}_1\ Wins]$.

Game 2: The game operation process is as below:

Initialization. $\mathcal{C}$ runs Setup algorithm to generate master secret key msk and system public parameter $Params$. and outputs $Params$ and msk to $\mathcal{A}_2$.

Queries. $\mathcal{A}_2$ issues the following queries in this stage.

- *Creation User*: When $\mathcal{C}$ receives the creation user query from $\mathcal{A}_1$ with inputting identity ID_i, $\mathcal{C}$ executes PPKey algorithm to generate d, executes SecretValue to generate x, executes KeyGen to create (PK_i, SK_i), then outputs PK_i to $\mathcal{A}_2$.
- *Reveal Secret Value*: When $\mathcal{C}$ receives the query from $\mathcal{A}_2$ with inputting identity ID_i, $\mathcal{C}$ executes SecretValue to generate x for $\mathcal{A}_2$.
- *Reveal Private Key*: When $\mathcal{C}$ receives the query from $\mathcal{A}_2$ with inputting identity ID_i, $\mathcal{C}$ executes PPKey to generate d, SecretValue to generate x, and KeyGen to create (PK_i, SK_i). Finally $\mathcal{C}$ outputs SK_i to $\mathcal{A}_2$.
- *Sign*: When $\mathcal{C}$ receives the query from $\mathcal{A}_2$ with tuple (ID_i, m_i), $\mathcal{C}$ executes Sign algorithm to generate δ_i for $\mathcal{A}_2$.

Forgery. For (ID_i^*, m_i^*), $\mathcal{A}_2$ forges a signature δ_i^*. If the following conditions are true, then $\mathcal{A}_2$ wins the game, (1) $\mathcal{A}_2$ never submits *Reveal Partial Private Key* and *Reveal Private Key* queries for the challenge identity ID_i^* in any stage. (2) $\mathcal{A}_2$ never executes *Sign* query for (ID_i^*, m_i^*).

Therefore, the advantage that $\mathcal{A}_2$ wins this game is $\mathsf{Adv}_{\mathcal{A}_2}(\kappa) = \Pr[\mathcal{A}_2\ wins]$.

For probability polynomial time (PPT) adversaries $\mathcal{A}_1$ and $\mathcal{A}_2$, if the above advantages $\mathsf{Adv}_{\mathcal{A}_1}(\kappa)$ and $\mathsf{Adv}_{\mathcal{A}_2}(\kappa)$ are negligible, then we can think that the corresponding CLAS scheme has unforgeability.

3 Our Proposed CLAS Scheme

3.1 Concrete Construction

Our CLAS scheme includes the following algorithms:

- **Setup**. With inputting the security parameter κ, KGC chooses a group G of order q and generator P, defines four hash functions $H_1, H_2, H_3, H_4 : \{0,1\}^* \to Z_q^*$. Then select $s \in Z_q^*$ as the system master secret key and calculates $P_{pub} = sP$. Finally, KGC sets $Params = \{G, q, p, P_{pub}, H_1, H_2, H_3, H_4\}$ as system public parameters.
- **Partial Private Key**. When receiving the tuple (ID_i, m_i) from the user U_i, KGC chooses $r_i \in Z_q^*$, calculates $R_i = r_iP$ and $d_i = (r_i + sh_{1i}) \bmod q$, where $h_{1i} = H_1(P_{pub}, ID_i, R_i)$. Finally, KGC outputs partial key (d_i, R_i) to the user U_i.
- **Public/Private Key**. If $d_iP = R + h_{i1}P_{pub}$ holds, the user U_i accepts the partial key. After that, U_i selects the secret value $x_i \in Z_q^*$, calculates $X_i = x_iP$. Output public key $PK_i = (X_i, R_i)$ and private key $SK_i = (x_i, d_i)$.
- **Signature**. To create a signature on the message $m_i \in \{0,1\}^*$, the user U_i chooses $t_i \in Z_q^*$, calculates $T_i = t_iP$ and $\sigma_i = h_{i4}t_i + h_{i3}d_i + h_{i2}x_i \bmod q$, where $h_{i2} = H_2(ID_i, PK_i, m_i, T_i)$, $h_{i3} = H_3(ID_i, PK_i, m_i, T_i)$ and $h_{i4} = H_4(ID_i, PK_i, m_i, T_i)$. Then U_i outputs the signature $\delta_i = (T_i, \sigma_i)$ to the verifier.
- **Verification**. After receiving $\delta_i = (T_i, \sigma_i)$, for $h_{i1} = H_1(P_{pub}, ID_i, R_i)$, $h_{i2} = H_2(ID_i, PK_i, m_i, T_i)$, $h_{i3} = H_3(ID_i, PK_i, m_i, T_i)$ and $h_{i4} = H_4(ID_i, PK_i, m_i, T_i)$, if $\sigma_iP = h_{i4}T_i + h_{i3}(R_i + h_{i1}P_{pub}) + h_{i2}X_i$ holds, then the verifier accepts it; Otherwise, the verifier rejects it.
- **Aggregate Signature**. When receiving the $(ID_i, PK_i, m_i, \delta_i)$, for i from 1 to n, the aggregator calculates $\sigma = \sum_{i=1}^{n}\sigma_i$. Finally, sets $\mathbf{T} = (T_1, \cdots, T_n)$, and outputs $\delta = (\mathbf{T}, \sigma)$ to the aggregate verifier.
- **Aggregate Verification**. With the signature $\delta = (\mathbf{T}, \sigma)$ and the identity message set $(ID_i, PK_i, m_i)_{i=1,2,\cdots,n}$, for i from 1 to n, the verifier calculates $h_{i1} = H_1(P_{pub}, ID_i, R_i)$, $h_{i2} = H_2(ID_i, PK_i, m_i, T_i)$, $h_{i3} = H_3(ID_i, PK_i, m_i, T_i)$ and $h_{i4} = H_4(ID_i, PK_i, m_i, T_i)$. Then verify the correctness of $\sigma P = \sum_{i=1}^{n} h_{i4}T_i + \sum_{i=1}^{n} h_{i3}(R_i + h_{i1}P_{pub}) + \sum_{i=1}^{n} h_{i2}X_i$, if it is correct, accept it; Otherwise, reject it.

3.2 Security Proof

We demonstrate that our underlying CLS scheme can resist attacks from Type-I and Type-II adversaries by building games between the challenger $\mathcal{C}$ and the adversaries $\mathcal{A}_1$, $\mathcal{A}_2$, respectively. The specific details are following.

Theorem 1. *If there exists a Type-I adversary $\mathcal{A}_1$ who can win Game 1 in polynomial time, then there exists a challenger $\mathcal{C}$ who can solve the hardness of DL problem with advantage $(1 - \frac{1}{e})\frac{\varepsilon_1}{e(q_1+q_2+1)q_h}$ in probability polynomial time, where q_1 is the number of partial private key generation queries, q_2 is he number of private key generation queries, and q_h is the number of H_3 oracle query. Let e express the base of the natural log.*

Proof. With tuple $(P, Q = bP)$ where $b \in Z_q^*$, the challenger $\mathcal{C}$ aims to know b solving DL problem.

Setup. $\mathcal{C}$ sets $P_{pub} = bP$ and sends $Params = \{G, q, P, P_{pub}, H_1, H_2, H_3, H_4\}$ to the adversary $\mathcal{A}_1$, and maintains four lists L_1, L_2, L_3, L_4, L_u for H_1, H_2, H_3, H_4 oracle queries and creation user queries, initially, each list is empty.

Queries. $\mathcal{A}_1$ conducts the following inquiries. Specially, $\mathcal{C}$ adaptively randomly selects an identity ID^* as the challenge identity.

- *Creation User Query.* With a identity ID_i from $\mathcal{A}_1$ for a creation user query, if $(ID_i, X_i, R_i, x_i, d_i)$ belongs to L_u, $\mathcal{C}$ outputs $PK_i = (X_i, R_i)$ to $\mathcal{A}_1$; Otherwise, $\mathcal{C}$ does the following computation.
  If $ID_i = ID^*$, $\mathcal{C}$ selects random values $r_i^*, x_i^*, h_{i1}^* \in Z_q^*$, computes $R_i^* = r_i^* P$ and $X_i^* = x_i^* P$. $\mathcal{C}$ stores (ID^*, R_i^*, h_{i1}^*) in the list L_1 and $(ID^*, X_i^*, R_i^*, x_i^*, \perp)$ in the list L_u. Finally, $\mathcal{C}$ outputs $PK^* = (X^*, R^*)$ to $\mathcal{A}_1$.
  Otherwise, $\mathcal{C}$ selects random values $d_i, x_i, h_{i1} \in Z_q^*$, computes $R_i = d_i P - h_{i1} P_{pub}$ and $X_i = x_i P$, and stores (ID_i, R_i, h_{i1}) in the list L_1 and $(ID_i, X_i, R_i, x_i, d_i)$ in the list L_u. Finally, $\mathcal{C}$ outputs $PK_i = (X_i, R_i)$ to $\mathcal{A}_1$.
- *H_1 Query.* With receiving (ID_i, R_i, P_{pub}) from $\mathcal{A}_1$, $\mathcal{C}$ outputs h_{i1} to $\mathcal{A}_1$ by searching the tuple $(ID_i, R_i, P_{pub}, h_{i1})$ from L_1. Notice that, the adversary $\mathcal{A}_1$ has completed the creation user query for the identity id_i before submitting the H_1 query.
- *H_2 Query.* With receiving $(ID_i, PK_i, P_{pub}, m_i, T_i)$ from $\mathcal{A}_1$, if $(ID_i, PK_i, P_{pub}, m_i, T_i, h_{i2})$ belongs to L_2, $\mathcal{C}$ outputs h_{i2} to $\mathcal{A}_1$; Otherwise $\mathcal{C}$ selects a random value $h_{i2} \in Z_q^*$, stores $(ID_i, PK_i, P_{pub}, m_i, T_i, h_{i2})$ in the list L_2 and sends it to $\mathcal{A}_1$.
- *H_3 Query.* With receiving $(ID_i, PK_i, P_{pub}, m_i, T_i)$ from $\mathcal{A}_1$, if $(ID_i, PK_i, P_{pub}, m_i, T_i, h_{i3})$ belongs to L_3, $\mathcal{C}$ outputs h_{i3} to $\mathcal{A}_1$; Otherwise $\mathcal{C}$ selects a random value $h_{i3} \in Z_q^*$, stores $(ID_i, PK_i, P_{pub}, m_i, T_i, h_{i3})$ in the list L_3 and sends it to $\mathcal{A}_1$.
- *H_4 Query.* With receiving $(ID_i, PK_i, P_{pub}, m_i, T_i)$ from $\mathcal{A}_1$, if $(ID_i, PK_i, P_{pub}, m_i, T_i, h_{i3})$ belongs to L_4, $\mathcal{C}$ outputs h_{i4} to $\mathcal{A}_1$; Otherwise $\mathcal{C}$ selects a random value $h_{i4} \in Z_q^*$, stores $(ID_i, PK_i, P_{pub}, m_i, T_i, h_{i4})$ in the list L_4 and sends it to $\mathcal{A}_1$.
- *Partial Private Key Query.* With a identity ID_i from $\mathcal{A}_1$ for a partial private key query, $\mathcal{C}$ finds whether $(ID_i, X_i, R_i, x_i, d_i)$ belongs to L_u, if it belongs, sends (d_i, R) to $\mathcal{A}_1$; Otherwise, $\mathcal{C}$ performs the creation user query with ID_i as input and outputs (d_i, R_i) to $\mathcal{A}_1$. Specially, in this query, if $ID_i = ID^*$, then $\mathcal{C}$ aborts, and this game is over.
- *Secret Value Query.* With a identity ID_i from $\mathcal{A}_1$ for a secret value query, $\mathcal{C}$ finds whether $(ID_i, X_i, R_i, x_i, d_i)$ belongs to L_u, if it belongs, sends x_i to $\mathcal{A}_1$; Otherwise, $\mathcal{C}$ performs the creation user query with ID_i as input and outputs x_i to $\mathcal{A}_1$. Specially, in this query, if $ID_i = ID^*$, then $\mathcal{C}$ aborts, and this game is over.
- *Private Key Query.* With a identity ID_i from $\mathcal{A}_1$ for a private key query, $\mathcal{C}$ finds whether $(ID_i, X_i, R_i, x_i, d_i)$ belongs to L_u, if it belongs, sends $SK_i =$

(x_i, d_i) to $\mathcal{A}_1$; Otherwise, $\mathcal{C}$ performs the creation user query with ID_i as input and outputs $SK_i = (x_i, d_i)$ to $\mathcal{A}_1$. Specially, in this query, if $ID_i = ID^*$, then $\mathcal{C}$ aborts, and this game is over.
- *Public Key Replacement Query.* With $(ID_i, PK_i' = (X', R'))$ from $\mathcal{A}_1$ for a public key replacement query, if $ID_i = ID^*$, $\mathcal{C}$ ignores this query; Otherwise, $\mathcal{C}$ replaces the tuple $(ID_i, X_i, R_i, x_i, d_i)$ with $(ID_i, X', R', \perp, \perp)$. Notice that, if the tuple $(ID_i, X_i, R_i, x_i, d_i)$ does not belong to L_u, then, $\mathcal{C}$ performs the creation user query with ID_i as input, after that, $\mathcal{C}$ replaces the tuple $(ID_i, X_i, R_i, x_i, d_i)$ with $(ID_i, X', R', \perp, \perp)$.
- *Signature Query.* With (ID_i, m_i) from $\mathcal{A}_1$ for a signature query, $\mathcal{C}$ can obtain the corresponding tuple $(ID_i, X_i, R_i, x_i, d_i)$ from L_u, and does the following computation.
If $ID_i \neq ID^*$ and $d_i \neq \perp$, $\mathcal{C}$ randomly chooses $t_i \in Z_q^*$, and calculates $T_i = t_iP$, $h_{i2} = H_2(ID_i, m_i, PK_i)$, $h_{i3} = H_3(ID_i, m_i, PK_i)$ and $h_{i4} = H_4(ID_i, m_i, PK_i, T_i)$. Next $\mathcal{C}$ computes $\sigma_i = h_{i4}t_i + h_{i3}d_i + h_{i2}x_i$ and outputs signature $\delta_i = (T_i, \sigma_i)$ to $\mathcal{A}_1$. Otherwise, $\mathcal{C}$ chooses $\sigma_i, h_{i2}, h_{i3}, h_{i4} \in Z_q^*$, and computes $T_i = h_{i4}^{-1}[\sigma_i P - h_{i3}(R_i + h_{i1}P_{pub}) - h_{i2}X_i]$. After that, $\mathcal{C}$ stores $(ID_i, PK_i, m_i, h_{i2})$ in the list L_2, $(ID_i, PK_i, m_i, h_{i3})$ in the list L_3, and $(ID_i, PK_i, m_i, T_i, h_{i4})$ in the list L_4. Finally, $\mathcal{C}$ returns signature $\delta_i = (T_i, \sigma_i)$ to $\mathcal{A}_1$. Notice that, h_{i1} can be obtained from the tuple (ID_i, R_i, P_{pub}) of L_1. Specially, in the signature query, the queried tuple (ID_i, m_i) will be added into a list L_S, which is used to record the signature query submitted by $\mathcal{A}_1$.

Forgery. In this stage, $\mathcal{A}_1$ forges a signature $\delta_{i1}^* = (T^*, \sigma_{i1}^*)$ for the identity message pair (ID_i^*, m_i^*), where $T^* = t_i^*P$. If $ID_i^* \neq ID^*$ or $(ID_i^*, m_i^*) \in L_S$, then $\mathcal{C}$ aborts. Otherwise, based on Forking lemma [15], under the replay operation of $\mathcal{C}$ on the H_3 oracle, $\mathcal{A}_1$ can forge a new signature $\delta_{i2}^* = (T^*, \sigma_{i2}^*)$ with different response $\hat{h}_{i3}$ of H_3 oracle and the same random value t_i^*. Then, these two equations $\sigma_{i1}^* = h_{i4}^*t_i^* + h_{i3}^*(r_i^* + bh_{i1}^*) + h_{i2}^*x^*$ and $\sigma_{i2}^* = h_{i4}^*t_i^* + \hat{h}_{i3}^*(r_i^* + bh_{i1}^*) + h_{i2}^*x^*$ are held.

Though computation getting $b = \frac{1}{h_{i1}^*}\left(\frac{\sigma_{i1}^* - \sigma_{i2}^*}{h_{i3}^* - \hat{h}_{i3}^*} - r_i^*\right)$, causing a contradiction with the DL problem. Let $\mathcal{F}_1$ express that the above game does not abort in the query stage; $\mathcal{F}_2$ express the above game does not abort in the forgery stage; $\mathcal{F}_3$ express $\mathcal{A}_1$ generates two valid signatures δ_{i1}^* and δ_{i2}^*. Based on the above, we have $\Pr[\mathcal{F}_1] = \left(1 - \frac{1}{q_1+q_2+1}\right)^{q_1+q_2}$ and $\Pr[\mathcal{F}_2] = (\frac{1}{q_1+q_2+1})$. According to Forking lemma, the probability that $\mathcal{A}_1$ generates two valid signatures δ_{i1}^* and δ_{i2}^* is $\Pr[\mathcal{F}_3] \geq \left(1 - \frac{1}{e}\right)\frac{\varepsilon_1}{q_h}$. Then, we have $\Pr[\mathcal{F}_1 \wedge \mathcal{F}_2 \wedge \mathcal{F}_3] \geq \left(1 - \frac{1}{e}\right)\frac{\varepsilon_1}{e(q_1+q_2+1)q_h}$.

To sum up, if there exists a Type-I adversary $\mathcal{A}_1$ who can win Game 1 with advantage ε_1, then there exists a challenger $\mathcal{C}$ who can solve the hardness of DL problem with advantage $(1 - \frac{1}{e})\frac{\varepsilon_1}{e(q_1+q_2+1)q_h}$.

Theorem 2. *If there exists a Type-II adversary $\mathcal{A}_2$ who can win Game 2 in probability polynomial time, then there exists a challenger $\mathcal{C}$ who can solve the hardness of DL problem.*

The proof of the above theorem is similar to the proof of Theorem 1.

4 Conclusions

In this paper, we propose a new scheme and prove its security based on the hardness of DL problem. Through comprehensive comparison, it is pointed out that our proposal has high efficiency and unforgeability. Aggregated signatures effectively reduce the communication traffic for signature delivery and the verification overhead, enabling efficient batch authentication. Therefore, our solution is suitable for smart home environments for limited resources.

References

1. Al-Riyami, S.S., Paterson, K.G.: Certificateless public key cryptography. In: Laih, C.-S. (ed.) ASIACRYPT 2003. LNCS, vol. 2894, pp. 452–473. Springer, Heidelberg (2003). https://doi.org/10.1007/978-3-540-40061-5_29
2. Boneh, D., Gentry, C., Lynn, B., Shacham, H.: Aggregate and verifiably encrypted signatures from bilinear maps. In: Biham, E. (ed.) EUROCRYPT 2003. LNCS, vol. 2656, pp. 416–432. Springer, Heidelberg (2003). https://doi.org/10.1007/3-540-39200-9_26
3. Zheng Gong, Yu., Long, X.H., Chen, K.: Practical certificateless aggregate signatures from bilinear maps. J. Inf. Sci. Eng. **26**(6), 2093–2106 (2010)
4. Zhang, Y., Zhang, Y., Li, Y., Wang, C.: Strong designated verifier signature scheme resisting replay attack. Inform. Technol. Control **44**(2), 165–171 (2015)
5. Kumar, P., Kumari, S., Sharma, V., Li, X., Sangaiah, A.K., Islam, S.K.H.: Secure CLS and CL-AS schemes designed for VANETs. J. Supercomput. **75**(6), 3076–3098 (2018). https://doi.org/10.1007/s11227-018-2312-y
6. Kumar, P., Kumari, S., Sharma, V., Sangaiah, A.K., Wei, J., Li, X.: A certificateless aggregate signature scheme for healthcare wireless sensor network. Sustain. Comput.: Inform. Syst. **18**, 80–89 (2018)
7. Wu, L., Xu, Z., He, D., Wang, X.: New certificateless aggregate signature scheme for healthcare multimedia social network on cloud environment. Security Commun. Netw. **2018** (2018)
8. Kamil, I.A., Ogundoyin, S.O.: An improved certificateless aggregate signature scheme without bilinear pairings for vehicular ad hoc networks. J. Inform. Secur. Appl. **44**, 184–200 (2019)
9. Zhao, Y., Hou, Y., Wang, L., Kumari, S., Khan, M.K., Xiong, H.: An efficient certificateless aggregate signature scheme for the internet of vehicles. Trans. Emerg. Telecommun. Technol. **31**(5), e3708 (2020)
10. Gayathri, N.B., Thumbur, G., Kumar, P.R., Rahman, M.Z.U., Reddy, P.V.: Efficient and secure pairing-free certificateless aggregate signature scheme for healthcare wireless medical sensor networks. IEEE Internet Things J. **6**(5), 9064–9075 (2019)
11. Liu, J., Wang, L., Yong, Yu.: Improved security of a pairing-free certificateless aggregate signature in healthcare wireless medical sensor networks. IEEE Internet Things J. **7**(6), 5256–5266 (2020)
12. Gong, Z., Gao, T., Guo, N.: Pcas: Cryptanalysis and improvement of pairing-free certificateless aggregate signature scheme with conditional privacy-preserving for vanets. Ad Hoc Networks, p. 103134 (2023)

13. Yang, X., Wen, H., Diao, R., Du, X., Wang, C.: Improved security of a pairing-free certificateless aggregate signature in healthcare wireless medical sensor networks. IEEE Internet of Things Journal (2023)
14. Zhan, Yu., Wang, B., Rongxing, L.: Cryptanalysis and improvement of a pairing-free certificateless aggregate signature in healthcare wireless medical sensor networks. IEEE Internet Things J. **8**(7), 5973–5984 (2021)
15. Qiao, Z., Yang, Q., Zhou, Y., Zhang, M.: Improved secure transaction scheme with certificateless cryptographic primitives for Iot-based mobile payments. IEEE Syst. J. **16**(2), 1842–1850 (2021)

Constant-Size Group Signatures with Message-Dependent Opening from Lattices

Simin Chen[1], Jiageng Chen[1(✉)], Atsuko Miyaji[2], and Kaiming Chen[2]

[1] School of Computer Science, Central China Normal University, Wuhan, China
chinkako@gmail.com

[2] Graduate School of Engineering, Osaka University, Osaka, Japan

Abstract. Group signatures allow users to sign messages on behalf of the group without prevealing their identities. However, the opening authority can trace signatures back to their source, raising concerns about privacy. To address this issue, Sakai *et al.* proposed a cryptographic primitive called Group Signature with Message-Dependent Opening (GS-MDO), which balances privacy and traceability. Libert et al. introduced GS-MDO using lattices, but the scheme's signature sizes vary with the number of group users. In this paper, we present the first constant-size group signature with message-dependent opening using lattices. Our scheme's signature, public key, and secret key sizes are reduced to $\widetilde{\mathcal{O}}(\lambda)$, and are independent of the number of group users.

Keywords: Lattice-Based Cryptography · Group Signature · Message-dependent Opening

1 Introduction

Group signature. Group signature is a fundamental cryptographic primitive proposed by Chaum *et al.* [9] in 1991, which enables users to sign messages on behalf of a group while preserving anonymity. To prevent abuse by anonymous group users, the opening authority can identify the user who generated the signature using the opening key [1]. However, this power has been criticized as excessive since it allows the authority to trace any well-behaved user. To address this issue, Sakai *et al.* [37] proposed a privacy-preserving extension called *Group Signature with Message-Dependent Opening* (GS-MDO). The scheme employs two distinct authorities: the opening authority and the admitter, who need to work in tandem to trace signatures. To reveal a signature, the admitter creates a message-specific token and shares it with the opening authority. The opening authority, in turn, utilizes the token and the opening key to expose the signature. It is worth noting that the admitter's consent is mandatory for each opening operation. It is not feasible for the admitter to trace the signature independently, as it lacks the opening key.

M. Zhang et al. (Eds.): ProvSec 2023, LNCS 14217, pp. 166–185, 2023.
https://doi.org/10.1007/978-3-031-45513-1_10

Many previous group signature schemes suffered from the drawback that their signature sizes or public key sizes depended on the number of group users. However, this disadvantage was addressed by Camenisch and Stadelr [6] who proposed a group signature scheme that was independent of the group size. Several other schemes [5,15,23] also have constant signature sizes, meaning that the signature sizes are determined only by the security parameters. However, it is worth noting that these schemes are not quantum-resistant.

LATTICE-BASED CRYPTOGRAPHY. Lattice-based cryptography has received significant attention since the pioneering contributions of Regev [35] and Gentry *et al.* [12]. Lattices offer several advantages over conventional number-theoretic cryptography, including conjectured security against quantum attacks, faster and more efficient arithmetic operations, and strong security guarantees based on worst-case hardness. Furthermore, lattices allow for the construction of versatile and powerful cryptographic primitives [11,13,39,42] that are difficult to implement in traditional cryptography. In this paper, we investigate the constant-size group signature with message-dependent opening (GS-MDO) based on lattices.

RELATED WORKS. In 2010, Gordon *et al.* [14] constructed the first lattice-based group signature based on *Learning With Errors* (LWE). However, the signature sizes of this scheme were linearly related to the number of group users, resulting in an increase in signature sizes as the number of group users increased. Later, Laguillaumie *et al.* [17] proposed a solution where the signature size grew logarithmically with the group size. Subsequently, Nguyen *et al.* [32] and Ling *et al.* [25] proposed more efficient solutions with parameter size $\mathcal{O}(\log N)$. Libert *et al.* [21] eliminated the need for GPV trapdoor [12] and improved efficiency via the Merkle hash tree. Ling *et al.* [27] proposed the first constant-size group signature whose size is only $\mathcal{O}(\lambda)$ (λ is the security parameter). Luo *et al.* [28] presented a constant-size group signature scheme, which followed the sign-hybrid-encrypt protocol and employed the Lyubashevsky signature scheme. In 2020, Canard *et al.* [7] gave a forward-secure group signature in the standard model with a constant signature size in group size N. However, the schemes mentioned above do not effectively address the enrollment and revocation of group members. To address these issues, Sahin *et al.* [36] proposed a constant-size group signature that only allows for the enrollment of new users into the group.

The message-dependent opening functionality was introduced by Sakai *et al.* [37] in 2012. Their scheme implied identity-based encryption [3,38]. To improve the efficiency, Ohara *et al.* [33] developed the GS-MDO scheme under the random oracle model. Libert and Joye [18] employed bilinear maps and Groth-Sahai proof systems [16] to construct the GS-MDO scheme based on complexity assumptions. Soon later, Libert *et al.* [22] proposed the first GS-MDO based on lattices, which combined Ling-Nguyen-Wang group signature [25] with Gentry-Peikert-Vaikuntanathan (GPV) identity-based encryption [12]. His scheme generated secret keys for users by a variant of Boyen signature [30]. In 2019, Emura *et al.* [10] presented formal definitions and constructions. Recently, Sun [41] presented a full dynamic GS-MDO from lattice, which combined the group signature by Ling [26] and double encryption paradigm [8]. And this scheme had a smaller soundness error than Libert's scheme which employed the Stern-like protocol [40]. However, this paper required an interaction between the group member and the admitter in the signing process, which does not match the usual definition of group signatures. And the signature size is still dependent of ℓ.

Our Contribution. We propose the first constant-size group signature with message-dependent opening from lattices (CSGS-MDO). Our scheme differs from previous works with message-dependent opening from lattices in that our signature size, public key size, and signer's secret key size are of order $\widetilde{\mathcal{O}}(\lambda)$, which does not increase as the number of group members increase. Our scheme is constant-size because we do not need to set the size of the group during the set-up phase, while others do. In previous works, one has to fix the group member N for security reduction or functional reasons. Table 1 is the comparison between our scheme and other schemes.

Table 1. Comparison of lattice-based schemes, based on their efficiencies and functionalities. $N = 2^\ell$ is the maximum number of group members and λ is the security parameter.

Schemes	Group PK size	Signer's SK size	Signature size	Dynamical	MDO
(Libert *et al.* 2016 [19])	$\widetilde{\mathcal{O}}(\lambda^2 \cdot \ell)$	$\widetilde{\mathcal{O}}(\lambda)$	$\widetilde{\mathcal{O}}(\lambda \cdot \ell)$	partially	no
(Libert *et al.* 2016 [22])	$\widetilde{\mathcal{O}}(\lambda^2 \cdot \ell)$	$\widetilde{\mathcal{O}}(\lambda)$	$\widetilde{\mathcal{O}}(\lambda \cdot \ell)$	static	yes
(Ling *et al.* 2017 [26])	$\widetilde{\mathcal{O}}(\lambda^2 + \lambda \cdot \ell)$	$\widetilde{\mathcal{O}}(\lambda) + \ell$	$\widetilde{\mathcal{O}}(\lambda \cdot \ell)$	fully	no
(Ling *et al.* 2018 [27])	$\widetilde{\mathcal{O}}(\lambda)$	$\widetilde{\mathcal{O}}(\lambda)$	$\widetilde{\mathcal{O}}(\lambda)$	partially	no
(Sun *et al.* 2021 [41])	$\widetilde{\mathcal{O}}(\lambda^2)$	$\widetilde{\mathcal{O}}(\lambda) + \ell$	$\widetilde{\mathcal{O}}(\lambda^2 \cdot \ell)$	fully	yes
Ours	$\widetilde{\mathcal{O}}(\lambda)$	$\widetilde{\mathcal{O}}(\lambda)$	$\widetilde{\mathcal{O}}(\lambda)$	partially	yes

† A scheme is classified as fully dynamical if it can both enroll and revoke members from a group. In contrast, a partially dynamical scheme is capable of enrolling members, but not revoking them. Lastly, a static scheme denotes a system where the number of group members is predetermined and remains fixed over time.

Our scheme is proven to satisfy traceability, full anonymity, and non-frameability, based on the underlying assumptions of *Ring Learning With Errors* (RLWE) and the *Ring Short Integer Solution* (RSIS). To sign a message M, a user first encrypts their public key p twice, followed by encrypting one of the ciphertexts using the Identity-Based Encryption (IBE) [12], achieving message-dependent opening. Subsequently, the user provides a Zero-Knowledge Argument of knowledge(ZKAoK), certifying that he is a legitimate group user and that they have encrypted the corresponding message accurately. The message-specific token t_M serves as the secret key of the second encryption. Upon receiving t_M, the open authority can disclose the signature of message M. To prove these statements, we translate these into the form $\mathbf{M} \cdot \mathbf{w} = \mathbf{u} \bmod q$. To achieve a shorter signature size, we also employ the refined technique that Ling *et al.* [27] first proposed in this process.

Organization. In Sect. 2, we provide a review of pertinent definitions and security assumptions. The supporting ZKAoK is designed in Sect. 3, while Sect. 4 presents the constant-size GS-MDO based on the lattice scheme. In Sect. 5, we analyze our scheme from three aspects: security, correctness, and efficiency. Finally, the conclusion of our group signature is presented in Sect. 6.

2 Background

NOTATIONS. Bold upper-case letters $\mathbf{A}$ represent matrices and bold lower-case letters $\mathbf{x}$ represent vectors. $(\mathbf{x} \| \mathbf{y}) \in \mathbb{R}^{m+k}$ which represents the concatenation of column vectors $\mathbf{x} \in \mathbb{R}^m$ and $\mathbf{y} \in \mathbb{R}^k$. $[\mathbf{A} | \mathbf{B}]$ is the column concatenation of matrices $\mathbf{A} \in \mathbb{R}^{n \times k}$ and $\mathbf{B} \in \mathbb{R}^{n \times m}$. Define $[n]$ as the set $\{1, ..., n\}$. $x \xleftarrow{\$} S$ means that uniformly randomly sample x from S, where S is a finite set.

2.1 Decompositions

In this subsection, we recall the protocol from [24] which we will employ in the underlying zero-knowledge argument system. In our paper, we will employ the decomposistion procedure when working with polynomials in the ring R_q. For any positive integer B, we define $\delta_B := \lfloor \log_2 B \rfloor + 1 = \lceil \log_2(B+1) \rceil$ and the sequence $B_1, ..., B_{\delta_B}$, where $B_i = \left\lfloor \frac{B+2^{i-1}}{2^i} \right\rfloor$ for $i \in [1, \delta_B]$. As indicated in [24], this sequence satisfies the equation: $\sum_{i=1}^{\delta_B} B_i = B$. For any integer $w \in [0, B]$, it can be expressed as $\mathbf{idec}_B(w) = (w^{(1)}, ..., w^{(\delta_B)})^{\mathrm{T}} \in \{0,1\}^{\delta_B}$ such that $\sum_{i=1}^{\delta_B} B_i \cdot w^{(i)} = w$.

In particular, when we work with the ring element in R_q, for any positive integer B, we use an injective function $\mathbf{redc}_B$ that maps $b \in R_q$ to $\mathbf{b} \in R^{\delta_B}$ where $\|b\|_\infty \leq B$ and $\|\mathbf{b}\|_\infty \leq 1$. The following describes how this works.

1. Let $\tau(b) = (b_0, ..., b_{n-1})^{\mathrm{T}}$. For each j, if $b_j = 0$ let $\sigma(b_j) = 0$; If $b_j > 0$ let $\sigma(b_j) = 1$; Otherwise, let $\sigma(b_j) = -1$.
2. $\forall j$, compute $\mathbf{v}_j = \sigma(b_j) \cdot \mathbf{idec}_B(|b_j|) = (\mathbf{v}_{j,1}, ..., \mathbf{v}_{j,\delta_B})^{\mathrm{T}} \in \{-1,0,1\}^{\delta_B}$.
3. We set the vector $\mathbf{v} = (\mathbf{v}_0 \| ... \| \mathbf{v}_{n-1}) \in \{-1,0,1\}^{n\delta_B}$, and compute $\mathbf{b} \in R^{\delta_B}$ such that $\tau(\mathbf{b}) = \mathbf{v}$.
4. Output $\mathbf{redc}_B(b) = \mathbf{b}$.

For any $\mathbf{w} = (w_1, ..., w_m)^{\mathrm{T}}$ such that $\|\mathbf{w}\|_\infty \leq B$, let $\mathbf{redc}_B(\mathbf{w}) = (\mathbf{redc}_B(w_1) \| ... \| \mathbf{redc}_B(w_m)) \in R^{m\delta_B}$. For positive integers m, B, the matrices $\mathbf{H}_B \in \mathbb{Z}^{n \times n\delta_B}$ and $\mathbf{H}_{m,B} \in \mathbb{Z}^{nm \times nm\delta_B}$ can be defined as follows.

$$\mathbf{H}_B = \begin{bmatrix} B_1 \dots B_{\delta_B} & & \\ & \ddots & \\ & & B_1 \dots B_{\delta_B} \end{bmatrix} \quad \text{and} \quad \mathbf{H}_{m,B} = \begin{bmatrix} \mathbf{H}_B & & \\ & \ddots & \\ & & \mathbf{H}_B \end{bmatrix}.$$

Then the following equations hold that $\tau(b) = \mathbf{H}_B \cdot \tau(\mathbf{redc}_B(b)) \bmod q$ and $\tau(\mathbf{w}) = \mathbf{H}_{m,B} \cdot \tau(\mathbf{redc}_B(\mathbf{w}))$.

Specially, If $B = \frac{q-1}{2}$, we replace $\mathbf{redc}_{\frac{q-1}{2}}$ with $\mathbf{redc}$, and replace $\mathbf{H}_{\frac{q-1}{2}}$ with $\mathbf{H}$.

2.2 Lattice Problems

Let q and $\mathbb{Z}_q$ be a prime and $[-\frac{q-1}{2}, \frac{q-1}{2}]$ respectively. We set the ring $R = \mathbb{Z}[X]/(X^n+1)$ and $R_q = (R/qR)$, where n is a power of 2. For $a = a_0 + a_1 \cdot X + ... + a_{n-1} \cdot X^{N-1} \in R$, we define $\|a\|_\infty = \max_i(|a_i|)$. We set $\|\mathbf{b}\|_\infty = \max_j(\|b_j\|_\infty)$ where $\mathbf{b} = (b_1, ..., b_m)^{\mathrm{T}}$.

We recall $\tau : R_q \to \mathbb{Z}_q^n$ that maps ring element $w = w_0 + w_1 \cdot X + ... + w_{n-1} \cdot X^{N-1} \in R_q$ to vector $\tau(w) = (w_0, w_1, ...w_{n-1})^{\mathrm{T}} \in \mathbb{Z}_q^n$ and $\mathsf{rot} : R_q \to \mathbb{Z}_q^{n\times n}$ that maps $b \in R_q$ to matrix $\mathsf{rot}(b) = [\tau(b) \,|\tau(b \cdot X)|... \,|\tau(b \cdot X^{n-1})] \in \mathbb{Z}_q^{n\times n}$. If $y = b \cdot w$ over R_q is true, then $\tau(y) = \mathsf{rot}(b) \cdot \tau(w) \bmod q$ is true.

If $\mathbf{B} = [b_1 |... |b_m] \in R_q^{1\times m}$, then we denote by $\mathsf{rot}(\mathrm{B})$ the matrix $\mathsf{rot}(\mathsf{B}) = [\mathbf{rot}(b_1) |... |\mathsf{rot}(b_m)] \in \mathbb{Z}_q^{n\times mn}$. If $\mathbf{w} = (w_1, ..., w_m)^{\mathrm{T}} \in R_q^m$, then we let $\tau(w) = (\tau(w_1) \|...\| \tau(w_m)) \in \mathbb{Z}_q^{mn}$. And if $y = \mathbf{B} \cdot \mathbf{w}$ over R_q is true, then $\tau(y) = \mathsf{rot}(\mathbf{B}) \cdot \tau(\mathbf{w}) \bmod q$ is true.

Definition 1 ([25,34]). *Let m and β be functions of a parameter n. Given a uniformly random $\mathbf{A} = [a_1 |... |a_m] \in R_q^{1\times m}$, The $\mathsf{RSIS}_{n,m,q,\beta}$ problem is to find a non-zero vector $\mathbf{w} = (w_1, ..., w_m)^{\mathrm{T}} \in R^m$ such that $\|\mathbf{w}\|_\infty \leq \beta$ and $\mathbf{A} \cdot \mathbf{w} = a_1 \cdot w_1 + ... + a_m \cdot w_m = 0$.*

For $m > \frac{\log q}{\log(2\beta)}$, $\gamma = 16\beta mn\log^2 n$, and $q \geq \frac{\gamma\sqrt{n}}{4\log n}$, the $\mathsf{RSIS}_{n,m,q,\beta}$ problem is at least as hard as $\mathsf{SVP}_\gamma^\infty$.

Definition 2 ([29]). *Let n and $m \geq 1$. Define a distribution $A_{\mathbf{s},\chi}$ for $\mathbf{s} \in R_q^n$ over $R_q^n \times R_q$ as follows: it outputs a pair $(\mathbf{a}, b = \mathbf{a}^\top \cdot \mathbf{s} + e) \in R_q^n \times R_q$ where $\mathbf{a} \xleftarrow{\$} R_q^n$ and $e \leftarrow \chi$. The decision $\mathsf{LWE}_{n,m,q,\chi}$ problem is to distinguish m samples $(\mathbf{a}, b = \mathbf{a}^\top \cdot \mathbf{s} + e) \in R_q^n \times R_q$, which are from the distribution $A_{\mathbf{s},\chi}$ for the secret $\mathbf{s} \in R_q^n$, and from the uniform distribution in $R_q^n \times R_q$.*

Let $q = \mathsf{poly}(n)$ be a prime power, $B = \tilde{\mathcal{O}}(n^{5/4})$, and χ be a B-bounded distribution on R, then for $\gamma = n^2(q/B)(nm/\log(nm))^{1/4}$, the $\mathsf{LWE}_{n,m,q,\chi}$ problem is at least as hard as $\mathsf{SVP}_\gamma^\infty$.

2.3 Constant-Size Group Signature with Message-Dependent Opening from Lattices

A partially dynamic GS-MDO from lattices scheme consists of a tuple of algorithms, which we employ the definitions of Libert *et al.* [22]:

Keygen(λ): The algorithm produces four important keys: the group public key gpk, the issuer key ik, the opening key ok, and the admitter's private key msk. Upon receipt of the issuer key, the issuer initializes the internal state S to zero and creates the registration table **reg**.

Join: The proposed algorithm involves an interaction between the issuer and a user seeking to become a member of the group. Upon successful completion of the protocol, the user is granted membership and obtains its secret key, while the issuer updates the registration table by adding the user's public key to the entry **reg**[S+1] and incrementing the internal state S by one.

Sign(gpk, gsk, M): A group member signs the message M by running this algorithm. The algorithm outputs a signature Σ of the message M.

Verify(gpk, M, Σ): Given a set of input variables, the algorithm verifies the validity of a signature with respect to a message M. If the verification is successful, the output is 1. Otherwise, the output is 0.

TrapGen(gpk, msk, M): The admitter operates this algorithm, generating a message-specific token t_M of the message M.

Open(gpk, ok, t_M, **reg**, M, Σ): Given a set of input variables, the opener operates this algorithm to obtain a pair (p', Π_{open}). If p' is not included in **reg**, return $(\perp, \perp)$. Otherwise,return (p', Π_{open}).

Judge(gpk, M, Σ, p', Π_{open}): This algorithm verifies that Π_{open} is a proof that group member p' generated Σ.

In order to establish the correctness and security of this scheme, we begin by expanding upon the oracles available to the adversary as defined by Bellare et al. [1].

AddU(i): Add an honest user into the group and return the user public key upk.

CruptU(i, upk_i): An adversary is able to corrupt a user by using this oracle. The adversary can choose the upk_i as the user's public key.

SndToI(i, M_{in}): In this oracle, the adversary interacts with an honest issuer as a user i. If this oracle is completed, M_{out} is returned to the adversary and the registration information is stored in **reg**[i].

SndToU(i, M_{in}): In this oracle, the adversary interacts with a legitimate user i as the issuer. If this oracle is completed, M_{out} is returned to the adversary and $\mathbf{gsk}_i$ is stored.

RevealU(i): This oracle returns the secret key $\mathbf{gsk}_i$ of user i to the adversary.

RReg(i): This oracle returns the registration information **reg**[i] to the adversary.

WReg(i, ρ): The adversary is able to change the registration information **reg**[i] by any string ρ.

QSign(i, M): The adversary is able to query the signature of message M, if user i is an honest user and $\mathbf{gsk}_i$ is defined.

Ch$_b(i_0, i_1, M)$: The adversary inputs (i_0, i_1, M), then this oracle outputs a signature Σ on message M by using the secret key $\mathbf{gsk}_{i_b}$ and stores (M, Σ) in CL.

QTrapGen(M): Return the message token t_M of message M.

QOpen(M, Σ): The adversary is able to trace the signature Σ, if CL does not include (M, Σ).

A partially dynamic group signature must need to verify traceability, non-frameability, and anonymity. Since there are two entities towards opening capability, therefore we define the two definitions of anonymity towards the admitter and the opener. Following the approach proposed by Ling et al. [27], we provide formal definitions for both types of anonymity in Fig. 1.

Definition 3. *The experiments for correctness and security, as defined in Figure 1, apply to any polynomial-time (*PPT*) adversary $\mathcal{A}$ and any value of λ.*

For anonymity against admitter, the advantage is defined as

$$\mathbf{Adv}_{\mathcal{A}}^{anon\text{-}adm}(\lambda) = \left|\Pr\left[\mathbf{Exp}_{\mathcal{A}}^{anon\text{-}adm\text{-}0}(\lambda) = 1\right] - 1/2\right|.$$

And for anonymity against opener, the advantage is defined as

$$\mathbf{Adv}_{\mathcal{A}}^{anon\text{-}oa}(\lambda) = \left|\Pr\left[\mathbf{Exp}_{\mathcal{A}}^{anon\text{-}oa\text{-}0}(\lambda) = 1\right] - 1/2\right|.$$

For other properties: correctness, traceability, and non-frameability, the advantage is the probability of outputting 1 *in the corresponding experiments. If all the advantages are negligible, then the above group signature scheme satisfies the above properties.*

2.4 Stern-Like Protocols for Lattices

The statistical ZKAoK utilized in our scheme is based on the Stern-like protocols [40] proposed by Stern in 1996. They are $\Sigma-$protocols in the generalized sense defined in [2,16], and they require three valid transcripts for extraction as opposed to the usual two. To understand Stern's protocol, it is helpful to first consider its abstract representation.

Let $L, D, q > 1$ be integers and $L \geq D$. VALID is defined as a subset of $\{-1, 0, 1\}^L$. Suppose that S_L is the symmetric group of all permutations of L elements, satisfying the following condition:

$$\pi \in S_L, \mathbf{x} \in \mathsf{VALID} \iff \pi(\mathbf{x}) \in \mathsf{VALID}. \tag{1}$$

If $\mathbf{x} \in \mathsf{VALID}$ and π is uniform in S_L, then $\pi(\mathbf{x})$ is also uniform in VALID. Our objective is to create a sZKAoK for the given relation.

$$R_{abstract} = \{(\mathbf{A}, \mathbf{u}), \mathbf{x} \in \mathbb{Z}_q^{D\times L} \times \mathbb{Z}_q^D \times \mathsf{VALID} : \mathbf{A} \cdot \mathbf{x} = \mathbf{u} \; mod \; q.\}$$

The conditions (1) is critical to proving that $\mathbf{x} \in \mathsf{VALID}$ in ZK: First $\mathcal{P}$ samples $\pi \xleftarrow{\$} S_L$ and sends $\pi(\mathbf{x})$ to $\mathcal{V}$. Then $\mathcal{V}$ checks that $\pi(\mathbf{x}) \in \mathsf{VALID}$. As a result of the randomized nature of π, $\mathcal{V}$ is unable to acquire any supplementary information regarding $\mathbf{x}$. Moreover, to verify the validity of the equation, $\mathcal{P}$ initially generates

$\underline{\mathbf{Exp}_{\mathcal{A}}^{corr}(\lambda)}$
$(\mathsf{gpk}, \mathsf{ik}, \mathsf{ok}, \mathsf{msk}) \leftarrow \mathbf{Keygen}(\lambda)$; CU $\leftarrow \emptyset$; HU$\leftarrow \emptyset$
$(i, M) \leftarrow \mathcal{A}(\mathsf{gpk} : \mathbf{AddU}, \mathbf{RReg})$
If $i \notin$HU then return 0; If $\mathsf{gsk}_i = \epsilon$ then return 0
$\Sigma \leftarrow \mathbf{Sign}(\mathsf{gpk}, \mathsf{gsk}_i, M)$; If $\mathbf{Verify}(\mathbf{gpk}, M, \Sigma) = 0$ then return 1
$(j, \Pi_{open}) \leftarrow \mathbf{Open}(\mathsf{gpk}, \mathsf{ok}, t_M, \mathbf{reg}, M, \Sigma)$; If $j \neq i$ then return 1
If $\mathbf{Judge}(\mathsf{gpk}, M, \Sigma, i, \mathbf{upk}_i, \Pi_{open})$ then return 1 else return 0

$\underline{\mathbf{Exp}_{\mathcal{A}}^{trace}(\lambda)}$
$(\mathsf{gpk}, \mathsf{ik}, \mathsf{ok}, \mathsf{msk}) \leftarrow \mathbf{Keygen}(\lambda)$;CU $\leftarrow \emptyset$; HU$\leftarrow \emptyset$; $SL \leftarrow \emptyset$
$(M, \Sigma) \leftarrow \mathcal{A}(\mathsf{gpk}, \mathsf{ok}, \mathsf{msk} : \mathbf{SndTol}, \mathbf{AddU}, \mathbf{RReg}, \mathbf{RevealU}, \mathbf{CruptU})$
If $\mathbf{Verify}(\mathsf{gpk}, M, \Sigma) = 0$ then return 0
$(i, \Pi_{open}) \leftarrow \mathbf{Open}(\mathsf{gpk}, \mathsf{ok}, t_M, \mathbf{reg}, M, \Sigma)$
If $i = \perp$ or $\mathbf{Judge}(\mathsf{gpk}, M, \Sigma, i, \mathsf{upk}_i, \Pi_{open}) = 0$ then return 1 else return 0

$\underline{\mathbf{Exp}_{\mathcal{A}}^{nf}(\lambda)}$
$(\mathsf{gpk}, \mathsf{ik}, \mathsf{ok}, \mathsf{msk}) \leftarrow \mathbf{Keygen}(\lambda)$;CU $\leftarrow \emptyset$; HU$\leftarrow \emptyset$
$(M, \Sigma, i, \Pi_{open}) \leftarrow \mathcal{A}(\mathsf{gpk}, \mathsf{ok}, \mathsf{msk} : \mathbf{SndTol}, \mathbf{WReg}, \mathbf{Sign}, \mathbf{RevealU}, \mathbf{CruptU})$
$\mathbf{Verify}(\mathsf{gpk}, M, \Sigma) = 0$ then return 0;
if the following are all true then return 1 else return 0:

- $i \in$HU and $\mathsf{gsk}_i \notin \epsilon$ and $\mathbf{Judge}(\mathsf{gpk}, M, \Sigma, i, \mathsf{upk}_i, \Pi_{open}) = 1$
- $\mathcal{A}$ did not query $\mathbf{RevealU}(i)$ and $\mathbf{Sign}(i, M)$

$\underline{\mathbf{Exp}_{\mathcal{A}}^{anon-adm-b}(\lambda)}$ // $b \in \{0, 1\}$
$(\mathsf{gpk}, \mathsf{ik}, \mathsf{ok}, \mathsf{msk}) \leftarrow \mathbf{Keygen}(\lambda)$;CU $\leftarrow \emptyset$; HU$\leftarrow \emptyset$; $SL \leftarrow \emptyset$
$b' \leftarrow \mathcal{A}(\mathsf{gpk}, \mathsf{msk} : \mathbf{Ch}_b, \mathbf{QOpen}, \mathbf{SndTol}, \mathbf{WReg}, \mathbf{RevealU}, \mathbf{CruptU})$
Return b'

$\underline{\mathbf{Exp}_{\mathcal{A}}^{anon-op-b}(\lambda)}$ // $b \in \{0, 1\}$
$(\mathsf{gpk}, \mathsf{ik}, \mathsf{ok}, \mathsf{msk}) \leftarrow \mathbf{Keygen}(\lambda)$;CU $\leftarrow \emptyset$; HU$\leftarrow \emptyset$; $SL \leftarrow \emptyset$
$b' \leftarrow \mathcal{A}(\mathsf{gpk}, \mathsf{msk} : \mathbf{Ch}_b, \mathbf{QTrapGen}, \mathbf{SndTol}, \mathbf{WReg}, \mathbf{RevealU}, \mathbf{CruptU})$
Return b'

Fig. 1. Experiments to define correctness and security for our scheme.

a vector $\mathbf{r}_x \xleftarrow{\$} \mathbb{Z}_q^D$ to obscure $\mathbf{x}$. Then $\mathcal{P}$ sends the vector $\mathbf{y} = \mathbf{x} + \mathbf{r}_x$ to $\mathcal{V}$, and convinces $\mathcal{V}$ that the equation $\mathbf{A} \cdot \mathbf{y} = \mathbf{A} \cdot \mathbf{r}_x + \mathbf{u}$ holds.

Due to the page limit, we omit the interaction between prover $\mathcal{P}$ and verifier $\mathcal{V}$. A statistically hiding and computationally binding string commitment scheme COM is employed in the protocol.

Theorem 1 ([19]). *The Stern-like protocol is a zero-knowledge argument of knowledge with statistical soundness and perfect completeness for the relation* $\mathsf{R}_{abstract}$. *The protocol has a soundness error of* $2/3$ *and a communication cost of* $\tilde{\mathcal{O}}(L \log q)$. *Specifically, the protocol includes simulators that can generate transcripts that are statistically indistinguishable from those produced by the actual prover when presented with the input* $(\mathbf{A}, \mathbf{u})$. *Additionally, there are knowledge extractors that can produce a valid output,* $\mathbf{x}' \in \mathsf{VALID}$, *satisfying the* *equation* $\mathbf{A} \cdot \mathbf{x}' = \mathbf{u} \bmod q$, *given a commitment* CMT *and three valid responses* $(\mathsf{RSP}_1, \mathsf{RSP}_2, \mathsf{RSP}_3)$ *to all* three *possible values of the challenge.*

3 The Underlying Zero-Knowledge Argument System

In this section, we outline the construction of our ZKAoK with statistical soundness. In our paper, the prover $\mathcal{P}$ aims to convince the verifier $\mathcal{V}$ of the following several facts.

1. He is a valid group member, in other word, he knows the triple $(t, \mathbf{v})$ which satisfies the following conditions:

$$\begin{cases} \mathbf{A}_t \cdot \mathbf{v} = p \\ \|\mathbf{v}\|_\infty \leq \beta. \end{cases} \tag{2}$$

   where $\mathbf{A}_t = \left[\mathbf{A} \middle| \mathbf{A}_{[0]} + \sum_{i=1}^{d} t_{[i]}\mathbf{A}_{[i]}\right] \in R_q^{1\times(\bar{m}+k)}$, $p \in R_q$, $\mathbf{v} \in R_q^{1\times(\bar{m}+k)}$, and $t_{[i]} = \sum_{j=c_{i-1}}^{c_i-1} t_j X^j \in R$.
2. He knows a secret key $\mathbf{x} \in R^m$ which satisfies

$$\begin{cases} \mathbf{B} \cdot \mathbf{x} = p, \\ \|\mathbf{x}\|_\infty \leq 1, \end{cases} \tag{3}$$

   where $p \in R_q$ and $\mathbf{B} \in R_q^{1\times m}$.
3. The vector $\mathbf{redc}(p) \in R^\ell$ is correctly encrypted and ciphertexts $(\mathbf{c}_{1,1}, \mathbf{c}_{1,2}, \mathbf{c}_{2,1}, \mathbf{c}_{2,2}) \in (R_q^\ell)^4$ are generated. Then prove that the following equations hold.

$$\mathbf{c}_{i,1} = \mathbf{b} \cdot g_i + \mathbf{e}_{i,1}, \mathbf{c}_{i,2} = \mathbf{a}_i \cdot g_i + e_{i,2} + \lfloor q/4 \rfloor \cdot \mathbf{rdec}(p)), \tag{4}$$

   hold for B-bounded randomness $g_1, g_2 \in R$, and $\mathbf{e}_{1,1}, \mathbf{e}_{2,1}, \mathbf{e}_{1,2}, \mathbf{e}_{2,2} \in R^\ell$.
4. $\mathbf{c}_{1,2}$ is also correctly encrypted and ciphertexts $(\mathbf{c}_{3,1}, \mathbf{c}_{3,2}) \in (R_q^k \times R_q^\ell)$ are generated. In the end, prove that the following equations hold.

$$\mathbf{c}_{3,1} = \mathbf{C}^\top \cdot \mathbf{g}_3 + \mathbf{e}_{3,1}, \mathbf{c}_{3,2} = \mathbf{G}^\top \cdot \mathbf{g}_3 + \mathbf{e}_{3,2} + \lfloor q/4 \rfloor \cdot \mathbf{c}_{1,2}, \tag{5}$$

   hold for B-bounded randomness $\mathbf{g}_3 \in R^m$, $\mathbf{e}_{3,1} \in R^k$, and $\mathbf{e}_{3,2} \in R^\ell$.

In the process, we will employ the refined permuting technique [27] and the integer decomposition technique from [24] to construct our zero-knowledge protocol.

3.1 Zero-Knowledge Protocol for the CSGS-MDO Scheme

Through the above protocol, we now transform equations (2,3,4,5) into a unified equation $\mathbf{M} \cdot \mathbf{w} = \mathbf{u} \bmod q$, where $\mathbf{M}$ and $\mathbf{u}$ are public, and the coefficients of vector $\mathbf{w}$ are in the set $\{-1, 0, 1\}$.

Firstly, let $\mathbf{v} = (\mathbf{v}_0|\mathbf{v}_1)$ where $\mathbf{v}_0 \in R_q^{\bar{m}}, \mathbf{v}_1 \in R_q^k$, $\mathbf{v}_0^* = \tau(\mathbf{redc}_\beta(\mathbf{v}_0)) \in \{-1, 0, 1\}^{n\bar{m}\delta_\beta}$, and $\mathbf{v}_1^* = \tau(\mathbf{redc}_\beta(\mathbf{v}_1)) \in \{-1, 0, 1\}^{nk\delta_\beta}$.

Then the equation (2) can be transformed into

$$\sum_{i=1}^{d} \sum_{j=c_{i-1}}^{c_i-1} \left[\mathbf{rot}(\mathbf{A}_{[i]} \cdot X^j) \cdot \mathbf{H}_{k,\beta}\right] \cdot t_j \cdot \mathbf{v}_1^* + \left[\mathbf{rot}(\mathbf{A}) \cdot \mathbf{H}_{\bar{m},\beta}\right] \cdot \mathbf{v}_0^* +$$

$$\left[\mathbf{rot}(\mathbf{A}_{[0]}) \cdot \mathbf{H}_{k,\beta}\right] \cdot \mathbf{v}_1^* - [\mathbf{H}] \cdot \tau(\mathbf{redc}(p)) = \mathbf{0}^n \bmod q.$$

Next, we transform equations (3), (4), and (5). Firstly, we let $\mathbf{x}^* = \tau(x) \in \{-1, 0, 1\}^{nm}$, $\mathbf{b} = (b_1, ..., b_\ell)^{\mathrm{T}}$ and $\mathbf{a}_i = (a_{i,1}, ..., a_{i,\ell})^{\mathrm{T}}$ with i in set $\{1, 2\}$. For $i \in \{1, 2\}$, compute $\mathbf{g}_i^* = \tau(\mathbf{redc}_B(g_i)) \in \{-1, 0, 1\}^{n\delta_B}$, $\mathbf{e}_{i,1}^* = \tau(\mathbf{redc}_B(\mathbf{e}_{i,1})) \in \{-1, 0, 1\}^{nl\delta_B}$ and $\mathbf{e}_{i,2}^* = \tau(\mathbf{redc}_B(\mathbf{e}_{i,2})) \in \{-1, 0, 1\}^{n\ell\delta_B}$. let $\mathbf{g}_3^* = \tau(\mathbf{redc}_B(\mathbf{g}_3)) \in \{-1, 0, 1\}^{nm\delta_B}$, $\mathbf{e}_{3,1}^* = \tau(\mathbf{redc}_B(\mathbf{e}_{3,1})) \in \{-1, 0, 1\}^{nk\delta_B}$, and $\mathbf{e}_{3,2}^* = \tau(\mathbf{redc}_B(\mathbf{e}_{3,2})) \in \{-1, 0, 1\}^{n\ell\delta_B}$.

Then the equation (3) can be transformed into

$$[\mathbf{rot}(\mathbf{B})] \cdot \mathbf{x}^* - [\mathbf{H}] \cdot \tau(\mathbf{redc}(p)) = \mathbf{0}^n \bmod q.$$

Meanwhile, the equations in (4) can be transformed into, for $i \in \{1, 2\}$,

$$\begin{bmatrix} \mathbf{rot}(b_1) \ldots \mathbf{H}_B \\ \vdots \\ \mathbf{rot}(b_\ell) \ldots \mathbf{H}_B \end{bmatrix} \cdot \mathbf{g}_i^* + [\mathbf{H}_{\ell,B}] \cdot \mathbf{e}_{i,1}^* = \tau(\mathbf{c}_{i,1}) \bmod q,$$

$$\begin{bmatrix} \mathbf{rot}(a_{1,1}) \ldots \mathbf{H}_B \\ \vdots \\ \mathbf{rot}(a_{1,\ell}) \ldots \mathbf{H}_B \end{bmatrix} \cdot \mathbf{g}_1^* + [\mathbf{H}_{\ell,B}] \cdot \mathbf{e}_{1,2}^* + \lfloor q/4 \rfloor \cdot \tau(\mathbf{redc}(p)) - \tau(\mathbf{c}_{1,2}) = \mathbf{0}^{n\ell} \bmod q,$$

and

$$\begin{bmatrix} \mathbf{rot}(a_{2,1}) \ldots \mathbf{H}_B \\ \vdots \\ \mathbf{rot}(a_{2,\ell}) \ldots \mathbf{H}_B \end{bmatrix} \cdot \mathbf{g}_2^* + [\mathbf{H}_{\ell,B}] \cdot \mathbf{e}_{2,2}^* + \lfloor q/4 \rfloor \cdot \tau(\mathbf{redc}(p)) = \tau(\mathbf{c}_{2,2}) \bmod q.$$

Finally, for the equations (5), let $\hat{\mathbf{C}} = \mathbf{C}^\top$ and $\hat{\mathbf{G}} = \mathbf{G}^\top$, then we can transform them as follows:

$$\left[\mathbf{rot}(\hat{\mathbf{C}})\right] \cdot [\mathbf{H}_{m,B}] \cdot \mathbf{g}_3^* + [\mathbf{H}_{k,B}] \cdot \mathbf{e}_{3,1}^* = \tau(\mathbf{c}_{3,1}) \bmod q,$$

and

$$\left[\mathbf{rot}(\hat{\mathbf{G}})\right] \cdot [\mathbf{H}_{m,B}] \cdot \mathbf{g}_3^* + [\mathbf{H}_{\ell,B}] \cdot \mathbf{e}_{3,2}^* + \lfloor q/4 \rfloor \cdot \tau(\mathbf{c}_{1,2}) = \tau(\mathbf{c}_{3,2}) \bmod q;$$

Now, we concatenate the public matrices, rearrange the secret vectors and combine them. And we can get the following equation:

$$\mathbf{M}_0 \cdot \mathbf{w}_0 = \mathbf{u} \bmod q,$$

where $\mathbf{u} = (\mathbf{0}^n \| \mathbf{0}^n \| \mathbf{0}^n \| \tau(\mathbf{c}_{1,1}) \| \tau(\mathbf{c}_{2,1}) \| \mathbf{0}^{nl} \| \tau(\mathbf{c}_{2,2}) \| \tau(\mathbf{c}_{3,1}) \| \tau(\mathbf{c}_{3,2}))$ and $\mathbf{M}_0$ (namely, those written inside $[\cdot]$) are public, and $\mathbf{w}_0 = (\mathbf{w}_1 \| \mathbf{w}_2 \| \mathbf{w}_3)$, with

$$\begin{cases} \mathbf{w}_1 = (\mathbf{v}_1^* \| t_0 \cdot \mathbf{v}_1^* \| \cdots \| t_{c_d-1} \cdot \mathbf{v}_1^*) \in \{-1,0,1\}^{(k\delta_\beta + c_d k \delta_\beta)n}, \\ \mathbf{w}_2 = (\mathbf{v}_0^* \| \tau(\mathbf{redc}(p)) \| \mathbf{x}^* \| \mathbf{g}_1^* \| \mathbf{e}_{1,1}^* \| \mathbf{g}_2^* \| \mathbf{e}_{2,1}^* \| \mathbf{e}_{1,2}^*) \in \{-1,0,1\}^{nm+2n\delta_B+3n\ell\delta_B+n\ell+n\bar{m}\delta_\beta}, \\ \mathbf{w}_3 = (\tau(\mathbf{c}_{1,2}) \| \mathbf{e}_{2,2}^* \| \mathbf{g}_3^* \| \mathbf{e}_{3,1}^* \| \mathbf{e}_{3,2}^*) \in \{-1,0,1\}^{n\ell+nm\delta_B+nk\delta_B+2n\ell\delta_B}. \end{cases}$$

Since the coefficients in the $\mathbf{w}_1$ vector are closely relate, we need to extend the blocks of the vectors $\mathbf{w}_0 = (\mathbf{w}_1 \| \mathbf{w}_2 \| \mathbf{w}_3)$ through the refined permuting technique [27].

For $x \in \{-1,0,1\}$, $\mathbf{enc}(x) = ([x+1]_3, [x]_3, [x-1]_3) \in \{-1,0,1\}^3$ where $[x]_3$ be the integer $x' \in \{-1,0,1\}$ such that $x' = x \bmod 3$. For $\mathbf{x} \in \{-1,0,1\}^\ell$, $\mathbf{enc}(\mathbf{x}) = (\mathbf{enc}(x_1) \| \ldots \| \mathbf{enc}(x_n)) \in \{-1,0,1\}^{3n}$.

For any $k \in \{0,1\}$ and $x \in \{-1,0,1\}$, the vector $\mathbf{ext}(k,x) = \mathbf{ext}(k,x) = (\bar{k} \cdot [x+1]_3, k \cdot [x+1]_3, \bar{k} \cdot [x]_3, k \cdot [x]_3, \bar{k} \cdot [x-1]_3, k \cdot [x-1]_3)^{\mathrm{T}} \in \{-1,0,1\}^6$. The protocol defines the permutation Π_x where $\mathbf{x} = (x_1, \ldots, x_n)^{\mathrm{T}} \in \{-1,0,1\}^n$, which transforms vector $\mathbf{k} = (\mathbf{k}_1, \ldots, \mathbf{k}_n) \in \mathbb{Z}^{3n}$ which contains n blocks of size 3 into vector: $\Pi_v(\mathbf{k}) = (\pi_{x_1}(\mathbf{k}_1) \| \ldots \| \pi_{x_n}(\mathbf{k}_n))$.

The protocol also defines the permutation $\psi_{b,x}$ where $\mathbf{b} = (b_0, \ldots, b_{c_d-1})^{\mathrm{T}} \in \{0,1\}^{c_d}$ and $\mathbf{x} = (x_1, \ldots, x_n) \in \{-1,0,1\}^n$, which transforms vector

$$\mathbf{k} = (\mathbf{k}_{-1} \| \mathbf{k}_{0,1} \| \ldots \| \mathbf{k}_{0,n} \| \ldots \| \mathbf{k}_{c_d-1,1} \| \ldots \| \mathbf{k}_{c_d-1,n}) \in \mathbb{Z}^{3n+6nc_d}$$

into vector

$$\Psi_{\mathbf{b},\mathbf{x}}(\mathbf{k}) = (\Pi_{\mathbf{k}}(\mathbf{k}_{-1}) \| \psi_{b_0,x_1}(\mathbf{k}_{0,1}) \| \cdots \| \psi_{b_0,x_n}(\mathbf{k}_{0,n}) \| \cdots \| \psi_{b_{c_d-1},x_1}(\mathbf{k}_{c_d-1,1}) \| \cdots \| \psi_{b_{c_d-1},x_n}(\mathbf{k}_{c_d-1,n})).$$

Next, we will transform the equation $\mathbf{M}_0 \cdot \mathbf{w}_0 = \mathbf{u} \bmod q$ into an equation $\mathbf{M} \cdot \mathbf{w} = \mathbf{u} \bmod q$. We propose to make the secret key $\mathbf{w}$ comply with the abstract protocol's requirements.

$$\mathbf{w}_1 \mapsto \mathbf{w}_1{}' = \mathbf{mix}(t, \mathbf{v}_1^*) =$$

$$(\mathbf{enc}(\mathbf{v}_1^*) \| \mathbf{ext}(t_0, (v_{1,1}^*)) \| \cdots \| \mathbf{ext}(t_0, (v_{1,nk\delta_B}^*)) \| \cdots \| \mathbf{ext}(t_{c_d-1}, (v_{1,nk\delta_B}^*))) \in \{-1,0,1\}^{L_1};$$

$$\mathbf{w}_2 \mapsto \mathbf{w}_2{}' = \mathbf{enc}(\mathbf{w}_2) \in \{-1,0,1\}^{L_2};$$

$$\mathbf{w}_3 \mapsto \mathbf{w}_3{}' = \mathbf{enc}(\mathbf{w}_3) \in \{-1,0,1\}^{L_3}.$$

Then, we let vector $\mathbf{w} = (\mathbf{w}_1' \| \mathbf{w}_2' \| \mathbf{w}_3') \in \{-1, 0, 1\}^L$, where

$$L = L_1 + L_2 + L_3; L_1 = 3nk\delta_\beta + 6nk\delta_\beta c_d;$$

$$L_2 = 3nm + 6n\delta_B + 9n\ell\delta_B + 3n\bar{m}\delta_\beta + 3n\ell;$$

$$L_3 = 3n\ell + 3nm\delta_B + 3nk\delta_B + 6n\ell\delta_B.$$

$$L = L_1 + L_2 + L_3; L_1 = 3nk\delta_\beta + 6nk\delta_\beta c_d;$$
$$L_2 = 3nm + 6n\delta_B + 9n\ell\delta_B + 3n\bar{m}\delta_\beta + 3n\ell;$$
$$L_3 = 3n\ell + 3nm\delta_B + 3nk\delta_B + 6n\ell\delta_B.$$

The matrix $\mathbf{M}$ is obtained by inserting zero-columns to matrix $\mathbf{M}_0$ in order to make $\mathbf{M} \cdot \mathbf{w} = \mathbf{M}_0 \cdot \mathbf{w}_0$. Now, we define the set VALID and the set S_L of all permutations of L elements such that the conditions in (1) hold.
VALID is defined as the set of all vectors $\mathbf{z}' = (\mathbf{z}_1' \| \mathbf{z}_2' \| \mathbf{z}_3') \in \{-1, 0, 1\}^L$, satisfying the following:

- There exist $t \in \{0, 1\}^{c_d}$ and $\mathbf{v}_1^* = \{-1, 0, 1\}^{nk\delta_\beta}$ such that $\mathbf{z}_1' = \mathbf{mix}(t, \mathbf{v}_1^*)$.
- There exists $\mathbf{w}_2 \in \{-1, 0, 1\}^{nm + 2n\delta_B + 3n\ell\delta_B + n\ell + n\bar{m}\delta_\beta}$ such that $\mathbf{z}_2' = \mathbf{enc}(\mathbf{w}_2)$.
- There exists $\mathbf{w}_3 \in \{-1, 0, 1\}^{n\ell + nm\delta_B + nk\delta_B + 2n\ell\delta_B}$ such that $\mathbf{z}_3' = \mathbf{enc}(\mathbf{w}_3)$.

Clearly, $\mathbf{w}$ is in the set of VALID. Now, we set $S_L = \{0, 1\}^{c_d} \times \{-1, 0, 1\}^{nk\delta_\beta} \times \{-1, 0, 1\}^{nm + 2n\delta_B + 3n\ell\delta_B + n\ell + n\bar{m}\delta_\beta} \times \{-1, 0, 1\}^{n\ell + nm\delta_B + nk\delta_B + 2n\ell\delta_B}$, for $\pi = (\mathbf{b}, \mathbf{e}, \mathbf{f}, \mathbf{h}) \in S_L$ and $\mathbf{z}^* = (\mathbf{z}_1 * \| \mathbf{z}_2^* \| \mathbf{z}_3^*) \in \mathbb{Z}^L$, where $\mathbf{z}_1^* \in \mathbb{Z}^{L_1}$, $\mathbf{z}_2^* \in \mathbb{Z}^{L_2}$ and $\mathbf{z}_3^* \in \mathbb{Z}^{L_3}$, we define $\pi(z^*) = (\Psi_{\mathbf{b},\mathbf{e}}(\mathbf{z}_1^*) \| \Pi_{\mathbf{f}}(\mathbf{z}_2^*) \| \Pi_{\mathbf{h}}(\mathbf{z}_3^*))$.

Therefore, the considered statement has been reduced to an instance of the abstract protocol described in Sect. 2.4.

Theorem 2 **([20]).** *The Stern-like protocol is a zero-knowledge argument of knowledge with statistical soundness and perfect completeness for the relation* $\mathsf{R}_{abstract}$. *The protocol has a soundness error of* $2/3$ *and a communication cost of* $\widetilde{\mathcal{O}}(L \log q)$. *Specifically, the protocol includes simulators that can generate transcripts that are statistically indistinguishable from those produced by the actual prover when presented with the input* $(\mathbf{M}, \mathbf{u})$. *Additionally, there are knowledge extractors that can produce a valid output,* $\mathbf{w}' \in \mathsf{VALID}$, *satisfying the equation* $\mathbf{M} \cdot \mathbf{w}' = \mathbf{u} \bmod q$, *given a commitment* CMT *and three valid responses* $(\mathsf{RSP}_1, \mathsf{RSP}_2, \mathsf{RSP}_3)$ *to all* three *possible values of the challenge.*

According to Sect. 2.4, the protocol has a perfect completeness and soundness error. It is worth mentioning that the communication cost is:

$$\mathcal{O}(L \cdot \log q) = \mathcal{O}(((3nk(\delta_\beta + 2\delta_\beta c_d) + 3n(m + 2\ell + (2 + m + k + \bar{m})\delta_B + 5\ell\delta_B)) \cdot \log q),$$

which is equal with $\mathcal{O}(n \cdot \log^4 n) = \widetilde{\mathcal{O}}(\lambda)$.

4 Scheme Construction

To enroll group members, we utilize a modified version of Boyen's signature [4]. The admitter secret key is used for generating the token t_M for message M. The issue key is the signing key which is used for enrolling group members. The opening key is used to trace the signature by one of the corresponding secret keys of two public keys.

To join the group, a user generates a secret key $\mathbf{x}$ and a public key p using matrix $\mathbf{B}$, and then interacts with the issuer to receive a Boyen's signature on his public key. Upon completion of this interaction, the user is enrolled in the group and receives the signature from the issuer. When a user signs a message M on behalf of the group, he first encrypts his public key p twice using the two public keys and then encrypts the resulting ciphertext using GPV-IBE. The user also generates a ZKAoK to prove the validity of his signature, the short vector corresponding to his public key, and that he computed the ciphertexts correctly. To open a signature of message M, the opener must first obtain the message token t_M from the admitter. The opener generates a NIZKAoK of correct opening Π_{open} to ensure the opening is legitimate, which is then verified by the judger. The opening result is only accepted if Π_{open} is a valid proof.

Let parameter $n = \mathcal{O}(\lambda)$ being a power of 2 and modulus $q = \widetilde{\mathcal{O}}(n^4)$, where $q = 3^k$ for some positive integer k, $\ell = \lfloor \log \frac{q-1}{2} \rfloor + 1$ and $\bar{m} = m + k$ where $m \geq 2\lceil \log q \rceil + 2$. let $\beta = \tilde{\mathcal{O}}(n)$ and $B = \tilde{\mathcal{O}}(n^{5/4})$ be integer bounds and χ be error distribution. Also let $d \geq \log_c(\omega(\log n))$ be an integer and $\{c_0, ..., c_d\}$ be a strictly increasing integer sequence, which $c_0 = 0$ and $c_i = \lfloor \alpha_0 c^i \rfloor$ for $i \in [d]$. Then we set $\mathcal{T}_i = \{0,1\}^{c_i}$ for $i \in [d]$. Let $t_{[i]} = (t_{c_{i-1}}, ..., t_{c_i - 1})^T$ for $t = (t_0, ..., t_{c_d - 1})^{\mathrm{T}} \in \mathcal{T}_d$. And we can get that $t = (t_{[1]} \| t_{[2]} \| ... \| t_{[d]})$. Set tag $t \in \mathcal{T}_d$ as $t(X) = \sum_{j=0}^{c_d - 1} t_j X^j \in R$ and $t_{[i]}$ as $t_{[i]}(X) = \sum_{j=c_{i-1}}^{c_i - 1} t_j X^j \in R$. The scheme is described in more detail below.

Keygen(λ): Steps involved in this algorithm are as follows:

1. Choose integer d and strictly increasing sequence of integers $c_0, ... c_d$. Then generate a verification key $\mathbf{A} \in R_q^{1\times\bar{m}}$; $\mathbf{A}_{[0]}, \mathbf{A}_{[1]}, ..., \mathbf{A}_{[d]} \in R_q^{1\times k}$;$\mathbf{F}_0 \in R_q^{1\times\bar{m}}$; $\mathbf{F}, \mathbf{F}_1 \in R_q^{1\times\ell}$; $u \in R_q$ and signing key $\mathbf{R} \in R_q^{m\times k}$ for Ducas's signature scheme.
2. Select collision-resistant hash functions $\mathcal{H} : \{0,1\}^* \to \{1,2,3\}^\kappa$ where $\kappa = \omega(\log \lambda)$ and $\mathcal{H}_1 : \{0,1\}^* \to R_q^{m\times\ell}$.
3. Let COM be a commitment scheme that has the following properties: statistically hiding and computationally binding.
4. Generate two encryption and decryption keys for Naor-Yung double-encryption mechanism [31], where the group manager will send any one of the decryption keys to the opener. Sample $s_1, s_2 \hookleftarrow \chi$, $\mathbf{e}_1, \mathbf{e}_2 \hookleftarrow \chi^\ell$, $\mathbf{b} \xleftarrow{\$} R_q^\ell$, and compute $\mathbf{a}_1 = \mathbf{b} \cdot s_1 + \mathbf{e}_1 \in R_q^\ell$, $\mathbf{a}_2 = \mathbf{b} \cdot s_2 + \mathbf{e}_2 \in R_q^\ell$.

5. Generate the matrix $\mathbf{C} \in R_q^{m\times k}$ with trapdoor basis $\mathbf{T_C} \in R_q^{k\times k}$ for GPV-IBE and generate the matrix $\mathbf{B} \in R_q^{1\times m}$. The trapdoor basis $\mathbf{T_C}$ is the secret key of the admitter, and the matrix $\mathbf{B}$ is the public parameter.
6. Output $\mathsf{gpk} = \{\mathbf{A}, \mathbf{A}_{[0]}, \mathbf{A}_{[1]}, ..., \mathbf{A}_{[d]}, \mathbf{C}, \mathbf{B}, u, \mathbf{b}, \mathbf{a}_1, \mathbf{a}_2\}$, $\mathsf{ik} = \mathbf{R}$, $\mathsf{ok} = (s_1, \mathbf{e}_1)$ and $\mathsf{msk} = \mathbf{T_C}$.

After receiving the ik, the issuer needs to initialize $S = 0$ and establish the registration table **reg**.

Join: The issuer and prospective user run the following interactive protocol:

1. User chooses the secret key $\mathbf{x} \in R^m$ and the coefficients of the secret key are in the set $\{-1, 0, 1\}$. Then the user computes his public key p using public parameter $\mathbf{B}$ such that $p = \mathbf{B} \cdot \mathbf{x}$.
2. When the issuer receives the registration from the user with $\mathsf{upk} = p$, he makes a verification to ensure p was not used by a registered user. If p is valid, the issuer performs the following steps. Choose the tag $t = (t_0, t_1, ...t_{c_d-1})^\top \in \mathcal{T}_d$, where $S = \sum_{j=0}^{c_d-1} 2^j \cdot t_j$, and compute $\mathbf{A}_t = \left[\mathbf{A} \middle| \mathbf{A}_{[0]} + \sum_{i=1}^{d} t_{[i]}\mathbf{A}_{[i]}\right] \in R_q^{1\times(\bar{m}+k)}$. Then use the signing key $\mathbf{R}$ to generate a short vector $\|\mathbf{v}\|_\infty \leq \beta$ such that $\mathbf{A}_t \cdot \mathbf{v} = p$. Then the signature of message p is $(t, \mathbf{v})$. The following equations are hold.
$$\begin{cases} \mathbf{A}_t \cdot \mathbf{v} = p, \\ \|\mathbf{v}\|_\infty \leq \beta. \end{cases}$$
Then the issuer sends the signature to the user. User sets his secret key as $\mathsf{gsk} = (\mathbf{x}, t, \mathbf{v})$. The issuer adds $\mathbf{reg}[S] = p$ into the registration table and updates S to $S + 1$.

Sign$(\mathsf{gpk}, \mathsf{gsk}, M)$: The group user uses his secret key to sign the message $M \in \{0,1\}^*$. And he executes the following algorithms:

1. The group user samples $g_1 \hookleftarrow \chi$, $g_2 \hookleftarrow \chi$, $\mathbf{e}_{1,1} \hookleftarrow \chi^\ell$, $\mathbf{e}_{2,1} \hookleftarrow \chi^\ell$, $\mathbf{e}_{2,2} \hookleftarrow \chi^\ell$, and $\mathbf{e}_{2,2} \hookleftarrow \chi^\ell$. Then encrypt $\mathbf{redc}(p) \in R_q^\ell$ to get ciphertexts $\mathbf{c}_i = (\mathbf{c}_{i,1}, \mathbf{c}_{i,2})$ for $i \in 1, 2$.
$$(\mathbf{c}_{i,1} = \mathbf{b} \cdot g_i + \mathbf{e}_{i,1}, \mathbf{c}_{i,2} = \mathbf{a}_i \cdot g_i + \mathbf{e}_{i,2} + \lfloor q/4 \rfloor \cdot \mathbf{rdec}(p)) \in R_q^\ell \times R_q^\ell.$$
2. The group user computes $\mathbf{G} = \mathcal{H}_1(M) \in R_q^{m\times\ell}$. Sample $\mathbf{g}_3 \hookleftarrow \chi^m$, $\mathbf{e}_{3,1} \hookleftarrow \chi^k$, and $\mathbf{e}_{3,2} \hookleftarrow \chi^\ell$, then encrypt $\mathbf{c}_{1,2}$.
$$\mathbf{c}_3 = (\mathbf{c}_{3,1}, \mathbf{c}_{3,2}) = (\mathbf{C}^\top \cdot \mathbf{g}_3 + \mathbf{e}_{3,1}, \mathbf{G}^\top \cdot \mathbf{g}_3 + \mathbf{e}_{3,2} + \lfloor q/4 \rfloor \cdot \mathbf{c}_{1,2}) \in R_q^k \times R_q^\ell.$$
3. The group user generates a NIZKAoK Π_{gs} to prove that he owns a tuple
$$\zeta = (\mathbf{x}, t, \mathbf{v}, p, g_1, g_2, \mathbf{g}_3, \mathbf{e}_{1,1}, \mathbf{e}_{2,1}, \mathbf{e}_{3,1}, \mathbf{e}_{1,2}, \mathbf{e}_{2,2}, \mathbf{e}_{3,2})$$
such that the condition from (2) hold, $\mathbf{c}_1$ and $\mathbf{c}_2$ are correct encryptions of $\mathbf{redc}(p)$, $\mathbf{c}_3$ is a correct encryption of $\mathbf{c}_{1,2}$ under the identity M, $\|\mathbf{x}\| \leq 1$, and $\mathbf{B} \cdot \mathbf{x} = p$.

To generate this, run the argument system in Sect. 3. To achieve negligible soundness error, the protocol is repeated $\kappa = \omega(\log \lambda)$ times. Employing the Fiat-Shamir heuristic makes the interactive system non-interactive, which gives $\Pi_{gs} = (\{\mathsf{CMT}_i\}_{i=1}^{\kappa}, \mathsf{CH}, \{\mathsf{RSP}_i\}_{i=1}^{\kappa})$ where $\mathsf{CH} = \mathcal{H}(M, \{\mathsf{CMT}_i\}_{i=1}^{\kappa}, \xi)$ with

$$\xi = (\mathbf{A}, \mathbf{A}_{[0]}, \mathbf{A}_{[1]}, ..., \mathbf{A}_{[d]}, \mathbf{C}, \mathbf{B}, \mathbf{G}, u, \mathbf{b}, \mathbf{a}_1, \mathbf{a}_2, \mathbf{c}_{1,1}, \mathbf{c}_2, \mathbf{c}_3).$$

4. The group user outputs the group signature $\Sigma = (\Pi_{gs}, \mathbf{c}_{1,1}, \mathbf{c}_2, \mathbf{c}_3)$.

Verify(gpk, M, Σ): This algorithm includes the following steps: parse $\Sigma = (\Pi_{gs}, \mathbf{c}_{1,1}, \mathbf{c}_2, \mathbf{c}_3)$. Verify that the proof Π_{gs} is valid, if not, return 0. Otherwise, return 1.

TrapGen(gpk, msk, M): This algorithm runs the following steps to generate a token for message M.

1. Answer as before if message M has already been asked.
2. Otherwise, use the trapdoor basis $\mathbf{T_C} \in R_q^{k\times k}$ to compute a small-norm matrix $\mathbf{E}_M \in R_q^{k\times \ell}$ such that $\mathbf{C} \cdot \mathbf{E}_M = \mathbf{G}$, where $\mathbf{G} = \mathcal{H}_1(M) \in R_q^{m\times \ell}$.
3. Set $t_M = \mathbf{E}_M$ and output the token t_M for message M.

Open(gpk, ok, t_M, **reg**, M, Σ): In this algorithm, the opener uses ok and t_M to open the signature Σ.

1. Use t_M to decrypt $\mathbf{c}_3 = (\mathbf{c}_{3,1}, \mathbf{c}_{3,2})$:

$$\mathbf{c}_{1,2} = \frac{(\mathbf{c}_{3,2} - {t_M}^{\top} \cdot \mathbf{c}_{3,1})}{\lfloor q/4 \rfloor}.$$

2. Use s_1 to decrypt $\mathbf{c}_1 = (\mathbf{c}_{1,1}, \mathbf{c}_{1,2})$:

$$\mathbf{p}'' = \frac{(\mathbf{c}_{1,2} - \mathbf{c}_{1,1} \cdot s_1)}{\lfloor q/4 \rfloor}.$$

3. For each coefficient of $\mathbf{p}''$,
   (a) If compared to -1 and 1, it is closer to 0, then round it to 0;
   (b) If compared to 0 and 1, it is closer to -1, then round it to -1;
   (c) If compared to -1 and 0, it is closer to 1, then round it to 1;
4. After rounding the coefficient of $\mathbf{p}''$, we set $\mathbf{p}''$ as $\mathbf{p}' \in R_q^{\ell}$ and we have $\tau(p') = \mathbf{H} \cdot \tau(\mathbf{p}')$ for $p' \in R_q$.
5. If the table **reg** does not include the registration information of p', then return $(\perp, \perp)$.
6. A NIZKAoK Π_{open} should be generated to prove that the opener owns a tuple $(s_1, \mathbf{e}_1, t_M, \mathbf{y}_1, \mathbf{y}_2) \in R_q \times R_q^{\ell} \times R_q^{k\times \ell} \times R_q^{\ell} \times R_q^{\ell}$.

$$\begin{cases} \|s_1\|_\infty \leq B; \|\mathbf{e}_1\|_\infty \leq B; \\ \|\mathbf{y}_1\|_\infty \leq \lceil q/10 \rceil; \|\mathbf{y}_2\|_\infty \leq \lceil q/10 \rceil; \\ \mathbf{b} \cdot s_1 + \mathbf{e}_1 = \mathbf{a}_1; \\ \mathbf{C} \cdot \mathbf{E}_M = \mathbf{G}; \\ \mathbf{c}_{1,2} - \mathbf{c}_{1,1} \cdot s_1 = \mathbf{y}_1 + \lfloor q/4 \rfloor \cdot \mathbf{redc}(p'); \\ \mathbf{c}_{3,2} - {t_M}^{\top} \cdot \mathbf{c}_{3,1} = \mathbf{y}_2 + \lfloor q/4 \rfloor \cdot \mathbf{c}_{1,2}. \end{cases}$$

We can use the same way that was used to generate the underlying zero-knowledge argument protocol to obtain the NIZKAoK Π_{open} for the considered statement. To achieve negligible soundness error, the protocol is repeated $\kappa = \omega(\log \lambda)$ times. Employing the Fiat-Shamir heuristic makes the interactive system non-interactive, which gives $\Pi_{open} = (\{\mathsf{CMT}_i\}_{i=1}^{\kappa}, \mathsf{CH}, \{\mathsf{RSP}_i\}_{i=1}^{\kappa})$ where $\mathsf{CH} = \mathcal{H}(\{\mathsf{CMT}_i\}_{i=1}^{\kappa}, \mathbf{b}, \mathbf{C}, \mathbf{G}, \mathbf{a}_1, M, \Sigma, p') \in \{1,2,3\}^{\kappa}$.

7. Output (p', Π_{open}).

Judge(gpk, M, Σ, p', Π_{open}): This algorithm returns 0 if **Verify** algorithm outputs 0. Otherwise, verify the proof Π_{open}, and if it is valid, then return 1; If not, return 0.

5 Analysis of the Scheme

In this section, we analyze our scheme from three aspects: security, correctness, and efficiency.

5.1 Security

The following theorems prove the security of our scheme under the assumptions that RSIS and RLWE are hard in the ROM. Due to space restrictions, the full proofs of Theorem 3-6 are provided in the full version.

Theorem 3. *If* RLWE *and* RSIS *are hard, the above group signature scheme satisfies traceability.*

Firstly, we assume that $\mathcal{A}$ breaks the traceability of the given group signature scheme with an advantage ϵ that cannot be ignored. Then we can construct a PPT algorithm $\mathcal{B}$ that produces a forged signature for Boyen's signature with an advantage that cannot be ignored. The security of Boyen's signature is under the assumptions of RSIS and RLWE.

Theorem 4. *Given the assumption that* $\mathsf{RLWE}_{n,\ell,q,\chi}$ *problem is hard, the aforementioned group signature scheme provides full anonymity against the Opening Authority.*

Since the adversary has access to the secret key of the first layer of **Sign** algorithm, we only need to consider the anonymity of the second layer of encryption to the opener. First, we program the random oracle $\mathcal{H}_1$ and change the way the challenger responds to the adversary's token queries. Then we modify the generation of the challenged signature Σ^*. The statistical zero-knowledge property of the argument system makes the simulated signature statistically indistinguishable from a real signature. Finally, the challenger samples uniformly random ciphertexts by using the hardness assumption of RLWE problem.

Theorem 5. *Given the assumption that* $\mathsf{RLWE}_{n,\ell,q,\chi}$ *problem is hard, the aforementioned group signature scheme provides fully anonymous against the Admitter.*

Since the adversary has access to the secret key of the external encryption layer of **Sign** algorithm, we only need to consider the anonymity of the first layer of encryption to the admitter. First, we implement a random oracle $\mathcal{H}$ and modify the behavior of the challenger towards the QOpen oracle of the adversary by simulating proofs. Then we modify the generation of the challenged signature Σ^*. The statistical zero-knowledge property of the argument system makes the simulated signature statistically indistinguishable from a real signature. Finally, the challenger samples uniformly random ciphertexts by using the hardness assumption of RLWE problem.

Theorem 6. *Given the assumption that* $\mathsf{RLWE}_{n,\ell,q,\chi}$ *problem is hard, the aforementioned group signature scheme provides non-frameability.*

Firstly, we assume that $\mathcal{A}$ breaks the non-frameability with a non-negligible advantage. Then we can construct a PPT algorithm $\mathcal{B}$ that solves the RSIS problem with an advantage that cannot be ignored.

5.2 Efficiency and Correctness

Efficiency. It is easy to compute that the size of gpk is $\mathcal{O}(\lambda \cdot \log^2(\lambda)) = \widetilde{\mathcal{O}}(\lambda)$ and the size of gsk_i is $\mathcal{O}(\lambda \cdot \log^2(\lambda)) = \widetilde{\mathcal{O}}(\lambda)$. The Stern-like NIZKAoK is decisive for the size of the signature. And we computed in Subsect. 3.1 that the size of this NIZKAoK is $\mathcal{O}(\lambda \cdot \log^4(\lambda))$. So the size of Π_{gs} is $\mathcal{O}(\lambda \cdot \log^4(\lambda)) \cdot \omega(\log \lambda) = \widetilde{\mathcal{O}}(\lambda)$.

Correctness. If the signature is generated by a legitimate user, the perfect completeness of the underlying protocol makes the signature be accepted by **Verify** algorithm. If the opener recovers $\mathbf{redc}(p)$ and p, it also will be accepted by Judger for the same reason. Regarding whether the **Open** algorithm is correct, we note that

$$\mathbf{c}_{3,2} - t_M{}^\top \cdot \mathbf{c}_{3,1} = \mathbf{e}_{3,2} + \lfloor q/4 \rfloor \cdot \mathbf{c}_{1,2} - t_M{}^\top \cdot \mathbf{e}_{3,1}$$

where $\|\mathbf{e}_{3,2}\| \leq B$, $\|\mathbf{e}_{3,1}\| \leq B$, and $t_M{}^\top$ is a small-norm matrix. Since $B = \widetilde{\mathcal{O}}(n^{5/4})$ and $q = \widetilde{\mathcal{O}}(n^4)$, we have $\mathbf{e}_{3,2} - t_M{}^\top \cdot \mathbf{e}_{3,1} \leq \widetilde{\mathcal{O}}(n^{5/4})$. Then for

$$\mathbf{c}_{1,2} - \mathbf{c}_{1,1} \cdot s_1 = \mathbf{e}_1 \cdot g_1 + \mathbf{e}_{1,2} + \lfloor q/4 \rfloor \cdot \mathbf{redc}(p) - \mathbf{e}_{1,1} \cdot s_1,$$

we also have $\mathbf{e}_1 \cdot g_1 + \mathbf{e}_{1,2} - \mathbf{e}_{1,1} \cdot s_1 \leq \widetilde{\mathcal{O}}(n^{5/4})$.

6 Conclusion

In this paper, we introduce the initial constant-size group signature with message-dependent opening derived from lattice-based cryptography. The proposed constant-size group signature with message-dependent opening scheme is demonstrated to be secure in the random oracle model. Furthermore, our scheme offers the benefit of not requiring the size of the group to be fixed, thereby expanding the potential applications of group signatures. The group signature size, public key size, and user's secret key size are of order $\widetilde{\mathcal{O}}(\lambda)$.

Acknowledgements. This work has been partly supported by the Fundamental Research Funds for the Central Universities (No. 30106220482), JSPS KAKENHI Grant Number JP21H03443, and SECOM Science and Technology Foundation.

References

1. Bellare, M., Micciancio, D., Warinschi, B.: Foundations of group signatures: formal definitions, simplified requirements, and a construction based on general assumptions. In: Biham, E. (ed.) EUROCRYPT 2003. LNCS, vol. 2656, pp. 614–629. Springer, Heidelberg (2003). https://doi.org/10.1007/3-540-39200-9_38
2. Benhamouda, F., Camenisch, J., Krenn, S., Lyubashevsky, V., Neven, G.: Better zero-knowledge proofs for lattice encryption and their application to group signatures. In: Sarkar, P., Iwata, T. (eds.) ASIACRYPT 2014. LNCS, vol. 8873, pp. 551–572. Springer, Heidelberg (2014). https://doi.org/10.1007/978-3-662-45611-8_29
3. Boneh, D., Franklin, M.: Identity-based encryption from the weil pairing. In: Kilian, J. (ed.) CRYPTO 2001. LNCS, vol. 2139, pp. 213–229. Springer, Heidelberg (2001). https://doi.org/10.1007/3-540-44647-8_13
4. Boyen, X.: Lattice mixing and vanishing trapdoors: a framework for fully secure short signatures and more. In: Nguyen, P.Q., Pointcheval, D. (eds.) Public Key Cryptography - PKC 2010, pp. 499–517. Springer, Berlin Heidelberg, Berlin, Heidelberg (2010)
5. Boyen, X., Waters, B.: Full-domain subgroup hiding and constant-size group signatures. In: Okamoto, T., Wang, X. (eds.) PKC 2007. LNCS, vol. 4450, pp. 1–15. Springer, Heidelberg (2007). https://doi.org/10.1007/978-3-540-71677-8_1
6. Camenisch, J., Stadler, M.: Efficient group signature schemes for large groups. In: Kaliski, B.S. (ed.) CRYPTO 1997. LNCS, vol. 1294, pp. 410–424. Springer, Heidelberg (1997). https://doi.org/10.1007/BFb0052252
7. Canard, S., Georgescu, A., Kaim, G., Roux-Langlois, A., Traoré, J.: Constant-size lattice-based group signature with forward security in the standard model. In: Nguyen, K., Wu, W., Lam, K.Y., Wang, H. (eds.) ProvSec 2020. LNCS, vol. 12505, pp. 24–44. Springer, Cham (2020). https://doi.org/10.1007/978-3-030-62576-4_2
8. Canetti, R., Halevi, S., Katz, J.: Chosen-ciphertext security from identity-based encryption. In: Cachin, C., Camenisch, J.L. (eds.) EUROCRYPT 2004. LNCS, vol. 3027, pp. 207–222. Springer, Heidelberg (2004). https://doi.org/10.1007/978-3-540-24676-3_13
9. Chaum, D., van Heyst, E.: Group signatures. In: Davies, D.W. (ed.) EUROCRYPT 1991. LNCS, vol. 547, pp. 257–265. Springer, Heidelberg (1991). https://doi.org/10.1007/3-540-46416-6_22
10. Emura, K., et al.: Group signatures with message-dependent opening: Formal definitions and constructions. Security Commun. Netw. **2019** (2019)
11. Gentry, C.: Fully homomorphic encryption using ideal lattices. In: Proceedings of the Forty-first Annual ACM Symposium on Theory of Computing, pp. 169–178 (2009)
12. Gentry, C., Peikert, C., Vaikuntanathan, V.: Trapdoors for hard lattices and new cryptographic constructions. In: Proceedings of the Fortieth Annual ACM Symposium on Theory of Computing, pp. 197–206 (2008)
13. Gorbunov, S., Vaikuntanathan, V., Wee, H.: Predicate encryption for circuits from LWE. In: Gennaro, R., Robshaw, M. (eds.) CRYPTO 2015. LNCS, vol. 9216, pp.

503–523. Springer, Heidelberg (2015). https://doi.org/10.1007/978-3-662-48000-7_25
14. Gordon, S.D., Katz, J., Vaikuntanathan, V.: A group signature scheme from lattice assumptions. In: Abe, M. (ed.) ASIACRYPT 2010. LNCS, vol. 6477, pp. 395–412. Springer, Heidelberg (2010). https://doi.org/10.1007/978-3-642-17373-8_23
15. Groth, J.: Fully anonymous group signatures without random oracles. In: Kurosawa, K. (ed.) ASIACRYPT 2007. LNCS, vol. 4833, pp. 164–180. Springer, Heidelberg (2007). https://doi.org/10.1007/978-3-540-76900-2_10
16. Groth, J., Sahai, A.: Efficient non-interactive proof systems for bilinear groups. In: Smart, N. (ed.) EUROCRYPT 2008. LNCS, vol. 4965, pp. 415–432. Springer, Heidelberg (2008). https://doi.org/10.1007/978-3-540-78967-3_24
17. Laguillaumie, F., Langlois, A., Libert, B., Stehlé, D.: Lattice-based group signatures with logarithmic signature size. In: Sako, K., Sarkar, P. (eds.) ASIACRYPT 2013. LNCS, vol. 8270, pp. 41–61. Springer, Heidelberg (2013). https://doi.org/10.1007/978-3-642-42045-0_3
18. Libert, B., Joye, M.: Group signatures with message-dependent opening in the standard model. In: Benaloh, J. (ed.) CT-RSA 2014. LNCS, vol. 8366, pp. 286–306. Springer, Cham (2014). https://doi.org/10.1007/978-3-319-04852-9_15
19. Libert, B., Ling, S., Mouhartem, F., Nguyen, K., Wang, H.: Signature schemes with efficient protocols and dynamic group signatures from lattice assumptions. In: Cheon, J.H., Takagi, T. (eds.) ASIACRYPT 2016. LNCS, vol. 10032, pp. 373–403. Springer, Heidelberg (2016). https://doi.org/10.1007/978-3-662-53890-6_13
20. Libert, B., Ling, S., Mouhartem, F., Nguyen, K., Wang, H.: Zero-knowledge arguments for matrix-vector relations and lattice-based group encryption. In: Cheon, J.H., Takagi, T. (eds.) ASIACRYPT 2016. LNCS, vol. 10032, pp. 101–131. Springer, Heidelberg (2016). https://doi.org/10.1007/978-3-662-53890-6_4
21. Libert, B., Ling, S., Nguyen, K., Wang, H.: Zero-knowledge arguments for lattice-based accumulators: logarithmic-size ring signatures and group signatures without trapdoors. In: Fischlin, M., Coron, J.-S. (eds.) EUROCRYPT 2016. LNCS, vol. 9666, pp. 1–31. Springer, Heidelberg (2016). https://doi.org/10.1007/978-3-662-49896-5_1
22. Libert, B., Mouhartem, F., Nguyen, K.: A lattice-based group signature scheme with message-dependent opening. In: Manulis, M., Sadeghi, A.-R., Schneider, S. (eds.) ACNS 2016. LNCS, vol. 9696, pp. 137–155. Springer, Cham (2016). https://doi.org/10.1007/978-3-319-39555-5_8
23. Libert, B., Peters, T., Yung, M.: Short group signatures via structure-preserving signatures: standard model security from simple assumptions. In: Gennaro, R., Robshaw, M. (eds.) CRYPTO 2015. LNCS, vol. 9216, pp. 296–316. Springer, Heidelberg (2015). https://doi.org/10.1007/978-3-662-48000-7_15
24. Ling, S., Nguyen, K., Stehlé, D., Wang, H.: Improved zero-knowledge proofs of knowledge for the isis problem, and applications. In: Kurosawa, K., Hanaoka, G. (eds.) PKC 2013. LNCS, vol. 7778, pp. 107–124. Springer, Heidelberg (2013). https://doi.org/10.1007/978-3-642-36362-7_8
25. Ling, S., Nguyen, K., Wang, H.: Group signatures from lattices: simpler, tighter, shorter, ring-based. In: Katz, J. (ed.) PKC 2015. LNCS, vol. 9020, pp. 427–449. Springer, Heidelberg (2015). https://doi.org/10.1007/978-3-662-46447-2_19
26. Ling, S., Nguyen, K., Wang, H., Xu, Y.: Lattice-based group signatures: achieving full dynamicity with ease. In: Gollmann, D., Miyaji, A., Kikuchi, H. (eds.) ACNS 2017. LNCS, vol. 10355, pp. 293–312. Springer, Cham (2017). https://doi.org/10.1007/978-3-319-61204-1_15

27. Ling, S., Nguyen, K., Wang, H., Xu, Y.: Constant-size group signatures from lattices. In: Abdalla, M., Dahab, R. (eds.) PKC 2018. LNCS, vol. 10770, pp. 58–88. Springer, Cham (2018). https://doi.org/10.1007/978-3-319-76581-5_3
28. Luo, Q., Jiang, C.Y.: A new constant-size group signature scheme from lattices. IEEE Access **8**, 10198–10207 (2020)
29. Lyubashevsky, V., Peikert, C., Regev, O.: On ideal lattices and learning with errors over rings. In: Gilbert, H. (ed.) EUROCRYPT 2010. LNCS, vol. 6110, pp. 1–23. Springer, Heidelberg (2010). https://doi.org/10.1007/978-3-642-13190-5_1
30. Micciancio, D., Peikert, C.: Trapdoors for lattices: simpler, tighter, faster, smaller. In: Pointcheval, D., Johansson, T. (eds.) EUROCRYPT 2012. LNCS, vol. 7237, pp. 700–718. Springer, Heidelberg (2012). https://doi.org/10.1007/978-3-642-29011-4_41
31. Naor, M., Yung, M.: Public-key cryptosystems provably secure against chosen ciphertext attacks. In: Proceedings of the Twenty-second Annual ACM Symposium on Theory of Computing, pp. 427–437 (1990)
32. Nguyen, P.Q., Zhang, J., Zhang, Z.: Simpler efficient group signatures from lattices. In: Katz, J. (ed.) PKC 2015. LNCS, vol. 9020, pp. 401–426. Springer, Heidelberg (2015). https://doi.org/10.1007/978-3-662-46447-2_18
33. Ohara, K., Sakai, Y., Emura, K., Hanaoka, G.: A group signature scheme with unbounded message-dependent opening. In: Proceedings of the 8th ACM SIGSAC Symposium on Information, Computer and Communications Security, pp. 517–522 (2013)
34. Peikert, C., et al.: A decade of lattice cryptography. Found. Trends® Theor. Comput. Sci. **10**(4), 283–424 (2016)
35. Regev, O.: On lattices, learning with errors, random linear codes, and cryptography. J. ACM (JACM) **56**(6), 1–40 (2009)
36. Şahin, M.S., Akleylek, S.: A constant-size lattice-based partially-dynamic group signature scheme in quantum random oracle model. J. King Saud Univ.-Comput. Inform. Sci. **34**(10), 9852–9866 (2022)
37. Sakai, Y., Emura, K., Hanaoka, G., Kawai, Y., Matsuda, T., Omote, K.: Group signatures with message-dependent opening. In: Abdalla, M., Lange, T. (eds.) Pairing 2012. LNCS, vol. 7708, pp. 270–294. Springer, Heidelberg (2013). https://doi.org/10.1007/978-3-642-36334-4_18
38. Shamir, A.: Identity-based cryptosystems and signature schemes. In: Blakley, G.R., Chaum, D. (eds.) CRYPTO 1984. LNCS, vol. 196, pp. 47–53. Springer, Heidelberg (1985). https://doi.org/10.1007/3-540-39568-7_5
39. Stehlé, D., Steinfeld, R.: Faster fully homomorphic encryption. In: Abe, M. (ed.) ASIACRYPT 2010. LNCS, vol. 6477, pp. 377–394. Springer, Heidelberg (2010). https://doi.org/10.1007/978-3-642-17373-8_22
40. Stern, J.: A new paradigm for public key identification. IEEE Trans. Inf. Theory **42**(6), 1757–1768 (1996)
41. Sun, Y., Liu, Y.: An efficient fully dynamic group signature with message dependent opening from lattice. Cybersecurity **4**(1), 1–15 (2021)
42. Yousuf, H., Lahzi, M., Salloum, S.A., Shaalan, K.: Systematic review on fully homomorphic encryption scheme and its application. In: Al-Emran, M., Shaalan, K., Hassanien, A.E. (eds.) Recent Advances in Intelligent Systems and Smart Applications. SSDC, vol. 295, pp. 537–551. Springer, Cham (2021). https://doi.org/10.1007/978-3-030-47411-9_29

Post-quantum Sigma Protocols and Signatures from Low-Rank Matrix Completions

Jiaming Wen, Houzhen Wang, and Huanguo Zhang(✉)

Key Laboratory of Aerospace Information Security and Trusted Computing, Ministry of Education, School of Cyber Science and Engineering, Wuhan University, Wuhan 430072, China
{wenjm,whz,liss}@whu.edu.cn

Abstract. We introduce a new hard problem to cryptography, named Low-Rank Matrix Completion (LRMC), whose hardness is equivalence with MinRank in multivariate cryptography (NP-Complete and quantum-resistant). We present a Sigma Protocol to prove the knowledge of LRMC. Comparing with the need for several matrices in the public key of MinRank-based constructions such as Courtois (ASIACRYPT 2001) and Bellini et al. (PQCrypto 2022), the benefits of using LRMC are that only one matrix is required, leading to smaller public key sizes, lower computation and communication costs, and fewer operations and time-consuming. In addition, it is more intuitive and succinct in the system setup. Then, we take full advantage of recent progresses to reduce the soundness error, including the Sigma Protocol with Helper (EUROCRYPT 2020), the cut-and-choose techniques (CCS 2018), and so on. When applying the Fiat-Shamir transform to convert the improved sigma protocol to a signature scheme, with more optimizations, the sizes are competitive with SPHINCS+, which has been determined to be standardized by the NIST after three rounds of evaluation, and is the only one that does not rely on (structural) lattice problems. This work increases the diversity of provable and practical post-quantum signatures, as the NIST is calling.

Keywords: Post-Quantum Cryptography · Multivariate Cryptography · Zero-Knowledge Proof · Sigma Protocol · Signature

1 Introduction

In July 2022, the National Institute of Standards and Technology (NIST) announced the results of the Third Round Post-Quantum Cryptography (PQC) Project and identified algorithms that will be standardized. The most recommended are CRYSTALS-Kyber (KEM) [2] and CRYSTALS-Dilithium (Digital Signature) [3], both of which are based on lattice problems. In addition, another lattice-based signature scheme, Falcon [21], and a hash-based signature scheme,

M. Zhang et al. (Eds.): ProvSec 2023, LNCS 14217, pp. 186–206, 2023.
https://doi.org/10.1007/978-3-031-45513-1_11

SPHINCS+ [1] will also be standardized. In terms of digital signature, according to the materials submitted to NIST by the design teams and the official evaluations, Dilithium is based on problems with the structural lattice called module lattice to reduce sizes, which may leave adversaries more chances to attack. Falcon is also constructed from module lattice and uses the hash-and-sign paradigm. Although it has a slightly better size, its signing algorithm has more complex internal logic and is therefore unfriendly to implement. SPHINCS+ is a kind of stateless signature scheme based on hash, whose security depends on the security of the underlying hash function and provides a reliable security guarantee. However, it will lead to relatively large sizes and performance costs.

During the PQC standardization process, the number of digital signature proposals was significantly lower than that of KEM proposals. The existing signature schemes suffer from a lack of diversity, and the NIST is calling for new proposals that will also be taken into account throughout the standardization process. For example, additional general-purpose signature schemes that do not rely on structural lattice, or signatures with short sizes and quick verification for certain uses, such as certificate transparency. Generally speaking, designing signature schemes based on abundantly established hardness assumptions, including but not limited to lattice, is still an exigent and significant assignment.

Sigma Protocol. Zero-Knowledge Proof of Knowledge (ZKPoK), and the more concrete Sigma Protocol, which refers to when input common x, Prover who owns witness w satisfied $(w, x) \in$ Relation R, can convince Verifier that he/she knows w, without leaking any additional information about w.

Sigma Protocols have been used to create a wide range of cryptographic primitives like digital signatures, group/ring signatures, and cryptographic applications such as electronic voting systems, privacy-preserving cryptocurrencies. However, some of them are not Perfect Soundness, that is to say, there is a non-negligible probability that Cheater without the witness w can deceive Verifier into thinking he/she knows w. The famous cases are Stern's protocol [35] and its variants on Lattice [25,30], MinRank [14] and MQ [34], all of which have the soundness error $\epsilon = 2/3$. There are also some works [9,13] that optimize the soundness error to $\epsilon = q/2(q-1) > 1/2$.

In order to decrease the soundness error of the Sigma Protocol, a straight but valid approach is to repeat the protocol for k times, and the soundness error of the entire protocol will become ϵ^k. Eventually, one can obtain a protocol with a negligible soundness error. However, a large number of repeated rounds will incur enormous communication overhead and time cost. Taking Stern's protocol with the soundness error $\epsilon = 2/3$ as an example, it requires $k = 219$ repetitions to get the soundness error down to less than 2^{-128}.

In recent years, with the process of standardizing post-quantum cryptography algorithms, various new techniques to reduce the soundness error of such Sigma Protocols have also been studied. One important progress is the Sigma Protocol with Helper, proposed by Beullens [8], is a standard Sigma Protocol attached to a trusted third party. When combined with the idea of cut-and-choose proposed by

Katz, Kolesnikov, and Wang [24] to remove the trusted third party, it successfully reduces the soundness error from 2/3 to $1/q'$, where q' is related to the size of the corresponding finite field.

From Sigma Protocol to Signature. Making a zero-knowledge identification protocol into a non-interactive signature scheme via a transformation like the Fiat-Shamir transform in ROM [20] or the Unruh transform in QROM [36] is mainstream approaches to creating signature schemes. For example, three of the second round shortlisted signature schemes in the NIST PQC project, MQDSS [13], Picnic [12], and Dilithium [3], all employ this strategy.

Unfortunately, in the past results, applying the above transforms directly to the Sigma Protocol with soundness error $\epsilon = 2/3$ to the signature lead enormous sizes. Drawing support from the Sigma Protocol with Helper and removing Helper by cut-and-choose, the soundness error can be reduced markedly. When combining with some further optimizations and the transforms, a new digital signature scheme with competitive size and signing time can be attained [5,8].

Our Contributions. In order to add diversity to post-quantum cryptographic construction, this work has contributions as follows.

- Firstly, we introduce the new hard problem called Low-Rank Matrix Completion (LRMC) to cryptographic designing, whose hardness is equivalent to the thoroughly researched MinRank in multivariate cryptography (quantum resistant and NP-Complete), but which enjoys a lot better sizes and looks more succinct and intuitive.
- Secondly, we provide a Sigma Protocol to prove the knowledge of a solution for LRMC, and give formal proof about Completeness, Soundness, and Special Honest-Verifier Zero-Knowledge (SHVZK). On the premise of equal security, the public key sizes, computation, and communication costs can be noticeably decreased compared with MinRank-based constructions [5,14]. We then utilize recent techniques to further decrease the soundness error.
- Finally, we converted the improved Sigma Protocol with lower soundness error to a signature scheme using the Fiat-Shamir transform. After further optimizations, the sizes are aggressive with SPHINCS+ [1], which has been determined as the standard by NIST after three rounds of assessment and selection, and is the only one that not relied on structural lattice problems.

Roadmap. In Sect. 2 we introduce notations and hard problems, followed by a recap of properties of commitment schemes. Subsequently, in Sect. 3 we recall the definitions and properties about Sigma Protocol and present a Sigma Protocol based on LRMC, with formal proof, and use recent techniques to decrease the soundness error. Moreover, in Sect. 4, we give a signature scheme based on LRMC that includes analysis, recommended parameters, and comparisons. Lastly, we summarize the whole paper in Sect. 5.

2 Preliminaries

For prime q, we let $\mathbb{F}_q$ to represent the finite field whose order is q, and q can be dropped when there is no ambiguity, i.e., finite field $\mathbb{F}$. For positive integer k, l, we use $\mathrm{Mat}_{k,l}(\mathbb{F})$ to represent the set consists of $k \times l$-dimension matrices with entries in $\mathbb{F}$, and denote it as $\mathrm{Mat}_k(\mathbb{F})$ for short when $k = l$. In addition, $\mathrm{GL}_k(\mathbb{F})$ is the group consists of invertible matrices in $\mathrm{Mat}_k(\mathbb{F})$. We let λ be the security parameter and all logarithms are base 2.

2.1 Hard Problems

MinRank. Stern constructed a Sigma Protocol based on Syndrome Decoding Problem in [35], the problem refers to given a public parity check matrix $\mathbf{H} \in \mathbb{F}_2^{k\times l}$ and a syndrome $\mathbf{s} \in \mathbb{F}_2^k$, finding a small weight vector $\mathbf{e} \in \mathbb{F}_2^l$ in the affine subspace of a linear space such that $\mathbf{He} = \mathbf{s}$, and Berlekamp et al. [6] provided a proof that it is a NP-Complete Problem. Similar to the Syndrome Decoding Problem, the MinRank Problem aims to find a linear combination of a given set of matrices that owns the small rank, which is also NP-Complete [10,14]. In fact, the MinRank problem contains the Syndrome Decoding Problem, and the conventional definition of MinRank is as follows.

Definition 1 (MinRank, [14]). *Given positive integers k, l, s, r, and $k \times l$-dimension matrices $\boldsymbol{M}_0; \boldsymbol{M}_1, \cdots, \boldsymbol{M}_s \in \mathrm{Mat}_{k,l}(\mathbb{F})$ over finite field $\mathbb{F}$, MinRank Problem is to find $\alpha_1, \cdots, \alpha_s \in \mathbb{F}$, such that*

$$rank(\boldsymbol{M}_0 + \sum_{i=1}^{s} \alpha_i \boldsymbol{M}_i) \leq r.$$

In cryptanalysis, breaking multivariate-based and code-based cryptographic schemes can always be converted into solving a MinRank instance. The method has been used to destroy schemes such as Hidden Field Equations (HFE) [7, 15,28] and TTM [22]. Besides, the NIST candidates Rainbow [18] and HFEv- [17,31] hence require larger parameters. However, what caught our attention most is that Courtois utilized MinRank to design a Sigma Protocol [14] followed the framework of Stern [35], which has been improved by Bellini et al. [5] recently.

1-MinRank. 1-MinRank can be viewed as a special case of MinRank, Derksen proved the equivalence between them [16].

Definition 2 (1-MinRank). *The problem is defined similar with MinRank, but requires the rank of matrices $\boldsymbol{M}_1, \cdots, \boldsymbol{M}_s$ are 1.*

Lemma 1 (Equivalence between MinRank and 1-MinRank, [16]). *The adversary can solve MinRank if and only if it can solve 1-MinRank.*

Low-Rank Matrix Completion (LRMC). Low-Rank Matrix Completion Problem, which fire up because Netflix's movie recommendation system [29]. To be more specific, given a large matrix where each row corresponds to a user and each column corresponds to a movie, every user has only watched and rated some of those movies, so this leads to a partially filled matrix. Because different user preferences can be divided into cliques, the large matrix will be sparse and low-rank, and predicting whether users would like to complete the matrix. LRMC has also been widely used in image processing [23], Internet of Things (IoT) localization [27], and so on.

There are some algorithms [11,26,32] attempted to solve the LRMC Problem. However, it has been proven equivalent to (1-)MinRank Problem [16], in other words, the LRMC Problem is also NP-Complete, and there is no effective (quantum) algorithm to solve these three problems for appropriate parameters. We describe the LRMC Problem with an example here.

Definition 3 (Low-Rank Matrix Completion, LRMC). *Given positive integers k, l, s, r, and a $k \times l$-dimension matrix $\boldsymbol{M} \in \mathrm{Mat}_{k,l}(\mathbb{F})$ which is only partially filled with s unfilled entries, LRMC is to complete the remaining (ordered from top to bottom and left to right), such that the resulting matrix has rank $\leq r$.*

Example 1. For $\mathbb{F} = \mathbb{F}_7$, choose a random partially filled matrix $\boldsymbol{M} \leftarrow \mathrm{Mat}_{3,4}(\mathbb{F}_7)$ with $s = 4$ unfilled entries and target rank $r = 2$, such as

$$\boldsymbol{M} = \begin{bmatrix} 1\,2\,4\,3 \\ 2\,4\,*\,* \\ *\,*\,5\,2 \end{bmatrix}$$

The symbol $*$ means entries that to be filled, and the problem ask to complete all the $*$ with elements in $\mathbb{F}_7$ such that $rank(\boldsymbol{M}) \leq r$. For example, $\boldsymbol{M}$ can be filled with $(4,3,1,3)$, $(1,6,4,1)$ and $(1,6,3,6)$ to obtain

$$\boldsymbol{M}_1 = \begin{bmatrix} 1\,2\,4\,3 \\ 2\,4\,4\,3 \\ 1\,3\,5\,2 \end{bmatrix}, \quad \boldsymbol{M}_2 = \begin{bmatrix} 1\,2\,4\,3 \\ 2\,4\,1\,6 \\ 4\,1\,5\,2 \end{bmatrix}, \quad \boldsymbol{M}_3 = \begin{bmatrix} 1\,2\,4\,3 \\ 2\,4\,1\,6 \\ 3\,6\,5\,2 \end{bmatrix}$$

easy to calculate $rank(\boldsymbol{M}_1) = 3 > 2, rank(\boldsymbol{M}_2) = 2 \leq 2, rank(\boldsymbol{M}_3) = 1 \leq 2$. As a result, $(1,6,4,1)$ and $(1,6,3,6)$ are solutions for this LRMC Problem.

Lemma 2 (Equivalence between 1-MinRank and LRMC, [16]**).** *The adversary can solve 1-MinRank if and only if it can solve LRMC.*

Theorem 1 (Equivalence between MinRank and LRMC, [16]**).** *The adversary can solve MinRank if and only if it can solve LRMC.*

Proof. It could be derived from Lemma 1 and Lemma 2 directly.

Remark 1. Since LRMC and MinRank can be reduced to each other, we can use attack methods for MinRank [5] to estimate the security for LRMC-based construction and choose the appropriate parameters. Essentially, each unfilled entry of the matrix $\boldsymbol{M}$ in LRMC can be corresponded to a matrix $\in \{\boldsymbol{M}_1, \cdots, \boldsymbol{M}_s\}$ in MinRank according to 1-MinRank [16], while the value that will be filled in LRMC is closely related to the coefficient α_i in MinRank.

2.2 Commitment Schemes

Many Sigma Protocols [5,8,25,30] and ours, relies on non-interactive commitment schemes $\mathsf{Com} : \{0,1\}^{\lambda} \times \{0,1\}^{*} \rightarrow \{0,1\}^{2\lambda}$, where λ is the security parameter. The commitment Com inputs a λ-bit string r which is uniformly random and a arbitrary length message m, outputs a 2λ-bit commitment value $\mathsf{Com}(r, m)$.

The commitment scheme should not reveal any information about the message m, and it should prevent denial, in other words, $\mathsf{Com}(r, m)$ can not be open to different message, these properties are formalized as follows. Furthermore, Com can be implemented by a secure cryptographic hash function in practice.

Definition 4 (Computational Hinding). *The advantage of a probabilistic polynomial time adversary $\mathcal{A}$ in breaking the Hiding property of the commitment scheme is defined as*

$$\mathsf{Adv}^{\mathsf{Hiding}}(\mathcal{A}, m_0, m_1) := \left| \Pr_{r \leftarrow\$ \{0,1\}^{\lambda}} [\mathcal{A}(\mathsf{Com}(r, m_0) = 1)] - \Pr_{r \leftarrow\$ \{0,1\}^{\lambda}} [\mathcal{A}(\mathsf{Com}(r, m_1) = 1)] \right|$$

We say Com *is Computationally Hiding, if for all polynomial time algorithms $\mathcal{A}$, and messages m_0, m_1, the advantage $\mathsf{Adv}^{\mathsf{Hiding}}(\mathcal{A}, m_0, m_1)$ is a negligible function of the security parameter λ.*

Definition 5 (Computational Binding). *The advantage of a probabilistic polynomial time adversary $\mathcal{A}$ in breaking the Binding property of the commitment scheme is defined as*

$$\mathsf{Adv}^{\mathsf{Binding}}(\mathcal{A}) := \Pr\left[(r_0, m_0, r_1, m_1) \leftarrow \mathcal{A}(1^{\lambda}); \mathsf{Com}(r_0, m_0) = \mathsf{Com}(r_1, m_1)\right]$$

We say Com *is Computationally Binding, if for all polynomial time algorithms $\mathcal{A}$, the advantage $\mathsf{Adv}^{\mathsf{Binding}}(\mathcal{A})$ is a negligible function of the security parameter λ.*

3 Sigma Protocol and LRMC-Based Construction

In this section, we firstly recap basic definitions of the standard Sigma Protocol, and present a zero-knowledge proof of the solution for an instance of the LRMC Problem. Then, we make use of Sigma Protocol with Helper [8], which is a technique developed in recent years, to decrease the soundness error and achieves 2-Special Soundness. Subsequently, we remove helper by cut-and-choose technique generalized from [24]. Eventually, we will obtain a LRMC-based Sigma Protocol with desirable soundness error.

3.1 Standard Sigma Protocol Based on LRMC

A standard (3-move) Sigma Protocol is in the form of Fig. 1, where x is the common input to Prover and Verifier, and witness w such that $(x, w) \in$ Relation R is the private input to Prover. $\mathcal{P}_1, \mathcal{P}_2, \mathcal{V}$ are polynomial-time algorithms, and $\mathsf{P}_{\mathsf{state}}$ represents the state of Prover.

Prover(x, w)		**Verifier**(x)
$(\mathsf{com}, \mathsf{P}_{\mathsf{state}}) \leftarrow \mathcal{P}_1(x, w)$	$\xrightarrow{\mathsf{com}}$	
	$\xleftarrow{\mathsf{ch}}$	$\mathsf{ch} \leftarrow_\$ \mathcal{C}$
$\mathsf{rsp} \leftarrow \mathcal{P}_2(\mathsf{P}_{\mathsf{state}}, \mathsf{ch})$	$\xrightarrow{\mathsf{rsp}}$	
		$\mathcal{V}(x, \mathsf{com}, \mathsf{ch}, \mathsf{rsp}) = \text{Accept/Reject}$

Fig. 1. The structure of a standard Sigma Protocol

Definition 6 (Sigma Protocol). *An interactive protocol between Prover and Verifier is said to be a Sigma Protocol for Relation R, if it is in the structure of* Fig. 1, *where w is the witness and x is the common input, such that:*

- **Completeness.** *If Prover and Verifier execute the protocol on the common input x, with the private input w to Prover satisfied $(x, w) \in R$, Verifier will always return Accept.*
- **Soundness.** *For any common input x with a valid transcript $(x, \mathsf{com}, \mathsf{ch}, \mathsf{rsp})$, there exists a polynomial-time knowledge extractor $\mathcal{E}$ that can extract the witness w, such that $(x, w) \in R$.*
- **Special Honest-Verifier Zero-Knowledge.** *There exists a polynomial-time simulator $\mathcal{S}$, on input common x with a challenge $\mathsf{ch} \leftarrow_\$ \mathcal{C}$, outputs a transcript of the form $(x, \mathsf{com}, \mathsf{ch}, \mathsf{rsp})$, which is computationally indistinguishable from the transcripts of honest executing the protocol on input (x, w), where w satisfied $(x, w) \in R$.*

Similar to Stern [35] and Courtois [14], we propose a zero-knowledge proof of a solution for the LRMC Problem in Fig. 2, which follows the above Sigma Protocol with challenge space $\mathcal{C} = \{0, 1, 2\}$, and the soundness error is $2/3$.

The system parameters include k, l, s, r and the finite field $\mathbb{F} = \mathbb{F}_q$. During the Key Generation phase, Prover chooses a random matrix $\mathbf{A} = (a_{i,j}) \leftarrow \mathrm{Mat}_{k,l}(\mathbb{F})$, such that $rank(\mathbf{A}) = r$, and removes s entries $(a_{i_1,j_1}, a_{i_2,j_2}, \cdots, a_{i_s,j_s})$ to obtain a partially filled matrix $\mathbf{A}^-$. Then he/she breaks it into $\mathbf{A}^- = \mathbf{A}_1^- + \mathbf{A}_2^-$, where $\mathbf{A}_1^-, \mathbf{A}_2^-$ are also partially filled. Prover can set $\mathbf{A}_1^-$ with all 1 at its filled entries, so $\mathbf{A}^-$ and $\mathbf{A}_2^-$ can be transformed to each other when knowing either of them. The public key is $\mathbf{A}^-$ (equivalent to the pair $(\mathbf{A}_1^-, \mathbf{A}_2^-)$), and the secret key is $(a_{i_1,j_1}, a_{i_2,j_2}, \cdots, a_{i_s,j_s}) = (a_{i_t,j_t})$ for $1 \leq t \leq s$.

Theorem 2 (LRMC-based Sigma Protocol). *Let* Com *be the commitment scheme which is Computational Hinding and Binding, then the protocol in* Fig. 2 *satisfied* Definition 6 *for challenge* $\mathsf{ch} \in \{0, 1, 2\}$, *with soundness error* $2/3$.

Proof. We prove the protocol in Fig. 2 achieves Perfect Completeness, Soundness with error $2/3$, and Special Honest-Verifier Zero-Knowledge in Definition 6.

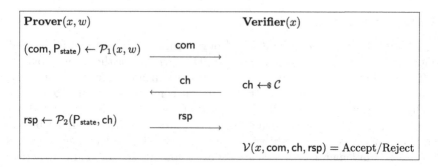

Prover		Verifier
Prover$(\mathbf{A}_1^-, \mathbf{A}_2^-, a_{i_t,j_t})$		**Verifier**$(\mathbf{A}_1^-, \mathbf{A}_2^-)$
Chooses $\mathbf{Y} \leftarrow\$ \mathrm{Mat}_{k,l}(\mathbb{F}), \mathbf{P} \leftarrow\$ \mathrm{GL}_k(\mathbb{F}), \mathbf{Q} \leftarrow\$ \mathrm{GL}_l(\mathbb{F})$ Divides $a_{i_t,j_t} = \alpha_{i_t,j_t} + \beta_{i_t,j_t} (1 \le t \le s)$ randomly Completes $\mathbf{A}_1^-$ with α_{i_t,j_t} to get $\mathbf{A}_1$ Completes $\mathbf{A}_2^-$ with β_{i_t,j_t} to get $\mathbf{A}_2$ $(r_0, r_1, r_2) \leftarrow\$ \{0,1\}^\lambda \times \{0,1\}^\lambda \times \{0,1\}^\lambda$ $\mathbf{c}_0 := \mathsf{Com}(r_0, \mathbf{P}, \mathbf{Q}, \mathbf{Y})$ $\mathbf{c}_1 := \mathsf{Com}(r_1, \mathbf{PA}_1\mathbf{Q} + \mathbf{Y})$ $\mathbf{c}_2 := \mathsf{Com}(r_2, \mathbf{PA}_2\mathbf{Q} - \mathbf{Y})$		
$\mathsf{com} := (\mathbf{c}_0, \mathbf{c}_1, \mathbf{c}_2)$	$\xrightarrow{\mathsf{com}}$	
	$\xleftarrow{\mathsf{ch}}$	$\mathsf{ch} \leftarrow\$ \mathcal{C} = \{0, 1, 2\}$
If $\mathsf{ch} = 0$, then reveals $\mathbf{c}_1, \mathbf{c}_2$ $\mathsf{rsp} := (r_1, r_2, \mathbf{PA}_1\mathbf{Q} + \mathbf{Y}, \mathbf{PA}_2\mathbf{Q} - \mathbf{Y})$ If $\mathsf{ch} = 1$, then reveals $\mathbf{c}_0, \mathbf{c}_2$ $\mathsf{rsp} := (r_0, r_2, \mathbf{P}, \mathbf{Q}, \mathbf{Y}, \beta = (\beta_{i_t,j_t}))$ If $\mathsf{ch} = 2$, then reveals $\mathbf{c}_0, \mathbf{c}_1$ $\mathsf{rsp} := (r_0, r_1, \mathbf{P}, \mathbf{Q}, \mathbf{Y}, \alpha = (\alpha_{i_t,j_t}))$		
	$\xrightarrow{\mathsf{rsp}}$	
		If $\mathsf{ch} = 0$, Computes and checks $\mathbf{c}_1 = \mathsf{Com}(r_1, \mathbf{PA}_1\mathbf{Q} + \mathbf{Y})$ $\mathbf{c}_2 = \mathsf{Com}(r_2, \mathbf{PA}_2\mathbf{Q} - \mathbf{Y})$ $rank(\mathbf{PA}_1\mathbf{Q} + \mathbf{Y} + \mathbf{PA}_2\mathbf{Q} - \mathbf{Y}) = r$ If $\mathsf{ch} = 1$, Recovers $\mathbf{A}_2$ with $\mathbf{A}_2^-$ and β Computes and checks $\mathbf{c}_0 = \mathsf{Com}(r_0, \mathbf{P}, \mathbf{Q}, \mathbf{Y})$ $\mathbf{c}_2 = \mathsf{Com}(r_2, \mathbf{PA}_2\mathbf{Q} - \mathbf{Y})$ If $\mathsf{ch} = 2$, Recovers $\mathbf{A}_1$ with $\mathbf{A}_1^-$ and α Computes and checks $\mathbf{c}_0 = \mathsf{Com}(r_0, \mathbf{P}, \mathbf{Q}, \mathbf{Y})$ $\mathbf{c}_1 = \mathsf{Com}(r_1, \mathbf{PA}_1\mathbf{Q} + \mathbf{Y})$
In each case, Verifier outputs Accept if and only if all conditions hold. Otherwise, it outputs Reject.		

Fig. 2. Standard Sigma Protocol for proving the knowledge of LRMC

Completeness. During an honest execution of the protocol, we have $\mathbf{A} = \mathbf{A}_1 + \mathbf{A}_2$, and $\mathbf{P}, \mathbf{Q}$ are invertible, which derives

$$rank(\mathbf{PA}_1\mathbf{Q} + \mathbf{Y} + \mathbf{PA}_2\mathbf{Q} - \mathbf{Y}) = rank(\mathbf{PAQ}) = rank(\mathbf{A}) = r,$$

Combining with the Completeness of the commitment scheme Com, we know Verifier will always output Accept, i.e., the protocol has Perfect Completeness.

Soundness (with Error $2/3$**).** A Sigma Protocol with soundness error $2/3$ means a dishonest prover can answer at most two of three challenges. We will prove if there exists Cheater who can answer all the $\mathsf{ch} \in \{0, 1, 2\}$, then it could be used to break the binding property of Com, or construct a polynomial-time knowledge extractor $\mathcal{E}$, which can be used to extract Prover's secret key, i.e., obtain a solution for the LRMC problem.

Since Com was used for committing $(r_1, \mathbf{PA}_1\mathbf{Q} + \mathbf{Y})$ and $(r_2, \mathbf{PA}_2\mathbf{Q} - \mathbf{Y})$. For ch $= 1$ and ch $= 2$, Cheater proves it has indeed generated them, and the binding property of Com guarantees the $(\mathbf{P}, \mathbf{Q}, \mathbf{Y})$ are the same. Subsequently, when ch $= 0$, it is not hard to see that $rank(\mathbf{P}(\mathbf{A}_1 + \mathbf{A}_2)\mathbf{Q}) = rank(\mathbf{PA}_1\mathbf{Q} + \mathbf{Y} + \mathbf{PA}_2\mathbf{Q} - \mathbf{Y}) = r$. Combining with $\mathbf{P}, \mathbf{Q}$ are invertible, thus Cheater can be used to obtain a solution $(\mathbf{A}_1 + \mathbf{A}_2)$ for the LRMC Problem.

Therefore, Cheater without the witness (a solution for the LRMC Problem) in the protocol in Fig. 2 will be rejected with probability $1/3$, and the soundness error is $2/3$.

Special Honest-Verifier Zero-Knowledge. We construct a polynomial-time simulator $\mathcal{S}$, on input public key $(\mathbf{A}_1^-, \mathbf{A}_2^-)$, and a challenge $\mathsf{ch} \leftarrow_\$ \mathcal{C} = \{0, 1, 2\}$, then it outputs a transcript $(\mathbf{A}_1^-, \mathbf{A}_2^-, \mathsf{com}' = (\mathbf{c}_0', \mathbf{c}_1', \mathbf{c}_2'), \mathsf{ch}, \mathsf{rsp}')$ as follows:

1. Chooses random $(r_0', r_1', r_2') \leftarrow_\$ \{0,1\}^\lambda \times \{0,1\}^\lambda \times \{0,1\}^\lambda$, as well as matrices $\mathbf{Y}' \leftarrow_\$ \mathrm{Mat}_{k,l}(\mathbb{F}), \mathbf{P}' \leftarrow_\$ \mathrm{GL}_k(\mathbb{F})$, and $\mathbf{Q}' \leftarrow_\$ \mathrm{GL}_l(\mathbb{F})$.
2. Simulates $\mathsf{com}' = (\mathbf{c}_0', \mathbf{c}_1', \mathbf{c}_2')$ and rsp' as follows:
   (a) Chooses $\alpha_{i_t,j_t}' = (\alpha_{i_1,j_1}', \cdots \alpha_{i_s,j_s}') \leftarrow_\$ \mathbb{F}^s$ and completes $\mathbf{A}_1^-$ with α_{i_t,j_t}' to obtain $\mathbf{A}_1'$.
   (b) Chooses a random matrix $\mathbf{R} \in \mathrm{Mat}_{k,l}(\mathbb{F})$, satisfied $rank(\mathbf{R}) = r$, and computes $\mathbf{A}_2' = \mathbf{R} - \mathbf{A}_1'$.
   (c) Computes $\mathbf{c}_0' = \mathsf{Com}(r_0', \mathbf{P}', \mathbf{Q}', \mathbf{Y}'), \mathbf{c}_1' = \mathsf{Com}(r_1', \mathbf{P}'\mathbf{A}_1'\mathbf{Q}' + \mathbf{Y}'), \mathbf{c}_2' = \mathsf{Com}(r_2', \mathbf{P}'\mathbf{A}_2'\mathbf{Q}' - \mathbf{Y}')$, and outputs $\mathsf{com}' = (\mathbf{c}_0', \mathbf{c}_1', \mathbf{c}_2')$.
   (d) Computes responses

$$\mathsf{rsp}'_{\mathsf{ch}=0} = (r_1', r_2', \mathbf{P}'\mathbf{A}_1'\mathbf{Q}' + \mathbf{Y}', \mathbf{P}'\mathbf{A}_2'\mathbf{Q}' - \mathbf{Y}');$$
$$\mathsf{rsp}'_{\mathsf{ch}=1} = (r_0', r_2', \mathbf{P}', \mathbf{Q}', \mathbf{Y}', \beta' = (\beta_{i_t,j_t}'));$$
$$\mathsf{rsp}'_{\mathsf{ch}=2} = (r_0', r_1', \mathbf{P}', \mathbf{Q}', \mathbf{Y}', \alpha' = (\alpha_{i_t,j_t}')).$$

Combining with the Computational Hiding of the commitment scheme Com, the simulated transcript $(\mathbf{A}_1^-, \mathbf{A}_2^-, \mathsf{com}' = (\mathbf{c}_0', \mathbf{c}_1', \mathbf{c}_2'), \mathsf{ch}, \mathsf{rsp}')$ satisfied:

1. ch $= 0$: $\mathsf{rsp}'_{\mathsf{ch}=0}$ is uniformly distributed in $\{0,1\}^\lambda \times \{0,1\}^\lambda \times \{(\mathbf{U}, \mathbf{V}) \in \mathrm{Mat}_{k,l}(\mathbb{F}) \times \mathrm{Mat}_{k,l}(\mathbb{F}),$ such that $rank(\mathbf{U} + \mathbf{V}) = r\}$.
2. ch $= 1$: $\mathsf{rsp}'_{\mathsf{ch}=1}$ is uniformly distributed in $\{0,1\}^\lambda \times \{0,1\}^\lambda \times \mathrm{GL}_k(\mathbb{F}) \times \mathrm{GL}_l(\mathbb{F}) \times \mathrm{Mat}_{k,l}(\mathbb{F}) \times \mathbb{F}^s$.
3. ch $= 2$: $\mathsf{rsp}'_{\mathsf{ch}=2}$ is uniformly distributed in $\{0,1\}^\lambda \times \{0,1\}^\lambda \times \mathrm{GL}_k(\mathbb{F}) \times \mathrm{GL}_l(\mathbb{F}) \times \mathrm{Mat}_{k,l}(\mathbb{F}) \times \mathbb{F}^s$.

That is to say, rsp′ is computationally indistinguishable from rsp in transcripts of honest executing the protocol on input the public-secret keypair $((\mathbf{A}_1^-, \mathbf{A}_2^-), (a_{i_1,j_1}, \cdots, a_{i_s,j_s}))$, where completes $\mathbf{A}^- = \mathbf{A}_1^- + \mathbf{A}_2^-$ with $(a_{i_1,j_1}, \cdots, a_{i_s,j_s})$ to obtain a rank r matrix $\mathbf{A}$.

Furthermore, since $\mathsf{com} = (\mathbf{c}_0, \mathbf{c}_1, \mathbf{c}_2)$ is totally determined by rsp in the same way that $\mathsf{com}' = (\mathbf{c}_0', \mathbf{c}_1', \mathbf{c}_2')$ is totally determined by rsp′, it can derive that the simulated transcript is computationally indistinguishable with the honest executing transcript. As a result, the simulator $\mathcal{S}$ is constructed successfully.

3.2 Sigma Protocol with Helper Based on LRMC

Beullens proposed the Sigma Protocol with Helper [8]. Informally, it extended the standard Sigma Protocol by adding a trusted third party. The trusted third party takes part in the protocol's execution. Firstly, it runs a Setup algorithm by seed to obtain auxiliary value aux, as well as seed to Prover and aux to Verifier, respectively. The variant (3-move) Sigma Protocol of the form of Fig. 3, where x is the common input to Prover and Verifier, and a witness w such that $(x, w) \in$ Relation R is the private input to Prover. It is worth noting that the Sigma Protocol with Helper can be converted into a standard Sigma Protocol through the idea of cut-and-choose [24].

Helper(x)
$\mathsf{seed} \leftarrow\!\!\$\ \{0,1\}^\lambda$
$\mathsf{aux} \leftarrow \mathsf{Setup}(\mathsf{seed})$
Sends seed to **Prover** and aux to **Verifier**

Prover(x, w, seed)		**Verifier**(x, aux)
$(\mathsf{com}, \mathsf{P_{state}}) \leftarrow \mathcal{P}_1(x, w, \mathsf{seed})$	com $\longrightarrow$	
	$\longleftarrow$ ch	$\mathsf{ch} \leftarrow\!\!\$\ \mathcal{C}$
$\mathsf{rsp} \leftarrow \mathcal{P}_2(\mathsf{P_{state}}, \mathsf{ch})$	rsp $\longrightarrow$	
		$\mathcal{V}(x, \mathsf{aux}, \mathsf{com}, \mathsf{ch}, \mathsf{rsp}) = \mathrm{Accept/Reject}$

Fig. 3. The structure of a Sigma Protocol with Helper

Definition 7 (Sigma Protocol with Helper, [8]). *An interactive protocol between Prover and Verifier is said to be a Sigma Protocol with Helper for Relation R, if it in the structure of* Fig. 3, *where w is the witness and x is the common input, such that:*

- **Completeness.** *If Prover and Verifier execute the protocol on the common input x, with the private input w to Prover satisfied $(x, w) \in R$, Verifier will always return Accept.*
- **2-Special Soundness.** *For any common input x with two valid transcripts $(x, \mathsf{aux}, \mathsf{com}, \mathsf{ch}, \mathsf{rsp})$ and $(x, \mathsf{aux}, \mathsf{com}, \mathsf{ch}', \mathsf{rsp}')$, where $\mathsf{aux} = \mathsf{Setup}(\mathsf{seed})$ for some* seed *(only Helper and Prover know the value of* seed*), and $\mathsf{ch} \neq \mathsf{ch}'$, there exists a polynomial-time knowledge extractor $\mathcal{E}$ that can extract the witness w, such that $(x, w) \in R$.*
- **Special Honest-Verifier Zero-Knowledge.** *There exists a polynomial-time simulator $\mathcal{S}$, on input common x, a random seed* seed*, with a challenge $\mathsf{ch} \leftarrow\!\!\$\ \mathcal{C}$, outputs a transcript of the form $(x, \mathsf{aux} = \mathsf{Setup}(\mathsf{seed}), \mathsf{com}, \mathsf{ch}, \mathsf{rsp})$,*

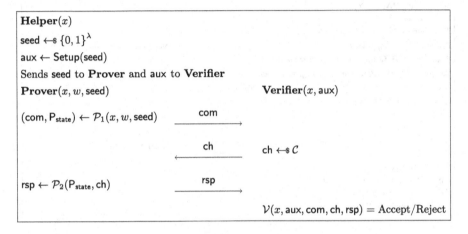

which is computationally indistinguishable from the transcripts of honest executing the protocol on input (x, w), where w satisfied $(x, w) \in R$.

Now, we present Sigma Protocol with Helper based on LRMC in Fig. 4, the system setting is same as the standard Sigma Protocol in Fig. 2.

Helper$(\mathbf{A}_1^-, \mathbf{A}_2^-)$

seed $\leftarrow\$ \{0,1\}^\lambda$

Generates $\mathbf{Y} \leftarrow\$ \mathrm{Mat}_{k,l}(\mathbb{F}), \mathbf{P} \leftarrow\$ \mathrm{GL}_k(\mathbb{F}), \mathbf{Q} \leftarrow\$ \mathrm{GL}_l(\mathbb{F})$, and $\alpha_{i_t,j_t} \leftarrow\$ \mathbb{F}^s$ from seed

Generates $(r_0, r_1) \leftarrow\$ \{0,1\}^\lambda \times \{0,1\}^\lambda$ from seed

Completes $\mathbf{A}_1^-$ with α_{i_t,j_t} to get $\mathbf{A}_1$

$\mathbf{c}_0 := \mathsf{Com}(r_0, \mathbf{P}, \mathbf{Q}, \mathbf{Y})$

$\mathbf{c}_1 := \mathsf{Com}(r_1, \mathbf{P}\mathbf{A}_1\mathbf{Q} + \mathbf{Y})$

aux $:= (\mathbf{c}_0, \mathbf{c}_1)$

Sends seed to **Prover** and aux to **Verifier**

Prover$(\mathbf{A}_1^-, \mathbf{A}_2^-, a_{i_t,j_t}, \text{seed})$ — **Verifier**$(\mathbf{A}_1^-, \mathbf{A}_2^-, \text{aux})$

Regenerates $\mathbf{Y}, \mathbf{P}, \mathbf{Q}, \alpha_{i_t,j_t}$, and r_0, r_1 from seed

Completes $\mathbf{A}_2^-$ with $\beta_{i_t,j_t} = a_{i_t,j_t} - \alpha_{i_t,j_t}$ to get $\mathbf{A}_2$.

$r_2 \leftarrow\$ \{0,1\}^\lambda$

$\mathbf{c}_2 := \mathsf{Com}(r_2, \mathbf{P}\mathbf{A}_2\mathbf{Q} - \mathbf{Y})$

$\xrightarrow{\mathbf{c}_2}$

$\xleftarrow{\mathsf{ch}}$ $\mathsf{ch} \leftarrow\$ \mathcal{C} = \{0,1\}$

If $\mathsf{ch} = 0$, then reveals $\mathbf{c}_1, \mathbf{c}_2$

rsp $:= (r_1, r_2, \mathbf{P}\mathbf{A}_1\mathbf{Q} + \mathbf{Y}, \mathbf{P}\mathbf{A}_2\mathbf{Q} - \mathbf{Y})$

If $\mathsf{ch} = 1$, then reveals $\mathbf{c}_0, \mathbf{c}_2$

rsp $:= (r_0, r_2, \mathbf{P}, \mathbf{Q}, \mathbf{Y}, \beta = (\beta_{i_t,j_t}))$

$\xrightarrow{\mathsf{rsp}}$

If $\mathsf{ch} = 0$, Computes and checks

$\mathbf{c}_1 = \mathsf{Com}(r_1, \mathbf{P}\mathbf{A}_1\mathbf{Q} + \mathbf{Y})$

$\mathbf{c}_2 = \mathsf{Com}(r_2, \mathbf{P}\mathbf{A}_2\mathbf{Q} - \mathbf{Y})$

$rank(\mathbf{P}\mathbf{A}_1\mathbf{Q} + \mathbf{Y} + \mathbf{P}\mathbf{A}_2\mathbf{Q} - \mathbf{Y}) = r$

If $\mathsf{ch} = 1$,

Recovers $\mathbf{A}_2$ with $\mathbf{A}_2^-$ and β

Computes and checks

$\mathbf{c}_0 = \mathsf{Com}(r_0, \mathbf{P}, \mathbf{Q}, \mathbf{Y})$

$\mathbf{c}_2 = \mathsf{Com}(r_2, \mathbf{P}\mathbf{A}_2\mathbf{Q} - \mathbf{Y})$

In each case, Verifier outputs Accept if and only if all conditions hold. Otherwise, it outputs Reject.

Fig. 4. Sigma Protocol with Helper for proving the knowledge of LRMC

Theorem 3 (LRMC-based Sigma Protocol with Helper). *Let* Com *be the commitment scheme which is Computational Hinding and Binding, then the protocol in Fig. 4 satisfied Definition 7 for challenge* $\mathsf{ch} \in \{0,1\}$.

Proof. We prove the protocol of Fig. 4 achieves Perfect Completeness, 2-Special Soundness, and Special Honest-Verifier Zero-Knowledge in Definition 7.

We denote $\mathsf{rsp} = (r_0, r_2, \mathbf{P}', \mathbf{Q}', \mathbf{Y}', \gamma = (\gamma_{i_t,j_t}))$ as the response for $\mathsf{ch} = 1$. An honest Prover fulfills $(\mathbf{P}', \mathbf{Q}', \mathbf{Y}') = (\mathbf{P}, \mathbf{Q}, \mathbf{Y})$ and $\gamma = \beta$.

Completeness. During an honest execution of the protocol, we have $\mathbf{A} = \mathbf{A}_1 + \mathbf{A}_2$, and $\mathbf{P}, \mathbf{Q}$ are invertible, which derives

$$rank(\mathbf{PA}_1\mathbf{Q} + \mathbf{Y} + \mathbf{PA}_2\mathbf{Q} - \mathbf{Y}) = rank(\mathbf{PAQ}) = rank(\mathbf{A}) = r$$

Combining with the Completeness of the commitment scheme Com, we know Verifier will always output Accept, i.e., the protocol has Perfect Completeness.

2-Special Soundness. For any input public key $(\mathbf{A}_1^-, \mathbf{A}_2^-)$, suppose an adversary knows two valid transcripts $(\mathbf{A}_1^-, \mathbf{A}_2^-, \mathsf{aux}, \mathsf{com} = \mathbf{c}_2, \mathsf{ch}, \mathsf{rsp})$ and $(\mathbf{A}_1^-, \mathbf{A}_2^-, \mathsf{aux}, \mathsf{com} = \mathbf{c}_2, \mathsf{ch}', \mathsf{rsp}')$, where $\mathsf{aux} = \mathsf{Setup}(\mathsf{seed})$ for given seed (only knows by Helper and Prover), and $\mathsf{ch} \neq \mathsf{ch}'$, we use it to construct a polynomial-time knowledge extractor $\mathcal{E}$ which can extract Prover's secret key, i.e., obtain a solution for the LRMC Problem.

Since $\mathsf{ch}, \mathsf{ch}' \in \{0, 1\}$ and $\mathsf{ch} \neq \mathsf{ch}'$, without loss of generality, we can assume $\mathsf{ch} = 1$ and $\mathsf{ch}' = 0$. Due to Verifier could answer all rsp, we complete $\mathbf{A}_2^-$ with γ to obtain $\mathbf{A}_2'$, the following is established for $\mathsf{ch} = 1$:

$$\mathbf{c}_0 = \mathsf{Com}(r_0, \mathbf{P}', \mathbf{Q}', \mathbf{Y}'), \quad \mathbf{c}_2 = \mathsf{Com}(r_2, \mathbf{P}'\mathbf{A}_2'\mathbf{Q}' - \mathbf{Y}').$$

According to the Computational Binding of the commitment scheme Com and $\mathbf{c}_0 = \mathsf{Com}(r_0, \mathbf{P}, \mathbf{Q}, \mathbf{Y})$, we have

$$\mathbf{P}' = \mathbf{P}, \quad \mathbf{Q}' = \mathbf{Q}, \quad \mathbf{Y}' = \mathbf{Y}.$$

On the other hand, note that for $\mathsf{ch}' = 0$, Verifier returns Accept only if $\mathbf{c}_2 = \mathsf{Com}(r_2, \mathbf{P}'\mathbf{A}_2'\mathbf{Q}' - \mathbf{Y}') = \mathsf{Com}(r_2, \mathbf{PA}_2'\mathbf{Q} - \mathbf{Y})$ as well as $r = rank(\mathbf{P}'\mathbf{A}_1\mathbf{Q}' + \mathbf{Y}' + \mathbf{P}'\mathbf{A}_2'\mathbf{Q}' - \mathbf{Y}') = rank(\mathbf{PA}_1\mathbf{Q} + \mathbf{PA}_2'\mathbf{Q}) = rank(\mathbf{P}(\mathbf{A}_1 + \mathbf{A}_2')\mathbf{Q})$, combining with $\mathbf{P}, \mathbf{Q}$ are invertible, we know the rank of $\mathbf{A}_1 + \mathbf{A}_2'$ is r. In addition to $\mathbf{c}_1 = \mathsf{Com}(r_1, \mathbf{PA}_1\mathbf{Q} + \mathbf{Y})$ from Helper's honest execution, we can obtain $\mathbf{A}_1 + \mathbf{A}_2'$, i.e., completing $\mathbf{A}_1^- + \mathbf{A}_2'^-$ with $\alpha + \gamma$, is a solution for the LRMC Problem.

Special Honest-Verifier Zero-Knowledge. We construct a polynomial-time simulator $\mathcal{S}$, on input public key $(\mathbf{A}_1^-, \mathbf{A}_2^-)$, a random seed seed, and a challenge $\mathsf{ch} \leftarrow_{\$} \mathcal{C} = \{0, 1\}$, it outputs a transcript $(\mathbf{A}_1^-, \mathbf{A}_2^-, \mathsf{aux} = \mathsf{Setup}(\mathsf{seed}), \mathsf{com}' = \mathbf{c}_2', \mathsf{ch}, \mathsf{rsp}')$ as follows:

1. Generates matrices $\mathbf{Y} \leftarrow_{\$} \mathrm{Mat}_{k,l}(\mathbb{F}), \mathbf{P} \leftarrow_{\$} \mathrm{GL}_k(\mathbb{F}), \mathbf{Q} \leftarrow_{\$} \mathrm{GL}_l(\mathbb{F})$, as well as $\alpha_{i_t,j_t} \leftarrow_{\$} \mathbb{F}^s, (r_0, r_1) \leftarrow_{\$} \{0,1\}^\lambda \times \{0,1\}^\lambda, \mathbf{c}_0 = \mathsf{Com}(r_0, \mathbf{P}, \mathbf{Q}, \mathbf{Y}), \mathbf{c}_1 = \mathsf{Com}(r_1, \mathbf{PA}_1\mathbf{Q} + \mathbf{Y}), \mathsf{aux} = (\mathbf{c}_0, \mathbf{c}_1)$ from seed as Helper's honest execution;
2. Simulates $\mathsf{com}' = \mathbf{c}_2'$ and rsp' according to ch :
   - $\mathsf{ch} = 0$: Chooses a random $r' \leftarrow_{\$} \{0,1\}^\lambda$ and a random matrix $\mathbf{R} \in \mathrm{Mat}_{k,l}(\mathbb{F})$ with $rank(\mathbf{R}) = r$, using $\mathbf{A}_1$ (completes $\mathbf{A}_1^-$ with α_{i_t,j_t}) to compute $\mathbf{A}_2' = \mathbf{R} - \mathbf{A}_1$, along with $\mathbf{c}_2' = \mathsf{Com}(r', \mathbf{PA}_2'\mathbf{Q} - \mathbf{Y})$, $\mathsf{rsp}' = (r_1, r', \mathbf{PA}_1\mathbf{Q} + \mathbf{Y}, \mathbf{PA}_2'\mathbf{Q} - \mathbf{Y})$.

- $\mathsf{ch} = 1$: Chooses a random $r' \leftarrow_{\$} \{0,1\}^\lambda$ and $\gamma \leftarrow_{\$} \mathbb{F}^s$, completes $\mathbf{A}_2^-$ with γ to obtain $\mathbf{A}_2'$, computes $\mathbf{c}_2' = \mathsf{Com}(r', \mathbf{P}\mathbf{A}_2'\mathbf{Q} - \mathbf{Y})$, as well as $\mathsf{rsp}' = (r_0, r', \mathbf{P}, \mathbf{Q}, \mathbf{Y}, \gamma)$.

Combining with the Computational Hiding of the commitment scheme Com, the simulated transcript $(\mathbf{A}_1^-, \mathbf{A}_2^-, \mathsf{aux} = (\mathbf{c}_0, \mathbf{c}_1), \mathsf{com} = \mathbf{c}_2', \mathsf{ch}, \mathsf{rsp}')$ satisfied:

1. When $\mathsf{ch} = 0$, rsp' is uniformly distributed in $\{0,1\}^\lambda \times \{0,1\}^\lambda \times \{(\mathbf{U}, \mathbf{V}) \in \mathrm{Mat}_{k,l}(\mathbb{F}) \times \mathrm{Mat}_{k,l}(\mathbb{F})$, such that $rank(\mathbf{U} + \mathbf{V}) = r\}$.
2. When $\mathsf{ch} = 1$, rsp' is uniformly distributed in $\{0,1\}^\lambda \times \{0,1\}^\lambda \times \mathrm{GL}_k(\mathbb{F}) \times \mathrm{GL}_l(\mathbb{F}) \times \mathrm{Mat}_{k,l}(\mathbb{F}) \times \mathbb{F}^s$.

That is to say, rsp' is computationally indistinguishable from rsp in transcripts of honest executing the protocol on input the public-secret keypair $((\mathbf{A}_1^-, \mathbf{A}_2^-), (a_{i_1,j_1}, \cdots, a_{i_s,j_s}))$, where completes $\mathbf{A}^- = \mathbf{A}_1^- + \mathbf{A}_2^-$ with $(a_{i_1,j_1}, \cdots, a_{i_s,j_s})$ to obtain a rank r matrix $\mathbf{A}$.

Furthermore, since $\mathbf{c}_2$ is totally determined by rsp in the same way that $\mathbf{c}_2'$ is totally determined by rsp', it can derive that the simulated transcript is computationally indistinguishable with the honest executing transcript. As a result, the simulator $\mathcal{S}$ is constructed successfully.

3.3 Removing the Helper

In order to remove the helper, we follow Beullens's spirit [8], which used the cut-and-choose approach proposed by Katz, Kolesnikov and Wang to dispense with the pre-processing [24], and was proven secure by Baum and Nof [4]. To be concrete, the procedure is described schematically in Fig. 5 and following.

Prover picks n seeds $\mathsf{seed}_1, \cdots, \mathsf{seed}_n$ and executes Setup algorithm to generate corresponding auxiliary value $\mathsf{aux}_i = (\mathbf{c}_{i,0}, \mathbf{c}_{i,1}), 1 \le i \le n$. Then, Prover sends all aux_i with $\mathbf{c}_{i,2} = \mathcal{P}_1(x, w, \mathsf{seed}_i)$ to Verifier. On receiving $(\mathsf{aux}_i, \mathbf{c}_{i,2}), 1 \le i \le n$, Verifier picks a random index $I \leftarrow_{\$} \{1, \cdots, n\}$ with a challenge $\mathsf{ch} \in \mathcal{C}$, and returns (I, ch) back to Prover. Prover sends seed_i for $i \in \bar{I} = \{1, \cdots, n\} \backslash I$ and rsp_I for $i = I$ to Verifier. Using seed_i for $i \in \bar{I}$, Verifier could checks if $\mathsf{aux}_{i \in \bar{I}}$ are generated legitimately, as well as if rsp_I is correct response for $i = I$.

3.4 Optimizations

Some optimizations can be also considered to diminish the communication cost of the protocol in Fig. 5, as follows.

Merkle Tree for Commitments. For the protocol in Fig. 5, $\mathbf{c}_{i,2} (1 \le i \le n)$ will be sent to Verifier in the commitment phase, but only one of which will be used in an honest execution of the whole protocol. Therefore, we can put $\mathbf{c}_{i,2}$ in a Merkle Tree, where $\mathbf{c}_{i,2}$ is the i-th leaf, and the root value is v_{root}. Instead of sending $\mathbf{c}_{i,2} (1 \le i \le n)$, Prover can send v_{root} as the commitment, and provide Verifier with the brother node of the path to recover v_{root}. Then, $\log n$ nodes of the Merkle Tree are required to reconstruct the root node and calculate v_{root}.

Prover(x, w)		**Verifier**(x)
for $i \in \{1, \cdots, n\}$ **do**		
$\mathsf{seed}_i \leftarrow_\$ \{0,1\}^\lambda$		
$(\mathbf{c}_{i,0}, \mathbf{c}_{i,1}) \leftarrow \mathsf{Setup}(\mathsf{seed}_i)$		
$\mathsf{aux}_i = (\mathbf{c}_{i,0}, \mathbf{c}_{i,1})$		
$\mathbf{c}_{i,2} \leftarrow \mathcal{P}_1(x, w, \mathsf{seed}_i)$		
end for		
	$\xrightarrow{\mathsf{aux}_i, \mathbf{c}_{i,2}, 1 \le i \le n}$	
		$I \leftarrow_\$ \{1, \cdots, n\}$
		$\mathsf{ch} \leftarrow_\$ \mathcal{C}$
	$\xleftarrow{I, \mathsf{ch}}$	
$\mathsf{rsp}_I \leftarrow \mathcal{P}_2(x, w, \mathsf{seed}_I, \mathsf{ch})$	$\xrightarrow{\mathsf{seed}_i, \forall i \in \bar{I}, \text{ and } \mathsf{rsp}_I}$	
		Computes and checks
		$\mathsf{aux}_i = \mathsf{Setup}(\mathsf{seed}_i), \forall i \in \bar{I}$
		$\mathcal{V}(x, \mathsf{aux}_I, \mathbf{c}_{I,2}, \mathsf{ch}, \mathsf{rsp}_I)$
Verifier outputs Accept if and only if all conditions hold. Otherwise, it outputs Reject.		

Fig. 5. Removing Helper from the Sigma Protocol with Helper

Additionally, commitments v_{root} and $\mathsf{aux}_1, \cdots, \mathsf{aux}_n$ can also be compressed by Merkle Tree. In the commitment phase, it only needs to send the commitment $\mathsf{Com}(r, (v_{\mathsf{root}}, \mathsf{aux}_1, \cdots, \mathsf{aux}_n))$, with missing inputs, and Verifier can recompute it like missing nodes of the Merkle Tree.

Binary Tree for Seeds. For the protocol in Fig. 5, Prover generates and sends seed_i for $i \in \bar{I} = \{1, \cdots, n\} \backslash I$ to Verifier. We can also optimize the transmission by using a Binary Tree. Prover picks the value of the root node randomly, and then expands to its two children nodes through Pseudo-Random Number Generator (PRNG), until it reaches the depth of $\lceil \log n \rceil$, i.e., it contains at least n leaf nodes, and each leaf node corresponds to seed_i $(i \in \bar{I})$. In this way, seed_i can be recomputed by $\lceil \log n \rceil$ node values rather than $k-1$ seed values.

Improvement in Parallel Repetition. Assume $\frac{1}{q}$ is the soundness error of a single execution of the Sigma Protocol in Fig. 5, in order to decrease the soundness error to $2^{-\lambda}$, the protocol needs to be repeated $REP = \lceil \frac{\lambda}{\log q} \rceil$ times. Katz, Kolesnikov and Wang [24] provide a more efficient method as follows.

The underlying idea is that instead of verifying 1 out of n, let Verifier choose τ out of n to verify in each round, as shown in Fig. 6. To be concrete, denote the index set as $I \subseteq \{1, \cdots, n\}$ with $|I| = \tau$, $\bar{I} = \{1, \cdots, n\} \backslash I$. Prover computes a total of M dishonest Setup and provides valid rsp_i. It is because Prover reveals $\mathsf{seed}_i, \forall i \in \bar{I}$ to Verifier at last, Prover can convince Verifier only when

Prover(x, w)		**Verifier**(x)
for $i \in \{1, \cdots, n\}$ **do**		
$\mathsf{seed}_i \leftarrow\!\$\ \{0,1\}^\lambda$		
$(\mathbf{c}_{i,0}, \mathbf{c}_{i,1}) \leftarrow \mathsf{Setup}(\mathsf{seed}_i)$		
$\mathsf{aux}_i = (\mathbf{c}_{i,0}, \mathbf{c}_{i,1})$		
$\mathbf{c}_{i,2} \leftarrow \mathcal{P}_1(x, w, \mathsf{seed}_i)$		
end for		
	$\mathsf{aux}_i, \mathbf{c}_{i,2}, 1 \leq i \leq n$ $\longrightarrow$	
		$I \subseteq \{1, \cdots, n\}, \lvert I \rvert = \tau$
		$\mathsf{ch}_i \leftarrow\!\$\ \mathcal{C}, \forall i \in I$
	$\longleftarrow$ $I, \mathsf{ch}_i, \forall i \in I$	
$\mathsf{rsp}_i \leftarrow \mathcal{P}_2(x, w, \mathsf{seed}_i, \mathsf{ch}_i), \forall i \in I$	$\mathsf{seed}_i, \forall i \in \bar{I}$; $\mathsf{rsp}_i, \forall i \in I$ $\longrightarrow$	
		Computes and checks
		$\mathsf{aux}_i = \mathsf{Setup}(\mathsf{seed}_i), \forall i \in \bar{I}$
		$\mathcal{V}(x, \mathsf{aux}_i, \mathbf{c}_{i,2}, \mathsf{ch}, \mathsf{rsp}_i), \forall i \in I$

Verifier outputs Accept if and only if all conditions hold. Otherwise, it outputs Reject.

Fig. 6. Improvement in Parallel Repetition in Fig. 5

all M dishonest Setup belongs to I. Therefore, the probability of this happening is $\binom{n-M}{\tau-M}\binom{n}{\tau}^{-1}$, and Prover needs to provide valid responses for the remaining $\tau - i$ honest Setup, the success probability is $\left(\frac{1}{q}\right)^{\tau-i}$. As a result, the soundness error of the whole protocol is

$$\max_{0 \leq M \leq \tau} \frac{\binom{n-M}{\tau-M}}{\binom{n}{\tau} q^{(\tau-M)}}$$

For the more rigorous proof, please refer to [4].

4 Signature and LRMC-Based Construction

In this section, we transform the improved Sigma Protocol into a Digital Signature Scheme using the Fiat-Shamir transform directly. Then, we evaluated the public key sizes and signature sizes after the above optimizations. Finally, we choose the parameters and compare them with the best schemes available.

4.1 From Sigma Protocol to Signature

The Fiat-Shamir transform [20] allows us to convert the Sigma Protocol based on LRMC Problem straight into the Signature Scheme. The underlying motivation is that instead of being chosen by the Verifier, challenge can be determined by the commitment and the message to sign. Concretely, to sign on the message μ, Signer executes the first move of the Sigma Protocol in Fig. 1 to generate com, then derives ch by $\mathsf{H}(\mathsf{com}, \mu)$, where μ is the message and H is random oracle. Finally, Signer executes the third move of the Sigma Protocol to obtain rsp, and the signature on μ is $(\mathsf{com}, \mathsf{rsp})$. Verifier can compute ch by querying the random oracle with (com, μ), and return Accept if and only if $(\mathsf{com}, \mathsf{ch}, \mathsf{rsp})$ is a valid transcript of the Sigma Protocol.

According to [19], we can also directly derive a signature scheme based on LRMC which is strongly unforgeable in the QROM.

4.2 Evaluation of the Signature Scheme

Public Key Size. The public key of the scheme is $(\mathbf{A}_1^-, \mathbf{A}_2^-)$, both are $k \times l$-dimension matrices with s entries unfilled. As is shown in the Key Generation phase in Sect. 3.1, we set $\mathbf{A}_1^-$ with all 1 at its filled entries, then $\mathbf{A}^-$ and $\mathbf{A}_2^-$ can be converted to each other without difficulty. As for the transmission of the public key, only $\mathbf{A}_2^-$ is necessary, because Verifier can change all filled entries of $\mathbf{A}_2^-$ to 1 to obtain $\mathbf{A}_1^-$. Therefore, the public key size is $(kl - s)\log q$ bits.

Our scheme's public key size is smaller when compared with recent MinRank-based signature scheme [5], even though they utilize seeds to reduce it, not to mention the additional time and storage costs they suffer when using seeds and other compression techniques. In fact, their method to compress is time-consuming and storage-occupied because it involves computing linear combinations of hundreds of matrices with several matrix-vector multiplications. The detailed comparisons are in Table 1.

Signature Size. The signature size of the signature scheme transformed from our improved sigma protocol, is determined by the communication cost of messages send from Prover to Verifier in Fig. 5 after optimizations in Sect. 3.4, it includes: $\mathsf{com} = \{\mathsf{aux}_i, \mathbf{c}_{i,2}(1 \le i \le n)\}$ and $\mathsf{rsp} = \{\mathsf{seed}_i(i \in \bar{I}), \mathsf{rsp}_i(i \in I)\}$.

1. $\mathbf{c}_{i,2}(1 \le i \le n)$: Due to Verifier will compute and check all $\mathbf{c}_{i,2}(i \in I)$ at the end, a total of τ. Using Merkle Tree for commitments in Sect. 3.4, Prover needs to send at most $\tau \log \frac{n}{\tau}$ tree-nodes with each size 2λ, for Verifier to reconstruct the root node and calculate v_{root}, and the commitment $\mathsf{Com}(r, (v_{\mathsf{root}}, \mathsf{aux}_1, \cdots, \mathsf{aux}_n))$ with size 2λ, so the total size is $2\lambda \cdot \tau \log\lceil \frac{n}{\tau} \rceil + 2\lambda$ bits.
2. $\mathsf{seed}_i(i \in \bar{I})$: Using Binary Tree for seeds in Sect. 3.4, Prover needs to send at most $\tau \log \frac{n}{\tau}$ tree-nodes with each size λ, for Verifier to recalculate seed_i for $i \in \bar{I}$, the total size is $\lambda \cdot \tau \log\lceil \frac{n}{\tau} \rceil$ bits.

3. $\mathsf{aux}_i(1 \leq i \leq n)$: $\mathsf{seed}_i(i \in \bar{I})$ have allowed Verifier to compute $\mathsf{aux}_i(i \in \bar{I})$, Verifier still need to check $\mathsf{aux}_i(i \in I)$. Note that one of each $\mathsf{aux}_i = (\mathbf{c}_{i,0}, \mathbf{c}_{i,1})$ can be parsed and computed from $\mathsf{rsp}_i(i \in I)$ in Fig. 4, so only τ values need to be provided by Prover (the rest $\mathbf{c}_{i,0}$ or $\mathbf{c}_{i,1}$ in aux_i for $i \in I$), and each size of the commitment output is 2λ, the total size is $\tau \cdot 2\lambda$ bits.
4. $\mathsf{rsp}_i(i \in I)$:
   rsp_i for $\mathsf{ch} = 0$ in Fig. 5 and Fig. 6, due to $\mathbf{A} = \mathbf{A}_1 + \mathbf{A}_2$, instead of sending $\mathbf{PA}_1\mathbf{Q}+\mathbf{Y}, \mathbf{PA}_2\mathbf{Q}-\mathbf{Y}$, Prover can send $\mathbf{PA}_1\mathbf{Q}+\mathbf{Y}$ with $\mathbf{PAQ}$ as rsp, carries the same information.
   - $\mathbf{PA}_1\mathbf{Q} + \mathbf{Y}$: Requires $kl \log q$ bits.
   - $\mathbf{PAQ}$: The advantage is $rank(\mathbf{PAQ}) = rank(\mathbf{A}) = r$, so it can be represented as $\mathbf{PAQ} = \mathbf{XY}$, where $\mathbf{X} \in \mathrm{Mat}_{k,r}(\mathbb{F})$ and $\mathbf{Y} \in \mathrm{Mat}_{r,l}(\mathbb{F})$. Using this method, instead of sending entries of $\mathbf{PA}_2\mathbf{Q} - \mathbf{Y}$ of $kl \log q$ bits, Prover only need to send $\mathbf{X}, \mathbf{Y}$, requires $(k+l)r \log q$ bits, which leads an improvement when $r < \frac{kl}{k+l}$.

   rsp_i for $\mathsf{ch} = 1$ in Fig. 5 and Fig. 6,
   - $\mathbf{P}, \mathbf{Q}, \mathbf{Y}$: Generated from seeds, requires λ bits.
   - $\beta = (\beta_{i_t,j_t}) : 1 \leq t \leq s$, β consists of s elements in $\mathbb{F} = \mathbb{F}_q$, requires $s \log q$ bits.

   The average size of the τ responses is

$$\frac{kl \log q + (k+l)r \log q}{2} + \frac{\lambda + s \log q}{2} \text{ bits} \tag{1}$$

From $1 \sim 4$ we have the signature size (total communication cost of messages send from Prover to Verifier) is:

$$\lambda \cdot (3\tau \log \left\lceil \frac{n}{\tau} \right\rceil + 2\tau + 2) + \tau \cdot \left(\frac{kl \log q + (k+l)r \log q}{2} + \frac{\lambda + s \log q}{2} \right) \text{ bits} \tag{2}$$

Parameters and Size Comparisons. Since the equivalence between the LRMC and MinRank shown in Theorem 1 and *Remark* 1 in Sect. 2, we can choose the corresponding set of parameters of [5], which is a very recent study on MinRank-based scheme. The concrete parameter sets and size comparisons is in Table 1.

1. We obtain optimal signature sizes for proposed scheme with cut-and-choose parameters $\tau = \lambda$ and $n = 2\lambda$ in Fig. 6 in Sect. 3.4.
2. **Comparing with MinRank-based signature schemes** [5,14]**.** Apart from shorter public key sizes, our signature scheme has advantages as follows.
   - Storage-Lower: Our signature scheme does not need to use seeds to generate the public key matrices $(\mathbf{A}_1^-, \mathbf{A}_2^-)$. While [5,14] used seeds to compress $s > 100$ matrices in $\mathrm{Mat}_{k,l}(\mathbb{F}_q)$ (more than 10 KiloBytes) into 20 Bytes. In the actual signing process, these seeds still need to be restored into matrices, and sufficient storage overhead is still required. We have a significant reduction in total storage costs of the public key and signature in actual signing, e.g., more than 30% for the Parameter Set I.

Table 1. Public key sizes (in Bytes) and signature sizes (in KiloBytes) for suggested parameters of LRMC-based signature in comparison to the MinRank-based signature, where Bellini et al. [5] is the state-of-the-art and Courtois [14] is the pioneering.

Parameter Set		I	II	III
λ [Security parameter]		128	192	256
q [Order of finite field $\mathbb{F} = \mathbb{F}_q$]		16	16	16
(k, l) [Dimensions of matrix $\mathbf{A}$]		(14, 14)	(17, 17)	(20, 20)
r [Rank of matrix $\mathbf{A}$]		4	6	6
s [Unfilled number of matrix $\mathbf{A}$]		108	130	208
Public Key Size (B)	This work	44	80	96
	Bellini et al. [5]	60 (by seeds)	104 (by seeds)	128 (by seeds)
	Courtois [14]	114 (by seeds)	169 (by seeds)	232 (by seeds)
Signature Size (KB)	This work	24	54	97
	Bellini et al. [5]	24	54	97
	Courtois [14]	55	118	221

- Time-Shorter: In [5,14], Verifier needs to calculate linear combinations of hundreds of matrices and several matrix vector multiplications in $\mathrm{Mat}_{k,l}(\mathbb{F}_q)$ to recover Signer's public key before verifying each time. We omit this step and save considerable time compared with them.
- Conceptually-Simpler: Our systems are more intuitive and succinct, only one (partially filled) matrix $\mathbf{A} \in \mathrm{Mat}_{k,l}(\mathbb{F}_q)$ will be defined in the system parameters, rather than $s+1$ matrices in the same dimensions in [5,14].

3. **Comparing with NIST Standards.** The sizes of our LRMC-based signature scheme are in the proximity of SPHINCS+ [1], which achieves $\lambda = 128$ at the cost of Public Key Size = 32 B and Signature Size ≈ 17 KB. SPHINCS+ is the only one that will be standardized but not based on the computational hardness of problems involving structural lattices. Lattice-based cryptographic constructions have many advantages, however, the attack methods using the special structure of lattices (e.g., module or ring), and the hardness of structural lattice problems are worth further study.

Running Time. To evaluate the efficiency of our scheme, we run experiments on the renowned number theory library Python3-cypari2 [33], and the hardware platform consists of a 2.3 GHz Quad-Core Intel Core i5, 16 GB RAM, macOS BigSur for 64 bit operation system. The commitment scheme com is instantiated as the SHAKE-3 hash function, and results are the average of different challenge values after enough times. Briefly, in our Signature Scheme without optimizations for the Parameter Set I ($\lambda = 128$, corresponding to NIST Security Level 2), the Signing phase runs in 21.344 ms, and the Verification phase runs in 2.207 ms, which are also competitive with NIST candidate signature schemes.

5 Conclusion

In this paper, we introduce a brand-new hard problem, Low-Rank Matrix Completion (LRMC), to build cryptographic primitives. The hardness of LRMC is equivalent to MinRank, which has been thoroughly studied to be NP-Complete and quantum-resistant. In order to increase the diversity of post-quantum cryptography, we present a (3-move) Sigma Protocol based on the LRMC Problem. After utilizing several optimization techniques, we transform the improved protocol into a Signature Scheme which is better than MinRank-based constructions in most aspects. The proposed Signature Scheme is also competitive with NIST candidate SPHINCS+, which is the only one determined to be standardized but does not rely on structural problems.

Acknowledgements. This work is supported by the National Key R&D Program of China (No. 2022YFB4500800), the Key R&D projects in Hubei Province (No.2022BAA041), and the Fundamental Research Funds for the Central Universities (No. 2042022kf0021). The authors are grateful to the committees and anonymous reviewers of PKC 2023 and ProvSec 2023 for their insightful comments that refine this work, and generous help from the shepherd. Furthermore, Jiaming Wen appreciates Lu Bai's assistance during the experiments.

References

1. Aumasson, J.P., et al.: SPHINCS+. http://sphincs.org/
2. Avanzi, R., et al.: CRYSTALS-Kyber. https://pq-crystals.org/kyber/
3. Bai, S., et al.: CRYSTALS-Dilithium. https://pq-crystals.org/dilithium/
4. Baum, C., Nof, A.: Concretely-efficient zero-knowledge arguments for arithmetic circuits and their application to lattice-based cryptography. In: Kiayias, A., Kohlweiss, M., Wallden, P., Zikas, V. (eds.) PKC 2020. LNCS, vol. 12110, pp. 495–526. Springer, Cham (2020). https://doi.org/10.1007/978-3-030-45374-9_17
5. Bellini, E., Esser, A., Sanna, C., Verbel, J.A.: MR-DSS - smaller minrank-based (ring-)signatures. In: Cheon, J.H., Johansson, T. (eds.) PQCrypto 2022, LNCS, vol. 13512, pp. 144–169. Springer, Heidelberg (2022). https://doi.org/10.1007/978-3-031-17234-2_8
6. Berlekamp, E.R., McEliece, R.J., van Tilborg, H.C.A.: On the inherent intractability of certain coding problems (corresp.). IEEE Trans. Inf. Theory **24**(3), 384–386 (1978). https://doi.org/10.1109/TIT.1978.1055873
7. Bettale, L., Faugère, J., Perret, L.: Cryptanalysis of HFE, multi-HFE and variants for odd and even characteristic. Des. Codes Cryptogr. **69**(1), 1–52 (2013). https://doi.org/10.1007/s10623-012-9617-2
8. Beullens, W.: Sigma protocols for MQ, PKP and SIS, and fishy signature schemes. In: Canteaut, A., Ishai, Y. (eds.) EUROCRYPT 2020. LNCS, vol. 12107, pp. 183–211. Springer, Cham (2020). https://doi.org/10.1007/978-3-030-45727-3_7
9. Beullens, W., Faugère, J.-C., Koussa, E., Macario-Rat, G., Patarin, J., Perret, L.: PKP-based signature scheme. In: Hao, F., Ruj, S., Sen Gupta, S. (eds.) INDOCRYPT 2019. LNCS, vol. 11898, pp. 3–22. Springer, Cham (2019). https://doi.org/10.1007/978-3-030-35423-7_1
10. Buss, J.F., Frandsen, G.S., Shallit, J.O.: The computational complexity of some problems of linear algebra. J. Comput. Syst. Sci. **58**(3), 572–596 (1999). https://doi.org/10.1006/jcss.1998.1608
11. Candès, E.J., Tao, T.: The power of convex relaxation: near-optimal matrix completion. IEEE Trans. Inf. Theory **56**(5), 2053–2080 (2010). https://doi.org/10.1109/TIT.2010.2044061

12. Chase, M., et al.: Post-quantum zero-knowledge and signatures from symmetric-key primitives. In: Thuraisingham, B., Evans, D., Malkin, T., Xu, D. (eds.) ACM CCS 2017, pp. 1825–1842. ACM (2017). https://doi.org/10.1145/3133956.3133997
13. Chen, M.-S., Hülsing, A., Rijneveld, J., Samardjiska, S., Schwabe, P.: From 5-pass $\mathcal{MQ}$-based identification to $\mathcal{MQ}$-based signatures. In: Cheon, J.H., Takagi, T. (eds.) ASIACRYPT 2016. LNCS, vol. 10032, pp. 135–165. Springer, Heidelberg (2016). https://doi.org/10.1007/978-3-662-53890-6_5
14. Courtois, N.T.: Efficient zero-knowledge authentication based on a linear algebra problem MinRank. In: Boyd, C. (ed.) ASIACRYPT 2001. LNCS, vol. 2248, pp. 402–421. Springer, Heidelberg (2001). https://doi.org/10.1007/3-540-45682-1_24
15. Courtois, N.T.: The security of hidden field equations (HFE). In: Naccache, D. (ed.) CT-RSA 2001. LNCS, vol. 2020, pp. 266–281. Springer, Heidelberg (2001). https://doi.org/10.1007/3-540-45353-9_20
16. Derksen, H.: On the equivalence between low-rank matrix completion and tensor rank. Linear Multilinear Algebra **66**(4), 645–667 (2018)
17. Ding, J., Perlner, R., Petzoldt, A., Smith-Tone, D.: Improved cryptanalysis of HFEv- via projection. In: Lange, T., Steinwandt, R. (eds.) PQCrypto 2018. LNCS, vol. 10786, pp. 375–395. Springer, Cham (2018). https://doi.org/10.1007/978-3-319-79063-3_18
18. Ding, J., Schmidt, D.: Rainbow, a new multivariable polynomial signature scheme. In: Ioannidis, J., Keromytis, A., Yung, M. (eds.) ACNS 2005. LNCS, vol. 3531, pp. 164–175. Springer, Heidelberg (2005). https://doi.org/10.1007/11496137_12
19. Don, J., Fehr, S., Majenz, C., Schaffner, C.: Security of the Fiat-Shamir transformation in the quantum random-oracle model. In: Boldyreva, A., Micciancio, D. (eds.) CRYPTO 2019. LNCS, vol. 11693, pp. 356–383. Springer, Cham (2019). https://doi.org/10.1007/978-3-030-26951-7_13
20. Fiat, A., Shamir, A.: How to prove yourself: practical solutions to identification and signature problems. In: Odlyzko, A.M. (ed.) CRYPTO 1986. LNCS, vol. 263, pp. 186–194. Springer, Heidelberg (1987). https://doi.org/10.1007/3-540-47721-7_12
21. Fouque, P.A., et al.: Falcon. https://falcon-sign.info/
22. Goubin, L., Courtois, N.T.: Cryptanalysis of the TTM cryptosystem. In: Okamoto, T. (ed.) ASIACRYPT 2000. LNCS, vol. 1976, pp. 44–57. Springer, Heidelberg (2000). https://doi.org/10.1007/3-540-44448-3_4
23. Han, B., Sim, J.: Reflection removal using low-rank matrix completion. In: CVPR 2017, pp. 3872–3880. IEEE Computer Society (2017). https://doi.org/10.1109/CVPR.2017.412
24. Katz, J., Kolesnikov, V., Wang, X.: Improved non-interactive zero knowledge with applications to post-quantum signatures. In: Lie, D., Mannan, M., Backes, M., Wang, X. (eds.) ACM CCS 2018, pp. 525–537. ACM (2018). https://doi.org/10.1145/3243734.3243805
25. Kawachi, A., Tanaka, K., Xagawa, K.: Concurrently secure identification schemes based on the worst-case hardness of lattice problems. In: Pieprzyk, J. (ed.) ASIACRYPT 2008. LNCS, vol. 5350, pp. 372–389. Springer, Heidelberg (2008). https://doi.org/10.1007/978-3-540-89255-7_23
26. Keshavan, R.H., Montanari, A., Oh, S.: Matrix completion from a few entries. IEEE Trans. Inf. Theory **56**(6), 2980–2998 (2010). https://doi.org/10.1109/TIT.2010.2046205
27. Kim, S., Nguyen, L.T., Shim, B.: Deep neural network based matrix completion for internet of things network localization. In: ICASSP 2020, pp. 3427–3431. IEEE (2020). https://doi.org/10.1109/ICASSP40776.2020.9053773

28. Kipnis, A., Shamir, A.: Cryptanalysis of the HFE public key cryptosystem by relinearization. In: Wiener, M. (ed.) CRYPTO 1999. LNCS, vol. 1666, pp. 19–30. Springer, Heidelberg (1999). https://doi.org/10.1007/3-540-48405-1_2
29. Koren, Y.: Collaborative filtering with temporal dynamics. In: Elder IV, J.F., Fogelman-Soulié, F., Flach, P.A., Zaki, M.J. (eds.) ACM SIGKDD 2009, pp. 447–456. ACM (2009). https://doi.org/10.1145/1557019.1557072
30. Ling, S., Nguyen, K., Stehlé, D., Wang, H.: Improved zero-knowledge proofs of knowledge for the ISIS problem, and applications. In: Kurosawa, K., Hanaoka, G. (eds.) PKC 2013. LNCS, vol. 7778, pp. 107–124. Springer, Heidelberg (2013). https://doi.org/10.1007/978-3-642-36362-7_8
31. Petzoldt, A., Chen, M.-S., Yang, B.-Y., Tao, C., Ding, J.: Design principles for HFEv-based multivariate signature schemes. In: Iwata, T., Cheon, J.H. (eds.) ASIACRYPT 2015. LNCS, vol. 9452, pp. 311–334. Springer, Heidelberg (2015). https://doi.org/10.1007/978-3-662-48797-6_14
32. Saade, A., Krzakala, F., Zdeborová, L.: Matrix completion from fewer entries: spectral detectability and rank estimation. In: Cortes, C., Lawrence, N.D., Lee, D.D., Sugiyama, M., Garnett, R. (eds.) NeurlPS 2015, pp. 1261–1269 (2015). https://proceedings.neurips.cc/paper/2015/hash/a8e864d04c95572d1aece099af852d0a-Abstract.html
33. SageMath: Python3-cypari2. https://github.com/sagemath/cypari2
34. Sakumoto, K., Shirai, T., Hiwatari, H.: Public-key identification schemes based on multivariate quadratic polynomials. In: Rogaway, P. (ed.) CRYPTO 2011. LNCS, vol. 6841, pp. 706–723. Springer, Heidelberg (2011). https://doi.org/10.1007/978-3-642-22792-9_40
35. Stern, J.: A new identification scheme based on syndrome decoding. In: Stinson, D.R. (ed.) CRYPTO 1993. LNCS, vol. 773, pp. 13–21. Springer, Heidelberg (1994). https://doi.org/10.1007/3-540-48329-2_2
36. Unruh, D.: Non-interactive zero-knowledge proofs in the quantum random oracle model. In: Oswald, E., Fischlin, M. (eds.) EUROCRYPT 2015. LNCS, vol. 9057, pp. 755–784. Springer, Heidelberg (2015). https://doi.org/10.1007/978-3-662-46803-6_25

Threshold Ring Signature Scheme from Cryptographic Group Action

Minh Thuy Truc Pham, Dung Hoang Duong(✉), Yannan Li(✉), and Willy Susilo(✉)

Institute of Cybersecurity and Cryptology, School of Computing and Information Technology, University of Wollongong, Northfields Avenue, Wollongong, NSW 2522, Australia

mttp907@uowmail.edu.au, {hduong,yannan,wsusilo}@uow.edu.au

Abstract. A threshold ring signature (t-out-of-N) is an extension of ring signatures that allow t users jointly sign a message on the behalf of N users, selected in an arbitrary manner, while keeping their identities anonymous. This paper presents a construction of threshold ring signature from cryptographic group action, based on the OR proof of group action and the idea of creating a threshold ring signature scheme from a ring signature scheme. We instantiate the proposed protocols in both isogeny and lattice settings. The signature size of our isogeny-based construction is smaller than the existing threshold ring signature scheme (e.g. 65 KB signatures compared to 187 KB for the same ring size).

Keywords: Threshold Ring Signature scheme · Group Action · Isogeny · Lattice

1 Introduction

In recent years, the quantum computer era is reaching its peak with several developments which pose a considerable threat to numerous widely used cryptographic constructions. As a result, a new era of cryptography, known as the post-quantum era, has emerged. This era focuses on developing cryptographic algorithms that can withstand quantum attacks. In 2016, the US National Institute of Standards and Technology (NIST) held a Post-Quantum Cryptography Standardization [2] with the goal of standardizing quantum-resistant cryptographic methods for the future. Since then, various cryptographic methods have been proposed, using different building blocks such as code-based, hash-based, multivariate-based, lattice-based, and isogeny-based techniques.

Ring Signatures, is one of the most important cryptographic primitives in this upcoming science future. In a ring signature scheme, a user can sign a

This work is partially funded by the Australian Research Council (ARC) Linkage Project LP220100332, Discovery Project DP220100003 and the RevITAlise (RITA) Research Grant 2021.

M. Zhang et al. (Eds.): ProvSec 2023, LNCS 14217, pp. 207–227, 2023.
https://doi.org/10.1007/978-3-031-45513-1_12

signature on behalf of the whole "ring" of users without revealing a single piece of information about the identity. The anonymity provided by ring signatures has a wide range of applications, including secure communication, online privacy , voting systems, and anonymous cryptocurrency transactions [4,39]. Notably, in constructing many practical anonymous cryptocurrencies, anonymity property can be used to maintain the security property of the transactions and the identity of the actual money user. Since the first ring signature scheme proposal, many constructions have been in reach in the literature based on a wide range of assumptions with additional properties and many forms of extensions, such as linkable ring signatures [12,31], revocable ring signatures [42] and threshold ring signatures in both the random oracle model and standard model [8,9,35] just to name a few. Our work will only focus on developing threshold ring signature schemes.

Threshold Ring Signature. In 2002, Bresson, Stern, and Szydloin et al. [13] presented the definition of Threshold Ring Signatures (TRS) scheme by extending the previous concept of ring signature scheme, which mandates a user to sign anonymously a message on behalf of a group of users. In the same manner, a **t-out-of-N threshold ring signature** scheme allows t users to create a joint signature on behalf of a larger group of N users without revealing the set of signer's identity. Inheriting the properties of the Ring Signature scheme, a TRS scheme must satisfy the *existential unforgeability* and *anonymity* (so-called source-hiding) properties. The *unforgeability* property ensures that any set of fewer than t users cannot collaborate to create a signature on behalf of any ring of users. The *anonymity* property ensures that if a signature σ is associated with a ring R of N users, then any possible subset of t users in that ring R have the same probability of being the set of signers. Another way of stating the source-hiding property is that the two subsets of t users SK_0^t and SK_1^t of a ring of N users R are likely to be the set of secret keys that signs a signature σ.

The benefit of the TRS lies in the fact that TRS is ideal for decentralized settings where users can join and leave the system dynamically. This feature has many applications in the field of Blockchain and cryptocurrencies. Specifically, the signature can be generated in a multi-user system even when some users are offline, as long as a minimum of t users are still online. Furthermore, inheriting from the application of the ring signature schemes, TRS also has many applications in the scenario of e-cash, e-voting and privacy-preserving cryptocurrencies where signers must protect their identities hidden from their fellow signers.

Motivated by the wide range of usage, several TRS constructions have recently been proposed in the literature. Based on Bresson's introductory definition, several constructions were proposed using non-post-quantum resistant hard problems such as Discrete Logarithm, RSA or bilinear maps [13,26,30,33,40,41]. In 2008, Aguilar, Cayrel and Gaborit et al. [1] proposed the first post-quantum code-based TRS scheme that is efficient in terms of its complexity. After that turning point, many other code-based TRS schemes were proposed with many improvements in efficiency and the complexity of the constructions, for example, [16] and [6].

Regarding lattice-based cryptography, in 2010, Cayrel et al. [17] proposed a lattice-based version of the initial work by Bresson [13]. Three years later, Bettaieb et.al. [8] enhanced Cayrel's scheme by generalizing the same identification scheme as in [17] but significantly reducing the size of the public key and signature by simply using a different way to achieve the anonymity property. Some efficient multivariate-based TRS constructions are also in reach [24,35] in recent years. Lately, Li and Maozhi et al. [29] proposed a post-quantum isogeny-based TRS scheme called "RippleSign" using trapdoor commitments combining with the technique of Bresson's construction [13]. However, their scheme still suffers the same disadvantages in a $\mathcal{O}(Nt)$ signature size.

One notable work recently is the paper [27] proposed by Haque and Scafuro, which describes new security definitions for the t-out-of-N threshold ring signature scheme in the presence of an "*active*" adversary. The authors also proposed a general construction of the TRS in the Quantum random oracle model (QROM) based on any post-quantum secure trapdoor commitment scheme. In 2022, Aranha et.al. [5] introduced a new property of TRS called *extendability*, which allows anyone to enlarge the set of potential signers of a given signature. The work also builds extendable (threshold) ring signature constructions from Signature of Knowledge and Discrete Log. However, these two topics exceed the scope of this paper.

Cryptographic Group Action. In general, cryptographic group action constructions are gaining attention as an effective method for developing cryptographic protocols, thanks to their strong mathematical properties. Specifically, schemes based on cryptographic group action can be applied in various settings, such as lattice and isogeny, and can address newly proposed challenges like the Isomorphism Problems of Trilinear Forms. [38]. The initial idea of using group action can be found in Couveignes' work [18] in which he used the action of the class group $\mathcal{C}\ell(\mathcal{O})$ on the set of $\mathbb{F}_q$-isomorphism class of ordinary elliptic curves with endomorphism ring $\mathcal{O}$. Stobunov and Rostovseve also proposed an independent work with a similar idea in [36]. Despite impractical performance and vulnerability under the quantum attack, these constructions laid the first foundation for the field. In 2018, the paper [15] was proposed as the first efficient post-quantum group action construction by adapting previous techniques but restricting the class group's action on the set of $\mathbb{F}_q$-isomorphism classes of *supersingular* curves.

In the isogeny-based setting of CSIDH [15], the hardness assumption is the computational problem of finding the inverse the action of an ideal, known as the "Group Action Inverse Problem (GAIP)" as described by Stolbunov [37]. Since the introduction of the CSIDH, many related research works have emerged, ranging from improving the performance of CSIDH [11,32,34] to developing ring signature schemes [10,20,22] to linkable ring signature [9] and threshold signature schemes [7,19,21], among others. It's worth mentioning that the recent attack proposed by Thomas Decru [14] does not apply to CSIDH as it relies on the isogeny-finding problem.

In recent studies [11,34], it has been demonstrated that the suggested parameters for CSIDH, although not broken under quantum polynomial time attacks, are still considered inefficient in terms of their claimed quantum security. Nonetheless, our focus will be on developing a comprehensive construction using cryptographic group action. This approach aims to encourage the exploration of more constructions based on group action, which serves as a connection between isogeny-based cryptography and lattice-based cryptography.

Two years after the publication of the crucial contribution paper [15], the paper [3] expanded the definitions of Couveignes's work on *hard homogeneous space* [18] to introduce various concepts and applications of cryptographic group actions, which they then instantiated using CSIDH. Also in that year, Bellens, Katsumata and Pintore et.al. [9] developed an efficient (linkable) ring signature scheme from OR proof of group action which can be applied in both isogeny and lattice settings. One of the key contributions of their research was the introduction of the concepts *admissible group action* and *admissible pair of group action.*

Our Contribution. In this paper, we develop a construction of threshold ring signature scheme using cryptographic group action, building on the idea of the OR proof of group action in [9] and combining with the idea of creating a threshold ring signature scheme from a ring signature scheme. To the best of our knowledge, this is the first TRS construction base on cryptographic group action. We also provide two instantiation of our TRS scheme using the CSIDH group action and the MLWE group action. Moreover, the isogeny-based instantiation is the most efficient construction in terms of the signature size. In Sect. 3, we specifically propose a base threshold Σ-protocol derived from the OR-proof of group action by adding a vector of positions for each user $\delta_i = (0, \ldots, 1, \ldots, 0) \in \{0,1\}^N$ in which the i coordinate is 1 and blurring the user's information by using a random permutation ϕ. Eventually, by using the Fiat-Shamir transform on the Σ-protocol, Sect. 4 present a group action-based threshold ring signature scheme. In comparison to the existing isogeny-based TRS scheme RippleSign [29], our scheme offers a more efficient and compact design, with shorter public and secret key sizes. Additionally, our scheme generates smaller signature sizes, where the signature size of the (2, 100)-threshold ring signature is just 65 KB compare to 187 KB of the RippleSign one. On the other hand, in comparison to the previous proposed lattice-based threshold ring signatures, our scheme may have a larger signature size for a small signer group. Still, the signature size grows at a slower rate as the number t of signers increases. We acknowledge that addressing this limitation is an open problem for us to improve in our scheme.

Table 1 provides a comparison between ours group action-based t-out-of-N threshold ring signature schemes and the previous notable constructions in the literature in term of signature size.

Table 1. Comparison of the signature size (KB) of this work's schemes and some existing TRS schemes

N	100	100	100	100	200	200	200	1000	1000	1000	
t	2	10	30	50	2	10	50	2	10	50	Security Assumption
[6]	50	250	750	1250	54	270	1350	82	410	2050	Syndrome decoding
CLRS [8]	520	2560	7680	12800	540	2680	13390	730	3630	18110	ISIS
Our lattice-based TRS	1414	1470	1611	1750	2815	2871	3151	14015	14071	14351	MLWE
[29]	187	✗	✗	✗	✗	✗	✗	✗	✗	✗	GAIP
Our isogeny-based TRS	65	66	68.5	71	129	130	135	641	642	647	GAIP

Organization. The paper is organized as follows. In Sect. 2, we present some preliminaries on Σ-protocols, definition and security model of threshold ring signature, as well as some notions on group actions, from both lattices and isogenies. In Sect. 3, we first present a construction of a base threshold OR-proof Σ-protocol whose the challenge space is only binary. This base protocol is the basic for the construction of the full threshold OR-proof protocol presented in Sect. 3.2, together with its security proofs in Sect. 3.3. Our threshold ring signature's construction and security proofs are presented in Sect. 4, and the instantiations in lattices and isogenies are presented in Sect. 5.

2 Preliminaries

2.1 Σ-Protocol

A Σ-protocol is a special type of public-coin three-move interactive protocol that involve a prover $\mathcal{P}$ and a verifier $\mathcal{V}$ who exchange messages according to a set of rules defined by the protocol. The prover aims to persuade the verifier of a statement's validity or knowledge of the secret, while the verifier tries to ascertain whether the proof is valid.

Definition 1 (Σ-protocol). *A Σ-protocol for a relation $\mathcal{R}$ between a prover $\mathcal{P}$ and a verifier $\mathcal{V}$ consists of four PPT algorithms $\mathcal{P} = (P_1, P_2)$ and $\mathcal{V} = (V_1, V_2)$. We assume that P_1 and P_2 share the same state and V_2 is a deterministic algorithm. The protocol proceeds as follows:*

1. *The prover $\mathcal{P}$ on input $(X, W) \in \mathcal{R}$, runs $\mathsf{com} \leftarrow P_1(X, W)$ and send the commitment com to the verifier $\mathcal{V}$.*
2. *The verifier runs $\mathsf{chall} \leftarrow V_1(\mathsf{com})$ to obtain a random challenge chall and sends it to the prover.*
3. *Given chall from the verifier, the prover $\mathcal{P}$ runs $\mathsf{resp} \leftarrow P_2(X, W, \mathsf{chall})$ and sends to the verifier. Here we allow P_2 to abort with some probability δ. In such cases, P_2 returns $\perp$.*
4. *The verifier runs $V_2(X, \mathsf{com}, \mathsf{chall}, \mathsf{resp})$ and returns 1 if it $\mathsf{accepts}$ and 0 if it $\mathsf{rejects}$.*

A Σ-protocol must satisfy the following properties:

Correctness with Abort. Assuming that the prover does not abort, we require that the Σ-protocol be correct. In particular, we require the following hold for all $(X, W) \in \mathcal{R}$

$$\Pr\left[V_2(X, \mathsf{com}, \mathsf{chall}, \mathsf{resp}) = 1 \;\middle|\; \begin{array}{c} \mathsf{com} \leftarrow P_1(X, W) \\ \mathsf{chall} \leftarrow V_1(\mathsf{com}) \\ \mathsf{resp} \leftarrow P_2(\mathsf{com}, \mathsf{chall}) \text{ s.t. } \mathsf{resp} \neq \perp \end{array} \right] = 1.$$

It's essential to note that the probability of the prover's aborting probability, denoted as δ, can have a non-negligible value.

Non-abort Special Zero-Knowledge. The Σ-protocol is non-abort special zero-knowledge if there exists a polynomial time simulator Sim such that for any (X, W) in the relation $\mathcal{R}$, a chall in the challenge space and an adversary $\mathcal{A}$, we have

$$|\Pr[\mathcal{A}(\tilde{P}(X, W, \mathsf{chall})) \rightarrow 1] - \Pr[\mathsf{Sim}((X, W, \mathsf{chall})) \rightarrow 1]| = \mathsf{negl}(\lambda).$$

Special Soundness. A Σ-protocol satisfies the special soundness property if there exists an extractor $\mathsf{Extract}$ such that, given a statement X and any two valid transcripts $(\mathsf{com}, \mathsf{chall}_1, \mathsf{resp}_1)$ and $(\mathsf{com}, \mathsf{chall}_2, \mathsf{resp}_2)$ such that $\mathsf{chall}_1 \neq \mathsf{chall}_2$, outputs a witness W satisfying $(X, W) \in \mathcal{R}$.

2.2 Threshold Ring Signature Scheme

This section will provide a review of the definition of a t-out-of-N threshold ring signature scheme, as well as its security model.

Let $\mathsf{PK}^N = \{\mathsf{pk}_1, \dots, \mathsf{pk}_N\}$ be a set of public keys and $\mathsf{SK}^N = \{\mathsf{sk}_1, \dots, \mathsf{sk}_N\}$ is the set of corresponding secret keys. Similarly, PK^t and SK^t be a set of public and secret keys of the t users. For a ring of N users, a t-out-of-N TRS scheme allows a set of t users to jointly sign a signature on behalf of that ring of users while preserving the anonymity of the set of signers.

Definition 2 (TRS). *A t-out-of-N TRS scheme consists of the three following polynomial-time algorithms:*

- $\mathsf{Th.KeyGen}(1^\lambda)$*: is a probabilistic algorithm which outputs N pairs of public and secret key for N users $(\mathsf{pk}_1, \mathsf{sk}_1), \dots, (\mathsf{pk}_N, \mathsf{sk}_N)$.*
- $\mathsf{Th.Sign}(t, m, \mathsf{PK}^N = \{\mathsf{pk}_1, \dots, \mathsf{pk}_N\}, \mathsf{SK}^t = \{\mathsf{sk}_{i_1}, \dots, \mathsf{sk}_{i_t}\}) \rightarrow \sigma$*: An interactive protocol between t users that takes on input a set of N public keys PK^N, a set of t users with secret keys $\mathsf{SK}^t = \{\mathsf{sk}_{i_1}, \dots, \mathsf{sk}_{i_t}\})$ with $\{i_1, \dots, i_t\} \subseteq \{1, \dots, N\}$ and a message m. The algorithm outputs a threshold ring signature σ on m.*

- $\mathsf{Th.Verify}(t, \sigma, m, \mathsf{PK}^N = \{\mathsf{pk}_1, \ldots, \mathsf{pk}_N\}) \to 1/0$: *a deterministic algorithm which on input a value* $t \leq N$, *a set of* N *public keys* PK^N, *a pair of signature and message* (σ, m); *outputs* 1 *if* σ *is a valid* t*-out-of-*N *TRS, and outputs* 0 *otherwise.*

A threshold ring signature scheme must adhere to three properties: *completeness*, *anonymity* and *unforgeable.*

Correctness. The *correctness* of the TRS scheme requires that if for the security parameter $\lambda \in \mathbb{N}$, $N = p(\lambda)$ where $p(\lambda)$ is a polynomial, $i \in [N]$, all key pairs $(\mathsf{pk}_i, \mathsf{sk}_i)$ outputted by $\mathsf{Th.KeyGen}$, and all messages $m \in \{0,1\}$, it holds that

$$\Pr\left[\mathsf{Th.Verify}(t, \sigma, m, \mathsf{PK}^N) = 1 \;\middle|\; \begin{array}{c} \{(\mathsf{pk}_1, \mathsf{sk}_1), \ldots, (\mathsf{pk}_N, \mathsf{sk}_N)\} \leftarrow \mathsf{Th.KeyGen}(1^\lambda) \\ \mathsf{PK}^N = \{\mathsf{pk}_1, \ldots, \mathsf{pk}_N\} \\ \mathsf{SK}^t = \{\mathsf{sk}_{i_1}, \ldots, \mathsf{sk}_{i_t}\} \\ \sigma \leftarrow \mathsf{Th.Sign}(t, m, \mathsf{PK}^N, \mathsf{SK}^t) \end{array} \right] = 1$$

Indistinguishable Source Hiding (Anonymity). The indistinguishable source hiding property, also known as anonymity, states that it is infeasible for an attacker to identify the subset of t users that collaborated to produce a signature σ. To formally define this property, we consider the anonymity game, which involves a t-out-of-N TRS and a probabilistic polynomial time adversary $\mathcal{A}$.

- **Setup.** The challenger generates N pairs of keys $(\mathsf{pk}_i, \mathsf{sk}_i)$ then sends the set of public keys $\mathsf{PK}^N = (\mathsf{pk}_1, \ldots, \mathsf{pk}_N)$ to the adversary $\mathcal{A}$.
- **Queries.** The adversary $\mathcal{A}$ has the access to queries a signing oracle $\mathcal{O}^{\mathsf{Th.Sign}(\cdot)}(\cdot)$ that returns a signature $\sigma \leftarrow \mathsf{Th.Sign}(m, \mathsf{PK}^N, \mathsf{SK}^t)$.
- **Challenge.** $\mathcal{A}$ outputs a message m^* and two distinct sets $\{i_{1,0}, \ldots, i_{t,0}\}$, $\{i_{1,1}, \ldots, i_{t,1}\}$ such that $\mathsf{pk}_{i_{j,\ell}} \in \mathsf{PK}^N$ for $j \in \{1, \ldots, t\}$ and $\ell \in \{0,1\}$.
- **Respond.** $\mathcal{C}$ chooses a random bit $b \in \{0,1\}$ then computes

$$\sigma^* \leftarrow \mathsf{Th.Sign}(m^*, \mathsf{PK}^N, \{\mathsf{sk}_{i_{1,b}}, \ldots, \mathsf{sk}_{i_{t,b}}\})$$

  The adversary $\mathcal{A}$ is also given $\mathsf{SK}^N \setminus \{\mathsf{sk}_{i_{1,0}}, \ldots, \mathsf{sk}_{i_{t,0}}\}$.
- **Guess.** The adversary outputs its guess b' and wins if $b' = b$.

The advantage of the adversary $\mathcal{A}$ is defined as $\mathsf{Adv}^{source-hiding}_{ThRS,\mathcal{A}}(\lambda) = |\Pr[\mathcal{A} \text{ wins }] - 1/2|$.

The TRS scheme is source-hiding (or anonymous) if the adversary $\mathcal{A}$'s advantage $\mathsf{Adv}^{source-hiding}_{ThRS,\mathcal{A}}(\lambda)$ for any adversary $\mathcal{A}$ is negligible.

Existential Unforgeability. The existential unforgeability, states that an attacker $\mathcal{A}$ cannot produce a valid t-out-of-N TRS without the knowledge the set of at least t signers' secret keys. To define this property formally, we consider the existential unforgeability game, which involves a t-out-of-N TRS scheme and a probabilistic polynomial time forger $\mathcal{F}$:

- **Setup.** The challenger generates N pairs of keys $(\mathsf{pk}_i, \mathsf{sk}_i)$ then send the set of public keys $\mathsf{PK}^N = (\mathsf{pk}_1, \ldots, \mathsf{pk}_N)$ to $\mathcal{F}$.
- **Queries.** The forger $\mathcal{F}$ is given access to a signing oracle $\mathcal{O}^{\mathsf{Th.Sign}(\cdot)}(\cdot)$ that returns a signature $\sigma \leftarrow \mathsf{Th.Sign}(m, \mathsf{PK}^N, \mathsf{SK}^t)$ on input $(m, \mathsf{PK}^N, \mathsf{PK}^t)$. The forger $\mathcal{F}$ also has access to a corrupt oracle $\mathcal{O}^{\mathsf{Th.KeyGen}(\cdot)}(\cdot)$ that on input an index $i \in [1, N]$ exposures a secret key sk_i of a public key $\mathsf{pk}_i \in \mathsf{PK}^N$. Note that the number of corrupted users should strictly less than t.
- **Forging.** The forger $\mathcal{F}$ outputs a t-out-of-N TRS σ^* for a message m^* that has not been queries and wins if $\mathsf{Th.Verify}(t, \sigma^*, m^*, \mathsf{PK}^N)$ outputs 1.

The advantage of the forger $\mathcal{F}$ is defined as $\mathsf{Adv}^{exist-unforg}_{\mathsf{ThRS},\mathcal{F}} = \Pr[\mathcal{F} \text{ wins}]$. A threshold ring signature scheme is said to be existential unforgeability if the forger $\mathcal{F}$'s advantage $\mathsf{Adv}^{exist-unforg}_{\mathsf{ThRS},\mathcal{F}}$ of successfully forges a signature σ^* for a message m^* is negligible.

2.3 Group Actions

This section will briefly review the definitions of Cryptographic Group Action and Admissible Group Action; further details can be found in [3,9].

Cryptographic Group Action

Definition 3 (Group Action [3]). *A group G is said to act on a set $\mathcal{X}$ if there is a map $\star : G \times \mathcal{X} \to \mathcal{X}$ that satisfies the following properties:*

- *Identity: If e is the identity element of G, then for any $x \in \mathcal{X}$, we have $e \star x = x$.*
- *Compatibility: For any $g, h \in G$ and any $x \in \mathcal{X}$, we have $(gh) \star x = g \star (h \star x)$.*

We use the notation $(G, \mathcal{X}, \star)$ to denote the group action.

Admissible Group Actions

Definition 4 (Admissible group action [9]). *Let G be additive group, S_1, S_2 two symmetric subsets of G, $\mathcal{X}$ a finite set, $\delta \in [0, 1]$ and $D_{\mathcal{X}}$ be a distribution over a set of group actions $\star : G \times \mathcal{X} \to \mathcal{X}$. We say that $\mathsf{AdmGA} = (G, \mathcal{X}, S_1, S_2, D_{\mathcal{X}})$ is a δ-admissible group action with respect to $X_0 \in \mathcal{X}$ if the following holds:*

1. *One can efficiently compute $g \star X$ for all $g \in S_1 \cup S_2$ and all $X \in \mathcal{X}$, sample uniformly from S_1, S_2 and $D_{\mathcal{X}}$, and represent elements of G and $\mathcal{X}$ uniquely.*

2. *The intersection of the sets S_2+g, $g \in S_1$, is sufficiently large. More formally, let $S_3 = \bigcap_{g \in S_1} S_2 + g$, then*
$$|S_3| = \delta |S_2|.$$
Furthermore, it is efficient to check whether an element $g \in G$ belongs to $|S_3|$.
3. *It is difficult to output $g' \in S_2 + S_3$ such that $g' \star X_0 = X$ with non-negligible probability, given $X = g \star X_0$ for some g sampled uniformly from S_1. That is, for any efficient adversary $\mathcal{A}$ we have*
$$\Pr\left[\begin{array}{c|c} & \star \leftarrow D_{\mathcal{X}} \\ g' \in S_2 + S_3 & g \leftarrow S_1 \\ g' \star X_0 = X & X \leftarrow g \star X_0 \\ & g' \leftarrow \mathcal{A}(\star, X) \end{array}\right] \leq \mathsf{negl}(\lambda).$$

Henceforth, we omit the description of the group action $\star$ and assume the probability is taken over the random choice of $\star$ when the context is clear.

2.4 Isogenies and Ideal Class Group Actions

The primary emphasis of this research is on the CSIDH setting, and for a comprehensive overview of this setting, the recommended source is the paper [15].

Let E denotes an elliptic curve over a finite field $\mathbb{F}_p$ where p is a large prime. E is called *supersingular* if $\#E(\mathbb{F}_p) \equiv 1(\mod p)$. An isogeny between two elliptic curves E and E' is a non-constant rational map that send the distinguished point of E to the distinguished point of E'. In this work, we focus only on the *separable* isogenies (which induce separable extensions of function fields) where the set of rational points $E(\mathbb{F}_p)$ has cardinality $p+1$. Isogenies from a curve E to itself are called endomorphisms. The set of all endomorphisms of the elliptic curve E that are defined over $\mathbb{F}_p$ together with the multiplication-by-0 map form a ring under the operations of addition and composition, denoted by $\mathsf{End}_{\mathbb{F}_p}(E)$. The endomorphism ring $\mathsf{End}_{\mathbb{F}_p}(E)$ is isomorphic to an order $\mathcal{O}$ of the quadratic field $\mathbb{Q}(\sqrt{-p})$ according to the paper CSIDH. The quotient of the group of fractional invertible ideals $\mathcal{I}(\mathcal{O})$ by the the subgroup of principal ideals $\mathcal{P}(\mathcal{O})$ is called the ideal class group of $\mathcal{O}$, denoted by $\mathcal{C}\ell(\mathcal{O})$.

Denote by $\mathcal{E}\ell\ell_p(\mathcal{O})$ the set of elliptic curves defined over $\mathbb{F}_p$ with complex multiplication by $\mathcal{O}$, then the above-mentioned class group $\mathcal{C}\ell(\mathcal{O})$ acts freely and transitively on $\mathcal{E}\ell\ell_p(\mathcal{O})$ i.e., there is a map
$$\begin{array}{ll} \mathcal{C}\ell(\mathcal{O}) \times \mathcal{E}\ell\ell_p(\mathcal{O}) & \rightarrow \mathcal{E}\ell\ell_p(\mathcal{O}) \\ (\mathfrak{a}, E) & \mapsto \mathfrak{a} \star E \end{array}$$

such that $\mathfrak{a} \star (\mathfrak{b} \star E)$ for all $\mathfrak{a}$, such that $\mathfrak{a} \star (\mathfrak{b} \star E)$ for all $\mathfrak{a}, \mathfrak{b} \in \mathcal{C}\ell(\mathcal{O})$ and $E \in \mathcal{E}\ell\ell_p(\mathcal{O})$, and such that for any $E, E' \in \mathcal{E}\ell\ell_p(\mathcal{O})$ there is a unique element $\mathfrak{a} \in \mathcal{C}\ell(\mathcal{O})$ such that $E' = \mathfrak{a} \star E$.

At present, various cryptographic protocols have been developed using isogenies between supersingular elliptic curves, where the security of these protocols depends on the Group Action Inverse Problem (GAIP) and its variants.

Definition 5 (Group Action Inverse Problem (GAIP)). *Let E_0 be an element in $\mathcal{E}\ell\ell_p(\mathcal{O})$, where p is an odd prime. Given E sample from the uniform distribution over $\mathcal{E}\ell\ell_p(\mathcal{O})$, the GAIP_p problem consists in finding an element $\mathfrak{a} \in \mathcal{C}\ell(\mathcal{O})$ such that $\mathfrak{a} \star E_0 = E$.*

2.5 Lattices

In this paper, we let R and R_p respectively denote the rings $\mathbb{Z}[X]/(X^n + 1)$ and $\mathbb{Z}[X]/(q, X^n + 1)$ for integers n and q. We will consider the norms of elements in R using the coefficient vectors in $\mathbb{Z}^n$. Meanwhile, the norm over R_q by representing coefficients of elements over R_q using elements in the range $(-q/2, q/2]$ when q is even and $[-(q-1)/2, (q-1)/2]$ when q is odd as in [9].

Regarding the lattice-based instantiation, we will recall the definitions of the *Module Short Integer Solution* (MSIS) problem and the *Module Learning with Errors* (MLWE) problem, which can be found in detail in [28].

Definition 6 (Module short integer solution). *Let n, q, k, ℓ, γ be integers. The advantage for the (Hermite normal form) module short integer solution problem $\mathsf{MSIS}_{n,q,k,\ell,\gamma}$ for an algorithm $\mathcal{A}$ is defined as*

$$\mathsf{Adv}^{\mathsf{MSIS}}_{n,q,k,\ell,\gamma}(\mathcal{A}) = \Pr[0 < \|\mathbf{u}\|_\infty < \gamma \wedge [\mathbf{A}|\mathbf{I}] \cdot \mathbf{u} = \mathbf{0} | \mathbf{A} \leftarrow \mathbf{R}_\mathbf{p}^{\mathbf{k}\times\ell}; \mathbf{u} \leftarrow \mathcal{A}(\mathbf{A})].$$

Definition 7 (Module learning with errors). *Let n, q, k, ℓ be integers and D a probability distribution over R_q. The advantage for the decision module learning with errors problem $\mathsf{dMLWE}_{m,q,k,\ell,D}$ for an algorithm $\mathcal{A}$ is defined as*

$$\mathsf{Adv}^{\mathsf{dMLWE}}_{n,q,k,\ell,D}(\mathcal{A}) = |\Pr[\mathcal{A}(\mathbf{A}, \mathbf{As} + \mathbf{e}) \to 1] - \Pr[\mathcal{A}(\mathbf{A}, \mathbf{v}) \to 1]|$$

where $\mathbf{A} \leftarrow \mathbf{R}_\mathbf{q}^{\mathbf{k}\times\ell}$, $\mathbf{s} \leftarrow \mathbf{D}^\ell$, $\mathbf{e} \leftarrow \mathbf{D}^\mathbf{k}$ and $\mathbf{v} \leftarrow \mathbf{R}_\mathbf{q}^\mathbf{k}$.

The advantage for the search Learning with errors problem $\mathsf{sMLWE}_{n,q,k,\ell,D}$ is defined analogously to above as the probability that $\mathcal{A}(\mathbf{A}, \mathbf{v} := \mathbf{As} + \mathbf{e})$ outputs $(\tilde{\mathbf{s}}, \tilde{\mathbf{e}})$, such that $\mathbf{A}\tilde{\mathbf{s}} + \tilde{\mathbf{e}} = \mathbf{v}$ and $(\tilde{\mathbf{s}}, \tilde{\mathbf{e}}) \in \mathsf{Supp}(D^\ell) \times \mathsf{Supp}(D^k)$.

3 Threshold Σ-Protocol from OR-Proof of Group Action

In this section, we present the construction of the Threshold OR Σ-protocol from OR-proof of group action, along with its corresponding security proof.

3.1 Base Threshold OR-Proof of Group Action

The concept of OR proof was initially introduced in a 2015 paper [25]. Ward Beullens then adapted their technique to develop a ring signature scheme based on group actions in [9]. In this subsection, we will provide a brief overview of the *Base Threshold OR-proof of group action* for the binary challenge space $\{0, 1\}$ by generalizing previous idea in the threshold setting. For a detailed explanation of the base OR-proof of group action, please refer to [9].

The important point to note here is the term of "Threshold" in our Threshold Σ-protocol refer for a set of no under the threshold of t out of some N users that act as the prover. The set of t users in the Threshold Σ-protocol selects a leader $\mathcal{L}$ who acts as an intermediary between the verifier and this set of users. The leader $\mathcal{L}$ is responsible for collecting the commitments and responses of the other members in S^t and transmitting them to the verifier. It is important to note that $\mathcal{L}$ is simply one of the users and has no access to any confidential information belonging to the other $t-1$ users.

We consider the base Threshold Σ-protocol for a ring of N users with $N+1$ elements $X_0, X_1, \ldots, X_N \in \mathcal{X}$ in which there exists $a_i \in \mathcal{G}$ such that $X_i = a_i \star X_0$ for all $i \in [1, N]$. Here each index $i \in [1, N]$ represents a user in a ring of N users. The prover $\mathcal{P}$ wants to claim that he knows a set of t group elements $\{a_{i_1}, \ldots, a_{i_t}\}$ such that $X_{i_j} = a_{i_j} \star X_0$ for all $j \in [1, t]$ (note that $i_j \in [1, N]$). For more convenience, we denote the index of elements in this set briefly by $\mathsf{S}^t = \{i_1, \ldots, i_t\} \subseteq \{1, \ldots, N\}$. The prover $\mathcal{P}$ first creates the commitments for all X_i by choosing n random group elements $b_i \in \mathcal{G}$ and computing $R_i = r_i \star X_i$. $\mathcal{P}$ then send $\{R_i, \ldots, R_n\}$ in random order to the verifier $\mathcal{V}$. After receiving the challenge $c \in \{0, 1\}$ from the verifier $\mathcal{V}$, the prover $\mathcal{C}$ creates the response resp based on the actual value of c. If the challenge bit c is 1, $\mathcal{C}$ sets $\{r_i = b_i\}_{i \in [1,N]}$ then sends the response $\mathsf{resp} = \{r_1, \ldots, r_n\}$ to the verifier to check whether $r_i \star X_i = R_i$ for all $i \in \{1, \ldots, N\}$. If the challenge c is equal to 0, $\mathcal{P}$ computes $r_i = b_i + a_i$ for all $i \in \mathsf{S}^t$ and sets the response $\mathsf{resp} = \{r_i\}_{i \in \mathsf{S}^t}$. The verifier now must check whether $r_i \star X_0 \in \{R_i, \ldots, R_n\}$. We note that the commitments $\{R_1, \ldots, R_n\}$ are sent in a random order, so the response hides the index of all elements in S^t when $c = 1$.

Following the Base OR Σ-protocol of [9], our Base Threshold OR Σ-protocol is also *commitment recoverable.*

Remark 8 (Commitment recoverable [9]). *Given the statement* X, *the challenge* chall *and response* resp, *there is an efficient deterministic algorithm* $\mathsf{RecoverCom}(\mathsf{X}, \mathsf{chall}, \mathsf{rsp})$ *that recovers the unique commitment* com *that leads the verifier to accept. This property allows the signer of a Fiat-Shamir type signature to include the challenge rather than the commitment, which shortens the signature size. Our sigma protocol is commitment recoverable.*

3.2 Construction

Let $\mathsf{AdmGA} = (G, \mathcal{X}, S_1, S_2, D_{\mathcal{X}})$ be an admissible group action with respected to $X_0 \in \mathcal{X}$, and suppose that $\{X_{i,0} = X_0, X_{i,1} = a_i \star X_{i,0}\}_{i \in [N]}$ are N public keys where the corresponding secret keys $a_1, \ldots, a_N$ are sample uniformly random from S_1.

Here and subsequently, we denote $\mathsf{PK}^N = \{\mathsf{pk}_1, \ldots, \mathsf{pk}_N\}$, $S^t = \{i_1, \ldots, i_t\} \subseteq \{1, 2, \ldots, N\}$, $\mathsf{SK}^t = \{\mathsf{sk}_{i_1}, \ldots, \mathsf{sk}_{i,t}\}$ are the set of all public keys of N users, the sets of t users and the corresponding secret keys, respectively.

Define the relation $\mathcal{R} = \{((X_{1,1}, \ldots, X_{N,1}), (a_{i_1}, i_1), (a_{i_2}, i_2), \ldots, (a_{i_t}, i_t) | a_{i_j} \in S_1, X_{i,1} = a_{i_j} \star X_0 \in \mathcal{X}, j \in [t]\}$. We will consider the threshold OR Σ-protocol between the prover $\mathcal{P} = (P_1, P_2)$ and the verifier $\mathcal{V} = (V_1, V_2)$ where $\mathcal{P}$ has the knowledge of $\{(a_{i_1}, i_1), \ldots, (a_{i_t}, i_t)\} \in S_1^t \times [N]^t$ such that $a_{i_j} \star X_0 = X_{i_j,1}$ for all $j \in [1, t]$.

Our group action-based OR-Σ protocol is described as follows:

KeyGen(λ)

On input the security parameter λ, the algorithm generates the public and secret keys pair for the i-th user as follows:

1. Sample $a_i \xleftarrow{R} S_1$;
2. Set $X_{i,0} := X_0$ and compute $X_{i,1} = a_i \star X_{i,0}$.
3. Output $\mathsf{pk}_i = (X_{i,0}, X_{i,1})$ and $\mathsf{sk}_i = a_i$.

$\mathsf{P}_1(\mathsf{PK}^N, \mathsf{SK}^t)$

On input the set of public keys of N users and the set of t signer, the algorithm proceed as follows:

1. Let $\mathcal{L}$ be the leader of the t signers who plays the role of intermediate between the t signers and a verifier $\mathcal{V}$ - note that $\mathcal{L}$ is one of the signer.
2. For i from 1 to N do:
   - Sample $b_i \in S_2$;
   - Compute $R_i = b_i \star X_{i,1}$ and send R_i to the leader $\mathcal{L}$.
3. The leader $\mathcal{L}$:
   - Choose a random permutation ϕ and a random bit string bits;
   - Compute $\{R_i'\}_{i \in [N]} = \phi\{R_i\}_{i \in [N]}$;
   - Compute $\mathsf{per} = \mathsf{Com}(\phi, \mathsf{bits})$.
4. The leader $\mathcal{L}$ sends the commitment $\mathsf{com} = (\{R_i'\}_{i \in [N]}, \mathsf{per})$ to the verifier $\mathcal{V}$.

$\mathsf{V}_1(\mathsf{PK}^N, \mathsf{com} = (\{R_i'\}_{i \in [N]}, \mathsf{per}))$

On input the set of public keys of N users and the commitment $\{R_i'\}_{i \in [N]}, \mathsf{per})$, the algorithm choose $c \xleftarrow{R} \{0, 1\}$ and sends c to the prover $\mathcal{P}$.

$\mathsf{P}_2(\mathsf{PK}^N, \mathsf{SK}^t, c)$

After receiving the challenge c from the verifier $\mathcal{V}$, the prover performs as follows:

- If $c = 1$:
  1. For i from 1 to N: Set $r_i = b_i$ then send r_i to the leader $\mathcal{L}$;
  2. The leader $\mathcal{L}$ sends $\mathsf{resp} = (\{r_i'\}_{i \in [N]} = \phi\{r_i\}_{i \in [N]}, \phi, \mathsf{bits})$ to the verifier.
- If $c = 0$:
  1. For all $i \in S^t$:
     - Let $\delta_i = (0, \ldots, \overset{i\text{-th}}{1}, \ldots, 0)$ be the vector position of the i-th user;
     - Compute $r_i = b_i + a_i$ and send (δ_i, r_i) to the leader $\mathcal{L}$.
  2. The leader $\mathcal{L}$ performs as follows:
     - If $r_i \notin S_3$ then abort;
     - Else $\mathcal{L}$ set $\delta_i = \mathbf{0} = (0, \ldots, 0), \forall i \notin S^t$. After that $\mathcal{L}$ computes $\phi\{\delta_i\}_{i \in [N]}$ and sends $\mathsf{resp} = (\{r_i\}_{i \in S^t}, \phi\{\delta_i\}_{i \in [N]})$ to the verifier.

$\mathsf{V}_2(\mathsf{PK}^N, \mathsf{com} = (\{R'_i\}_{i\in[N]}, \mathsf{per}), c, \mathsf{resp})$
The verification phrase is proceed as follows:
- If $c = 1$:
  - Compute $\{X'_{i,1}\}_{i\in[N]} = \phi\{X_{i,1}\}_{i\in[N]}$;
  - Check whether $r'_i \star X'_{i,1} \stackrel{?}{=} R'_i$, $\forall i \in [N]$ and $\mathsf{Com}(\phi, \mathsf{bits}) \stackrel{?}{=} \mathsf{per}$.
- If $c = 0$:
  - Check whether $r_i \star X_0 \stackrel{?}{\in} \{R'_i\}$ and $\mathsf{wt}(\phi\{\delta_i\}) \stackrel{?}{=} t$.
- Return 1 if all the condition are satisfied else return 0.

3.3 Security Proof

In this section, we will demonstrate that the security of the Threshold OR Σ-protocol holds.

Correctness with Abort. If the protocol is executed honestly:

- If $c = 1$, then the prover $\mathcal{P}$ does not abort.
- If $c = 0$, the prover aborts if there exists $r_i = b_i + a_i \in S_3$, $i \in S^t$. Since b_i is chosen uniformly at random in S_2, we have that r_i distributed uniformly at random in $S_2 + a_i$. The probability that $r_i \in S_3$ is

$$\frac{|S_3|}{|S_2 + a_i|} = \frac{|S_3|}{|S_2|} = \delta.$$

  Hence the probability that the prover aborts in the Σ-protocol above is $\dfrac{1-\delta^t}{2}$.

Non-abort Honest Verifier Zero-Knowledge. In this part, we consider the non-abort prover $\tilde{\mathcal{P}}$. Assume that the challenge c is given before the commitment com; the simulator Sim is defined as follows:

- If $c = 1$, Sim picks random $\{r_i\}_{i\in[N]}$, where $r_i \stackrel{R}{\leftarrow} S_2$ then computes $\{R_i = r_i \star X_{i,1}\}_{i\in[N]}$. Sim chooses a random permutation ϕ and a random bit string bits then computes $\mathsf{per} = \mathsf{Com}(\phi, \mathsf{bits})$. Sim then outputs the transcript $(\{R_i\}_{i\in[N]}, \mathsf{per}, c = 1, \{r_i\}_{i\in[N]}, \phi, \mathsf{bits})$.
- If $c = 0$, Sim picks t random elements $r_i \stackrel{R}{\leftarrow} S_2, i \in S^t$ then sets $R_i = r_i \star X_{i,1}$. Sim chooses a permutation Sim and a random bit string bits then computes $\mathsf{per} = \mathsf{Com}(\phi, \mathsf{bits})$ and $\phi\{\delta_i\}$. Finally, the simulator Sim outputs the transcript $(\{R'_i\}_{i\in[N]}, \mathsf{per}, c = 0, \{r_i\}_{i\in S^t}, \phi\{\delta_i\})$.

It is clear that both the real transcripts and the simulated transcripts have uniformly distributed values $\{r_i\}$ and satisfy the completeness property. Hence, the real and simulated transcripts are indistinguishable.

Special Soundness. Given two valid transcripts $(\mathsf{com}, \mathsf{chall}_1, \mathsf{resp}_1)$ and $(\mathsf{com}, \mathsf{chall}_2, \mathsf{resp}_2)$ where $\mathsf{chall}_1 \neq \mathsf{chall}_2$, there exists an extractor Extract that can recover the secret.

The two accepting transcripts of the Threshold OR Σ-protocol are: $(\{R'_i\}_{i\in[N]}, \mathsf{per}, c = 1, \{r'_{i,c=1}\}_{i\in[N]} = \phi\{r_i = b_i\}_{i\in[N]}, \phi, \mathsf{bits})$ and $(\{R'_i\}_{i\in[N]}, \mathsf{per}, c = 0, \{r_{i,c=0} = b_i + a_i\}_{i\in S^t}, \phi\{\delta_i\}_{i\in[N]})$. The extractor first computes $R''_i = r_{i,c=0} \star X_0$ for all $\{r_{i,c=0}\}_{i\in S^t}$ (note that $R''_i \in \{R'_i\}_{i\in[N]}$).

Beside $(\{R'_i\}_{i\in[N]}, \mathsf{per}, c = 1, \{r'_{i,c=1}\}_{i\in[N]} = \phi\{r_i = b_i\}_{i\in[N]}, \phi, \mathsf{bits})$ is also a valid transcript. The extractor then use ϕ to find the identity of all t signers and their actual position where $r_i = b_i$. The extractor finally outputs $w_i = r_{i,c=0} - r'_{i,c=1} = b_i + a_i - b_i = a_i$ for all $i \in [1, t]$ which are the secret keys of all signers in S^t.

4 Threshold Ring Signature Scheme from OR-Proof of Group Action

To obtain the threshold ring signature from group action, we apply the Fiat-Shamir transform where a hash function H is used to generate the challenge c. In order to reach the required security level, we will have to execute the base Threshold Σ-protocol λ times. Additionally, we will make a standing assumption regarding our TRS scheme: let $\mathcal{H}$ be a family of hash functions, we sample a uniformly random hash function H from $\mathcal{H}$ and set

$$\mathsf{H}(\mathsf{com}, m) = \mathsf{H}(\{\{R_{i,j}\}_{i\in[N],j}, \mathsf{per}_j\}_{j\in[\lambda]}, m) = \mathbf{c} \in \{\mathbf{0}, \mathbf{1}\}^{\lambda}.$$

The signature σ for the message m is the transcript of the Threshold Σ-protocol from OR-proof of group action. The remainder of this section will be devoted to prove the security of the TRS scheme.

Indistinguishable Source-Hiding (Anonymity). Recall that the source-hiding property holds that it is infeasible for an adversary to guess which subset of t signers collaborate to generate the joint threshold ring signature. The proof of this property employs the same methodology as in the paper [9]. Therefore, in this part, we will outline the main ideas of the proof.

Generally speaking, the indistinguishable source-hiding property can be derived from the unique zero-knowledge property of the Threshold OR Σ-protocol. Concretely, no matter which value of b is selected, the challenger in the game will utilize the special zero-knowledge simulator Sim to generate a simulated signature for each signature query made by the adversary $\mathcal{A}$. Since the proof is produced independently of the set of secret keys S_0^t, S_1^t, the anonymity property follows.

Unforgeability. The unforgeability property of the signature scheme follows from the zero-knowledge property of the Σ-protocol and the rewinding argument.

Theorem 9. *Let* H *be a hash function modelled as a random oracle and assume that the Threshold* Σ*-protocol from OR-proof of group action satisfies the zero knowledge and special soundness properties. Then the TRS scheme is existential unforgeability under the hardness of the underlying hardness problem due to the properties of the Admissible Group Action.*

Proof. We can now proceed the security proof of the TRS scheme in a similar manner as demonstrated in the paper [25].

In particular, we first assume that there exists a forger $\mathcal{F}$ who has a probability of at least $1/p(\lambda)$ of breaking the unforgeability property of the TRS scheme, where p is a positive polynomial and infinitely many $\lambda \in \mathbb{N}$. We will demonstrate the existence of an adversary $\mathcal{A}$ who can utilize $\mathcal{F}$ as a black box to violate the third property of the Admissible Group Action specified in **Definition** 4 in polynomial time. The success probability of $\mathcal{A}$ will be approximately $1/(2p(\lambda) \cdot N^2)$. Suppose that the forger $\mathcal{F}$ can make no more than $t-1$, $q_s(\lambda)$ and $q_{\mathsf{H}}(\lambda)$ queries to $\mathcal{O}^{\mathsf{Th.KeyGen}(\cdot)}(\cdot)$, $\mathcal{O}^{\mathsf{Th.Sign}(\cdot)}(\cdot)$ and the random oracle H, respectively.

At the beginning of the game, the adversary $\mathcal{A}$ is provided with two elements X_0 and X_1 from the set $\mathcal{X}$, and it aims to find an element $a \in S_1$ such that $X_1 = a \star X_0$. $\mathcal{A}$ first selects a random index $k \in [1, N]$ and sets $\mathsf{pk}_k = (X_{k,0}, X_{k,1}) = (X_1, X_0)$. Using $\mathcal{F}$ as a black box and the rewinding technique, $\mathcal{A}$ attempts to obtain two forgeries for the same set of t signers SK^t, which includes the user k, on the same message m.The special soundness property of the Threshold Σ-protocol from OR-proof of group action may permit extraction of the secret key sk_k, which is the answer of $\mathcal{A}$ to the underlying hardness problem. The adversary $\mathcal{A}$ proceeds by generating the remaining $N-1$ pair of keys for $i \in [1, N]$, where $i \neq k$, by sampling $a_i \in S_1$ and setting $X_{i,0} = X_0, X_{i,1} = a_i \star X_{i,0}$. For each $i \neq k$, $\mathcal{A}$ sets $(\mathsf{pk}_i, \mathsf{sk}_i) = ((X_{i,0}, X_{i,1}), a_i)$ and sends the entire set of public key $\mathsf{PK}^N = (\mathsf{pk}_1, \ldots, \mathsf{pk}_N)$ to the forger $\mathcal{F}$.

Let the Type I abort be the event that the simulation aborts related to pk_k and the Type II abort be the event that the simulation aborts related to the queries to the random oracles.

The Type I abort refers to the scenario where the game is terminated due to the queries to the keys of the user k, while the Type II abort related to the case where the simulation is stopped because of queries made to the random oracles.

After completing the previous step, the forger $\mathcal{F}$ can now ask for his needed information through the $\mathcal{O}^{\mathsf{Th.KeyGen}(\cdot)}(\cdot)$, $\mathcal{O}^{\mathsf{Th.Sign}(\cdot)}(\cdot)$ queries. The forger $\mathcal{F}$ can call the corruption oracle $\mathcal{O}^{\mathsf{Th.KeyGen}(\cdot)}(\cdot)$ at most $t-1$ times, which, given an index i, returns the secret key $sk_i = a_i$ of user i. It is important to note that if the forger $\mathcal{F}$ ever queries $\mathcal{O}^{\mathsf{Th.KeyGen}(\cdot)}(k)$, the game is immediately aborted (Type I). It follows that, the probability that the adversary $\mathcal{A}$ aborts the game in this step is $1/N$.

To respond to queries to the signing oracles $\mathcal{O}^{\mathsf{Th.Sign}(\cdot)}(\mathsf{PK}^N, \mathsf{PK}^t, m)$ made by $\mathcal{F}$, the adversary $\mathcal{A}$ picks a random string $\mathbf{c} \leftarrow \{\mathbf{0}, \mathbf{1}\}^\lambda$. Then, it uses the non-abort special honest verifier simulator Sim to simulate the commitment $\mathsf{com} = \{\{R_{i,j}\}_{i\in[N],j}, \mathsf{per}_j\}_{j\in[\lambda]}$. The hash function $\mathsf{H}(\cdot)$ is programmed as a random oracle with

$$\mathsf{H}(\mathsf{com}, m) = \mathsf{H}(\{\{R_{i,j}\}_{i\in[N],j}, \mathsf{per}_j\}_{j\in[\lambda]}, m) = \mathbf{c} \in \{\mathbf{0}, \mathbf{1}\}^\lambda,$$

except the case when the tuple $(\mathsf{PK}^N, \mathsf{PK}^t, m, \{\{R_{i,j}\}_{i\in[N],j}, \mathsf{per}_j\}_{j\in[\lambda]})$ has been queries before. If this ever happens, the game is aborted (Type II). The adversary $\mathcal{A}$ now uses Sim to generate a response resp according to the challenge $\mathbf{c}$. Finally, the signature σ is constructed as the transcript of the Σ-protocol generated by Sim. It follows immediately that the resulting signature σ is indistinguishable from the actual signature generated by a set of t honest users by the non-abort special zero-knowledge property of the above Σ-protocol.

Having queried to obtain information from $\mathcal{A}$, $\mathcal{F}$ attempts to produce a forged signature σ^* with some set of uncorrupted signers PK^{t^*} in the ring PK^N in which the signature does not come from the signing oracle $\mathcal{O}^{\mathsf{Th.Sign}(\cdot)}(\cdot)$. If the public key $\mathsf{pk}_k \notin \mathsf{PK}^{t^*}$then the game is aborted (Type I). The probability that k is a member of the set of t signers PK^t that $\mathcal{F}$ is trying to forge is t/N.

If $\mathcal{F}$ fails to generate a valid pair of the message - signature (m^*, σ^*), we halt the game. If $\mathcal{F}$ create a successful forge threshold ring signature $\sigma_0^* = (\mathsf{com}^*, \mathbf{c}_0^*, \mathsf{resp}_0^*)$ on m^* by the set of t signers PK^{t^*} on the ring PK^N from a random oracle queries $\mathsf{H}(\mathsf{com}^*, m^*) = \mathbf{c}_0$, we will save this pair of message-signature and use the rewinding technique to rewind $\mathcal{F}$ back to the point where it made the query to $\mathsf{H}(\mathsf{com}^*, m^*)$ and give it random answers to the oracle query until it produces an additional signature $\sigma^{*\prime}$ for the challenge $\mathbf{c}_1$. If there exists a query to a random oracle that had been asked before, we abort the game (Type II). Besides, we will halt the game if the number of rewinding overreaches $2p(\lambda)$ times. Now, the adversary $\mathcal{A}$ obtain two valid transcripts $(\sigma_0^* = (\mathsf{com}^*, \mathbf{c}_0^*, \mathsf{resp}_0^*), \mathbf{m}^*)$ and $(\sigma^* = (\mathsf{com}^*, \mathbf{c}_1^*, \mathsf{resp}_1^*), \mathbf{m}^*)$ where $\mathbf{c}_0^* \neq \mathbf{c}_1^*$ on the same commitment com^*. Let $j \in [\lambda]$ be the index such that $c_{0,j} \neq c_{1,j}$ in which $c_{0,j}$ and $c_{1,j}$ are the j-th elements of the two challenge vectors $\mathbf{c}_0^*$ and $\mathbf{c}_1^*$, respectively. There is no loss of generality in assuming that $(c_{0,j}, c_{1,j}) = (0, 1)$. Since both transcripts are valid, we have that $V_2(\mathsf{com}_j^*, 0, \mathsf{resp}_{0,j}^*) = 1$ and $V_2(\mathsf{com}_j^*, 1, \mathsf{resp}_{1,j}^*) = 1$. The adversary $\mathcal{A}$ can now use the special soundness property to retrieve a secret key sk_k and solve the underlying hard problem.

It is therefore of interest to look at the explanation of the game given above.

To understand the game, it is important to note that based on the presented assumption, the adversary $\mathcal{F}$ has at least $1/p(\lambda)$ chance of creating a successful forgery where $p(\lambda)$ is a polynomial and $\lambda \in \mathbb{N}$ is the security parameter. On average, it is evident that the forger $\mathcal{F}$ will have to rewind $p(\lambda)$ times to sample a successful forgery. Therefore, an adversary $\mathcal{A}$ must execute approximately $2p(\lambda)$ times to obtain two successful forgeries using a specific oracle query, with a success probability of at least $1/2p(\lambda)$.

Note that we have proved that the simulator Sim has a negligible probability of colliding with another oracle query $\mathsf{H}(\cdot)$ that has been used before due to the property of the Σ-protocol. Without loss of generality, we can denote this probability by a negligible function $\nu(\lambda)$. Under the conditions specified at the beginning of the game, including a maximum of $q_S(\lambda)$ signing queries and a total of $q_S(\lambda) + q_{\mathsf{H}}(\lambda)$ random oracle queries for each run of the adversary $\mathcal{A}$, the probability of aborting in Type II is bounded by $(2p(\lambda)+1)q_S(\lambda)(q_S(\lambda)+q_{\mathsf{H}}(\lambda))\nu(\lambda)$. As $\nu(\lambda)$ is negligible, this term is also negligible.

What is left is to show that the collision probability in the second challenge we get after rewinding is negligible. With a maximum of $q_S(\lambda) + q_{\mathsf{H}}(\lambda)$ queries to the random oracle in each run of the adversary $\mathcal{A}$, we get a total risk of $\frac{((q_S(\lambda)+q_{\mathsf{H}}(\lambda))(2p(\lambda)+1))^2}{2^{2\lambda}}$ of having a collision.

By avoiding type I and type II aborts, as well as collisions, the adversary $\mathcal{A}$ is left with a probability of approximately $\frac{1}{N} \cdot \frac{1}{2p(\lambda)} \cdot \frac{t}{N} - (2p(\lambda)+1)q_S(\lambda)(q_S(\lambda)+q_{\mathsf{H}}(\lambda))\nu(\lambda) - \frac{((q_S(\lambda)+q_{\mathsf{H}}(\lambda))(2p(\lambda)+1))^2}{2^{2\lambda}} \approx \frac{t}{2p(\lambda)\cdot N^2}$ in succeed in using the special soundness property to extract the information of the secret keys of all t signers and solve the underlying hard problem, which is the desired conclusion. □

5 Instantiations

The isogeny-based and lattice-based instantiations follow easily by applying the Admissible Group Action from the paper by Beullens [9].

5.1 Isogeny-Based

Our isogeny-based TRS scheme follows the Theorem 5.1 [9] by Beullens (the CSIDH paradigm) and focuses on the *Admissible Group Action form CSIDH-512*. We assume that the ideal class group $\mathcal{C}\ell(\mathcal{O})$ is cyclic with generator $\mathfrak{g}$ of order M where $M = \#\mathcal{C}\ell(\mathcal{O})$. We now have the group $\mathbb{Z}_M$ acts freely and transitively on $\mathcal{E}\ell\ell_p(\mathcal{O})$ via the group action $\star$ defined as $a \star X = \mathfrak{g}^a * X$.

Theorem 10 (AdmGA from CSIDH − 512.). *We use* CSIDH − 512 *prime p and define the group action $\star : G \times \mathcal{X} \to \mathcal{X}$ as in* CSI − FiSh *and suppose that the* GAIP_p *is hard. Then* $\mathsf{AdmGA}_{\mathsf{GAIP}_{512}} = (G, \mathcal{X}, S_1, S_2, D_{\mathcal{X}})$ *is a δ-admissible group action with respect to $X_0 \in \mathcal{X}$, where $G, \mathcal{X}, X_0, S_1, S_2$ and δ are defined as follows:*

- $G, S_1, S_2 := \mathbb{Z}_M$;
- $\mathcal{X} := \mathcal{E}$;
- X_0;
- $\delta = 1$.

Parameters Selection. In our isogeny-based construction, a user's public key contains the information of two supersingular elliptic curves, each with a size of 64B. As per CSI-FiSh, the secret key is roughly half the size of the public key, which is 16B.

We use 128 bits for storing the information of the permutation ϕ and the randomness. To meet the security requirement of the scheme, we need to execute the threshold identification protocol λ times. If the challenge $c_i = 1$ ($i \in [1, \lambda]$), the transcript of the protocol has the total size of $(16N + 48)$B. If the challenge $c_i = 0$ ($i \in [1, \lambda]$), this number is $(64N + 16t + 32)$B. To sum up, the size of the signature is $(640N + 128t + 640)$B.

5.2 Lattice-Based

The lattice-based TRS scheme also follows the work by Beullens and adapts the Admissible Group Action under the MSIS and MLWE assumptions. We now recall Theorem 5.7 from [9] about AdmGA from lattices.

Theorem 11 (AdmGA from lattices.). *Let n be a power of 2 , $q = 5 \mod 8$ and let k, ℓ be integers. Let B_1, B_2 be integers such that $B_1 < B_2 < q$ and assume the $\mathsf{MSIS}_{k,\ell,2B_2}$ and $\mathsf{sMLWE}_{k,\ell,B_1}$ assumptions hold. Then, $\mathsf{AdmGA}_{\mathsf{MLWE}} = (G, \mathcal{X}, S_1, S_2, D_{\mathcal{X}})$ is a δ-admissible group action with respect to any $X_0 \in \mathcal{X}$, where $(G, \mathcal{X}, S_1, S_2, D_X)$ are defined as follows:*

- $(G, \mathcal{X}) := (R_q^\ell \times R_q^k, R_q^k)$;
- *For* $b \in \{0, 1\}$, $S_b := \{(\mathbf{s}, \mathbf{e}) \in G | \|\mathbf{s}\|_\infty, \|\mathbf{e}\|_\infty \leq B_b\}$;
- *The group action* $\star_\mathbf{A} : G \times \mathcal{X} \to \mathcal{X}$, *uniquely defined by a matrix* $\mathbf{A} \in R_q^{k\times\ell}$, *is defined as* $(\mathbf{s}, \mathbf{e}) \star_\mathbf{A} \mathbf{w} := (\mathbf{A}\mathbf{s} + \mathbf{e}) + \mathbf{w}$;
- $D_\mathcal{X}$ *is the uniform distribution over* $R_q^{k\times\ell}$;
- $\delta := \left(\dfrac{2(B_2 - B_1) + 1}{2B_2 + 1}\right)^{n(k+\ell)}$.

Parameters Selection. We follow the Falafl scheme and choose the ring $R_q = \mathbb{Z}_q/(X^{256}+1)$, $q = 8380417$. We use the medium parameter set of Dilithium where the dimension of the MLWE problem is $(k, \ell) = (3, 4)$ and the coefficients of the secrets vectors are chosen uniformly random from $[-6, 6]$. Following the parameter calculation of [23], the secret key of a user in the lattice-based construction is a pair of vector $(\mathbf{s}, \mathbf{e}) \in \mathbf{R_q^\ell} \times \mathbf{R_q^k}$ that size is 0.896KB. The public key $\mathsf{pk} = (X_0, X_1)$'s size is 1.728KB. Similar to the isogeny-based construction, we use 128 bits for saving the information of ϕ and the randomness. The size of the Σ-protocol's transcript when $c_i = 1$ ($i \in [1, \lambda]$) is $(896N + 48)$B and when $c_i = 0$ is $(864N + 896t + 32)$B. To meet the security requirements, the signature size is approximately $(14N + 7t + 0.64)$KB.

References

1. Aguilar Melchor, C., Cayrel, P.-L., Gaborit, P.: A new efficient threshold ring signature scheme based on coding theory. In: Buchmann, J., Ding, J. (eds.) PQCrypto 2008. LNCS, vol. 5299, pp. 1–16. Springer, Heidelberg (2008). https://doi.org/10.1007/978-3-540-88403-3_1
2. Alagic, G., et al.: Status report on the third round of the nist post-quantum cryptography standardization process (2022)
3. Alamati, N., De Feo, L., Montgomery, H., Patranabis, S.: Cryptographic group actions and applications. In: Moriai, S., Wang, H. (eds.) ASIACRYPT 2020. LNCS, vol. 12492, pp. 411–439. Springer, Cham (2020). https://doi.org/10.1007/978-3-030-64834-3_14
4. Alberto Torres, W.A., et al.: Post-Quantum one-time linkable ring signature and application to ring confidential transactions in blockchain (Lattice RingCT v1.0). In: Susilo, W., Yang, G. (eds.) ACISP 2018. LNCS, vol. 10946, pp. 558–576. Springer, Cham (2018). https://doi.org/10.1007/978-3-319-93638-3_32
5. Aranha, D.F., Hall-Andersen, M., Nitulescu, A., Pagnin, E., Yakoubov, S.: Count me in! extendability for threshold ring signatures. In: PKC 2022, pp. 379–406 (2022)
6. Assidi, H., Ayebie, E.B., Souidi, E.M.: An efficient code-based threshold ring signature scheme. J. Inf. Secur. Appl. **45**(C), 52–60 (2019)
7. Atapoor, S., Baghery, K., Cozzo, D., Pedersen, R.: CSI-shark: CSI-FiSh with sharing-friendly Keys. ePrint 2022/1189 (2022)
8. Bettaieb, S., Schrek, J.: Improved lattice-based threshold ring signature scheme. In: Gaborit, P. (ed.) PQCrypto 2013. LNCS, vol. 7932, pp. 34–51. Springer, Heidelberg (2013). https://doi.org/10.1007/978-3-642-38616-9_3
9. Beullens, W., Katsumata, S., Pintore, F.: Calamari and falafl: logarithmic (linkable) ring signatures from isogenies and lattices. In: Moriai, S., Wang, H. (eds.) ASIACRYPT 2020. LNCS, vol. 12492, pp. 464–492. Springer, Cham (2020). https://doi.org/10.1007/978-3-030-64834-3_16
10. Beullens, W., Kleinjung, T., Vercauteren, F.: CSI-FiSh: efficient isogeny based signatures through class group computations. In: Galbraith, S.D., Moriai, S. (eds.) ASIACRYPT 2019. LNCS, vol. 11921, pp. 227–247. Springer, Cham (2019). https://doi.org/10.1007/978-3-030-34578-5_9
11. Bonnetain, X., Schrottenloher, A.: Quantum security analysis of CSIDH. In: Canteaut, A., Ishai, Y. (eds.) EUROCRYPT 2020. LNCS, vol. 12106, pp. 493–522. Springer, Cham (2020). https://doi.org/10.1007/978-3-030-45724-2_17
12. Branco, P., Mateus, P.: A code-based linkable ring signature scheme. In: Baek, J., Susilo, W., Kim, J. (eds.) ProvSec 2018. LNCS, vol. 11192, pp. 203–219. Springer, Cham (2018). https://doi.org/10.1007/978-3-030-01446-9_12
13. Bresson, E., Stern, J., Szydlo, M.: Threshold ring signatures and applications to ad-hoc groups. In: Yung, M. (ed.) CRYPTO 2002. LNCS, vol. 2442, pp. 465–480. Springer, Heidelberg (2002). https://doi.org/10.1007/3-540-45708-9_30
14. Castryck, W., Decru, T.: An efficient key recovery attack on sidh (preliminary version). Cryptology ePrint Archive, Paper 2022/975 (2022)
15. Castryck, W., Lange, T., Martindale, C., Panny, L., Renes, J.: CSIDH: an efficient post-quantum commutative group action. In: Peyrin, T., Galbraith, S. (eds.) ASIACRYPT 2018. LNCS, vol. 11274, pp. 395–427. Springer, Cham (2018). https://doi.org/10.1007/978-3-030-03332-3_15

16. Cayrel, P.-L., El Yousfi Alaoui, S.M., Hoffmann, G., Véron, P.: An improved threshold ring signature scheme based on error correcting codes. In: Özbudak, F., Rodríguez-Henríquez, F. (eds.) WAIFI 2012. LNCS, vol. 7369, pp. 45–63. Springer, Heidelberg (2012). https://doi.org/10.1007/978-3-642-31662-3_4
17. Cayrel, P.-L., Lindner, R., Rückert, M., Silva, R.: A lattice-based threshold ring signature scheme. In: Abdalla, M., Barreto, P.S.L.M. (eds.) LATINCRYPT 2010. LNCS, vol. 6212, pp. 255–272. Springer, Heidelberg (2010). https://doi.org/10.1007/978-3-642-14712-8_16
18. Couveignes, J.-M.: Hard homogeneous spaces. ePrint 2006/291 (2006)
19. Cozzo, D., Smart, N.P.: Sashimi: cutting up CSI-FiSh secret keys to produce an actively secure distributed signing protocol. In: Ding, J., Tillich, J.-P. (eds.) PQCrypto 2020. LNCS, vol. 12100, pp. 169–186. Springer, Cham (2020). https://doi.org/10.1007/978-3-030-44223-1_10
20. De Feo, L., Galbraith, S.D.: SeaSign: compact isogeny signatures from class group actions. In: Ishai, Y., Rijmen, V. (eds.) EUROCRYPT 2019. LNCS, vol. 11478, pp. 759–789. Springer, Cham (2019). https://doi.org/10.1007/978-3-030-17659-4_26
21. De Feo, L., Meyer, M.: Threshold schemes from isogeny assumptions. In: Kiayias, A., Kohlweiss, M., Wallden, P., Zikas, V. (eds.) PKC 2020. LNCS, vol. 12111, pp. 187–212. Springer, Cham (2020). https://doi.org/10.1007/978-3-030-45388-6_7
22. Decru, T., Panny, L., Vercauteren, F.: Faster SeaSign signatures through improved rejection sampling. In: Ding, J., Steinwandt, R. (eds.) PQCrypto 2019. LNCS, vol. 11505, pp. 271–285. Springer, Cham (2019). https://doi.org/10.1007/978-3-030-25510-7_15
23. Ducas, L., et al.: Crystals-dilithium: a lattice-based digital signature scheme. In: TCHES, pp. 238–268 (2018)
24. Duong, D.H., Tran, H.T., Susilo, W., Luyen, L.V.: An efficient multivariate threshold ring signature scheme. Comput. Stand. Interfaces **74**, 103489 (2021)
25. Groth, J., Kohlweiss, M.: One-out-of-many proofs: or how to leak a secret and spend a coin. In: Oswald, E., Fischlin, M. (eds.) EUROCRYPT 2015. LNCS, vol. 9057, pp. 253–280. Springer, Heidelberg (2015). https://doi.org/10.1007/978-3-662-46803-6_9
26. Haque, A., Krenn, S., Slamanig, D., Striecks, C.: Logarithmic-size (linkable) threshold ring signatures in the plain model. In: PKC 2022, pp. 437–467 (2022)
27. Haque, A., Scafuro, A.: Threshold ring signatures: new definitions and post-quantum security. In: Kiayias, A., Kohlweiss, M., Wallden, P., Zikas, V. (eds.) PKC 2020. LNCS, vol. 12111, pp. 423–452. Springer, Cham (2020). https://doi.org/10.1007/978-3-030-45388-6_15
28. Langlois, A., Stehlé, D.: Worst-case to average-case reductions for module lattices. Des. Codes Cryptogr. **75**(3), 565–599 (2015)
29. Li, L., Xu, M.: Ripplesign: isogeny-based threshold ring signatures with combinatorial methods. In: CSP 2022, pp. 11–15 (2022)
30. Liu, J.K., Wong, D.S.: On the security models of (threshold) ring signature schemes. In: Park, C., Chee, S. (eds.) ICISC 2004. LNCS, vol. 3506, pp. 204–217. Springer, Heidelberg (2005). https://doi.org/10.1007/11496618_16
31. Lu, X., Au, M.H., Zhang, Z.: Raptor: a practical lattice-based (linkable) ring signature. In: Deng, R.H., Gauthier-Umaña, V., Ochoa, M., Yung, M. (eds.) ACNS 2019. LNCS, vol. 11464, pp. 110–130. Springer, Cham (2019). https://doi.org/10.1007/978-3-030-21568-2_6
32. Meyer, M., Reith, S.: A faster way to the CSIDH. ePrint 2018/782 (2018)
33. Okamoto, T., Tso, R., Yamaguchi, M., Okamoto, E.: A k-out-of-n ring signature with flexible participation for signers. ePrint 2018/728 (2018)

34. Peikert, C.: He gives C-Sieves on the CSIDH. In: Canteaut, A., Ishai, Y. (eds.) EUROCRYPT 2020. LNCS, vol. 12106, pp. 463–492. Springer, Cham (2020). https://doi.org/10.1007/978-3-030-45724-2_16
35. Petzoldt, A., Bulygin, S., Buchmann, J.: A multivariate based threshold ring signature scheme. ePrint 2012/194 (2012)
36. Stolbunov, A.: Constructing public-key cryptographic schemes based on class group action on a set of isogenous elliptic curves. Adv. Math. Commun. **4**(2), 215–235 (2010)
37. Stolbunov, A.: Cryptographic schemes based on isogenies (2012)
38. Tang, G., Duong, D.H., Joux, A., Plantard, T., Qiao, Y., Susilo, W.: Practical post-quantum signature schemes from isomorphism problems of trilinear forms. In: EUROCRYPT 2022, pp. 582–612. Springer, Heidelberg (2022). https://doi.org/10.1007/978-3-031-07082-2_21
39. Tsang, P.P., Wei, V.K.: Short linkable ring signatures for E-Voting, E-Cash and attestation. In: Deng, R.H., Bao, F., Pang, H.H., Zhou, J. (eds.) ISPEC 2005. LNCS, vol. 3439, pp. 48–60. Springer, Heidelberg (2005). https://doi.org/10.1007/978-3-540-31979-5_5
40. Tsang, P.P., Wei, V.K., Chan, T.K., Au, M.H., Liu, J.K., Wong, D.S.: Separable linkable threshold ring signatures. In: Canteaut, A., Viswanathan, K. (eds.) INDOCRYPT 2004. LNCS, vol. 3348, pp. 384–398. Springer, Heidelberg (2004). https://doi.org/10.1007/978-3-540-30556-9_30
41. Yuen, T.H., Liu, J.K., Au, M.H., Susilo, W., Zhou, J.: Threshold ring signature without random oracles. In: ASIACCS 2011, pp. 261–267 (2011)
42. Zhang, X., Liu, J.K., Steinfeld, R., Kuchta, V., Yu, J.: Revocable and linkable ring signature. In: Liu, Z., Yung, M. (eds.) Inscrypt 2019. LNCS, vol. 12020, pp. 3–27. Springer, Cham (2020). https://doi.org/10.1007/978-3-030-42921-8_1

Encryption

Homomorphic Witness Encryption from Indistinguishable Obfuscation

Yuzhu Wang[1], Xingbo Wang[1], and Mingwu Zhang[1,2](✉)

[1] School of Computer Science and Information Security, Guilin University of Electronic Technology, Guilin 541004, China
csmwzhang@gmail.com

[2] School of Computer Science, Hubei University of Technology, Wuhan 430068, China

Abstract. Witness encryption (WE) is a new encryption paradigm that allows encrypting a message using the instance of a particular NP problem, and someone who knows a solution to this problem (i.e., a witness) can effectively decrypt the ciphertext. Traditional witness encryption is built from multi-linear encodings. In this work, we put forth the concept of homomorphic witness encryption (HWE), where one can evaluate functions over ciphertexts of the same instance without decrypting them, i.e., one can manipulate a set of ciphertexts with messages $(m_1, \cdots, m_n)$ to obtain the evaluation of $f(m_1, \cdots, m_n)$, for any function f. We declare that such homomorphic witness encryption schemes can be generically constructed from indistinguishable obfuscation ($i\mathcal{O}$) for any classes of functions. Then we propose an instantiate of multiplicative homomorphic witness encryption (MHWE) using an $i\mathcal{O}$, homomorphic encryption for NP problems such as Subset-Sum and a batch-processed GS-proof system, which enables us to evaluate multiplication operations over ciphertext. Furthermore, we give the security and efficiency of our candidate schemes.

Keywords: Witness Encryption · Homomorphism · Subset-Sum Problem · Indistinguishable Obfuscation · Noninteractive Zero-Knowledge Proof

1 Introduction

Witness Encryption. Witness encryption (WE) is a new encryption paradigm introduced by Garg, Gentry, Sahai, and Waters [1], which defines for some NP-language $\mathcal{L}$ with witness relation R so that $\mathcal{L} = \{x \mid \exists\ w : R(x, w) = 1\}$. In a witness encryption scheme, the encryption algorithm takes as input an instance x along with a message M and produces a ciphertext C. Using a witness w such that $R(x, w) = 1$, the decryptor can recover the message M from the ciphertext

M. Zhang—This work is partially supported by the National Natural Science Foundation of China under grants 62072134 and U2001205, the Key projects of Guangxi Natural Science Foundation under grant 2019JJD170020.

M. Zhang et al. (Eds.): ProvSec 2023, LNCS 14217, pp. 231–250, 2023.
https://doi.org/10.1007/978-3-031-45513-1_13

C. Decryption is only possible if x is actually in the language $\mathcal{L}$ and a ciphertext C hides the message M if C has been computed with respect to some $x \notin \mathcal{L}$.

Since its introduction, witness encryption has been subject to intense study which can broadly be categorized into two areas. Firstly, works that consider for all NP problem and thereby mostly focusing on a speical NP-complete problem, i.e., Exact Cover problem [1], Hamilton Cycle problem [2], SAT problem [3], and Subset-Sum problem [4], Sudoku problem [5]. This typically results in constructions beyond practical interest, as they rely on strong assumptions, such as multilinear mapping (MMap) [6] or obfuscation techniques ($i\mathcal{O}$) [7,8]. Secondly, works that restrict the power by only supporting limited classes of NP languages that are of particular interest for practical applications, i.e., algebraic languages [9], commitments [10], and signature [11]. Here, the main focus is on well-studied cryptographic assumptions and efficient constructions. The applications of witness encryption are mainly used to construct cryptographic primitives from WE, including indeed novel constructions of known primitives public-key encryption, identity-based encryption (IBE) [12], attribute-based encryption (ABE) [13,14], and Multiparty Computation (MPC) [15,16] or new primitives [17–19]. Moreover, Bellare and Hoang [20] proposed to use WE to realize asymmetric password-based encryption (A-PBE), where the hash of a password (as a public key) can be used to encrypt a message, which can then be decrypted using the respective password.

Our Work: Homomorphic Witness Encryption. Considering that most of the existing WE constructions [21–24] are built on MMap or obfuscation, they are far from practical. Therefore, in this paper, we construct a WE scheme where encryption is very efficient, and we do so by moving the heavy computational work of the encryption phase to the setup phase, and where the ciphertext generated for the same instance can be processed in a batch. This setup algorithm is run by the trusted party once and everyone can use the same parameters, a situation identical to the standard homomorphic public key encryption.

We call this concept homomorphic witness encryption (HWE): Loosely speaking, an HWE is an augmented witness encryption that allows anyone with witness w to evaluate a circuit $\mathcal{C}$ over sets of ciphertexts $(CT_1, \cdots, CT_n)$ homomorphically, without necessarily knowing the secret messages $(m_1, \cdots, m_n)$ encapsulated within these ciphertexts. The resulting output (which is also a ciphertext) contains the circuit output $\mathcal{C}(m_1, \cdots, m_n)$.

Next, we outline the four algorithms in our homomorphic witness encryption scheme from $i\mathcal{O}$. The syntax follows the standard notation for witness encryption, except that we consider an additional setup phase to generate public parameters for encryption and decryption. Furthermore, HWE is augmented with an evaluation algorithm that allows one to manipulate ciphertexts in a meaningful way. The Setup algorithm (which is not present in standard WE) takes as input only a security parameter 1^λ and outputs public parameters $(pp_e, pp_d) \leftarrow \mathsf{Setup}(1^\lambda)$. To encrypt a message m for an instance x, one runs an encryption algorithm $CT \leftarrow \mathsf{Enc}(pp_e, x, m)$. Such ciphertext CT can then be decrypted given a witness w, i.e., for which $R(x, w)$ =1 holds, as $m = \mathsf{Dec}(pp_d, CT, w)$.

To evaluate n ciphertext messages $(CT_1, \cdots, CT_n)$, one runs an Eval algorithm $CT' \leftarrow \mathsf{Eval}(\mathcal{C}, CT_1, \cdots, CT_n)$. The goal of homomorphic witness encryption is to keep the parameters pp_e for encryption and ciphertexts small and the Enc and Eval algorithm efficient.

In this work we put forward the concept of HWE and we formally characterize their security guarantees. Then, we propose a general construction that supports homomorphic evaluation of all types of circuits and instantiate the MHWE scheme that supports homomorphic evaluation of multiplicative circuits.

Our Contribution. The main contributions of this paper are as follows:

- **Modeling:** We formally define a new primitive homomorphic witness encryption (HWE) with security notion in the indistinguishability setting. Within HWE, one can evaluate functions over ciphertext of the same instance without decrypting them, i.e., one can manipulate a set of ciphertexts with messages $(m_1, \cdots, m_n)$, and someone who has the witness can decrypt to obtain $f(m_1, \cdots, m_n)$, for any functions f.
- **Constructions:** We propose a general construction of homomorphic witness encryption for any functions f, which relies on the existence of indistinguishability obfuscation ($i\mathcal{O}$). In addition, we provide a multiplicative homomorphic witness encryption (MHWE) scheme for Subset-Sum problem.
- **Techniques:** To instantiate our MHWE scheme, we develop two main technical contributions. The first one is finding a useful variant of homomorphic encryption for our purposes. We define the notion of homomorphic encryption for NP problem and construct this primitive based on variant of ElGamal encryption. The second one is to apply the batching technique to the Groth-Sahai proof system, which resorts to the small exponent batching technique [GL89] to achieve batching in bilinear groups.

Technical Overview. Since its inception, witness encryption has been inexorably linked with multilinear mapping (MMap) [6] or obfuscation techniques ($i\mathcal{O}$) [7,8], which are known to be equivalent [25]. In [26], Garg et al. showed that indistinguishability obfuscation implies witness encryption for an NP-Complete language. Indistinguishability obfuscation (i$\mathcal{O}$) requires that given any two equivalent circuits $\mathcal{C}_0$ and $\mathcal{C}_1$ of similar size, the obfuscations of $\mathcal{C}_0$ and $\mathcal{C}_1$ should be computationally indistinguishable. The most direct application is to give the adversary access to computations using secret keys without having to reveal the keys themselves. It is exactly this property that we will use to build our homomorphic witness encryption.

Next, we follow the blueprint in [26] and construct homomorphic witness encryption from indistinguishability obfuscation. Recall that building witness encryption from $i\mathcal{O}$ also requires a CPA-secure public key encryption scheme and a statistically simulation sound NIZK proof system. However, here we encounter the first key problem that we must tackle: if (x, m) is encoded as M in [27] for encryption, it will not satisfy the homomorphism of witness encryption. We address this problem by introducing the notion of homomorphic encryption for NP problem, which requires homomorphism for different message ciphertexts encrypted using the same NP instance. Specifically, we construct IND-CPA-secure multiplicative homomorphic encryption based on a variant of ElGamal encryption.

The second element we need to achieve homomorphism is a batch-verifiable NIZK proof system. We adopt the GS proof system proposed by Groth et al. [28] and implement the batch verification proof system needed for our MHWE scheme based on the small exponent batching technique [29,30]. Batch verification techniques typically consist of two phases: the first phase, where all the equations are combined into a single one, and the second phase, where the cost of verifying the combined claim is optimized. In the bilinear pairings, the latter implies reducing the number of pairing operations, which are the most expensive operations, but also trying to minimize the total cost, taking into account the relative cost of other operations (the cost of exponentiations $G_T > G_2 > G_1$). For example, for the second phase, one of the rules of Ferrara et al. [30] is to "move the exponent into the pairing," i.e., one should replace terms of the form $e(g_1, g_2)^{\gamma}$ by $e(g_1^{\gamma}, g_2)$ in the combined expression.

Related Work. Witness Encryption was introduced by Garg, Gentry, Sahai, and Waters [1]. They provide the first construction of WE for the NP-complete problem Exact Cover and uses approximate multilinear maps (MMap). Subsequently, Garg et al. [26] showed that indistinguishability obfuscation [7,8] implies WE. Subsequently, Zhandry [31] gave a constructure of reusable WE using witness pseudorandom functions (witness PRFs) and provided a witness PRFs instantiation from MMap. To achieve more efficient encryption procedure, Abusalah et al. [27] introduced an interesting variant of WE, i.e., Offline WE (OWE), where the encryption algorithm uses neither multilinear maps nor obfuscation. They achieved efficient encryption by outsourcing the resource-heavy computations to a setup phase that processes necessary tools to produce public parameters for encryption and decryption. Later, several other works [22,24,32] built upon [27,31] and proposed the selectively secure OWE scheme, or semi-adaptive security OWE scheme for any NP-language.

Our approach is a follow-up to the work of [27]. Abusalah et al. [27] propose the notion of offline witness encryption from Indistinguishable obfuscation, which is similar to our homomorphic witness encryption. Apart from being a standard public key encryption scheme (which does not homomorphically encrypt messages based on NP problem instances), the main difference is that Enc algorithm outputs parameter π which cannot perform batch verification on the NIZK proof.

2 Preliminaries

In this section, we will start by giving our definition of public key encryption for NP instance scheme Σ and the notions of indistinguishability obfuscation ($i\mathcal{O}$) and statistically simulation sound NIZK proof system Π that will be needed in the realization of our witness encryption candidate.

2.1 Notations and Conventions

We use $[n]$ to denote the set $\{1, \cdots, n\}$, and let $\lambda \in \mathbb{N}$ be the security parameter. Let $x \leftarrow S$ denote the process of sampling x uniformly at random from the finite set S. By $y \leftarrow \mathsf{A}(\lambda, x)$, we denote that y is assigned the output of the potentially probabilistic (PPT) algorithm A on input (λ, x) with access to uniformly random coins. To make the random coins r explicit, we write $\mathsf{A}(\lambda, x; r)$. A function $\mu : \mathbb{N} \rightarrow \mathbb{R}$ is called negligible if $\mu(n) \leq \frac{1}{p(n)}$ holds for every positive polynomial $p(\cdot)$ and all sufficiently large $n \in \mathbb{N}$. We use μ to denote such a negligible function.

2.2 Public Key Encryption for NPInstance

Definition 1. *A public key encryption for NP language $\mathcal{L}$ scheme Σ = (Setup, Enc, Dec, Eval) with message space $\mathcal{M}$ consists of the following PPT algorithms:*

- $\mathsf{Setup}(1^\lambda)$: *On input a security parameter 1^λ, Setup outputs a public key pk and a secret key sk.*
- $\mathsf{Enc}(pk, x, m)$: *On input a public key pk, an instance $x \in \mathcal{L}$ and a message $m \in \mathcal{M}$, Enc outputs a ciphertext CT.*
- $\mathsf{Dec}(sk, CT)$: *On input a ciphertext CT and a secret key sk, Dec outputs a message $m \in \mathcal{M} \cup \{\perp\}$.*
- $\mathsf{Eval}(op, x, CT_1, \cdots, CT_n)$: *On input a homomorphic operation op, an instance $x \in \mathcal{L}$ and a set of n ciphertexts $(CT_1, \cdots, CT_n)$, Eval outputs a ciphertext CT'.*

We require Σ scheme to be correct and to provide ciphertext indistinguishable under chosen plaintext attacks (IND-CPA security).

Definition 2 (Correctness). *A Σ scheme is correct, if for any $\lambda \in \mathbb{N}$, any $x \in \mathcal{L}$, any $m \in \mathcal{M}$, any (pk, sk) in the support of $\mathsf{Setup}(1^\lambda)$, and all CT in the support of $\mathsf{Enc}(pk, x, m)$, such that,*

$$|Pr[\mathsf{Dec}(sk, CT) = m] - 1| \leqslant \mu(\lambda)$$

Definition 3 (IND-CPA Security). *A Σ scheme is secure, if for all valid PPT adversaries $\mathcal{A}$ there is a negligible function $\mu(\lambda)$ it holds that*

$$Pr\left[\begin{array}{c} pk, sk \leftarrow \mathsf{Setup}(1^\lambda), \\ (x, m_0, m_1, st) \leftarrow \mathcal{A}(pk), b \leftarrow \{0,1\}, : b = b^* \\ c \leftarrow \mathsf{Enc}(pk, x, m_b), b^* \leftarrow \mathcal{A}(c, st) \end{array}\right] \leq \frac{1}{2} + \mu(\lambda).$$

2.3 Indistinguishability Obfuscation

Definition 4 (Indistinguishability Obfuscation [26]). *A uniform PPT algorithm $i\mathcal{O}$ is an indistinguishability obfuscator for a circuit class $\{\mathcal{C}_\lambda\}$, if it satisfies the following conditions:*

- *For all* $\lambda \in \mathbb{N}$, *for all* $C \in \mathcal{C}_\lambda$, *for all* $x \in \{0,1\}^\lambda$, *we have that*

$$\Pr\left[C'(x) = C(x) : C' \leftarrow i\mathcal{O}(\lambda, C)\right] = 1$$

- *For all PPT distinguisher* $\mathcal{D}$, *all security parameters* $\lambda \in \mathbb{N}$, *and all pairs of circuits* $C_0, C_1 \in \mathcal{C}_\lambda$, *such that for any input* x, $C_0(x) = C_1(x)$ *and* $|C_0| = |C_1|$, *it holds that*

$$\left|\Pr\left[\mathcal{D}\left(i\mathcal{O}\left(1^\lambda, C_0\right)\right) = 1\right] - \Pr\left[\mathcal{D}\left(i\mathcal{O}\left(1^\lambda, C_1\right)\right) = 1\right]\right| \leq \mu(\lambda)$$

2.4 SSS-Noninteractive Zero-Knowledge Proofs

Let R be an efficiently computable binary relation, where for a pair $(x', w') \in R$ we call x' the statement and w' the witness. Let $\mathcal{L}$ denote the language consisting of statements in R. A non-interactive zero-knowledge (NIZK) proof system [28, 33] for a language $\mathcal{L} \in \mathsf{NP}$ allows proving that some statements are in $\mathcal{L}$ without leaking information about the corresponding witnesses w in a noninteractive manner. We note that we require the proof system to support batch verify. This can be done by using the batch techniques of the proof system described in [29,34,35]. We employ a batch processing technique similar to that in [34], but our NIZK has an additional batch processing algorithm compared to the standard proof system, which is mainly used to pre-process the proofs before batch verification.

Definition 5 (SSS-Noninteractive Zero-Knowledge Proof System). *A statistically simulation sound non-interactive zero-knowledge (SSS-NIZK) proof system* Π *for a language* $\mathcal{L} \in \mathsf{NP}$ *with witness relation* R *consists of the following PPT algorithms:*

- *Setup*(1^λ): *On input a security parameter* λ, *Setup outputs a common reference string* crs.
- *Prove*(crs, x', w'): *On input a common reference string* crs *and* $(x', w') \in R$, *Prove outputs a proof* π.
- *Verify*(crs, x', π): *On input a common reference string* crs, *an instance* x' *and a proof* π, *Verify outputs* 1 *(accept) or* 0 *(reject).*
- *Batch*$(x', \pi_1, \cdots, \pi_n)$: *On input an instance* x' *and a set of proofs* $\pi_1, \cdots, \pi_n$, *Batch outputs a proof* π'.

Perfect Completeness. *A* Π *scheme is perfect complete, if for all* $(x', w') \in R$ *such that* $R(x', w') = 1$, *it holds that*

$$\Pr[crs \leftarrow \mathsf{Setup}(1^\lambda); \pi \leftarrow \mathsf{Prove}(crs, x', w') : \mathsf{Verify}(crs, x', \pi) = 1] = 1$$

Statistical Soundness. *A* Π *scheme is sound, if for all* $x' \notin \mathcal{L}$, *and all non-uniform polynomial time adversaries* $\mathcal{A}$, *it holds that*

$$\Pr\left[\begin{array}{c} crs \leftarrow \mathsf{Setup}\left(1^\lambda\right); \\ x' \notin \mathcal{L};\ (x', \pi) \leftarrow \mathcal{A}(crs) \end{array} : \mathsf{Verify}(crs, x', \pi) = 1\right] \leq \mu(\lambda)$$

Computational Zero-Knowledge. *A Π scheme is computational zero knowledge, if exists a PPT algorithm $Sim = (S_1, S_2)$, where S_1 returns a simulated common reference string crs together with a simulation trapdoor τ that enables S_2 to simulate proofs without access to the witness, for all $\lambda \in \mathbb{N}$, all $x' \in \mathcal{L}$, and all non-uniform polynomial time adversaries $\mathcal{A}$, it holds that*

$$\Pr[crs \leftarrow \mathsf{Setup}(1^\lambda); \pi \leftarrow \mathsf{Prove}(crs, x', w') : \mathcal{A}(crs, \pi) = 1]$$
$$\approx \Pr[(crs, \tau) \leftarrow S_1(1^\lambda, x'); \pi \leftarrow S_2(\tau, crs, x') : \mathcal{A}(crs, \tau, \pi) = 1]$$

Statistical Simulation Soundness. *A Π scheme is said to be statistically simulation sound if it is infeasible to convince an honest verifier of a false statement even when the adversary itself is provided with a simulated proof. For all statements x' and all (even unbounded) adversaries $\mathcal{A}$, it holds that*

$$Pr\left[\begin{matrix}(crs,\tau) \leftarrow S_1\left(1^\lambda, x'\right) \\ \pi \leftarrow S_2\left(crs, \tau, x'\right)\end{matrix} : \begin{matrix}\exists\,(y', \pi')\ s.t.\ y' \neq x' \wedge y' \notin L \\ \wedge\ \mathsf{Verify}(crs, y', \pi') = 1\end{matrix}\right] \leq \mu(\lambda)$$

ElGamal Commitments. Garg et al. [26] provide a SSS-NIZK proof system from non-interactive and perfectly binding commitment scheme, and the NIZK proof system. In the following we will review a detailed description of the ElGamal commitment scheme Com with perfect binding.

Let us consider $\mathbb{G} =< g >$, a cyclic group of prime order p, and two random generators $ck \leftarrow (g, k) \in \mathbb{G}^2$. The ElGamal commitment scheme allows to commit to group elements from $\mathbb{G}$:

Commitment: A commitment $\mathsf{Com}(g, k, M)$ to a message $M \in \mathbb{G}$ is computed by picking $r \leftarrow \mathbb{Z}_p$ and setting $cm \leftarrow (cm_1 = g^r, cm_2 = M \cdot k^r)$, while the opening value is set to h^r;

Opening: If $e(cm_2 \cdot M^{-1}, h) = e(k, h^r)$ and $e(cm_1, h) = e(g, h^r)$, the receiver accepts the opening to M, otherwise it refuses.

This yields a perfectly binding commitment scheme for messages from $\mathbb{G}$, and, as the commitment is an ElGamal encryption, it is perfecly binding and computationally hiding.

3 Homomorphic Witness Encryption

We present our definitional framework of homomorphic witness encryption (HWE). Loosely speaking, an HWE is an augmented witness encryption that allows anyone with witness w to homomorphically evaluate a circuit C on ciphertexts $(CT_1, \cdots, CT_n)$ generated using the same instance x. The syntax follows the standard notation for witness encryption, except that we consider an additional setup phase to generate public parameters for encryption and decryption. Furthermore, HWE is augmented with an evaluation algorithm that allows one to manipulate ciphertexts in a meaningful way.

Definition 6 (Homomorphic Witness encryption). *A homomorphic witness encryption (HWE) scheme for an NP language $\mathcal{L}$ with a relation R is a tuple of four algorithms (Setup, Enc, Dec, Eval) defined as follows.*

- $\mathsf{Setup}(1^\lambda)$: *On input a security parameter 1^λ, Setup outputs a public parameter pp_e for encryption and a public parameter pp_d for decryption.*
- $\mathsf{Enc}(pp_e, x, m)$: *On input an encryption parameter pp_e, an instance $x \in \mathcal{L}$ and a message $m \in \mathcal{M}$, Enc outputs a ciphertext CT.*
- $\mathsf{Dec}(pp_d, CT, w)$: *On input a ciphertext CT and a witness w, Dec outputs a message $m \in \mathcal{M} \cup \{\perp\}$.*
- $\mathsf{Eval}(op, x, CT_1, \cdots, CT_n)$: *On input a homomorphic operation op, an instance $x \in \mathcal{L}$ and a set of n ciphertexts $(CT_1, \cdots, CT_n)$, Eval outputs a ciphertext CT'.*

We require an HWE scheme (Setup, Enc, Dec, Eval) to be correct and selectively secure, as defined below.

Definition 7 (Correctness). *An HWE scheme is correct, if for any $\lambda \in \mathbb{N}$, any $x \in \mathcal{L}$, any $(m_1, \cdots, m_n) \in \mathcal{M}^n$, any (pp_e, pp_d) in the support of $\mathsf{Setup}(1^\lambda)$, and all CT_i in the support of $\mathsf{Enc}(pp_e, x, m_i)$, such that,*

$$|Pr[\mathsf{Dec}(pp_d, \mathsf{Eval}(op, x, CT_1, \cdots, CT_n), w) = op(m_1, \cdots, m_n)] - 1| \leqslant \mu(\lambda)$$

Definition 8 (Security of HWE). *An HWE scheme is secure, if for any PPT adversaries $\mathcal{A} = (\mathcal{A}_1, \mathcal{A}_2)$ in $\mathsf{Exp}^{Sel-b}_{\mathsf{HWE},\mathcal{A}}(\lambda)$ (Fig. 1) it holds that*

$$\left|\Pr[\mathsf{Exp}^{Sel-0}_{\mathsf{HWE},\mathcal{A}}(\lambda) = 1] - \Pr[\mathsf{Exp}^{Sel-1}_{\mathsf{HWE},\mathcal{A}}(\lambda) = 1]\right| \leqslant \mu(\lambda)$$

$\mathsf{Exp}^{Sel-b}_{\mathsf{HWE},\mathcal{A}}(\lambda)$:
$-(x, m_0, m_1, st) \leftarrow \mathcal{A}_1(1^\lambda, R) // \lvert m_0\rvert = \lvert m_1\rvert$
$-(pp_e, pp_d) \leftarrow \mathsf{Setup}(1^\lambda)$
$-b \leftarrow \{0,1\}; CT_b \leftarrow \mathsf{Enc}(pp_e, x, m_b)$
$-b' \leftarrow \mathcal{A}_2(CT_b, pp_e, pp_d, st)$
$-if\ x \in \mathcal{L},\ return\ 0$

Fig. 1. Selective-security game of HWE

4 HWE from Indistinguishability Obfuscation

In this section, we present our generic construction of an HWE scheme from indistinguishability obfuscation, which borrows construction ideas from indistinguishability obfuscation by Garg et al. [26]. Our construction uses indistinguishability obfuscator $i\mathcal{O}$, public-key encryption based NP instance scheme Σ, and statistically simulation sound non-interactive zero-knowledge (SSS-NIZK) proof system Π. The algorithms are described below.

$\mathsf{HWE.Setup}(1^\lambda)$:
- Generate $(pk_1, sk_1) \leftarrow \Sigma.\mathsf{Setup}(1^\lambda)$ and $(pk_2, sk_2) \leftarrow \Sigma.\mathsf{Setup}(1^\lambda)$.
- Set $crs \leftarrow \Pi.\mathsf{Setup}(1^\lambda, R)$.
- Compute an obfuscation $\mathcal{O}_{P_1[sk_1,crs]}$ for the program $P_1[sk_1, crs]$ using the circuit size value equal to the value $\max\{|P_1[sk_1, crs]|, |P_2[sk_2, crs]|\}$.
- Output $pp_e = (crs, pk_1, pk_2)$ and $pp_d = \mathcal{O}_{P_1[sk_1,crs]}$.

$\mathsf{HWE.Enc}(pp_e, x, M)$:
- Compute $c_1 = \Sigma.\mathsf{Enc}(pk_1, x, m, r_1)$ and $c_2 = \Sigma.\mathsf{Enc}(pk_2, x, m, r_2)$.
- Generate $\pi \leftarrow \Pi.\mathsf{Prove}(crs, (pk_1, pk_2, c_1, c_2), (x, m, r_1, r_2))$.
- Output $CT = (x, c_1, c_2, \pi)$.

$\mathsf{HWE.Dec}(pp_d, CT, w)$:
- Parse $pp_d = \mathcal{O}_{P_1[sk_1,crs]}$ as a circuit.
- Output $M = \mathcal{O}_{P_1[sk_1,crs]}(CT, w)$.

$\mathsf{HWE.Eval}(op, CT_1, \cdots, CT_n)$:
- Parse $CT_i := (c_{i,1}, c_{i,2}, \pi_i)$ for $i = 1, \cdots, n$.
- Generate $c'_j \leftarrow \Sigma.\mathsf{Eval}(op, x, c_{1,j}, \cdots, c_{n,j})$ for $j = 1, 2$.
- Compute $\pi' \leftarrow \Pi.\mathsf{Batch}(x, \pi_1, \cdots, \pi_n)$.
- Output $CT' = (c'_1, c'_2, \pi')$.

Correctness. The correctness of our construction follows immediately from the correctness of the obfuscators $i\mathcal{O}$, IND-CPA security Σ scheme, SSS-NIZK proof system Π, and the description of the programs template P_1. We describe the two program classes in the figures below.

P_1

Constants: pk_1, pk_2, sk_1, crs
Input: $CT := (x, c_1, c_2, \pi), w$
- If $\Pi.\mathsf{Verify}(crs, (pk_1, pk_2, c_1, c_2), \pi) \neq 1 \vee R(x, w) \neq 1$, output $\perp$.
- Else output $m \leftarrow \Sigma.\mathsf{Dec}(sk_1, c_1)$.

P_2

Constants: pk_1, pk_2, sk_2, crs
Input: $CT := (x, c_1, c_2, \pi), w$
- If $\Pi.\mathsf{Verify}(crs, (pk_1, pk_2, c_1, c_2), \pi) \neq 1 \vee R(x, w) \neq 1$, output $\perp$.
- Else output $m \leftarrow \Sigma.\mathsf{Dec}(sk_2, c_2)$.

Security Proof

Theorem 1. *Let Σ be an IND-CPA secure scheme, Π be an SSS-NIZK proof system, and $i\mathcal{O}$ be an indistinguishability obfuscator for the circuit class $\mathcal{C}_\lambda$. Then, our generic construction is a selectively IND-HWE-CPA secure HWE scheme.*

Proof. We present the proof of IND-HWE-CPA security of our generic construction by organizing a sequence of hybrids. In the first hybrid the challenger encrypts m_0. We then gradually change the encryption in multiple hybrid steps into an encryption of m_1. We show that each successive hybrid experiment is indistinguishable from the last, thus showing our construction to have indistinguishability security. Consider the following sequence of hybrids.

Sequence of Hybrids

- Hybrid $\mathcal{H}_0$: Is defined as the original scheme.
- Hybrid $\mathcal{H}_1$: This hybrid is identical to $\mathcal{H}_0$ with the exception that (crs, π^*) is simulated as

$$(\text{crs},\pi^*) \leftarrow \mathsf{Sim}\left(1^\lambda, \exists x, m, r_1, r_2 : \begin{array}{c} c_1^* \leftarrow \Sigma.\mathsf{Enc}\left(pk_1, x, m; r_1\right) \\ \wedge c_2^* \leftarrow \Sigma.\mathsf{Enc}\left(pk_2, x, m; r_2\right) \end{array}\right),$$

  where c_1^* and c_2^* are part of the challenge ciphertext CT^* .
- Hybrid $\mathcal{H}_2$: This hybrid is identical to the last hybrid, $\mathcal{H}_1$, with the exception that the challenge ciphertext is generated as $c_1^* = \Sigma.\mathsf{Enc}(pk_1, x, m_0; r_1)$ and $c_2^* = \Sigma.\mathsf{Enc}(pk_2, x, m_1; r_2)$.
- Hybrid $\mathcal{H}_3$: This hybrid is identical to the last hybrid, $\mathcal{H}_2$, with the exception that the program $P_2[sk_2, crs]$ is obfuscated rather than $P_1[sk_1, crs]$.
- Hybrid $\mathcal{H}_4$: This hybrid is identical to the hybrid $\mathcal{H}_3$ with the exception that the challenge ciphertext is generated as $c_1^* = \Sigma.\mathsf{Enc}(pk_1, x, m_1; r_1)$ and $c_2^* = \Sigma.\mathsf{Enc}(pk_2, x, m_1; r_2)$,where the NIZK is still simulated and keys all created from $P_2[sk_2, crs]$.
- Hybrid $\mathcal{H}_5$: This hybrid is identical to the last hybrid, $\mathcal{H}_3$, with the exception that the program $P_1[sk_1, crs]$ is obfuscated rather than $P_2[sk_2, crs]$.
- Hybrid $\mathcal{H}_6$: This hybrid is the same as Hybrid $\mathcal{H}_5$ with the exception that the crs is generated from an honest run of the Π.Setup algorithm and that the NIZK proof component, π^*, of the challenge ciphertext is generated from the witness (r_1, r_2). This corresponds to the security game when message m_1 is encrypted for the challenge ciphertext.

Proofs of Hybrid Arguments

Lemma 1. *If SSS-NIZK proof system Π is computationally zero knowledge, then no poly-time attacker can distinguish with non-negligible probability between $\mathcal{H}_0$ and $\mathcal{H}_1$.*

Proof. We show that if there is a non-uniform PPT adversary $\mathcal{A}$ that can distinguish between $\mathcal{H}_0$ and $\mathcal{H}_1$ with non-negligible advantage, then there is a non-uniform PPT adversary $\mathcal{B}$ that breaks the zero knowledge security of our NIZK scheme. $\mathcal{B}$ runs $\mathcal{A}$ and works as follows.

First, $\mathcal{B}$ is given an NP instance x and a pair of messages m_0, m_1 by $\mathcal{A}$. Next, $\mathcal{B}$ generates both public keys itself (keeping the first secret key) and computes the encryptions $c_1^* = \Sigma.\mathsf{Enc}(pk_1, x, m_0; r_1)$, $c_2^* = \Sigma.\mathsf{Enc}(pk_2, x, m_0; r_2)$. Then, $\mathcal{B}$ submits to challenger of Π the statement

$$x' := \{\exists x, m, r_1, r_2 : c_1^* \leftarrow \Sigma.\mathsf{Enc}(pk_1, x, m; r_1) \wedge c_2^* \leftarrow \Sigma.\mathsf{Enc}(pk_2, x, m; r_2)\}$$

as well as the witness (x, m_0, r_1, r_2). It receives back (crs', π'), sets $crs = crs'$, $\pi^* = \pi'$ and the challenge ciphertext as $CT := (c_1^*, c_2^*, \pi^*)$.

If the zero knowledge challenger used the honest setup algorithm and prover to generate crs' and π^*, then we are exactly in hybrid $\mathcal{H}_0$; if it simulated the proof, then we are in hybrid $\mathcal{H}_1$. Therefore, if a non-uniform PPT adversary $\mathcal{A}$ can distinguish between the two hybrids with non-negligible advantage, then $\mathcal{B}$ can break the zero-knowledge property of the Π scheme.

Lemma 2. *If our Σ scheme is IND-CPA secure, then no poly-time attacker can distinguish with non-negligible probability between $\mathcal{H}_1$ and $\mathcal{H}_2$.*

Proof. We show that if there is a non-uniform PPT adversary $\mathcal{A}$ that can distinguish between $\mathcal{H}_1$ and $\mathcal{H}_2$ with non-negligible advantage, then there is a non-uniform PPT adversary $\mathcal{B}$ that breaks the IND-CPAsecurity of Σ scheme. $\mathcal{B}$ runs $\mathcal{A}$ and works as follows.

First, $\mathcal{B}$ is given an NP instance x and a pair of messages m_0, m_1 by $\mathcal{A}$. Next, $\mathcal{B}$ generates the first public key itself (keeping the secret key) and computes the encryption $c_1^* = \Sigma.\mathsf{Enc}(pk_1, x, m_0; r_1)$. Then, $\mathcal{B}$ receives a public key pk from the IND-CPA challenger of Σ and sets $pk_2 := pk$. Next, $\mathcal{B}$ submits the messages m_0, m_1 to the challenger and receives back c' 0 . It sets $c_2^* = c'$. Finally, it uses the simulation algorithm to get:

$$(\mathrm{crs}, \pi^*) \leftarrow \mathsf{Sim}\left(1^\lambda, \exists x, m, r_1, r_2 : \begin{array}{c} c_1^* \leftarrow \Sigma.\mathsf{Enc}\left(pk_1, x, m; r_1\right) \\ \wedge c_2^* \leftarrow \Sigma.\mathsf{Enc}\left(pk_2, x, m; r_2\right) \end{array}\right).$$

The parameters and challenge ciphertext are now given out as $pp_e = (pk_1, pk_2, crs)$ and $CT := (c_1^*, c_2^*, \pi^*)$.

If the IND-CPA challenger of Σ gave an encryption of m_0, then we are exactly in hybrid $\mathcal{H}_1$, and if it gave an encryption of m_1, then we are in hybrid $\mathcal{H}_2$. Therefore, if a non-uniform PPT adversary $\mathcal{A}$ can distinguish the two hybrids with non-negligible advantage, then $\mathcal{B}$ can break the IND-CPA security of Σ scheme.

Lemma 3. *If $i\mathcal{O}$ is an indistinguishability obfuscator for the circuit class $\mathcal{C}_\lambda$ and Π scheme is statistically simulation-sound, then no poly-time attacker can distinguish between $\mathcal{H}_2$ and $\mathcal{H}_3$. $\mathcal{B}$ runs $\mathcal{A}$ and works as follows.*

Proof. We show that if there is a non-uniform PPT adversary $\mathcal{A}$ that that can distinguish between $\mathcal{H}_2$ and $\mathcal{H}_3$ with non-negligible advantage, then there is a non-uniform PPT adversary $\mathcal{B}$ that breaks the indistinguishability obfuscator security of our obfuscation scheme.

First, $\mathcal{B}$ is given an NP instance x and a pair of messages m_0, m_1 by $\mathcal{A}$. Next, $\mathcal{B}$ generates both public keys (keeping both secret keys) and computes the encryptions $c_1^* = \Sigma.\mathsf{Enc}(pk_1, x, m_0; r_1)$, $c_2^* = \Sigma.\mathsf{Enc}(pk_2, x, m_0; r_2)$. it uses the simulation algorithm to get:

$$(\mathrm{crs}, \pi^*) \leftarrow \mathsf{Sim}\left(1^\lambda, \exists x, m, r_1, r_2 : \begin{array}{c} c_1^* \leftarrow \Sigma.\mathsf{Enc}\,(pk_1, x, m; r_1) \\ \wedge c_2^* \leftarrow \Sigma.\mathsf{Enc}\,(pk_2, x, m; r_2) \end{array}\right).$$

The parameters and challenge ciphertext are now given out as $pp_e = (pk_1, pk_2, crs)$ and $CT := (c_1^*, c_2^*, \pi^*)$.

Next, we check that both programs have the same input/output behavior. We break these down by cases on the input. In case the inputs (c_1, c_2, π) where c_1, c_2 are valid encryptions of the same message and π is a valid proof, then both programs decrypt to the same message m. Hence, the output is the same on all inputs of this class. The second set of inputs we consider are when the proof π does not pass the verification. In this case, both circuits output $\perp$. Finally, we can consider cases where the verification check passes, but c_1, c_2 are not valid encryptions of the same message. Due to the statistical simulation soundness property of the Π scheme this can only happen if $c_1 = C_1^*$ and $c_1 = C_1^*$. In this case, we have $x' = (pk_1, pk_2, c_1, c_2) \notin \mathcal{L}$. Since we have $\Pi.\mathsf{Verify}(crs, x', \pi) = 0$, which means that bboth circuits output $\perp$. This concludes that both programs have the same output on all inputs.

If the $i\mathcal{O}$ challenger chose the first program, then we are exactly in hybrid $\mathcal{H}_2$, and if it chose the second program, then we are in hybrid $\mathcal{H}_3$. Therefore, if non-uniform PPT adversary $\mathcal{A}$ can distinguish the two hybrids with non-negligible advantage, then $\mathcal{B}$ can break the security of $i\mathcal{O}$ for the circuit class $\mathcal{C}_\lambda$.

Lemma 4. *If our Σ scheme is IND-CPA secure, then no poly-time attacker can distinguish with non-negligible probability between $\mathcal{H}_3$ and $\mathcal{H}_4$.*

Proof. The proof of this lemma follows analogously to that of Lemma 2.

Lemma 5. *If $i\mathcal{O}$ is an indistinguishability obfuscator for the circuit class $\mathcal{C}_\lambda$ and Π scheme is statistically simulation-sound, then no poly-time attacker can distinguish between $\mathcal{H}_4$ and $\mathcal{H}_5$.*

Proof. The proof of this lemma follows analogously to that of Lemma 3.

Lemma 6. *If SSS-NIZK proof system Π is computationally zero knowledge, then no poly-time attacker can distinguish with non-negligible probability between $\mathcal{H}_5$ and $\mathcal{H}_6$.*

Proof. The proof of this lemma follows analogously to that of Lemma 1.

Theorem 2. *Under the assumptions listed above our HWE scheme is selectively secure in the indistinguishability game of Sect. 3.*

Proof. Theorem 2 follows from Lemmas 1–6. The first hybrid $\mathcal{H}_0$ corresponds to encrypting a message m_0 in the selective functional encryption indistinguishability game and the last hybrid $\mathcal{H}_6$ corresponds to encrypting the message m_1. Security in the indistinguishability game follows.

5 MHWE for Subset-Sum

In this section, we present our multiplicative homomorphic witness encryption (MHWE) scheme based on the subset-sum problem. An instance of subset-sum problem consists of a subset $A = \{a_1, \cdots, a_n\}$ and a target value a_0, where $a_0, a_1, \cdots, a_n \in \mathbb{Z}^{n+1}$. A witness is a set $I \subseteq A$ such that $\sum_{i \in I} i = a_0$. We encode the subset-sum problem instances using Horner's law and construct a homomorphic encryption scheme Σ for the instances based on a variant of Elgamal encryption.

5.1 Multiplicatively Homomorphic Witness Encryption

In the following we describe our MHWE scheme for language $\mathcal{L}_{ss} := \{x = \{A, a_0, \overline{R}\} \mid \exists w = I \subseteq A : \sum_{i \in I} i = a_0\}$. The algorithms are described below.

$\mathsf{MH.Setup}(1^\lambda)$:
- Sample a safe prime p, and compute $Y_1 := g_1^{\alpha_1}$, $Y_2 := g_2^{\alpha_2}$, where $g_1, g_2 \in \mathbb{G}^2$, $\alpha_1, \alpha_2 \leftarrow \mathbb{Z}_q^2$.
- Set $sk_1 = \alpha_1$, $pk_1 = (p, g_1, Y_1)$, and $sk_2 = \alpha_2$, $pk_1 = (p, g_2, Y_2)$.
- Generate $crs = (crs_{\mathsf{GS}} \leftarrow \mathsf{GS.Setup}(1^\lambda), ck, cm \leftarrow \mathsf{Com}(ck, 1^l))$.
- Compute an obfuscation $\mathcal{O}_{P_3[sk_1,crs]}$ for the program $P_3[sk_1, crs]$ using the circuit size value equal to the value $\max\{|P_3[sk_1, crs]|, |P_4[sk_2, crs]|\}$.
- Output $pp_e = (crs, pk_1, pk_2)$ and $pp_d = \mathcal{O}_{P_3[sk_1,crs]}$.

$\mathsf{MH.Enc}(pp_e, x, m)$:
- Compute the encoding $R(x) = a_0 + a_1 \cdot \overline{R} + a_2 \cdot \overline{R}^2 + \cdots + a_n \cdot \overline{R}^n$.
- Sample $r_1, r_2 \leftarrow \mathbb{Z}_p^2$ and compute $c_1 = (u_1, v_1) = (g^{r_1} \bmod p,\ Y_1^{r_1} \cdot R(x)m \bmod p)$, $c_2 = (u_2, v_2) = (g_2^{r_2} \bmod p,\ Y_2^{r_2} R(x)m \bmod p)$.
- Generate $\pi = (\pi' \leftarrow \mathsf{GS.Prove}(crs_{\mathsf{GS}}, x', w'), h, h^{r_1}, h^{r_2})$.
- Output $CT = (x, c_1, c_2, \pi)$.

$\mathsf{MH.Dec}(pp_d, CT, w)$:
- Parse $pp_d = \mathcal{O}_{P_3[sk_1,crs]}$ as a circuit.
- Output $m \leftarrow \mathcal{O}_{P_3[sk_1,crs]}(CT, w)$.

$\mathsf{MH.Eval}(\times, CT_1, \cdots, CT_n)$:
- Parse every $CT_i := (c_{i,1}, c_{i,2}, \pi_i)$, $c_{i,j} := (u_{i,j}, v_{i,j})$, for $i = 1, 2, \cdots n$, $j = 1, 2$.
- Compute $u'_j := \prod_{i=1}^n u_{i,j} \bmod p$, and $v'_j := \prod_{i=1}^n v_{i,j} \cdot R(x)^{1-n} \bmod p$, where $j = 1, 2$.
- Set $\pi' \leftarrow \mathsf{GS.Batch}(CT_1, \cdots, CT_n)$.
- Output $CT' = (c'_1 = (u'_1, v'_1), c'_2 = (u'_2, v'_2), \pi')$.

Remarkably, The Prover algorithm of the GS proof system generates a proof π for x', where x' is the following statement: $\exists\ w' = (x, m, r_1, r_2), r$ such that $R(x^*, w') = 1 \vee cm = \text{Com}(x^*; r)$. Consider the following set of linear pairing-product equations in variables $H_1, H_2, H_3, H_4, H_5 \in \mathbb{H}$:

$$e(g, H_3)e(g, H_4) = e(g, h) \tag{1}$$

$$e(cm_2^{(i)} c_{i,j}^{-1}, H_4) = e(ck_{i,j}, H_5),\ for\ i = 1, 2,\ j = 1, 2 \tag{2}$$

$$e(cm_1, H_4) = e(g, H_5) \tag{3}$$

$$e(Y_1, H_1)e(Y_2^{-1}, H_2) = e(u_1 \cdot u_2^{-1}, H_3) \tag{4}$$

$$e(g, H_i) = e(u_i, H_3),\ for\ i = 1, 2 \tag{5}$$

A proof of our SSS-NIZK proof system is a GS proof of satisfiability of the above equation system and is computed by using witness $(r1, r2)$ and setting the variables to

$$H_1 = h^{r_1},\ H_2 = h^{r_2},\ H_3 = h,\ H_4 = 1,\ H_5 = 1 \tag{6}$$

Given a statement (c_1, c_2), the simulator sets up the crs by choosing $r_c \leftarrow \mathbb{Z}_p$ and setting $cm \leftarrow \mathsf{Com}(ck, (c_1, c_2); r_c)$. It simulates a proof for statement $(c_1, c_2) \in \mathcal{L}_{GS}$ by computing a GS proof for Eqs. (1)–(5) by instantiating the variables as

$$H_1 = 1,\ H_2 = 1,\ H_3 = 1,\ H_4 = h,\ H_5 = h^{r_c} \tag{7}$$

Applying small exponent batching, which is the standard approach [29,30]. This yields:

$$e(g, H_3^{\sum_{k=1}^n r_k})e(g, H_4^{\sum_{k=1}^n r_k}) = e(g, h^{\sum_{k=1}^n r_k})$$

$$e((cm_2^{(i)} c_{i,j}^{-1})^{\sum_{k=1}^n r_k}, H_4) = e(ck_{i,j}, H_5^{\sum_{k=1}^n r_k}),\ for\ i = 1, 2,\ j = 1, 2$$

$$e(cm_1^{\sum_{k=1}^n r_k}, H_4) = e(g, H_5^{\sum_{k=1}^n r_k})$$

$$e(Y_1, H_1^{\sum_{k=1}^n r_k})e(Y_2^{-1}, H_2^{\sum_{k=1}^n r_k}) = e((u_1 u_2^{-1})^{\sum_{k=1}^n r_k}, H_3)$$

$$e(g, H_i^{\sum_{k=1}^n r_k}) = e(u_i^{\sum_{k=1}^n r_k}, H_3),\ for\ i = 1, 2$$

Correctness. The correctness of our construction follows immediately from the correctness of the obfuscators $i\mathcal{O}$, IND-CPA security Σ scheme, SSS-NIZK proof system Π, and the description of the programs template P_3. We describe the two program classes in the figures below.

$$m' = \frac{v'}{R(x)u'^{\alpha}} = \frac{\prod_{i=1}^n v_i}{\prod_{i=1}^n u_i^{\alpha} \cdot R(x)^n} = \frac{\prod_{i=1}^n Y^r \cdot m_i}{\prod_{i=1}^n g^{\alpha r}} = \prod_{i=1}^n m_i.$$

P_3

Constants: pk_1, pk_2, sk_1, crs
Input: $CT := (x, c_1, c_2, \pi), w$
1. If $\mathsf{NIZK.Verify}(crs, x', \pi) = 1$
2. If $w = I \subseteq A \bigwedge \sum_{a \in I} a = a_0$
3. Output $m \leftarrow \Sigma.\mathsf{Dec}(sk_1, c_1)$.
4. Output $\perp$.

P_4

Constants: pk_1, pk_2, sk_2, crs
Input: $CT := (x, c_1, c_2, \pi), w$
1. If $\mathsf{NIZK.Verify}(crs, x', \pi) = 1$
2. If $w = I \subseteq A \bigwedge \sum_{a \in I} a = a_0$
3. Output $m \leftarrow \Sigma.\mathsf{Dec}(sk_2, c_2)$.
4. Output $\perp$.

Security Proof

Theorem 3. *If our Σ scheme is IND-CPA secure, the Π system is statistically simulation sound secure, and $i\mathcal{O}$ is indistinguishability confusing. Then, our multiplicatively homomorphic witness encryption construction is selectively IND-MHWE-CPA secure MHWE scheme.*

Proof. Our MHWE scheme is a instantiation of the generic HWE construction, and thus the security proof is similar to Theorem 1. Our scheme uses Garg et al. [26] to provide an $i\mathcal{O}$ candidate construction for polynomial-size circuit families that achieves indistinguishability confusion. Thus, in the following we will show that our Σ scheme is IND-CPA secure and the Π system is statistically simulation sound secure.

Lemma 7. *If the DDH assumption is hard, our Σ scheme is provably secure in the IND-CPA security model.*

Proof. We show that if there is a non-uniform PPT adversary $\mathcal{A}$ that can (t, μ)-break the Σ scheme in the IND-CPA security model, then there is a non-uniform PPT adversary $\mathcal{B}$ that solves the DDH problem. Given as input a problem instance (g, g^a, g^b, Z) over the cyclic group $(\mathbb{G}, g, p)$, $\mathcal{B}$ runs $\mathcal{A}$ and works as follows.

First, $\mathcal{B}$ sets the public key as $Y = g^a$ where $\alpha = a$. The public key is available from the problem instance. Next, $\mathcal{B}$ is given an NP instance x and a pair of messages m_0, m_1 by $\mathcal{A}$. Then, $\mathcal{B}$ randomly chooses $b' \in \{0, 1\}$ and sets the challenge ciphertext CT^* as $CT^* = (g^b, Z \cdot R(x)m'_b)$, where g^b and Z are from the problem instance. Finally, the parameters and challenge ciphertext are now given out as $pk = (g, Y)$ and $CT^* = (g^b, Z \cdot R(x)m'_b)$.

If Z is true, i.e., a DDH four-tuple, the simulation is indistinguishable from the real attack, and thus the adversary has probability $\frac{1}{2} + \frac{1}{\mu}$ of guessing the encrypted message correctly. If Z is false, i.e., a random four-tuple, it is easy to see that the challenge ciphertext is a one-time pad because the message is encrypted using Z, which is random and cannot be calculated from the other parameters given to the adversary. Therefore, the adversary only has probability $\frac{1}{2}$ of guessing the encrypted message correctly. Thus, if $\mathcal{A}$ can attack our Σ scheme with non-negligible advantage, then $\mathcal{B}$ can the same advantage break DDH assumption.

Lemma 8. *If the elgamal commitment scheme* Com *is perfectly binding and the* NIZK *scheme is computationally zero-knowledge and statistically sound, then our* Π *scheme is statistically simulationally sound.*

Proof. The proof of this Lemma 8 is as follows:

Computational Zero-Knowledge. We will start by describing our simulator $S' = (S'_1, S'_2)$ assuming the simulator $S = (S_1, S_2)$ for $\mathsf{GS} = (\mathsf{Setup}, \mathsf{Prove}, \mathsf{Verify})$.

$S'_1(1^\lambda, \widetilde{x} = (c_1, c_2, pk_1, pk_2))$ generates the common random string $crs = (crs^*, cm)$ where $cm \leftarrow \mathsf{Com}(\widetilde{x}; \widetilde{r})$.

S_2 generates the proof for x' using the randomness $\widetilde{r}$, where x' is the following statement: $\exists\ \widetilde{w}, \widetilde{r}$ such that $(\widetilde{x}, \widetilde{w}) \in R \vee cm = \mathrm{Com}(\widetilde{x}; \widetilde{r})$. More specifically, it just outputs $\mathsf{Prove}(crs^*, x', \widetilde{r})$.

The computational zero-knowledge property of our simulator follows from the following simple hybrid argument.

- Hybrid $\mathcal{H}_0$: This hybrid corresponds to the honest generation of the proof.
- Hybrid $\mathcal{H}_1$: We start generating cm as a commitment to x rather that 1^l.
- Hybrid $\mathcal{H}_2$: We start using the randomness used in generation of the commitment cm for generating the proof rather than the real witness. In other words, we use the simulation strategy.

Proof. Indistinguishability between hybrids $\mathcal{H}_0$ and $\mathcal{H}_1$ follows from the computational hiding property of our commitment scheme Com.

Indistinguishability between hybrids $\mathcal{H}_1$ and $\mathcal{H}_2$ follows from the computational zero-knowledge property of our NIZK system.

Statistical Simulation-Soundness. An $\mathsf{SSS\text{-}NIZK}$ proof for the statement

$$c_1 \text{ and } c_2 \text{ encrypt the same message} \vee cm \text{ commits to } (c_1, c_2). \tag{8}$$

We will start by describing our simulator $S' = (S'_1, S'_2)$ assuming the simulator $S = (S_1, S_2)$ for $\mathsf{GS} = (\mathsf{Setup}, \mathsf{Prove}, \mathsf{Verify})$.

$S'_1(1^\lambda, \widetilde{x} = (c_1, c_2, pk_1, pk_2))$ generates the common random string $crs = (crs^*, cm)$ where $cm \leftarrow \mathsf{Com}(\widetilde{x}; \widetilde{r})$.

S_2 generates the proof for x' using the randomness $\widetilde{r}$, where x' is the following statement: $\exists\ \widetilde{w}, \widetilde{r}$ such that $(\widetilde{x}, \widetilde{w}) \in R \vee cm = \text{Com}(\widetilde{x}; \widetilde{r})$. More specifically, it just outputs $\mathsf{Prove}(crs^*, x', \widetilde{r})$.

The statistical simulation-soundness property of our simulator follows from the following simple hybrid argument.

- Hybrid $\mathcal{H}_0$: This hybrid corresponds to the honest generation of the proof.
- Hybrid $\mathcal{H}_1$: We sets up the crs by choosing $r_c \leftarrow \mathbb{Z}_p$ and setting $cm := \mathsf{Com}(ck, (c_1, c_2); r_c)$.
- Hybrid $\mathcal{H}_2$: We start using a proof of satisfiability of Eqs. (1)–(5) proves that $cm = \text{Com}(\widetilde{x}; \widetilde{r})$. It simulates a proof for statement $(c_1, c_2, pk_1, pk_2) \in \mathcal{L}_{\mathsf{GS}}$ by computing a GS proof for Eqs. (1)–(5) by instantiating the variables as Eq. (7).

Proof. Indistinguishability between hybrids $\mathcal{H}_0$ and $\mathcal{H}_1$ follows from the commitment in the crs is hiding under DDH in $\mathbb{G}$ and the computational hiding property of our commitment scheme Com.

Indistinguishability between hybrids $\mathcal{H}_1$ and $\mathcal{H}_2$ follows from the GS proofs are witnessindistinguishable under **SXDH**, this simulation is also indistinguishable under **SXDH**. Therefore, statistical simulation-soundness holds, since once the crs is set up, $(c_1, c_2, pk_1, pk_2) \in \mathcal{L}_{\mathsf{GS}}$ is the only statement for which a proof using the 2nd clause in Eq. (8) can be computed. Any other proof must use the first clause, meaning the statement must be in the language.

6 Discussion

Cost of Our MHWE. In standard implementations of bilinear groups for 128-bit security, $\mathbb{G}$ elements are of size 256 bits and $\mathbb{H}$ elements are of size 512 bits.

In the encryption phase: An encryption in our MHWE scheme then consists of two ElGamal ciphertexts (each in $\mathbb{G}^2$) and a GS proof with 5 variables in $\mathbb{H}$ (requiring 10 elements from $\mathbb{H}$) and 9 linear equations (requiring 18 elements from $\mathbb{G}$). Computing an ElGamal encryption requires 2 exponentiations and 1 group operations in $\mathbb{G}$. The 2 elements from $\mathbb{H}$ required for each variable require 2 exponentiations and one group operation in $\mathbb{H}$. The 2 elements from $\mathbb{G}$ required for each equation are computed using together 4 exponentiations and 2 group operations in $\mathbb{G}$.

In the batching phase: An batching in our MHWE scheme then consists of two ElGamal ciphertexts (each in $\mathbb{G}^2$) and a GS proof with 5 variables in $\mathbb{H}$ and 9 linear equations. Aggregation n ElGamal ciphertexts requires $2n - 2$ group operations in $\mathbb{G}$.

Similar to our scheme is the proposed by Abusalah et al. [27], but their encryption in the WE scheme consists of two ElGamal ciphertexts (each in $\mathbb{G}^{l+1}$) and a GS proof with 5 variables in $\mathbb{H}$. Since the scheme of [27] encodes (x, m) in $\mathbb{G}$ and then encrypts it by bit, it has a larger ciphertext length than our homomorphic encryption scheme Σ.

7 Conclusion

In this paper, We present and formally define for the first to construct a general framework for homomorphic witness encryption that do cover all languages in NP. We formally showed that such HWE constructions can be instantiated from indistinguishable obfuscation and statistically simulation sound non-interactive zero-knowledge proof system. In addition, we construct a Subset-Sum problem homomorphic encryption scheme based on the ElGamal encryption variant to instantiate our multiplicative homomorphic witness encryption scheme. And we formally prove its indistinguishability security under the assumption that $i\mathcal{O}$ exists. In all cases, we have constant size ciphertexts and need only two ciphertexts and a NIZK proof.

References

1. Garg, S., Gentry, C., Sahai, A., Waters, B.: Witness encryption and its applications. In: Proceedings of the Forty-Fifth Annual ACM Symposium on Theory of Computing, pp. 467–476 (2013)
2. Arita, S., Handa, S.: Two applications of multilinear maps: group key exchange and witness encryption. In: Proceedings of the 2nd ACM Workshop on ASIA Public-Key Cryptography, pp. 13–22 (2014)
3. Liu, J., Garcia, F., Ryan, M.: Time-release protocol from bitcoin and witness encryption for sat. Korean Circ. J. **40**(10), 530–535 (2015)
4. Liu, J., Jager, T., Kakvi, S.A., Warinschi, B.: How to build time-lock encryption. Des. Codes Cryptogr. **86**(11), 2549–2586 (2018). https://doi.org/10.1007/s10623-018-0461-x
5. Uberti, G., Luo, K., Cheng, O., Goh, W.: Building usable witness encryption. arXiv preprint arXiv:2112.04581 (2021)
6. Garg, S., Gentry, C., Halevi, S.: Candidate multilinear maps from ideal lattices. In: Johansson, T., Nguyen, P.Q. (eds.) EUROCRYPT 2013. LNCS, vol. 7881, pp. 1–17. Springer, Heidelberg (2013). https://doi.org/10.1007/978-3-642-38348-9_1
7. Barak, B., et al.: On the (Im)possibility of obfuscating programs. In: Kilian, J. (ed.) CRYPTO 2001. LNCS, vol. 2139, pp. 1–18. Springer, Heidelberg (2001). https://doi.org/10.1007/3-540-44647-8_1
8. Bartusek, J., Ishai, Y., Jain, A., Ma, F., Sahai, A., Zhandry, M.: Affine determinant programs: a framework for obfuscation and witness encryption. In: 11th Innovations in Theoretical Computer Science Conference (2020)
9. Derler, D., Slamanig, D.: Practical witness encryption for algebraic languages or how to encrypt under groth-sahai proofs. Des. Codes Cryptogr. **86**(11), 2525–2547 (2018)
10. Campanelli, M., David, B., Khoshakhlagh, H., Konring, A., Nielsen, J.B.: Encryption to the future: a paradigm for sending secret messages to future (anonymous) committees. In: Advances in Cryptology-ASIACRYPT 2022: 28th International Conference on the Theory and Application of Cryptology and Information Security, Taipei, Taiwan, 5–9 December 2022, Proceedings, Part III, pp. 151–180. Springer, Heidelberg (2023). https://doi.org/10.1007/978-3-031-22969-5_6
11. Döttling, N., Hanzlik, L., Magri, B., Wohnig, S.: Mcfly: verifiable encryption to the future made practical. Cryptology ePrint Archive (2022)

12. Boneh, D., Franklin, M.: Identity-based encryption from the weil pairing. In: Kilian, J. (ed.) CRYPTO 2001. LNCS, vol. 2139, pp. 213–229. Springer, Heidelberg (2001). https://doi.org/10.1007/3-540-44647-8_13
13. Sahai, A., Waters, B.: Fuzzy identity-based encryption. In: Cramer, R. (ed.) EUROCRYPT 2005. LNCS, vol. 3494, pp. 457–473. Springer, Heidelberg (2005). https://doi.org/10.1007/11426639_27
14. Garg, S., Gentry, C., Halevi, S., Zhandry, M.: Fully secure attribute based encryption from multilinear maps. Cryptology ePrint Archive (2014)
15. Benhamouda, F., Lin, H.: Mr NISC: multiparty reusable non-interactive secure computation. In: Pass, R., Pietrzak, K. (eds.) TCC 2020. LNCS, vol. 12551, pp. 349–378. Springer, Cham (2020). https://doi.org/10.1007/978-3-030-64378-2_13
16. Campanelli, M., Fiore, D., Khoshakhlagh, H.: Witness encryption for succinct functional commitments and applications. Cryptology ePrint Archive (2022)
17. Badrinarayanan, S., Miles, E., Sahai, A., Zhandry, M.: Post-zeroizing obfuscation: new mathematical tools, and the case of evasive circuits. In: Fischlin, M., Coron, J.-S. (eds.) EUROCRYPT 2016. LNCS, vol. 9666, pp. 764–791. Springer, Heidelberg (2016). https://doi.org/10.1007/978-3-662-49896-5_27
18. Badrinarayanan, S., Garg, S., Ishai, Y., Sahai, A., Wadia, A.: Two-message witness indistinguishability and secure computation in the plain model from new assumptions. In: Takagi, T., Peyrin, T. (eds.) ASIACRYPT 2017. LNCS, vol. 10626, pp. 275–303. Springer, Cham (2017). https://doi.org/10.1007/978-3-319-70700-6_10
19. Faonio, A., Nielsen, J.B., Venturi, D.: Predictable arguments of knowledge. In: Fehr, S. (ed.) PKC 2017. LNCS, vol. 10174, pp. 121–150. Springer, Heidelberg (2017). https://doi.org/10.1007/978-3-662-54365-8_6
20. Bellare, M., Hoang, V.T.: Adaptive witness encryption and asymmetric password-based cryptography. In: Katz, J. (ed.) PKC 2015. LNCS, vol. 9020, pp. 308–331. Springer, Heidelberg (2015). https://doi.org/10.1007/978-3-662-46447-2_14
21. Chen, Y., Vaikuntanathan, V., Wee, H.: GGH15 beyond permutation branching programs: proofs, attacks, and candidates. In: Shacham, H., Boldyreva, A. (eds.) CRYPTO 2018. LNCS, vol. 10992, pp. 577–607. Springer, Cham (2018). https://doi.org/10.1007/978-3-319-96881-0_20
22. Pal, T., Dutta, R.: Semi-adaptively secure offline witness encryption from puncturable witness PRF. In: Nguyen, K., Wu, W., Lam, K.Y., Wang, H. (eds.) ProvSec 2020. LNCS, vol. 12505, pp. 169–189. Springer, Cham (2020). https://doi.org/10.1007/978-3-030-62576-4_9
23. Goyal, R., Vusirikala, S., Waters, B.: Collusion resistant broadcast and trace from positional witness encryption. In: Lin, D., Sako, K. (eds.) PKC 2019. LNCS, vol. 11443, pp. 3–33. Springer, Cham (2019). https://doi.org/10.1007/978-3-030-17259-6_1
24. Chvojka, P., Jager, T., Kakvi, S.A.: Offline witness encryption with semi-adaptive security. In: Conti, M., Zhou, J., Casalicchio, E., Spognardi, A. (eds.) ACNS 2020. LNCS, vol. 12146, pp. 231–250. Springer, Cham (2020). https://doi.org/10.1007/978-3-030-57808-4_12
25. Albrecht, M.R., Farshim, P., Han, S., Hofheinz, D., Larraia, E., Paterson, K.G.: Multilinear maps from obfuscation. J. Cryptol. **33**(3), 1080–1113 (2020)
26. Garg, S., Gentry, C., Halevi, S., Raykova, M., Sahai, A., Waters, B.: Candidate indistinguishability obfuscation and functional encryption for all circuits. In: 2013 IEEE 54th Annual Symposium on Foundations of Computer Science, pp. 40–49 (2013)

27. Abusalah, H., Fuchsbauer, G., Pietrzak, K.: Offline witness encryption. In: Manulis, M., Sadeghi, A.-R., Schneider, S. (eds.) ACNS 2016. LNCS, vol. 9696, pp. 285–303. Springer, Cham (2016). https://doi.org/10.1007/978-3-319-39555-5_16
28. Groth, J., Sahai, A.: Efficient non-interactive proof systems for bilinear groups. In: Smart, N. (ed.) EUROCRYPT 2008. LNCS, vol. 4965, pp. 415–432. Springer, Heidelberg (2008). https://doi.org/10.1007/978-3-540-78967-3_24
29. Blazy, O., Fuchsbauer, G., Izabachène, M., Jambert, A., Sibert, H., Vergnaud, D.: Batch Groth–Sahai. In: Zhou, J., Yung, M. (eds.) ACNS 2010. LNCS, vol. 6123, pp. 218–235. Springer, Heidelberg (2010). https://doi.org/10.1007/978-3-642-13708-2_14
30. Ferrara, A.L., Green, M., Hohenberger, S., Pedersen, M.Ø.: Practical short signature batch verification. In: Fischlin, M. (ed.) CT-RSA 2009. LNCS, vol. 5473, pp. 309–324. Springer, Heidelberg (2009). https://doi.org/10.1007/978-3-642-00862-7_21
31. Zhandry, M.: How to avoid obfuscation using witness PRFs. In: Kushilevitz, E., Malkin, T. (eds.) TCC 2016. LNCS, vol. 9563, pp. 421–448. Springer, Heidelberg (2016). https://doi.org/10.1007/978-3-662-49099-0_16
32. Pal, T., Dutta, R.: Offline witness encryption from witness PRF and randomized encoding in CRS model. In: Jang-Jaccard, J., Guo, F. (eds.) ACISP 2019. LNCS, vol. 11547, pp. 78–96. Springer, Cham (2019). https://doi.org/10.1007/978-3-030-21548-4_5
33. Feige, U., Lapidot, D., Shamir, A.: Multiple noninteractive zero knowledge proofs under general assumptions. SIAM J. Comput. **29**(1), 1–28 (1999)
34. Camenisch, J., Hohenberger, S., Pedersen, M.Ø.: Batch verification of short signatures. In: Naor, M. (ed.) EUROCRYPT 2007. LNCS, vol. 4515, pp. 246–263. Springer, Heidelberg (2007). https://doi.org/10.1007/978-3-540-72540-4_14
35. Jutla, C.S., Roy, A.: Switching lemma for bilinear tests and constant-size NIZK proofs for linear subspaces. In: Garay, J.A., Gennaro, R. (eds.) CRYPTO 2014. LNCS, vol. 8617, pp. 295–312. Springer, Heidelberg (2014). https://doi.org/10.1007/978-3-662-44381-1_17

Identity-Based Matchmaking Encryption Secure Against Key Generation Center

Sohto Chiku[1(✉)], Keisuke Hara[1,2], and Junji Shikata[1]

[1] Yokohama National University, Yokohama, Japan
chiku-sohto-tw@ynu.jp

[2] National Institute of Advanced Industrial Science and Technology, Tokyo, Japan

Abstract. Identity-based matchmaking encryption (IB-ME) is a generalization of identity-based encryption (IBE), in which both the sender and receiver can specify the target identity. The key escrow problem, in which the authority is concentrated in the key generation center, has been pointed out as one of the most important issues, when implementing IBE in the real world. Recently, an approach to solve the key escrow problem in IBE has been proposed by introducing a new entity called an Identity Certificate Authority (ICA), which decentralizes the authority.

In this paper, we extend the above approach to solve the key escrow problem for IBE to the IB-ME setting. Specifically, we first propose a new formalization of IB-ME solving the key escrow problem (by introducing ICA in its formulation). This new type of IB-ME is called *blind IB-ME with certified identities*. Then, we provide a concrete construction of blind IB-ME with certified identities based on the standard assumptions over bilinear groups. Finally, we implement our proposed scheme and demonstrate that it is practically efficient compared with existing schemes.

Keywords: Identity-based matchmaking encryption · Key escrow problem · Bilinear groups

1 Introduction

1.1 Background and Motivation

(Identity-Based) Matchmaking Encryption. The concept of matchmaking encryption (ME) is a new form of encryption proposed by Ateniese et al. [3]. Using ME, both sender and receiver can specify appropriate policies which the other party must satisfy in order for the message to be revealed. One of the primary applications of ME is to implement a non-interactive secret handshake (SH) protocol among agents belonging to different organizations. For example, by using ME, when a sender generates a ciphertext, it can specify the (encapsulated) secret message is intended for FBI agents. Then, when a receiver decrypts the ciphertext, it can also specify that it wants to read messages only if these

M. Zhang et al. (Eds.): ProvSec 2023, LNCS 14217, pp. 251–273, 2023.
https://doi.org/10.1007/978-3-031-45513-1_14

are sent by NSA agents. If any of these two requirements does not hold, it is guaranteed that the message remains hidden as its security requirement.

One of the most practical and important policies in ME is the *identity-based setting*. An ME in identity-based setting is called *identity-based matchmaking encryption (IB-ME)* [3,10,17,24], whose access policies are simply bit-strings to present identities. More specifically, in IB-ME, each sender (resp., receiver) is provided a secret encryption (resp., decryption) key associated to its identity σ (resp., ρ) by the authority called *key generation center (KGC)*. When a sender generates a ciphertext C, in addition to a plaintext m, it selects the the target identity of receiver ρ. Upon receiving a ciphertext C from the sender with σ, a receiver who has a decryption key of ρ and selects a sender identity σ can decrypt the ciphertext. We require two types of security for IB-ME called *privacy* and *authenticity*. If some policy on identities among senders and receivers does not hold, privacy guarantees that any information about the corresponding plaintext and identity does not leak from a ciphertext. Also, authenticity ensures that only the sender who has an encryption key associated to σ can generate a ciphertext associated to σ.

As a practical application of IB-ME, Ateniese et al. [3] showed that IB-ME can be used to implement a privacy-preserving bulletin board over a Tor network. There, agents (who belong to different organizations) can communicate secretly through this bulletin board or parties can collect information from anonymous sources.

Key Escrow Problem on Identity-Based Encryption. One of the most important primitives in identity-based cryptography is *identity-based encryption (IBE)* [7]. While IBE has a merit that we can solve a problem on public-key encryption of distributing public key certificates, it has the *key escrow problem* in the security aspects, which is one of the most critical barrier when using it in real-world applications. More precisely, in the IBE setting, the KGC has an ability to decrypt all ciphertexts since it can get secret keys for any identity. To overcome this problem, several attempts to reduce the amount of trust on the KGC on IBE have already been proposed. Among these attempts, one of the main approaches is to introduce an independent notion of security against the KGC for (standard) IBE [12,15,21]. In this line of research, Emura et al. [15,16] recently proposed a new formalization of IBE to address the key escrow problem (which is inspired by the Chow's work [12]). Their new formalization for IBE is called *blind IBE with certified identities* and they provided two constructions of this primitive based on lattices or bilinear groups. Roughly, their formalization is based on an idea of creating an additional authority called *identity-certifying authority (ICA)* to authenticate the system users and realizing anonymous key-issuing protocol between users and the KGC.

Motivation. Since both of a sender and receiver can specify the identity of the counterpart, we can see that IB-ME is a generalization of IBE. Then, similar to IBE, IB-ME inherits the key escrow problem that the KGC has the potential to decrypt all ciphertexts. Also, in IB-ME setting, the KGC has an additional power to forge valid ciphertexts corresponding to all identities. In this aspect, we can see that the key escrow problem in the IB-ME setting is more serious than one in (standard) IBE.

Furthermore, as mentioned above, IB-ME is expected to be useful for secret communications between users different organizations, such as FBI agents and NSA agents. When considering such a real-world application, current IB-ME is not preferable since both of senders and receivers (who belong to different organizations) are authenticated and their secret keys are generated, by the single KGC. In other words, it is more realistic that the users from different organizations are authenticated by their own authority center respectively and the KGC works for just issuing secret keys for users (without getting the information of their secret keys). Note that, while existing IB-ME has risk that the KGC might leak users' secret keys (e.g., when it is get infected with malware), this approach also prevents such a vulnerability.

1.2 Our Contribution

In this paper, based on the above motivation, we give the following three technical contributions.

New Formalization of IB-ME Preventing the Key Escrow Problem. Firstly, we consider a new formalization of IB-ME addressing the key escrow problem, which is inspired by the work [15,16]. Specifically, we introduce the new concept of IB-ME called *blind IB-ME with certified identities*. In blind IB-ME with certified identities, in addition to the KGC and users (senders and receivers), a new authority called the *sender/receiver ICA* is created. Roughly, while the KGC works to (blindly) generate secret keys for senders and receivers, the sender/receiver ICA is responsible for authenticating senders/receivers by issues certificates for senders/receivers. By creating each (different) ICA for senders and receivers, we capture a scenario that senders and receivers belonging to two different organizations have non-interactive SH in a more reasonable manner. Regarding security aspects, we define privacy and authenticity for each of three entities: users, the KGC, and the (sender/receiver) ICA. More precisely, we define privacy for the users (priv-users), the KGC (priv-KGC), and the (receiver) ICA (priv-ICA).[1] In addition, we define authenticity for the users (auth-users), the KGC (auth-KGC), and the (sender) ICA (auth-ICA).

Concrete Construction of Blind IB-ME with Certified Identities. Based on our formalization of IB-ME, we propose a concrete construction of blind IB-ME with certified identities based on Bilinear Diffie-Hellman (BDH) assumption over bilinear groups in the random oracle model (ROM). One can see that our concept is the combination of the EKW-IBE scheme [15,16] and the AFNV-IB-

[1] Note that, similar to the previous works [3,15,16], our privacy notion captures both indistinguishability and anonymity (for senders and receivers) against chosen plaintext attacks.

ME scheme [3], where both schemes are extensions of the Boneh-Franklin IBE scheme [7].

Performance Evaluation of Our Scheme. To show the practical efficiency of our blind IB-ME scheme with certified identities, we implement and evaluate our scheme in Python. From this experimentation result, we can see that our scheme is as efficient as the EKW-IBE scheme and the AFNV-IB-ME scheme [3,16].[2] Note that both compared schemes has the almost same efficiency with the Boneh-Franklin IBE scheme, which is one of the most practically efficient IBE schemes. Here, an important point is that our scheme has highly practical efficiency, while it has stronger security than previous ones.

1.3 Related Works

In this section, we recall some related works on IB-ME. As mentioned above, Ateniese et al. [3] firstly introduced a notion of IB-ME. They provided an efficient IB-ME scheme based on the (standard) BDH assumption over bilinear groups in the ROM. Following their works, we now have concrete constructions of IB-ME from pairings in the standard model [10,17]. Very recently, Wang et al. [24] proposed a generic construction of IB-ME from 2-level hierarchical IBE and identity-based signature, which provides the first IB-ME scheme from lattices.

Identity-Based Encryption. The idea of using some unique information about the identity of a user as its public encryption key was conceived by Shamir [23] and is known as IBE. We now have constructions of IBE schemes from pairings, quadratic residuosity, and lattices in the random oracle model [7,13,18] to more recent constructions in the standard model [1,5,6,9,11].

(Identity-based) Matchmaking Encryption. As mentioned above, Ateniese et al. [3] firstly introduced a notion of ME to realize non-interactive SH. They proposed two generic constructions of (general) ME based on 2-input functional encryption (FE) [19] or FE for randomized functionalities [20]. They also addressed the question of obtaining efficient ME in the simple (that is, identity-based) setting, which is called IB-ME. More precisely, they provided an efficient IB-ME scheme based on the (standard) BDH assumption over bilinear groups in the ROM.

Following their works, we now have concrete constructions of IB-ME from pairings in the standard model [10,17]. Very recently, Wang et al. [24] proposed a generic construction of IB-ME from 2-level hierarchical IBE and identity-based signature, which provides the first IB-ME scheme from lattices.

[2] In this paper implements their schemes with symmetric pairing, but there have been papers in the past that have implemented EKW-IBE with asymmetric pairing [14].

1.4 Organization

The remainder of the paper is organized as follows: In Sect. 2, we introduce preliminaries that will be used later. Then, in Sect. 3, we give the relevant definitions including syntax and security definition. Next, the construction and proof of our IB-ME are given in Sect. 4 and Sect. 5, respectively. In Sect. 6 presents the performance evaluation of schemes.

2 Preliminaries

2.1 Notation

In this paper, we use the following notaions. For $n \in \mathbb{N}$, we denote $[n] = \{1, .., n\}$. $x \leftarrow X$ denotes the operation of sampling an element x from a finite set X. $y \leftarrow \mathcal{A}(x; r)$ denotes that a probabilistic Turing machine $\mathcal{A}$ outputs y for an input x using a randomness r, and we simply denote $y \leftarrow \mathcal{A}(x)$ when we need not write an internal randomness explicitly. For interactive Turing machines $\mathcal{A}$ and $\mathcal{B}$, $v \leftarrow \langle \mathcal{A}(x_a), \mathcal{B}(x_b) \rangle$ denotes that $\mathcal{A}$ outputs v at the end of an execution of an interactive protocol between $\mathcal{A}$ and $\mathcal{B}$, where $\mathcal{A}$ and $\mathcal{B}$ take x_a and x_b as input respectively. PPT stands for probabilistic polynomial time. $x := y$ denotes that x is defined by y. $\hat{e}$ denotes the base of the natural logarithm. We say a function $\varepsilon(\lambda)$ is negligible in λ, if $\varepsilon(\lambda) = o(1/\lambda^c)$ for every $c \in \mathbb{Z}$, and we write $negl(\lambda)$ to denote a negligible function in λ. $\emptyset$ denotes the empty set. If $\mathcal{O}$ is a function or an algorithm and $\mathcal{A}$ is an algorithm, $\mathcal{A}^{\mathcal{O}}$ means $\mathcal{A}$ has oracle access to $\mathcal{O}$.

2.2 Digital Signature

In this section, we recall the definition of digital signature.

Definition 1 (Digital Signature). *A digital signature scheme with a plaintext space* $\mathbb{M}$ *consists of a tuple of three PPT algorithms* $\mathsf{Sig} = (\mathsf{Sig.KeyGen}, \mathsf{Sig.Sign}, \mathsf{Sig.Verify})$. $\mathsf{Sig.KeyGen}$ *is the key generation algorithm that, given a security parameter* 1^λ, *outputs a verification key* $\mathsf{vk_{sig}}$ *and a signing key* $\mathsf{sk_{sig}}$. $\mathsf{Sig.Sign}$ *is the signing algorithm that, given a signing key* $\mathsf{sk_{sig}}$ *and a plaintext* $m \in \mathbb{M}$, *outputs a signature* Σ_{sig}. $\mathsf{Sig.Verify}$ *is the (deterministic) verification algorithm that, given a verification key* $\mathsf{vk_{sig}}$, *a message* m, *and a signature* Σ_{sig}, *outputs either* 1 *(meaning "accept") or* 0 *(meaning "reject").*

As the correctness for Sig, we require that $\mathsf{Sig.Verify}(\mathsf{vk_{sig}}, m, \mathsf{Sig.Sign}(\mathsf{sk_{sig}}, m)) = 1$ holds for all $\lambda \in \mathbb{N}$, $m \in \mathbb{M}$, and $(\mathsf{vk_{sig}}, \mathsf{sk_{sig}}) \leftarrow \mathsf{Sig.KeyGen}(1^\lambda)$.

We require digital signature to satisfy (standard) existential unforgeability under chosen-message attacks (EUF-CMA security). Due to the space limitation, we omit the detail definition here.

2.3 Bilinear Groups

In this section, we recall some notations for bilinear groups and the Bilinear Diffie-Hellman (BDH) assumption (over bilinear groups).

Definition 2 (Bilinear Groups). *Let q be a λ-bit prime, $\mathbb{G}$ and $\mathbb{G}_T$ groups of order q, $e : \mathbb{G} \times \mathbb{G} \rightarrow \mathbb{G}_T$ a bilinear map (pairing), and p a generator of $\mathbb{G}$. We require that bilinearlity: for all $g_1, g_2 \in \mathbb{G}$ and $a, b \in \mathbb{Z}_q$, $e(g_1^a, g_2^b) = e(g_1, g_2)^{ab}$, and non-degeneracy: $e(g, g) \neq 1$ hold. We say that $(\mathbb{G}, \mathbb{G}_T, p, q, e)$ is a bilinear group.*

Definition 3 (Bilinear Diffie-Hellman (BDH) Assumption). *Let $G = (\mathbb{G}, \mathbb{G}_T, p, q, e)$ be a bilinear group. We say that the BDH assumption holds if for any PPT adversary $\mathcal{A}$, $\mathsf{Adv}^{\mathsf{BDH}}_{G,\mathcal{A}}(\lambda) := \Pr[\mathcal{A}(G, p^a, p^b, p^c) = e(p, p)^{abc}] = negl(\lambda)$ holds, where $a, b, c \leftarrow \mathbb{Z}_q$.*

3 Blind Identity-Based Matchmaking Encryption with Certified Identities

In this section, we present a new formalization of IB-ME that resolves the key escrow problem. As mentioned in the introduction, we refer to this primitive as blind IB-ME with certified identities, since the sender (resp., receiver) key-generation process can be seen as (blind) IB-ME with a sender (resp., receiver) ICA to certify a sender's (resp., receiver's) identity.

In blind IB-ME with certified identities, a sender with an identity σ (resp., receiver with an identity ρ) first authenticates itself with the ICA for senders (resp., receivers) to obtain its certificate. Then, a sender (resp., receiver) uses its certificate to run an interactive protocol with the KGC, and get a sender key ek_σ (resp., receiver key dk_ρ) for use as in standard IB-ME. Here, the KGC never knows the sender identity σ and receiver identity ρ which it is interacting with. That is, this implies that the KGC does not know ek_σ and dk_ρ. We assume that senders (resp., receivers) communicate with the ICA for senders (resp., receivers) and the KGC via secure channels. Note that, as in standard IB-ME, senders and receivers use the same encryption and decryption algorithm.

Definition 4 (Blind IB-ME with Certified Identities). *A Blind IB-ME scheme with certified identities* IB-ME *consists of the following PPT algorithms:*

$\mathsf{Setup}(1^\lambda) \rightarrow \mathsf{params}$: *The setup algorithm takes as input a security parameter 1^λ, and outputs a public parameter* params*. We assume the identity space $\mathcal{ID}$ and the message space $\mathcal{M}$ are defined by* params*. Moreover, we assume* params *are implicitly provided as input to the following algorithms.*

$\mathsf{KGC.KeyGen}(\mathsf{params}) \rightarrow (\mathsf{mpk}, \mathsf{msk})$: *The KGC key-generation algorithm takes as input* params*, and outputs a master public key* mpk *and a master secret key* msk.

$\mathsf{ICA.SKGen}(\mathsf{params}) \rightarrow (\mathsf{vk}_{\mathsf{snd}}, \mathsf{ik}_{\mathsf{snd}})$: *The sender ICA key-generation algorithm takes as input* params*, and outputs a sender certificate verfication key $\mathsf{vk}_{\mathsf{snd}}$ and a sender certificate-issuing key $\mathsf{ik}_{\mathsf{snd}}$.*

$\mathsf{ICA.RKGen}(\mathsf{params}) \rightarrow (\mathsf{vk}_{\mathsf{rcv}}, \mathsf{ik}_{\mathsf{rcv}})$: *The receiver ICA key-generation algorithm takes as input* params*, and outputs a receiver certificate verfication key* $\mathsf{vk}_{\mathsf{rcv}}$ *and a receiver certificate issuing key* $\mathsf{ik}_{\mathsf{rcv}}$.

$\mathsf{ICA.SCert}(\mathsf{vk}_{\mathsf{snd}}, \mathsf{ik}_{\mathsf{snd}}, \sigma) \rightarrow (\mathsf{scert}, \mathsf{td}_\sigma)$: *The sender certificate-issuing algorithm run by ICA takes as inputs a sender certificate verification key* $\mathsf{vk}_{\mathsf{snd}}$*, a sender certificate issuing key* $\mathsf{ik}_{\mathsf{snd}}$*, and a sender's identity* $\sigma \in \mathcal{ID}$*, and outputs a sender certificate* scert *and a trapdoor information* td_σ.

$\mathsf{ICA.RCert}(\mathsf{vk}_{\mathsf{rcv}}, \mathsf{ik}_{\mathsf{rcv}}, \rho) \rightarrow (\mathsf{rcert}, \mathsf{td}_\rho)$: *The receiver certificate-issuing algorithm run by ICA takes as inputs a receiver certificate verification key* $\mathsf{vk}_{\mathsf{rcv}}$*, a receiver certificate issuing key* $\mathsf{ik}_{\mathsf{rcv}}$*, and a receiver's identity* $\rho \in \mathcal{ID}$*, and outputs a receiver certificate* rcert *and a trapdoor information* td_ρ.

$\mathsf{IB\text{-}ME.Enc}(\mathsf{mpk}, \mathsf{ek}_\sigma, \rho, m) \rightarrow C$: *The encryption algorithm run by a sender takes as inputs the master public key* mpk*, an encryption key* ek_σ*, a target identity* $\rho \in \mathcal{ID}$*, and a message* $m \in \mathcal{M}$*, and outputs a ciphertext* C.

$\mathsf{IB\text{-}ME.Dec}(\mathsf{mpk}, \mathsf{dk}_\rho, \sigma, C) \rightarrow m$ *or* $\perp$: *The decryption algorithm run by receiver takes as input the master public key* mpk*, a decryption key* dk_ρ*, a target identity* $\sigma \in \mathcal{ID}$*, and a ciphertext* C*, and outputs* m *or* $\perp$.

$\langle \mathsf{ObtainSK}(\mathsf{mpk}, \sigma, \mathsf{scert}, \mathsf{td}_\sigma), \mathsf{IssueSK}(\mathsf{mpk}, \mathsf{msk}, \mathsf{vk}_{\mathsf{snd}}) \rangle$: *The interactive sender key issuing protocol between a sender and the KGC involves two interactive algorithms* $\mathsf{ObtainSK}$ *and* $\mathsf{IssueSK}$*. The sender and the KGC interactively run the* $\mathsf{ObtainSK}$ *algorithm and the* $\mathsf{IssueSK}$ *algorithm, respectively as follows.*

- **Sender:** *The sender takes as input* $(\mathsf{mpk}, \sigma, \mathsf{scert}, \mathsf{td}_\sigma)$ *as specified by the input of* $\mathsf{ObtainSK}$*, and sends a first-round message* $\mathsf{M}_{\mathsf{snd}}$ *to the KGC.*
- **KGC:** *The KGC takes as input* $(\mathsf{mpk}, \mathsf{msk}, \mathsf{vk}_{\mathsf{snd}})$ *as specified by the input of* $\mathsf{IssueSK}$ *along with the message* $\mathsf{M}_{\mathsf{snd}}$ *sent by the sender, and returns a second-round message* $\mathsf{M}^{\mathsf{snd}}_{\mathsf{KGC}}$ *to the sender.*
- **Sender:** *On input the message* $\mathsf{M}^{\mathsf{snd}}_{\mathsf{KGC}}$ *from the KGC, the sender (locally) outputs either* ek_σ *or* $\perp$.

$\langle \mathsf{ObtainRK}(\mathsf{mpk}, \rho, \mathsf{rcert}, \mathsf{td}_\rho), \mathsf{IssueRK}(\mathsf{mpk}, \mathsf{msk}, \mathsf{vk}_{\mathsf{rcv}}) \rangle$: *The interactive receiver key issuing protocol between a receiver and the KGC involves two interactive algorithms* $\mathsf{ObtainRK}$ *and* $\mathsf{IssueRK}$*. The receiver and the KGC interactively run the* $\mathsf{ObtainRK}$ *algorithm and the* $\mathsf{IssueRK}$ *algorithm, respectively as follows.*

- **Receiver:** *The receiver takes as input* $(\mathsf{mpk}, \rho, \mathsf{rcert}, \mathsf{td}_\rho)$ *as specified by the input of* $\mathsf{ObtainRK}$*, and sends a first-round message* $\mathsf{M}_{\mathsf{rcv}}$ *to the KGC.*
- **KGC:** *The KGC takes as input* $(\mathsf{mpk}, \mathsf{msk}, \mathsf{vk}_{\mathsf{rcv}})$ *as specified by the input of* $\mathsf{IssueRK}$ *along with the message* $\mathsf{M}_{\mathsf{rcv}}$ *sent by the receiver, and returns a second-round message* $\mathsf{M}^{\mathsf{rcv}}_{\mathsf{KGC}}$ *to the reveiver.*
- **Receiver:** *On input the message* $\mathsf{M}^{\mathsf{rcv}}_{\mathsf{KGC}}$ *from the KGC, the receiver (locally) outputs either* dk_ρ *or* $\perp$.

Correctness. For all $\lambda \in \mathbb{N}$, all $\sigma, \rho \in \mathcal{ID}$, and all $m \in \mathcal{M}$, $\Pr[\mathsf{IB\text{-}ME.Dec}(\mathsf{mpk}, \mathsf{dk}_\rho, \sigma, C) = m] = 1 - negl(\lambda)$ holds, where it is taken over the randomness used in running $\mathsf{params} \leftarrow \mathsf{Setup}(1^\lambda)$, $(\mathsf{mpk}, \mathsf{msk}) \leftarrow \mathsf{KGC.KeyGen}(\mathsf{params})$, $(\mathsf{vk}_{\mathsf{snd}}, \mathsf{ik}_{\mathsf{snd}}) \leftarrow \mathsf{ICA.SKGen}(\mathsf{params})$, $(\mathsf{vk}_{\mathsf{rcv}}, \mathsf{ik}_{\mathsf{rcv}}) \leftarrow \mathsf{ICA.RKGen}(\mathsf{params})$, $(\mathsf{scert}, \mathsf{td}_\sigma) \leftarrow \mathsf{ICA.SCert}(\mathsf{vk}_{\mathsf{snd}}, \mathsf{ik}_{\mathsf{snd}}, \sigma)$, $(\mathsf{rcert}, \mathsf{td}_\rho) \leftarrow \mathsf{ICA.RCert}(\mathsf{vk}_{\mathsf{rcv}}, \mathsf{ik}_{\mathsf{rcv}}, \rho)$, $\mathsf{ek}_\sigma \leftarrow$

$\langle \mathsf{ObtainSK}(\mathsf{mpk}, \sigma, \mathsf{scert}, \mathsf{td}_\sigma), \mathsf{IssueSK}(\mathsf{mpk}, \mathsf{msk}, \mathsf{vk}_{\mathsf{snd}})\rangle$, $\mathsf{dk}_\rho \leftarrow \langle \mathsf{ObtainRK}(\mathsf{mpk}, \rho, \mathsf{rcert}, \mathsf{td}_\rho), \mathsf{IssueRK}(\mathsf{mpk}, \mathsf{msk}, \mathsf{vk}_{\mathsf{rcv}})\rangle$, and $C \leftarrow \mathsf{IB\text{-}ME.Enc}(\mathsf{mpk}, \mathsf{ek}_\sigma, \rho, m)$.

Security. We define privacy and authenticity against (corrupted) users, the KGC, and the (sender/receiver) ICA. Roughly, privacy guarantees that nothing is leaked to an unintended party who does not match the sender's policy. Moreover, authenticity guarantees that no adversary who does not have the encryption key of the corresponding identity can generate a valid ciphertext corresponding to the identity.

Firstly, as in standard IB-ME, we consider privacy and authenticity against (corrupted) users. In this setting, we do not consider an adversary (corrupted user) $\mathcal{A}$ who can obtain a certificate for σ^* and ρ^*, since this will allow $\mathcal{A}$ to trivially break security, where σ^* and ρ^* is the target identities.

Next, we consider privacy and authenticity against the honest-but-curious KGC (who follows the protocol execution but try to leak some information of the underlying plaintexts from the ciphertexts or to generate a valid ciphertext of an unknown sender). In brief, our privacy (resp., authenticity) against the KGC guarantees that, when the KGC runs honestly (that is, generates secret keys honestly), it cannot get any information about the corresponding identities or plaintexts from target ciphertexts (resp., forge valid ciphertexts by the target sender), even if it uses knowledge obtained via the key-issuing protocol. Note that we do not consider the KGC colluding with the sender's ICA (resp. receiver's ICA) in the privacy (resp. authenticity) game, since this will be not able to guarantee sender anonymity (resp. receiver anonymity).

Finally, we consider the notion of security against the malicious (sender/receiver) ICA. A malicious sender (resp., receiver) ICA can generate certificates for any sender (resp., receiver), and thereby obtain the corresponding secret keys by impersonating the user and interacting with the (honest) KGC. Therefore, in principle, we do not allow the sender (resp., receiver) ICA to have arbitrary access to the encryption (resp., decryption) key-generation oracle (that is, interacting with the KGC). Then, we model the malicious ICA to have the capability of generating a potentially malicious key pair $(\mathsf{vk}_{\mathsf{snd}}, \mathsf{ik}_{\mathsf{snd}})$ in the authenticity experiment (auth-ICA) and $(\mathsf{vk}_{\mathsf{rcv}}, \mathsf{ik}_{\mathsf{rcv}})$ in the privacy experiment (priv-ICA), while disallowing it to have access to the encryption/decryption key-generation oracle.

In the following, we provide the formal security definitions. There, when introducing some oracle $\mathcal{O}$, we assume that the query list $\mathcal{Q}_\mathcal{O}$ is firstly initialized to $\emptyset$. Moreover, CTSamp be a sampling algorithm that takes a master public key and outputs an element in the ciphertext space.

Definition 5 (priv-users). *Let* IB-ME *be a blind IB-ME scheme. We consider the following game.*

Setup: *At the outset of the game, the challenger runs* $\mathsf{params} \leftarrow \mathsf{Setup}(1^\lambda)$, $(\mathsf{mpk}, \mathsf{msk}) \leftarrow \mathsf{KGC.KeyGen}(\mathsf{params})$, $(\mathsf{vk}_{\mathsf{snd}}, \mathsf{ik}_{\mathsf{snd}}) \leftarrow \mathsf{ICA.SKGen}(\mathsf{params})$. $(\mathsf{vk}_{\mathsf{rcv}}, \mathsf{ik}_{\mathsf{rcv}}) \leftarrow \mathsf{ICA.RKGen}(\mathsf{params})$, *and initializes an empty list* $\sigma\mathsf{List} := \emptyset$,

ρList := $\emptyset$. *The challenger further picks a random coin* coin $\leftarrow \{0,1\}$ *and keeps it secret. The challenger gives* (params, mpk, $\mathsf{vk_{snd}}$, $\mathsf{vk_{rcv}}$) *to* $\mathcal{A}$. *After this,* $\mathcal{A}$ *can adaptively make the following five types of queries to the challenger in arbitrary order: sender certificate, receiver certificate, encryption key, decryption key, and challenge queries.* $\mathcal{A}$ *can query the first four arbitrarily polynomially many times and the fifth only once.*

Sender Certificate Query: *If* $\mathcal{A}$ *submits* $\sigma \in \mathcal{ID}$ *to the challenger, the challenger computes* $(\mathsf{scert}, \mathsf{td}_\sigma) \leftarrow \mathsf{ICA.SCert}(\mathsf{vk_{snd}}, \mathsf{ik_{snd}}, \sigma)$ *and returns* $(\mathsf{scert}, \mathsf{td}_\sigma)$ *to* $\mathcal{A}$. *It then stores* σ *to* σList.

Receiver Certificate Query: *If* $\mathcal{A}$ *submits* $\rho \in \mathcal{ID}$ *to the challenger, the challenger computes* $(\mathsf{rcert}, \mathsf{td}_\rho) \leftarrow \mathsf{ICA.RCert}(\mathsf{vk_{rcv}}, \mathsf{ik_{rcv}}, \rho)$ *and returns* $(\mathsf{rcert}, \mathsf{td}_\rho)$ *to* $\mathcal{A}$. *It then stores* ρ *to* ρList.

Encryption Key Query: *If* $\mathcal{A}$ *submits a first-round message* $\mathsf{M_{snd}}$ *to the challenger, the challenger runs the IssueKey algorithm taking as inputs* $(\mathsf{mpk}, \mathsf{msk}, \mathsf{vk_{snd}})$ *and the message* $\mathsf{M_{snd}}$, *and obtains a second-round message* $\mathsf{M^{snd}_{KGC}}$. *It then returns* $\mathsf{M^{snd}_{KGC}}$ *to* $\mathcal{A}$.

Decryption Key Query: *If* $\mathcal{A}$ *submits a first-round message* $\mathsf{M_{rcv}}$ *to the challenger, the challenger runs the* IssueKey *algorithm taking as inputs* $(\mathsf{mpk}, \mathsf{msk}, \mathsf{vk_{rcv}})$ *and the message* $\mathsf{M_{rcv}}$, *and obtains a second-round message* $\mathsf{M^{rcv}_{KGC}}$. *It then returns* $\mathsf{M^{rcv}_{KGC}}$ *to* $\mathcal{A}$.

Challenge Query: *If* $\mathcal{A}$ *submits* (σ^*, ρ^*, m^*) *to the challenger where* $\sigma^* \in \mathcal{ID}$, $\rho^* \in \mathcal{ID}$, $\rho^* \notin \rho\mathsf{List}$ *and* $m^* \in \mathcal{M}$, *the challenger proceeds as follows: If* coin $= 0$, *the challenger returns* $C^* \leftarrow \mathsf{IB\text{-}ME.Enc}(\mathsf{mpk}, \mathsf{ek}_\sigma, \rho, m^*)$. *Otherwise, if* coin $= 1$, *the challenger returns* $C^* \leftarrow \mathsf{CTSamp}(\mathsf{mpk})$.

Guess: $\mathcal{A}$ *outputs a guess* $\widehat{\mathsf{coin}} \in \{0,1\}$ *for coin.*

We say that IB-ME *is* priv-users *secure if the advantage* $\mathsf{Adv}^{\mathsf{priv\text{-}users}}_{\mathsf{IB\text{-}ME},\mathcal{A}}(\lambda) = |\Pr[\mathsf{coin} = \widehat{\mathsf{coin}}] - 1/2|$ *is negligible for any PPT adversary* $\mathcal{A}$.

Definition 6 (auth-users). *Let* IB-ME *be a blind IB-ME scheme. We consider the following game.*

Setup: *At the outset of the game, the challenger runs* params $\leftarrow \mathsf{Setup}(1^\lambda)$, $(\mathsf{mpk}, \mathsf{msk}) \leftarrow \mathsf{KGC.KeyGen}(\mathsf{params})$, $(\mathsf{vk_{snd}}, \mathsf{ik_{snd}}) \leftarrow \mathsf{ICA.SKGen}(\mathsf{params})$. $(\mathsf{vk_{rcv}}, \mathsf{ik_{rcv}}) \leftarrow \mathsf{ICA.RKGen}(\mathsf{params})$, *and initializes an empty list* σList := $\emptyset$, ρList := $\emptyset$. *The challenger gives* (params, mpk, $\mathsf{vk_{snd}}$, $\mathsf{vk_{rcv}}$) *to* $\mathcal{A}$. *After this,* $\mathcal{A}$ *can adaptively make the following four types of queries to the challenger in arbitrary order: sender certificate, receiver certificate, encryption key, and decryption key.* $\mathcal{A}$ *can every query arbitrarily polynomially many times.*

Sender Certificate Query: *If* $\mathcal{A}$ *submits* $\sigma \in \mathcal{ID}$ *to the challenger, the challenger computes* $(\mathsf{scert}, \mathsf{td_{snd}}) \leftarrow \mathsf{ICA.SCert}(\mathsf{vk_{snd}}, \mathsf{ik_{snd}}, \sigma)$ *and returns* $(\mathsf{scert}, \mathsf{td_{snd}})$ *to* $\mathcal{A}$. *It then stores* σ *to* σList.

Receiver Certificate Query: *If* $\mathcal{A}$ *submits* $\rho \in \mathcal{ID}$ *to the challenger, the challenger computes* $(\mathsf{rcert}, \mathsf{td_{rcv}}) \leftarrow \mathsf{ICA.RCert}(\mathsf{vk_{rcv}}, \mathsf{ik_{rcv}}, \rho)$ *and returns* $(\mathsf{rcert}, \mathsf{td_{rcv}})$ *to* $\mathcal{A}$. *It then stores* ρ *to* ρList.

Encryption Key Query: *If $\mathcal{A}$ submits a first-round message* $\mathsf{M}_{\mathsf{snd}}$ *to the challenger, the challenger runs the IssueKey algorithm taking as inputs* $(\mathsf{mpk}, \mathsf{msk}, \mathsf{vk}_{\mathsf{snd}})$ *and the message* $\mathsf{M}_{\mathsf{snd}}$*, and obtains a second-round message* $\mathsf{M}^{\mathsf{snd}}_{\mathsf{KGC}}$*. It then returns* $\mathsf{M}^{\mathsf{snd}}_{\mathsf{KGC}}$ *to* $\mathcal{A}$.

Decryption Key Query: *If $\mathcal{A}$ submits a first-round message* $\mathsf{M}_{\mathsf{rcv}}$ *to the challenger, the challenger runs the* IssueKey *algorithm taking as inputs* $(\mathsf{mpk}, \mathsf{msk}, \mathsf{vk}_{\mathsf{rcv}})$ *and the message* $\mathsf{M}_{\mathsf{rcv}}$*, and obtains a second-round message* $\mathsf{M}^{\mathsf{rcv}}_{\mathsf{KGC}}$*. It then returns* $\mathsf{M}^{\mathsf{rcv}}_{\mathsf{KGC}}$ *to* $\mathcal{A}$.

Forgery: *If $\mathcal{A}$ submits (C^*, ρ^*, σ^*) to the challenger where $\sigma^* \in \mathcal{ID}$, $\sigma^* \notin \sigma\mathsf{List}$, $\rho^* \in \mathcal{ID}$ and C^* is an element in the ciphertext space. Then, challenger runs* ObtainRK *and* IssueRK *to get* dk_{ρ^*}*, and get* $m \leftarrow \mathsf{IB\text{-}ME.Dec}(\mathsf{mpk}, \mathsf{dk}_{\rho^*}, \sigma^*, C^*)$*. Finally, $\mathcal{A}$ wins if there exists a tuple (σ, ρ^*, m) so that $\sigma \neq \sigma^*$, $\rho^* \notin \rho\mathsf{List}$ and $m \neq \perp$.*

We say that IB-ME *is* auth-users *secure if the advantage* $\mathsf{Adv}^{\mathsf{auth\text{-}users}}_{\mathsf{IB\text{-}ME},\mathcal{A}}(\lambda) = \Pr[\mathcal{A}\,\mathrm{wins}]$ *is negligible for any PPT adversary* $\mathcal{A}$.

Definition 7 (priv-KGC). *Let* IB-ME *be a blind IB-ME scheme. We consider the following game.*

Setup: *At the outset of the game, the challenger runs* $\mathsf{params} \leftarrow \mathsf{Setup}(1^\lambda)$, $(\mathsf{mpk}, \mathsf{msk}) \leftarrow \mathsf{KGC.KeyGen}(\mathsf{params})$, $(\mathsf{vk}_{\mathsf{snd}}, \mathsf{ik}_{\mathsf{snd}}) \leftarrow \mathsf{ICA.SKGen}(\mathsf{params})$. $(\mathsf{vk}_{\mathsf{rcv}}, \mathsf{ik}_{\mathsf{rcv}}) \leftarrow \mathsf{ICA.RKGen}(\mathsf{params})$*, and initializes two empty list* $\sigma\mathsf{List} := \emptyset, \rho\mathsf{List} := \emptyset$ *and two counter* $Q_{\mathsf{sk}} := 0, Q_{\mathsf{dk}} := 0$*. The challenger further picks a random coin* $\mathsf{coin} \leftarrow \{0,1\}$ *and keeps it secret. The challenger gives* $(\mathsf{params}, \mathsf{mpk}, \mathsf{msk}, \mathsf{vk}_{\mathsf{snd}}, \mathsf{vk}_{\mathsf{rcv}})$ *to $\mathcal{A}$. After this, $\mathcal{A}$ can adaptively make the following four types of queries to the challenger in arbitrary order: encryption, issue sender's key, issue receiver's key, and challenge queries. $\mathcal{A}$ can query the first three arbitrarily polynomially many times and the fourth only once.*

Encryption Query: *If $\mathcal{A}$ submits two index i, j and a message $m \in \mathcal{M}$ to the challenger, the challenger first checks if $i \in [Q_{\mathsf{sk}}]$ and $j \in [Q_{\mathsf{dk}}]$ where $[0]$ is defined as the empty set. If not, the challenger aborts the game and outputs a random coin* $\widehat{\mathsf{coin}} \in \{0,1\}$*. Otherwise, the challenger retrieves the $i-th$ entry $\sigma \in \sigma\mathsf{List}$ and the $j-th$ entry $\rho \in \rho\mathsf{List}$, and returns* $C \leftarrow \mathsf{IB\text{-}ME.Enc}(\mathsf{mpk}, \mathsf{ek}_\sigma, \rho, m)$*. Where,* ek_σ *be set by* IssueSK *and* ObtainSK.

IssueSK Query: *If* A *makes an IssueSK query, the challenger first randomly samples $\sigma \leftarrow \mathcal{ID}$ and computes* $(\mathsf{scert}, \mathsf{td}_{\mathsf{snd}}) \leftarrow \mathsf{ICA.SCert}(\mathsf{vk}_{\mathsf{snd}}, \mathsf{ik}_{\mathsf{snd}}, \sigma)$*. It then runs* ObtainSK *on inputs* $(\mathsf{mpk}, \sigma, \mathsf{scert}, \mathsf{td}_{\mathsf{snd}})$ *to generate the first-round message* $\mathsf{M}_{\mathsf{snd}}$ *and returns* $\mathsf{M}_{\mathsf{snd}}$ *to $\mathcal{A}$. Finally, the challenger stores σ to* $\sigma\mathsf{List}$ *and updates* $Q_{\mathsf{sk}} \leftarrow Q_{\mathsf{sk}} + 1$.

IssueRK Query: *If* A *makes an IssueRK query, the challenger first randomly samples $\rho \leftarrow \mathcal{ID}$ and computes* $(\mathsf{rcert}, \mathsf{td}_{\mathsf{rcv}}) \leftarrow \mathsf{ICA.RCert}$ $(\mathsf{vk}_{\mathsf{rcv}}, \mathsf{ik}_{\mathsf{rcv}}, \rho)$*. It then runs* ObtainRK *on inputs* $(\mathsf{mpk}, \rho, \mathsf{rcert}, \mathsf{td}_{\mathsf{rcv}})$ *to generate the first-round message* $\mathsf{M}_{\mathsf{rcv}}$ *and returns* $\mathsf{M}_{\mathsf{rcv}}$ *to $\mathcal{A}$. Finally, the challenger stores ρ to* $\rho\mathsf{List}$ *and updates* $Q_{\mathsf{dk}} \leftarrow Q_{\mathsf{dk}} + 1$.

Challenge Query: *If $\mathcal{A}$ submits (i^*, j^*, m^*) to the challenger where $m^* \in \mathcal{M}$, the challenger first checks if $i^* \in [Q_{\mathsf{sk}}]$ and $j^* \in [Q_{\mathsf{dk}}]$. If not, the challenger aborts the game and outputs random $\widehat{\mathsf{coin}} \in \{0,1\}$. Otherwise, the challenger proceeds as follows: The challenger first retrieves the i^*-th entry $\sigma^* \in \sigma\mathsf{List}[i]$ and the j^*-th entry $\rho^* \in \rho\mathsf{List}[j]$. Then, if $\mathsf{coin} = 0$, the challenger returns $C^* \leftarrow \mathsf{IB\text{-}ME.Enc}(\mathsf{mpk}, \mathsf{ek}^*_{\sigma}, \rho^*, m^*)$. Otherwise, if $\mathsf{coin} = 1$, the challenger returns $C^* \leftarrow \mathsf{CTSamp}(\mathsf{mpk})$.*

Guess: *$\mathcal{A}$ outputs a guess $\widehat{\mathsf{coin}} \in \{0,1\}$ for coin.*

We say that IB-ME *is* priv-KGC *secure if the advantage $\mathsf{Adv}^{\mathsf{priv\text{-}KGC}}_{\mathsf{IB\text{-}ME},\mathcal{A}}(\lambda) = |\Pr[\mathsf{coin} = \widehat{\mathsf{coin}}] - 1/2|$ is negligible for any PPT adversary $\mathcal{A}$.*

Definition 8 (auth-KGC). *Let* IB-ME *be a blind IB-ME scheme. We consider the following game.*

Setup: *At the outset of the game, the challenger runs $\mathsf{params} \leftarrow \mathsf{Setup}(1^\lambda)$, $(\mathsf{mpk}, \mathsf{msk}) \leftarrow \mathsf{KGC.KeyGen}(\mathsf{params})$, $(\mathsf{vk}_{\mathsf{snd}}, \mathsf{ik}_{\mathsf{snd}}) \leftarrow \mathsf{ICA.SKGen}(\mathsf{params})$. $(\mathsf{vk}_{\mathsf{rcv}}, \mathsf{ik}_{\mathsf{rcv}}) \leftarrow \mathsf{ICA.RKGen}(\mathsf{params})$, and initializes two empty list $\sigma\mathsf{List} := \emptyset, \rho\mathsf{List} := \emptyset$ and two counter $Q_{\mathsf{sk}} := 0, Q_{\mathsf{dk}} := 0$. The challenger gives $(\mathsf{params}, \mathsf{mpk}, \mathsf{msk}, \mathsf{vk}_{\mathsf{snd}}, \mathsf{vk}_{\mathsf{rcv}})$ to $\mathcal{A}$. After this, $\mathcal{A}$ can adaptively make the following three types of queries to the challenger in arbitrary order: decryption, issue sender's key, issue receiver's key. $\mathcal{A}$ can every query arbitrarily polynomially many times.*

Encryption Query: *If $\mathcal{A}$ submits two index i, j and a message $m \in \mathcal{M}$ to the challenger, the challenger first checks if $i \in [Q_{\mathsf{sk}}]$ and $j \in [Q_{\mathsf{dk}}]$ where $[0]$ is defined as the empty set. If not, the challenger aborts and outputs $\widehat{\mathsf{coin}} \in \{0,1\}$. Otherwise, the challenger retrieves the $i-th$ entry $\sigma \in \sigma\mathsf{List}$ and $j-th$ entry $\rho \in \rho\mathsf{List}$, and returns $C \leftarrow \mathsf{IB\text{-}ME.Enc}(\mathsf{mpk}, \mathsf{ek}_\sigma, \rho, m)$. Where, ek_σ be set by* IssueSK *and* ObtainSK.

IssueSK Query: *If* A *makes an IssueSK query, the challenger first randomly samples $\sigma \leftarrow \mathcal{ID}$ and computes $(\mathsf{scert}, \mathsf{td}_{\mathsf{snd}}) \leftarrow \mathsf{ICA.SCert}(\mathsf{vk}_{\mathsf{snd}}, \mathsf{ik}_{\mathsf{snd}}, \sigma)$. It then runs* ObtainSK *on inputs $(\mathsf{mpk}, \sigma, \mathsf{scert}, \mathsf{td}_{\mathsf{snd}})$ to generate the first-round message $\mathsf{M}_{\mathsf{snd}}$ and returns $\mathsf{M}_{\mathsf{snd}}$ to $\mathcal{A}$. Finally, the challenger stores σ to $\sigma\mathsf{List}$ and updates $Q_{\mathsf{sk}} \leftarrow Q_{\mathsf{sk}} + 1$.*

IssueRK Query: *If* A *makes an IssueRK query, the challenger first randomly samples $\rho \leftarrow \mathcal{ID}$ and computes $(\mathsf{rcert}, \mathsf{td}_{\mathsf{rcv}}) \leftarrow \mathsf{ICA.RCert}(\mathsf{vk}_{\mathsf{rcv}}, \mathsf{ik}_{\mathsf{rcv}}, \rho)$. It then runs* ObtainRK *on inputs $(\mathsf{mpk}, \rho, \mathsf{rcert}, \mathsf{td}_{\mathsf{rcv}})$ to generate the first-round message $\mathsf{M}_{\mathsf{rcv}}$ and returns $\mathsf{M}_{\mathsf{rcv}}$ to $\mathcal{A}$. Finally, the challenger stores ρ to $\rho\mathsf{List}$ and updates $Q_{\mathsf{dk}} \leftarrow Q_{\mathsf{dk}} + 1$.*

Forgery: *If $\mathcal{A}$ submits (C^*, i^*, j^*) to the challenger where C^* is an element in the ciphertext space. the challenger first checks if $i^* \in [Q_{\mathsf{sk}}]$ and $j^* \in [Q_{\mathsf{dk}}]$. If not, the challenger aborts the game and outputs $\widehat{\mathsf{coin}} \in \{0,1\}$. Otherwise, the challenger proceeds as follows: The challenger first retrieves the i^*-th entry $\sigma^* \in \sigma\mathsf{List}$ and the j^*-th entry $\rho^* \in \rho\mathsf{List}$. Then, the challenger runs* ObtainRK *and* IssueRK *to get dk_{ρ^*}, and get $m \leftarrow \mathsf{IB\text{-}ME.Dec}(\mathsf{mpk}, \mathsf{dk}_{\rho^*}, \sigma^*, C^*)$. Finally, $\mathcal{A}$ wins if there exists a tuple (σ, ρ^*, m) so that $\sigma \neq \sigma^*$ and $m \neq \perp$.*

We say that IB-ME *is* auth-KGC *secure if the advantage* $\mathsf{Adv}^{\mathsf{auth\text{-}KGC}}_{\mathsf{IB\text{-}ME},\mathcal{A}}(\lambda) = \Pr[\mathcal{A}\,\text{wins}]$ *is negligible for any PPT adversary* $\mathcal{A}$.

Definition 9 (priv-ICA). *Let* IB-ME *be a blind IB-ME scheme. We consider the following game.*

Setup: *At the outset of the game, the challenger runs* $\mathsf{params} \leftarrow \mathsf{Setup}(1^\lambda)$, $(\mathsf{mpk}, \mathsf{msk}) \leftarrow \mathsf{KGC.KeyGen}(\mathsf{params})$ *and* $(\mathsf{vk_{snd}}, \mathsf{ik_{snd}}) \leftarrow \mathsf{ICA.SKGen}(\mathsf{params})$. *The challenger further picks a random coin* $\mathsf{coin} \leftarrow \{0, 1\}$ *and keeps it secret. The challenger gives* $(\mathsf{params}, \mathsf{mpk}, \mathsf{vk_{snd}})$ *to* $\mathcal{A}$. *After this,* $\mathcal{A}$ *can adaptively make the following two types of queries to the challenger in arbitrary order: sender certificate, and challenge queries.* $\mathcal{A}$ *can query the first one arbitrarily polynomially many times and the second only once.*

Sender Certificate Query: *If* $\mathcal{A}$ *submits* $\sigma \in \mathcal{ID}$ *to the challenger, the challenger computes* $(\mathsf{scert}, \mathsf{td}_\sigma) \leftarrow \mathsf{ICA.SCert}(\mathsf{vk_{snd}}, \mathsf{ik_{snd}}, \sigma)$ *and returns* $(\mathsf{scert}, \mathsf{td}_\sigma)$ *to* $\mathcal{A}$.

Challenge Query: *If* $\mathcal{A}$ *submits* (σ^*, ρ^*, m^*) *to the challenger where* $\sigma^* \in \mathcal{ID}$, $\rho^* \in \mathcal{ID}$ *and* $m^* \in \mathcal{M}$, *the challenger proceeds as follows: If* $\mathsf{coin} = 0$, *the challenger returns* $C^* \leftarrow \mathsf{IB\text{-}ME.Enc}(\mathsf{mpk}, \mathsf{ek}_{\sigma^*}, \rho^*, m^*)$. *Otherwise, if* $\mathsf{coin} = 1$, *the challenger returns* $C^* \leftarrow \mathsf{CTSamp}(\mathsf{mpk})$.

Guess: $\mathcal{A}$ *outputs a guess* $\widehat{\mathsf{coin}} \in \{0, 1\}$ *for coin.*

We say that IB-ME *is* priv-ICA *secure if the advantage* $\mathsf{Adv}^{\mathsf{priv\text{-}ICA}}_{\mathsf{IB\text{-}ME},\mathcal{A}}(\lambda) = |\Pr[\mathsf{coin} = \widehat{\mathsf{coin}}] - 1/2|$ *is negligible for any PPT adversary* $\mathcal{A}$.

Definition 10 (auth-ICA). *Let* IB-ME *be a blind IB-ME scheme. We consider the following game.*

Setup: *At the outset of the game, the challenger runs* $\mathsf{params} \leftarrow \mathsf{Setup}(1^\lambda)$, $(\mathsf{mpk}, \mathsf{msk}) \leftarrow \mathsf{KGC.KeyGen}(\mathsf{params})$ *and* $(\mathsf{vk_{rcv}}, \mathsf{ik_{rcv}}) \leftarrow \mathsf{ICA.RKGen}(\mathsf{params})$. *The challenger gives* $(\mathsf{params}, \mathsf{mpk}, \mathsf{vk_{rcv}})$ *to* $\mathcal{A}$. *After this,* $\mathcal{A}$ *can make the following receiver certificate query polynomially many times.*

Receiver Certificate Query: *If* $\mathcal{A}$ *submits* $\rho \in \mathcal{ID}$ *to the challenger, the challenger computes* $(\mathsf{rcert}, \mathsf{td}_\rho) \leftarrow \mathsf{ICA.RCert}(\mathsf{vk_{rcv}}, \mathsf{ik_{rcv}}, \rho)$ *and returns* $(\mathsf{rcert}, \mathsf{td}_\rho)$ *to* $\mathcal{A}$..

Forgery: *If* $\mathcal{A}$ *submits* (C^*, ρ^*, σ^*) *to the challenger where* $\sigma^* \in \mathcal{ID}$, $\rho^* \in \mathcal{ID}$ *and* C^* *is an element in the ciphertext space. Then, challenger runs* ObtainRK *and* IssueRK *to get* dk_{ρ^*}, *and get* $m \leftarrow \mathsf{IB\text{-}ME.Dec}(\mathsf{mpk}, \mathsf{dk}_{\rho^*}, \sigma^*, C^*)$. *Finally,* $\mathcal{A}$ *wins if there exists a tuple* (σ, ρ^*, m) *so that* $m \neq \perp$.

We say that IB-ME *is* auth-ICA *secure if the advantage* $\mathsf{Adv}^{\mathsf{auth\text{-}ICA}}_{\mathsf{IB\text{-}ME},\mathcal{A}}(\lambda) = \Pr[\mathcal{A}\,\text{wins}]$ *is negligible for any PPT adversary* $\mathcal{A}$.

4 Construction Based on Bilinear Groups

In this section, we present our blind IB-ME scheme with certified identities based on bilinear groups. Inspired by the construction of the blind IBE scheme with certified identities by Emura et al. [16] (In the following, we call this scheme the EKW-IBE), our scheme combines the IB-ME scheme by Ateniese et al. [3] (In the following, we call this scheme the AFNV-IB-ME scheme.) with the Boldyreva's blind signature scheme [4]. Roughly, we are able to combine the AFNV-IB-ME scheme with Boldyreva's blind signature scheme since the signature generated by the Boldyreva's scheme is a BLS signature [8] which can be interpreted as a secret key of the AFNV-IB-ME scheme. Note that, similar to the EKW-IBE, we cannot construct this scheme in a black-box way using any IB-ME and any blind signature since these two primitives does not necessarily have compatibility.

Construction. Let $\mathbb{G}$ and $\mathbb{G}_T$ be groups with prime order q, $p \in \mathbb{G}$ a generator, and $e : \mathbb{G} \times \mathbb{G} \to \mathbb{G}_T$ a pairing. Let $\Phi : \mathbb{G}_T \to \{0,1\}^l$ be a polynomial-time computable padding function. We require that, for all $m \in \mathbb{G}_T$, anyone can verify in polynomial time whether m is padded correctly and there exists an invertible function Φ^{-1}. Let $\mathsf{Sig} = (\mathsf{Sig.KeyGen}, \mathsf{Sig.Sign}, \mathsf{Sig.Verify})$ be a digital signature scheme with a message space $\mathbb{G}$.

$\mathsf{Setup}(1^\lambda)$: Choose $(\mathbb{G}, \mathbb{G}_T, p, q, e)$ where q be a λ-bit prime number. Output $\mathsf{params} = (1^\lambda, (\mathbb{G}, \mathsf{H}', \mathbb{G}_T, p, q, e), \mathsf{H}, \hat{\mathsf{H}}, \Phi)$ where $\mathsf{H} : \{0,1\}^* \to \mathbb{G}, \mathsf{H}' : \{0,1\}^* \to \mathbb{G}, \hat{\mathsf{H}} : \mathbb{G}_T \to \{0,1\}^l$ are hash function modeled as random oracles.

$\mathsf{KGC.KeyGen}(\mathsf{params})$: Choose $x, y \leftarrow \mathbb{Z}_q$ and compute $X = p^x$ and $Y = p^y$, Then output a master public key $\mathsf{mpk} = (X, Y)$ and a master secret key $\mathsf{msk} = (x, y)$.

$\mathsf{ICA.SKGen}(\mathsf{params})$: Run $(\mathsf{vk_{snd}}, \mathsf{sk_{snd}}) \leftarrow \mathsf{Sig.KeyGen}(1^\lambda)$. Then output a certificate verification key $\mathsf{vk_{snd}} = \mathsf{vk_{snd}}$ and a certificate issuing key $\mathsf{ik_{snd}} = \mathsf{sk_{snd}}$.

$\mathsf{ICA.RKGen}(\mathsf{params})$: Run $(\mathsf{vk_{rcv}}, \mathsf{sk_{rcv}}) \leftarrow \mathsf{Sig.KeyGen}(1^\lambda)$. Then output a certificate verification key $\mathsf{vk_{rcv}} = \mathsf{vk_{rcv}}$ and a certificate issuing key $\mathsf{ik_{rcv}} = \mathsf{sk_{rcv}}$.

$\mathsf{ICA.SCert}(\mathsf{ck_{snd}}, \mathsf{ik_{snd}}, \sigma)$: Parse $\mathsf{ik_{snd}} = \mathsf{sk_{snd}}$ and compute $u_\sigma = \mathsf{H}'(\sigma)$. Then, choose $v_{\sigma,1} \leftarrow \mathbb{Z}_q$ and compute $u_{\sigma,1} = p^{v_{\sigma,1}}$. Furthermore, compute $u_{\sigma,2} = u_\sigma u_{\sigma,1} \in \mathbb{G}$ and $\Sigma_{\mathsf{snd}} \leftarrow \mathsf{Sig.Sign}(\mathsf{sk_{snd}}, u_{\sigma,2})$. Finally, output a sender certificate $\mathsf{scert} = (u_{\sigma,2}, \Sigma_{\mathsf{snd}})$ and trapdoor information $\mathsf{td_{snd}} = v_{\sigma,1}$.

$\mathsf{ICA.RCert}(\mathsf{ck_{rcv}}, \mathsf{ik_{rcv}}, \rho)$: Parse $\mathsf{ik_{rcv}} = \mathsf{sk_{rcv}}$ and compute $u_\rho = \mathsf{H}(\rho)$. Then, choose $v_{\rho,1} \leftarrow \mathbb{Z}_q$ and compute $u_{\rho,1} = p^{v_{\rho,1}}$. Furthermore, compute $u_{\rho,2} = u_\rho u_{\rho,1} \in \mathbb{G}$ and $\Sigma_{\mathsf{rcv}} \leftarrow \mathsf{Sig.Sign}(\mathsf{sk_{rcv}}, u_{\rho,2})$. Finally, output a receiver certificate $\mathsf{rcert} = (u_{\rho,2}, \Sigma_{\mathsf{rcv}})$ and trapdoor information $\mathsf{td_{rcv}} = v_{\rho,1}$.

$\mathsf{IB\text{-}ME.Enc}(\mathsf{mpk}, \mathsf{ek}_\sigma, \mathsf{rcv}, m)$: On input encryption key ek_σ, a target identity $\mathsf{rcv} = \rho$, and a message $m \in \{0,1\}^n$, compute $u_\rho = \mathsf{H}(\rho)$. Next, sample $s, r \leftarrow \mathbb{Z}_q$, compute $c_0 = p^r$, $c_1 = p^s$ and $c = \Phi(m) \oplus \hat{\mathsf{H}}(e(u_\rho, X^s)) \oplus \hat{\mathsf{H}}(e(u_\rho, p^r \cdot \mathsf{ek}_\sigma))$. Finally, output a ciphertext $C = (c_0, c_1, c)$.

$\mathsf{IB\text{-}ME.Dec}(\mathsf{mpk}, \mathsf{dk}_\rho, \mathsf{snd}, C)$: On input decryption key dk_ρ, a target identity $\mathsf{snd} = \sigma$, and a ciphertext C, parse $C = (c_0, c_1, c)$. Next, compute $u_\sigma = \mathsf{H}'(\sigma)$, and compute

$$m = \Phi^{-1}(c \oplus \hat{\mathsf{H}}(e(\mathsf{dk}_\rho^1, c_1)) \oplus \hat{\mathsf{H}}(e(\mathsf{dk}_\rho^2, u_\sigma) \cdot e(\mathsf{dk}_\rho^3, c_0))).$$

Finally, output m.

$\langle\mathsf{ObtainSK}(\mathsf{mpk}, \sigma, \mathsf{scert}, \mathsf{td}_{\mathsf{snd}}), \mathsf{IssueSK}(\mathsf{mpk}, \mathsf{msk}, \mathsf{vk}_{\mathsf{snd}})\rangle$: The sender and the KGC interactively runs ObtainSK and IssueSK, respectively.

Sender: On input $(\mathsf{mpk}, \sigma, \mathsf{scert}, \mathsf{td}_{\mathsf{snd}})$, set the first-round message $\mathsf{M}_{\mathsf{snd}} = \mathsf{scert}$ and send $\mathsf{M}_{\mathsf{snd}}$ to the KGC. Here, $\mathsf{scert} = (u_{\sigma,2}, \Sigma_{\mathsf{snd}})$.

KGC: On input $(\mathsf{mpk}, \mathsf{msk}, \mathsf{vk}_{\mathsf{snd}})$ and the first-round message $\mathsf{M}_{\mathsf{snd}}$, parse $\mathsf{vk}_{\mathsf{snd}} = \mathsf{vk}_{\mathsf{snd}}$ and $\mathsf{M}_{\mathsf{snd}} = (u_{\sigma,2}, \Sigma_{\mathsf{snd}})$. If $\mathsf{Sig.Verify}(\mathsf{vk}_{\mathsf{snd}}, u_{\sigma,2}, \Sigma_{\mathsf{snd}}) = \perp$, then set $\mathsf{M}_{\mathsf{KGC}}^{\mathsf{snd}} = \perp$ and send $\mathsf{M}_{\mathsf{KGC}}^{\mathsf{snd}}$ to the sender. Otherwise, parse $\mathsf{mpk} = (X, Y)$ and $\mathsf{msk} = (x, y)$. Then, compute $v_{\sigma,2} = u_{\sigma,2}^y$, set $\mathsf{M}_{\mathsf{KGC}}^{\mathsf{snd}} = v_{\sigma,2}$, and send $\mathsf{M}_{\mathsf{KGC}}^{\mathsf{snd}}$ to the sender.

Sender: If $\mathsf{M}_{\mathsf{KGC}}^{\mathsf{snd}} = \perp$, then output $\perp$. Otherwise, parse $\mathsf{td}_{\mathsf{snd}} = v_{\sigma,1}$ and $\mathsf{M}_{\mathsf{KGC}}^{\mathsf{snd}} = v_{\sigma,2}$, compute $\mathsf{e}_\sigma = v_{\sigma,2} \cdot Y^{-v_{\sigma,1}}$ and (locally) output the sender-key $\mathsf{ek}_\sigma = \mathsf{e}_\sigma$.

$\langle\mathsf{ObtainRK}(\mathsf{mpk}, \rho, \mathsf{rcert}, \mathsf{td}_{\mathsf{rcv}}), \mathsf{IssueRK}(\mathsf{mpk}, \mathsf{msk}, \mathsf{vk}_{\mathsf{rcv}})\rangle$: The receiver and the KGC interactively runs ObtainRK and IssueRK, respectively.

Receiver: On input $(\mathsf{mpk}, \rho, \mathsf{rcert}, \mathsf{td}_{\mathsf{rcv}})$, set the first-round message $\mathsf{M}_{\mathsf{rcv}} = \mathsf{rcert}$ and send $\mathsf{M}_{\mathsf{rcv}}$ to the KGC. Here, $\mathsf{rcert} = (u_{\rho,2}, \Sigma_{\mathsf{rcv}})$.

KGC: On input $(\mathsf{mpk}, \mathsf{msk}, \mathsf{vk}_{\mathsf{rcv}})$ and the first-round message $\mathsf{M}_{\mathsf{rcv}}$, parse $\mathsf{vk}_{\mathsf{rcv}} = \mathsf{vk}_{\mathsf{rcv}}$ and $\mathsf{M}_{\mathsf{rcv}} = (u_{\sigma,2}, \Sigma_{\mathsf{rcv}})$. If $\mathsf{Sig.Verify}(\mathsf{vk}_{\mathsf{rcv}}, u_{\rho,2}, \Sigma_{\mathsf{rcv}}) = \perp$, then set $\mathsf{M}_{\mathsf{KGC}}^{\mathsf{rcv}} = \perp$ and send $\mathsf{M}_{\mathsf{KGC}}^{\mathsf{rcv}}$ to the receiver. Otherwise, parse $\mathsf{mpk} = (X, Y)$ and $\mathsf{msk} = (x, y)$. Then, compute $v_{\rho,2}^1 = u_{\rho,2}^x$, $v_{\rho,2}^2 = u_{\rho,2}^y$ and $v_{\rho,2}^3 = u_{\rho,2}$, set $\mathsf{M}_{\mathsf{KGC}}^{\mathsf{rcv}} = v_{\rho,2} = (v_{\rho,2}^1, v_{\rho,2}^2, v_{\rho,2}^3)$, and send $\mathsf{M}_{\mathsf{KGC}}^{\mathsf{rcv}}$ to the receiver.

Receiver: If $\mathsf{M}_{\mathsf{KGC}}^{\mathsf{rcv}} = \perp$, then output $\perp$. Otherwise, parse $\mathsf{td}_{\mathsf{rcv}} = v_{\rho,1}$ and $\mathsf{M}_{\mathsf{KGC}}^{\mathsf{rcv}} = v_{\rho,2} = (v_{\rho,2}^1, v_{\rho,2}^2, v_{\rho,2}^3)$, compute $\mathsf{e}_\rho^1 = v_{\rho,2}^1 \cdot X^{-v_{\rho,1}}$, $\mathsf{e}_\rho^2 = v_{\rho,2}^2 \cdot Y^{-v_{\rho,1}}$ and $\mathsf{e}_\rho^3 = v_{\rho,2}^3 \cdot p^{-v_{\rho,1}}$ and (locally) output the receiver-key $\mathsf{dk}_\rho = (\mathsf{dk}_\rho^1, \mathsf{dk}_\rho^2, \mathsf{dk}_\rho^3) = (\mathsf{e}_\rho^1, \mathsf{e}_\rho^2, \mathsf{e}_\rho^3)$.

Correctness. Here, we confirm that our scheme IB-ME satisfies correctness. In the following, we assume that Setup, KGC.KeyGen, ICA.SKGen, and ICA.RKGen are run correctly. If the key issuing protocol between a sender σ (resp., a receiver ρ) and the KGC is run correctly, the sender (resp., receiver) gets a secret encryption (resp., decryption) key $\mathsf{ek}_\sigma = v_{\sigma,2} \cdot Y^{-v_{\sigma,1}} = u_{\sigma,2}^y \cdot (p^y)^{-v_{\sigma,1}} = (\mathsf{H}'(\sigma)^y p^{v_{\sigma,1} y}) p^{-v_{\sigma,1} y} = \mathsf{H}'(\sigma)^y$ (resp., $\mathsf{dk}_\rho = (\mathsf{dk}_\rho^1, \mathsf{dk}_\rho^2, \mathsf{dk}_\rho^3) = (v_{\rho,2}^1 \cdot X^{-v_{\rho,1}}, v_{\rho,2}^2 \cdot Y^{-v_{\rho,1}}, v_{\rho,2}^3 \cdot p^{-v_{\rho,1}}) = (u_{\rho,2}^x \cdot (p^x)^{-v_{\sigma,1}}, u_{\rho,2}^y \cdot (p^y)^{-v_{\rho,1}}, u_{\rho,2} \cdot p^{-v_{\rho,1}}) = (\mathsf{H}(\rho)^x, \mathsf{H}(\rho)^y, \mathsf{H}(\rho))$). Let $C(= c_0, c_1, c) \leftarrow \mathsf{IB\text{-}ME.Enc}(\mathsf{mpk}, \mathsf{ek}_\sigma, \rho, m)$. Then, when IB-ME.Dec is run with dk_ρ, we have $\Phi^{-1}(c \oplus \hat{\mathsf{H}}(e(\mathsf{dk}_\rho^2, u_\sigma) \cdot e(\mathsf{dk}_\rho^3, c_0)) \oplus \hat{\mathsf{H}}(e(\mathsf{dk}_\rho^1, c_1)) = \Phi^{-1}(c \oplus \hat{\mathsf{H}}(e(u_\rho, p^r \cdot \mathsf{ek}_\sigma)) \oplus \hat{\mathsf{H}}(e(u_\rho, X^s))) = m$.

5 Security Analysis

In this section, we provide the security analysis for our scheme. Before diving into the analysis of the security of our scheme, we recall a blind IBE with certified identities scheme by Emura et al. [16]. Please refer to the paper [15,16] for the definition of blind IBE with certified identities. Emura et al. construct Blind-IBE based on the DBDH assumption, but in this paper, in order to reduce our scheme to the BDH assumption, we give a minor changed version of Blind-IBE $\mathsf{Blind\text{-}IBE}^+$ from BDH assumption. The construction of $\mathsf{Blind\text{-}IBE}^+$ is below:

Let $\mathbb{G}$ and $\mathbb{G}_T$ be groups with prime order q, $p \in \mathbb{G}$ a generator, and $e : \mathbb{G} \times \mathbb{G} \rightarrow \mathbb{G}_T$ a pairing. Let $\mathsf{Sig} = (\mathsf{Sig.KeyGen}, \mathsf{Sig.Sign}, \mathsf{Sig.Verify})$ be a digital signature scheme with a message space $\mathbb{G}$.

$\mathsf{IBE.Setup}(1^\lambda)$: Choose $(\mathbb{G}, \mathbb{G}_T, p, q, e)$ where q be a λ-bit prime number. Output $\mathsf{params} = (1^\lambda, (\mathbb{G}, \mathbb{G}_T, p, q, e), \mathsf{H}, \hat{\mathsf{H}})$ where $\mathsf{H} : \{0,1\}^* \rightarrow \mathbb{G}, \hat{\mathsf{H}} : \mathbb{G}_T \rightarrow \{0,1\}^l$ are hash function modeled as random oracles.

$\mathsf{KGC.KGen}(\mathsf{params})$: Choose $x \leftarrow \mathbb{Z}_q$ and compute $Y = p^x$. Then, output a master public key $\mathsf{mpk} = Y$ and a master secret key $\mathsf{msk} = x$.

$\mathsf{ICA.KeyGen}(\mathsf{params})$: Run $(\mathsf{vk}_{\mathsf{Sig}}, \mathsf{sk}_{\mathsf{Sig}}) \leftarrow \mathsf{Sig.Sign}(1^\lambda)$. Then, output a certificate verification key $\mathsf{vk} = \mathsf{vk}_{\mathsf{Sig}}$ and a certificate issuing key $\mathsf{ik} = \mathsf{sk}_{\mathsf{Sig}}$.

$\mathsf{ICA.Cert}(\mathsf{vk}, \mathsf{ik}, \mathsf{ID})$: Parse $\mathsf{ik} = \mathsf{sk}_{\mathsf{Sig}}$ and compute $u_{\mathsf{ID}} = \mathsf{H}(\mathsf{ID})$. Then, choose $v_{\mathsf{ID},1} \leftarrow \mathbb{Z}_q$ and compute $u_{\mathsf{ID},1} = p^{v_{\mathsf{ID},1}}$. Furthermore, compute $u_{\mathsf{ID},2} = u_{\mathsf{ID}} u_{\mathsf{ID},1} \in \mathbb{G}$ and $\Sigma_{\mathsf{Sig}} \leftarrow \mathsf{Sig.Sign}(\mathsf{sk}_{\mathsf{Sig}}, u_{\mathsf{ID},2})$. Finally, output a certificate $\mathsf{cert} = (u_{\mathsf{ID},2}, \Sigma_{\mathsf{Sig}})$ and trapdoor information $\mathsf{td} = v_{\mathsf{ID},1}$.

$\mathsf{IBE.Enc}(\mathsf{mpk}, \mathsf{ID}, m)$: Compute u_{ID}. To encrypt a message $m \in \{0,1\}^l$, sample $s \leftarrow \mathbb{Z}_q$, and compute $c_0 = g^s$ and $c = m \oplus \hat{\mathsf{H}}(e(u_{\mathsf{ID}}, Y^s))$. Finally output a cipher text $C = (c_0, c)$.

$\mathsf{IBE.Dec}(\mathsf{mpk}, \mathsf{sk}_{\mathsf{ID}}, C)$: Parse $\mathsf{sk}_{\mathsf{ID}} = \mathsf{H}(\mathsf{ID})^x$ and $C = (c_0, c)$. Compute $m = c_1 \oplus \hat{\mathsf{H}}(e(\mathsf{sk}_{\mathsf{ID}}, c_0))$ and output m.

$\langle \mathsf{ObtainKey}(\mathsf{mpk}, \sigma, \mathsf{cert}, \mathsf{td}), \mathsf{IssueSK}(\mathsf{mpk}, \mathsf{msk}, \mathsf{vk}) \rangle$: The sender and the KGC interactively runs $\mathsf{ObtainKey}$ and $\mathsf{IssueKey}$, respectively.

User: On input $(\mathsf{mpk}, \mathsf{ID}, \mathsf{cert}, \mathsf{td})$, set the first-round message $\mathsf{M}_{\mathsf{user}} = \mathsf{cert}$ and send $\mathsf{M}_{\mathsf{user}}$ to the KGC. Here, $\mathsf{cert} = (u_{\mathsf{ID},2}, \Sigma_{\mathsf{Sig}})$.

KGC: On input $(\mathsf{mpk}, \mathsf{msk}, \mathsf{vk})$ and the first-round message $\mathsf{M}_{\mathsf{user}}$, parse $\mathsf{vk} = \mathsf{vk}_{\mathsf{Sig}}$ and $\mathsf{M}_{\mathsf{user}} = (u_{\mathsf{ID},2}, \Sigma_{\mathsf{Sig}})$. If $\mathsf{Sig.Verify}(\mathsf{vk}_{\mathsf{Sig}}, u_{\mathsf{ID},2}, \Sigma_{\mathsf{Sig}}) = \perp$, then set $\mathsf{M}_{\mathsf{KGC}} = \perp$ and send $\mathsf{M}_{\mathsf{KGC}}$ to the user. Otherwise, parse $\mathsf{mpk} = Y$ and $\mathsf{msk} = x$. Then, compute $v_{\mathsf{ID},2} = u_{\mathsf{ID},2}^x$, set $\mathsf{M}_{\mathsf{KGC}} = v_{\mathsf{ID},2}$, and send $\mathsf{M}_{\mathsf{KGC}}$ to the user.

User: If $\mathsf{M}_{\mathsf{KGC}} = \perp$, then output $\perp$. Otherwise, parse $\mathsf{td} = v_{\mathsf{ID},1}$ and $\mathsf{M}_{\mathsf{KGC}} = v_{\mathsf{ID},2}$, compute $\mathsf{e}_{\mathsf{ID}} = v_{\sigma,2} \cdot Y^{-v_{\mathsf{ID},1}}$ and (locally) output the secret key $\mathsf{sk}_{\mathsf{ID}} = \mathsf{e}_{\mathsf{ID}}$.

Theorem 1. *Our Blind IB-ME scheme with certified identity* $\mathsf{IB\text{-}ME}$ *satisfies* $\mathsf{priv\text{-}users}$ *in the random oracle model if the underlying signature scheme* Sig *is EUF-CMA secure and the BDH assumption holds.*

Proof. Firstly, we show that if $\mathsf{Blind\text{-}IBE}^+$ is $\mathsf{IND\text{-}ANON\text{-}CPA}$ secure, then our scheme satisfies $\mathsf{priv\text{-}users}$.

Lemma 2. *Let* $\mathcal{A}^{\mathsf{IB\text{-}ME}}$ *be an adversary that breaks* $\mathsf{priv\text{-}user}$ *of our IB-ME. Then, there is an adversary* $\mathcal{B}^{\mathsf{IBE}}$ *that breaks* $\mathsf{IND\text{-}ANON\text{-}CPA}$ *security of* $\mathsf{Blind\text{-}IBE}^+$.

Proof. Let q_{dk} be the maximum number which $\mathcal{A}$ makes decryption key queries. Using the adversary $\mathcal{A}^{\textsf{IB-ME}}$, we construct adversary $\mathcal{B}^{\textsf{IBE}}$ so that $\textsf{Adv}^{\textsf{priv-users}}_{\textsf{IB-ME},\mathcal{A}^{\textsf{IB-ME}}}(\lambda) = \hat{e} \cdot (1 + q_{\textsf{dk}})\textsf{Adv}^{\textsf{IND-ANON-CPA}}_{\textsf{IBE},\mathcal{B}^{\textsf{IBE}}}(\lambda)$ as follows.

1. Upon receiving $((1^\lambda, (\mathbb{G}, \mathbb{G}_T, p, q, e), \textsf{H}, \hat{\textsf{H}}), Y, \textsf{vk})$, $\mathcal{B}^{\textsf{IBE}}$ samples a secret value $x \leftarrow \mathbb{Z}_q$, computes a public value $X = p^x$. Next, $\mathcal{B}^{\textsf{IBE}}$ prepares $(\textsf{vk}_{\textsf{snd}}, \textsf{ik}_{\textsf{snd}})$ by running ICA.SKGen algorithm, a random oracle $\textsf{H}'$ and the padding function, and gives $((1^\lambda, (\mathbb{G}, \mathbb{G}_T, p, q, e), \textsf{H}, \textsf{H}', \hat{\textsf{H}}), (X, Y), \textsf{vk}_{\textsf{snd}}, \textsf{vk}_{\textsf{rcv}} (= \textsf{vk}))$. Note that the master secret key y and the issuing key ik remain unknown to $\mathcal{B}^{\textsf{IBE}}$.
2. When $\mathcal{A}^{\textsf{IB-ME}}$ makes oracle queries, $\mathcal{B}^{\textsf{IBE}}$ answers to these as follows:
   (a) When $\mathcal{A}^{\textsf{IB-ME}}$ makes a H query on ρ, with probability $1 - \delta$, $\mathcal{B}^{\textsf{IBE}}$ runs the H oracle of Blind-IBE$^+$ to obtain $u_\rho = u_{\textsf{ID}}$, and updates $\textsf{HList} \leftarrow \textsf{HList} \cup \{(\rho, u_\rho, \perp, 0)\}$. Otherwise, $\mathcal{B}^{\textsf{IBE}}$ samples $\hat{b} \leftarrow \mathbb{Z}_q$, computes $u_\rho = p^{\hat{b}}$, and updates $\textsf{HList} \leftarrow \textsf{HList} \cup \{(\rho, u_\rho, \hat{b}, 1)\}$. Then, $\mathcal{B}^{\textsf{IBE}}$ returns u_ρ to $\mathcal{A}^{\textsf{IB-ME}}$.
   (b) When $\mathcal{A}^{\textsf{IB-ME}}$ makes a $\textsf{H}'$ query on σ, $\mathcal{B}^{\textsf{IBE}}$ samples $\hat{b} \leftarrow \mathbb{Z}_q$, computes $u_\sigma = p^{\hat{b}}$, and updates $\textsf{H}'\textsf{List} \leftarrow \textsf{H}'\textsf{List} \cup \{(\rho, u_\rho, \hat{b})\}$. Then, $\mathcal{B}^{\textsf{IBE}}$ returns u_σ to $\mathcal{A}^{\textsf{IB-ME}}$.
   (c) When $\mathcal{A}^{\textsf{IB-ME}}$ queries for a sender certificate corresponding to σ, the $\mathcal{B}^{\textsf{IBE}}$ runs $((u_{\sigma,2}, \Sigma_{\textsf{snd}}), v_{\sigma,1}) = (\textsf{scert}, \textsf{td}_\sigma) \leftarrow \textsf{ICA.SCert}(\textsf{vk}_{snd}, \textsf{ik}_{snd}, \sigma)$ and returns $(\textsf{scert}, \textsf{td}_\sigma)$ to $\mathcal{A}^{\textsf{IB-ME}}$. Furthermore, $\mathcal{B}^{\textsf{IBE}}$ updates $\sigma\textsf{List} \leftarrow \sigma\textsf{List} \cup \{\sigma\}$ and $\textsf{SCList} \leftarrow \textsf{SCList} \cup \{(\textsf{scert}, \textsf{td}_\sigma, \sigma)\}$.
   (d) When $\mathcal{A}^{\textsf{IB-ME}}$ queries for a receiver certificate corresponding to ρ, the $\mathcal{B}^{\textsf{IBE}}$ runs certificate query of Blind-IBE$^+$ to obtain $((u_{\rho,2}, \Sigma_{\textsf{snd}}), v_{\rho,1}) = (\textsf{rcert}, \textsf{td}_\rho) = (\textsf{cert}, \textsf{td})$ and returns $(\textsf{rcert}, \textsf{td}_\rho) = ((u_{\rho,2}, \Sigma_{\textsf{rcv}}), \textsf{td}_\rho$ to $\mathcal{A}^{\textsf{IB-ME}}$. Furthermore, $\mathcal{B}^{\textsf{IBE}}$ updates $\rho\textsf{List} \leftarrow \rho\textsf{List} \cup \{\rho\}$ and $\textsf{RCList} \leftarrow \textsf{RCList} \cup \{(\textsf{rcert}, \textsf{td}_\rho, \rho)\}$.
   (e) When $\mathcal{A}^{\textsf{IB-ME}}$ queries for a encryption key with a first-round message $\textsf{M}_{\textsf{snd}} = (u_{\sigma,2}, \Sigma_{\textsf{snd}})$, $\mathcal{B}^{\textsf{IBE}}$ extracts $u_{\rho,2}$ and $v_{\rho,1}$ from $((u_{\sigma,2}, \Sigma_{\textsf{snd}}), v_{\sigma,1}, \sigma) \in \textsf{SCList}$ and $\hat{b}$ from $(\sigma, u_\sigma, \hat{b}) \in \textsf{H}'\textsf{List}$. Then, $\mathcal{B}^{\textsf{IBE}}$ returns the second-round message $\textsf{M}^{\textsf{snd}}_{\textsf{KGC}} = v_{\sigma,2} = Y^{v_{\sigma,1}+\hat{b}}$ or $\perp$ to $\mathcal{A}^{\textsf{IB-ME}}$.
   (f) When $\mathcal{A}^{\textsf{IB-ME}}$ queries for a decryption key with a first-round message $\textsf{M}_{\textsf{rcv}}$, $\mathcal{B}^{\textsf{IBE}}$ extracts $u_{\rho,2}$ and $v_{\rho,1}$ from $((u_{\rho,2}, \Sigma_{\textsf{rcv}}), v_{\rho,1}, \rho) \in \textsf{RCList}$ and $\hat{b}$ from $(\rho, u_\rho, \hat{b}, \hat{d}) \in \textsf{HList}$. If $\hat{d} = 0$, then $\mathcal{B}^{\textsf{IBE}}$ aborts the game. Otherwise, if $\hat{d} = 1$, then $\mathcal{B}^{\textsf{IBE}}$ computes $v_{\rho,2} = (v^1_{\rho,2}, v^2_{\rho,2}, v^3_{\rho,2}) = (u^x_{\rho,2}, (Y)^{v_{\rho,2}+\hat{b}} u_{\rho,2})$. Finally, $\mathcal{B}^{\textsf{IBE}}$ returns the second-round message $\textsf{M}^{\textsf{rcv}}_{\textsf{KGC}} = v_{\rho,2}$ or $\perp$ to $\mathcal{A}^{\textsf{IB-ME}}$.
   (g) When $\mathcal{A}^{\textsf{IB-ME}}$ queries for a challenge ciphertext on σ^*, ρ^* and message m^*, $\mathcal{B}^{\textsf{IBE}}$ extracts the entry $(\rho^*, u_{\rho^*}, \hat{b}^*, \hat{d}^*) \in \textsf{HList}$. If $\hat{d}^* = 1$, then $\mathcal{B}$ aborts the game and output guess coin $\widehat{\textsf{coin}} \leftarrow \{0, 1\}$. Otherwise, if $\hat{d}^* = 0$, then $\mathcal{B}^{\textsf{IBE}}$ samples random $r \leftarrow \mathbb{Z}_q$ and computes $c^*_0 = p^r$ and $m^*_0 = \Phi(m) \oplus \hat{\textsf{H}}(e(u_{\rho^*}, c^*_0 \cdot ek_{\sigma^*}))$. Next, $\mathcal{B}$ sends (m^*_0, ρ^*) to its challenger and receives $C^*_0 = (c^*_1, c^*)$. Finally, $\mathcal{B}^{\textsf{IBE}}$ sends $C^* = (c^*_0, c^*_1, c^*)$ to $\mathcal{A}^{\textsf{IB-ME}}$.
3. When $\mathcal{A}^{\textsf{IB-ME}}$ outputs a guess $\widehat{\textsf{coin}}$, $\mathcal{B}^{\textsf{IBE}}$ returns the same guess $\widehat{\textsf{coin}}$.

From the above simulation, we can see that $\mathcal{B}^{\mathsf{IBE}}$ can break the IND-ANON-CPA security if it does not abort. Thus, in the following, we estimate the probability that $\mathcal{B}^{\mathsf{IBE}}$ does not abort. First, the probability that $\mathcal{B}^{\mathsf{IBE}}$ does not abort for the decryption key queries is $\delta^{q_{dk}}$. Then, $\mathcal{B}^{\mathsf{IBE}}$ does not abort in the challenge with probability $(1-\delta)$. Hence, the overall probability of $\mathcal{B}^{\mathsf{IBE}}$ does not abort in the challenge with probability $\delta^{q_{dk}}(1-\delta)$, which is maximized at $\delta_{opt} = q_{dk}/(q_{dk}+1)$. In this case, the probability that $\mathcal{B}^{\mathsf{IBE}}$ does not abort is at least $(\hat{e}\cdot(1+q_{dk}))^{-1}$. From the above, we have $\mathsf{Adv}^{\mathsf{priv\text{-}users}}_{\mathsf{IB\text{-}ME},\mathcal{A}^{\mathsf{IB\text{-}ME}}}(\lambda) = \hat{e}\cdot(1+q_{\mathsf{dk}})\mathsf{Adv}^{\mathsf{IND\text{-}ANON\text{-}CPA}}_{\mathsf{IBE},\mathcal{B}^{\mathsf{IBE}}}(\lambda)$.

□(Lemma 2)

Then, we show that $\mathsf{Blind\text{-}IBE}^{+}$ is IND-ANON-CPA secure.

Lemma 3. *$\mathsf{Blind\text{-}IBE}^{+}$ is IND-ANON-CPA secure in the random oracle model if the underlying signature scheme Sig is eu-cma secure, and assuming the hardness of the BDH problem.*

Proof. Let $\mathcal{A}^{\mathsf{IBE}}$ be a PPT adversary against the IND-ANON-CPA security game. In the following let X_i denote the event that $\mathcal{A}^{\mathsf{IBE}}$ wins in Game_i.

Game_0 : This is the original IND-ANON-CPA security game of $\mathsf{Blind\text{-}IBE}^{+}$.
Game_1*:* In this game, we change how $\mathcal{B}^{\mathsf{BDH}}$ answers the secret key queries.

- When $\mathcal{A}^{\mathsf{IBE}}$ queries for a secret key with input a first-round message $\mathsf{M}_{\mathsf{user}} = (u_{\mathsf{ID},2}, \Sigma_{\mathsf{Sig}})$, $\mathcal{B}^{\mathsf{BDH}}$ first checks whether $\mathsf{Sig.Verify}(\mathsf{vk}, u_{\mathsf{ID},2}, \Sigma_{\mathsf{Sig}}) = \top$. If not, it returns the second-round message $\mathsf{M}_{\mathsf{KGC}} = \bot$ to $\mathcal{A}^{\mathsf{IBE}}$. Next, it sets $\mathsf{cert} = (u_{\mathsf{ID},2}, \Sigma_{\mathsf{Sig}})$ and checks whether $(\mathsf{cert}, \star, \star) \in \mathsf{CList}$, where $\star$ represents an arbitrary value. If not, $\mathcal{B}^{\mathsf{BDH}}$ aborts the game. Otherwise, $\mathcal{B}^{\mathsf{BDH}}$ parses $\mathsf{M}_{\mathsf{user}} = (u_{\mathsf{ID},2}, \Sigma_{\mathsf{Sig}})$ and returns the second-round message $\mathsf{M}_{\mathsf{KGC}} = v_{\mathsf{ID},2}$ or $\bot$ to $\mathcal{A}^{\mathsf{IBE}}$ depending on $\mathsf{M}_{\mathsf{user}}$.

At the end of the game, $\mathcal{A}^{\mathsf{IBE}}$ outputs a guess $\widehat{\mathsf{coin}}$ for coin, $\mathcal{B}^{\mathsf{BDH}}$ outputs the solution of BDH problem. As in [15, Lemma 6], we have $|\Pr[X_0] - \Pr[X_1]| = negl(\lambda)$ by the EUF-CMA security of the underlying signatures scheme. We omit the proof since it is almost the same as that of [15, Lemma 6]. As the end of the proof, we will show that $|\Pr[X_1] - 1/2| = negl(\lambda)$ due to the hardness of the BDH problem. (Due to the space limitation, the formal proof will be given in full version.)

Claim 4. *If the BDH assumption holds, then $|\Pr[X_1] - 1/2| = negl(\lambda)$ holds.*

From the above, we have $\mathsf{Adv}^{\mathsf{IND\text{-}ANON\text{-}CPA}}_{\mathsf{IBE},\mathcal{A}^{\mathsf{IBE}}}(\lambda) \le |\Pr[X_0] - \Pr[X_1]| + |\Pr[X_1] - 1/2| = negl(\lambda)$. That is, $\mathsf{Blind\text{-}IBE}^{+}$ is IND-ANON-CPA secure. □(Lemma 3)

Putting everything together, we have $\mathsf{Adv}^{\mathsf{priv\text{-}users}}_{\mathsf{IB\text{-}ME},\mathcal{A}^{\mathsf{IB\text{-}ME}}}(\lambda) = negl(\lambda)$. That is, our blind IB-ME scheme with certified identity IB-ME satisfies priv-users.

□(Theorem 1)

Theorem 5. *Our blind IB-ME scheme with certified identity* IB-ME *satisfies* auth-user *in the random oracle model if the underlying signature scheme* Sig *is EUF-CMA secure and the BDH assumption holds.*

Proof. Let $\mathcal{A}^{\mathsf{IB\text{-}ME}}$ be a PPT adversary against the auth-users security game. In the following let X_i denote the event that $\mathcal{A}^{\mathsf{IB\text{-}ME}}$ wins in Game_i.
Game_0 : This is the original auth-users security game of IB-ME.
Game_1 : In this game, we change how $\mathcal{B}^{\mathsf{BDH}}$ answers to the encryption key queries and the decryption key queries, as Game_1 in Lemma 3.

We have $|\Pr[X_0] - \Pr[X_1]| = negl(\lambda)$ by the eu-cma security of underlying signature scheme. We omit the proof since it is similar to [15, Lemma 6].

Finally, we will show that $\Pr[X_1] = negl(\lambda)$ by the BDH assumption. (Due to the space limitation, the formal proof will be given in full version.)

Lemma 6. *If the BDH assumption holds, then* $\Pr[X_1] = negl(\lambda)$ *holds.*

From the above, $\mathsf{Adv}^{\mathsf{auth\text{-}users}}_{\mathsf{IB\text{-}ME},\mathcal{A}^{\mathsf{IB\text{-}ME}}}(\lambda) \leq |\Pr[X_0] - \Pr[X_1]| + \Pr[X_1] = negl(\lambda)$ holds, that is, IB-ME satisfies auth-user. □(Theorem 5)

Theorem 7. *Our blind IB-ME scheme with certified identity* IB-ME *satisfies* priv-KGC *in the random oracle model assuming the hardness of the BDH assumption holds.*

Proof. To prove Theorem 7, we use $\mathsf{Blind\text{-}IBE}^+$ again. Now, we show that if Blind-IBE is IND-ANON-KGC secure, then our scheme satisfies priv-KGC.

Lemma 8. *Let* $\mathcal{A}^{\mathsf{IB\text{-}ME}}$ *be an adversary that breaks* priv-KGC *of our IB-ME. Then, there is an adversary* $\mathcal{B}^{\mathsf{IBE}}$ *that breaks* IND-ANON-KGC *security of* $\mathsf{Blind\text{-}IBE}^+$.

By using the similar argument in Lemma 2, we have $\mathsf{Adv}^{\mathsf{priv\text{-}KGC}}_{\mathsf{IB\text{-}ME},\mathcal{A}^{\mathsf{IB\text{-}ME}}}(\lambda) = \hat{e}(1 + q_{idk})\mathsf{Adv}^{\mathsf{IND\text{-}ANON\text{-}KGC}}_{\mathsf{IBE},\mathcal{B}^{\mathsf{IBE}}}(\lambda)$. (Due to the space limitation, the formal proof will be given in full version.)

Then, we show that $\mathsf{Blind\text{-}IBE}^+$ is IND-ANON-KGC secure. (Due to the space limitation, the formal proof will be given in full version.)

Lemma 9. $\mathsf{Blind\text{-}IBE}^+$ *is* IND-ANON-KGC *secure in the random oracle model assuming the hardness of BDH assumption.*

Putting everything together, we have $\mathsf{Adv}^{\mathsf{priv\text{-}KGC}}_{\mathsf{IB\text{-}ME},\mathcal{A}^{\mathsf{IB\text{-}ME}}}(\lambda) = negl(\lambda)$. That is, our blind IB-ME scheme with certified identity IB-ME satisfies priv-KGC.
□(Theorem 7)

Theorem 10. *Our blind IB-ME scheme with certified identity* IB-ME *satisfies* auth-KGC *in the random oracle model assuming the hardness of the BDH assumption holds.*

Proof. Let $\mathcal{A}^{\mathsf{IB\text{-}ME}}$ be an adversary that breaks auth-KGC of our IB-ME. We use $\mathcal{A}^{\mathsf{IB\text{-}ME}}$ to construct an adversary $\mathcal{B}^{\mathsf{BDH}}$ against the BDH problem. Now, we assume $\mathcal{A}$ makes at most Q IssueSK queries, where $Q(\lambda)$ can be arbitrary large polynomials. $\mathcal{B}^{\mathsf{BDH}}$ receives the challenge $(p, p^\alpha, p^\beta, p^\gamma)$. (The solution is

$D = p^{\alpha\beta\gamma}$.) Looking ahead, $\mathcal{B}^{\mathsf{BDH}}$ implicitly sets $\mathsf{H}(\sigma_I) = p^{\alpha\gamma}$. At begining the game, $\mathcal{B}^{\mathsf{BDH}}$ prepares $I \leftarrow [Q_{sk}]$ and two integers $Q_{sk} := 0$ and $Q_{rk} := 0$, samples $x, y \leftarrow \mathbb{Z}_q$, and computes $X = p^x$ and $Y = p^y$. Moreover, $\mathcal{B}^{\mathsf{BDH}}$ prepares $(\mathsf{vk}_{\mathsf{snd}}, \mathsf{ik}_{\mathsf{snd}})$ and $(\mathsf{vk}_{\mathsf{rcv}}, \mathsf{ik}_{\mathsf{rcv}})$ by running ICA.SKGen algorithm and ICA.RKGen algorithm. It then provides $((X,Y),(x,y),\mathsf{vk}_{\mathsf{snd}},\mathsf{vk}_{\mathsf{rcv}})$ to $\mathcal{A}^{\mathsf{IB\text{-}ME}}$ and answers to queries by $\mathcal{A}^{\mathsf{IB\text{-}ME}}$:

- When $\mathcal{A}^{\mathsf{IB\text{-}ME}}$ makes H query on ρ, $\mathcal{B}^{\mathsf{BDH}}$ first check $(\rho, u_\rho, \star) \in \mathsf{HList}$. If so, $\mathcal{B}^{\mathsf{BDH}}$ returns u_ρ. If not, $\mathcal{B}^{\mathsf{BDH}}$ samples $\hat{\beta} \leftarrow \mathbb{Z}_q$ and computes $u_\rho = p^{\beta\hat{\beta}}$. Finally, returns u_ρ to $\mathcal{A}^{\mathsf{IB\text{-}ME}}$ and updates $\mathsf{HList} \leftarrow \{(\rho, u_\rho, \hat{\beta})\}$.
- When $\mathcal{A}^{\mathsf{IB\text{-}ME}}$ makes an H' query on σ, $\mathcal{B}^{\mathsf{BDH}}$ first checks if $\sigma \in \sigma\mathsf{List}$. If not, $\mathcal{B}^{\mathsf{BDH}}$ samples $u_\sigma \in \mathbb{G}$ and updates $\mathsf{H'List} \leftarrow \mathsf{H'List} \cup \{(\sigma, u_\sigma)\}$. If $\sigma = \sigma\mathsf{List}[I]$, $\mathcal{B}^{\mathsf{BDH}}$ aborts.
- When $\mathcal{A}^{\mathsf{IB\text{-}ME}}$ makes $\hat{\mathsf{H}}$ query on χ, $\mathcal{B}^{\mathsf{BDH}}$ samples a random $\hat{h} \leftarrow \{0,1\}^n$, and updates $\hat{\mathsf{H}}\mathsf{List} \leftarrow \hat{\mathsf{H}}\mathsf{List} \cup \{(\chi, \hat{h})\}$. Finally, it returns $\hat{h}$ to $\mathcal{A}^{\mathsf{IB\text{-}ME}}$.
- When $\mathcal{A}^{\mathsf{IB\text{-}ME}}$ makes encryption query on index i, j and a message m, $\mathcal{B}^{\mathsf{BDH}}$ checks $i \in [Q_{sk}] \wedge j \in [Q_{rk}]$. If not, $\mathcal{B}^{\mathsf{BDH}}$ returns $\perp$. Otherwise, it retrieves $\sigma_i = \sigma\mathsf{List}[i]$, $\rho_j = \rho\mathsf{List}[j]$, and the unique tuples $(\sigma, u_\sigma) \in \mathsf{H'List}$ and $(\rho, u_\rho) \in \mathsf{HList}$. Then, the challenger samples $r, s \leftarrow \mathbb{Z}_q$. We know that $ek_{\sigma_i} = \mathsf{H}'(\sigma_i)^y$. Next $\mathcal{B}^{\mathsf{BDH}}$ computes the ciphertext as $c_0 = p^s$, $c_1 = p^r$ and $c = \Phi(m) \oplus \hat{\mathsf{H}}(e(u_{\rho_j}, X^s)) \oplus \hat{\mathsf{H}}(e(u_{\rho_j}, p^r \cdot \mathsf{ek}_{\sigma_i}))$ as specified by the scheme, and returns the ciphertext $C = (c_0, c_1, c)$ to $\mathcal{A}^{\mathsf{IB\text{-}ME}}$.
- When $\mathcal{A}^{\mathsf{IB\text{-}ME}}$ makes an IssueSK query, $\mathcal{B}^{\mathsf{IBE}}$ first samples $\sigma \leftarrow \mathcal{ID}$. $\mathcal{B}^{\mathsf{IBE}}$ makes H' query on input σ and receives back u_σ. $\mathcal{B}^{\mathsf{BDH}}$ proceeds with generating $(\mathsf{scert}, \mathsf{td}_\sigma)$ by running $\mathsf{ICA.SCert}(\mathsf{vk}_{\mathsf{snd}}, \mathsf{ik}_{\mathsf{snd}}, \sigma)$, and sets the first-round message $\mathsf{M}_{\mathsf{snd}} = \mathsf{scert} = (u_{\sigma,2}, \Sigma_{\mathsf{snd}})$. It then returns $\mathsf{M}_{\mathsf{snd}}$ to $\mathcal{A}^{\mathsf{IB\text{-}ME}}$. Finally, the challenger updates $Q_{sk} \leftarrow Q_{sk} + 1$ and then set $\sigma\mathsf{List}[Q_{sk}] = \sigma$.
- When $\mathcal{A}^{\mathsf{IB\text{-}ME}}$ makes an IssueRK query, $\mathcal{B}^{\mathsf{IBE}}$ first samples $\rho \leftarrow \mathcal{ID}$. $\mathcal{B}^{\mathsf{IBE}}$ makes H query on input ρ and receives back u_ρ. $\mathcal{B}^{\mathsf{BDH}}$ proceeds with generating $(\mathsf{rcert}, \mathsf{td}_\rho)$ by running $\mathsf{ICA.RCert}(\mathsf{vk}_{\mathsf{rcv}}, \mathsf{ik}_{\mathsf{rcv}}, \rho)$, and sets the first-round message $\mathsf{M}_{\mathsf{rcv}} = \mathsf{rcert} = (u_{\rho,2}, \Sigma_{\mathsf{rcv}})$. It then returns $\mathsf{M}_{\mathsf{rcv}}$ to $\mathcal{A}^{\mathsf{IB\text{-}ME}}$. Finally, $\mathcal{B}^{\mathsf{IBE}}$ updates $Q_{rk} \leftarrow Q_{rk} + 1$ and then set $\sigma\mathsf{List}[Q_{rk}] = \rho$.

Finally, $\mathcal{A}^{\mathsf{IB\text{-}ME}}$ sends (C^*, i^*, j^*) to $\mathcal{B}^{\mathsf{BDH}}$. Let $\sigma_{i^*} = \sigma\mathsf{List}[i^*]$ and $\rho_{j^*} = \rho\mathsf{List}[j^*]$. Now, $\mathcal{B}^{\mathsf{BDH}}$ extracts $u_{\sigma_{i^*}}$ from $(\sigma_{i^*}, u_{\sigma_{i^*}}) \in \mathsf{H'List}$ and $u_{\rho_{j^*}}$ from $(\rho_{j^*}, u_{\rho_{j^*}}) \in \mathsf{HList}$. We know $\mathsf{dk}^2_{\rho_{j^*}} = p^{\beta\hat{\beta}y}$, and if $i^* = I$, $H'(\sigma_{i^*}) = p^{\alpha\gamma}$, we have $e(\mathsf{dk}^2_{\rho_{j^*}}, \mathsf{H}'(\sigma_{i^*})) = e(p^{\beta\hat{\beta}y}, p^{\alpha\gamma}) = D^{y\hat{\beta}}$, and $u_{\rho_{j^*}} = \mathsf{dk}^3_{\rho_{j^*}}$. Next, $\mathcal{B}^{\mathsf{BDH}}$ computes $z = 1/y\hat{\beta}$, takes a random tuple $(\chi, \hat{h})$, and computes $D' = (\chi \cdot e(u_{\rho j^*}, c_0^*)^{-1})^z = (e(\mathsf{dk}^2_{\rho_{j^*}}, u_{\sigma_{i^*}}) e(\mathsf{dk}^3_{\rho_{j^*}}, c_0^*) e(u_{\rho_{j^*}}, c_0^*)^{-1})^z = e(\mathsf{dk}^2_{\rho_{j^*}}, u_{\sigma_{i^*}})^z = e(p^{y\beta\hat{\beta}}, p^{\alpha\gamma})^{1/y\hat{\beta}} = D$. First of all, note that the simulation of auth-KGC is done. By using the similar argument in [7, Lemma 4.2], $\mathcal{B}^{\mathsf{BDH}}$ outputs the correct solution D' with probability at least $2/Qq_{\hat{\mathsf{H}}}$, where $q_{\hat{H}}$ is number of $\hat{\mathsf{H}}$ queries and Q is the number of elements in $\sigma\mathsf{List}$. Hence, we have $\mathsf{Adv}^{\mathsf{auth\text{-}KGC}}_{\mathsf{IB\text{-}ME},\mathcal{A}^{\mathsf{IB\text{-}ME}}}(\lambda) = \frac{Q q_{\hat{\mathsf{H}}}}{2}\mathsf{Adv}^{\mathsf{BDH}}_{\mathcal{B}^{\mathsf{BDH}}}(\lambda)$. Since the BDH assumption holds, we have $\mathsf{Adv}^{\mathsf{auth\text{-}KGC}}_{\mathsf{IB\text{-}ME},\mathcal{A}^{\mathsf{IB\text{-}ME}}}(\lambda) = negl(\lambda)$, that is, IB-ME satisfies auth-KGC.

□(Theorem 10)

The security game against the ICA is a strictly weaker variant of the security game against corrupted users. Therefore, Theorem 1 proves Corollary 11 and Theorem 5 proves Corollary 12.

Corollary 11. *Our blind IB-ME scheme with certified identity* IB-ME *satisfies* priv-ICA *in the random oracle model if the underlying signature scheme* Sig *is EUF-CMA secure and the BDH assumption holds.*

Corollary 12. *Our blind IB-ME scheme with certified identity* IB-ME *satisfies* auth-ICA *in the random oracle model if the underlying signature scheme* Sig *is EUF-CMA secure and the BDH assumption holds.*

6 Experimental Result

In this section, we show that our proposed scheme does not lose efficiency compared to existing schemes. Specifically, the processing time and data size of our scheme are the almost same as ones of AFNV-IB-ME [3] and EKW-IBE [16]. To this end, we implement a proof of concept in Python 3.7.13 using Charm 0.50 [2], which is a framework for prototyping pairing-based cryptosystems. Since our IB-ME is constructed using symmetric pairings, we instantiate it with a supersingular curve with a 512-bit base field (curve `SS512` in Charm), which gives approximately 80 bits of security [22]. The experimental platform is performed on a personal computer running 64-bit Ubuntu 22.04 LTS with AMD Ryzen 5-3600 CPU@3.50 GH and 8 GB of RAM.

Table 1 presents a comparison result of the cost in milliseconds, associated to the main cryptographic operations among of AFNV-IB-ME, EKW-IBE, and our scheme. We executed these experiments in 50 different runs of 10 times each, and both the minimum and average timing was taken for each operation; we use the Python module `timeit` for these measurements. It can be seen that the efficiency of AFNV-IB-ME, EKW-IBE, and our scheme are comparable for the main high-level operations of IB-ME, namely Encryption and Decryption. Furthermore, the total average processing time of other operations in our scheme is about 28.689 ms, which is considered highly practical, while our scheme has additional security compared to EKW-IBE and AFNV-IB-ME. Finally, Table 2 shows a summary of the space costs associated to different elements of AFNV-IB-ME, EKW-IBE, and our scheme.

Table 1. Evaluation of Time Performances

	AFNV-IBME		EKW-IBE		Our-IBME	
	Min.(ms)	Ave.(ms)	Min.(ms)	Ave.(ms)	Min.(ms)	Ave.(ms)
KGC.KeyGen	1.698	1.866	0.919	0.961	1.674	1.801
ICA.SKGen	–	–	–	–	0.920	0.951
ICA.RKGen	–	–	0.920	0.961	0.925	0.947
ICA.SCert	–	–	–	–	5.876	6.011
ICA.RCert	–	–	5.860	5.962	5.864	5.946
SKGen	2.676	2.917	–	–	5.072	5.138
RKGen	3.428	3.837	5.072	5.146	7.740	7.905
Encryption	5.551	6.134	4.485	4.558	5.572	6.081
Decryption	3.568	3.872	0.621	0.643	3.566	3.727

Table 2. Evaluation of Space Costs

	AFNV-IB-ME	EKW-IBE	Our IB-ME
Eencryption Key	$\lvert\mathbb{G}\rvert$	–	$\lvert\mathbb{G}\rvert$
Decryption Key	$3\lvert\mathbb{G}\rvert$	$\lvert\mathbb{G}\rvert$	$3\lvert\mathbb{G}\rvert$
Message	n	n	n
Ciphertext	$2\lvert\mathbb{G}\rvert + l$	$\lvert\mathbb{G}\rvert + l$	$2\lvert\mathbb{G}\rvert + l$

Acknowledgement. This research was in part conducted under a contract of "Research and development on IoT malware removal/make it non-functional technologies for effective use of the radio spectrum" among "Research and Development for Expansion of Radio Wave Resources (JPJ000254)", which was supported by the Ministry of Internal Affairs and Communications, Japan. This work was in part supported by JSPS KAKENHI Grant Numbers JP21H03395, JP22H03590 and JST CREST JPMJCR2113.

References

1. Agrawal, S., Boneh, D., Boyen, X.: Efficient lattice (H)IBE in the standard model. In: Gilbert, H. (ed.) EUROCRYPT 2010. LNCS, vol. 6110, pp. 553–572. Springer, Heidelberg (2010). https://doi.org/10.1007/978-3-642-13190-5_28
2. Akinyele, J.A., et al.: Charm: a framework for rapidly prototyping cryptosystems. J. Cryptogr. Eng. **3**(2), 111–128 (2013)
3. Ateniese, G., Francati, D., Nuñez, D., Venturi, D.: Match me if you can: matchmaking encryption and its applications. In: Boldyreva, A., Micciancio, D. (eds.) CRYPTO 2019. LNCS, vol. 11693, pp. 701–731. Springer, Cham (2019). https://doi.org/10.1007/978-3-030-26951-7_24
4. Boldyreva, A.: Threshold signatures, multisignatures and blind signatures based on the gap-diffie-hellman-group signature scheme. In: Desmedt, Y.G. (ed.) PKC 2003. LNCS, vol. 2567, pp. 31–46. Springer, Heidelberg (2003). https://doi.org/10.1007/3-540-36288-6_3

5. Boneh, D., Boyen, X.: Efficient selective-ID secure identity-based encryption without random oracles. In: Cachin, C., Camenisch, J.L. (eds.) EUROCRYPT 2004. LNCS, vol. 3027, pp. 223–238. Springer, Heidelberg (2004). https://doi.org/10.1007/978-3-540-24676-3_14
6. Boneh, D., Boyen, X.: Secure identity based encryption without random oracles. In: Franklin, M. (ed.) CRYPTO 2004. LNCS, vol. 3152, pp. 443–459. Springer, Heidelberg (2004). https://doi.org/10.1007/978-3-540-28628-8_27
7. Boneh, D., Franklin, M.: Identity-based encryption from the weil pairing. In: Kilian, J. (ed.) CRYPTO 2001. LNCS, vol. 2139, pp. 213–229. Springer, Heidelberg (2001). https://doi.org/10.1007/3-540-44647-8_13
8. Boneh, D., Lynn, B., Shacham, H.: Short signatures from the Weil pairing. J. Cryptol. **17**(4), 297–319 (2001)
9. Cash, D., Hofheinz, D., Kiltz, E., Peikert, C.: Bonsai trees, or how to delegate a lattice basis. In: Gilbert, H. (ed.) EUROCRYPT 2010. LNCS, vol. 6110, pp. 523–552. Springer, Heidelberg (2010). https://doi.org/10.1007/978-3-642-13190-5_27
10. Chen, J., Li, Y., Wen, J., Weng, J.: Identity-based matchmaking encryption from standard assumptions. Cryptology ePrint Archive, Report 2022/1246 (2022)
11. Chen, J., Wee, H.: Fully, (almost) tightly secure IBE and dual system groups. In: Canetti, R., Garay, J.A. (eds.) CRYPTO 2013. LNCS, vol. 8043, pp. 435–460. Springer, Heidelberg (2013). https://doi.org/10.1007/978-3-642-40084-1_25
12. Chow, S.S.M.: Removing escrow from identity-based encryption. In: Jarecki, S., Tsudik, G. (eds.) PKC 2009. LNCS, vol. 5443, pp. 256–276. Springer, Heidelberg (2009). https://doi.org/10.1007/978-3-642-00468-1_15
13. Cocks, C.: An identity based encryption scheme based on quadratic residues. In: Honary, B. (ed.) Cryptography and Coding 2001. LNCS, vol. 2260, pp. 360–363. Springer, Heidelberg (2001). https://doi.org/10.1007/3-540-45325-3_32
14. Ema, S., Sato, Y., Emura, K., Ohigashi, T.: Implementation and evaluation of an identity-based encryption with security against the kgc. In: 2021 Ninth International Symposium on Computing and Networking Workshops (CANDARW), pp. 320–325 (2021)
15. Emura, K., Katsumata, S., Watanabe, Y.: Identity-based encryption with security against the KGC: a formal model and its instantiation from lattices. In: Sako, K., Schneider, S., Ryan, P.Y.A. (eds.) ESORICS 2019. LNCS, vol. 11736, pp. 113–133. Springer, Cham (2019). https://doi.org/10.1007/978-3-030-29962-0_6
16. Emura, K., Katsumata, S., Watanabe, Y.: Identity-based encryption with security against the KGC: a formal model and its instantiations. Theor. Comput. Sci. **900**, 97–119 (2022)
17. Francati, D., Guidi, A., Russo, L., Venturi, D.: Identity-based matchmaking encryption without random oracles. Cryptology ePrint Archive, Report 2021/1660 (2021)
18. Gentry, C., Peikert, C., Vaikuntanathan, V.: Trapdoors for hard lattices and new cryptographic constructions. In: 40th ACM STOC, pp. 197–206 (2008)
19. Goldwasser, S., et al.: Multi-input functional encryption. In: Nguyen, P.Q., Oswald, E. (eds.) EUROCRYPT 2014. LNCS, vol. 8441, pp. 578–602. Springer, Heidelberg (2014). https://doi.org/10.1007/978-3-642-55220-5_32
20. Goyal, V., Jain, A., Koppula, V., Sahai, A.: Functional encryption for randomized functionalities. In: Dodis, Y., Nielsen, J.B. (eds.) TCC 2015. LNCS, vol. 9015, pp. 325–351. Springer, Heidelberg (2015). https://doi.org/10.1007/978-3-662-46497-7_13

21. Izabachène, M., Pointcheval, D.: New anonymity notions for identity-based encryption. In: Ostrovsky, R., De Prisco, R., Visconti, I. (eds.) SCN 2008. LNCS, vol. 5229, pp. 375–391. Springer, Heidelberg (2008). https://doi.org/10.1007/978-3-540-85855-3_25
22. Rouselakis, Y., Waters, B.: Efficient statically-secure large-universe multi-authority attribute-based encryption. In: Böhme, R., Okamoto, T. (eds.) FC 2015. LNCS, vol. 8975, pp. 315–332. Springer, Heidelberg (2015). https://doi.org/10.1007/978-3-662-47854-7_19
23. Shamir, A.: Identity-based cryptosystems and signature schemes. In: Blakley, G.R., Chaum, D. (eds.) CRYPTO 1984. LNCS, vol. 196, pp. 47–53. Springer, Heidelberg (1985). https://doi.org/10.1007/3-540-39568-7_5
24. Wang, Y., Wang, B., Lai, Q., Zhan, Y.: Identity-based matchmaking encryption with stronger security and instantiation on lattices. Cryptology ePrint Archive, Report 2022/1718 (2022)

Multi-input Functional Encryption for Unbounded Inner Products

Bishnu Charan Behera(✉) and Somindu C. Ramanna

Department of Computer Science and Engineering, Indian Institute of Technology Kharagpur, Kharagpur, India
bishnu_charan_behera@iitkgp.ac.in, somindu@cse.iitkgp.ac.in

Abstract. In this work, we propose a construction for *Multi-Input Inner Product Encryption* (MIPFE) that can handle vectors of variable length in different encryption slots. This construction is the first of its kind, as all existing MIPFE schemes allow only equal length vectors. The scheme is constructed in the private key setting, providing privacy for both message as well as the function, thereby achieving the so-called *full-hiding* security. Our MIPFE scheme uses bilinear groups of prime order and achieves security under well studied cryptographic assumptions, namely, the symmetric external Diffie-Hellman assumption.

Keywords: Functional encryption (FE) · inner-product FE · multi-input FE · unbounded vectors

1 Introduction

Functional encryption (FE) [1–5] is a modern cryptographic primitive that generalizes *public key encryption* (PKE). Compared to traditional cryptographic approaches, FE offers more flexibility in sharing and dispersing information. As the name suggests, FE allows users to retrieve some function of the message, where an owner of a master secret key can generate a secret key sk_f for any function f, which can be used to recover $f(m)$ from the ciphertext ct_m of the message m.

In a *multi-input functional encryption* (MIFE) [6–9] there are multiple encryption slots to encrypt messages in different slots independently. The decryption key of MIFE decrypts n ciphertexts simultaneously to evaluate the joint functionality of the n messages. MIFE system is useful in scenarios when information to be processed together is supplied at different points of time or by multiple parties. Applications of MIFE include data mining over encrypted data coming from multiple sources, the multi-client delegation of computations to external servers, processing encrypted streaming data, non-interactive differentially private data releases, etc. The research on MIFE can be broadly characterized into two categories. The first category mainly emphasizes on the construction of MIFE for general multi-input functionalities such as Turing machines or arbitrary polynomial-size circuits. However, such construction relies on very strong cryptographic primitives like indistinguishability obfuscation, single-input FE

M. Zhang et al. (Eds.): ProvSec 2023, LNCS 14217, pp. 274–289, 2023.
https://doi.org/10.1007/978-3-031-45513-1_15

for general circuits, etc. On the other hand, the second approach focuses on the construction of efficient MIFE system based on standard cryptographic assumptions for specific multi-input functionalities like comparison or multi-input inner product.

In an *inner product functional encryption* (IPFE) [10–14], the secret key $\mathsf{sk}_{\mathbf{y}}$ for vector $\mathbf{y}$ can reveal $\langle \vec{x}, \mathbf{y} \rangle$ from the ciphertext $\mathsf{ct}_{\vec{x}}$ for the vector $\vec{x}$. The inner product is an interesting functionality because we can directly compute the weighted mean from the encrypted data. The inner product version of MIFE is called *multi-input inner product functional encryption* (MIPFE) [15–19]. In MIPFE, there are several encryption slots to encrypt vectors $\{\vec{x}_\iota\}_{\iota \in S}$ in different slots independently. The decryption key $\mathsf{sk}_{\{\mathbf{y}_\iota\}_{\iota \in S}}$ of MIPFE can reveal $\sum_{\iota \in S} \langle \vec{x}_\iota, \mathbf{y}_\iota \rangle$ from the ciphertext ct_ι for all $\iota \in S$. The FE schemes can be broadly categorized into two types. The first type specifically provides message confidentiality. On the other hand, the second type defines a unified notion called *full-hiding security* where function privacy in addition to message privacy is guaranteed. To motivate the utility of function privacy, we cite an example from [19]: Consider a scenario when a hospital subscribes to an external cloud server to store its patient's medical records. To ensure the confidentiality of the medical record while performing various computations on the outsourced data remotely from time to time, a promising option for the hospital is to use a FE scheme where data can be encrypted locally before uploading to the cloud server. Now, when the hospital wants the information of all patients suffering from a certain disease, it must provide a functional decryption key to the cloud server to retrieve all the required information. However, if function privacy is not ensured, it may leak certain confidential information of some public figures (if someone is on the hospital record). It may damage their publicity resulting in financial loss. This situation is clearly undesirable from a privacy perspective.

To address this issue, many recent works have been initiated both in the single-input and multi-input settings. However, it has been observed that the function privacy in private key settings provides better security in comparison to the public key settings. In order to achieve it in a public key setting, the function must be chosen from certain high-entropy distribution. Instead, the extent of function privacy is much stronger in the private key setting. Even though it is a potential tool for function privacy, only a handful number of research works exist in the literature.

The work of Lin [20] computes the inner products of arbitrary polynomial degrees, where the standard inner product is a degree 2 function. But, it is a multilinear map-based construction. However, the work of Datta et al. [19] is much more practical. They proposed two constructions of MIPFE. The first design is a MIPFE function private scheme supporting a polynomial number of encryption slots. And, the second design is capable of handling an apriori unbounded number of encryption slots and multi-input inner product functions with arbitrary slot index sets of any polynomial size. Both the constructions obtained security under standard k-LIN assumptions.

In all existing MIPFE construction, the size of vectors at different slots is pre-determined and all public parameters of the system are chosen based on that.

This makes them incapable of handling variable-length vectors at different slots. A layman approach to overcome this problem is to fix the size m to be arbitrarily large. This, however, would lead to large parameters whose size typically grows linearly in m. A natural question is whether there exists an MIPFE scheme with the parameters being completely unconstrained by the lengths of the vectors in keys and ciphertexts. In fact, MIPFE with variable-length vectors has many real-life applications. Consider n hospitals holding already shared private keys and each of these hospitals uses the FE system to store patient records on a cloud server. Suppose organization Z is curious about the weighted average of a specific medical outcome for all of the patients at these facilities. In that case, it can obtain a decryption key to bring up the needed outcome. But the existing constructions cannot handle this scenario, as it is not possible for these n hospitals to have the same number of patients. A solution to this problem is to use an MIPFE scheme that can handle variable length vectors at each slot.

Our Contributions In this work, we solve the above-mentioned problem in the private key setting. Our construction of private-key MIPFE scheme is based on bilinear groups of prime order and achieves a unified notion of security called *full-hiding* security. We closely follow techniques from [21]. Security relies on the standard SXDH assumption. We consider two standard indexing methods from [21], namely *consecutive* and *separate*. Each vector element gets indexed automatically according to its position in consecutive settings. For instance, in (a, b, c), a is indexed to 1, b to 2 and c to 3. On the other hand, in separate indexing, each vector is specified with an index set. Let's assume (a, b, c) is indexed according to set $\{2, 6, 7\}$, that means a is indexed at 2, b at 6 and c at 7. For decryption, we use a form, namely *ct-dominant*. In a ct-dominant scheme, the decryption process works only if the index set of the decryption vector is a subset of the index set of the encryption vector. That is, if D_{sk} is the index set for secret key sk and D_{ct} is the index set for ciphertext ct, then we have $D_{\mathsf{sk}} \subseteq D_{\mathsf{ct}}$ for each encryption slot ι.

We now provide a brief overview of the construction. Let $e : \mathbb{G}_1 \times \mathbb{G}_2 \to \mathbb{G}_T$ be an asymmetric bilinear map of prime order p. The master secret key is a pair of dual orthogonal bases $(\mathbf{B}_\iota, \mathbf{B}_\iota^*)$ for the vector spaces $\mathbb{G}_1^n$ and $\mathbb{G}_2^n$ along with scalars $\{s_\iota\}$ for each slot ι. For each slot ι, the ciphertext and secret key corresponding to vectors $\mathbf{x}_\iota$ and $\mathbf{y}_\iota$ respectively are of the form $(\pi_{\iota,i}(i, 1), s_\iota, x_{\iota,i}, z_\iota, 0, 0)\mathbf{B}_\iota$ and $(\rho_{\iota,i}(-1, i), u_\iota, y_{\iota,i}, r_{\iota,i}, 0, 0)\mathbf{B}_\iota^*$, respectively. The indexing technique from [4] is used in the first two prefixes. These two prefix dimensions specify the vector's index, and only if the indices of both the ciphertext and secret key are equal, correct decryption is possible. The last two dimensions are not used in the real scheme but reserved for defining semi-functional spaces in the proof of security. In [17], a secret key component of the form $k_T = e(P_1, P_2)^{\sum_\iota z_\iota r}$ is used to prevent partial leak of information. We follow the similar steps to avoid any partial leak, we use $k_T = e(P_1, P_2)^{-\sum_{\iota \in [n]} |D_\iota| s_\iota u_\iota}$, where $|D_\iota|$ is the cardinality of vectors in slot ι, s_ι is part of master secret and u_ι is the random scalar used for key generation.

The key and ciphertext are designed as shown above considering four main aspects. First, the slot matching is done through the dual orthogonal bases $(\mathbf{B}_\iota, \mathbf{B}^*_\iota)$. Next, index matching is done through the indexing technique in the first two prefixes. The fifth component is used to prevent the re-composition of ciphertext. Suppose, the slot size is 2 with encryption vectors $\vec{x}_1$ and $\vec{x}_2$ for slots 1 and 2, respectively. And decryption vectors $\mathbf{y}_1$ and $\mathbf{y}_2$. In the multi-input settings, the decryption algorithm should reveal $\langle \mathbf{x}_1, \mathbf{y}_1\rangle + \langle \mathbf{x}_2, \mathbf{y}_2\rangle$ but not the individual inner products $\langle \mathbf{x}_1, \mathbf{y}_1\rangle$ and $\langle \mathbf{x}_2, \mathbf{y}_2\rangle$. To prevent this partial leak of information, we add s_ι for each slot in the master secret key. And, there is a target $\mathbb{G}_T$-component k_T in the secret key as mentioned above, which cancels the other factors to reveal the desired result. More importantly, to obtain the joint evaluation over $\vec{x}_\iota$'s and $\mathbf{y}_\iota$'s, we need ciphertext for each slot $\iota \in [n]$.

Our indexing technique is inspired by the public key IPFE construction of [21]. On the other hand, the private key construction in [21] is more efficient. For each index, a dual orthonormal bases is generated using a pseudo-random function keyed by the master secret key k. It is natural to ask whether an extension of the same leads to a more efficient MIPFE scheme. Though we do not rule this out, observe that we need different dimensions in the dual orthonormal bases in order to match both slots and indices of vectors in each slot. We use n different dual orthonormal bases corresponding to the n slots in our construction, which are generated and stored as part of the master secret key in the setup phase.

2 Preliminaries

2.1 Notation

We write $x_1, \ldots, x_k \xleftarrow{\text{R}} \mathcal{X}$ to indicate that $x_1, \ldots, x_k$ are sampled independently from a set $\mathcal{X}$ according to some distribution R (U denotes uniform distribution). For a (probabilicstic) algorithm $\mathcal{A}$, $y \longleftarrow \mathcal{A}(x)$ means that y is chosen according to the output distribution of $\mathcal{A}$ on input x. A function $f : \mathbb{N} \rightarrow \mathbb{R}$ is called *negligible* in $m (\in \mathbb{N})$ if for every constant $c > 0$, $\exists m_0 \in \mathbb{N}$ such that $f(m) < 1/m^c$ for all $m \geq m_0$. We write a negligible function in m as $\mathsf{negl}(m)$. For a natural number n, denote the set $\{1, 2, \ldots, n\}$ by $[n]$. For a prime p, we denote by $\mathbb{Z}_p$ the field of order p. Vectors over $\mathbb{Z}_p$ will be represented by bold face lower case letters (e.g. $\mathbf{v}$). $\mathbb{Z}_p^{n\times n}$ denotes the set of all $n \times n$ matrices over $\mathbb{Z}_p$ and $\mathsf{GL}_n(\mathbb{Z}_p)$, the general linear group of degree n over $\mathbb{Z}_p$ consisting of all invertible $n \times n$ matrices over $\mathbb{Z}_p$. We denote matrices over $\mathbb{Z}_p$ by bold-face upper case letters (e.g. $\mathbf{A}$). $\mathbf{A}^T$ denotes the transpose of matrix $\mathbf{A}$ and $\mathbf{A}^* = (\mathbf{A}^{-1})^T$ denotes the orthonormal dual basis of $\mathbf{A}$. $\mathbf{I}_n$ denotes the identity matrix of dimension n. For vectors $\mathbf{u} = (u_1, \ldots, u_n)$ and $\mathbf{v} = (v_1, \ldots, v_n)$, $\langle \mathbf{u}, \mathbf{v}\rangle$ denotes their inner product $\sum_{i=1}^n u_i v_i$.

Inner Products of Unbounded Vectors. An unbounded vector is written as $\mathbf{x} = (x_i)_{i\in D}$ where D, a finite subset of $\mathbb{N}^*$ is called the domain of $\mathbf{x}$. In this paper, $x_i \in \mathbb{Z}_p$ for all $i \in D$, where p is defined by the bilinear map used in the construction of our encryption scheme. Given two vectors $\mathbf{x} = (x_i)_{i \in D}$ and $\mathbf{y} = (y_i)_{i \in D'}$, the inner product $\langle \mathbf{x}, \mathbf{y} \rangle$ is a function defined as:

$$\langle \mathbf{x}, \mathbf{y} \rangle = \sum_{i \in D \cap D'} x_i y_i$$

where the domains D and D' are non-empty finite subsets of $\mathbb{N}^*$. In the ct-dominant setting D' would be a subset of D. For simplicity we assume that $D = [m]$ for some $m \in \mathbb{N}$ and $D' \subseteq [m]$.

2.2 Bilinear Groups and Related Assumptions

A bilinear map $\mathcal{G} = (\mathbb{G}_1, \mathbb{G}_2, \mathbb{G}_T, P_1, P_2, e, p)$ consists of cyclic groups $\mathbb{G}_1, \mathbb{G}_2, \mathbb{G}_T$ of prime order p with the first two groups given by generators P_1, P_2 respectively and an *efficiently computable* map $e : \mathbb{G}_1 \times \mathbb{G}_2 \to \mathbb{G}_T$, with the following two properties:

Bilinearity: $e(aQ_1, bQ_2) = e(Q_1, Q_2)^{ab}$, for all $Q_1 \in \mathbb{G}_1$, $Q_2 \in \mathbb{G}_2$ and $a, b \in \mathbb{Z}_p$.
Non-degeneracy: $e(P_1, P_2)$ is a generator for $\mathbb{G}_T$ unless $P_1 = 0$ or $P_2 = 0$ where $P_1 \in \mathbb{G}_1$, $P_2 \in \mathbb{G}_2$.

The bilinear group generator $\mathsf{GroupGen}(\vartheta)$ takes a security parameter ϑ as input and returns a bilinear map $\mathcal{G}$ over a ϑ-bit prime p.

We represent an element $aP_\tau \in \mathbb{G}_\tau$ for $\tau \in \{1, 2\}$ as $[a]_\tau$ and an element $e(P_1, P_2)^a \in \mathbb{G}_T$ as $[a]_T$, where P_τ is a generator of G_τ. Given $[a]_\tau$ it is generally hard to obtain a. Observe that for $a, b \in \mathbb{Z}_p$, given $[a]_\tau, [b]_\tau$, one can compute $[a + b]_\tau$ as $[a]_\tau + [b]_\tau$. Furthermore, given $[a]_1, [b]_2$, one can compute $[ab]_T$ as $e([a]_1, [b]_2)$. For $\mathbf{A} = (a_{i,j})_{i,j \in [n]} \in \mathbb{Z}_p^{n \times n}$, $[\mathbf{A}]_\tau$ is defined as $([a_{i,j}]_\tau)_{i,j \in [n]}$. Similarly, for a vector $\mathbf{x} = (x_1, \ldots, x_n) \in \mathbb{Z}_p^n$, $[\mathbf{x}]_\tau$ is defined as $([x_1]_\tau, \ldots, [x_n]_\tau)$.

Dual Pairing Vector Spaces. Let $n \in \mathbb{N}$ and let $(\mathbf{B}, \mathbf{B}^*)$ be dual orthonormal bases for $\mathbb{Z}_p^n$. Then $[\mathbf{B}]_1$ and $[\mathbf{B}^*]_2$ are dual orthonormal bases of vector spaces $\mathbb{G}_1^n$ and $\mathbb{G}_2^n$ respectively. The following two properties hold:

- For vectors $\mathbf{x}, \mathbf{y} \in \mathbb{Z}_p^n$, $e([\mathbf{x}]_1, [\mathbf{y}]_2) = e(P_1, P_2)^{\langle \mathbf{x}, \mathbf{y} \rangle}$.
- Suppose that $\mathbf{B}$ is chosen at random from $\mathsf{GL}_n(\mathbb{Z}_p)$. Then for arbitrary vectors $\mathbf{x}_1, \ldots, \mathbf{x}_k, \mathbf{y}_1, \ldots, \mathbf{y}_l \in \mathbb{Z}_p^n$ and any matrix $\mathbf{M} \in \mathsf{GL}_n(\mathbb{Z}_p)$, the distributions $\left(\{\mathbf{x}_i \mathbf{B}\}_{i \in [k]}, \{\mathbf{y}_i \mathbf{B}^*\}_{i \in [l]}\right)$ and $\left(\{\mathbf{x}_i \mathbf{M} \mathbf{B}\}_{i \in [k]}, \{\mathbf{y}_i \mathbf{M}^* \mathbf{B}^*\}_{i \in [l]}\right)$ are identical.

Diffie-Hellman Assumption. Let $\tau \in \{1, 2\}$. Given an asymmetric bilinear map $\mathcal{G} \leftarrow \mathsf{GroupGen}(\vartheta)$, along with

$$[a]_\tau, [e]_\tau, [t_\beta]_\tau = [ae + \beta f]_\tau$$

where $a, e, f \xleftarrow{\text{U}} \mathbb{Z}_p$, the DDH$\tau$ problem asks to determine whether $\beta = 0$ or $\beta = 1$.
For a probabilistic polynomial time adversary $\mathscr{A}$, define

$$\mathsf{Adv}_{\mathscr{A}}^{\mathcal{G}}(\text{DDH}\tau)(\vartheta) = \left| \Pr[\mathscr{A}(\mathcal{G}, [a]_\tau, [e]_\tau, [t_0]_\tau) = 1] - \Pr[\mathscr{A}(\mathcal{G}, [a]_\tau, [e]_\tau, [t_1]_\tau) = 1] \right|.$$

The decisional Diffie-Hellman assumption in group G_T (DDHT) assumption holds if for all PPT adversaries $\mathscr{A}$, $\mathsf{Adv}^{\mathcal{G}}_{\mathscr{A}}(\text{DDH}T)(\vartheta) \leq \mathsf{negl}(\vartheta)$.

The symmetric external Diffie-Hellman (SXDH) assumption is said to hold if both DDH1 and DDH2 hold.

2.3 Multi-input IPFE with Variable Vector Size

Multi-input Inner Product Functionality. A bounded-arity multi-input inner product function family $\mathcal{F}^{\mathcal{B}}_{\vartheta} = \{\mathcal{F}^{\mathcal{B}}_n\}$ for some $\mathcal{B} \in \mathbb{N}$, where each sub-families $\mathcal{F}^{\mathcal{B}}_n$ consists of bounded-arity multi-input inner product functions $f_{\{\mathbf{y}_\iota\}_{\iota\in[n]}}$. Each function $f_{\{\mathbf{y}_\iota\}_{\iota\in[n]}} : \mathbb{Z}^{m_1} \times \mathbb{Z}^{m_2} \times ... \times \mathbb{Z}^{m_n} \to \mathbb{Z}$, with the associated vectors $\{y_\iota\}_{\iota\in[n]}$ each belonging to $\mathbb{Z}^{m'_i}$, is defined as

$$f_{\{\mathbf{y}_\iota\}\iota\in[n]}(\mathbf{x}_1, \ldots, \mathbf{x}_n) = \sum_{\iota\in[n]} \langle \mathbf{x}_\iota, \mathbf{y}_\iota \rangle$$

for all sets of vectors $\{\mathbf{x}_\iota\}_{\iota\in[n]}$ of variable length over $\mathbb{Z}$ and the value of the inner product $\langle \mathbf{x}_\iota, \mathbf{y}_\iota \rangle \leq \mathcal{B}$. Since we work on the ct-dominant setting, we define the inner product $\langle \mathbf{x}_\iota, \mathbf{y}_\iota \rangle = \sum_{i\in m'_\iota} x_{\iota,i} \cdot y_{\iota,i}$ assuming $[m'_\iota] \subseteq [m_\iota]$.

Private Key MIPFE Over Variable-Length Vectors. A private key *bounded-arity* multi-input inner product function encryption scheme over variable-length vectors associated with function family $\mathcal{F}^{\mathcal{B}}_n$ is specified by the following polynomial-time algorithms.

Setup$(1^\vartheta, n, \mathcal{B})$: Takes the security parameter 1^ϑ, the arity $n \in \mathbb{N}$ for the multi-input inner product functionality, and the upper bound $\mathcal{B}$ on the values of inner products. It generates and outputs the master secret key msk and the public parameters pp.

KeyGen$(\mathsf{pp}, \mathsf{msk}, \{\mathbf{y}_\iota\}_{\iota\in[n]})$: It takes as input pp, msk and the set of vectors $\{\mathbf{y}_\iota\}_{\iota\in[n]}$ of variable lengths such that $\mathbf{y}_\iota \in \mathbb{Z}^{m'_\iota}$ for all $\iota \in [n]$. Finally, it outputs the decryption key sk corresponding to the given set of vectors.

Encrypt$(\mathsf{pp}, \mathsf{msk}, \iota, \mathbf{x}_\iota)$: Takes as input pp, the master secret msk, an index $\iota \in [n]$ and a vector $\mathbf{x}_\iota \in \mathbb{Z}^{m_\iota}$ for slot ι. It outputs the ciphertext ct_ι.

Decrypt$(\mathsf{pp}, \mathsf{sk}, \{\mathsf{ct}_\iota\}_{\iota\in[n]})$: Takes as input pp, a decryption key sk and set of n ciphertexts $\{\mathsf{ct}_\iota\}_{\iota\in[n]}$. It outputs $d \in \mathbb{Z}$ or special symbol $\perp$ to indicate failure.

Correctness. The above scheme is said to be *correct* if for all security parameters 1^ϑ, for all n polynomial in ϑ, for all sets of n vectors $\{\mathbf{x}_\iota\}_{\iota\in[n]}, \{\mathbf{y}_\iota\}_{\iota\in[n]}$ with $\langle \mathbf{x}_\iota, \mathbf{y}_\iota \rangle \leq \mathcal{B}$, we have

$$\Pr\left[d = \sum_{\iota\in[n]} \langle \mathbf{x}_\iota, \mathbf{y}_\iota \rangle \;\middle|\; \begin{array}{l} (\mathsf{pp}, \mathsf{msk}) \leftarrow \mathsf{Setup}(1^\vartheta, n, \mathcal{B}) \\ \mathsf{sk} \leftarrow \mathsf{KeyGen}(\mathsf{pp}, \mathsf{msk}, \{\mathbf{y}_\iota\}_{\iota\in[n]}) \\ \{\mathsf{ct}_\iota \leftarrow \mathsf{Encrypt}(\mathsf{pp}, \mathsf{msk}, \iota, \mathbf{x}_\iota)\}_{\iota\in[n]} \\ d \leftarrow \mathsf{Decrypt}(\mathsf{pp}, \mathsf{sk}, \{\mathsf{ct}_\iota\}_{\iota\in[n]}) \end{array} \right] \geq 1 - \mathsf{negl}(\vartheta)$$

for some negligible function negl.

Full-Hiding Security. The notion of full-hiding security for private key MIPFE arity n can be formalized through the following experiment $\mathsf{Expt}_{\mathscr{A}}(\beta)$, for $\beta \xleftarrow{U} \{0,1\}$, where $\mathscr{A}$ is the adversary and $\mathscr{C}$ is the challenger.

Setup: $\mathscr{C}$ generates $(\mathsf{pp}, \mathsf{msk}) \leftarrow \mathsf{Setup}(1^{\vartheta}, n, \mathcal{B})$ and passes the public parameter pp to $\mathscr{A}$. $\mathscr{C}$ generates $\beta \xleftarrow{U} \{0,1\}$.

Key Query Phase: $\mathscr{A}$ adaptively makes (polynomially many in ϑ) key extraction queries: for the jth secret key query the $\mathscr{A}$ provides pair of vector sets $(\{\mathbf{y}_{j,\iota,0}\}_{\iota\in[n]}, \{\mathbf{y}_{j,\iota,1}\}_{\iota\in[n]})$ such that $\mathbf{y}_{j,\iota,0}, \mathbf{y}_{j,\iota,1} \in \mathbb{Z}^{m'_{j,\iota}}$; $\mathscr{C}$ then responds with the secret key $\mathsf{sk}_j^* \leftarrow \mathsf{KeyGen}(\mathsf{pp}, \mathsf{msk}, \{\mathbf{y}_{j,\iota,\beta})\}$.

Ciphertext Query Phase: $\mathscr{A}$ adaptively makes a polynomial number of ciphertext queries. Each query consists of a pair of vectors $(\mathbf{x}_{\mu_\iota,\iota,0}, \mathbf{x}_{\mu_\iota,\iota,1}) \in (\mathbb{Z}^{m_{\mu_\iota,\iota}})^2$ for slot ι. In response to μ_ι ciphertext query numbered μ_ι, $\mathscr{C}$ returns $\mathsf{ct}^*_{\mu_\iota,\iota} \leftarrow \mathsf{Encrypt}(\mathsf{pp}, \mathsf{msk}, \mathbf{x}_{\mu_\iota,\iota,\beta})$. We assume that the total number of decryption key queries made by $\mathscr{A}$ is q_{sk} and the total number of ciphertext queries for index ι is $q_{\mathsf{ct},\iota}$ with the restriction that the number of queries for each index be atleast one i.e., $q_{\mathsf{ct},\iota} \geq 1$ for all $\iota \in [n]$. Also, For all $j \in [q_{\mathsf{sk}}]$ and for all $(\mu_1, ..., \mu_n) \in [q_{\mathsf{ct},1}] \times ... \times [q_{\mathsf{ct},n}]$, we must have

$$\sum_{\iota\in[n]} \langle \mathbf{x}_{\mu_\iota,\iota,0}, \mathbf{y}_{j,\iota,0} \rangle = \sum_{\iota\in[n]} \langle \mathbf{x}_{\mu_\iota,\iota,1}, \mathbf{y}_{j,\iota,1} \rangle$$

Guess: $\mathscr{A}$ concludes the game with a guess $\beta' \in \{0,1\}$.

The MIPFE scheme is said to achieve fully hiding if for any PPT adversary $\mathscr{A}$ the advantage is,

$$\mathsf{Adv}^{\mathrm{MIPFE}}_{\mathscr{A}}(\vartheta) = |\Pr[\mathsf{Expt}^{\mathrm{MIPFE}}_{\mathscr{A}}(0) = 1] - \Pr[\mathsf{Expt}^{\mathrm{MIPFE}}_{\mathscr{A}}(1) = 1]| \leq \mathsf{negl}(\vartheta)$$

for some negligible function negl.

3 Our Variable Vector Length MIPFE Scheme

3.1 Construction

$\mathsf{Setup}(1^{\vartheta})$: Takes a security parameter 1^{ϑ}, generates bilinear group $(\mathcal{G} = (\mathbb{G}_1, \mathbb{G}_2, \mathbb{G}_T, P_1, P_2, e, p)) \leftarrow \mathsf{GroupGen}(1^{\vartheta})$, chooses $s_\iota \xleftarrow{U} \mathbb{Z}_p, \mathbf{B}_\iota \xleftarrow{U} \mathsf{GL}_7(\mathbb{Z}_p)$ $\forall \iota \in [n]$. And it sets,

$$\mathsf{pp} = \mathcal{G}, \mathsf{msk} = \{s_\iota, \mathbf{B}_\iota, \mathbf{B}^*_\iota\}_{\iota\in[n]}$$

$\mathsf{Encrypt}(\mathsf{pp}, \mathsf{msk}, \iota, \mathbf{x}_\iota = (x_{\iota,i})_{i\in[m_\iota]})$: The size of vector $\mathbf{x}_\iota$ is m_ι. Choose $\pi_{\iota,i}, z_\iota \xleftarrow{U} \mathbb{Z}_p$, $\forall i \in [m_\iota]$. Compute

$$\mathbf{c}_{\iota,i} = (\pi_{\iota,i}(i,1), s_\iota, x_{\iota,i}, z_\iota, 0, 0)\,\mathbf{B}_\iota, \ \forall i \in [m_\iota]$$

Output the ciphertext $\mathsf{ct}_\iota = (\iota, \{[\mathbf{c}_{\iota,i}]_1\}_{i\in m_\iota})$.

KeyGen$(\mathsf{pp}, \mathsf{msk}, \{D_\iota, y_\iota = (y_{\iota,i})_{i\in D_\iota}\}_{\iota\in[n]})$: On input a set of vectors $\mathbf{y}_\iota$ defined over index set D_ι for $\iota \in [n]$, choose $u_\iota, \rho_{\iota,i}, r_{\iota,i} \xleftarrow{\text{U}} \mathbb{Z}_p$, $\forall \iota \in [n], i \in D_\iota$ such that $\sum_{i\in D_\iota} r_{\iota,i} = 0$. It sets

$$\mathbf{k}_{\iota,i} = (\rho_{\iota,i}(-1,i), u_\iota, y_{\iota,i}, r_{\iota,i}, 0, 0)\,\mathbf{B}_\iota^*, \ \ \forall \iota \in [n], i \in D_\iota$$
$$\hat{k} = e(P_1, P_2)^{-\sum_{\iota\in[n]}|D_\iota|u_\iota s_\iota}$$

where $|D_\iota|$ represents the cardinality of the domain D_ι. Output the secret key $\mathsf{sk} = (\hat{k}, \{D_\iota, \{[\mathbf{k}_{\iota,i}]_2\}_{i\in D_\iota}\}_{\iota\in[n]})$.

Decrypt$(\mathsf{pp}, \mathsf{sk}, \{\mathsf{ct}_\iota\}_{\iota\in[n]})$: If $D_\iota \subseteq [m_\iota], \forall \iota \in [n]$, then compute

$$h = \hat{k} \prod_{\iota\in[n]} \prod_{i\in D_\iota} e([\mathbf{c}_{\iota,i}]_1, [\mathbf{k}_{\iota,i}]_2)$$

Then compute and output the discrete logarithm of h to base $e(P_1, P_2)$.

Correctness. For any set of n ciphertexts $\{\mathsf{ct}_\iota = (\iota, \{[\mathbf{c}_{\iota,i}]_1\}_{i\in m_\iota})\}_{\iota\in[n]}$, and decryption key $\mathsf{sk} = (\hat{k}, \{D_\iota, \{[\mathbf{k}_{\iota,i}]_2\}_{i\in D_\iota}\}_{\iota\in[n]})$, if $D_\iota \subseteq [m_\iota]$ for all $\iota \in [n]$, we have

$$\begin{aligned}
h &= \hat{k} \prod_{\iota\in[n]} \prod_{i\in D_\iota} e([\mathbf{c}_{\iota,i}]_1, [\mathbf{k}_{\iota,i}]_2) \\
&= \hat{k} \prod_{\iota\in[n]} e(P_1, P_2)^{\sum_{i\in D_\iota}\langle \mathbf{c}_{\iota,i}, \mathbf{k}_{\iota,i}\rangle} \\
&= \hat{k} \prod_{\iota\in[n]} e(P_1, P_2)^{\sum_{i\in D_\iota} x_{\iota,i}y_{\iota,i} + u_\iota s_\iota + r_{\iota,i} z_\iota} \\
&= \hat{k} \prod_{\iota\in[n]} e(P_1, P_2)^{\sum_{i\in D_\iota} x_{\iota,i}y_{\iota,i} + u_\iota s_\iota} \\
&= \hat{k} \cdot e(P_1, P_2)^{\sum_{\iota\in[n]}\langle \mathbf{x}_\iota, \mathbf{y}_\iota\rangle + |D_\iota|u_\iota s_\iota} \\
&= e(P_1, P_2)^{-\sum_{\iota\in[n]}|D_\iota|u_\iota s_\iota} e(P_1, P_2)^{\sum_{\iota\in[n]}\langle \mathbf{x}_\iota, \mathbf{y}_\iota\rangle + |D_\iota|u_\iota s_\iota} \\
&= e(P_1, P_2)^{\sum_{\iota\in[n]}\langle \mathbf{x}_\iota, \mathbf{y}_\iota\rangle}
\end{aligned}$$

Computing discrete logarithm produces the desired result which is $\sum_{\iota\in[n]}\langle \mathbf{x}_\iota, \mathbf{y}_\iota\rangle$. Given that $\sum_{\iota\in[n]}\langle \mathbf{x}_\iota, \mathbf{y}_\iota\rangle \leq n\mathcal{B}$ which is polynomial in ϑ, it is feasible to compute discrete logarithm of h to base $e(P_1, P_2)$.

3.2 Proof of Security

Theorem 1. *Our* MIPFE *scheme is fully hiding under the restriction that the adversary makes atleast one ciphertext query for each slot provided the* SXDH *assumption holds in the underlying pairing groups. More formally, for any PPT* *adversary $\mathscr{A}$ against our* MIPFE *scheme, there exist a PPT adversary $\mathscr{B}$ for* SXDH *such that*

$$\mathsf{Adv}_{\mathscr{A}}^{\mathrm{MIPFE}}(\vartheta) \leq \left(2q_{\mathsf{sk}} + 3\sum_{\iota\in[n]} q_{\mathsf{ct},\iota}\right) \mathsf{Adv}_{\mathscr{B}}^{\mathrm{SXDH}}(\vartheta) + 2^{-\Omega(\vartheta)}$$

Proof. The proof starts with $\mathsf{Expt}_{\mathscr{A}}^{\mathrm{MIPFE}}(0)$ which is game 0 and ends with $\mathsf{Expt}_{\mathscr{A}}^{\mathrm{MIPFE}}(1)$. In the intermediate games, we change the ciphertext and secret key from $\beta = 0$ to $\beta = 1$ using both computational and information theoretic arguments. We assume that the adversary $\mathscr{A}$ makes atleast one ciphertext query for each slot ι. The sequence of games is as follows.

Game 0: This game is same as the real security game when $\beta = 0$. For all $\iota \in [n], \mu_\iota \in [q_{\mathsf{ct},\iota}]$, in response to μ_ι^{th} ciphertext query for the slot ι with a pair of vectors $(\mathbf{x}_{\mu_\iota,\iota,0}, \mathbf{x}_{\mu_\iota,\iota,1})$ of same length $m_{\mu_\iota,\iota}$, the challenger returns the ciphertext $\mathsf{ct}_{\mu_\iota,\iota} = (\iota, \{[\mathbf{c}_{\mu_\iota,\iota,i}]_1\}_{i\in[m_{\mu_\iota,\iota}]})$ where

$$\mathbf{c}_{\mu_\iota,\iota,i} = (\pi_{\mu_\iota,\iota,i}(i,1), s_\iota, x_{\mu_\iota,\iota,0,i}, z_{\mu_\iota,\iota}, 0, 0)\mathbf{B}_\iota, \;\; \forall i \in [m_{\mu_\iota,\iota}]$$

and for all $j \in [q_{\mathsf{sk}}]$, the jth secret key query with two sets of n vectors each, $(\{\mathbf{y}_{j,\iota,0}\}_{\iota\in[n]}, \{\mathbf{y}_{j,\iota,1}\}_{\iota\in[n]})$ with vectors for slot ι defined over domain $D_{j,\iota}$, the adversary is provided $\mathsf{sk}_j = (\hat{k}_j, \left(D_{j,\iota}, \{[\mathbf{k}_{j,\iota,i}]_2\}_{i\in D_{j,\iota}}\right)_{\iota\in[n]})$, where

$$\mathbf{k}_{j,\iota,i} = (\rho_{j,\iota,i}(-1,i), u_{j,\iota}, y_{j,\iota,0,i}, r_{j,\iota,i}, 0, 0)\mathbf{B}_\iota^*, \forall\iota \in [n], i \in D_{j,\iota}$$
$$\hat{k}_j = e(P_1, P_2)^{-\sum_{\iota\in[n]}|D_{j,\iota}|s_\iota u_{j,\iota}}$$

where $\sum_{i\in D_{j,\iota}} r_{j,\iota,i} = 0$.

Game 1-v-1, $v \in [q_{\mathsf{sk}}]$: Game 1-0-2 is same as Game 0. This game is same as Game 1-$(v-1)$-2, except that the v-th secret key query is responded as

$$\mathbf{k}_{v,\iota,i} = (\rho_{v,\iota,i}(-1,i), u_{v,\iota}, y_{v,\iota,0,i}, r_{v,\iota,i}, 0, \boxed{\bar{r}_{v,\iota,i}})\mathbf{B}_\iota^*, \forall\iota \in [n], i \in D_{v,\iota}$$
$$\hat{k}_v = e(P_1, P_2)^{-\sum_{\iota\in[n]}|D_{v,\iota}|s_\iota u_{v,\iota}}$$

where $\sum_{i\in D_{v,\iota}} \bar{r}_{v,\iota,i} = 0$.

Game 1-v-2, $v \in [q_{\mathsf{sk}}]$: This game is same as Game 1-v-1 except that the v-th secret key query is responded as

$$\mathbf{k}_{v,\iota,i} = (\rho_{v,\iota,i}(-1,i), u_{v,\iota}, y_{v,\iota,0,i}, r_{v,\iota,i}, \boxed{y_{v,\iota,1,i}}, \bar{r}_{v,\iota,i})\mathbf{B}_\iota^*, \forall\iota \in [n], i \in D_{v,\iota}$$
$$\hat{k}_v = e(P_1, P_2)^{-\sum_{\iota\in[n]}|D_{v,\iota}|s_\iota u_{v,\iota}}$$

Game 2-ι-μ_ι-1, $\iota \in [n], \mu_\iota \in [q_{\mathsf{ct},\iota}]$: Game 2-0-$q_{\mathsf{ct},0}$-3 is same as Game 1-$q_{\mathsf{sk}}$-2. This game is same as Game 2-$(\iota-1)$-$q_{\mathsf{ct},\iota-1}$-3 if $\mu_\iota = 1$ or Game 2-ι-$(\mu_\iota - 1)$-3 if $\mu_\iota > 1$ except that the μ_ι-th ciphertext query for ι-th slot corresponding to pair of vectors $(\mathbf{x}_{\mu_\iota,\iota,0}, \mathbf{x}_{\mu_\iota,\iota,1})$ with same length $m_{\mu_\iota,\iota}$ is responded with $\mathsf{ct}_{\mu_\iota,\iota} = (\iota, \{[\mathbf{c}_{\mu_\iota,\iota,i}]_1\}_{i\in m_{\mu_\iota,\iota}})$, where

$$\mathbf{c}_{\mu_\iota,\iota,i} = (\pi_{\mu_\iota,\iota,i}(i,1), s_\iota, x_{\mu_\iota,\iota,0,i}, z_{\mu_\iota,\iota}, 0, \boxed{z'_{\mu_\iota,\iota}})\mathbf{B}_\iota, \ \ \forall i \in [m_{\mu_\iota,\iota}]$$

Here, the random scalars are chosen as in Game 2-$(\iota-1)$-$q_{ct,\iota-1}$-3 or Game 2-ι-$(\mu_\iota - 1)$-3 according as $\mu_\iota = 1$ or $\mu_\iota > 1$.

Game 2-ι-μ_ι-2, $\iota \in [n], \mu_\iota \in [q_{\mathsf{ct},\iota}]$: This game is same as Game 2-ι-μ_ι-1 except that

$$\mathbf{c}_{\mu_\iota,\iota,i} = (\pi_{\mu_\iota,\iota,i}(i,1), s_\iota, \boxed{0}, z_{\mu_\iota,\iota}, \boxed{x_{\mu_\iota,\iota,1,i}}, z'_{\mu_\iota,\iota})\mathbf{B}_\iota, \ \ \forall i \in [m_{\mu_\iota,\iota}]$$

Game 2-ι-μ_ι-3, $\iota \in [n], \mu_\iota \in [q_{\mathsf{ct},\iota}]$: This game is same as Game 2-ι-μ_ι-2 except that

$$\mathbf{c}_{\mu_\iota,\iota,i} = (\pi_{\mu_\iota,\iota,i}(i,1), s_\iota, 0, z_{\mu_\iota,\iota}, x_{\mu_\iota,\iota,1,i}, \boxed{0})\mathbf{B}_\iota, \ \ \forall i \in [m_{\mu_\iota,\iota}]$$

Game 3: This game is same as Game 2-n-$q_{\mathsf{ct},n}$-3 except that all the ciphertext and secret key are responded as

$$\begin{aligned}
\mathbf{c}_{\mu_\iota,\iota,i} &= (\pi_{\mu_\iota,\iota,i}(i,1), s_\iota, \boxed{x_{\mu_\iota,\iota,1,i}}, z_{\mu_\iota,\iota}, \boxed{0}, 0)\mathbf{B}_\iota, \ \ \forall i \in [m_{\mu_\iota,\iota}] \\
\mathbf{k}_{j,\iota,i} &= (\rho_{v,\iota,i}(-1,i), u_{j,\iota}, \boxed{y_{j,\iota,1,i}}, r_{j,\iota,i}, \boxed{y_{j,\iota,0,i}}, \bar{r}_{j,\iota,i})\mathbf{B}^*_\iota, \ \ \forall \iota \in [n], i \in D_{j,\iota} \\
\hat{k}_j &= e(P_1, P_2)^{-\sum_{\iota\in[n]} |D_{j,\iota}| s_\iota u_{j,\iota}}
\end{aligned}$$

Game 4: This game is same as the real security game when $\beta = 1$. For all $\iota \in [n], \mu_\iota \in [q_{\mathsf{ct},\iota}]$, in response to μ_ι^{th} ciphertext query for the slot ι with a pair of vectors $(\mathbf{x}_{\mu_\iota,0,\iota}, \mathbf{x}_{\mu_\iota,\iota,1})$ of same length $m_{\mu_\iota,\iota}$, it returns the ciphertext $\mathsf{ct}_{\mu_\iota,\iota} = (\iota, \{[\mathbf{c}_{\mu_\iota,\iota,i}]_1\}_{i\in m_{\mu_\iota,\iota}})$ where

$$\mathbf{c}_{\mu_\iota,\iota,i} = (\pi_{t_\iota,\iota,i}(i,1), s_\iota, x_{\mu_\iota,\iota,1,i}, z_{\mu_\iota,\iota}, 0, 0)\mathbf{B}_\iota, \ \ \forall i \in [m_{\mu_\iota,\iota}]$$

and for all $j \in [q_{\mathsf{sk}}]$, the jth secret key query on two sets of n vectors each $\left(\{\mathbf{y}_{j,\iota,0}\}_{\iota\in[n]}, \{\mathbf{y}_{j,\iota,1}\}_{\iota\in[n]}\right)$ defined over domain $D_{j,\iota}$ for slot ι, is responded with $\mathsf{sk}_j = (\hat{k}_j, \left(D_{j,\iota}, \{[\mathbf{k}_{j,\iota,i}]_2\}_{i\in D_{j,\iota}}\right)_{\iota\in[n]})$, where

$$\begin{aligned}
\mathbf{k}_{j,\iota,i} &= (\rho_{j,\iota,i}(-1,i), u_{j,\iota}, y_{j,\iota,1,i}, r_{j,\iota,i}, \boxed{0,0})\mathbf{B}^*_\iota, \ \ \forall \iota \in [n], i \in D_{j,\iota} \\
\hat{k}_j &= e(P_1, P_2)^{-\sum_{\iota\in[n]} |D_{j,\iota}| s_\iota u_{j,\iota}}
\end{aligned}$$

where $\sum_{i\in D_{j,\iota}} r_{j,\iota,i} = 0$.

Let E_X denote the probability that the adversary $\mathscr{A}$ wins in game X.

Lemma 1. *There exists a PPT algorithm $\mathscr{B}$ for* DDH2 *such that*

$$\left|\Pr[\mathsf{E}_{1\text{-}(v-1)\text{-}2}] - \Pr[\mathsf{E}_{1\text{-}v\text{-}1}]\right| \leq \mathsf{Adv}_{\mathscr{B}}^{\mathrm{DDH2}}(\vartheta) + 2^{-\Omega(\vartheta)}$$

Proof. Adversary $\mathscr{B}$ receives an instance of DDH i.e., $(\mathcal{G}, [a]_2, [e]_2, [t_\beta]_2)$, and it sets $\mathsf{pp} = \mathcal{G}$. It samples $\mathbf{W}_\iota \xleftarrow{\text{U}} \mathsf{GL}_7(\mathbb{Z}_p),\ \forall \iota \in [n]$. It sets,

$$\mathbf{B}_\iota = \begin{pmatrix} \mathbf{I}_4 & & & \\ & 0 & 0 & 1 \\ & 0 & 1 & 0 \\ & 1 & 0 & -a \end{pmatrix} \mathbf{W}_\iota, \quad \mathbf{B}_\iota^* = \begin{pmatrix} \mathbf{I}_4 & & & \\ & a & 0 & 1 \\ & 0 & 1 & 0 \\ & 1 & 0 & 0 \end{pmatrix} \mathbf{W}_\iota^*, \forall \iota \in [n]$$

Then $\mathscr{B}$ simulates the ciphertext and secret key query in the following manner. All the ciphertext query is respond as follows:

$$[\mathbf{c}_{\mu_\iota,\iota,i}]_1 = [(\pi_{\mu_\iota,\iota,i}(i,1), s_\iota, x_{\mu_\iota,\iota,0,i}, z_{\mu_\iota,\iota}, 0, 0)\mathbf{B}_\iota]_1,\ \ \forall i \in [m_{\mu_\iota,\iota}]$$

And the secret key query is responded with $\hat{k}_j = e(P_1, P_2)^{-\sum_{\iota\in[n]} |D_{j,\iota}| s_\iota u_{j,\iota}}$ for all $j \in [q_{\mathrm{sk}}]$, and

$$[\mathbf{k}_{j,\iota,i}]_2 = \begin{cases} [(\rho_{j,\iota,i}(-1,i), u_{j,\iota}, y_{j,\iota,0,i}, r_{j,\iota,i}, y_{j,\iota,1,i}, \bar{r}_{j,\iota,i})\mathbf{B}_\iota^*]_2,\ \forall \in D_{j,\iota}, & (j < v) \\ [(\rho_{j,\iota,i}(-1,i), u_{j,\iota}, y_{j,\iota,0,i}, r_{j,\iota,i}, 0, 0)\mathbf{B}_\iota^*]_2,\ \forall \in D_{j,\iota}, & (j > v) \end{cases}$$

Now, for the v-th secret key query, $\mathscr{B}$ responds as follows:

$$r'_{v,\iota,i} \xleftarrow{\text{U}} \mathbb{Z}_p \text{ such that } \sum_{i\in D_{v,\iota}} r'_{v,\iota,i} = 0$$

$$\begin{aligned}[\mathbf{k}_{v,\iota,i}]_2 &= [(\rho_{v,\iota,i}(-1,i), u_{v,\iota}, y_{v,\iota,0,i}, 0, 0, 0)\mathbf{B}_\iota^* + r'_{v,\iota,i}(0,0,0,0,t_\beta,0,e)\mathbf{W}_\iota^*]_2 \\ &= [(\rho_{v,\iota,i}(-1,i), u_{v,\iota}, y_{v,\iota,0,i}, er'_{v,\iota,i}, 0, \beta f r'_{v,\iota,i})\mathbf{B}_\iota^*]_2\end{aligned}$$

implicitly setting $r_{v,\iota,i} = er'_{v,\iota,i}$. Now, $\mathscr{A}$'s view is same as Game 1-$(v-1)$-2 if $\beta = 0$, otherwise it is Game 1-v-1 with $\bar{r}_{v,\iota,i} = fr'_{v,\iota,i}$.

Lemma 2. $\left|\Pr[\mathsf{E}_{1\text{-}v\text{-}1}] - \Pr[\mathsf{E}_{1\text{-}v\text{-}2}]\right| \leq 2^{-\Omega(\vartheta)}$.

Proof. We choose $\mathbf{B}_\iota \xleftarrow{\text{U}} \mathsf{GL}_7(\mathbb{Z}_p), \forall \iota \in [n]$. Now, all the ciphertext query are responded as:

$$[\mathbf{c}_{\mu_\iota,\iota,i}]_1 = [(\pi_{\mu_\iota,\iota,i}(i,1), s_\iota, x_{\mu_\iota,\iota,0,i}, z_{\mu_\iota,\iota}, 0, 0)\mathbf{B}_\iota]_1,\ \ \forall i \in [m_{\mu_\iota,\iota}]$$

And the secret key query is responded with $\hat{k}_j = e(P_1, P_2)^{-\sum_{\iota\in[n]} |D_{j,\iota}| s_\iota u_{j,\iota}}$ for all $j \in [q_{sk}]$, and

$$[\mathbf{k}_{j,\iota,i}]_2 = \begin{cases} [(\rho_{j,\iota,i}(-1,i), u_{j,\iota}, y_{j,\iota,0,i}, r_{j,\iota,i}, y_{j,\iota,1,i}, \bar{r}_{j,\iota,i})\mathbf{B}_\iota^*]_2,\ \forall \in D_{j,\iota}, & (j < v) \\ [(\rho_{j,\iota,i}(-1,i), u_{j,\iota}, y_{j,\iota,0,i}, r_{j,\iota,i}, 0, 0)\mathbf{B}_\iota^*]_2,\ \forall \in D_{j,\iota}, & (j > v) \end{cases}$$

Now, for the v-th secret key query, we sample $w \xleftarrow{\text{U}} \{0,1\}$, and set

$$[\mathbf{k}_{v,\iota,i}]_2 = [(\rho_{v,\iota,i}(-1,i), u_{v,\iota}, y_{v,\iota,0,i}, r_{j,\iota,i}, wy_{v,\iota,1,i}, \bar{r}_{j,\iota,i})\mathbf{B}_\iota^*]_2$$

$\mathscr{A}$'s view is same as Game 1-v-1 if $w = 0$, otherwise it is Game 1-v-2.

Lemma 3. *There exist a PPT adversary* $\mathscr{B}$ *for* DDH1 *such that* $\forall \iota \in [n]$,

$$\left|\Pr[\mathsf{E}_{2\text{-}\iota\text{-}\mu_\iota\text{-}1}] - \Pr[\mathsf{E}_{2\text{-}(\iota-1)\text{-}q_{\mathsf{ct},\iota-1}\text{-}3}]\right| \leq \mathsf{Adv}_{\mathscr{B}}^{\mathrm{DDH1}}(\vartheta) + 2^{-\Omega(\vartheta)}, \text{if } \mu_\iota = 1$$
$$\left|\Pr[\mathsf{E}_{2\text{-}\iota\text{-}\mu_\iota\text{-}1}] - \Pr[\mathsf{E}_{2\text{-}\iota\text{-}(\mu_\iota-1)\text{-}3}]\right| \leq \mathsf{Adv}_{\mathscr{B}}^{\mathrm{DDH1}}(\vartheta) + 2^{-\Omega(\vartheta)}, \text{if } \mu_\iota > 1$$

Proof. Adversary $\mathscr{B}$ receives an instance of DDH1 $(\mathcal{G}, [a]_1, [e]_1, [t_\beta]_1)$ and it sets $\mathsf{pp} = \mathcal{G}$. It samples $\mathbf{W}_\iota \xleftarrow{\mathrm{U}} \mathsf{GL}_7(\mathbb{Z}_p), \forall \iota \in [n]$ and defines

$$\mathbf{B}_\iota = \begin{pmatrix} \mathbf{I}_4 & & & \\ & a & 0 & 1 \\ & 0 & 1 & 0 \\ & 1 & 0 & 0 \end{pmatrix} \mathbf{W}_\iota, \quad \mathbf{B}_\iota^* = \begin{pmatrix} \mathbf{I}_4 & & & \\ & 0 & 0 & 1 \\ & 0 & 1 & 0 \\ & 1 & 0 & -a \end{pmatrix} \mathbf{W}_\iota^*, \forall \iota \in [n].$$

All the secret key query are responded as,

$$r'_{j,\iota,i}, r''_{j,\iota,i} \xleftarrow{\mathrm{U}} \mathbb{Z}_p, \text{such that} \sum_{i \in D_{j,\iota}} r'_{j,\iota,i} = \sum_{i \in D_{j,\iota}} r''_{j,\iota,i} = 0$$

$$\begin{aligned}[\mathbf{k}_{j,\iota,i}]_2 &= [(\rho_{j,\iota,i}(-1,i), u_{j,\iota}, y_{j,\iota,0,i}, r'_{j,\iota,i}, y_{j,\iota,1,i}, 0)\mathbf{B}_\iota^* + (0,0,0,0,r''_{j,\iota,i},0,0)\mathbf{W}_\iota^*]_2 \\ &= [(\rho_{j,\iota,i}(-1,i), u_{j,\iota}, y_{j,\iota,0,i}, r'_{j,\iota,i} + ar''_{j,\iota,i}, y_{j,\iota,1,i}, r''_{j,\iota,i})\mathbf{B}_\iota^*]_2\end{aligned}$$

And sets $\hat{k}_j = e(P_1, P_2)^{-\sum_{\iota \in [n]} |D_{j,\iota}| s_\iota u_{j,\iota}}$. We can implicitly set $r_{j,\iota,i} = r'_{j,\iota,i} + ar''_{j,\iota,i}$ and $\bar{r}_{j,\iota,i} = r''_{j,\iota,i}$.
Now, all the ciphertext queries are responded as follows,

(i) If $(\iota', q_\iota) < (\iota, u_\iota)$, then the ciphertext is returned as,

$$[\mathbf{c}_{q_\iota,\iota',i}]_1 = [(\pi_{q_\iota,\iota',i}(i,1), s_\iota, 0, z_{q_\iota,\iota'}, x_{q_\iota,\iota',1,i}, 0)\mathbf{B}_{\iota'}]_1, \ \ \forall i \in [m_{q_\iota,\iota'}]$$

(ii) If $(\iota', q_\iota) = (\iota, u_\iota)$, then $\forall i \in [m_{u_\iota,\iota}]$ the ciphertext is returned as,

$$\begin{aligned}[\mathbf{c}_{u_\iota,\iota,i}]_1 &= [(\pi_{u_\iota,\iota,i}(i,1), s_\iota, x_{u_\iota,\iota,0,i}, 0,0,0)\mathbf{B}_\iota + z'_{u_\iota,\iota}(0,0,0,0,t_\beta,0,e)\mathbf{W}_\iota]_1 \\ &= [(\pi_{u_\iota,\iota,i}(i,1), s_\iota, x_{u_\iota,\iota,0,i}, ez'_{u_\iota,\iota}, 0, \beta f z'_{u_\iota,\iota})\mathbf{B}_\iota]_1\end{aligned}$$

(iii) If $(\iota', q_\iota) > (\iota, u_\iota)$, the ciphertext is returned as,

$$[\mathbf{c}_{q_\iota,\iota',i}]_1 = [(\pi_{q_\iota,\iota',i}(i,1), s_\iota, x_{q_\iota,\iota',0,i}, z_{q_\iota,\iota'}, 0, 0)\mathbf{B}_{\iota'}]_1, \ \ \forall i \in [m_{q_\iota,\iota'}]$$

Adversary $\mathscr{B}$ perfectly simulated the secret key and ciphertext queries. View of adversary $\mathscr{A}$ is equally distributed between Game 2-ι-μ_ι-1 and Game 2-$(\iota - 1)$-$q_{\mathsf{ct},\iota-1}$-3 or Game 2-ι-$(\mu_\iota - 1)$-3, depending on $\mu_\iota = 1$ or $\mu_\iota > 1$ according as $\beta = 0$ or $\beta = 1$.

Lemma 4. $\left|\Pr[\mathsf{E}_{2\text{-}\iota\text{-}\mu_\iota\text{-}1}] - \Pr[\mathsf{E}_{2\text{-}\iota\text{-}\mu_\iota\text{-}2}]\right| \leq 2^{-\Omega(\vartheta)}$.

Proof. We choose $\mathbf{B}_\iota \xleftarrow{\text{U}} \mathsf{GL}_7(\mathbb{Z}_p), \forall \iota \in [n]$. Now the j-th secret key is responded as,

$$\mathbf{k}_{j,\iota,i} = (\rho_{j,\iota,i}(-1,i), u_{j,\iota}, y_{j,\iota,0,i}, r_{j,\iota,i}, y_{j,\iota,1,i}, \bar{r}_{j,\iota,i})\mathbf{B}_\iota^*, \ \ \forall \iota \in [n], i \in D_{j,\iota}$$
$$\hat{k}_j = e(P_1, P_2)^{-\sum_{\iota\in[n]} |D_{j,\iota}| s_\iota u_{j,\iota}}$$

And for the μ_ι-th ciphertext query, we sample $\hat{w} \xleftarrow{\text{U}} \{0,1\}$ and set

$$[\mathbf{c}_{\mu_\iota,\iota,i}]_1 = [(\pi_{\mu_\iota,\iota,i}(i,1), s_\iota, (1-\hat{w})x_{\mu_\iota,\iota,0,i}, z_{\mu_\iota,\iota}, \hat{w}x_{\mu_\iota,\iota,1,i}, z'_{\mu_\iota,\iota})\mathbf{B}_\iota]_1, \ \ \forall i \in [m_{\mu_\iota,\iota}]$$

$\mathscr{A}$'s view is same as Game 2-ι-μ_ι-1 if $\hat{w} = 0$, otherwise it is Game 2-ι-μ_ι-2.

Lemma 5. *There exists a PPT adversary* $\mathscr{B}$ *for DDH1 s.t.*

$$\left| \Pr[\mathsf{E}_{2\text{-}\iota\text{-}\mu_\iota\text{-}2}] - \Pr[\mathsf{E}_{2\text{-}\iota\text{-}\mu_\iota\text{-}3}] \right| \le \mathsf{Adv}_{\mathscr{B}}^{\mathrm{SXDH}}(\vartheta) + 2^{-\Omega(\vartheta)}$$

Proof. $\mathscr{B}$ receives an instance of DDH1 $(\mathcal{G}, [a]_1, [e]_1, [t_\beta]_1)$ and it sets $\mathsf{pp} = \mathcal{G}$. It samples $\mathbf{W}_\iota \xleftarrow{\text{U}} \mathsf{GL}_7(\mathbb{Z}_p), \forall \iota \in [n]$ and defines

$$\mathbf{B}_\iota = \begin{pmatrix} \mathbf{I}_4 & & & \\ & a & 0 & 1 \\ & 0 & 1 & 0 \\ & 1 & 0 & 0 \end{pmatrix} \mathbf{W}_\iota, \quad \mathbf{B}_\iota^* = \begin{pmatrix} \mathbf{I}_4 & & & \\ & 0 & 0 & 1 \\ & 0 & 1 & 0 \\ & 1 & 0 & -a \end{pmatrix} \mathbf{W}_\iota^*, \forall \iota \in [n]$$

All the secret key query are responded as,

$$r'_{j,\iota,i}, r''_{j,\iota,i} \leftarrow \mathbb{Z}_p, \text{such that} \sum_{i\in D_{j,\iota}} r'_{j,\iota,i} = \sum_{i\in D_{j,\iota}} r''_{j,\iota,i} = 0$$

$$\begin{aligned}[\mathbf{k}_{j,\iota,i}]_2 &= [(\rho_{j,\iota,i}(-1,i), u_{j,\iota}, y_{j,\iota,0,i}, r'_{j,\iota,i}, y_{j,\iota,1,i}, 0)\mathbf{B}_\iota^* + (0,0,0,0,r''_{j,\iota,i},0,0)\mathbf{W}_\iota^*]_2 \\ &= [(\rho_{j,\iota,i}(-1,i), u_{j,\iota}, y_{j,\iota,0,i}, r'_{j,\iota,i} + ar''_{j,\iota,i}, y_{j,\iota,1,i}, r''_{j,\iota,i})\mathbf{B}_\iota^*]_2\end{aligned}$$

And sets $\hat{k}_j = e(P_1, P_2)^{-\sum_{\iota\in[n]} |D_{j,\iota}| s_\iota u_{j,\iota}}$. We can implicitly set $r_{j,\iota,i} = r'_{j,\iota,i} + ar''_{j,\iota,i}$ and $\bar{r}_{j,\iota,i} = r''_{j,\iota,i}$.
Now, all the ciphertext queries are responded as follows,

$$\begin{aligned}[\mathbf{c}_{u_\iota,\iota,i}]_1 &= [(\pi_{u_\iota,\iota,i}(i,1), s_\iota, 0, 0, x_{u_{\iota,\iota,1,i}}, 0)\mathbf{B}_\iota + \tilde{z}_{u_\iota,\iota}(0,0,0,0,t_\beta,0,e)\mathbf{W}_\iota]_1 \\ &= [(\pi_{u_\iota,\iota,i}(i,1), s_\iota, 0, e\tilde{z}_{u_\iota,\iota}, x_{u_{\iota,\iota,1,i}}, \beta f\tilde{z}_{u_\iota,\iota})\mathbf{B}_\iota]_1\end{aligned}$$

implicitly setting $z_{\mu_\iota,\iota} = e\tilde{z}_{u_\iota,\iota}$. Now $\mathscr{A}'s$ view is same as Game 2-ι-μ_ι-2 if $\beta = 1$ implicitly setting $z'_{u_\iota,\iota} = \beta f\tilde{z}_{u_\iota,\iota}$; otherwise it is Game 2-ι-μ_ι-3.

Lemma 6. $\Pr[\mathsf{E}_{2\text{-}n\text{-}q_{ct,n}\text{-}3}] = \Pr[\mathsf{E}_3]$.

Proof. We choose $\mathbf{B}_\iota \xleftarrow{\mathrm{U}} \mathsf{GL}_7(\mathbb{Z}_p), \forall \iota \in [n]$. And define,

$$\mathbf{W}_\iota = \begin{pmatrix} \mathbf{I}_3 & & & & \\ & & & 1 & \\ & & 1 & & \\ & 1 & & & \\ & & & & 1 \end{pmatrix} \mathbf{B}_\iota, \quad \mathbf{W}^*_\iota = \begin{pmatrix} \mathbf{I}_3 & & & & \\ & & & 1 & \\ & & 1 & & \\ & 1 & & & \\ & & & & 1 \end{pmatrix} \mathbf{B}^*_\iota, \forall \iota \in [n]$$

Then all the ciphertext and secret key query are responded as,

$$\begin{aligned} \mathbf{c}_{\mu_\iota,\iota,i} &= (\pi_{\mu_\iota,\iota,i}(i,1), s_\iota, 0, z_{\mu_\iota,\iota}, x_{\mu_\iota,\iota,1,i}, 0)\mathbf{B}_\iota \\ &= (\pi_{\mu_\iota,\iota,i}(i,1), s_\iota, x_{\mu_\iota,\iota,1,i}, z_{\mu_\iota,\iota}, 0, 0)\mathbf{W}_\iota \\ \mathbf{k}_{j,\iota,i} &= (\rho_{j,\iota,i}(-1,i), u_{j,\iota}, y_{j,\iota,0,i}, r_{j,\iota,i}, y_{j,\iota,1,i}, \bar{r}_{j,\iota,i})\mathbf{B}^*_\iota \\ &= (\rho_{j,\iota,i}(-1,i), u_{j,\iota}, y_{j,\iota,1,i}, r_{j,\iota,i}, y_{j,\iota,0,i}, \bar{r}_{j,\iota,i})\mathbf{W}^*_\iota \end{aligned}$$

So, $\mathscr{A}$'s view is identical to both the games.

Lemma 7. *For any* PPT *adversary* $\mathscr{A}$*, there exists a* PPT *adversary* $\mathscr{B}$ *for SXDH s.t.*

$$\left|\Pr[\mathrm{E}_3] - \Pr[\mathrm{E}_4]\right| \leq q_{\mathrm{sk}}\mathrm{Adv}^{\mathrm{SXDH}}_{\mathscr{B}} + 2^{-\Omega(\vartheta)}$$

Proof. The proof is done the same way as Game 0 to Game 1-q_{sk}-2 but in the reverse order.

4 Conclusion

In this work, we have proposed a construction of private-key MIPFE with an apriori bounded slot size that can handle variable-length vectors at each slot. We proved security under the SXDH assumption. It would be interesting to further explore whether there exist constructions of MIPFE that can withstand an *arbitrary* number of encryption slots with variable-length vectors at each slot.

Acknowledgments. The first author expresses thanks to University Grants Commission (UGC), India for their support.

References

1. Boneh, D., Sahai, A., Waters, B.: Functional encryption: definitions and challenges. In: Ishai, Y. (ed.) TCC 2011. LNCS, vol. 6597, pp. 253–273. Springer, Heidelberg (2011). https://doi.org/10.1007/978-3-642-19571-6_16
2. Boneh, D., Sahai, A., Waters, B.: Functional encryption: a new vision for public-key cryptography. Commun. ACM **55**(11), 56–64 (2012)
3. O'Neill, A.: Definitional issues in functional encryption. Cryptology ePrint Archive (2010)

4. Okamoto, T., Takashima, K.: Fully secure functional encryption with general relations from the decisional linear assumption. In: Rabin, T. (ed.) CRYPTO 2010. LNCS, vol. 6223, pp. 191–208. Springer, Heidelberg (2010). https://doi.org/10.1007/978-3-642-14623-7_11
5. Agrawal, S., Gorbunov, S., Vaikuntanathan, V., Wee, H.: Functional encryption: new perspectives and lower bounds. In: Canetti, R., Garay, J.A. (eds.) CRYPTO 2013. LNCS, vol. 8043, pp. 500–518. Springer, Heidelberg (2013). https://doi.org/10.1007/978-3-642-40084-1_28
6. Goldwasser, S., et al.: Multi-input functional encryption. In: Nguyen, P.Q., Oswald, E. (eds.) EUROCRYPT 2014. LNCS, vol. 8441, pp. 578–602. Springer, Heidelberg (2014). https://doi.org/10.1007/978-3-642-55220-5_32
7. Boneh, D., Lewi, K., Raykova, M., Sahai, A., Zhandry, M., Zimmerman, J.: Semantically secure order-revealing encryption: multi-input functional encryption without obfuscation. In: Oswald, E., Fischlin, M. (eds.) EUROCRYPT 2015. LNCS, vol. 9057, pp. 563–594. Springer, Heidelberg (2015). https://doi.org/10.1007/978-3-662-46803-6_19
8. Badrinarayanan, S., Gupta, D., Jain, A., Sahai, A.: Multi-input functional encryption for unbounded arity functions. In: Iwata, T., Cheon, J.H. (eds.) ASIACRYPT 2015. LNCS, vol. 9452, pp. 27–51. Springer, Heidelberg (2015). https://doi.org/10.1007/978-3-662-48797-6_2
9. Brakerski, Z., Komargodski, I., Segev, G.: Multi-input functional encryption in the private-key setting: stronger security from weaker assumptions. In: Fischlin, M., Coron, J.-S. (eds.) EUROCRYPT 2016. LNCS, vol. 9666, pp. 852–880. Springer, Heidelberg (2016). https://doi.org/10.1007/978-3-662-49896-5_30
10. Abdalla, M., Benhamouda, F., Kohlweiss, M., Waldner, H.: Decentralizing inner-product functional encryption. In: Lin, D., Sako, K. (eds.) PKC 2019. LNCS, vol. 11443, pp. 128–157. Springer, Cham (2019). https://doi.org/10.1007/978-3-030-17259-6_5
11. Agrawal, S., Libert, B., Maitra, M., Titiu, R.: Adaptive simulation security for inner product functional encryption. In: Kiayias, A., Kohlweiss, M., Wallden, P., Zikas, V. (eds.) PKC 2020. LNCS, vol. 12110, pp. 34–64. Springer, Cham (2020). https://doi.org/10.1007/978-3-030-45374-9_2
12. Abdalla, M., Catalano, D., Gay, R., Ursu, B.: Inner-product functional encryption with fine-grained access control. In: Moriai, S., Wang, H. (eds.) ASIACRYPT 2020. LNCS, vol. 12493, pp. 467–497. Springer, Cham (2020). https://doi.org/10.1007/978-3-030-64840-4_16
13. Agrawal, S., Libert, B., Stehlé, D.: Fully secure functional encryption for inner products, from standard assumptions. In: Robshaw, M., Katz, J. (eds.) CRYPTO 2016. LNCS, vol. 9816, pp. 333–362. Springer, Heidelberg (2016). https://doi.org/10.1007/978-3-662-53015-3_12
14. Datta, P., Dutta, R., Mukhopadhyay, S.: Functional encryption for inner product with full function privacy. In: Cheng, C.-M., Chung, K.-M., Persiano, G., Yang, B.-Y. (eds.) PKC 2016. LNCS, vol. 9614, pp. 164–195. Springer, Heidelberg (2016). https://doi.org/10.1007/978-3-662-49384-7_7
15. Tomida, J.: Tightly secure inner product functional encryption: multi-input and function-hiding constructions. Theor. Comput. Sci. **833**, 56–86 (2020)
16. Abdalla, M., Benhamouda, F., Gay, R.: From single-input to multi-client inner-product functional encryption. In: Galbraith, S.D., Moriai, S. (eds.) ASIACRYPT 2019. LNCS, vol. 11923, pp. 552–582. Springer, Cham (2019). https://doi.org/10.1007/978-3-030-34618-8_19

17. Abdalla, M., Gay, R., Raykova, M., Wee, H.: Multi-input inner-product functional encryption from pairings. In: Coron, J.-S., Nielsen, J.B. (eds.) EUROCRYPT 2017. LNCS, vol. 10210, pp. 601–626. Springer, Cham (2017). https://doi.org/10.1007/978-3-319-56620-7_21
18. Abdalla, M., Catalano, D., Fiore, D., Gay, R., Ursu, B.: Multi-input functional encryption for inner products: function-hiding realizations and constructions without pairings. In: Shacham, H., Boldyreva, A. (eds.) CRYPTO 2018. LNCS, vol. 10991, pp. 597–627. Springer, Cham (2018). https://doi.org/10.1007/978-3-319-96884-1_20
19. Datta, P., Okamoto, T., Tomida, J.: Full-hiding (unbounded) multi-input inner product functional encryption from the k-linear assumption. IACR Cryptol. ePrint Arch., p. 61 (2018)
20. Lin, H.: Indistinguishability obfuscation from sxdh on 5-linear maps and locality-5 prgs. Cryptology ePrint Archive, Paper 2016/1096 (2016). https://eprint.iacr.org/2016/1096
21. Tomida, J., Takashima, K.: Unbounded inner product functional encryption from bilinear maps. Jpn. J. Ind. Appl. Math. **37**(3), 723–779 (2020). https://doi.org/10.1007/s13160-020-00419-x

FleS: A Compact and Parameter-Flexible Supersingular Isogeny Based Public Key Encryption Scheme

Weihan Huang, Min Luo(✉), Cong Peng, and Debiao He

Key Laboratory of Aerospace Information Security and Trusted Computing of Ministry of Education, School of Cyber Science and Engineering, Wuhan University, Wuhan, China
{weihanhuang,mluo,cpeng}@whu.edu.cn

Abstract. Post-quantum public key encryption (PKE) is an important cryptographic primitive to handle the threat from quantum computer. Isogeny-based cryptography attracts great attention due to the most compact key size. At Asiacrypt 2020, Moriya *et al.* proposed (C)SiGamal without using hash functions or transformations. At PQCrypto 2021, Fouosta *et al.* proposed SimS by simplifying SiGamal and it achieves IND-CCA security. Both of them require the prime p satisfies that $p+1$ has the factor 2^r. This limits the choice of parameters and the class group action for such a parameter is slower than CSIDH.

Targeting on constructing an efficient, parameter-flexible and secure post-quantum PKE scheme based on CSIDH, we propose FleS. Compared to SimS, FleS has almost no requirement for the parameters and has smaller key size. We carefully design a point-choosing algorithm to make FleS suitable for any parameter. We give a proof of the IND-CCA security of FleS under the CSSIDDH and CSSIKoE (Fouosta *et al.* at PQCrypto 2021) assumptions. Finally we implement FleS using CSIDH-512 parameter set. The result shows that with the same message space the key generation of FleS is 1.74× faster than SimS, the encryption is 1.17× faster than SimS and the decryption is 1.05× faster than SimS.

Keywords: Post-quantum cryptography · supersingular isogeny · PKE · CSIDH · FleS

1 Introduction

The development of the quantum computer makes the traditional public key schemes such as RSA [27], ECC [2] and their variants insecure. As a response to it, the National Institute of Standards and Technology (NIST) started a standardization to call for post-quantum secure schemes around the world.

Isogeny-based cryptography system is the youngest and least studied among the post-quantum cryptography. The earlist isogeny-based scheme can be traced back to Couveignes [11], Rostovtsev and Stolbunov [29] to design a key exchange protocol.

M. Zhang et al. (Eds.): ProvSec 2023, LNCS 14217, pp. 290–308, 2023.
https://doi.org/10.1007/978-3-031-45513-1_16

The mother hard problem behind isogeny-based crgyptography is to find an isogeny between the supersingular elliptic curves [21]. This hard problem is believed to be computationally hard for both quantum and classical computers. The first attempt in isogeny-based cryptography can be tracked to the work of Couveignes in 1997 but is not officially published [11]. Later Rostovtsev and Stolbunov restudied the work of Couveignes and designed a key exchange protocol using the isogeny between ordinary elliptic curves [29]. The proposals of the CGL hash function [8] and the SIDH key exchange protocol [21] drew the world's attention. The submission of the SIKE [3] to NIST marked a new era of the study in isogeny-based cryptography. Unfortunately, SIDH was broken by a key recovery attack proposed by Castryck *et al.* [6] and was later improved by Robert [28] and Maino *et al.* [22] to arbitrary starting curve, which makes it impossible to fix SIDH by changing the parameter set. Compared to other post-quantum cryptographys, isogeny-based cryptography is less efficient but can provide the most compact key and ciphertext size.

At Asiacrypt 2018, Castryck *et al.* proposed CSIDH [7], where "C" means "commutative". In general, CSIDH is similar to the work of Couveignes except using the isogeny between supersingular elliptic curves. At Asiacrypt 2020, De Feo *et al.* proposed SQISign [14,15], a new signature scheme based on isogeny. SQISign constructs a new method for constructing cryptography schemes using supersingular isogenies. SQISign provides the most compact size of keys and signatures and its efficiency is almost within the acceptable limits. The isogeny-based PKE schemes include SIKE [3], Séta [13], SHeals and Heals [18], and the recently proposed SiGamal [24] and SimS [19]. Among them, Séta and the PKE schemes derived from SIDH can only achieve OW-CPA security. By using hash functions or transformations [4,20], some of them can achieve IND-CPA or IND-CCA security but the additional computation cost is too expensive, making them unpractical. Unfortunately, with SIDH broken, all of them and their derived variants are insecure. At Asiacrypt 2020, Moriya *et al.* proposed (C)SiGamal PKE scheme [24], which is the first PKE scheme derived from CSIDH structure and can achieve IND-CPA security under the assumptions without any use of hash functions or complex transformations. They thought that a variant of (C)SiGamal can achieve IND-CCA security but was proved wrong later [19]. At PQCrypto 2021, Fouotsa *et al.* proposed SimS [19], a simplification of SiGamal. SimS achieves the IND-CCA security without additional expensive computation cost.

Our Contribution. In this paper, we design a new isogeny-based PKE scheme modified from SimS which we call FleS. We modify SimS and get the new proposed PKE scheme FleS. We prove the IND-CCA security of FleS.

Compared with SimS, our scheme is more flexible in the choice of parameters. SimS requires that the big prime p must have the form of $2^r\ell_1\ell_2...\ell_n - 1$ and r must be big enough to ensure the message space. Our scheme only requires the big prime p satisfies that $p + 1$ has the factors to be distinct odd primes, which is the basic requirement to apply Pohlig-Hellman algorithm to solve discrete logarithm problem (DLP). When instantiating our scheme, the user can adapt the parameter set according to the security requirement and the usage scenario.

Table 1. Comparison between FleS, SimS, SiGamal and C-SiGamal. FleS is instantiated with CSIDH-512 parameter and the message space is 256 bit, where ρ means using the seed as private key. SimS and (C)SiGamal use p_{256}.

	FleS	SimS	SiGamal	C-SiGamal
Private key	ρ	$[\mathfrak{a}]$	$\mathfrak{a}$	$\mathfrak{a}$
Size of public key	$\log_2 p$	$\log_2 p$	$2\log_2 p$	$2\log_2 p$
Size of ciphertext	$2\log_2 p$	$2\log_2 p$	$4\log_2 p$	$2\log_2 p$
Cost of class group action	1.00×	2.31×	2.58×	2.58×
Security level	IND-CCA	IND-CCA	IND-CPA	IND-CPA

For the same size of parameters, FleS has bigger message space and smaller key size than SimS. More importantly, FleS is more efficient than SimS. For the first parameter $p_{128} = 2^{130}\ell_1\ell_2 ... \ell_{60} - 1$, the size of p_{128} is 522 bits but the message space is about 128 bits. Relatively speaking, when using the parameter set CSIDH-512, the size of the big prime is about 512 bits, slightly smaller than p_{128}, but our scheme's biggest space is approximately 510 bits, almost four times as SimS when using p_{128}. In general, our scheme's biggest message space is almost the same as the size of the big prime while SimS's message space is related to the power of 2 of the big prime. Even when using the same parameter set, FleS can also change the message space according to security and efficiency needs.

Finally, we implement FleS with CSIDH-512 parameter set and set the message space to be 256 bits. As the result shows, FleS is more efficient than SimS and (C)SiGamal.

Outline. The remainder of this paper is organized as follows: in Sect. 2, we recall some basic background knowledge. In Sect. 3, we present our proposed PKE scheme FleS and the ideas to design it. In Sect. 4, we present the proof of the security of FleS. In Sect. 5, we show the implementation result of FleS and compare it with SimS and CSIDH. We conclude the paper in Sect. 6.

2 Preliminaries

In this work, p represents a big prime number and $\mathbb{F}_q$ is a finite filed of size q. We are most interested in the case $\mathbb{F}_q = \mathbb{F}_{p^2}$.

2.1 Supersingular Elliptic Curves and Isogenies

We begin by recalling some basic knowledge of elliptic curve and isogeny. For the detailed introduction, we suggest the reader to [9,30]. For an overview, we suggest [12].

Elliptic Curve. In mathematics, an elliptic curve is a smooth, projective and algebraic curve of genus one with a special point called the infinity point. We denote an elliptic curve by E. For an elliptic curve E defined over a field k, we denote $E(k)$ as the set of k-rational points of E. All these points along with the infinity point forms an abelian group.

There are many forms of representations of elliptic curve such as Weierstrass equation, Montgomery curve, Edwards curve, Hessian curve and Jacobi quartics [1]. For the isogeny-based cryptography, we are most interested in the Montgomery curve. We introduce Montgomery curve in detail for our work.

Definition 1. *A montgomery curve over a finite field K is defined by the equation*

$$By^2 = x^3 + Ax^2 + x$$

for some $A, B \in K$ satisfying $B(A^2 - 4) \neq 0$.

Different from the Weierstrass form, Montgomery form has advantages for certain computation and has been widely used in isogeny-based cryptography. The most important advantage is that we can use one coordinate, *i.e.*, the x coordinate, to represent a point. Although there may be two points to have the same x coordinate, their y coordinates are just of different signs. This representation also takes huge advantages in the computations of point adding and ladder [23].

Isogeny. We introduce the concept of isogeny. For more detailed information, readers can refer to [10,26].

Definition 2. *Let $\phi : E_1 \rightarrow E_2$ be a map from E_1 to E_2. ϕ is said to be an isogeny if ϕ is a surjective group morphism satisfying $ker\phi$ is finite and ϕ maps the infinity point of E_1 to the infinity point of E_2. Two elliptic curves are said to be isogenous if there exists an isogeny between them.*

The degree of an isogeny is its degree as a rational map. Isogenies can be divided into two categories: purely inseparable isogeny and separable isogeny. The only purely inseparable isogeny is the Frobenius isogeny. Every isogeny can be factored as a composition of a series of purely inseparable isogenies and separable isogenies. If the decomposition of an isogeny only includes purely separable isogenies, this isogeny is said to be separable or otherwise inseparable.

Every isogeny $\phi : E_1 \rightarrow E_2$ comes up with an unique isogeny $\overline{\phi} : E_2 \rightarrow E_1$ defined in the opposite direction. This isogeny has the property that

$$\phi \circ \overline{\phi} = [deg\phi]_{E_2}, \overline{\phi} \circ \phi = [deg\phi]_{E_1} \quad (1)$$

where $[m]_E$ means the m-th scaling endomorphism in the elliptic curve E. It seems that the dual isogeny is similar to an inverse except a division by degree, but we know that the DLP in elliptic curve is believed to be computationally hard.

The existence of dual isogeny means that being isogenous is an equivalence relation. All elliptic curves can be divided into isogenous equivalence classes. Isogenous curves over a field have the same number of points and the converse holds as well [31].

Theorem 1 (Tate's Theorem [31]). *If two elliptic curves over a field are isogenous, they have the same number of points and the converse holds as well.*

In our work, we mainly focus on the separable isogenies. In this sense, the degree of the isogeny is equal to the cardinality of its kernel *i.e.*

$$deg\phi = |ker\phi| \tag{2}$$

An isogeny of degree 1 is an isomorphism and two curves are isomorphic if there exists an isomorphism between them. The isomorphic curves have the same j-invariant. Using j-invariant to represent elliptic curve can half the storage. In general, isomorphic curves can be considered the same.

Since an isogeny is a group morphism, its kernel must be a subgroup of E_1. Any subgroup G of an elliptic curve E can define an isogeny ϕ with $\ker\phi = G$. The isogeny and the image curve can be computed by Velu's Formule using $O(|G|(\log p)^2)$ bits opration. It is only practical for small size subgroup [17].

Endomorphism Ring. An endomorphism is an isogeny from an elliptic curve to itself. For example, the k-th scaling $k \in \mathbb{Z}$, *i.e.*, $[k] : P \to [k]P$. All endomorphisms form a ring called the endomorphism ring denoted by $\text{End}(E)$. According to [30], the endomorphism ring $\text{End}(E)$ is isomorphic to either a quadratic imaginary field or a maximal order in a quaternion algebra. In the former the curve is said to be ordinary and otherwise supersingular.

We denote $\text{End}_{\mathbb{F}_p}(E)$ as the endomorphism ring defined over $\mathbb{F}_p$. In general, the $\mathbb{F}_p$-endormorphism ring of a supersingular elliptic curve E is isomorphic to either $\mathbb{Z}[\pi]$ or $\mathbb{Z}[\frac{1+\pi}{2}]$ [16]. For the ordinary case, we have $\text{End}(E) = \text{End}_{\mathbb{F}_p}(E)$ but for the supersingular case $\text{End}_{\mathbb{F}_p}(E) \subsetneq \text{End}(E)$. For the supersingular curve it is known that its full endomorphism ring is isomorphic to a maximal order of quaternion algebra while its endomorphism ring over $\mathbb{F}_p$ is isomorphic to a order of quadratic field $\mathbb{Q}(\sqrt{p})$. In our work, we mainly focus on the $\mathbb{F}_p$-endormorphism ring $\text{End}_{\mathbb{F}_p}(E)$ and denote it as $\text{End}_{\mathbb{F}_p}(E) = \mathcal{O}$.

2.2 Class Group Action

In this subsection, we introduce the concept of ideal class group and the group action. For further details, readers can refer to [30,32].

Definition 3 (Ideal Class Group). *Let $\mathcal{O}$ be an order of a field K. We denote by*

- *$\mathcal{I}_{\mathcal{O}}$ be the group containing invertible fractional ideals of $\mathcal{O}$.*

- $\mathcal{P}_{\mathcal{O}}$ *be the group containing fractional principal invertible ideals of* $\mathcal{O}$, i.e., *all invertible ideals of the form* $\alpha\mathcal{O}$ *for* $\alpha \in K$.

Then the ideal class group of the order $\mathcal{O}$ *is defined as:*

$$Cl(\mathcal{O}) = \mathcal{I}_{\mathcal{O}}/\mathcal{P}_{\mathcal{O}}$$

By the definition, given a fraction ideal $\mathfrak{a} \in \mathcal{I}_{\mathcal{O}}$, we denote $[\mathfrak{a}]$ as its equivalence class in $Cl(\mathcal{O})$. For two elements $\mathfrak{a}, \mathfrak{b} \in \mathcal{I}_{\mathcal{O}}$, $[\mathfrak{a}] = [\mathfrak{b}]$ is equivalent to

$$\exists \alpha \in K, \mathfrak{b} = (\alpha)\mathfrak{a} \tag{3}$$

Group Action on Supersingular Ellpitic Curevs. In our work we will focus on the order $\mathcal{O} = \text{End}_{\mathbb{F}_p}(E)$. We denote its class group by $Cl(\mathcal{O})$. Given an ideal $\mathfrak{a}$, it is natural to get a subgroup of the elliptic curve by the intersection of the kernels of all the endomorphisms in $\mathfrak{a}$, *i.e.*,

$$S_{\mathfrak{a}} = \cap_{a \in \mathfrak{a}} ker(a) \tag{4}$$

Through the subgroup $S_{\mathfrak{a}}$, we can compute an isogeny starting from E to a new curve denoted by $E/S_{\mathfrak{a}}$ or simply $[\mathfrak{a}]E$. By denoting the set of the supersingular elliptic curves whose endomorphism rings in $\mathbb{F}_p$ are isomorphic to $\mathcal{O}$ by $\varepsilon(\mathcal{O})$, we obtain a group action:

$$Cl(\mathcal{O}) \times \varepsilon(\mathcal{O}) \to \varepsilon(\mathcal{O}) \tag{5}$$

Theorem 2 (Group Action on $Cl(\mathcal{O})$ **[7]).** $Cl(\mathcal{O})$ *acts transitively and freely on* $\varepsilon(\mathcal{O})$.

$$Cl(\mathcal{O}) \times \varepsilon(\mathcal{O}) \to \varepsilon(\mathcal{O})$$
$$([\mathfrak{a}], E) \to [\mathfrak{a}]E = E/S_{\mathfrak{a}}$$

The main hard problem behind the above group action is as follow [7]:

Definition 4 (Group Action Inverse Problem (GAIP)). *Given* E, E_0 *with* $End(E_0) = End(E) = \mathcal{O}$, *find* $\mathfrak{a} \subset \mathcal{O}$ *satisfying* $E = [\mathfrak{a}]E_0$

2.3 CSIDH

At Asiacrypt 2018, Castryck *et al.* proposed CSIDH [7]. For a supersingular elliptic curve E its cardinality satisfies $|E(\mathbb{F}_p)| = p + 1$. It is obviously that if p is of the form $p = 4\ell_1\ell_2...\ell_n - 1$, we have $|E(\mathbb{F}_p)| = 4\ell_1\ell_2...\ell_n$. Such a curve has ℓ_i-torsion subgroup for all $i \in [1, n]$. Since $p = -1 \bmod \ell_i$, we have in $\mathbb{Q}(\sqrt{p})$ the prime ℓ_i spilt into

$$\ell_i\mathcal{O} = (\ell_i, \pi - 1)(\ell_i, \pi + 1) = \mathfrak{l}_i\overline{\mathfrak{l}_i} \tag{6}$$

where $\pi = \sqrt{p}$ represents the Frobenius endomorphism. Note that the kernel of the endomorphism corresponding to $\mathfrak{l}_i$ is the intersection of kernel of $[\ell_i]$ and $\pi - 1$, *i.e.*, the ℓ_i-torsion subgroup which lies in the kernel of $\pi - 1$. To be more specific, it is just the subgroup of order ℓ_i defined over $\mathbb{F}_p$. Similarly for $\overline{\mathfrak{l}_i}$, it is the ℓ_i-torsion subgroup defined over $\mathbb{F}_{p^2}$ rather than $\mathbb{F}_p$. CSIDH simply computes the isogeny and the image curve corresponding to $\mathfrak{l}_i$ or $\overline{\mathfrak{l}_i}$ using Velu's Formule, which only requires $\mathcal{O}(\ell_i(\log p)^2)$ bit operations. Since all ℓ_i are small primes, the action $[\mathfrak{l}_i]$ and $[\overline{\mathfrak{l}_i}]$ can be computed efficiently.

The security of CSIDH and its derived variants relies on the so called Commutative Supersingular Isogeny Diffie-Hellman assumption. In our work we use its decisional version.

Assumption 1. *The CSSIDDH (Commutative Supersingular Isogeny Decisional Diffie-Hellman) assumption holds for any PPT algorithm $\mathcal{A}$ that given $[\mathfrak{a}], [\mathfrak{b}], [\mathfrak{c}]$ and $F_0 := [\mathfrak{b}][\mathfrak{a}]E_0, F_1 := [\mathfrak{c}]E_0$, it has negligible advantage to distinguish the couple $(E_0, [\mathfrak{a}]E_0, [\mathfrak{b}]E_0, F_0)$ and $(E_0, [\mathfrak{a}]E_0, [\mathfrak{b}]E_0, F_1)$.*

Computing the Group Action. In the original CSIDH scheme, Castryck *et al.* [7] mentioned three methods to compute the group action and suggested the last one which is to find a basis of the ℓ-torsion subgroup over $\mathbb{F}_p$ when computing $\mathfrak{l}$ or $\mathbb{F}_{p^2}/\mathbb{F}_p$ when computing $\overline{\mathfrak{l}}$ and then applying the Velu's formulas [17] to compute the isogeny and the image curve.

2.4 Public Key Encryption

Below, we describe the formal definition of standard PKE schemes.

Definition 5 (Public Key Encryption). *A public key encryption (PKE) scheme consists of four PPT algorithms as follows:*

- $\mathsf{SysGen}(\lambda)$: On input a security parameter λ, the *system parameter generation algorithm* outputs the system parameters par. For convenience, par is other algorithms' public and implicit input.
- $\mathsf{KeyGen}(\lambda)$: On input the system parameters par, the *key generation algorithm* outputs a private key sk and a public key pk.
- $\mathsf{Enc}(\mathsf{pk}, \mathsf{m})$: On inputs a public key pk and a plaintext $\mathsf{m} \in \{0,1\}^\tau$, the *encryption algorithm* outputs a ciphertext c. Here, τ is the maximum bit length of the plaintext space.
- $\mathsf{Dec}(\mathsf{sk}, \mathsf{c})$: On inputs a private key sk and a ciphertext c, the *decryption algorithm* outputs the plaintext $\mathsf{m} \in \{0,1\}^\tau$ or a decryption failure flag $\perp$.

Definition 6 (Correctness). *A public key encryption scheme $\Gamma =$ (KeyGen, Enc, Dec) is correct if for any message $\mathsf{m} \in \{0,1\}^\tau$ the following equation holds*

$$\Pr\left[m' \neq m \wedge m' \neq \perp \;\middle|\; \begin{array}{c} (\mathsf{sk}, \mathsf{pk}) \leftarrow \mathsf{KeyGen}(\lambda), \\ c \leftarrow \mathsf{Enc}(\mathsf{pk}, \mathsf{m}), \\ m' \leftarrow \mathsf{Dec}(\mathsf{sk}, \mathsf{c}) \end{array} \right] \leq \mathsf{negl}(\lambda). \tag{7}$$

Typically, we can use the indistinguishability model to define the security of PKE schemes.

Definition 7 (IND-CPA Security). *A public key encryption scheme Γ is secure in the security model of indistinguishability against chosen-plaintext attacks (IND-CPA) if the following advantage*

$$\mathsf{Adv}_{\Gamma,\mathcal{A}}^{\mathsf{IND-CPA}} = 2\left(\Pr\left[b = b^* \middle| \begin{array}{l}(\mathsf{sk},\mathsf{pk}) \leftarrow \mathsf{KeyGen}(\lambda), m_0, m_1 \leftarrow \mathcal{A}(\mathsf{pk}),\\ b \xleftarrow{\$} \{0,1\}, c \leftarrow \mathsf{Enc}(\mathsf{pk}, m_b), b^* \leftarrow \mathcal{A}(\mathsf{pk}, c)\end{array}\right] - \frac{1}{2}\right)$$

is negligible for any PPT adversary $\mathcal{A}$.

Definition 8 (IND-CCA Security). *A public key encryption scheme Γ is secure in the security model of indistinguishability against chosen-ciphertext attacks (IND-CCA) if the following advantage*

$$\mathsf{Adv}_{\Gamma,\mathcal{A}}^{\mathsf{IND-CCA}} = 2\left(\Pr\left[b = b^* \middle| \begin{array}{l}(\mathsf{sk},\mathsf{pk}) \leftarrow \mathsf{KeyGen}(\lambda), m_0, m_1 \leftarrow \mathcal{A}^{\mathcal{O}}(\mathsf{pk}),\\ b \xleftarrow{\$} \{0,1\}, c \leftarrow \mathsf{Enc}(\mathsf{pk}, m_b), b^* \leftarrow \mathcal{A}^{\mathcal{O}}(\mathsf{pk}, c)\end{array}\right] - \frac{1}{2}\right)$$

is negligible for any PPT adversary $\mathcal{A}$, where $\mathcal{A}$ is allow to query the decryption oracle $\mathcal{O}(.)$ with any ciphertext $c' \neq c$.

2.5 Pohlig-Hellman Algorithm

Pohlig and Hellman proposed an efficient algorithm in 1978 to solve the DLP [25]. The Pohlig-Hellman algorithm indicates that if the order n of a cyclic group G is of the form $n = \ell_1^{e_1}\ell_2^{e_2}...\ell_t^{e_t}$ where all ℓ_i are small primes, the DLP over G can be solved efficiently. In our work, we only focus on the case $n = \ell_1\ell_2...\ell_t$. The algorithm is described as following where $DL(x, y)$ means solving the discrete logarithm problem between x, y and $CRT(crs_1, crs_2, ..., crs_t)$ means applying Chinese Remainder Theorem. It is easy to verify that $crs_i = x \bmod \ell_i$ so the algorithm correctly return x.

Algorithm 1. Pohlig-Hellman algorithm

Input: a cyclic group G of smooth order $n = \ell_1\ell_2...\ell_t$ along with a generator g and an element $h \in G$
Output: $x \in [1, n]$ such that $h = g^x$
1: **for all** $i \in [1, t]$ **do**
2: $h_i = h^{n/\ell_i}$
3: $g_i = g^{n/\ell_i}$
4: Solve the discrete logarithm problem $crs_i = DL(h_i, g_i)$
5: **end for**
6: $x = CRT(crs_1, crs_2, ..., crs_t)$
7: return x

3 Our Scheme

Now we introduce our new post-quantum PKE scheme, called FelS in which "Fle" means "flexible" and "S" inherits from "SiGamal" and "SimS". This name highlights that our scheme has a flexible choice of parameters according to the security requirement and the practical needs. We propose a deterministic algorithm to find a point of wanted order.

3.1 Overlook

We observe that in SimS, the point choosing algorithm requires that the big prime p must be of the form $2^r\ell_1\ell_2...\ell_n - 1$, which all ℓ_i are distinct small odd primes and r must be big enough to ensure the message space. This requirement limits the choice of parameters and the message space. We must find the big prime p that $p+1$ has the big factor 2^r and the left to be distinct small odd primes. The factor 2^r limits the message space. For the parameters p_{128} and p_{256} recommended in SimS, their message space are approximately 128 bits and 256 bits respectively but both of them are almost 512 bits length.

We obtain FleS by adapting the point choosing process in such a way that we choose the parameters to be the CSIDH-512 parameter $p = 4\ell_1\ell_2...\ell_n - 1$ and we choose the point to be of the order $\ell_{t1}\ell_{t_2}...\ell_{t_s}$ where all $\ell_{t_i} \in \{\ell_1, \ell_2, ..., \ell_n\}$ are distinct. In this case, our scheme's biggest message space can be approximately $\{0,1\}^{512}$ when the order is $\ell_1\ell_2...\ell_n$, four times as SimS's p_{128} parameter and twice as SimS's p_{256} parameter. We can adjust the message space by changing the order of the point we choose according to the security and efficiency need. It is worth noting that the group action of CSIDH-512 is much faster than that in SimS, which gives much improvement in performance.

To choose a point of order $\ell_{t1}\ell_{t_2}...\ell_{t_s}$, our basic idea is to find points of order $\ell_{t_1}, \ell_{t_2},...,$ and ℓ_{t_s} and sum them up to get a new point of order we want. Having this point P, Bob can embed the message by computing $P_C = [m]P$ and Alice can decrypt the message by using the Pohlig-Hellman algorithm [25].

Lemma 1. *For two elements x_1 and x_2 in a group G, if x_1 has order ℓ_1 and x_2 has order ℓ_2 and $gcd(\ell_1, \ell_2) = 1$, then $x_1 + x_2$ has order $\ell_1\ell_2$.*

In general, the public parameter of FleS contains a big prime whose factors are many distinct odd primes, a public supersingular elliptic curve $E_0 : y^2 = x^3 + x$ and a randomizing function f_E along with its inverse g_E such that $bin(f_E(x)) = bin(x) \bigoplus bin(E)$ where $bin(x)$ means the binary representation of x. Alice randomly chooses an ideal class $[\mathfrak{a}]$ and computes $E_1 = [\mathfrak{a}]E_0$, then her public key is E_1 and private key is $[\mathfrak{a}]$. To encrypt a message m, Bob randomly chooses an ideal class $[\mathfrak{b}]$, computes $E_3 = [\mathfrak{b}]E_0, E_4 = [\mathfrak{b}]E_1$, and chooses a point P_{E_4} of order $\ell_{t1}\ell_{t_2}...\ell_{t_m}$ in E_4. He sends E_3 and $f_E(x(P_C))$ where $P_C = [m]P_{E_4}$. To decrypt the message m, Alice computes $E_4 = [\mathfrak{a}]E_3$ and runs the same point choosing algorithm to find the same point P_{E_4}. Then she runs Pohlig-Hellman algorithm [25] to solve the DL problem $P_c = [m]P_{E_4}$ to get m. Figure 1 depicts the whole process.

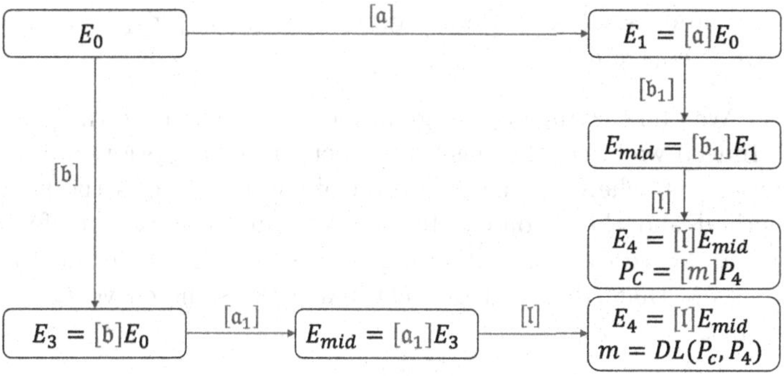

Fig. 1. FleS scheme

3.2 The FleS Public Key Encryption Scheme

Now let us concretly describe the FleS's key generation, encryption and decryption process (using the CSIDH-512 parameter set and setting the order of the point to be $\ell_1\ell_2...\ell_n$ as an example).

- **KeyGen**: Let $p = 4\ell_1\ell_2...\ell_n - 1$ be a big prime where $\ell_1, \ell_2, ..., \ell_n$ are all small dinstinct primes. Let $E_0 : y^2 = x^3 + x$ be the public supersingular ellipitic curves under the Montgomery forms. Alice randomly chooses an ideal class $[\mathfrak{a}] = [\mathfrak{l}_1]^{a_1}...[\mathfrak{l}_1]^{a_n} \in Cl(\mathcal{O})$ and computes $E_1 = [\mathfrak{a}]E_0$. Then the public key is the curve E_1 and the corresponding private key is the ideal class $[\mathfrak{a}]$. The message space is approximately $\mathcal{M} = \{0,1\}^{\log \ell_1\ell_2...\ell_n}$.
- **Enc**: Let $m \in \mathcal{M}$ be a message. Bob randomly chooses an ideal class $[\mathfrak{b}] = [\mathfrak{l}_1]^{b_1}...[\mathfrak{l}_n]^{b_n} \in Cl(\mathcal{O})$ and computes $E_3 = [\mathfrak{b}]E_0$ and $E_4 = [\mathfrak{b}]E_1$. In the process to compute $E_4 = [\mathfrak{b}]E_1$, Bob finds a point $P_{E_4} \in E_4$ such that P_{E_4} is of the order $\ell_1\ell_2...\ell_n$ and computes $P_c = [m]P_{E_4}$. Bob compute n bits $s = s_1s_2...s_n$ where

$$s_i = \begin{cases} 0, m \ mod \ \ell_i < \ell_i/2 \\ 1, m \ mod \ \ell_i > \ell_i/2 \end{cases}$$

  He sends the couple $(E_3, x^{'} = f_{E_4}(x(P_c)), s^{'} = f_{E_4,n}(s))$ to Alice, where $f_{E_4,n}$ means only using the n bits of E_4 to encode.
- **Dec**: Upon receiving the couple $(E_3, x^{'}, s^{'})$, Alice first verifies that E_3 is a supersingular elliptic curve. If not, then Alice aborts. Alice computes $E_4 = [\mathfrak{a}]E_3$ and in this process finds the same points P_{E_4} of order $\ell_1\ell_2...\ell_n$ as Bob. If $g_{E_4}(x^{'})$ is not a point in E_4, then she aborts. She decodes $s = g_{E_4,n}(s^{'})$ and solves the discrete logarithm problem between P_c and P_{E_4} by applying the Pohlig-Hellman algorithm [25] to get $\{crs_1, crs_2, ..., crs_n\}$. She changes $\{crs_1, crs_2, ..., crs_n\}$ by the equation

$$crs_i = \begin{cases} crs_i, s_i = 0 \\ \ell_i - crs_i, s_i = 1 \end{cases} = s_i \cdot \ell_i - (2s_i - 1)crs_i$$

Then Alice applies Chinese Remainder Thoerem to $\{crs_1, crs_2, ..., crs_n\}$ to recover the message m.

Remark 1. We don't change the original method to compute the group action in CSIDH. Indeed we break the class group action in encryption and decryption into two processes, where the computation of the first one is the same as the original method and the second is to compute an const isogeny for a vector $(1, 1, ..., 1)$ and we add a point choosing process into it. The aim to break it down is to assure that Alice and Bob can reach the same curve E_{mid} and find the same point.

Remark 2. The additional checking bit string s is necessary. In our work we use Montgomery curve and only x-coordinate to represent the point. For a point P of order ℓ, $[k]P$ and $[\ell - k]P$ have the same x-coordinate. So when applying Pohlig-hellman algorithm, if $m \ mod \ \ell_i > \ell_i/2$, the algorithm will compute $crs_i = \ell_i - (m \ mod \ \ell_i)$. The checking bit string s is used to correct this bias. Although this makes the ciphertext size a little bigger, it is within the acceptable range.

3.3 Finding the Point of Wanted Order

For the correctness of the scheme, Alice and Bob must find the same point P_{E_4}. In [19], they prove an ingenious way to find a deterministic point of order 2^r. But their method is based on mathematics theory and not suitable for our scheme to find point of order $\ell_1\ell_2...\ell_n$. To do this, in the computation of isogeny, we break the secret key of Bob $[\mathfrak{b}] = [\mathfrak{l}_1]^{b_1}...[\mathfrak{l}_n]^{b_n} \in Cl(\mathcal{O})$ into two parts, the first part $[\mathfrak{b}_1] = [\mathfrak{l}_1]^{b_1-1}...[\mathfrak{l}_n]^{b_n-1}$ and the second part $[\mathfrak{1}] = [\mathfrak{l}_1]...[\mathfrak{l}_n]$. During the encryption process, Bob first computes the group action by $[\mathfrak{b}_1]$ and reaches a middle curve $E_{mid} = [\mathfrak{b}_1]E_1$. Then he computes the second part $E_4 = [\mathfrak{1}]E_{mid}$ and during this process he finds a point P_{E_4} of order $\ell_1...\ell_n$. When receiving the ciphertext, Alice does the same as Bob, *i.e.*, breaking $[\mathfrak{a}] = [\mathfrak{l}_1]^{a_1}...[\mathfrak{l}_n]^{a_n}$ into $[\mathfrak{a}_1] = [\mathfrak{l}_1]^{a_1-1}...[\mathfrak{l}_n]^{a_n-1}$ and $[\mathfrak{1}] = [\mathfrak{l}_1]...[\mathfrak{l}_n]$. She can reach the same curve E_{mid} as Bob by computing $E_{mid} = [\mathfrak{a}_1]E_3$ and find the same point P_{E_4} during computing $E_4 = [\mathfrak{1}]E_{mid}$. The algorithm to find the point P_{E_4} is as follows:

In every iteration, we make sure that $T' = [k_i]S$ is a point of order ℓ_i by checking whether it is equal to infinity. We must point out that in the algorithm, we first finish the ℓ_i isogeny computation and then find the ℓ_i order point in the image curve and add it to P. The reason for this is that the ℓ_i isogeny will map a point of order ℓ_i to the infinity point of the image curve. So the point addition must follow the isogeny computation. By the Lemma 1, it is easy to see that by algorithm 2 we can find the point we want and the algorithm is deterministic.

Theorem 3. *The point P output by algorithm 2 is of order $\ell_1\ell_2...\ell_n$.*

Proof. we use ϕ_i to represent the ℓ_i isogeny and T_i to reprensent the point chosen in the i-th iteration, so ϕ can be factored into

$$\phi = \phi_1 \circ \phi_2 \circ ... \circ \phi_n$$

Then the output P is as follows:

$$P = \phi_2 \circ ... \circ \phi_n(T_1) + \phi_3 \circ ... \circ \phi_n(T_2) + ... + \phi_n(T_{n-1}) + T_n$$

It is easy to verify that the i-th part of P is a point of order ℓ_i. So by lemma 1, P is a point of $\ell_1\ell_2...\ell_n$.

Algorithm 2. Find point of wanted order

Input: a supersingular elliptic curve $E_A : y^2 = x^3 + Ax^2 + x$
Output: the image curve $E_B = [\mathfrak{l}_1]...[\mathfrak{l}_n]E_A : y^2 = x^3+Bx^2+x$ and a point in $P \in E_B$ of order $\ell_1\ell_2...\ell_n$

1: set $k = p + 1$
2: set P to be the infinity point in E_A
3: **for** $i \leftarrow 1, n$ **do**
4: set $k_i \leftarrow k/\ell_i$
5: $x \leftarrow \mathbb{F}_p$
6: if $x^3 + Ax^2 + x$ is not a square in $\mathbb{F}_p$, goto step 5
7: set $x(Q) \leftarrow x$
8: if $R = [k_i]Q$ is infinity, goto step 5
9: compute the isogeny $\phi : E_A \rightarrow E_B : y^2 = x^3 + Bx^2 + x$ with $ker\phi = (R)$
10: $A \leftarrow B, P \leftarrow \phi(P)$
11: set $t \leftarrow 1$
12: set $x \leftarrow t$
13: **while** $x^3 + Ax^2 + x$ is not a square in $\mathbb{F}_p$ **do**
14: set $t \leftarrow t + 1$, goto step 12
15: **end while**
16: set $x(S) \leftarrow x$
17: **while** $T = [k_i]S$ is infinity **do**
18: set $t \leftarrow t + 1$, goto step 12
19: **end while**
20: set $P \leftarrow P + T$
21: **end for**
22: return A and P

Remark 3 The above algorithm provides a method to find a point of order $\ell_1\ell_2...\ell_n$. In fact, we can optionally change the algorithm to suit our need. For example, if we want a point of order $\ell_1\ell_2...\ell_{n/2}$, we can just compute the action $[\mathfrak{l}_1][\mathfrak{l}_2]...[\mathfrak{l}_{n/2}]$ on the starting curve then we get a point of order $\ell_1\ell_2...\ell_{n/2}$ in the end curve.

We provide another simple method to construct the scheme. For using the CSIDH-512 parameter set, the bit length of the big prime p is 512 bits. Besides the factor 4, the bit length of the remainder small prime is 510 bits, almost 512 bits. For example, if we want to instantiate FleS for a message space of 128 bits. We can simply random choose a element $x \in \mathbb{F}_p$ and check whether it can be a point. If so, we check the order of this point, if the order of the point is bigger than 128 bits length, we can just use this point to encrypt the message. Or more general, we can use the method "Hash onto point". We hash the j-invariant of the shared elliptic curve E_4 to a element of $\mathbb{F}_p$ and do the same thing above. It is easy to verify that the probability to finding a point of order less than 128 bits is negligible. So this method is feasible.

3.4 Correctness Analysis

To prove the correctness of the proposed scheme, we need to verify that f_E is a bijection and g_E is its inverse. In [19], it is shown that f_E satisfies the following property:

- P1:f_E is a bijection and $g_E = f_E^{-1}$ can be computed efficiently when having access to E.
- P2:Any adversary having no access to E and x cannot distinguish $f_E(x)$ from a random element for any element $x \in F_p$.
- P3:For every $x \in F_p$ and $R \in \mathbb{F}_p(x)$, any adversary having no access to E and x cannot compute $f_E(R(x))$ from $f_E(x)$

When Alice receives the couple $(E_3, x^{'} = f_{E_4}(x(P_c)), s^{'} = f_{E_4,n}(s)$, she can efficiently compute E_4 and get the same point P_{E_4} as Bob. So

$$x(P_c) = g_{E_4}(x^{'}), s = g_{E_4,n}(s^{'}) \tag{8}$$

can be efficiently computed by Alice. Then the message can be decrypted efficiently by using Pohlig-Hellman algorithm to solve the discrete logarithm problem between P_c and P_{E_4} with the help of s as follows:

$$\{crs_1, crs_2, ..., crs_n\} = DL(P_c, P_{E_4}) \tag{9}$$

$$crs_i = s_i \cdot \ell_i - (2s_i - 1)crs_i \tag{10}$$

$$m = CRT(crs_1, crs_2, ..., crs_n). \tag{11}$$

Therefore, it is proved that the proposed scheme is implemented correctly.

4 Security Analysis

4.1 Some Concepts and Theorems

In [19], Fouotsa *et. al* proposed the CSSIKoE(Commutative Supersingular Isogeny Knowledge of Exponent) assumption to prove the IND-CCA security of SimS. We recall the CSSIKoE assumption and adjust it to our settings [19].

Assumption 2 (CSSIKoE). *The CSSIKoE assumption is stated as follow.*

Let $p = 4\ell_1\ell_2...\ell_n - 1$ *be a big prime and* $[\mathfrak{a}], [\mathfrak{b}]$ *be two element uniformly sampled from* $Cl(\mathcal{O})$ *and* $f_E(x)$ *be a function such that for any adversary having no access to* E *and* x *cannot compute* $f_E(R(x))$ *for* $R \in \mathbb{F}_p(X)$.

For every PPT adversary $\mathcal{A}$ *that takes* E_0,$[\mathfrak{a}]E_0$ *and* $([\mathfrak{b}]E_0, f_{[\mathfrak{a}][\mathfrak{b}]E_0}(x(P)))$ *where* $P \in [\mathfrak{a}][\mathfrak{b}]E_0$ *as input, and returns*

$$([\mathfrak{b}^{'}]E_0, f_{[\mathfrak{a}][\mathfrak{b}^{'}]E_0}(x(P^{'}))) \neq ([\mathfrak{b}]E_0, f_{[\mathfrak{a}][\mathfrak{b}]E_0}(x(P))) \tag{12}$$

where $P^{'} \in [\mathfrak{a}][\mathfrak{b}^{'}]E_0$ *has the same order as* P*, there exist a PPT adversary* $\mathcal{A}^{'}$ *that takes the same inputs and returns* $([\mathfrak{b}^{'}], [\mathfrak{b}^{'}]E_0, f_{[\mathfrak{a}][\mathfrak{b}]E_0}(x(P^{'})))$.

4.2 Security Proof

Now we prove the IND-CCA security of our scheme based on the proof of SimS [19]. we first prove the IND-CPA security based on Assumption 1. Then we prove the IND-CCA security based on the IND-CPA security and Assumption 2 modified from [19].

Theorem 4. *If Assumption 1 holds and* f_E *satifies (P2), then FleS is IND-CPA security.*

Proof. Suppose FleS cannot achieve IND-CPA security, there exists a PPT adversary $\mathcal{A}$ such that $\mathcal{A}$ can distinguish a ciphertext c is encrypted by m_0 or m_1 with a nonnegligible advantage γ.

Let $(E_0, [\mathfrak{a}]E_0, [\mathfrak{b}]E_0, F)$ be a CSSIDDH instance. We aim to distinguish a given input to be a correct tuple *i.e.* $F = [\mathfrak{a}][\mathfrak{b}]E_0$ or a bad tuple *i.e.* $F \neq [\mathfrak{a}][\mathfrak{b}]E_0$. We define the following test:

- **Simulation**: Simulating an instance by two messages m_0 and m_1 along with a tuple $(E_0, [\mathfrak{a}]E_0, [\mathfrak{b}]E_0, E)$. One chooses a point P_E of order $\ell_1\ell_2...\ell_n$, chooses a $b \in \{0, 1\}$ randomly and computes $c = ([\mathfrak{b}]E_0, f_E(x([m_b]P_E)), s^{'})$.
- **Query** $\mathcal{A}$: Querying $\mathcal{A}$ with $([\mathfrak{a}]E_0, c)$ and receiving a response $b^{'} \in \{0, 1\}$. The result of the test is 1 if $b = b^{'}$ or 0 otherwise.

Now we discuss in the following cases:

- **Case 1: $\mathcal{A}$ Can Distinguish the Validity of the Ciphertext.** We run the above test once. If the ciphertext is invalid, the adversary $\mathcal{A}$ will return abort. This means that $F \neq [\mathfrak{a}][\mathfrak{b}]E_0$. So we can construct the CSSIDDH solver $\mathcal{A}^{'}$ as follows:
  - If the adversary $\mathcal{A}$ returns abort, $\mathcal{A}^{'}$ returns bad.
  - If the adversary returns a bit $b^{'} \in \{0, 1\}$, $\mathcal{A}^{'}$ returns good.
- **Case 2: $\mathcal{A}$ Cannot Distinguish the Validity of the Ciphertext.** If the adversary has no ability to distinguish the validity, the return of the test will always be a bit. We can run the test for enough times and count the number of 0 and 1.

If the tuple is correct, the adversary $\mathcal{A}$ has the ability to corrctly returns $b^{'} = b$ with negligible advantage. The proportion of 1 of the total returns should be

$$Pr(1) = \frac{1}{2} + \gamma \tag{13}$$

If the tuple is a bad one, since the adversary A has no access to E and $x([m_b]P_E)$, so in the view of $\mathcal{A}$, it cannot distinguish $f_E(x([m_b]P_E))$ from a random bit strings because f_E satisfies P2. So $\mathcal{A}$ returns 0 or 1 both with equal probability $\frac{1}{2}$, the proportion of 0 and 1 of the total should both be almost $\frac{1}{2}$ *i.e.*

$$Pr(1) = \frac{1}{2} \pm \text{ngl}(\lambda) \tag{14}$$

So we can construct the CSSIDDH solver $\mathcal{A}^{'}$ as follows: if $Pr(1) \approx \frac{1}{2}$ the return is bad else correct.

Then we prove the IND-CCA security of the FleS.

Theorem 5. *If FleS is IND-CPA security and Assumption 2 holds, then FleS is IND-CCA security.*

Proof. If FleS is not IND-CCA security, there exists an adversary $\mathcal{A}$ which can successfully determine a given ciphertext ct is encrypted by m_0 or m_1 with negligible advantage γ.

Suppose $\mathcal{A} = (\mathcal{A}_1, O(.))$ where $O(.)$ represents the decryption oracle. When $\mathcal{A}$ queries the $O(.)$ with some tuples $ct_1 = (F_1, x_1, s_1^{'}), ..., ct_n = (F_n, x_n, s_n^{'})$ where all ct_i are valid ciphertext. By Assumption 2 there exists a PPT algorithm $\mathcal{A}_2$ that it outputs $ct_1^{'} = (F_1, x_1), ..., ct_n^{'} = (F_n, x_n)$ along with $\mathfrak{b}_1, ..., \mathfrak{b}_n \in Cl(\mathcal{O})$ such that $F_1 = [\mathfrak{b}_1]E_0, ..., F_n = [\mathfrak{b}_n]E_0$. With the knowledge of $\mathfrak{b}_1, ..., \mathfrak{b}_n$ and $[\mathfrak{a}]E_0$, $\mathcal{A}_2$ can decrypt $ct_1 = (F_1, x_1, s_1^{'}), ..., ct_n = (F_n, x_n, s_n^{'})$ correctly.

We can construct a new adversary $\mathcal{A}^{'} = (\mathcal{A}_1, \mathcal{A}_2)$. The adversary $\mathcal{A}^{'}$ is a PPT adversary which has the ability to determine whether a ciphertext ct is decrypted by m_0 or m_1 with negligible advantage γ without making queries to decryption oracle. This is opposed to the IND-CPA security of FleS. FleS is IND-CCA security.

5 Implementation Result

Here we present the experimentation results. The implementation is inistantiated using the parameter set CSIDH-512. Our code is published on github[1]. We compare our implementation results with SimS and (C)SiGamal.

We sum up all the costs including multiplication, square, addition and inverse and transform them all to multiplication under the coefficient relations that 1S=0.8M, 1A=0.05M and 1I=100M.

Here we compare the computation costs of C-SiGamal, SiGamal, SimS and our scheme. The Table 2 shows the performance of SiGamal, C-SiGamal [24] and

[1] https://github.com/hwh962682296/isogeny.

Table 2. Computation costs of C-SiGamal, SiGamal, SimS and FleS

	Kgen	Enc	Dec
C-SiGamal(p_{256})	1151447	2685714	1528020
SiGamal(p_{256})		2208530	1536829
SimS(p_{256})	1023827	2057297	1417401
FleS	589074	1756487	1347302

SimS [19]. Using the parameter p_{256}, the message space of SiGamal and SimS are approximately 128 bits and using p_{256},the message space is 256 bits.

We implement FleS using CSIDH-512 parameter set and set the message space to be 256 bits to facilitate comparison. This can be done by using the last 32 small primes $\ell_{43}, \ell_{44}, ..., \ell_{74}$ and set the order of point to be $\ell_{43}...\ell_{74}$. Also there are many choices to do this.

Design. SimS and (C)SiGamal use the structure derived from CSIDH while FleS can be instantiated using the structure of CSIDH or Csi-Fish [5] when using CSIDH-512 parameter set. When using CSIDH-1024 or other parameter sets to obtain a bigger message space, FleS can be instantiated under CSIDH. Indeed, FleS can obtain better performance if instantiated using the structure of CSIDH because the group structure of Csi-Fish is about 15% slower than that of CSIDH. In our work, we choose to use the structure of Csi-Fish to obtain a smaller public key size.

Security. For the security, FleS can achieve IND-CCA security as SimS relying on the CSSIKoE and CSSIDDH assumptions while (C)SiGamal can only reach the IND-CPA security.

Size. Because of the structure of Csi-Fish, FleS's private key size is only 128 bits. Both of SimS and (C)SiGamal use vector to represent ideal class, so their private key sizes are bigger than FleS's. The FleS's public key size is smaller than SimS and (SiGamal because the size of the prime of CSIDH-512 is smaller than p_{256}. The FleS's ciphertext size is about 26 bits larger than SimS and SiGamal because of the additional checking bits. But the ciphertext size of FleS and SimS is about 1000 bits, so the additional bits are acceptable.

Efficiency. FleS is more efficient compared to SimS, (C)SiGamal when the message space is same. From the results in the Table 2, FleS key generation process is 1.74× faster than that of SimS and 1.95× than that of SiGamal and C-SiGamal. For encryption, FleS is about 1.17× faster than SimS, 1.26× faster than SiGamal and 1.53× than C-SiGamal. For the decryption, there are also a speed up about 1.05× than SimS, 1,14× than SiGamal and C-SiGamal.

6 Conclusion and Future Work

In this paper, we review the protocols proposed by Fouotsa *et al.* at PQCrypto 2021. We construct a new isogeny-based PKE scheme called FleS by changing the point choosing method of SimS to make the scheme more flexible. Compared to SimS, FleS has the smaller key size with the same message space while the ciphertext size is a little bigger. FleS can be instantiated in almost any parameter set according to the actual demand for security and efficiency. We prove that FleS is IND-CCA security relying on the CSSIDDH assumption and the CSSIKoE assumption proposed in [19]. We implement our scheme using the parameter set CSIDH-512 and compare the performance with SimS and SiGamal. The result shows that FleS is more efficient when the message space is $\{0,1\}^{256}$.

More work on constructing a better method to find the point of wanted order is needed to gain better performance. Such a work can make our scheme more practical. The second direction is to compute the ideal class group structure for more parameter sets so there are more choices for us to instantiate FleS. Indeed, more parameter choices may bring better method to find point.

Acknowlegements. The work was supported by the National Key Research and Development Program of China (No. 2022YFB3102400), the National Natural Science Foundation of China (Nos. 62172307, 62202339, 62272350), and the Special Project on Science and Technology Program of Hubei Provience (Nos. 2020AEA013, 2021BAA025). We thank reviewers for valuable advice.

References

1. Elliptic Curve Database (2023). http://hyperelliptic.org
2. Alkhoraidly, A., Dominguez-Oviedo, A., Hasan, M.A.: Fault attacks on elliptic curve cryptosystems. In: Information Security and Cryptography, pp. 137–155. Springer, Heidelberg (2012). https://doi.org/10.1007/978-3-642-29656-7
3. Azarderakhsh, R., et al.: Supersingular isogeny key encapsulation. Submiss. NIST Post-Quant. Standard. Project **152**, 154–155 (2017)
4. Bellare, M., Rogaway, P.: Optimal asymmetric encryption. In: De Santis, A. (ed.) EUROCRYPT 1994. LNCS, vol. 950, pp. 92–111. Springer, Heidelberg (1995). https://doi.org/10.1007/BFb0053428
5. Beullens, W., Kleinjung, T., Vercauteren, F.: CSI-FiSh: efficient isogeny based signatures through class group computations. In: Galbraith, S.D., Moriai, S. (eds.) ASIACRYPT 2019. LNCS, vol. 11921, pp. 227–247. Springer, Cham (2019). https://doi.org/10.1007/978-3-030-34578-5_9
6. Castryck, W., Decru, T.: An efficient key recovery attack on SIDH. In: Hazay, C., Stam, M. (eds.) Advances in Cryptology - EUROCRYPT 2023, Part V. LNCS, vol. 14008, pp. 423–447. Springer, Heidelberg (2023). https://doi.org/10.1007/978-3-031-30589-4_15
7. Castryck, W., Lange, T., Martindale, C., Panny, L., Renes, J.: CSIDH: an efficient post-quantum commutative group action. In: Peyrin, T., Galbraith, S. (eds.) ASIACRYPT 2018. LNCS, vol. 11274, pp. 395–427. Springer, Cham (2018). https://doi.org/10.1007/978-3-030-03332-3_15

8. Charles, D.X., Lauter, K.E., Goren, E.Z.: Cryptographic hash functions from expander graphs. J. Cryptol. **22**(1), 93–113 (2007). https://doi.org/10.1007/s00145-007-9002-x
9. Cohen, H., et al.: Handbook of Elliptic and Hyperelliptic Curve Cryptography. CRC Press (2005)
10. Costello, C., Hisil, H.: A simple and compact algorithm for SIDH with arbitrary degree isogenies. In: Takagi, T., Peyrin, T. (eds.) ASIACRYPT 2017. LNCS, vol. 10625, pp. 303–329. Springer, Cham (2017). https://doi.org/10.1007/978-3-319-70697-9_11
11. Couveignes, J.M.: Hard homogeneous spaces. Cryptology ePrint Archive, Report 2006/291 (2006). https://eprint.iacr.org/2006/291
12. De Feo, L.: Mathematics of isogeny based cryptography. arXiv preprint arXiv:1711.04062 (2017)
13. De Feo, L., et al.: Séta: supersingular encryption from torsion attacks. In: Tibouchi, M., Wang, H. (eds.) ASIACRYPT 2021. LNCS, vol. 13093, pp. 249–278. Springer, Cham (2021). https://doi.org/10.1007/978-3-030-92068-5_9
14. De Feo, L., Kohel, D., Leroux, A., Petit, C., Wesolowski, B.: SQISign: compact post-quantum signatures from quaternions and isogenies. In: Moriai, S., Wang, H. (eds.) ASIACRYPT 2020. LNCS, vol. 12491, pp. 64–93. Springer, Cham (2020). https://doi.org/10.1007/978-3-030-64837-4_3
15. De Feo, L., Leroux, A., Wesolowski, B.: New algorithms for the deuring correspondence: SQISign twice as fast. Cryptology ePrint Archive, Report 2022/234 (2022). https://eprint.iacr.org/2022/234
16. Delfs, C., Galbraith, S.D.: Computing isogenies between supersingular elliptic curves over f _p f p. Des. Codes Crypt. **78**, 425–440 (2016)
17. Diédhiou, S.: Isogénie entre courbes elliptiques (2020)
18. Fouotsa, T.B., Petit, C.: SHealS and healS: isogeny-based PKEs from a key validation method for SIDH. In: Tibouchi, M., Wang, H. (eds.) ASIACRYPT 2021. LNCS, vol. 13093, pp. 279–307. Springer, Cham (2021). https://doi.org/10.1007/978-3-030-92068-5_10
19. Fouotsa, T.B., Petit, C.: SimS: a simplification of SiGamal. In: Cheon, J.H., Tillich, J.P. (eds.) Post-Quantum Cryptography - 12th International Workshop, PQCrypto 2021, pp. 277–295. Springer, Heidelberg (2021). https://doi.org/10.1007/978-3-030-81293-5_15
20. Fujisaki, E., Okamoto, T.: Secure integration of asymmetric and symmetric encryption schemes. In: Wiener, M. (ed.) CRYPTO 1999. LNCS, vol. 1666, pp. 537–554. Springer, Heidelberg (1999). https://doi.org/10.1007/3-540-48405-1_34
21. Jao, D., De Feo, L.: Towards quantum-resistant cryptosystems from supersingular elliptic curve isogenies. In: Yang, B.-Y. (ed.) PQCrypto 2011. LNCS, vol. 7071, pp. 19–34. Springer, Heidelberg (2011). https://doi.org/10.1007/978-3-642-25405-5_2
22. Maino, L., Martindale, C.: An attack on Sidh with arbitrary starting curve. Cryptology ePrint Archive (2022)
23. Montgomery, P.L.: Speeding the pollard and elliptic curve methods of factorization. Math. Comput. **48**(177), 243–264 (1987)
24. Moriya, T., Onuki, H., Takagi, T.: SiGamal: a supersingular isogeny-based PKE and its application to a PRF. In: Moriai, S., Wang, H. (eds.) ASIACRYPT 2020. LNCS, vol. 12492, pp. 551–580. Springer, Cham (2020). https://doi.org/10.1007/978-3-030-64834-3_19
25. Pohlig, S.C., Hellman, M.E.: An improved algorithm for computing logarithms over gf (p) and its cryptographic significance function

26. Renes, J.: Computing isogenies between montgomery curves using the action of (0, 0). In: Lange, T., Steinwandt, R. (eds.) PQCrypto 2018. LNCS, vol. 10786, pp. 229–247. Springer, Cham (2018). https://doi.org/10.1007/978-3-319-79063-3_11
27. Rivest, R.L., Shamir, A., Adleman, L.M.: A method for obtaining digital signatures and public-key cryptosystems. Commun. Assoc. Comput. Mach. **21**(2), 120–126 (1978). https://doi.org/10.1145/359340.359342
28. Robert, D.: Breaking SIDH in polynomial time. In: Hazay, C., Stam, M. (eds.) Advances in Cryptology - EUROCRYPT 2023, Part V. LNCS, vol. 14008, pp. 472–503. Springer, Heidelberg (2023). https://doi.org/10.1007/978-3-031-30589-4_17
29. Rostovtsev, A., Stolbunov, A.: Public-key cryptosystem based on isogenies. Cryptology ePrint Archive (2006)
30. Silverman, J.H.: The Arithmetic of Elliptic Curves, vol. 106. Springer (2009)
31. Tate, J.: Endomorphisms of Abelian Varieties Over Finite Fields. Invent. Math. **2**(2), 134–144 (1966)
32. Washington, L.C.: Elliptic Curves: Number Theory and Cryptography. CRC Press (2008)

A New Revocable Attribute Based Encryption on Lattice

Lifeng Guo(✉), Lingxia Wang, Xueke Ma, and Qianli Ma

School of Computer and Information Technology, Shanxi University, Taiyuan, China
lfguo@sxu.edu.cn

Abstract. In this paper we propose a new Lattice-based Revocable Attribute Based Encryption (RL-ABE) scheme in the cloud. We use Ciphertext-Policy Attribute Based Encryption (CP-ABE) in the scheme. This policy is implemented in the way that the data owner can define her/his own access control policy. And our access policy uses a linear secret sharing scheme (LSSS) converted by boolean formula to achieve fine-grained access control of user permissions. More importantly, we propose a new revocation mechanism. Different from the current revocation mechanism, data service manager in the cloud do not require key during the revocation process, thus avoiding the key leakage problem and improving the security of the solution. In addition, the difficult problem we based on is the learning with error (LWE) problem in lattice, which is resistant to quantum algorithm attacks. The scheme that is constructed in this paper using the LWE problem is proved to be secure under selective plaintext attacks.

Keywords: Lattice · Attribute based encryption · Revocation · LWE · Linear secret sharing scheme(LSSS)

1 Introduction

In the era of Big Data, where information is exploding, a large amount of data and information is outsourced to cloud servers. This gives more and more data to be stored and processed, reducing the amount of computing and storage space of local computers and saving a lot of resources. However, the outsourcing of large amount of data information to cloud servers also brings some security issues. Therefore, cloud servers are not completely trustworthy. Therefore, realizing data sharing and ensuring the security of outsourced data has become a hot topic of research in recent years.

After Identity-Based Encryption (IBE), Sahai and Waters proposed fuzzy Identity-Based Encryption (FIBE) [19]. In 2005, opening the fine-grained attribute-based encryption scheme [2,6,11,20,27]. It implements a one-to-many communication model where data owners encrypt messages based on attributes, reducing data overhead, protecting users' privacy, and preventing collusion attacks by users. Attribute-based encryption schemes include Key-Policy Attribute-Based Encryption (KP-ABE) and Ciphertext-Policy Attribute-Based Encryption (CP-ABE). In the CP-ABE scheme, the ciphertext is associated with

M. Zhang et al. (Eds.): ProvSec 2023, LNCS 14217, pp. 309–326, 2023.
https://doi.org/10.1007/978-3-031-45513-1_17

the access policy and the decryption key is associated with the user attributes. The data owner customizes the access structure to encrypt the plaintext according to the actual access requirements. It is more flexible and more suitable for ciphertext access control in cloud storage. This proposal studies exactly the use of CP-ABE.

With the arrival of quantum computers, traditional cryptographic schemes constructed based on discrete logarithms and large integer decomposition problems will no longer be secure. There is an urgent need for a cryptographic technique that can resist quantum attacks. Among the post-quantum cryptography, the properties of lattice make it stand out. Firstly, the lattice is considered to be resistant to quantum attacks. Secondly, the operations on the lattice are linear operations, which are efficient, parallelizable, and easy to implement in software and hardware, making them an excellent class of cryptographic mechanisms. More importantly, lattice also has the property that the worst-case difficulty can be reduced to the average case difficulty [17]. This property provides an important theoretical basis for the implementation of lattice, making it a hot research topic in the field of cryptography.

Currently, many revocable attribute-based encryption schemes have been constructed, first proposed in scheme [16]. There are three types of revocations according to the revocation granularity: system attribute revocation, i.e., revoking the access to a certain attribute in the system so that all users who have the attribute cannot decrypt it. User revocation, i.e., revoking a certain user's access to a ciphertext in the system. User attribute revocation, i.e., revoking a user's access to a certain attribute without affecting other attributes. Different revocation algorithms are suitable for different system performance. Based on the above introduction, it is important to study the application of revocation to lattice based attribute encryption.

1.1 Related Work

With the continuous breakthroughs in quantum computers, among which lattice-based cryptographic schemes are particularly prominent. In 1996, Ajtai et al. [5] introduced lattice-based encryption for the first time, proving that the time equivalent of the attack algorithm breaks the SVP problem. This ensured the security of the data, but the scheme was inefficient and had poor practicality. It was until 2005 that Regev proposed LWE [18], which gave the first cryptographic scheme based on LWE construction and reduced the worst-case lattice problem to the average case LWE problem. Subsequently, cryptographic researchers have proposed many encryption schemes constructed based on the LWE problem. In 2008, Gentry et al. [10] constructed the first lattice based identity encryption scheme using short bases on lattice, but constructed under the random prediction model. In 2009, Agrawal et al. [1] constructed a lattice based identity encryption scheme under the standard model. Agrawal and Boyen et al. [3,4] proposed (fuzzy) identity encryption scheme on a lattice and proved that the scheme is identity-secure by choice under the LWE assumption. In 2012, Zhang et al. [26]

proposed the first lattice based attribute based encryption scheme with ciphertext policy applying a gated access structure to achieve the most basic access structure in the lattice.In 2013, Boyen [7] proposed a lattice based attribute based encryption scheme with key policy applying a linear secret sharing technique in the access structure, further enhancing the lattice based attribute based encryption scheme's expression capability. In the same year, Xie [23] proposed a lattice based attribute based encryption scheme supporting "or restricted" circuit access control structures, but the number of circuit structures supported by this scheme is very limited. In 2014, Wang [22] proposed an attribute based encryption scheme based on the ciphertext policy under the LWE assumption in the standard model, which scheme implements a with gate access structure on multi-valued attributes. In 2021, Datta et al. [9] constructed the first provably secure lattice based CP-ABE scheme, which avoids the conversion from a generic circuit based key policy to a ciphertext policy. relies on linear secret sharing schemes with new properties, but the CP-ABE construction is not more efficient than existing schemes. Based on the above study, we propose a lattice based CP-ABE scheme for adaptive selection of plaintext attacks. The scheme relies on a linear secret sharing scheme converted from a Boolean formula.

When user leaves the system or secret key is compromised, it requires a user revocation mechanism to satisfy. Therefore for the large number of users in the system, an efficient revocable mechanism is very important. And in 2020 Han's revocable and traceable attribute-based encryption scheme [12] enables tracking and revocation of malicious users. Then the construction of revocable attribute-based encryption on lattice is still evolving. In 2012, Chen et al. [8] proposed an efficient revocable encryption scheme for identity-based encryption on lattice, which supports identity revocation but is difficult to achieve fine-grained access. In 2018, Wang et al. [21] proposed a revocable ciphertext policy attribute-based encryption scheme on lattice, which implements a multivalued attribute on with-gate access structure, with the drawback that the access structure is too simple.In 2020, Yang and Wu [24] proposed a revocable attribute-based encryption scheme on lattice, which supports fine-grained access and attribute revocation, and the access control structure uses a threshold access structure. In 2022, Yang and Sun [25] proposed a practical revocable multi-authority attribute-based encryption scheme, also based on R-LWE, using an access control structure with an access tree as well.In 2023, Luo et al. [14] proposed a lattice-based revocable attribute-based encryption scheme on standard lattice, but using a key policy for attribute-based encryption.

1.2 Contribution

Based on the above scheme, in this paper we construct a lattice revocable ciphertext policy based attribute base encryption scheme. The contributions of our scheme are as follows:

(1) The rapid development of quantum algorithms and quantum computers, post-quantum cryptography have also received great attention. Due to the uniqueness of lattice, its use is more maturely developed. And our RL-ABE

scheme uses exactly the LWE problem in lattice, which is resistant to quantum attacks.

(2) The efficient revocation mechanism fits increasingly well with our evolving network environment. Due to the different system environments, the granularity of revocation used is also different. Faced with users who need to be registered or malicious users, user revocation can be used to achieve this. Our scheme uses revocation binomial tree to update the ciphertext, and this revocation is a direct revocation performed by data service manager, which enhances the efficiency of revocation.

(3) We propose a novel revocation mechanism. In the revocation binomial tree, the node values are a set of associated random matrices. The ciphertext is updated by a simple operation, which in turn enables user revocation. In this process, there is no need to generate an update key, which enhances the security of the scheme.

(4) Monotonic Spanning Procedure (MSP). The access structure used in the scheme is a linear secret sharing scheme, and the monotonic access structure is a Boolean formula consisting of AND and OR operators. We apply this access structure to the lattice based attribute encryption scheme, which makes the scheme more efficient.

1.3 Paper Organization

The rest of the paper is structured as follows: Sect. 2 describes some preparatory knowledge, i.e., notation, lattice theory, related algorithms, hard problems, binary trees, and LSSS. Section 3 describes the system structure, model definition, and security proof. Section 4 elaborates the concrete construction of the scheme. Section 5 proves the correctness of the scheme and analysis of parameters. Section 6 describes security proof of the scheme. Section 7 compares with other related schemes for performance analysis. Finally, Sect. 8 presents the concluding remarks and the next steps of the paper.

2 Preliminaries

In this section, we will introduce the basics related to the lattice and some other essential knowledge.

2.1 Notations

The set of real numbers (integers) is denoted by $\mathbb{R}$ ($\mathbb{Z}$, resp.). Vector is represented by bold lowercase letters(e.g., $\mathbf{e}$) and are column vectors by default in this paper. The matrix is represented by bold uppercase letters(e.g., $\mathbf{A}$) and consists of a set of column vectors. For any integer $q \geq 2$, we let $\mathbb{Z}_q$ denote the ring of integers modulo q. We let $\mathbb{Z}_q^{n\times m}$ denote the set of $n \times m$ matrix with integers modulo q. The two-parametric and infinite-parametric numbers are denoted by l_2 and l_∞, respectively. Let $\|\mathrm{X}\| = \max_i \|x_i\|$ denotes the norm of the matrix

X. For two matrices $X \in \mathbb{Z}^{n\times m_1}$ and $Y \in \mathbb{Z}^{n\times m_2}$, $(X \| Y) \in {}^{n\times(m_1+m_2)}$ denote the concatenation of the columns of X followed by the columns of Y. Similarly, for two matrices $X \in \mathbb{Z}^{n\times m}$ and $Y \in \mathbb{Z}^{n'\times m}$, $(X;Y) \in \mathbb{Z}^{(n+n')\times m}$ denote the concatenation of the rows of X followed by the rows of Y.

2.2 Lattice

Definition 1 [3]: Let $b_1, b_2, \cdots, b_m \in \mathbb{R}^n$ be a set of linearly independent vectors. Define $B \in \mathbb{Z}_q^{n\times m}$ as the matrix consisting of the set of vectors $b_1, b_2, \cdots, b_m$. A full rank lattice $\mathcal{L}$ which is an integer span of B can be represented as:

$$\mathcal{L}(B) = \mathcal{L}(b_1, b_2, \cdots, b_m) = \left\{\sum x_i b_i \,|x_i \in \mathbb{Z}\right\}$$

Definition 2: For a matrix $A \in \mathbb{Z}^{n\times m}$, a vector $u \in \mathbb{Z}_q^n$, and a prime number q, then:

$$\Lambda_q^{\perp}(A) = \{x \in \mathbb{Z}^m : Ax = 0 \,(\mathrm{mod} q)\}$$

$$\Lambda_q^{u}(A) = \{x \in \mathbb{Z}^m : Ax = u \,(\mathrm{mod} q)\}$$

Definition 3 (Discrete Gaussian) [3]: For any real number $r > 0$, define the Gaussian function $\rho_{r,c}(x)$ to be centered on c with parameter r on $\mathcal{L} \subset \mathbb{Z}^n$:

$$\forall x \in \mathcal{L}, \rho_{r,c}(x) = \exp(-\pi \frac{\| x - c \|}{r^2})$$

Let $\rho_{r,c}(\mathcal{L}) = \sum_{x\in\mathcal{L}} \rho_{r,c}(x)$. For the real $r > 0$ and n-dimensional lattice $\mathcal{L}$, the discrete Gaussian distribution on lattice is defined as:

$$\forall y \in \mathcal{L}, D_{\mathcal{L},\mathrm{r,c}}(y) = \frac{\rho_{r,c}(y)}{\rho_{r,c}(\mathcal{L})}$$

When the values of c and $r > 0$ respectively are 0 and 1, the subscript can be omitted.

2.3 Related Algorithms

TrapGen(q, n) $\rightarrow$ **(A, T_A)** [10]: For a prime $q > 2$, a positive integer n and $m \geq 5n \log q$, there is a probabilistic polynomial time (PPT) algorithm TrapGen(q, n). The output a full rank matrix $A \in \mathbb{Z}_q^{n\times m}$ and $T_A \in \mathbb{Z}_q^{m\times m}$, where A is statistically uniform on $\mathbb{Z}_q^{n\times m}$, $T_A \in \mathbb{Z}_q^{m\times m}$ is the base of the lattice $\Lambda_q^{\perp}(A)$ and $\| \tilde{T}_A \| \leq m \cdot \omega(\sqrt{\log m})$.

SamplePre **(A, T_A, u, σ)** $\rightarrow$ ***e*** [10]: For a prime $q > 2$, a full rank matrix $A \in \mathbb{Z}_q^{n\times m}$, a basis for $T_A \in \mathbb{Z}_q^{m\times m}$, a vector $u \in \mathbb{Z}_q^n$ and a Gaussian parameter $\sigma > \left\|\tilde{T}_A\right\| \omega\left(\sqrt{\log m}\right)$, outputs a vector $e \in \mathbb{Z}^m$ sampled from a distribution statistically close to $D_{\Lambda_q^u(A),\sigma}$ and satisfied $e \in \Lambda_q^u(A)$.

SampleD $(\mathrm{A}, T_{\mathrm{A}}, \mathrm{U}, \sigma) \rightarrow \mathrm{X}$ [10]: For a prime $q > 2$, a full rank matrix $\mathrm{A} \in \mathbb{Z}_q^{n\times m}$, a basis $\mathrm{T_A} \in \mathbb{Z}_q^{m\times m}$ for $\Lambda_q^{\perp}(\mathrm{A})$, a matrix $\mathrm{U} \in \mathbb{Z}_q^{n\times k}$ and a Gaussian parameter $\sigma > \left\|\tilde{T}_{\mathrm{A}}\right\| \omega\left(\sqrt{\log m}\right)$, outputs a matrix $\mathrm{X} \in \mathbb{Z}^{m\times k}$ sampled from a distribution statistically close to $D_{\Lambda_q^U(\mathrm{A}),\sigma}$.

SampleLeft $(\mathrm{A},\mathrm{B}, T_{\mathrm{A}}, u, \sigma) \rightarrow e$ [10]: For a full rank matrix $\mathrm{A} \in \mathbb{Z}_q^{n\times m}$, a matrix $\mathrm{B} \in \mathbb{Z}_q^{n\times m_1}$, a basis $\mathrm{T_A} \in \mathbb{Z}_q^{m\times m}$ for $\mathrm{T_A} \in \mathbb{Z}_q^{m\times m}$, a vector $u \in \mathbb{Z}_q^n$ and a Gaussian parameter $\sigma > \left\|\tilde{T}_{\mathrm{A}}\right\| \omega\left(\sqrt{\log m + m_1}\right)$, outputs a vector $e \in \mathbb{Z}^{m+m_1}$ sampled from a distribution statistically close to $D_{\Lambda_q^u(\mathrm{A}||\mathrm{B}),\sigma}$ and satisfied $(\mathrm{A}||\mathrm{B}) \cdot e = u \bmod q$.

SampleRight $(\mathrm{A},\mathrm{B},\mathrm{R}, u, \sigma) \rightarrow e$ [10]: For a full rank matrix $\mathrm{A},\mathrm{B} \in \mathbb{Z}_q^{n\times m}$, a matrix $\mathrm{R} \in \{-1,1\}^{m\times m}$, a basis $\mathrm{T_B} \in \mathbb{Z}_q^{m\times m}$ for $\Lambda_q^{\perp}(\mathrm{B})$, a vector $u \in \mathbb{Z}_q^n$ and a Gaussian parameter $\sigma > \left\|\tilde{T}_{\mathrm{A}}\right\| \cdot \|\mathrm{R}\| \, \omega\left(\sqrt{\log m}\right)$, outputs a vector $e \in \mathbb{Z}^{2m}$ sampled from a distribution statistically close to $D_{\Lambda_q^u(\mathrm{A}||\mathrm{AR}+\mathrm{B}),\sigma}$ and satisfied $(\mathrm{A}||\mathrm{AR}+\mathrm{B}) \cdot e = u \bmod q$.

Leftover Hash Lemma [15]: For $m > (n+1)\log q + \omega(\log n)$, Uniform random matrix $\mathrm{S} \in \{-1,1\}^{m\times m}$ and $\mathrm{A},\mathrm{B} \in \mathbb{Z}_q^{n\times m}$, there is $\left(\mathrm{A},\mathrm{AS},\mathrm{S}^{\top}e\right) \overset{c}{\approx} (\mathrm{A},\mathrm{B},e)$ for a vector $e \in \mathbb{Z}_q^n$.

2.4 The LWE Hardness Assumption

Definition 4 [3]: **Decisional Learning With Errors (DLWE)** Given a prime number q and a positive integer n, defined a normal distribution $\Psi_\alpha\,(\alpha > 0)$. its center is 0 and variance is $\alpha/\sqrt{2\pi}$. Suppose the learning with error χ on $\mathbb{Z}_q$, define the distribution $\mathrm{A}_{s,\chi}$ on $(u_i, v_i) = \left(u_i, {u_i}^{\top}s + x_i\right) \in \mathbb{Z}_q^n \times \mathbb{Z}_q$, where $u_i \in \mathbb{Z}_q^n$ is a randomly selected vector, $x_i \in \mathbb{Z}_q$ is independently selected according to the distribution χ.

The decision $(\mathbb{Z}_q, n, \chi) - LWE$ is hard to distinguish between the pseudo-random distribution and the true random distribution on $\mathrm{A}_{s,\chi}$ and $\mathbb{Z}_q^n \times \mathbb{Z}_q$.

2.5 Binary Tree

The scheme uses the property of complete binary trees for revocation. Assuming that the set of system attributes is $Q = \{att_1, \cdots, att_{|S|}\}$ and the set of system users is $U = \{u_1, \cdots, u_{|U|}\}$. $|U|$ is the number of users, and constructing a binary tree with users as leaf nodes will result in $2|U| - 1$ nodes.

1. Generate a random matrix $\mathrm{B}_0 \in \mathbb{Z}_q^{n\times m}$ containing trapdoor as the root node.The non-leaf node is $\mathrm{B}_i = \mathrm{B}_0\mathrm{M}_i, i \in [1, |U| - 2]$ with $\mathrm{M}_i \in \{0,1\}^{m\times m}$. The leaf node is $\mathrm{B}_j = \mathrm{B}_0\mathrm{N}_j, j \in [|U| - 1, 2|U| - 2]$ with $\mathrm{N}_j \in \{-1,1\}^{m\times m}$. We let M_i be a reversible matrix with one and only one 1 in each row and column and all the rest 0s. N_j is also a revertible matrix. The binary tree is shown in Fig. 1.

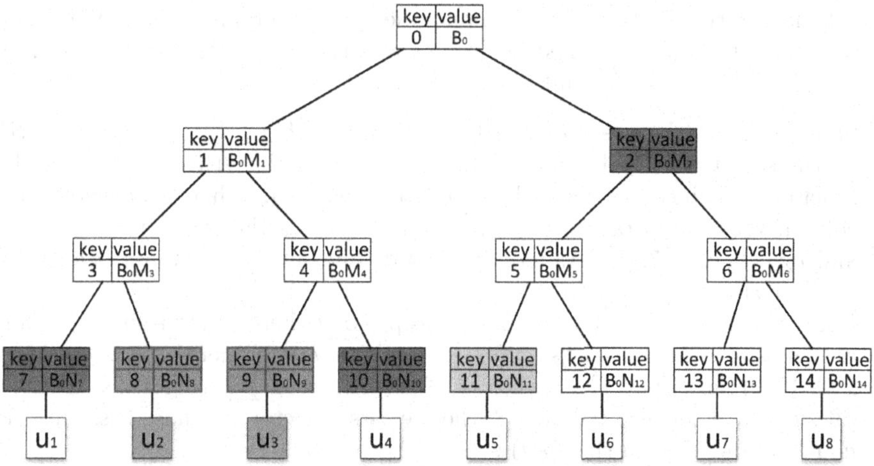

Fig. 1. Binary Tree.

2. We give Table 1 as an example of KUNodes algorithm. An example is as follows. If the user revocation list is $R = \{u_2, u_3\}$, the minimum set of coverage without revoked users is $\text{cover}(R) = \{2, 7, 10\}$. When the added revocation user is u_5, the updated revocation list is $R' = \{u_2, u_3, u_5\}$, and the minimum set of coverage without revoked users is $\text{cover}(R') = \{6, 7, 10, 12\}$. The path of user u_6 in a binary tree is $path(u_6) = path(12) = \{0, 2, 5, 12\}$. Therefore, there is one and only one node that satisfies $j = \text{cover}(R) \bigcap path(u_6) = \{2\}$. But the path of user u_2 in a binary tree is $path(u_2) = path(8) = \{0, 1, 3, 8\}$. There is $\text{cover}(R) \bigcap path(u_2) = \emptyset$.

Table 1. KUNodes.

Algorithm: KUNodes algorithm
Input: BT, RL.
Output: Y.
1. $X, Y \leftarrow \emptyset$; $\forall \gamma \in$ RL, set $X \leftarrow X \cup Path(\gamma)$.
2. $\forall \gamma \in X$:
If $\gamma_L \notin X$, set $Y \leftarrow Y \cup \{\gamma_L\}$;
If $\gamma_R \notin X$, set $Y \leftarrow Y \cup \{\gamma_R\}$.
3. $Y \leftarrow \emptyset$, set $Y \leftarrow Y \cup \{root\}$.
4. Return Y.

2.6 LSSS

Linear secret sharing scheme (LSSS) [2]: The LSSS matrices are transformed by Boolean formulae, and transformation is given through scheme [13](Appendix

G). Boolean formulae is called the monotone span programs(MSPs). We define the matrix L to be transformed by the access structure $\mathbb{A}$. An MSP is given by a matrix $L \in \{-1,0,1\}^{l \times n}$ and a mapping ρ.

1. Sharing: Let S be a set of attributes and $I = \{i | i \in \{1, \cdots, l\}, \rho(i) \in S\}$ be the set of rows in L that belong to S. For all the i-th row of L, let the function ρ defined the party labeling row i as $\rho(i)$. When we consider the column vector $v = (s, r_2, \cdots, r_n)$, where $s \in \mathbb{Z}_p$ is the secret to be shared, and $r_2, \cdots, r_n \in \mathbb{Z}_p$ are randomly chosen. The share $\lambda_i = L_i \cdot v$ belongs to party $\rho(i)$.
2. Reconstruction: We say that (L, π) accepts S if there exists a linear combination of rows in that gives $(1, 0, \cdots, 0)$. For $\rho(i) \in S$ there exist coefficients $\omega_i \in \{0,1\}$ such that $\sum_{i \in I} \omega_i L_i = (1, 0, \cdots, 0)$, then $\sum_{i \in I} \omega_i \lambda_i = s$. If it not satisfied by a set of attributes S, there exists a vector ϖ whose first entry is non-zero and $\forall i$ such that $\rho(i) \in S, \langle \varpi, L_i \rangle = 0$.

3 System Model and Security Model

3.1 System Architecture

In this section we describe our RL-ABE scheme through the system architecture, the model definition and the security model. The system architecture contains five main entities, as shown in Fig. 2:

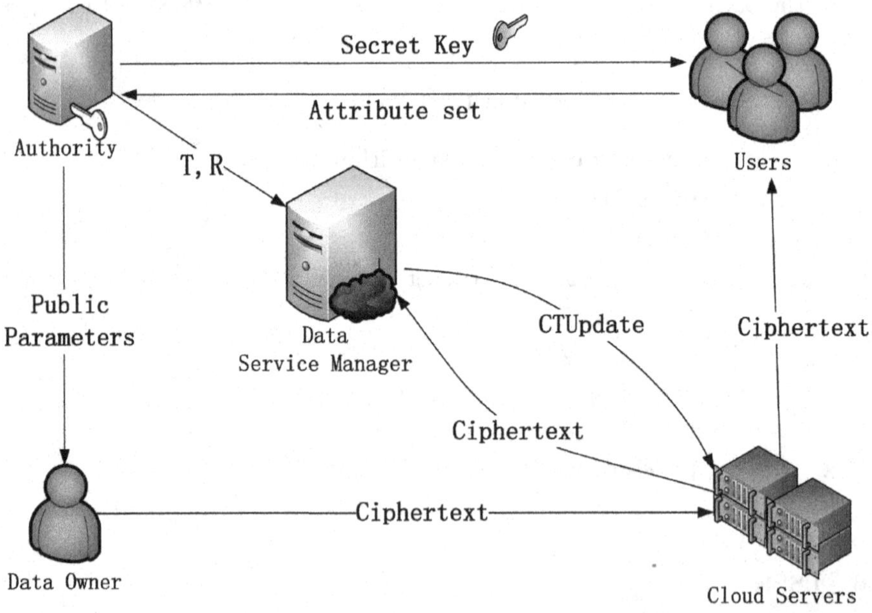

Fig. 2. System Model.

- **Authority**: The authority defines the corresponding attributes according to the user's identity and assigns the key corresponding to the attributes to the user. It is a fully trusted authority.
- **Data Owner**: The data owner defines the access control policy and encrypts the message, which in turn uploads the ciphertext to the cloud storage.
- **Cloud**: The cloud stores cryptographic data and provides data access for users.
- **User**: The user accesses the data in the cloud and downloads the ciphertext data to local. Only when the user's attributes satisfy the access policy and is not in the revocation list, he/she can use his/her private key to decrypt the ciphertext.
- **Data Service Manager**: Data Service Manager stores the binary tree and updates the user's ciphertext and revocation list at the time of revocation, i.e., the revocation function is implemented for users who need to be revoked.

3.2 Model Definition

The RL-ABE consists of five algorithms, as follows:

- ***Setup*** $(\lambda, Q, U) \rightarrow (PP, MSK)$: The authority runs the algorithm. And it inputs a security parameter λ, system attribute set Q and users set U. It outputs the public parameter PP that will be issued and the reserved system master key MSK. It also generates a complete binary tree $\mathcal{T}$ consisting of the user set and the revocation list R.
- ***KeyGen*** $(PP, S, MSK) \rightarrow SK$: The authority runs the algorithm. Input public parameter PP, the user's attribute set S and system master key MSK. Output the private key SK for that user and send it.
- ***Encrypt*** $(PP, W, \mu) \rightarrow CT$: The data owner runs the algorithm. Input public parameters PP, access policy W and plaintext message $\mu \in \{0, 1\}$. Output the ciphertext CT and upload to the cloud.
- ***Decrypt*** $(PP, CT, SK) \rightarrow \mu/\perp$: The user runs the algorithm. The public parameters PP, the ciphertext CT and user's private key SK are taken as input. If the user's attribute set S satisfies the access policy W and the user is not in the revocation list R, the decryption can be successful; otherwise the decryption fails.
- ***CTUpdate*** $(PP, R', CT) \rightarrow CT'$: The data service manager runs the algorithm. The public parameters PP, the latest revocation list R' and ciphertext CT are used as input. The updated ciphertext CT' is output based on the values of the nodes in the binary tree.

3.3 Security Model

The RL-ABE scheme we describe is with a selective security model. The security model is described by the game between the challenger $\mathcal{C}$ and the adversary $\mathcal{A}$ as follows:

Init. Adversary $\mathcal{A}$ selects an access policy W^* associated with a set of attributes and a revocation list R^*, and sends to challenger $\mathcal{C}$;
Setup. Challenger $\mathcal{C}$ runs the Setup algorithm and sends the public parameter PP to adversary $\mathcal{A}$, while retaining the MSK;
Phase1. Adversary $\mathcal{A}$ adaptively performs multiple key generation queries on the condition that the key is not satisfying the access policy;
Challenge. Adversary $\mathcal{A}$ sends two equal-length messages $\mu_0 \neq \mu_1$. Challenger $\mathcal{C}$ randomly flips a coin $b \in \{0, 1\}$, calculates the corresponding ciphertext and sends it to the adversary;
Phase2. Similar to phase 1, the adversary $\mathcal{A}$ continues to ask the challenger $\mathcal{C}$ for the private key;
Guess. Adversary $\mathcal{A}$ outputs guess $b' \in \{0, 1\}$ of b.

The advantage of adversary $\mathcal{A}$ is defined with the above IND-CPA game as follows:

$$Adv_{\mathcal{A}}^{IND-CPA}(\lambda) = \left| \Pr\left[b = b'\right] - \frac{1}{2} \right|$$

Definition 5: Ours RL-ABE scheme is secure if the advantage $Adv_{\mathcal{A}}^{IND-CPA}$ (λ) is negligible in λ for all polynomial time adversary $\mathcal{A}$.

4 Construction of RL-ABE Scheme

In this section, the specific steps of the RL-ABE scheme are described as follows:

Setup $(\boldsymbol{\lambda}, \boldsymbol{Q}, \boldsymbol{U})$: Input security parameters λ, the set of system attributes $Q = \{att_1, att_2, \cdots, att_{|S|}\}$ and the maximum set of users U. The system parameters are $n, m, q, l, \sigma, \alpha$:

1. For each att_i, the authority uses algorithm TrapGen(n, m, q) to generate a uniform random matrix $\mathrm{A}_i \in \mathbb{Z}^{n\times m}$ with a short base $T_{\mathrm{A}_i} \subseteq \Lambda_q^{\perp}(\mathrm{A}_i)$ such that $\| \tilde{T}_{\mathrm{A}_i} \| \leqslant o(\sqrt{n\log q})$.
2. Call the algorithm TrapGen(n, m, q) to generate a uniform random matrix $\mathrm{U} = \left[\mathrm{U}_1|\mathrm{U}_2|\cdots|\mathrm{U}_{|S|}\right] \in \mathbb{Z}^{n\times m}$ with $\mathrm{U}_i \in \mathbb{Z}^{n\times \eta}, m = \eta|S|$ and a short base $T_{\mathrm{U}} \subseteq \Lambda_q^{\perp}(\mathrm{U})$ such that $\| \tilde{T}_{\mathrm{U}} \| \leqslant o(\sqrt{n\log q})$. Meanwhile, it also generates a uniform random matrix $\mathrm{B}_0 \in \mathbb{Z}_q^{n\times m}$ and a short basis $T_{\mathrm{B}_0} \subseteq \Lambda_q^{\perp}(\mathrm{B}_0)$ such that $\| \tilde{T}_{\mathrm{B}_0} \| \leqslant o(\sqrt{n\log q})$.
3. Generate vector $u = (u_1, u_2, \cdots, u_n) \in \mathbb{Z}_q^n$ randomly. System users U construct a complete binary tree $\mathcal{T}$ as described in Sect. 2.5; and the initial revocation list is R.
4. Return the public parameters PP and the master key MSK:

$$\mathrm{PP} = \left(\{\mathrm{A}_i\}_{i\in|S|}, \mathrm{B}_0, \mathrm{U}, u, \{\mathrm{M}_i\}_{i\in[1,|U|-2]}, \{\mathrm{N}_j\}_{j\in[|U|-1,2|U|-2]}, R, \mathcal{T}\right)$$

$$MSK = \left(\{T_{\mathrm{A}_i}\}_{i\in|S|}, T_{\mathrm{B}_0}, T_{\mathrm{U}}\right)$$

KeyGen (S, PP, MSK): Input the public parameters PP, the master key MSK and the attribute set S corresponding to the user u, and output the user's private key SK:

1. For each $att_i \in Q$, the authority uses algorithm SampleD $(\mathrm{A}_i, T_{\mathrm{A}_i}, \mathrm{U}_i, \sigma)$ to output $\mathrm{X}_i \in \mathbb{Z}^{m \times \eta}$ so that $\mathrm{A}_i \cdot \mathrm{X}_i = \mathrm{U}_i(\mathrm{mod} q)$.
2. The set of attributes S corresponding to user u generates matrix $\mathrm{U}' = [\mathrm{U}'_1 | \mathrm{U}'_2 | \cdots | \mathrm{U}'_{|S|}] \in \mathbb{Z}^{n \times m}$ and $T_{\mathrm{U}'}$ with $\mathrm{U}'_i = \mathrm{U}_i, i \in S \cap Q; \mathrm{U}'_i = 0 \in \mathbb{Z}^{n \times \eta}, i \notin S \cap Q$. Then call algorithm SamplePre$(\mathrm{U}', T_{\mathrm{U}'}, u, \sigma)$ to output $e = (e_1, e_2, \cdots, e_{|S|})$ with $e_i \in \mathbb{Z}_q^{\eta \times 1}$ so that $\mathrm{U}' \cdot e = u(\mathrm{mod} q)$.
3. For user u, there is $Path(i) = \{i_0, \cdots, i_u\}$, where i_0 is the root node and i_u is the leaf node corresponding to the user. Run SampleLeft $(\mathrm{B}_0, \mathrm{B}_{i_u}, T_{\mathrm{B}_0}, \sigma, u)$ for the user's leaf node value B_{i_u} and output e_{i_u}. Noting $\mathrm{E}_{i_u} = (\mathrm{B}_0 \| \mathrm{B}_{i_u})$, there exists $\mathrm{E}_{i_u} \cdot e_{i_u} = u(\mathrm{mod} q)$.
4. Return the private key of user u who owns attribute set S is SK:

$$SK = \left(\{\mathrm{X}_i, e_i\}_{i \in |S|}, e_{i_u} \right)$$

Encrypt (PP, W, μ): The data owner inputs the public parameters PP, the access policy $W = (\mathrm{L}, \rho)$ and the encrypted message $\mu \in \{0, 1\}$.

1. The data owner defines an access policy $W = (\mathrm{L}, \rho)$, where $\mathrm{L} \in_q^{l \times n}$ is a linear secret sharing matrix and the mapping $\rho : [l] \to Q$ associates each row of the matrix L with an attribute in the attribute set Q. A secret vector $s \in \mathbb{Z}_q^n$ and a random vector $a = (a_1, a_2, \cdots, a_n) \in \mathbb{Z}_q^n$ are chosen to generate a random vector $v = (a^{\mathrm{T}} s, v_2, \cdots, v_n) \in \mathbb{Z}_q^n$ with random values $v_2, \cdots, v_n \in \mathbb{Z}_q$. Choose the noise vectors $e_1 \leftarrow \chi_{lwe}^m$ and $\{e_{i,2}\}_{i \in [l]} \leftarrow \chi_{lwe}^m$, there is $C_1 = Lv + e_1$. For each $i \in [l]$, there is $C_{i,1} = L_i v + e_{i,1}, C_{i,2} = \mathrm{A}_i^{\mathrm{T}} a + e_{i,2}$.
2. Select noise $\hat{e} \leftarrow \chi_{lwe}$ and $e_1 \leftarrow \chi_{lwe}$, encrypt message $\mu \in \{0, 1\}$ and then output ciphertexts $C = a^{\mathrm{T}} u + e + \mu \left\lfloor \frac{q}{2} \right\rfloor$ and $\hat{C} = a^{\mathrm{T}} s + \hat{e}$.
3. Take any random vector $b \in \mathbb{Z}_q^n$. For each $j \in \mathrm{cover}(R)$, choose the noise $\{e_j\}_{j \in \mathrm{cover}(R)} \leftarrow \chi_{lwe}^m$, $\tilde{e} \leftarrow \chi_{lwe}^m$ and $\bar{e} \leftarrow \chi_{lwe}$, output $C_j = B_j^{\top} \cdot b + e_j$, $C_0 = B_0^{\top} \cdot b + \tilde{e}$, $\bar{C} = u^{\top} b + \bar{e}$.
4. Return to ciphertext CT:

$$CT = \left(C_1, \{C_{i,2}\}_{i \in [l]}, \hat{C}, C, C_0, \{C_j\}_{j \in \mathrm{cover}(R)}, \bar{C} \right)$$

Decrypt (PP, SK, CT): Inputs public parameter PP, private key SK and ciphertext CT. If the set of attributes corresponding to the user $S \nvDash W$ or $u \in R$, the algorithm outputs $\perp$. If $S \vDash W$ and $u \notin R$, the algorithm runs as follows:

1. Define $I = \{i : \rho(i) \in S\}$. Then a set of numbers $\{\omega_i\}_{i \in I} \in \{0, 1\}^*$ can be reconstructed in polynomial time to satisfy $\sum_{i \in I} \omega_i \mathrm{L}_i = (1, 0, \cdots, 0)$.

2. For $j \in \text{cover}(R) \cap path(u)$, if j is a non-leaf node, then

$$y = \left(C_0; \mathrm{N}_{i_u}^{\top}\left(\mathrm{M}_j^{\top}\right)^{-1} C_j\right) = \begin{pmatrix} C_0 \\ C_{i_u} \end{pmatrix}$$
$$= \begin{pmatrix} \mathrm{B}_0^{\top} \cdot b \\ \mathrm{B}_{i_u}{}^{\top} \cdot b \end{pmatrix} + \begin{pmatrix} \tilde{e} \\ \mathrm{N}_{i_u}^{\top}\left(\mathrm{M}_j^{\top}\right)^{-1} e_j \end{pmatrix}$$
$$= \mathrm{E}_{i_u}{}^{\top} \cdot b + e'$$

If j is a leaf node, then

$$y = (C_0; C_{i_u}) = \begin{pmatrix} C_0 \\ C_{i_u} \end{pmatrix} = \begin{pmatrix} B_0^{\top} \cdot b \\ B_{i_u}{}^{\top} \cdot b \end{pmatrix} + \begin{pmatrix} \tilde{e} \\ e_j \end{pmatrix} = E_{i_u}{}^{\top} \cdot b + e'$$

3. The user runs the decryption algorithm and calculates: $x = C + \hat{C} - \sum_{i \in I} \omega_i \cdot C_{i,1} - \sum_{i \in I} C_{i,2}^{\top} \cdot \mathrm{X}_i \cdot e_i$ $x + \bar{C} - e_{i_u}^{\top} \cdot y$

CTUpdate (R', PP, CT): The data service manager runs the ciphertext update algorithm. The input public parameter PP, the latest revocation list R' and the ciphertext CT. cover(R') is the minimum coverage set associated with the latest revocation list R' and cover(R) is the minimum coverage set associated with the latest revocation list R.

If j' is a non-leaf node, then $C'_{j'} = \mathrm{M}_{j'}^{\top}\left(\mathrm{M}_j^{\top}\right)^{-1} C_j$. If j' is a leaf node, then $C'_{j'} = \mathrm{N}_{j'}^{\top}\left(\mathrm{M}_j^{\top}\right)^{-1} C_j$. The output is the updated ciphertext CT':

$$CT' = \left(C_1, \{C_{i,2}\}_{i \in [l]}, \hat{C}, C, C_0, \{C'_{j'}\}_{j' \in \text{cover}(R')}, \bar{C}\right)$$

5 Correctness and Parameter Analysis

5.1 Correctness

The following equation is calculated to achieve decryption.

$$\begin{aligned} x =& C + \hat{C} - \sum\nolimits_{i \in I} \omega_i \cdot C_{i,1} - \sum\nolimits_{i \in I} C_{i,2}^{\top} \cdot \mathrm{X}_i \cdot e_i \\ =& a^{\top} u + e + \mu \left\lfloor \tfrac{q}{2} \right\rfloor + a^{\top} s + \hat{e} - \sum\nolimits_{i \in I} \omega_i \cdot (\mathrm{L}_i v + e_{i,1}) - \sum\nolimits_{i \in I} \left(a^{\top} \mathrm{A}_i + e_{i,2}^{\top}\right) \mathrm{X}_i \cdot e_i \\ =& \cancel{a^{\top}} u + e + \mu \left\lfloor \tfrac{q}{2} \right\rfloor + \cancel{a^{\top}} s + \hat{e} - \cancel{a^{\top}} s - \sum\nolimits_{i \in I} \omega_i \cdot e_{i,1} - \left(\cancel{a^{\top}} u + \sum\nolimits_{i \in I} e_{i,2}^{\top} \cdot \mathrm{X}_i \cdot e_i\right) \\ =& \mu \left\lfloor \tfrac{q}{2} \right\rfloor + e + \hat{e} - \sum\nolimits_{i \in I} \omega_i \cdot e_{i,1} - \sum\nolimits_{i \in I} e_{i,2}^{\top} \cdot \mathrm{X}_i \cdot e_i \\ =& \mu \left\lfloor \tfrac{q}{2} \right\rfloor + x' \end{aligned}$$

Where x' means $e + \hat{e} - \sum_{i \in I} \omega_i e_{i,1} - \sum_{i \in I} e_{i,2}^{\top} \cdot \mathrm{X}_i \cdot e_i$.

$$\begin{aligned} x + \bar{C} - e_{i_u}^{\top} \cdot y &= \mu \left\lfloor \tfrac{q}{2} \right\rfloor + x' + u^{\top} b + \bar{e} - e_{i_u}^{\top}\left(\mathrm{E}_{i_u}{}^{\top} \cdot b + e'\right) \\ &= \mu \left\lfloor \tfrac{q}{2} \right\rfloor + x' + \cancel{u^{\top} b} + \bar{e} - \cancel{u^{\top} b} - e_{i_u}^{\top} \cdot e' \\ &= \mu \left\lfloor \tfrac{q}{2} \right\rfloor + x' + \bar{e} - e_{i_u}^{\top} \cdot e' \\ &= \mu \left\lfloor \tfrac{q}{2} \right\rfloor + x'' \end{aligned}$$

Where x'' means $x' + \bar{e} - e_{i_u}^{\top} \cdot e'$.

If $|x''| < \frac{q}{5}$ holds, then it can be decrypted correctly. And when $\left|x + \bar{C} - e_{i_u}^{\top} \cdot y\right| < \frac{q}{5}$, then the output is 0, otherwise the output is 1.

5.2 Update Ciphertext

If j' is a non-leaf node, then

$$\begin{aligned} C_{j'} &= \mathrm{M}_{j'}^{\top}\left(\mathrm{M}_j^{\top}\right)^{-1} C_j \\ &= \mathrm{M}_{j'}^{\top}\left(\mathrm{M}_j^{\top}\right)^{-1}\left(\mathrm{B}_j^{\top} s + e_j\right) \\ &= \mathrm{B}_{j'}^{\top} s + \mathrm{M}_{j'}^{\top}\left(\mathrm{M}_j^{\top}\right)^{-1} e_j \\ &= \mathrm{B}_{j'}^{\top} s + e_1' \end{aligned}$$

If j' is a leaf node, then

$$\begin{aligned} C_{j'} &= \mathrm{N}_{j'}^{\top}\left(\mathrm{M}_j^{\top}\right)^{-1} C_j \\ &= \mathrm{N}_{j'}^{\top}\left(\mathrm{M}_j^{\top}\right)^{-1}\left(\mathrm{B}_j^{\top} s + e_j\right) \\ &= \mathrm{B}_{j'}^{\top} s + \mathrm{N}_{j'}^{\top}\left(\mathrm{M}_j^{\top}\right)^{-1} e_j \\ &= \mathrm{B}_{j'}^{\top} s + e_2' \end{aligned}$$

In which $e_1' = \mathrm{M}_{j'}^{\top}\left(\mathrm{M}_j^{\top}\right)^{-1} e_j, e_2' = \mathrm{N}_{j'}^{\top}\left(\mathrm{M}_j^{\top}\right)^{-1} e_{j,}$.

5.3 Parameters

The safety parameter is λ and the upper bound on the number of attributes is $|S|$. (1) For the hard problem LWE, ensure that $\alpha q \geqslant 2\sqrt{m}$. (2) For TrapGen$(n, m, q)$, require $m > 5n \log q$. (3) For SampleGaussian$(\Lambda, \mathrm{B}, \sigma, c)$, have $\|e_j\| \leqslant \sigma\sqrt{m}$. (4) To ensure that correctness holds, it is necessary to make $|x''| < \frac{q}{5}$ hold.

$$\begin{aligned} |x''| &= \left|e + \hat{e} - \sum\nolimits_{i \in I} \omega_i e_{i,1} - \sum\nolimits_{i \in I} e_{i,2}^{\top} \mathrm{X}_i e_i + \bar{e} - e_{i_u}^{\top} e'\right| \\ &\leqslant \sigma + \sigma - l \cdot \sigma - l \cdot \sqrt{m}\sigma \cdot \sqrt{m\eta}\sigma \cdot \sqrt{\eta}\sigma + \sigma - \sqrt{2m}\sigma \cdot \sqrt{2m}\sigma \\ &\leqslant 3\sigma + l\sigma + lm\eta\sigma^3 + 2m\sigma^2 \end{aligned}$$

6 Security Analysis

Theorem: If there exists a probabilistic polynomial adversary $\mathcal{A}$ that solves our solution RL-ABE by a non-negligible advantage $\varepsilon > 0$, then there exists a probabilistic polynomial challenger $\mathcal{C}$ that distinguishes the decisional $\left(\mathbb{Z}_q, n, \bar{\Psi}_\alpha\right) -$

LWE problem with the advantage $\varepsilon/2$. ***Proof***: Provide an instance of the LWE problem as a sampling prediction machine $\mathcal{O}$. For some secret key $s \in \mathbb{Z}_q^n$, it can be either true random O_s' or noisy pseudo-random O_s. Challenger $\mathcal{C}$ uses adversary $\mathcal{A}$ to distinguish between the two. The proof is as follows:

Instance. Challenger $\mathcal{C}$ accesses LWE sampling predictor O to get samples: $(a, v_{a_1}, v_{a_2}) \in (\mathbb{Z}_q^n \times \mathbb{Z}_q \times \mathbb{Z}_q)$ $[(\mathrm{A}_1, x_1), \cdots (\mathrm{A}_{|S|}, x_{|S|})] \in (\mathbb{Z}_q^{n\times m} \times \mathbb{Z}_q^m)^{|S|}$ $(\mathrm{B}_0, \{x_0, \cdots, x_{2|U|-2}\}) \in \left(\mathbb{Z}_q^{n\times m} \times (\mathbb{Z}_q^m)^{2|U|-1}\right)$ ***Init***.Adversary $\mathcal{A}$ chooses an access policy $W^* = (\mathrm{L}^*, \rho^*)$ and a revocation list R^* for an attack and gives it to challenger $\mathcal{C}$. $\mathrm{L}^* \in \mathbb{Z}_q^{l^*\times n^*}$ the corresponding attribute sets I^*, and the mapping $\rho^*(i)$ corresponds to each row L_i^* in the matrix L^*. ***Setup***. Challenger $\mathcal{C}$ generates the integers n, m, q. For each att_i, call algorithms TrapGen $(n, m, q) \rightarrow (\mathrm{A}_i, T_{\mathrm{A}_i})$ and TrapGen $(n, m, q) \rightarrow (\mathrm{A}_i, T_{\mathrm{A}_i})$, where $\mathrm{U} = [\mathrm{U}_1 |\cdots |\mathrm{U}_{|S|}] \in \mathbb{Z}_q^{n\times m}$ and $m = \eta|S|$. For the revocation list R^*, there is $I_{R^*} = \{i \in path(u) | u \in R^*\}$. Generate public parameter $PP = \left(\{\mathrm{A}_i\}_{i\in|S|}, \mathrm{B}_0, \mathrm{U}, u\right)$ to send to adversary $\mathcal{A}$ and retain $MSK = \left(\{T_{\mathrm{A}_i}\}_{i\in|S|}, T_{\mathrm{U}}\right)$.

***Phase*1**. Adversary $\mathcal{A}$ sends the attribute set S^* of user u^* with private key query. *Case*1: If $S^* \models W^*$ and $u^* \notin R^*$, the challenger $\mathcal{C}$ outputs $\perp$; *Case*2: If $S^* \models W^*$ and $u^* \in R^*$, the challenger $\mathcal{C}$ runs as follows:

1. For each $att_i \in S^*$, call algorithm SampleD $(\mathrm{A}_i, T_{\mathrm{A}_i}, \mathrm{U}_i, \sigma) \rightarrow \mathrm{X}_i^*$, then $\mathrm{A}_i \cdot \mathrm{X}_i^* = \mathrm{U}_i (\mathrm{mod} q)$.
2. For the set of queried attributes S^*, generate matrices $\mathrm{U}_{S^*} = \left[\mathrm{U}_1^* | \mathrm{U}_2^* | \cdots | \mathrm{U}_{|S|}^*\right] \in \mathbb{Z}^{n\times m}$ and $T_{\mathrm{U}_{S^*}}$, where $\mathrm{U}_i^* = 0 \in \mathbb{Z}^{n\times\eta}, i \notin S^* \cap S$, $\mathrm{U}_i^* = \mathrm{U}_i, i \in S^* \cap S$.
3. Call algorithm SamplePre$(\mathrm{U}_{S^*}, T_{\mathrm{U}_{S^*}}, u, \sigma) \rightarrow e^*$ again, then we have $\mathrm{U}_{S^*} \cdot e^* = u(\mathrm{mod} q)$, where $e^* = (e_1^*, e_2^*, \cdots, e_{|S|}^*)$.
4. For user $u^* \in R^*$, there is $path(u^*) = \{i_0^*, \cdots, i_d^*\}$, $i_d^* \in I_{R^*}$, corresponding to leaf node matrix of $\mathrm{B}_{i_d^*} \in \mathbb{Z}_q^{n\times m}$. Define $\mathrm{E}_{i_d^*} = \mathrm{B}_0 || \mathrm{B}_{i_d^*}$. Choose $e_{i_d^*} \leftarrow D_{\mathbb{Z}_q^{2m}, \sigma}$ and compute $\mathrm{E}_{i_d^*} \cdot e_{i_d^*} = u$; Challenger $\mathcal{C}$ sends the private key of user u^*.

*Case*3: If $S^* \not\models W^*$ and $u^* \in R^*$, the challenger $\mathcal{C}$ runs as follows: For $I = \{i : \rho^*(i) \in S^*\}$, there exists a vector $\boldsymbol{\omega} = (\omega_1, \omega_2, \cdots, \omega_{n^*})$, where $\omega_1 \neq 0$, such that $\mathrm{L}_i^* \cdot \boldsymbol{\omega} = 0$. The rest of the runs are the same as *Case*2.

*Case*4: If $S^* \not\models W^*$ and $u^* \notin R^*$, the challenger $\mathcal{C}$ runs as follows: For user $u^* \notin R^*$, there is $path(u^*) = \{i_0^*, \cdots, i_d^*\}$, corresponding to leaf node matrix of $\mathrm{B}_{i_d^*} \in \mathbb{Z}_q^{n\times m}$. Call algorithm TrapGen $(n, m, q) \rightarrow \left(\mathrm{B}_{i_d^*}, T_{\mathrm{B}_{i_d^*}}\right)$. Choose a uniform random matrix $\mathrm{R}_0 \in \{-1, 1\}^{m\times m}$ and call right sampling algorithm SampleRight $(\mathrm{B}_0, \mathrm{B}_{i_d^*}, \mathrm{R}_0, \sigma, u) \rightarrow e_{i_d^*}$ with $\mathrm{E}_{i_d^*} \cdot e_{i_d^*} = u$, where $\mathrm{E}_{i_d^*} = \mathrm{B}_0 \| \mathrm{B}_0\mathrm{R}_0 + \mathrm{B}_{i_{d*}}$. The rest of the runs are the same as *Case*3.

$$SK = \left(\{\mathrm{X}_i^*\}_{i\in|S^*|}, e^*, e_{i_d^*}\right)$$

Challenge. Adversary $\mathcal{A}$ sends two equal-length messages μ_0, μ_1 to challenger $\mathcal{C}$. The challenger randomly chooses $b \in \{0, 1\}$ and encrypts μ_b under access policy W^*. The challenger chooses the secret value $s^* \in_q^n$ and the random vector $a \in_q^n$ to generate the random vector $v = (a^\top s, v_2, \cdots, v_{n^*}) \in_q^{n^*}$. For each $i \in I^*$, randomly select $\mathrm{R}, \mathrm{R}_{i,2} \in \{-1,1\}^{m\times m}$ and compute $C_1^* = L^* v$ and $C_{i,2} = \mathrm{R}_{i,1}^\top x_i$. For the selected μ_b, compute $C = v_{a_1} + \mu_b \lfloor q/2 \rfloor$ and $C_1 = v_{a_2}$.

For $\forall j \in \mathrm{cover}(R^*)$, randomly select $\mathrm{R}_j \in \{-1,1\}^{m\times m}$, $C_j = \mathrm{R}_j^\top \cdot x_j$, $\bar{C} = v_b$, $C_0 = \mathrm{R}_0^\top \cdot x_0$.

Return the challenge ciphertext:

$$CT = \left(C, C_0, C_1, C_1^*, \{C_{i,2}\}_{i\in[l]}, \{C_j\}_{j\in \mathrm{cover}(R)}, \bar{C}\right)$$

.

***Phase*2**. Similar to Phase1, the adversary continues to ask the challenger for the private key.

Guess. The adversary $\mathcal{A}$ outputs $b' \in \{0,1\}$ as a guess for b. If $b' = b$, then output $O = O_s$. If $b' \neq b$, then output $O = O_s'$.

Assuming that adversary $\mathcal{A}$ guesses the correct b with probability at least $1/2 + \varepsilon$, the challenger solves the decisional $({}_q, n, \bar{\Psi}_\alpha) - LWE$ problem with the following advantage:

$$\begin{aligned}
&\frac{1}{2}\Pr[b' = b | O = O_s] + \frac{1}{2}\Pr[b' = b | O = O_{s'}] - \frac{1}{2} \\
=&\frac{1}{2} \times \left(\frac{1}{2} + \varepsilon\right) + \frac{1}{2} \times \frac{1}{2} - \frac{1}{2} \\
=&\frac{\varepsilon}{2}
\end{aligned}$$

7 Performance Analysis

Table 2. The comparison of related schemes.

Scheme	ACS	Assumption	Revocable	not-UCK	QS
Datta [9]	LSSS	LWE	×	×	√
Han [12]	LSSS	q-BDHE	√	×	×
Chen [8]	—	LWE	√	×	√
Yang [24]	Threshold	LWE	√	×	√
Yang [25]	Access Tree	R-LWE	√	×	√
Ours	LSSS	LWE	√	√	√

In this paper, we compare the Access Control Structure(ACS), Assumption, whether revocation is supported, revocation without updating the ciphertext or key(not-UCK) and Quantum Security(QS) with schemes, as shown in Table 2.

Comparing from the ACS this scheme applied LSSS to improve the operational efficiency. Importantly, compared to other schemes, this scheme does not require the generation of associated keys or ciphertexts for revocation. The data service manager in the cloud uses the system public parameters to act on the cipher text to achieve user revocation. This in turn enhances the security and flexibility of the scheme. Both constructions [9] and [12] introduce LSSS, which allows user attributes to operate in matrices. In contrast, our scheme considers more features.

The performance in terms of storage overhead is given in Table 3. q, w, s and r denote system attributes, attributes in access structure, user attributes and revoked attributes respectively. And N denotes the number of authority. At the same time, let $k = q + w - s + 1$. We have compared the analysis with the schemes [8,24,25]. The storage space is smaller in terms of public parameters, ciphertext and key size comparison.

Table 3. Comparison of Storage Overhead.

Scheme	Public parameter size	Ciphertext Size	Decryption key size
Chen [8]	$(2qm + 2m + 1)\, n \lceil \log q \rceil$	$(km + m + 1)\, n \lceil \log q \rceil$	$4\,(q + s)\, mn \lceil \log q \rceil$
Yang [24]	$(2qm + 4m + 1)\, n \lceil \log q \rceil$	$(3km + 1) \lceil \log q \rceil$	$2\,(2q + 2s - r)\, m \lceil \log q \rceil$
Yang [25]	$(4qm + Nm + 2m + 1)\, n \lceil \log q \rceil$	$(2km + m + 1)\, n \lceil \log q \rceil$	$2\,(2q + 2s - r)\, mn \lceil \log q \rceil$
Ours	$(qm + 2m + 1)\, n \lceil \log q \rceil + \lvert U \rvert\,(m + 1)\, m$	$[(w + r + 1)\, m + l + 3] \lceil \log q \rceil$	$(qm + 2m + 3)\, m \lceil \log q \rceil$

8 Conclusion

In our lattice revocable ciphertext policy attribute based encryption scheme, linear secret sharing technique and user revocation are used to improve the efficiency of encryption and decryption in lattice. It further breaks the use of linear secret sharing technique in lattice. Also this scheme is resistant to quantum attacks, which is more widely used compared to other schemes. In the case of user revocation, different from the previous schemes where the node values are vector groups, this scheme uses node values that are matrix groups. The advantage is that it does not require authority to generate the relevant revocation key, which enhances the flexibility of revocation. However, the scheme uses a complete binary tree based implementation of user revocation. This revocation mechanism is not fine-grained and affects the normal access to other attributes of legitimate users. The attribute-level user revocation can be further implemented in subsequent research, which in turn enables the revocation of a user's certain attribute.

Acknowledgement. Lifeng Guo was supported by the National Science Foundation of Shanxi Province (202203021221012). The work is supported in part by the National Science Foundation of China (NSFC) under grants: 62002210.

References

1. Agrawal, S., Boyen, X.: Identity-based encryption from lattices in the standard model. manuscript (2009)
2. Agrawal, S., Chase, M.: FAME: fast attribute-based message encryption. In: Thuraisingham, B., Evans, D., Malkin, T., Xu, D. (eds.) ACM-CCS 2017, pp. 665–682. ACM (2017). https://doi.org/10.1145/3133956.3134014
3. Agrawal, S., Boneh, D., Boyen, X.: Lattice basis delegation in fixed dimension and shorter-ciphertext hierarchical IBE. In: Rabin, T. (ed.) CRYPTO 2010. LNCS, vol. 6223, pp. 98–115. Springer, Heidelberg (2010). https://doi.org/10.1007/978-3-642-14623-7_6
4. Agrawal, S., Boyen, X., Vaikuntanathan, V., Voulgaris, P., Wee, H.: Functional encryption for threshold functions (or fuzzy ibe) from lattices. In: Fischlin, M., Buchmann, J., Manulis, M. (eds.) PKC 2012. LNCS, vol. 7293, pp. 280–297. Springer, Heidelberg (2012). https://doi.org/10.1007/978-3-642-30057-8_17
5. Ajtai, M.: Generating hard instances of lattice problems (extended abstract). In: Miller, G.L. (ed.) STOC, pp. 99–108. ACM (1996). https://doi.org/10.1145/237814.237838
6. Ambrosin, M., Conti, M., Dargahi, T.: On the feasibility of attribute-based encryption on smartphone devices. In: Cirani, S., Dohler, M., Ferrari, G., Grieco, L.A., Picone, M., Watteyne, T. (eds.) Proceedings of the 2015 Workshop on IoT challenges in Mobile and Industrial Systems, 2015, pp. 49–54. ACM (2015). https://doi.org/10.1145/2753476.2753482
7. Boyen, X.: Attribute-based functional encryption on lattices. In: Sahai, A. (ed.) TCC 2013. LNCS, vol. 7785, pp. 122–142. Springer, Heidelberg (2013). https://doi.org/10.1007/978-3-642-36594-2_8
8. Chen, J., Lim, H.W., Ling, S., Wang, H., Nguyen, K.: Revocable identity-based encryption from lattices. In: Susilo, W., Mu, Y., Seberry, J. (eds.) ACISP 2012. LNCS, vol. 7372, pp. 390–403. Springer, Heidelberg (2012). https://doi.org/10.1007/978-3-642-31448-3_29
9. Datta, P., Komargodski, I., Waters, B.: Decentralized multi-authority ABE for DNFs from LWE. In: Canteaut, A., Standaert, F.-X. (eds.) EUROCRYPT 2021. LNCS, vol. 12696, pp. 177–209. Springer, Cham (2021). https://doi.org/10.1007/978-3-030-77870-5_7
10. Gentry, C., Peikert, C., Vaikuntanathan, V.: Trapdoors for hard lattices and new cryptographic constructions. In: Dwork, C. (ed.) STOC, pp. 197–206. ACM (2008). https://doi.org/10.1145/1374376.1374407
11. Goyal, V., Pandey, O., Sahai, A., Waters, B.: Attribute-based encryption for fine-grained access control of encrypted data. In: ACM-CCS 2006, pp. 89–98. ACM (2006). https://doi.org/10.1145/1180405.1180418
12. Han, D., Pan, N., Li, K.: A traceable and revocable ciphertext-policy attribute-based encryption scheme based on privacy protection. IEEE Trans. **19**(1), 316–327 (2022). https://doi.org/10.1109/TDSC.2020.2977646
13. Lewko, A., Waters, B.: Decentralizing attribute-based encryption. In: Paterson, K.G. (ed.) EUROCRYPT 2011. LNCS, vol. 6632, pp. 568–588. Springer, Heidelberg (2011). https://doi.org/10.1007/978-3-642-20465-4_31
14. Luo, F., Al-Kuwari, S.M., Wang, H., Wang, F., Chen, K.: Revocable attribute-based encryption from standard lattices. Comput. Stand. Interfaces **84**, 103698 (2023). https://doi.org/10.1016/j.csi.2022.103698

15. Micciancio, D., Peikert, C.: Trapdoors for lattices: simpler, tighter, faster, smaller. In: Pointcheval, D., Johansson, T. (eds.) EUROCRYPT 2012. LNCS, vol. 7237, pp. 700–718. Springer, Heidelberg (2012). https://doi.org/10.1007/978-3-642-29011-4_41
16. Pirretti, M., Traynor, P., McDaniel, P.D., Waters, B.: Secure attribute-based systems. J. Comput. Secur. **18**(5), 799–837 (2010). https://doi.org/10.3233/JCS-2009-0383
17. Regev, O.: New lattice-based cryptographic constructions. J. ACM **51**(6), 899–942 (2004). https://doi.org/10.1145/1039488.1039490
18. Regev, O.: On lattices, learning with errors, random linear codes, and cryptography. In: Gabow, H.N., Fagin, R. (eds.) STOC, pp. 84–93. ACM (2005). https://doi.org/10.1145/1060590.1060603
19. Sahai, A., Waters, B.: Fuzzy identity-based encryption. In: Cramer, R. (ed.) EUROCRYPT 2005. LNCS, vol. 3494, pp. 457–473. Springer, Heidelberg (2005). https://doi.org/10.1007/11426639_27
20. Wang, G., Liu, Q., Wu, J.: Hierarchical attribute-based encryption for fine-grained access control in cloud storage services. In: Al-Shaer, E., Keromytis, A.D., Shmatikov, V. (eds.) ACM-CCS 2010, pp. 735–737. ACM (2010), https://doi.org/10.1145/1866307.1866414
21. Wang, S., Zhang, X., Zhang, Y.: Efficient revocable and grantable attribute-based encryption from lattices with fine-grained access control. IET Inf. Secur. **12**(2), 141–149 (2018). https://doi.org/10.1049/iet-ifs.2017.0225
22. Wang, Y.: Lattice ciphertext policy attribute-based encryption in the standard model. Int. J. Netw. Secur. **16**(6), 444–451 (2014). https://ijns.jalaxy.com.tw/contents/ijns-v16-n6/ijns-2014-v16-n6-p444-451.pdf
23. Xie, X., Xue, R.: Attribute-based encryption for a subclass of circuits with bounded depth from lattices. IACR Cryptol. ePrint Arch., pp. 342 (2013). https://eprint.iacr.org/2013/342
24. Yang, K., Wu, G., Dong, C., Fu, X., Li, F., Wu, T.: Attribute based encryption with efficient revocation from lattices. Int. J. Netw. Secur. **22**(1), 161–170 (2020). https://ijns.jalaxy.com.tw/contents/ijns-v22-n1/ijns-2020-v22-n1-p161-170.pdf
25. Yang, Y., Sun, J., Liu, Z., Qiao, Y.: Practical revocable and multi-authority CP-ABE scheme from RLWE for cloud computing. J. Inf. Secur. Appl. **65**, 103108 (2022). https://doi.org/10.1016/j.jisa.2022.103108
26. Zhang, J., Zhang, Z., Ge, A.: Ciphertext policy attribute-based encryption from lattices. In: Youm, H.Y., Won, Y. (eds.) ACM-CCS 2012, pp. 16–17. ACM (2012). https://doi.org/10.1145/2414456.2414464
27. Zhang, Y., Chen, X., Li, J., Wong, D.S., Li, H.: Anonymous attribute-based encryption supporting efficient decryption test. In: Chen, K., Xie, Q., Qiu, W., Li, N., Tzeng, W. (eds.) ACM-CCS 2013, pp. 511–516. ACM (2013), https://doi.org/10.1145/2484313.2484381

An Efficient Keyword-Based Ciphertext Retrieval Scheme

Zihao Liu, Ruixuan Deng, Chongxi Guan, and Hua Shen(✉)

Hubei University of Technology, Wuhan, China
nancy78733@126.com

Abstract. This paper designs an efficient ciphertext retrieval scheme that can realize single-keyword and multi-keyword retrieval while resisting privacy leakage. The proposed scheme uses SM2 to verify the requester's identity and uses the SM4 algorithm to encrypt keywords to avoid leaking keyword information to the server. In addition, it utilizes SM3 to hash the ciphertext to improve attack resistance while ensuring efficient retrieval. The main highlights of the presented scheme are to transform a single-keyword or multi-keyword ciphertext retrieval into a secure vector inner-product problem and introduce an access priority algorithm based on the designed multi-level feedback priority queue model to improve retrieval speed. Experimental results show that, compared to the current commonly used ciphertext retrieval methods FBDSSE-CQ and VBTree, the retrieval speed of this scheme on 1000 keyword and 100000 file data sets is improved by 12 times and 6829 times, respectively.

Keywords: Ciphertext retrieval · single-keyword retrieval · multi-keyword retrieval · vector inner product · multi-level feedback priority queue

1 Introduction

With the rapid development of cloud technology, more companies and users migrate local data to cloud servers to reduce local overhead [1–3]. As a result, users submit the ciphertexts of their files to cloud servers for storage, protecting their privacy but making it challenging to search the object files according to the given keywords [7]. To solve this problem, Song et al. [8] proposed an SWP scheme, which implements searchable encryption, but the scheme could be more efficient since it needs to scan the entire file for a single-keyword query. Next, Shmueli et al. [9] proposed the Z-IDX scheme, which uses a bloom filter to track keywords in a file efficiently. However, the retrieval efficiency still needs to improve because the server search needs to be calculated and judged file by file. After that, [10] proposed the SSE-1 scheme to improve retrieval efficiency, but it did not support multi-keyword queries.

In practical applications, the volume of data is usually enormous, and efficiency is crucial. This paper presents a ciphertext retrieval method that supports fast single-keyword or multi-keyword queries to further improve the efficiency of multi-keyword queries and implements the corresponding prototype module. The main contributions are as follows:

M. Zhang et al. (Eds.): ProvSec 2023, LNCS 14217, pp. 327–341, 2023.
https://doi.org/10.1007/978-3-031-45513-1_18

- We propose a safe and effective ciphertext retrieval method by converting a single-keyword or multi-keyword ciphertext retrieval into a secure vector inner-product problem. The proposed method creates file-to-keyword vector correspondences. By applying vector inner-product operations in accordance with the vector correspondences, it completes ciphertext retrieval, lowering the computational cost of retrieval and resolving the redundancy issue in storage.
- We introduce an access priority algorithm based on a multi-level feedback priority sequence model into our retrieval method to improve the quality of retrieval services.
- The experimental results demonstrate that our method has a good average retrieval time.

2 Preliminaries

The National Cryptography Administration has formulated and promulgated a number of cryptography standards, including SM1, SM2, SM3, SM4, SM7, SM9, and ZUC. We utilize SM2, SM3, and SM4 to design our ciphertext retrieval method.

SM2 [11] is an elliptic curve public key cryptography algorithm, which consists of four parts: general principles, a digital signature algorithm, a key sharing protocol, and a public key encryption algorithm.

SM3 [12] is a cryptographic hash algorithm. As an improvement over SHA-256. It is appropriate for digital signature and verification in commercial cryptography applications, and its security is on par with SHA-256. Both SM3 and MD5 iterate similarly, and both use the Merkle-Damgard structure. The digest value length is 256 bits, and the data packet length is 512 bits. Four stages make up the execution of the entire algorithm: message filling, message expansion, iterative compression, and output results.

SM4 is a symmetric group cipher algorithm that has speed and security features. It was formally published as an ISO/IEC standard in June 2021 [13]. It has a 128 bit key length and a 128 bit package length. It uses a 32-round iteration method for both encryption and decryption. The round encrypt key is used in reverse sequence for decryption, which successfully yields the plaintext. SM4 has 5 basic encryption modes: ECB, CBC, CFB, OFB, and CTR. We adopt its CBC encryption mode in our work.

3 The Proposed Scheme

3.1 System Model

Our system model (shown in Fig. 1) includes multiple file providers (denoted as FP), one cloud server (denoted as CS), one file requester (denoted as FR), and one trusted third party (denoted as TTP). The TTP is responsible for initializing the system, generating system parameters, and securely sending a symmetric key

Table 1. Main Notations

Notation	Description
FP, CS, FR	File Provider, Cloud Server, File Requester
FV, FVL, RV	File Vector, FV List, Result Vector
kw, GKL	Keyword, Global Industry Keyword List
LKL	Local Keyword List (includes the industry keywords appearing in a FP's files)
GMR	a list recording Global keyword-based Mapping Relationships between GKL and all FPs' files
LMR	a list recording Local keyword-based Mapping Relationships between a FP's LKL and its files
MLQ	the Multi-Level feedback priority Queue model
m, FP_i	the number of FPs, the ith FP
n_i	the number of files provided by FP_i
$N = \sum_{i=1}^{m} n_i$	the total number of files of all File Providers
$file_1^{(i)}, \cdots, file_{n_i}^{(i)}$	the files provided by FP_i
$[[file_1^{(i)}]]_{key}, \cdots, [[file_{n_i}^{(i)}]]_{key}$	the ciphertexts of FP_i's files
key	the key that encrypt and decrypt files (a key of SM_4)
(pk, sk)	the public key and private key of the CS
K	the number of industry keywords in the GKL
kw_k	the kth keyword of the GKL, where $k = 1, 2, \cdots, K$
K_i	the number of keywords that appear in FP_i's files
$LKL^{(i)}$	FP_i's LKL, it is $\{LKL_1^{(i)}, \cdots, LKL_{K_i}^{(i)}\}$
$kw_{k_i}^{(i)}$	the k_ith keyword of LKL_i, where $k_i = 1, 2, \cdots, K_i$
$LMP^{(i)}$	FP_i's LMR, it is $\{LMP_1^{(i)}, \cdots, LMP_{K_i}^{(i)}\}$
Q	the number of the FR's search keywords, $1 \leq Q \leq K$
qkw_j	the jth search keyword, where $j = 1, 2, \cdots, Q$

to FPs for encrypting their files. FPs belong to the same industry, so they have the same global industry keyword list (denoted as GKL). Note, however, that the keywords appearing in a FP's files are a subset (denoted as LKL) of the GKL. FPs encrypt their files and construct their local keyword-based mapping relationships (denoted as LMR) between keywords on the keyword list and their files, then upload their encrypted files and LMRs to the CS. The CS stores the received encrypted files, integrates LMRs to obtain a global keyword-based mapping relationship (denoted as GMR), and generates the file vectors (denoted as FV) according to the GMR. Note that a mapping relationship is a list related to a keyword that stores the IDs of all files that include the keyword. Moreover, a FV is also related to a keyword that stores the storage addresses of the files that include the keyword in the database of the CS. FPs' files are stored in ciphertext in the CS's database. When file retrieval is required, the FR should first have its identity verified by the TTP. If the FR passes its identity authentication, it will receive the key that can be used to decrypt the returned encrypted files. After that, the FR will submit its query request related to one or more search keywords to the CS. CS calculates the corresponding result vector (denoted as RV) according to the search keywords and the GMR. RV will return the object files to it. The RV is related to FR's search keywords and records the storage addresses of the encrypted files that include all search keywords (Table 1).

Suppose there are m FPs ($FP_1, FP_2, \cdots, FP_m$), FP_i (where $i = 1, 2, \cdots, m$) has n_i files, and the size of the industry keyword list is K. We also assume that FP_i has K_i LMRs, where $K_i \leq K$. It is clear that each LMR of FP_i includes at most n_i file IDs and the GMR includes K mapping relationships, each GMR has at most $N = \sum_{i=1}^{m} n_i$ file IDs.

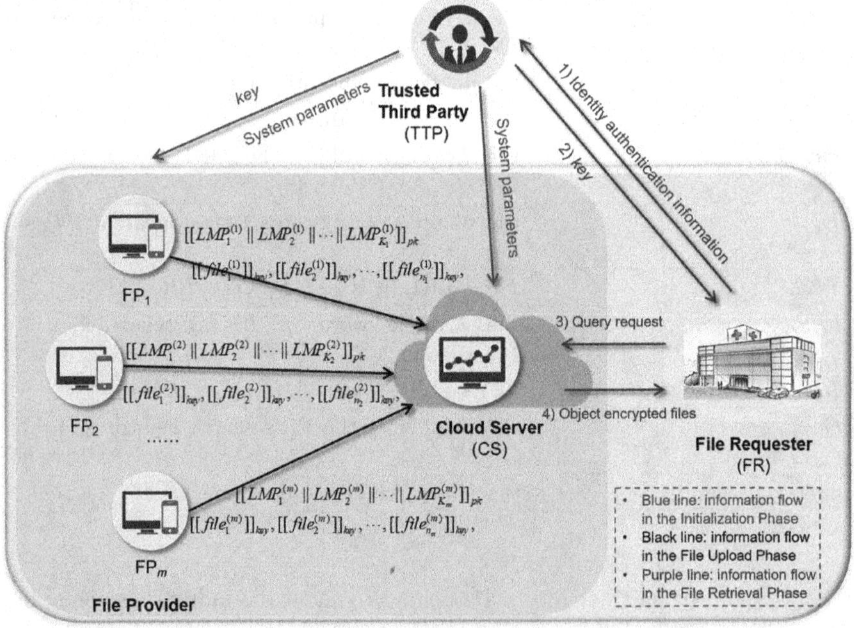

Fig. 1. System Model

3.2 Attack Model

The FPs, the CS, and the FR are honest-but-curious. They keep the retrieval smooth but try to infer files by analyzing the information obtained by them. Specifically, FPs cannot gain access to other FPs' files; the CS should know nothing about all FPs' files; the FR can only gain access to the files it needs. Moreover, $\mathscr{A}$ is an external adversary that tries to obtain the files and hash values of keywords through eavesdropping on communication channels. Furthermore, they cannot collude with each other.

3.3 Design Objects

Our design goal is to develop an efficient keyword-based ciphertext retrieval scheme. In particular, the following three desirable objectives need to be considered.

Confidentiality: The proposed retrieval scheme should ensure the confidentiality of files and query intent under the proposed attack model.

Correctness: The proposed retrieval scheme should return the correct results according to the query request.

Efficiency: The proposed retrieval scheme should have good retrieval performance.

3.4 Scheme Details

The proposed ciphertext retrieval scheme consists of three phases: Initialization, File Upload, File Retrieval.

1) Initialization Phase. In this phase, the TTP generates a key key for encryption and decryption by using SM4 scheme and securely transmits key to m FPs. Moreover, the TTP constructs the global keyword list GKL for a given industry and distributes it to all FPs and the CS. Suppose GKL consists of K keywords: $\{kw_1, kw_2, \cdots, kw_K\}$. The CS generates its public key pk and private key sk using an efficient asymmetric encryption scheme (such as the ECC-ElGamal scheme).

2) File Upload Phase. The process flow of this phase is shown in Fig. 2. This phase is to prepare for the next phase of the file retrieval services.

- File Provider-End
  Step 1: FP_i $(i = 1, 2, \cdots, m)$ generates its local mapping relationship list $LMP^{(i)}$ according to its files and GKL. For the sake of narration, we suppose $LKL^{(i)} = \{LKL_1^i, LKL_2^i, \cdots, LKL_{K_i}^i\} \subseteq GKL$ is FP_i's local keyword list. In other words, $LKL^{(i)}$ includes all keywords that belong to GKL and appear in FP_i's files. We assume that the size of $LKL^{(i)}$ is K_i and represent them as $\{kw_1^{(i)}, kw_2^{(i)}, \cdots, kw_{K_i}^{(i)}\}$. Therefore, we can represent $LMP^{(i)}$ as $\{LMP_1^i, LMP_2^i, \cdots, LMP_{K_i}^i\}$. $LMP_{k_i}^i\}$ $(k_i \in \{1, 2, \cdots, K_i\})$ is a keyword-based list that stores $H(kw_{k_i}^{(i)})$ (calculated by performing the SM3 algorithm) and

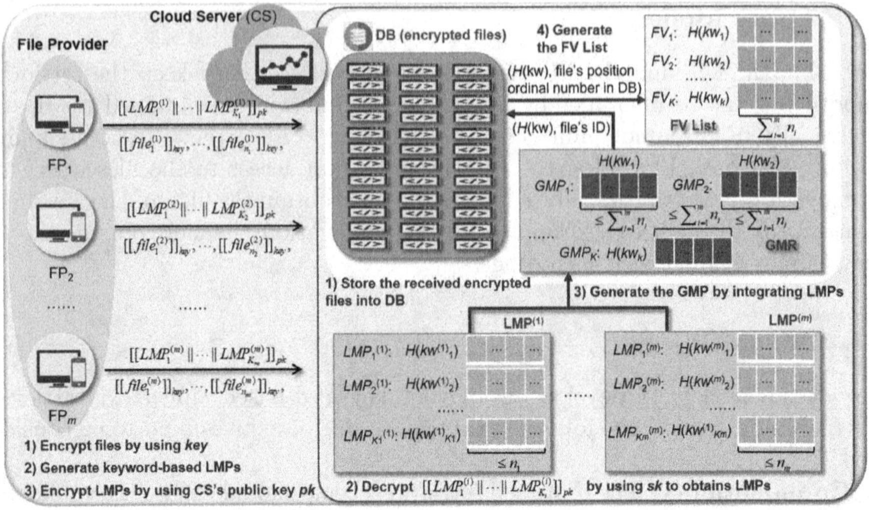

Fig. 2. The Process Flow of File Upload Phase

records IDs of its files containing the keyword $kw^{(i)}_{k_i}$. Clearly, the number of IDs contained in $LMP^i_{k_i}\}$ is at most n_i.
Step 2: FP_i encrypts its files by executing SM4's encryption algorithm with key to obtain $\{[[file^{(i)}_1]]_{key}$, $[[file^{(i)}_2]]_{key}$, $\cdots$, $[[file^{(i)}_{n_i}]]_{key}\}$.
Step 3: FP_i encrypts $LMP^{(i)}$ by using the CS's public key pk to gain $[[LMP^i_1$ $||$ $[[LMP^i_2$ $||$ $cdots$ $||$ $LMP^i_{K_i}]]_{pk}$.
Step 4: FP_i transmits the encrypted files and the encrypted $LMP^{(i)}$ to the CS.

- Cloud Server-End
Step 1: The CS stores received encrypted files $\{[[file^{(i)}_1]]_{key}$, $[[file^{(i)}_2]]_{key}$, $\cdots$, $[[file^{(i)}_{n_i}]]_{key}\}$ (i is from 1 to m) into its database DB.
Step 2: The CS decrypted $[[LMP^i_1$ $||$ $[[LMP^i_2$ $||$ $cdots$ $||$ $LMP^i_{K_i}]]_{pk}$ by using its private key sk to obtain $LMP^{(i)} = \{LMP^i_1, LMP^i_2, \cdots, LMP^i_{K_i}\}$ (i is from 1 to m).
Step 3: The CS generates the global keyword-base mapping relationship list $GMR = \{GMR_1, GMR_2, \cdots, GMR_K\}$ by carrying out the AL_{GMR} algorithm (Alg. 1). GMR_k ($k \in \{1, 2, \cdots, K\}$) is a keyword-based list that stores $H(kw_k)$ (calculated by performing the SM3 algorithm) and records IDs of all FPs' files containing the keyword kw_k. Clearly, the number of IDs in GMR_k is at most $N = \sum_{i=1}^{m} n_i$.

Step 4: The CS constructs a keyword-based file vector list $FVL = \{FV_1, FV_2, \cdots, FV_K\}$ based on GMR and the DB that stores all encrypted files by executing the AL_{FVL} (Alg. 2). Each FV records the hash value of one industry keyword (computed by executing the SM3 algorithm) and the position ordinal numbers in the DB of all files that contain this keyword. FV utilizes a bit vector

Algorithm 1. GMR Construction (AL_{GMR}).

Input: $GKL = \{kw_1, kw_2, \cdots, kw_K\}$, $LMP^{(i)} = \{LMP^i_1, LMP^i_2, \cdots, LMP^i_{K_i}\}$ (i is from 1 to m);
Output: the global mapping relationship list GMR.

for $k = 1$ to K **do**
  $GMR_k \leftarrow H(kw_k)$;
end for
for $i = 1$ to m **do**
  for $k_i = 1$ to K_i **do**
    if $H(kw_k) == H(kw^{(i)}_{k_i})$ **then**
      GMR_k $leftarrow$ files' IDs stored in $LMP^i_{(k_i)}$;
    end if
  end for
end for
return GMR;

of size $N = \sum_{i=1}^{m} n_i$ to record the file's position ordinal numbers. In other words, FV_k ($k = 1, 2, \cdots, K$) is corresponding to kw_k. FV_k consists of two parts: the one (denoted as $FV_k.Hash$) is used to store $H(kw_k)$, the other is a bit vector of size N (denoted as $FV_k.vector$). If a file contains the keyword kw_k and its position ordinal number in DB is t ($1 \leq t \leq N$), then $FV_k.vector[t] = 1$, otherwise $FV_k.vector[t] = 0$. In this way, $FV_k.vector$ can record the position ordinal numbers in the DB of all files that contain kw_k.

3) File Retrieval Phase. The process flow of this phase is shown as Fig. 3. This phase is to provide efficient query services for the FR.

- File Requester-End

Note that before making its first request for query services, the FR should acquire the qualification for asking queries. To acquire the qualification, the FR needs to send its identity authentication information to the TTP. The TTP verifies the FR's identity by using the SM2 algorithm. If the FR is approved, the TTP will return the key *key* to it, informing it that it can enjoy query request services. Suppose the FR's retrieval requirement is to obtain the files that contain Q ($1 \leq Q \leq K$) target keywords $qkw_1, qkw_2, \cdots, qkw_Q$.

Step 1: The FR calculates the hash values of its target keywords qkw_1, $qkw_2, \cdots, qkw_Q$ by calling SM3 algorithm to obtain $H(qkw_1), H(qkw_2), \cdots, H(qkw_Q)$.

Step 2: The FR encrypts $H(qkw_1), H(qkw_2), \cdots, H(qkw_Q)$ by using the CS's public key pk to gain $[[H(qkw_1) \mid\mid H(qkw_2) \mid\mid cdots \mid\mid H(qkw_Q)]]_{pk}$.

Step 3: The FR takes $[[H(qkw_1) \mid\mid H(qkw_2) \mid\mid cdots \mid\mid H(qkw_Q)]]_{pk}$ as its query request and send it to the CS.

- Cloud Server-End

Step 1: The CS decrypts $[[H(qkw_1) \mid\mid H(qkw_2) \mid\mid cdots \mid\mid H(qkw_Q)]]_{pk}$ by using its private key sk to obtain the hash values of the target keywords of the FR.

Algorithm 2. FVL Construction (AL_{FVL}).

Input: $GMR = \{GMR_1, GMR_2, \cdots, GMR_K\}$, DB;
Output: the file vector list FVL.

for $k = 1$ to K **do**
  for $t = 1$ to N **do**
    $FV_k.vector[t] = 0$;
  end for
end for
for $k = 1$ to K **do**
  $FV_k.Hash \leftarrow H(kw_k)$ of GMR_k;
  while GMR_k has IDs that have not been accessed **do**
    $ID \leftarrow$ an ID that has not been accessed;
    search DB according to ID to obtain the position ordinal number t of the corresponding file;
    $FV_k.vector[t] = 1$;
  end while
end for
return FVL;

Step 2: The CS generates the result vector RV by executing the AL_{RV} algorithm (Algorithm 3). The size of RV is also N. The AL_{RV} algorithm outputs RV by computing vector inner-product operations between the vectors in FVL that are indicated by $H(qkw_1)$, $H(qkw_2)$, $\cdots$, $H(qkw_Q)$.

To improve the quality of search services, the CS returns search results in decreasing order of priority of the search hit files. We define the priority of an encrypted file as the number of times that the encrypted file is retrieved. Therefore, the DB stores and maintains the priorities of encrypted files in addition to storing these encrypted files. Each time an encrypted file is retrieved, its priority is increased by 1. To prevent the priorities of files from being too large, clear the priorities of all files periodically. Moreover, we design a data structure (called the multi-level feedback priority queue, denoted as MLQ) to help the CS achieve this service objective. A $L - MLQ$ is an instance of MLQ, and it includes L priority queues that have different levels, where the priorities of the files belonging to the Level 1 queue are higher than those of the files belonging to the Level 2, the priorities of the files belonging to the Level 2 queue are higher than those of the files belonging to the Level 3, and so on. Note that every queue is itself a priority queue; for example, every queue is a given-size heap. If the Level 1 queue is not full, the fit files' position number will be inserted into the Level 1 queue. If the Level 1 queue is full, then delete the fit file's position number with the lowest priority from the Level 1 queue and insert it into the Level 2 queue, and so on. For convenience, we use $DB[t].pri$ to represent the priority of the encrypted file stored in the tth location of the DB and utilize $DB[t].file$ to represent this encrypted file.

Step 3: The CS optimizes the return order of search results by executing the AL_{OPT} algorithm (Algorithm 4).

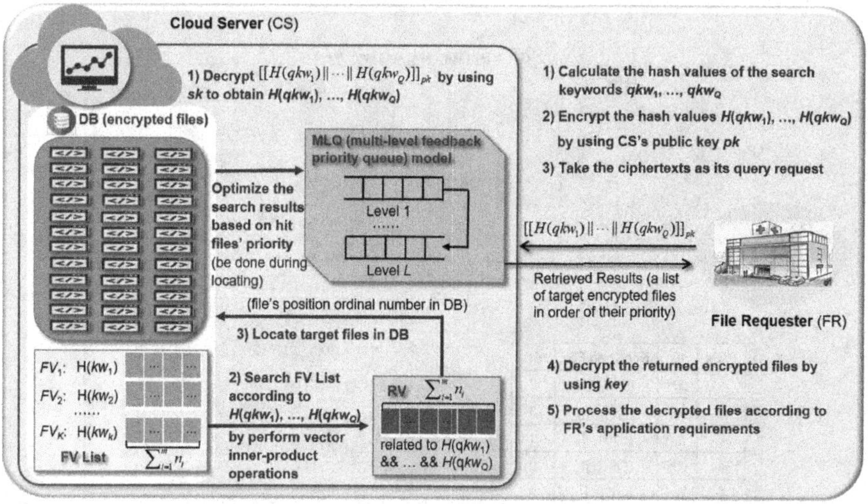

Fig. 3. The Process Flow of File Retrieval Phase

Step 4: The CS finds the fit encrypted files in the DB and returns them to FR in the order specified by MLQ_{FR}.

- File Requester-End

Step 4: The FR decrypted its received encrypted files using *key* to obtain the files containing Q target keywords with the order of files' popularity.

Step 5: The FR process the decrypted files according to its application requirements.

4 Correctness Analysis

We use the case method to verify the correctness of our scheme. Suppose $GKL = \{kw_1, kw_2, kw_3, kw_4, kw_5\}$, there are two FPs, FP_1 and FP_2. FP_1's $LKL_1 = \{kw_1, kw_2, kw_5\}$. FP_1 has four files $file_1^{(1)}$ with $ID_1^{(1)}$, $file_2^{(1)}$ with $ID_2^{(1)}$, $file_3^{(1)}$ with $ID_3^{(1)}$, and $file_4^{(1)}$ with $ID_4^{(1)}$. FP_2's $LKL_2 = \{kw_1, kw_2, kw_3\}$. FP_2 has five files $file_1^{(2)}$ with $ID_1^{(2)}$, $file_2^{(2)}$ with $ID_2^{(2)}$, $file_3^{(2)}$ with $ID_3^{(2)}$, $file_4^{(2)}$ with $ID_4^{(2)}$, and $file_5^{(2)}$ with $ID_5^{(2)}$. Suppose $file_1^{(1)}$, $file_2^{(1)}$, $file_3^{(1)}$, $file_1^{(2)}$, $file_3^{(2)}$, $file_5^{(2)}$ contain kw_1; $file_2^{(1)}$, $file_3^{(1)}$, $file_2^{(2)}$, $file_3^{(2)}$, $file_4^{(2)}$ contain kw_2; $file_1^{(2)}$, $file_3^{(2)}$, $file_4^{(2)}$ contain kw_3; $file_1^{(1)}$, $file_3^{(1)}$, $file_4^{(1)}$, $file_3^{(2)}$, $file_5^{(2)}$ contain kw_5. $LMR^{(1)}$ generated by FP_1, $LMR^{(2)}$ generated by FP_2, GMR and FVL generated by the CS, and the CS's DB are shown in Fig. 4.

Suppose the FR's target keywords are $\{qkw_1 = kw_1, qkw_2 = kw_5\}$. The retrieval process is shown in Fig. 5. According to Fig. 5, we can know that four files $file^{(1)_1}$, $file_3^{(1)}$, $file_3^{(2)}$, and $file_5^{(2)}$ contain $qkw_1 = kw_1$ and $qkw_2 = kw_5$

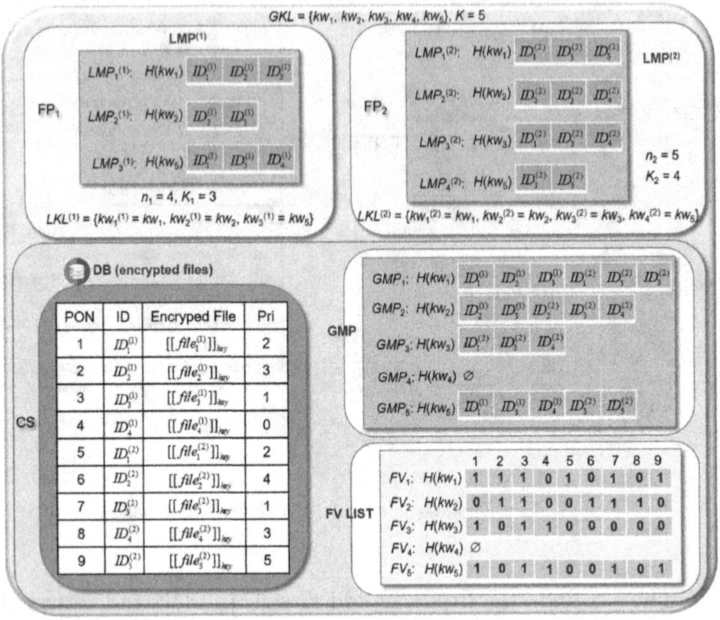

Fig. 4. The Instance for Verifying Correctness (Preparatory Phase)

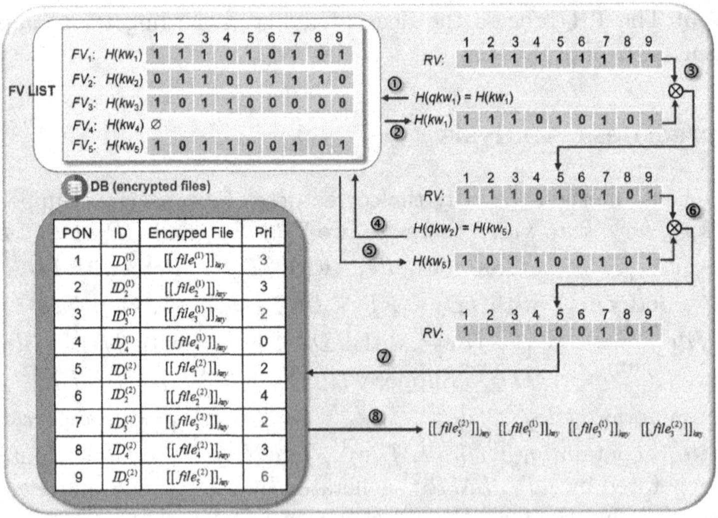

Fig. 5. The Instance for Verifying Correctness (Retrieval Phase)

Algorithm 3. FVL Construction (AL_{RV}).

Input: FVL, $H(qkw_1)$, $H(qkw_2)$, $\cdots$, $H(qkw_Q)$;
Output: the result vector RV.

for $t = 1$ to N **do**
  $RV[t] = 1$;
end for
for $j = 1$ to Q **do**
  for $k = 1$ to K **do**
    if $FV_k.Hash == H(qkw_j)$ **then**
      RV = Vector_Inner_Product_Operation(RV, $FV_k.vector$);
      break;
    end if
  end for
end for
return RV;

Algorithm 4. Optimize Search Results (AL_{OPT}).

Input: RV, DB;
Output: the instance MLQ_{FR} of multi-level feedback priority queue model corresponding to this service request.

$MLQ_{FR} \leftarrow$ Instantiate MQL;
for $t = 1$ to N **do**
  if RV[t] == 1 **then**
    Insert t into MLQ_{FR} according to $DB[t].pri$;
  end if
end for
return MLQ_{FR};

at the same time, which is consistent with the actuation situation of the given case. Therefore, our scheme can return the correct search results according to the query request.

5 Confidentiality Analysis

The key *key* used to encrypt and decrypt files is a key of the SM4 scheme. Because the CS and $\mathscr{A}$ cannot obtain *key*, the confidentiality of FPs' files is assured. Moreover, $LMP^{(}i)$ ($i = 1, 2, \cdots, m$) involves the sensitive of the FP_i's files. $LMP^{(}i)$ is encrypted using the CS's public key pk before transmitting it. Besides, the request intention of the FR is also encrypted using pk before submitting it to the CS. As a result, only CS can gain $LMP^{(}i)$ and the hash values of the target keywords. Therefore, the confidentiality of $LMP^{(}i)$ and the target keywords are also assured. Furthermore, in our scheme, the CS obtains the hash value of the keywords instead of the keywords, increasing the difficulty of the CS in obtaining the keywords. Therefore, our scheme for the CS also guarantees the confidentiality of the files' keywords and the target keywords to a certain extent.

6 Experiment

6.1 Experiment Evaluation

Conduct an experimental simulation on this model with experimental tools and an environment: Pycharm Python 3.7, MySQL database. CPU: AMD Ryzen 54600H 3.00 GHz, memory: 3 GB, Win 10 64-bit operating system.

Figure 6(a) shows the corresponding structure of a database, which has three attributes. The first attribute is the hash value corresponding to the keyword ciphertext. The second attribute is the file vector corresponding to the keyword and the relationship between each keyword and the file. The last attribute is the priority number set for the priority algorithm.

Figure 6(b) shows the corresponding structure of a database, which also has three attributes. The first attribute is the file identifier corresponding to the ciphertext file, used for file vector retrieval files; the second is the ciphertext corresponding to the file; and the third is the heat of each file, used for multi-level feedback sequence models.

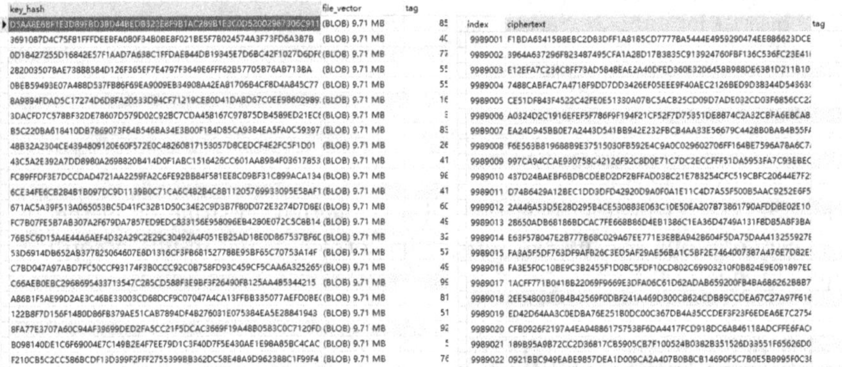

(a) ciphertext data (b) the ciphertext retrieval results

Fig. 6. The DB for Ciphertext Files

Figure 7 mainly shows the final experimental process and results of the module, including the initialization vector and symmetric key of the SM4, used to encrypt the search keywords, the hash value corresponding to the search keyword ciphertext, the finally retrieved ciphertext file, the plaintext file decrypted by using the SM4 key and initialization vector, and the total retrieval time.

A total of 5 keywords were used in this search, their plaintext and their HASH values were:
Keywords: plaintext
HASH
Test_KeyWord1
af0ee8795a23441cb495749169ac2f4ec51adf96e3e5dcb021ad1b666bae53dc
Test_KeyWord2
b3b566159a90f6bde97363404d2b14e482a232f3bbd54fba99c208cb814882e4
Test_KeyWord3
11e4672f1153c1d85e4fb9e97caa90e061a71f0324299a1742a1ca28387ce25b
Test_KeyWord4
8c30e1de9b46755b2538a43903c2a62284f73461a5c9ecbe1bc3b307a7ae1c95
Test_KeyWord5
4b3815487e553c0ed405a46855e9ff39e7324b8dclffb3c5ece126fd237b4eec
SM4 initial vector IV
354148a37d284e1d2ba552dd5690ae50
SM4 symmetric key KEY
d9aa44a12e87272deb0b40801bcc
A list of retrieved ciphertexts
973bf61f2e29f36e0401aca2298dc06fbd2373049560f0bbd6086f3f90ad1a0d
ac653d1e5bb45c34d8068ccd891fa748c142c77f679d4a16bd60f1258b3b705e59866d92a8eed6666df55c774c675c5931dde2da0d25e4b5f263c5e8015da57
996bbc337203e7b4457a12e3ea2765d49f044af9cf69677d4daa2b90b24621f48fb595042a99e18a72384ef0dfd918b3542938b9f4e58ff93fe651bdc1d5f35
Decrypted plaintext information
File1_TestMessage_0123456789
File2_TestMessage_0123456789abcdefghijklmnopqrstuvwxyz
File3_TestHessage_0123456789abcdefghijklmnopqrstuvWxyzABCDEFGHIJKLNNOPQRSTUVWXY
The time consumed by this search was: 25.007 ms

Fig. 7. A Ciphertext Retrieval Model

6.2 Performance Analysis

To test the retrieval efficiency of this module, we selected different numbers of keywords and documents and measured the retrieval time results as shown in the Table 2.

Table 2. Running time under different parameters

Number of keywords	Number of files	Time
1,000	100,000	15.97 ms
1,000	1,000,000	27.04 ms
10,000	100,000	32.42 ms
10,000	1,000,000	38.35 ms
10,000	10,000,000	223.75 ms

When the number of keywords and files is large enough, the retrieval time is measured in milliseconds, indicating that the retrieval efficiency of this module is high and can sufficiently meet user needs.

In order to better illustrate the retrieval stability and efficiency of the module, this article compares two retrieval schemes, FBDSSE-CQ [14] and VBTree [15], with this scheme (with a dataset of 1000 keywords and 100000 files). The statistical results obtained are shown in Fig. 8.

7 Conclusion

In this paper, we develop a retrieval method based on vector products, use vector products to realize a multi-keyword ciphertext search, and use multi-level feedback sequence to realize parallel search and sorting, which significantly

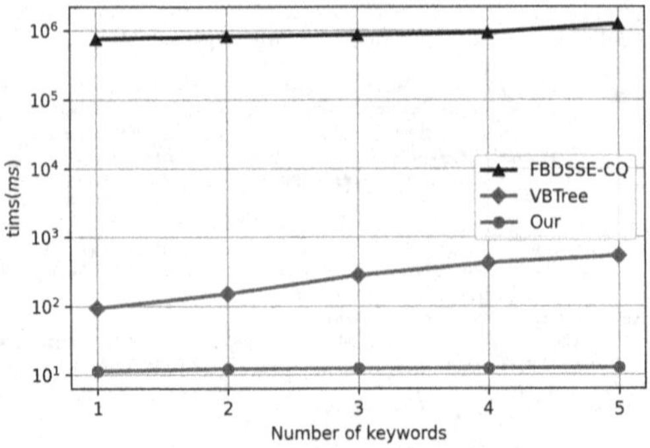

Fig. 8. A Ciphertext retrieval model

improves the retrieval efficiency. The experimental results show that the proposed scheme ensures high retrieval efficiency and accuracy while ensuring the security of data. In future work, we will investigate how to implement fuzzy retrieval without reducing efficiency so that semantic search can be performed and accurate results can be returned quickly.

Acknowledgement. This work is supported in part by the National Natural Science Foundation of China (61702168, U2001205) and in part by the Green Industry Technology Leading Program of Hubei University of Technology (XJ2021000901).

References

1. Liang, K., Susilo, W.: Searchable attribute-based mechanism with efficient data sharing for secure cloud storage. IEEE Trans. Inf. Forensics Secur. **10**(9), 1981–1992 (2015)
2. Shen, H., Zhang, M., Wang, H., et al.: Efficient and privacy-preserving massive data processing for smart grids. IEEE Access **9**, 70616–70627 (2021)
3. Zhang, M., Yang, M., Shen, G., et al.: A verifiable and privacy-preserving cloud mining pool selection scheme in blockchain of things. Inf. Sci. **623**, 293–310 (2023)
4. Zhang, M., Huang, S., Shen, G., et al.: PPNNP: a privacy-preserving neural network prediction with separated data providers using multi-client inner-product encryption. Comput. Stand. Interfaces **84**, 103678 (2023)
5. Shen, H., Li, J., Wu, G., et al.: Data release for machine learning via correlated differential privacy. Inf. Process. Manag. **60**(3), 103349 (2023)
6. Zhang, M., Chen, Y., Susilo, W.: Decision tree evaluation on sensitive datasets for secure e-healthcare systems. IEEE Trans. Depend. Secure Comput. **20**, 3988–4001 (2022)
7. Fu, Z., Ren, K., Shu, J., et al.: Enabling personalized search over encrypted outsourced data with efficiency improvement. IEEE Trans. Parallel Distrib. Syst. **27**(9), 2546–2559 (2016)
8. Song, X.D., Wagner, D., Perrig, A.: Practical techniques for searches on encrypted data. In: Proceedings of the IEEE Symposium on Security and Privacy, pp. 44–55. IEEE Press (2000)

9. Shmueli, E., Waisenberg, R., Elovici, Y., Gudes, E.: Designing secure indexes for encrypted databases. In: Jajodia, S., Wijesekera, D. (eds.) DBSec 2005. LNCS, vol. 3654, pp. 54–68. Springer, Heidelberg (2005). https://doi.org/10.1007/11535706_5
10. Curtmola, R., Garay, J., Kamara, S., Ostrovsky, R.: Searchable symmetric encryption: improved definitions and efficient constructions. In: Proceedings of the 13th ACM Conference on Computer and Communications Security (CCS 2006), pp. 79–88. ACM Press, New York (2006)
11. State Cryptography Administration. The State Cryptography Administration issued the "SM2 Elliptic Curve Public Key Cryptography Algorithm". Accessed 17 Dec 2010
12. State Cryptography Administration. The State Cryptography Administration issued an announcement on the "SM3 Cryptographic Hash Algorithm". Accessed 17 Dec 2010
13. Feng, Y., Zhu, Z., Feng, Z.: Principle and implementation of SM4 algorithm. Cable TV Technol. **6**, 94–96 (2019)
14. Zuo, C., Sun, S., Liu, J.K., et al.: Forward and backward private dynamic searchable symmetric encryption for conjunctive queries. IACR Cryptology EPrint Archive (2020)
15. Wu, Z.Q., Li, K.L.: VBTree: forward secure conjunctive queries over encrypted data for cloud computing. VLDB J. **28**(1), 25–46 (2019)

Privacy Preservation

Privacy Preserving Outsourced K-means Clustering Using Kd-tree

Yanxiang Deng[1(✉)], Lin Liu[1], Shaojing Fu[1], Yuchuan Luo[1], Wei Wu[1], and Shixiong Wang[2]

[1] College of Computer, National University of Defense Technology, Changsha, China
{dengyanxiang20,liulin16,fushaojing,luoyuchuan09}@nudt.edu.cn
[2] Academy of Military Sciences, Beijing, China

Abstract. Nowadays, more and more resource-constrained individuals and corporations tend to outsource their data and machine learning tasks to cloud servers, enjoying high-quality data storage and computing services ubiquitously. However, outsourcing sensitive data can bring data security and privacy issues, arousing public concerns. In this work, we propose an efficient privacy-preserving outsourced scheme of K-means clustering on encrypted data in the twin-cloud model using the paradigm of secret sharing. The state-of-the-art outsourced K-means clustering scheme using fully homomorphic encryption is efficient but not secure enough. To better solve this problem, we utilize the kd-tree data structure and design a set of secure protocols, presenting a new scheme that is almost as efficient as the state-of-the-art schemes but more secure. In our scheme, the clustering process is performed by two cloud servers without leaking any intermediate information. We provide formal security analyses and evaluate the performance of our scheme on both synthetic and real-world datasets. The experiment results show that our scheme is efficient and practical.

Keywords: Privacy-preserving · K-means clustering · Outsourced computing · Secret sharing

1 Introduction

Over the past few years, we have witnessed the rapid development and deployment of cloud computing, offering plenty of benefits for real-world applications, such as rapid resource elasticity, file storage platforms, data storage applications, and outsourcing computation. One of the most important benefits of cloud computing is outsourcing computation. Clients with resource-constraint devices can outsource workloads that require heavy computation and communication power to the cloud servers, enjoying almost unlimited computing resources after payment [20]. As machine learning usually requires a lot of computing resources and storage space, clients with limited resources often outsource model training tasks to cloud servers, saving local implementation costs. However, for clients

M. Zhang et al. (Eds.): ProvSec 2023, LNCS 14217, pp. 345–364, 2023.
https://doi.org/10.1007/978-3-031-45513-1_19

from domains such as financial companies and medical organizations, both original data and intermediate results in the process of performing machine learning tasks can be very sensitive and significant [31]. As a result, outsourcing computation inevitably suffers from some new security challenges due to untrusted cloud servers.

K-means clustering, one of the most widely used techniques for statistical data analysis and data mining, has been used in many areas, e.g., diagnosis in medical imaging [1] and market segmentation [2]. To preserve data security in cloud computing, one straightforward way is to utilize cryptographic tools such as homomorphic encryption (HE) and secret sharing (SS), which support arithmetical operations on ciphertext without decryption. In the past few years, many works have been proposed to address the privacy-preserving K-means clustering problem [3–7]. Some of them are quite efficient but lack security [3], while others are secure but with huge computational and communication overhead [33].

For both efficiency and data security, we implement a privacy-preserving scheme based on a simple and efficient implementation of the K-means clustering algorithm [8]. The plaintext scheme uses kd-tree as data structure to store data records, accelerating the clustering process and reducing redundant and time-consuming ciphertext operations such as comparisons. Different from previous works, our scheme is not only efficient but also secure, which is meaningful in real-world applications.

1.1 Our Contribution

In this work, we propose a privacy-preserving K-means clustering scheme using the kd-tree structure on outsourced data in a twin-cloud model. The main contributions of our work are summarized as follows:

- With secret sharing technology and millionaires' protocol in [9], we design a set of secure protocols, which can find minimal value, compute Euclidean distance, and compare ciphertexts in a privacy-preserving way. Based on these sub-protocols, we propose a novel privacy-preserving outsourced K-means clustering (PPOKC) scheme which efficiently performs outsourced K-means clustering over the kd-tree data structure.
- By using the kd-tree data structure to store data, the proposed scheme reduces redundant calculations and improves efficiency. Besides, all intermediate values are kept secure. In our scheme, users could stay offline once they construct the kd-tree and upload data. As a result, our scheme minimizes users' computation and communication overhead, which is a vital requirement for resource-constrained users.
- We test the performance of our scheme on several real-world and synthetic datasets and compare them with the most related works. The experimental results show that our scheme is as efficient as state-of-the-art [3] but with a higher security level.

2 Preliminary

In this section, we will introduce some essential preliminary concepts, such as additive secret sharing, K-means clustering algorithm, and kd-tree data structure.

2.1 Additive Secret Sharing

We use the Secret Sharing (SS) paradigm to achieve privacy and efficiency. All user data and intermediate values are secret-shared between the two cloud servers. We employ two different sharing schemes: Additive sharing and Boolean sharing [30]. In the following, if not specifically pointed out, we assume that all data are within a ring $\mathbb{Z}_N$.

To additively share l-bit value x to two cloud servers, the user first generates $\langle x \rangle_0^A \in \mathbb{Z}_N$ uniformly at random and calculates $\langle x \rangle_1^A = x - \langle x \rangle_0^A \pmod N$, sending $\langle x \rangle_i^A, i \in [0, 1]$ to cloud server C_0 and C_1 respectively. We omit the modular operation in the protocol descriptions for ease of presentation. In this paper, additive shares are denoted by $\langle \cdot \rangle$ for short.

- **Addition**: To calculate the sum of value $\langle x \rangle$ and a constant number c, cloud C_0 locally computes $\langle z \rangle_0 = \langle x \rangle_0 + c$, while cloud C_1 computes $\langle z \rangle_1 = \langle x \rangle_1$. In addition, to calculate $\langle z \rangle = \langle x + y \rangle = \langle x \rangle + \langle y \rangle$, we let C_i computes $\langle z \rangle_i = \langle x \rangle_i + \langle y \rangle_i$.
- **Multiplication**: To multiply $\langle x \rangle$ and $\langle y \rangle$, we use Beaver's pre-computed multiplication triplet technique [23]. Suppose we have $\langle c \rangle = \langle a \rangle \cdot \langle b \rangle$, C_i locally calculates $\langle e \rangle_i = \langle x \rangle_i - \langle a \rangle_i$ and $\langle f \rangle_i = \langle y \rangle_i - \langle b \rangle_i, i \in [0, 1]$. Both clouds reconstruct e and f, and C_i calculates $\langle z \rangle_i = i \cdot e \cdot f + f \cdot \langle a \rangle_i + e \cdot \langle b \rangle_i + \langle c \rangle_i, i \in [0, 1]$. To be precise, we use **MUL** to denote secure multiplication. If the input is two secret shared values, then the output is the secret shared product. If the input is two secret shared arrays, then the output is a secret shared array, with each element being the product of corresponding elements.

Pre-computed arithmetic triples must be refreshed every multiplication and can be generated offline by the two cloud servers using Oblivious Transfer (OT) or a trusted third party. In this work, we mainly consider the computation and communication overhead of the online stage.

Boolean sharing can be seen as additive sharing in $\mathbb{Z}_2$, and thus all the protocols introduced above carry over. The addition operation is replaced by the XOR operation ($\bigoplus$), and multiplication is replaced by the AND operation. We denote Boolean shares of x as $\langle x \rangle^B$ for short.

2.2 K-means Clustering Based on Kd-tree

One of the most commonly used clustering algorithms is K-means clustering which divides n data records into k disjoint subsets [33]. In addition, each cluster has a center, and compared with other clusters, each data record has a shorter distance to the center of the cluster it belongs to. There are many implementations of K-means clustering to make the process more efficient, one of which is using kd-tree as the major data structure and designing a filtering algorithm to cluster data records [8].

Kd-tree is a space-partitioning data structure, putting spatially close points together in the same node [24]. It has been used in many applications to accelerate calculations related to point space, such as the k nearest neighbor algorithm [25] and creating point clouds.

Here, we choose the following method to form a kd-tree.

- In the k-dimensional data set, we calculate the variance of each dimension and select the dimension d_{max} with maximal variance to divide the data set.
- Finding the median value m on dimension d_{max} as the pivot to divide this data set, obtaining two sub-datasets.

Repeat the above process until all leaf nodes are generated. The kd-tree data structure has two main advantages. On the one hand, it groups data that may be in the same cluster into one node. On the other hand, it uses an optimized way to divide the initial space into two subspaces to accelerate subsequent data processing.

3 System Model and Design Goal

3.1 System Model

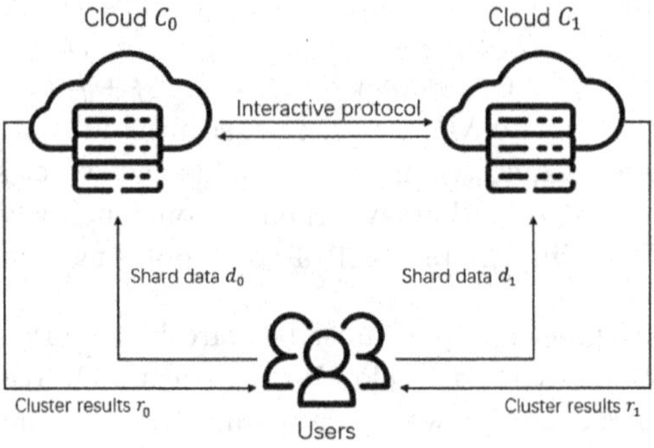

Fig. 1. System Model

As shown in Fig. 1, our privacy-preserving K-means clustering system involves two non-colluding cloud servers and multiple users.

- **Two Clouds:** We have two non-colluding cloud servers in this system, denoted as cloud C_0 and cloud C_1, both of which maintain the kd-tree secretly shared by the users. They perform a series of secure protocols to do K-means clustering in a privacy-preserving way, returning the secret shared cluster centers to the users in the end.

- **Users:** Users perform kd-tree construction on original data and then choose random numbers to secretly divide the result into two parts, sending them to two clouds. After K-means clustering, users will receive the secret shared result and restore the final clustering centers.

Since kd-tree is easy to construct on plaintext but difficult to construct efficiently on ciphertext, we let users construct kd-tree, which brings little communication and computation overhead but accelerates later processes.

3.2 Threat Model

In our work, we suppose that two cloud servers C_0 and C_1 are semi-honest (a.k.a., honest-but-curious), which means they will not deviate from the defined protocol, but attempt to collect private information about the other party during the clustering process. In addition, we assume that C_0 and C_1 cannot collude with each other. Such a non-colluding model between two cloud servers has been widely used in a lot of works to support interactive protocols over encrypted data [3,26].

3.3 Design Goals

The privacy-preserving outsourced K-means clustering scheme proposed in this work achieves the following design goals:

- **Privacy and Security.** All outsourced data and intermediate values computed during the clustering process could not be learned by the two cloud servers. In our scheme, the results of the clustering process are kept secret.
- **Efficiency.** Our scheme should be efficient for the data owners. The whole training process is mainly done by the two cloud servers, which have more computation and communication resources, bringing little overhead to users.
- **Correctness.** Our primary goal is to obtain correct clustering results. The two cloud servers should be able to return the same results compared with plaintext K-means clustering scheme.

4 Building Blocks

In this section, we provide a set of building blocks that will be used as subprotocols in our scheme. Our privacy-preserving scheme is designed based on Secret Sharing and secure comparison protocol in [9]. We stress that all the data are within $\mathbb{Z}_N$ in the following algorithm. As mentioned, we omit the "mod N" in the following context. The notations used in our scheme are given in Table 1.

Table 1. Notations

Notation	Definition
$x_i = \{x_{i1}, ..., x_{im}\}$	Point i with m attributes
$C = \{c_1, ..., c_m\}$	Centor of each node in kd-tree
$c_{min/max}$	Minimal and maximal value of every dimension in each node
$Z = \{z_1, ..., z_k\}$	k candidate centers
$\langle x \rangle / \langle x \rangle^A$	Additive secret shares of x in $\mathbb{Z}_N$
$\langle x \rangle^B$	Boolean secret shares of x in $\mathbb{Z}_2$
$\langle x \rangle_{0/1}$	Cloud $C_{0/1}$ additive secret shares of x
MUL	Secure Multiplication
SED	Secure Eclidean Distance
SC	Secure Comparison
SMin(S/L)	Secure Minimum on small or large datasets
SF	Secure Filtering

4.1 Secure Euclidean Distance (SED)

To calculate the Euclidean distance between cluster z_i and point x for $i \in [k]$, we have the following equation:

$$dist = \sqrt{\sum_{j=1}^{m} (z_i[j] - x[j])^2} \tag{1}$$

where $x[j]$ denotes the jth attribute of x. After all data records are assigned to the corresponding cluster, we have updated cluster centers z_i' by computing the mean values of the data contained in certain clusters. Suppose the size of the new cluster z_i' is $|z_i'|$ and it contains data records $\{x_1, ..., x_{|z_i'|}\}$, then we have the jth attribute of z_i' represented as

$$z_i'[j] = \frac{x_1[j] + \cdots + x_{|z_i'|}[j]}{|z_i'|} = \frac{s_i'[j]}{|z_i'|}, 1 \leq j \leq m \tag{2}$$

where $s_i'[j]$ denotes the sum of the jth attribute values of data records contained in cluster z_i'.

Since it is difficult to do division directly on secret sharing values, we adopt the scaling method proposed in [7] to turn the division in Eq. 2 into multiplication. First, we calculate the scaling factors α and α_i for cluster z_i, represented as

$$\alpha = \prod_{j=1}^{k} |z_j|, \alpha_i = \prod_{j=1 \wedge i \neq j}^{k} |z_j| \tag{3}$$

For the convenience of calculation, we omit the radical operation in Eq. 1. Then, we modify the Euclidean distance formula to be

$$dist = \sum_{j=1}^{m}(\alpha x[j] - \alpha_i z_i[j])^2 \tag{4}$$

According to the characteristics of the secret-sharing scheme, we can make some improvements to the formula and simplify the calculations. During one iteration, no matter what distances we calculate, values of α, α_i, and related calculation results are the same, so we can calculate these values at the beginning of one iteration, reducing a lot of redundant calculations. What's more, irrelevant calculations can be performed simultaneously in secret sharing, reducing the number of interactions.

4.2 Secure Comparison (SC)

Party P_i holds arithmetic secret sharing values $\langle x \rangle_i$ and $\langle y \rangle_i$, $i \in [0, 1]$. We want to securely compare x and y, obtaining arithmetic secret sharing results $\delta = LT(x, y), \delta = \langle \delta \rangle_0 + \langle \delta \rangle_1$.

$$\mathrm{LT}(x, y) = \begin{cases} 1, & \text{if } x < y \\ 0, & \text{if } x \geq y \end{cases} \tag{5}$$

Recently, an efficient and secure comparison protocol was proposed in [9] to solve the millionaires' problem with less communication complexity. After a few rounds of OT, P_0 and P_1 hold boolean secret sharing result of $\delta = LT(x, y), \delta = \langle \delta \rangle_0^B \bigoplus \langle \delta \rangle_1^B$ respectively.

Since the input and output are different from what we want, we add some modifications to make use of the millionares' protocol properly. Details of our Secure Comparison (SC) are shown in Algorithm 1.

Algorithm 1 SC

Input: C_0, C_1 hold $\langle x \rangle_i$ and $\langle y \rangle_i$, $i \in [0, 1]$.
Output: C_0, C_1 learn $\langle \delta \rangle_0$ and $\langle \delta \rangle_1$.
Performed by: C_0 **and** C_1

1: C_0 generates random integer $a, a \in \mathbb{Z}_N$, $\langle r \rangle_0 = \langle x \rangle_0 - \langle y \rangle_0 + a$, sending $\langle r \rangle_0$ to C_1
2: C_1 lets $\langle r \rangle_1 = \langle x \rangle_1 - \langle y \rangle_1$, and add $\langle r \rangle_0$ to $\langle r \rangle_1$, $r = \langle r \rangle_0 + \langle r \rangle_1 = x - y + a$
3: C_0 and C_1 use millionares' protocol to compare a and r, obtaining $\langle v \rangle_i^B, i \in [0, 1]$. $\langle v \rangle_i^B$ represents $\langle LT(a, r) \rangle_i^B$.
4: C_i pick random integer t_i, $\langle v' \rangle_{1-i}^B = \langle v \rangle_i^B \bigoplus t_i$, C_i send $\langle v' \rangle_{1-i}^B$ to C_{1-i}. Then $\langle v \rangle_i^B$ is secret shared between C_0 and C_1.
5: C_0 and C_1 performs $\langle v \rangle_0^B \langle v \rangle_1^B \leftarrow \mathrm{MUL}(\langle v \rangle_1^B, \langle v \rangle_0^B)$
6: $\delta_i = v_i - 2[v_0 v_1]_i, i \in [0, 1]$

When the inputs are secretly shared, the millionaires' protocol can't be used to compare x and y directly. So we let one party C_0 generate a random integer

a, making the comparison between x and y change to the comparison between a and $x - y + a$, and the latter way is easier to achieve in the secret sharing scheme, requiring one round of interaction.

For the output, we need to transfer boolean sharing ($v = \langle v\rangle_0^B \bigoplus \langle v\rangle_1^B$) to arithmetic sharing ($v = \langle v\rangle_0^A + \langle v\rangle_1^A$) based on the observation that $v = \langle v\rangle_0^B + \langle v\rangle_1^B - 2\langle v\rangle_0^B\langle v\rangle_1^B$ is feasible. To compute $\langle v\rangle_0^B\langle v\rangle_1^B$, we need to let party C_i secret share value $\langle v\rangle_i^B$ to party C_{1-i} and then do MUL operation.

4.3 Secure Minimum (SMin(S/L))

Secure Minimum(SMin(S/L)) can be used to securely find the minimum value or value index from a data vector. The traditional way of finding minimum value among n numbers is using bubble sort, which needs $(n-1)$ comparisons and can not be done in parallel. Since the secure comparison protocol can compare multiple pairs of numbers at once, we propose two algorithms to find the minimum depending on the size of the datasets.

When dealing with small datasets, we can increase the number of data pairs that need to be compared in one round, reducing the number of comparisons to one. Take a data set containing three integers $x_i \in \mathbb{Z}_N, i \in [1,3]$ for example. We compare each integer x_i with the other two integers. As a result, we now have six pairs of integers $(x_i, x_{j\neq i}), i, j \in [1,3]$, which can be compared in one round using SC.

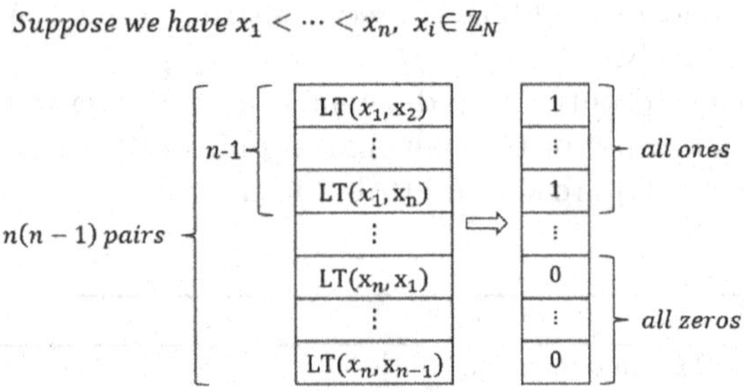

Fig. 2. Secure minimal on small dataset (SMin(S))

The results are denoted as $\{\langle\delta_1\rangle, ..., \langle\delta_6\rangle\}$ secret shared by C_0 and C_1. Then we use MUL to multiply the comparing results related to $x_i, i \in [1,3]$, obtaining $\{\langle m_1\rangle, \langle m_2\rangle, \langle m_3\rangle\}$. Suppose $x_1 < x_2 < x_3$, comparing results related to x_1 are all ones, while the results of x_2, x_3 contain at least one zero. So naturally, we know that $m_1 = 1, m_2 = 0, m_3 = 0$. The whole process can be seen in Fig. 2.

On large data sets, the number of comparing pairs increases by square level. As a result, we give up the idea of increasing comparing pairs and use a tree structure to reduce comparison rounds, requiring $\log n$ rounds of comparisons.

Suppose our dataset contains n integers, we first compare $n/2$ pairs of integers and then multiply comparing results with comparing pairs to obtain smaller values, resulting in a smaller dataset containing $n/2$ integers to repeat the above process until the minimum is obtained. An example is shown in Fig. 3.

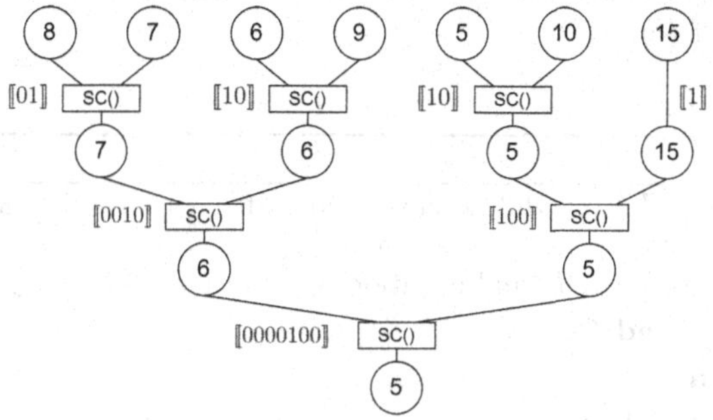

Fig. 3. Secure minimal on large dataset (SMin(L))

There is little difference in the algorithm of finding minimum and maximum values, so we omit the description of the Secure Maximum SMax (S/L) protocol here.

4.4 Secure Filtering (SF)

This section will discuss how to cluster data on the kd-tree structure, and correctness is based on the observation in [8].

Starting from the root node, we traverse each node to determine whether points in that node can be divided into a certain cluster. For each node, we have a set of candidate clusters. During iteration, we continuously delete candidate cluster that does not meet requirements until only one remains. The detailed process is shown in Algorithm 2.

For the Input, $\langle c\rangle$ is the current node to be processed, and $\langle p_i\rangle, i \in [k]$ is an identifier to determine whether the $i-$th candidate cluster has been pruned. In Lines 1 to 4, we use SED protocol to calculate the distance between tree node $\langle c\rangle$ and candidate cluster $\langle z_i\rangle$. With the help of identifier $\langle p_i\rangle$, the distance of the noncandidate cluster is set to maximum value $\langle max\rangle$. And then SMin(S) protocol is used to find the closest candidate cluster $\langle z^*\rangle$.

The core of the secure filtering algorithm is performing a series of sub-protocols to exclude candidate clusters that do not meet the candidate criteria. The condition for filtering candidate cluster $\langle z_j\rangle$ is that all data points contained in node $\langle c\rangle$ are closer to $\langle z^*\rangle$ compared with $\langle z_j\rangle$. In Lines 7 to 15, we will elaborate on how to determine whether to exclude a candidate cluster. First, we subtract $\langle z_j\rangle$ from $\langle z^*\rangle$ by dimension, obtaining $\langle \mu\rangle$, and then compare each dimension data of $\langle \mu\rangle$ with 0. $\langle c_i\rangle_{min}$ and $\langle c_i\rangle_{max}$ denotes the projection of node $\langle c\rangle$ on the i-th coordinate axis, which are calculated and secret shared by users. If $\langle r_i\rangle$ is less than 0, $\langle v_i\rangle$ is set to $\langle c_i\rangle_{min}$, otherwise $\langle c_i\rangle_{max}$. We calculate the distance from $\langle z^* \rangle$ and $\langle z_j \rangle$ to $\langle v \rangle$, obtaining $\langle d^* \rangle$ and $\langle d_j \rangle$ respectively. If $\langle d^* \rangle < \langle d_j \rangle$, then $\langle z_j \rangle$ is filtered and $\langle p_j \rangle$ is set to 0. We accumulate $\langle p_j \rangle, j \in [k]$ and use the secure comparison protocol to determine whether there is only one cluster left in the candidate cluster group. f determines whether to stop iterating over child notes of $\langle c \rangle$.

Algorithm 2 SF

Input: Kd-tree node $\langle c \rangle$, candidate cluster identifier $\langle p_i \rangle, i \in [k]$, and initial cluster center $\langle z_i \rangle, i \in [k]$

Output: Updated $\langle p_i \rangle, i \in [k]$ and iteration termination identifier f

Performed by: C_0 **and** C_1

for $i = 1$ to n **do**
  $\langle d_i \rangle \leftarrow \text{SED}(\langle z_i \rangle, \langle c \rangle)$
  $\langle d_i \rangle \leftarrow \text{MUL}(\langle d_i \rangle, \langle p_i \rangle) + \text{MUL}(\langle max \rangle, 1 - \langle p_i \rangle)$
end for
$\{\langle r_1 \rangle, ..., \langle r_k \rangle\} \leftarrow \text{SMin}(\langle d_1 \rangle, ..., \langle d_k \rangle)$
$\langle z^* \rangle \leftarrow \sum_{i=1}^{k} \text{MUL}(\langle r_i \rangle, \langle z_i \rangle)$
for $j = 1$ to k **do**
  $\langle \mu \rangle \leftarrow \langle z_j \rangle - \langle z^* \rangle$
  $\langle r \rangle \leftarrow \text{SC}(\langle \mu \rangle, 0)$
  $\langle v \rangle \leftarrow \text{MUL}(\langle r \rangle, \langle c \rangle_{min}) + \text{MUL}(1 - \langle r \rangle, \langle c \rangle_{max})$
  $\langle d^* \rangle \leftarrow \text{SED}(\langle z^* \rangle, \langle v \rangle)$
  $\langle d_j \rangle \leftarrow \text{SED}(\langle z_j \rangle, \langle v \rangle)$
  $\langle d_j \rangle \leftarrow \text{MUL}(\langle d_j \rangle, \langle p_j \rangle) + \text{MUL}(\langle max \rangle, 1 - \langle p_j \rangle)$
  $\langle p_j \rangle \leftarrow \text{SC}(\langle d_j \rangle, \langle d^* \rangle)$
end for
$\langle f \rangle \leftarrow \text{SC}(\sum_{j=1}^{k} \langle p_j \rangle, 2)$
$f \leftarrow \text{Rec}(\langle f \rangle_0, \langle f \rangle_1)$

---

5 The Proposed Secure Clustering Scheme

In this section, we proposed Privacy-Preserving Outsourced K-means Clustering (PPOKC) scheme using the kd-tree data structure and secret sharing paradigm. We assume that the original data is additively secret shared between C_0 and C_1, and the two cloud servers cannot collude. We apply the building blocks given in Sect. 4 as the sub-protocols in our scheme, which consists of two main stages: (1) Initialization, (2) Filtering.

- **Initialization**: First, users generate a kd-tree on their datasets. Then, they split the data into two shares and sent these secret shared values to C_0 and C_1, respectively. Moreover, they also split the parameters of the kd-tree into two shared parts and sent them to C_0 and C_1, respectively. In this work, we use $\langle tree \rangle$ to represent the shared kd-tree.

- **Filtering**: The kd-tree is secret shared between C_0 and C_1. The candidate set for the root node contains all cluster centers. We perform the filtering algorithm for each node in the tree until all data are divided into the corresponding cluster. At the end of one iteration, we update the cluster center and compare old cluster centers with new cluster centers to determine whether the termination condition has been met.

5.1 Privacy-Preserving Outsourced K-means Clustering Scheme

The detailed PPOKC scheme is shown in Algorithm 3. First, users construct the kd-tree on the plaintext, which brings little computation overhead. Then, initial clusters are selected, and all related data are secret shared to cloud servers. Upon receiving secret shared data, cloud servers started clustering until termination criteria were satisfied.

Algorithm 3 PPOKC

Input: Secret shared data $x_{ij}, i \in [n], j \in [m]$, iteration termination parameter ϵ
Output: Secret shared cluster Centers $\langle z'_j \rangle, j \in [k]$

1: **Initialization (User)**
2: Construct kd-tree on plaintext
3: Secret shared all related data, including raw data x_{ij}, kd-tree and random initial cluster centers $z_j, j \in [k]$ and send above data to C_0 and C_1
4: **Clustering** (C_0, C_1)
5: For root node, we have candidate cluster identifier array $\{\langle p_1 \rangle, ..., \langle p_k \rangle\}$, with all value set to 1.
6: Traverse nodes in kd-tree until all nodes are clustered.
7: $f \leftarrow \mathrm{SF}(\langle c \rangle, \langle p \rangle, \langle z_1 \rangle, ..., \langle z_k \rangle)$
8: **if** $f == 1$ **then**
9:     Update cluster $\langle z'_j \rangle \leftarrow \langle z'_j \rangle + \mathrm{MUL}(\langle p_j \rangle, \langle c \rangle), j \in [k]$
10: **else**
11:     Repeat above process to child nodes of $\langle c \rangle$
12: **end if**
13: $\langle r \rangle \leftarrow \mathrm{SC}(\sum_{i=1}^{k} \mathrm{SED}(\langle z_i \rangle, \langle z'_i \rangle), \epsilon)$
14: **if** $\langle r \rangle_0 + \langle r \rangle_1 == 1$ **then**
15:     Finish clustering and return the secret shared results.
16: **else**
17:     $\{\langle z_1 \rangle, ..., \langle z_k \rangle\} \leftarrow \{\langle z'_1 \rangle, ..., \langle z'_k \rangle\}$
18:     Go back to step 5.
19: **end if**

After all nodes are clustered, we calculate the distance between the new cluster centers and the original cluster centers and determine whether to stop iteration according to ϵ. If the termination criteria are not satisfied, we update cluster centers and start a new iteration. In Line 14, we leak one bit of data to determine whether to terminate the iteration, but we can also fix the number of iterations to avoid such operation. The number of iterations required for the convergence of different datasets is usually different. Some privacy-preserving schemes [3,4] adopt similar methods to determine whether to stop the iteration.

It is worth mentioning that the data contained in different nodes are disjoint, and the filtering process of different nodes in the same layer will not affect each other. Thus, parallel processing can be used to further improve efficiency.

5.2 Discussion

Most recently, Wu *et al.* [3] proposed an efficient privacy-preserving K-means clustering scheme in the two-cloud model. However, we found that even though this work is efficient, there are serious security issues existing in this work. In line 11 of the S3ED algorithm from ref. [3], we can find that "$Dst_{aj} \leftarrow Dst_{aj} * r_1^a + r_1^a$, for $j \in [k]$", meaning that all distances between two vectors for the same row a are added the same noise. From the analyses in Sect. 7.3 from [26], we can see that this kind of way cannot protect the distribution of the distances between two vectors for the same row a. In this proposed scheme, different random noises are added to different distance data, which cannot leak any information from the original data.

6 Security Analysis

In this section, according to the standard simulation argument [20], we assume cloud server C_0 and C_1 to be the potential adversaries and provide formal security proof for the proposed building blocks, including SED, SC, SMin(S/L), and SF protocols. Then, according to the Composition Theorem, we prove that PPOKC is also secure under the semi-honest model. In addition, to show our system's security under the semi-honest model, we adopt some theorem and lemmas in our security analysis.

Lemma 1. If we have a random variable x uniformly distributed on $\mathbb{Z}_N$ and independent from any variable $y \in \mathbb{Z}_N$, then $x \pm y$ is also uniformly random and independent from y [21,22].

Theorem 1. The SED algorithm proposed is secure under the semi-honest model.

Proof 1. In our SED, most of the operations are performed locally by C_1 and C_0. The interactions only occur in the MUL algorithm, which is secure and proved in reference [23]. Therefore, it's trival to demonstrate the security of our SED.

Theorem 2. The SC algorithm proposed is secure under the semi-honest model.

Proof 2. This algorithm is designed based on the millionaires' protocol, which has been proved security in [9]. C_0 scramble the data with different random numbers and send it to C_1, which is secure given lemma 1. The security proof of converting boolean sharing to additive sharing is based on the security of MUL. Thus, we can conclude that the SC is secure.

Theorem 3. The SMin(S/L) proposed is secure under the semi-honest model.

Proof 3. The SMin(S) protocol on small dataset is simply another version of the SC. The only difference is that we add some MUL operations at the end. Thus, its security can be directly obtained from the security of the SC protocol. For our SMin(L) protocol, we denote the execution image of cloud server C_1 as $\Pi_A(SMin(L)) = \{\langle x_i^A \rangle, \langle r_i^A \rangle, \langle \alpha_i^A \rangle\}$, where $\langle x_i^A \rangle$ is the input value, $\langle r_i^A \rangle$ is intermediate value and $\langle \alpha_i^A \rangle$ is the comparing result, for $i \in [n]$. All these items are secret shared values. We also assume that the simulated image of C_1 can be denoted as $\Pi_A^S(SMin(L)) = \{x_i', r_i', \alpha_i'\}$, where all the simulated item are random numbers generated from $\mathbb{Z}_N$. Since the additive shares are random in $\mathbb{Z}_N$, the $\{\langle x_i^A \rangle, \langle r_i^A \rangle, \langle \alpha_i^A \rangle\}$ are computationally indistinguishable from $\{x_i', r_i', \alpha_i'\}$. From the above analysis, we can draw a conclusion that $\Pi_A(SMin(L))$ is computationally indistinguishable from $\Pi_A^S(SMin(L))$. C_1 performs the same work as C_0 does, so we omit the security analysis here for simplicity.

Theorem 5. The efficient privacy-preserving K-means clustering scheme is secure under the semi-honest model without leaking any intermediate information.

Proof 5. As shown in algorithm 6, the proposed PPOKC scheme is a sequential composition of the secure protocols given before. Since we have already proved the security for all the building blocks, according to the Composition Theorem [20], we claim that our PPOKC scheme is secure against C_0 and C_1 under the semi-honest model. In addition, since the two clouds cannot collude with each other, C_0 and C_1 cannot figure out which cluster the data records are divided into. Therefore, data access patterns are hidden from the cloud servers. Due to the characteristics of the kd-tree data structure, the number of data records contained in each tree node is known but which data it contains remains unknown. So both cloud servers cannot track back the relationship between a data record and its corresponding tree node.

7 System Evaluation and Performance Analysis

We implement an efficient privacy-preserving K-means clustering system based on our proposed protocols and report the experimental results in this section. We have run our experiments on a large number of synthetic data sets to show the practicality and scalability. We also compare the performance of our scheme on real-world data sets with the state-of-the-art privacy-preserving clustering schemes [3,5].

7.1 Experimental Setup

To understand the scalability of our protocols, we conduct experiments on synthetic data sets on a single server that has Intel Core i9-10980XE 3.00 GHz CPU and 64 GB RAM.

For the most direct comparison to the work of [3], we matched the test system's computational performance to that of [3]. We evaluate our protocol on a machine that has Inter Core i7-7700HQ 2.80 GHz CPU and 16 GB RAM.

In our scheme, the secure comparison protocol is implemented using the Millionaires' Protocol in [9]. The whole system is implemented in C++.

7.2 Datasets

For fair comparisons, we use three datasets, each of which was evaluated in some relevant works:

- The first dataset is the real-world dataset KEGG Metabolic Reaction Network (Undirected) [5] in the UCI KDD archive. We run experiments over a small database consisting of 8192 data records with five attributes ($n = 8192, m = 5$), and the number of clusters is 3 ($k = 3$). This dataset was evaluated in [3] and [6], whose schemes are based on homomorphic encryption.
- The second dataset is a 2-dimensional dataset from [29], which consists of 400 data points and 3 clusters. The dataset was evaluated in [11].
- We also generate a synthetic dataset that contains n data records with m attributes randomly generated from integer domain $[0, 1000]$ with uniform distribution.

7.3 Experiments for Real-World Dataset

Comparison with Wu's Scheme. For the most direct comparison, we perform a comparison on a small database, which comes from the UCI KDD dataset [5] to match the dataset used in [3], using the same experimental machine. The experiment results are shown in Table 2, which gives the computation and communication overheads of one iteration during the outsourced clustering process.

Table 2. scheme comparison ($n = 8192, m = 5, k = 3$)

Performance	PPCOM	SEOKC	PPOKC
Computation cost	401 min	17 s	20 s
Communication cost	1430 MB	148 MB	405MB

As shown in the table above, the PPCOM and SEOKC schemes need 401 min and 17 s, respectively, to perform one iteration, while our PPOKC scheme takes 20 s, which is much more efficient than PPCOM (1203 times faster) and almost as fast as SEOKC.

For communication cost, the previous work needs 1430 MB and 148 MB separately, while our scheme requires 405MB. By comparing the previous work, we find that our scheme can reach speeds similar to the current state-of-the-art scheme [3] but more securely, disclosing no data distribution information and intermediate results.

Comparison with Jaschke and Armknecht's Scheme. To conduct a fair comparison, we now perform a comparison on a small 2-dimensional dataset Lsun to match the dataset used in [11]. Since paper [11] ran experiments on Inter i7-3770, 3.4 GHz, 20 GB RAM, we use a similar (1.13x slower) machine as reported before.

Paper [11] presents three different versions of privacy-preserving K-means clustering algorithms (exact, stabilized and approximate), of which took 545.91 days, 48.9 h, and 15.47 h to complete 15 iterations, respectively. For our scheme, it took 20.94 s to complete the same iterations, which is much faster than their versions.

In addition, we use the same initial cluster centers to run the plaintext K-means clustering algorithm and our privacy-preserving scheme on the Lsun dataset and present the obtained centroids in Figs. 4 and 5, respectively. All protocols employed in our framework are the same as the original protocols used in the efficient plaintext K-means clustering algorithm [8]. As a result, our scheme obtains the same model accuracy compared with the original algorithm.

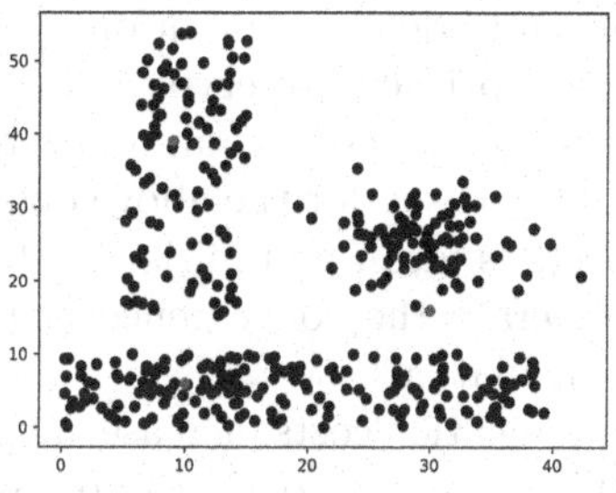

Fig. 4. Plaintext K-means model

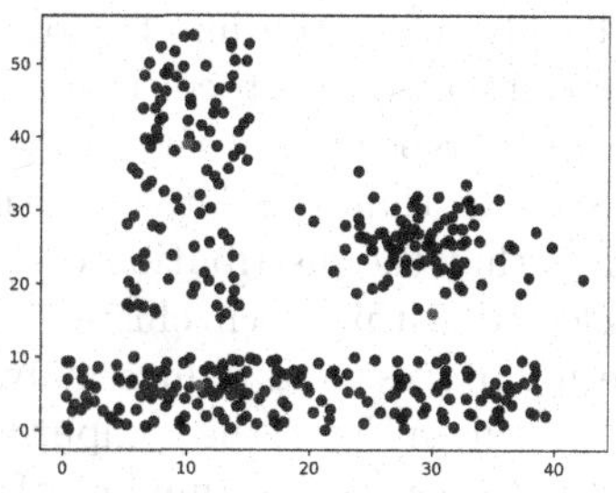

Fig. 5. Privacy Preserving model

7.4 Experiments for Synthetic Dataset

We use d-dimensional synthetic data sets on the range of set sizes $n \in [10000, 60000]$, of which data records are generated in integer domain $[0, 1000]$. Our synthetic data set generator takes several clusters $k \in [3, 15]$. There exist various criteria to stop iterations in K-means. In this experiment, we simply set the number of iterations to a fixed value ($T = 20$) to have a better observation of the experiment results. In order to reduce the impact of random factors on the experiments, initial cluster centers are randomly generated within each cluster.

We consider three parameters that mainly affect the implementation, i.e., the number of data records n, the number of dimensions m, and the number of clusters k. To explore the impact of the target factor independently, our experiment is based on the following strategy, fixing one parameter and varying the other two parameters. The running results, which include computation and communication costs, are shown in Figs. 6 and 7.

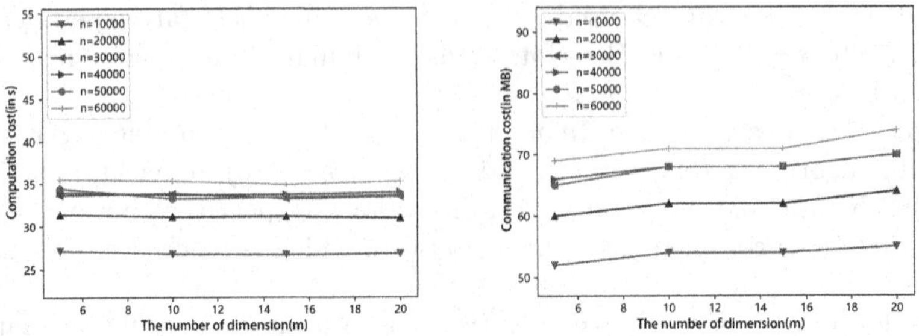

Fig. 6. $k = 3, T = 20$

From Fig. 6, we can see the effect of dimension m on computation and communication costs. Compared with the number of the data set n, dimension m has little impact on computation and communication costs. The reason is that m will only affect the number of multiplication and addition operations. The secure comparison protocol is the bottleneck of our privacy-preserving scheme. From the perspective of time span, the dataset with $n = 60000$ only costs ten more seconds than the dataset with $n = 10000$. The reason for the above observation is that the distribution of synthetic datasets is ideal, and initial clusters are selected within each cluster, which will accelerate the convergence of the clustering process and reduce many redundant calculations.

As shown in Fig. 7, the computation and communication costs increase almost linearly along with the number of clusters k. When k is set to 15, the dataset with 60000 data spends about 4000 s more than the dataset with 10000 data. The experiment results are consistent with the analysis of our scheme. When k increases, we will execute more secure comparison protocols, which brings more computation and communication overhead.

By analyzing the experiment results, we find that our scheme is not only efficient but also secure and adapts to large data sets. Compared with previous work [3, 11], our scheme performs much better when k is large. The advantage of the efficient K-means algorithm allows us to reduce redundant calculations and further accelerate the clustering process. In addition, SIMD operations can be easily implemented to greatly improve the efficiency of our scheme.

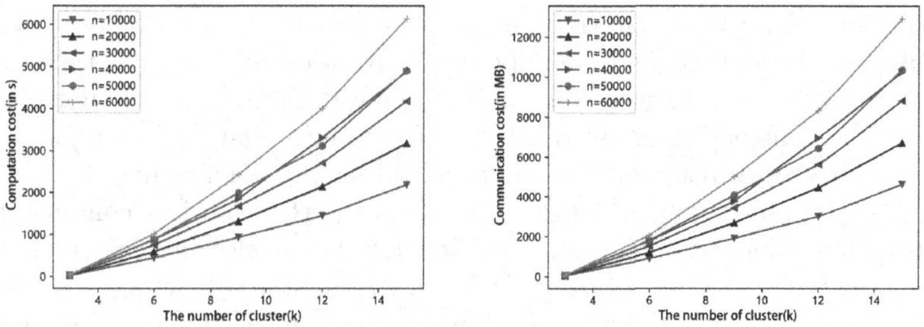

Fig. 7. $m = 5, T = 20$

8 Related Work

In recent years, a lot of research has focused on privacy-preserving K-means clustering protocols, which can be applied in many real-world applications. Generally, these protocols are designed mainly for two scenarios, which are multi-party computation [6,10] and outsourced computation [3,11,27,28]. The first type requires two or more data owners to jointly perform secure protocols, which brings non-negligible computational and communicational overhead to users with limited resources. However, in outsourced computation, data owners are not involved in the execution of the protocols.

Provided that data are held by multiple parties, it can be partitioned in mainly two ways: horizontally partitioned and vertically partitioned. Considering different attributes for the same entity can be stored at different sites (vertically partitioned), Doganay et al. [16] presented a scheme using additive secret sharing to perform K-means clustering without revealing local databases. Lin et al. [17] proposed an approximate comparison protocol combining homomorphic encryption and additive secret sharing and achieved an accuracy of clustering similar to the standard K-means algorithm.

Over horizontally partitioned dataset, Patel et al. [18] use Elliptic Curve cryptography based ElGamal scheme to avoid multiple cipher operations at each site, hence being efficient in terms of computational cost. By allowing parties to communicate in a ring topology, communication cost was reduced. However, the schemes mentioned above inevitably leak intermediate values, which are considered not secure enough. Mohassel et al. [4] proposed a communication-efficient secure multiplication method based on 1-out-of-N Oblivious Transfer, presenting a scalable privacy-preserving clustering algorithm without any security issues. The scheme is both efficient and secure in two-party computation scenario.

Various research has been done in the outsourced scenario. Liu [12] uses Liu's encryption algorithm [13] and Paillier encryption algorithm to encrypt data and then outsource it to one cloud. However, users are highly involved in each iteration, sending trapdoor information and receiving their part in each cluster. In addition, the whole process leaks intermediate values, such as cluster sizes and centroids. To fix this, Jaschke et al. [11] proposed a secure scheme to implement K-means clustering on encrypted data using fully homomorphic encryption. Although this scheme does not have security issues, it takes about 500 days to complete 15 iterations over a small dataset, which is not efficient enough. The schemes mentioned above all outsource data to a single server, which avoids the security issue of collusion but sacrifices efficiency.

Kim et al. [14] designs a secure protocol that performs a fast comparison on encrypted data and considers data distribution when selecting centroids, making the clustering process secure and efficient. The state-of-the-art outsourcing scheme of K-means was proposed by Wu [3], which utilized fully homomorphic encryption and ciphertext packing technique, spending 17 s to complete one iteration on 8192 data records. However, they decrypt the distances after adding the same random noise, comparing them on the plaintext, which may leak the distribution information of data [15]. Different from the existing works, by using the paradigm of secret sharing and millionaires' protocol [9], our proposed PPOKC scheme can efficiently perform the outsourced K-means clustering without leaking any intermediate values, which is suitable to be applied in real world.

9 Conclusion

We proposed a novel efficient PPOKC scheme addressing the problem of privacy-preserving clustering in the context of outsourced computing. The scheme we design protects data security and privacy of cluster information, hiding data access patterns. In addition, we provide a formal security analysis of our protocols, such as SC and SED, evaluating the scheme's performance with extensive experiments both on real-world and synthetic datasets. The experimental results show that our scheme is as efficient as the state-of-the-art scheme but more secure without leaking data distribution characteristics, making our scheme more suitable for real-world applications. For future work, we prepare to advance our research to approximate a privacy-preserving machine learning scheme on a larger dataset. As many machine learning tasks are performed on massive data, their requirements for calculation accuracy are not so high, which can be used to improve efficiency in the privacy-preserving scheme.

Acknowledgment. This work is supported by the National Nature Science Foundation of China (No. 62102429, No. 62072466, No. 62102430, No. 62102440), Natural Science Foundation of Hunan Province, China (Grant No. 2021JJ40688), the NUDT Grants (No. ZK19-38, No. ZK22-50).

References

1. Masulli, F., Schenone, A.: A fuzzy clustering based segmentation system as support to diagnosis in medical imaging. Artif. Intell. Med. **16**(2), 129–147 (1999)
2. Chaturvedi, A., Carroll, J.D., Green, P.E., Rotondo, J.A.: A feature-based approach to market segmentation via overlapping k-centroids clustering. J. Mark. Res. **34**(3), 370–377 (1997)

3. Wu, W., Liu, J., Wang, H., Hao, J., Xian, M.: Secure and efficient outsourced k-means clustering using fully homomorphic encryption with ciphertext packing technique. IEEE Trans. Knowl. Data Eng. **33**(10), 3424–3437 (2020)
4. Mohassel, P., Rosulek, M., Trieu, N.: Practical privacy-preserving k-means clustering. Proc. Priv. Enh. Technol. **2020**(4), 414–433 (2020)
5. Naeem, M., Asghar, S.: KEGG metabolic reaction network data set. The UCI KDD Archive (2011)
6. Rong, H., Wang, H., Liu, J., Hao, J., Xian, M.: Privacy-preserving-means clustering under multiowner setting in distributed cloud environments. Secur. Commun. Netw. **2017** (2017)
7. Rao, F.-Y., Samanthula, B.K., Bertino, E., Yi, X., Liu, D.: Privacy-preserving and outsourced multi-user k-means clustering. In: 2015 IEEE Conference on Collaboration and Internet Computing (CIC), pp. 80–89. IEEE (2015)
8. Kanungo, T., Mount, D.M., Netanyahu, N.S., Piatko, C.D., Silverman, R., Wu, A.Y.: An efficient k-means clustering algorithm: analysis and implementation. IEEE Trans. Pattern Anal. Mach. Intell. **24**(7), 881–892 (2002)
9. Rathee, D., et al.: Cryptflow2: practical 2-party secure inference. In: Proceedings of the 2020 ACM SIGSAC Conference on Computer and Communications Security, pp. 325–342 (2020)
10. Gheid, Z., Challal, Y.: Efficient and privacy-preserving k-means clustering for big data mining. In: 2016 IEEE Trustcom/BigDataSE/ISPA, pp. 791–798. IEEE (2016)
11. Jäschke, A., Armknecht, F.: Unsupervised machine learning on encrypted data. In: Cid, C., Jacobson, M., Jr. (eds.) SAC 2018. LNCS, vol. 11349, pp. 453–478. Springer, Cham (2018). https://doi.org/10.1007/978-3-030-10970-7_21
12. Liu, X., et al.: Outsourcing two-party privacy preserving k-means clustering protocol in wireless sensor networks. In: 2015 11th International Conference on Mobile Ad-hoc and Sensor Networks (MSN), pp. 124–133. IEEE (2015)
13. Liu, D., Bertino, E., Yi, X.: Privacy of outsourced k-means clustering. In: Proceedings of the 9th ACM Symposium on Information, Computer and Communications Security, pp. 123–134 (2014)
14. Kim, H.-J., Chang, J.-W.: A privacy-preserving k-means clustering algorithm using secure comparison protocol and density-based center point selection. In: 2018 IEEE 11th International Conference on Cloud Computing (CLOUD), pp. 928–931. IEEE (2018)
15. Kargupta, H., Datta, S., Wang, Q., Sivakumar, K.: On the privacy preserving properties of random data perturbation techniques. In: Third IEEE International Conference on Data Mining, pp. 99–106. IEEE (2003)
16. Doganay, M.C., Pedersen, T.B., Saygin, Y., Savaş, E., Levi, A.: Distributed privacy preserving k-means clustering with additive secret sharing. In: Proceedings of the 2008 International Workshop on Privacy and Anonymity in Information Society, pp. 3–11 (2008)
17. Lin, Z., Jaromczyk, J.W.: Privacy preserving two-party k-means clustering over vertically partitioned dataset. In: Proceedings of 2011 IEEE International Conference on Intelligence and Security Informatics, pp. 187–191. IEEE (2011)
18. Patel, S.J., Punjani, D., Jinwala, D.C.: An efficient approach for privacy preserving distributed clustering in semi-honest model using elliptic curve cryptography. Int. J. Netw. Secur. **17**(3), 328–339 (2015)
19. Chen, X.: Introduction to secure outsourcing computation. Synth. Lect. Inf. Secur. Priv. Trust **8**(2), 1–93 (2016)

20. Goldreich, O.: Encryption schemes. The foundations of cryptography, vol. 2 (2004)
21. Bogdanov, D., Laur, S., Willemson, J.: Sharemind: a framework for fast privacy-preserving computations. In: Jajodia, S., Lopez, J. (eds.) ESORICS 2008. LNCS, vol. 5283, pp. 192–206. Springer, Heidelberg (2008). https://doi.org/10.1007/978-3-540-88313-5_13
22. Bogdanov, D., Niitsoo, M., Toft, T., Willemson, J.: High-performance secure multi-party computation for data mining applications. Int. J. Inf. Secur. **11**(6), 403–418 (2012)
23. Beaver, D.: Efficient multiparty protocols using circuit randomization. In: Feigenbaum, J. (ed.) CRYPTO 1991. LNCS, vol. 576, pp. 420–432. Springer, Heidelberg (1992). https://doi.org/10.1007/3-540-46766-1_34
24. El Malki, N., Ravat, F., Teste, O.: KD-means: clustering method for massive data based on KD-tree. In: 22nd International Workshop on Design, Optimization, Languages and Analytical Processing of Big Data-DOLAP 2020, vol. 2572. CEUR-WS (2020)
25. Cover, T., Hart, P.: Nearest neighbor pattern classification. IEEE Trans. Inf. Theory **13**(1), 21–27 (1967)
26. Liu, L., et al.: Toward highly secure yet efficient KNN classification scheme on outsourced cloud data. IEEE Internet Things J. **6**(6), 9841–9852 (2019)
27. Cheng, K., Hou, Y., Wang, L.: Secure similar sequence query on outsourced genomic data. In: Proceedings of the 2018 on Asia Conference on Computer and Communications Security, pp. 237–251 (2018)
28. Liu, X., Deng, R.H., Choo, K.-K.R., Weng, J.: An efficient privacy-preserving outsourced calculation toolkit with multiple keys. IEEE Trans. Inf. Forensics Secur. **11**(11), 2401–2414 (2016)
29. Fränti, P., Sieranoja, S.: K-means properties on six clustering benchmark datasets. Appl. Intell. **48**(12), 4743–4759 (2018)
30. Beimel, A.: Secret-sharing schemes: a survey. In: Chee, Y.M., Guo, Z., Ling, S., Shao, F., Tang, Y., Wang, H., Xing, C. (eds.) IWCC 2011. LNCS, vol. 6639, pp. 11–46. Springer, Heidelberg (2011). https://doi.org/10.1007/978-3-642-20901-7_2
31. Papernot, N., McDaniel, P., Sinha, A., Wellman, M.P.: SoK: security and privacy in machine learning. In: 2018 IEEE European Symposium on Security and Privacy (EuroS&P), pp. 399–414. IEEE (2018)
32. Xu, R., Wunsch, D.: Survey of clustering algorithms. IEEE Trans. Neural Networks **16**(3), 645–678 (2005)
33. Hegde, A., Möllering, H., Schneider, T., Yalame, H.: SoK: efficient privacy-preserving clustering. Proc. Priv. Enh. Technol. **2021**(4), 225–248 (2021)
34. Bozdemir, B., Canard, S., Ermis, O., Möllering, H., Önen, M., Schneider, T.: Privacy-preserving density-based clustering. In: Proceedings of the 2021 ACM Asia Conference on Computer and Communications Security, pp. 658–671 (2021)
35. Boldyreva, A., Tang, T.: Privacy-preserving approximate k-nearest-neighbors search that hides access, query and volume patterns. Cryptology ePrint Archive (2021)

Fuzzy Deduplication Scheme Supporting Pre-verification of Label Consistency

Zehui Tang[1], Shengke Zeng[1(✉)], Tao Li[2,3], Shuai Cheng[1], and Haoyu Zheng[1]

[1] School of Computer and Software Engineering, Xihua University, Chengdu 610039, China
zengshengke@gmail.com
[2] State Key Laboratory of Public Big Data, College of Computer Science and Technology, Guizhou University, Guiyang 550025, China
[3] School of Computer Science, Qufu Normal University, Rizhao 276825, China

Abstract. Efficiently and securely removing encrypted redundant data with cross-user in the cloud is challenging. Convergent Encryption (CE) is difficult to resist dictionary attacks for its deterministic tag. Server-aided mechanism is against such attacks while it may exist collusion. Focus on multimedia data, this paper proposes an efficient and secure fuzzy deduplication system without any additional servers. We also propose a notion of pre-verification of label consistency to compensate for the irreparable post-verification loss. Compared with other fuzzy deduplication schemes, our work has apparent advantages in deduplication efficiency and security based on a natural data set.

1 Introduction

People use big data to describe and define the massive data generated in the information age. This data enables applications such as video, audio, images, logs, health records, social network interactions, scientific data, etc. [20]. IBM has pointed out that the 2.5EB of data created daily is also 90% of the data generated in the past two years [12]. In order to solve the problem of duplicate data redundancy and reduce expensive storage waste, deduplication technology was born, including the detection of near-duplicate images [10], the elimination of similar or nearly identical audio and video, and other methods [12,14]. The same or similar files encrypted by different clients are uploaded as completely independent ciphertexts, so basic or naive encryption applications can severely hinder near-duplicate data deduplication. This conflicts with deduplication because comparing the ciphertexts encrypted by users with different private keys is difficult. To address this challenge, some deduplication mechanisms have been proposed, such as Convergent Encryption (CE) [4], Message Lock Encryption (MLE) [2] and its variants [18].

Li *et al.'s* [7] proposed the first secure client-side similar image deduplication scheme for cloud storage to efficiently reduce data redundancy in memory. However, this scheme relies on a trusted third party, and the key sharing among

M. Zhang et al. (Eds.): ProvSec 2023, LNCS 14217, pp. 365–384, 2023.
https://doi.org/10.1007/978-3-031-45513-1_20

groups does not apply to public cloud storage platforms with a large number of users (such as Huawei Cloud). Chen *et al.'s* [3] also proposed a similar secure image deduplication scheme based on group key sharing, although this scheme can provide some security against external adversary attacks (such as server collusion attacks). However, at the cost of compromising the privacy of group members, using such a scheme makes it difficult to defend against social engineering attacks. For systems with multi-user and cross-domain interaction, this data deduplication mechanism is embarrassing. Jiang *et al.'s* [6] proposed a combination of FuzzyMLE and FuzzyPoW so that the cloud server can safely deduplicate encrypted multimedia data within a certain distance (i.e. Hamming distance) while reducing data overhead from client to server over the network. However, FuzzyMLE is based on the auxiliary server to avoid a guessing attack in which these two servers may collude for each other to leak data, and FuzzyPoW can indeed verify whether there is similar ciphertext between clients, still, its shortcoming is that in the case that FuzzyPoW fails to pass. The server cannot distinguish which client provided incorrect information, and cannot play a tracking role. Our scheme uses a zero-knowledge proof label consistency pre-verification method to solve the problem of FuzzyPoW.

Liu *et al.'s* [9] proposed a single server data deletion scheme for the first time. This scheme relies on the strong collision nature of the short hash to resist the dictionary attack of the storage server and calls similar users to recover the key by uploading users with the help of the cloud storage server. In addition, it is very regrettable that the secure deduplication scheme of Liu *et al.'s* is exact deduplication, which only applies to the exact same files. Takeshia *et al.'s* [13] aim to solve almost the same image deduplication problem, but their scheme cannot resist the brute force attack by repeated queries from the server and the client. The deduplication of fuzzy data based on a single server still has a long way to go.

These deduplication schemes up to date only achieve post-verification of label consistency (verify through the deduplication phase or the download phase). Although they can handle the tag-matching problem, it can not make up for the loss after the integrity compromise. Therefore, we propose a notion of pre-verification to check the label consistency in advance, which effectively solving the irreversible loss problem in post-verification.

In general, we construct a fuzzy deduplication for the similar multimedia data with single server to be against various attacks. Our contribution mainly includes the following 4 items, and the comparison of the related deduplication schemes is listed in Table 1.

- We propose a fuzzy deduplication strategy for approximate data which fits multimedia data. Our scheme does not depend on any additional servers to resist the brute-force attacks. Therefore, it is not necessary to assume the server is honest.
- We propose a notion of pre-verification to avoid the difficulty of tracking malicious users for schemes which are post-verification. As a result, our work compensates for the irreparable loss of post-verification.

- We consider the underlying collusion attacks between the clients and the cloud server and make use of a variable-length short hash technology to handle it.
- Our experimental results show that our scheme achieves high deduplication of fuzzy data by comparing the similarity of tags. With a threshold of 1, our deduplication rate is 20.8% higher than that of Jiang *et al.'s* [6]

Table 1. Comparison of related programss

Test Group	SS	FD	CR	BFAR	RAR	TC	CG
Jiang *et al.'s* [6]	×	√	×	√	√	×	√
chen *et al.'s* [3]	√	×	×	√	×	×	×
Takeshita *et al.'s* [13]	√	√	√	×	√	×	√
Our'scheme	√	√	√	√	√	√	√

'√' = **Satisfied** '×' = **Unsatisfied** SS = Single Server
FD = Fuzzy Deduplication CR = Collusion Resistance BFAR = Brute-Force Attacks Resistance RAR = Replay Attacks Resistance TC = Tag Consistency
CG = Cross Group

2 Preliminaries

In this section, we summarize the Hamming distance, perceptual hash [8], hash collision [9], and zero-knowledge proof, which constitute the primary supporting knowledge of our system.

2.1 Hamming Distance and Threshold

Hamming Distance. Hamming distance is a common distance measurement method, which is usually used to compare the distance between two characters. Let $\mathtt{X} = (\mathtt{x}_1, \mathtt{x}_2, ..., \mathtt{x}_n)$ and $\mathtt{Y} = (\mathtt{y}_1, \mathtt{y}_2, ..., \mathtt{y}_n)$, then the Hamming distance between X and Y is as shown in the Eq. (1):

$$\mathtt{H}(\mathtt{X}, \mathtt{Y}) = \sum_{\mathtt{i}=0}^{\mathtt{n}} \mathtt{d}(\mathtt{x}_\mathtt{i}, \mathtt{y}_\mathtt{i}) \tag{1}$$

Here, $\mathtt{d}(\mathtt{x}_\mathtt{i}, \mathtt{y}_\mathtt{i})$ means that when the characters in each corresponding position of X and Y are the same, they are equal to 0, and vice versa, they are equal to 1. For binary coded numbers, the Hamming distance can be calculated by XOR operation, as shown in Eq. (2):

$$\mathtt{H}(\mathtt{X}, \mathtt{Y}) = \sum_{\mathtt{i}=0}^{\mathtt{n}} \mathtt{d}(\mathtt{x}_\mathtt{i} \oplus \mathtt{y}_\mathtt{i}) \tag{2}$$

Threshold. The threshold has a direct impact on the deduplication rate of the deduplication scheme. We set D to represent the threshold between Hamming distances to judge the similarity of data, as shown below:

1) if $d(X,Y) \leq D \Rightarrow$ X and Y are recognized as similar strings.

2) if $d(X,Y) = 0 \Rightarrow$ X and Y are recognized as identical strings.

3) if $d(X,Y) > D \Rightarrow$ X and Y are recognized as dissimilar strings.

2.2 Perceptual Hashing

Perceptual Hashing. The Perceptual Hash function can be used to determine whether the original data is similar. Perceptual Hash describes a type of hash value that can be compared, which is a digital signature calculated based on multimedia content and features. Standard Perceptual Hashing algorithms [17] are mainly divided into `ahash`, `phash` and `dhash`. Zauner *et al.'s* pointed out that although the speed of `phash` is slightly slower than that of `ashah` and `dhash`, the recognition effect is the best. Therefore, in order to achieve more effective image feature matching, many deduplication systems select `phash` as the feature vector of massive image data. A common `phash` processes images as follows:

1. Size reduction: To avoid the impact of image size on deduplication, we uniformly scale the image to $N \times N$ (high frequency gives details, low frequency gives structure).
2. Adjust colour: Simplify the colour of the image and convert it to grayscale using the following Eq. (3). Red (R), Green (G), Blue (B).

$$\mathtt{Gray} = \mathtt{R} \times 0.299 + \mathtt{G} \times 0.587 + \mathtt{B} \times 0.114 \tag{3}$$

3. Discrete cosine transform (DCT): DCT is a special Fourier transform that transforms a picture from the pixel domain to the frequency domain.
4. Calculate DCT average value: calculate the average value of 64 reserved low frequencies.
5. `Phash` calculation: compare each DCT value with the average value. Equation (4) e.g.,

$$\begin{aligned} &\mathtt{if}\ (\mathtt{DCT'value} \geq \mathtt{Avg}) \longmapsto \mathtt{Output}\ \ 1 \\ &\mathtt{if}\ (\mathtt{DCT'value} < \mathtt{Avg}) \longmapsto \mathtt{Output}\ \ 0 \end{aligned} \tag{4}$$

6. Hamming distance: Perform the XOR operation on the `phash` of the file to determine the number of different characters in the corresponding position of the string.

2.3 Hash Collisions

The hash function is an irreversible mapping from message space to image space and compresses a any input length into a fixed output length. The hash function accepts a string $\mathtt{X} \in \{0,1\}^*$ as input and outputs a string $\mathtt{H(x)} \in \{0,1\}^{\mathtt{n}}$, where n is the length. Hash functions with longer outputs are less collision-resistant, while hash functions with shorter outputs are more collision-resistant.

We use a short hash to avoid guessing attacks and improve efficiency. We obtain **phash** from the original data and select the fingerprints with odd (or even) serial numbers in **phash** to reorganize into a new short **phash**. The assembly process is shown in Fig. 1.

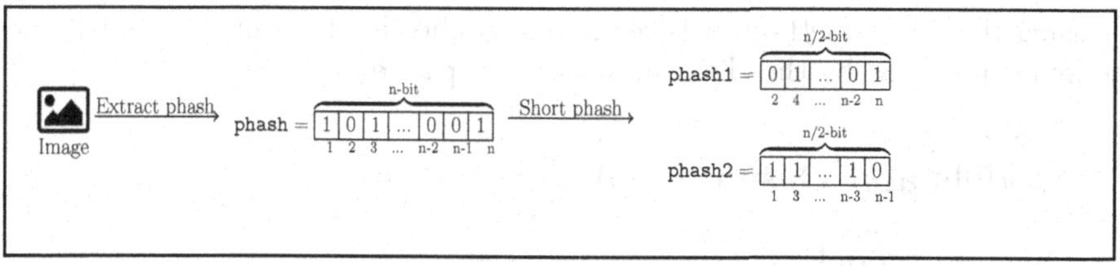

Fig. 1. A hash of length n constructs a short hash

2.4 Zero-Knowledge Proof

Zero-knowledge system is a cryptographic protocol. One side of the protocol is called the prover (PR), and the other side of the protocol is the verifier (VE). In our paper, we use the zero-knowledge proof of graph isomorphism to propose a verification method for the cloud server to check whether the client's tags are consistent or not, which realizes the pre-verification and avoids the defect of irreparable losses caused by post-verification. In the proof of label consistency, we need to prove that the image matches with the corresponding **phash**, therefore we only need to prove that image (I) and **phash** (P) satisfy the relationship of $\mathtt{I} = \varphi\mathtt{P}$, where φ is the mapping relationship. The proof process is shown in Fig. 2.

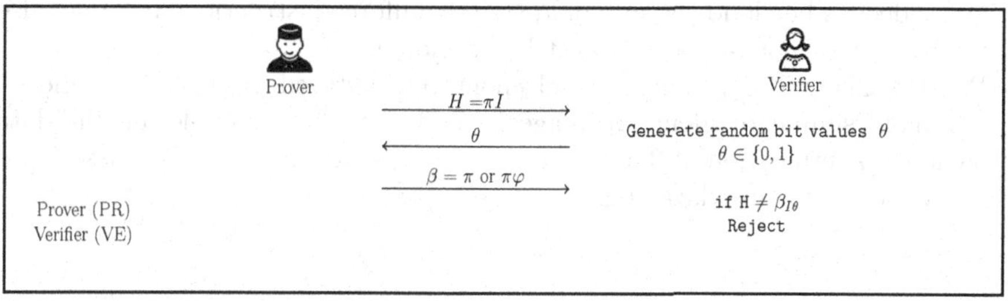

Fig. 2. Zero-knowledge Proofs for Label Consistency

1. PR randomly generates a permutation π, calculates the graph $\mathtt{H} = \pi\mathtt{I}$, and then sends H to VE.
2. VE generates a bit value $\theta \in \{0, 1\}$ and sends θ to PR.
3. PR reacts differently according to θ. As shown in the Eq. (5)

$$\begin{aligned} \mathtt{if}\ (\theta = 1) \Rightarrow \mathtt{PR} \quad \mathtt{sends} \quad \beta = \pi \\ \mathtt{if}\ (\theta = 0) \Rightarrow \mathtt{PR} \quad \mathtt{sends} \quad \beta = \pi\varphi \end{aligned} \tag{5}$$

4. VE calculation. As shown in the Eq. (6)

$$\begin{aligned} \mathtt{if}\ (\theta = 0) \Rightarrow \beta\mathtt{I}_\theta = \pi\varphi\mathtt{P} = \pi\mathtt{I} = \mathtt{H} \\ \mathtt{if}\ (\theta = 1) \Rightarrow \beta\mathtt{I}_\theta = \pi\mathtt{I} = \mathtt{H} \end{aligned} \tag{6}$$

By using the above method, it is realized that the cloud server verifies whether the image provided by the client matches with phash.

3 Models and Design Goals

3.1 System Model

Unlike the server-aided schemes [6,13], our scheme does not rely on any additional servers (single server only) to solve the brute-force guessing attacks. We adopt a client-side deduplication strategy, in which the files are unnecessary to be uploaded if the duplicates are checked. Therefore, our scheme comprises three kinds of roles: an uploading client, a cloud server, and parallel client $\mathtt{PC_i} = \{\mathtt{PC_1}, \mathtt{PC_2}, ..., \mathtt{PC_n}\}$, where n is the number of clients that have stored data similar to the uploading file. The system framework is shown in Fig. 3, and each entity is described as follows:

- Uploading Client (C): The uploading client is a user who needs to outsource its data to a cloud server. The stored files should be encrypted for the data privacy. In order to save storage and bandwidth, C would check the existence of the uploading file on the server(by sending the file's fingerprint). Duplicate files are not uploaded.
- Cloud Server (CS): The cloud server stores the client's private data. In order to save storage costs, it needs to deduplicate multimedia data such as pictures and videos. The cloud server would strictly enforce instructions but may also try to guess client privacy (honest but curious).
- Parallel Client ($\mathtt{PC_i}$): The parallel clients have stored data on CS. When C may hold similar or identical images, $\mathtt{PC_i}$ assists CS in completing the data ownership verification of C. C is defined as a new $\mathtt{PC_i}$ member if it passes, and a key for decrypting data is given.

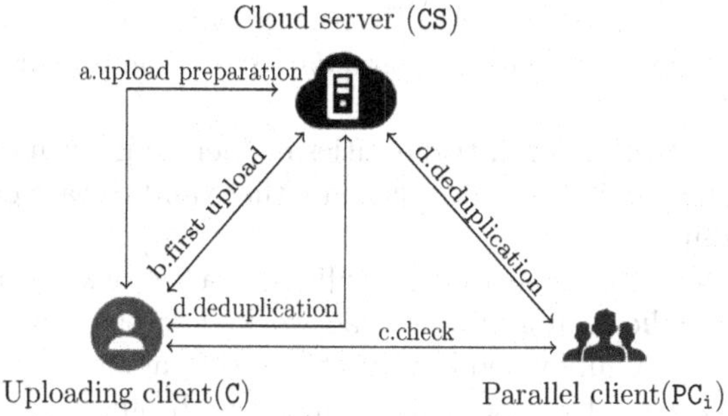

Fig. 3. System model

3.2 Threat Model

In our scheme, none of the three entities is absolutely trustworthy, and we analyze the hazards of each entity according to the characteristics of each entity, as shown below:

A Malicious Uploading Client. C attempts to launch a data ownership spoofing attack using the file's fingerprint. In addition, it may carry out a forgery attack, where C uses the correct label to repeatedly check but uploads the forged ciphertext (inconsistent with the label) to damage the integrity of other client files.

An Honest-But-Curious Cloud Service. CS faithfully executes storage instructions and deduplication instructions, however it may also try to steal and understand the underlying content of stored ciphertexts. We also consider that CS may collude with C or PC_i to guess the storage content, thereby stealing user data information.

A Malicious Parallel Client. PC_i falsely reports information in the hash compared with C resulting in duplicate data not being deduplicated, resulting in a waste of CS storage space. PC_i also may conspire with CS to steal C's private information.

The probability of pairwise conspiracy among the three entities is low, but it does not mean that it will not happen [15,16], and it is difficult for ordinary users to detect whether their privacy has been leaked (such as CS can guess the stored information without making it public). The security of the above system needs to be improved.

3.3 Design Goals

We design the following security goals by analyzing the threat model in Sect. 3.2.

- Data privacy: Even if the data is transmitted in an unsafe channel and stolen by the adversary, the adversary will never know the plaintext of the data without the decryption key.

- Resistance to brute-force attacks: Even if the adversary obtains all the data plaintext, it cannot guess the encrypted data stored on CS through the specific tag data.
- Anti-collusion attack: Even if two entities cooperate in exchanging communication parameters and other information, other valid private data information cannot be obtained.
- Tag consistency: Tag inconsistency will have a serious negative impact on subsequent deduplication and download work. Therefore, we need to strictly check whether the C uploaded data matches the tag.
- Track the adversary: Data security cannot be absolutely guaranteed in the security system, but there must be a way to track the adversary after being attacked.
- Efficiency: The main goal of our scheme is to efficiently detect and delete duplicate data while ensuring user privacy and security. We strive to achieve maximum efficiency in deduplication while maintaining low overhead.

4 Proposed Scheme

We present our scheme in this section. It includes 4 main stages in total: Upload Preparation, First Upload, Deduplication and Download. We illustrate the description of the required symbols in Table 2 below.

Table 2. Notations used in the proposed scheme

Notation	Description
$\mathtt{ID}$	the identity of $\mathtt{C}$
$\mathtt{pk_c}$	the public key of $\mathtt{C}$
$\mathtt{sk_C}$	the private key of $\mathtt{C}$
$\mathtt{k_C}$	Symmetric encryption key
$\mathtt{ID_i}$	the identity of $\mathtt{PC_i}$
$\mathtt{pk_{Pc_i}}$	the public key of $\mathtt{PC_i}$
$\mathtt{sk_{Pc_i}}$	the private key of $\mathtt{PC_i}$
$\mathtt{pk_{c_i}}$	the public key of $\mathtt{CS}$
$\mathtt{sk_{C_i}}$	the private key of $\mathtt{CS}$
$\mathtt{ph_c}$	the image fingerprint from $\mathtt{C}$
$\mathtt{ph_{c_i}}$	the image fingerprint from $\mathtt{PC_i}$
$\mathtt{d}(\cdot)$	the Hamming distance calculation operation
$\mathtt{D}$	the threshold in deduplication
$\mathtt{url}$	the storage address of C
$\mathtt{OutPut}(\cdot)$	short hash constructor
$\mathtt{Enc}(\cdot)$	public-key encryption algorithm
$\mathtt{E}(\cdot)$	symmetric encryption algorithm

4.1 Upload Preparation

As shown in Fig. 4, the client must follow the steps below to determine whether its files need to be deduplicated.
Client:

1. CS needs to check whether the I and P match, as shown in Fig. 2. The verification is passed, and the subsequent process is carried out.
2. C needs to extract **phash** from the image and convert the **phash** into $\mathbf{phash_i}$, as shown in Fig. 1 (For the convenience of CS to calculate similar fingerprints, C should select $\mathbf{phash_1}$ or $\mathbf{phash_2}$).
3. C generates the public key $\mathbf{pk_c}$, secret key $\mathbf{sk_c}$ and **id**, obtains the public key $\mathbf{pk_{c_i}}$ of the cloud storage server and uses $\mathbf{pk_{c_i}}$ to encrypt $\mathbf{phash_i}$.
4. C sends M_1 to CS: $M_1 = \mathbf{Enc}_{\mathbf{pk}_{c_i}}(\mathbf{id}, \mathbf{phash}_1)$.

Cloud Service:

1. Generate a public key $\mathbf{pk_{c_i}}$ and a secret key $\mathbf{sk_{c_i}}$.
2. Accept M_1 and decrypt M_1 with $\mathbf{sk_{c_i}}$.
3. Perform a deduplication check. Confirm whether the uploaded image is an approximate duplicate file, and determine whether to perform further deduplication operations.
   - if $d > D$ Execute First Upload .
   - if $d \leq D$ Execute Deduplication.

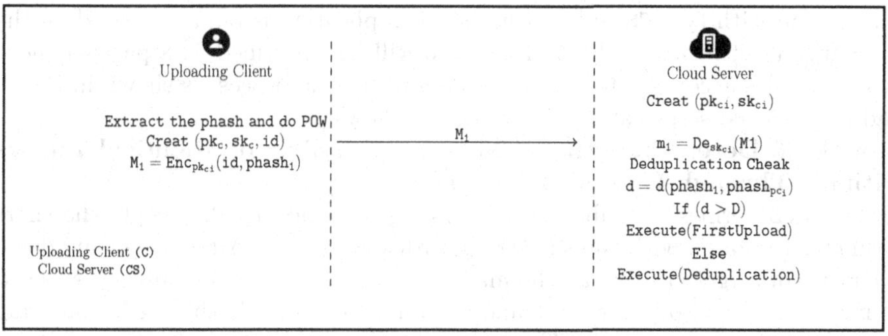

Fig. 4. Upload Preparation

4.2 First Upload

If there are no duplicate files in CS, then C is asked to upload the image after the duplicate data deletion check, as shown in Fig. 5. The specific steps are as follows:

1. CS creates a public resource locator URL to store C's encrypted file as $\mathtt{URL} = \mathtt{Enc}_{pk_c}(\mathtt{url})$.
2. C accepts URL and decrypts URL with $\mathtt{sk_c}$.
3. C encrypts image (img) with k_c and sends I_c to CS as $I_c = E_{k_c}(\mathtt{img})$.
4. CS accepts I_c and records $\{I_c, \mathtt{phash_i}, \mathtt{id}\}$.

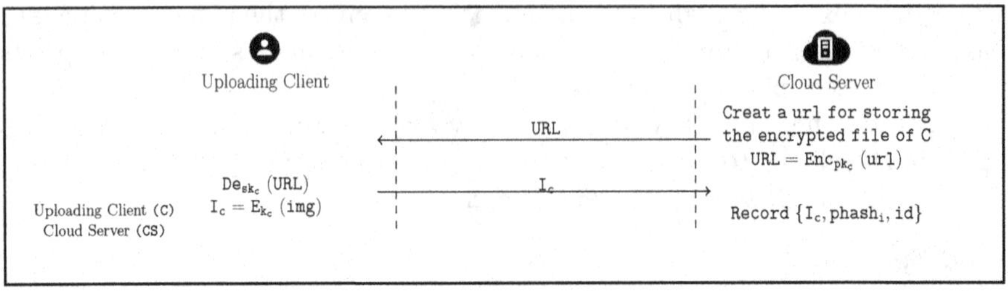

Fig. 5. First Upload

4.3 Deduplication

When C enters the deduplication phase, it means that CS may have stored an image similar to the uploaded image, therefore it needs to interact with CS and PC_i at this stage. Specifically, C needs to perform a new round of phash value comparison with PC_i, CS judges whether deduplication is required based on the comparison between C and PC_i. Finally, C will be confirmed as a parallel client or upload files according to the above judgment. The process is shown in Fig. 6, and the detailed steps can be described as follows.

Step 1: CS Determines that C May have Similar or Identical Images with PC_i Through Hamming Distance

After CS verifies the labelling consistency provided by C, accepts the short hash of C to match with the short hash provided by PC_i. After narrowing down the range of target customers who may have similar or identical images, we need to make a comparison between C and PC_i improved short hash lengths, allowing for more precise comparisons. Therefore, we need a new round of communication.

1. CS needs find PC_i from the cloud database.
2. CS needs build an n' bit OutPut function, n' is the length of output phash

$$\mathtt{OutPut}(n', \mathtt{phash}) \qquad n' \in (n/2, n].$$

3. CS encrypts ID_{c_i} and D' with pk_c, D' is the threshold for the current round of agreement to determine whether the image is similar

$$ID_i = \mathtt{Enc}_{pk_c}(ID_{c_i} || D').$$

4. CS encrypts $\mathtt{ID_c}$ and $\mathtt{D'}$ with $\mathbf{pk}_{\mathtt{p_{c_i}}}$

$$\mathtt{ID_c} = \mathtt{Enc}_{\mathbf{pk}_{\mathtt{p_{c_i}}}}(\mathtt{ID_c}||\mathtt{D'}).$$

5. CS sends $\mathtt{ID_i}$ to C, and sends $\mathtt{ID_c}$ to $\mathtt{PC_i}$.

Step 2: Communication Between C and $\mathtt{PC_i}$ to Determine Whether the File of C is Similar to the File of $\mathtt{PC_i}$

C and $\mathtt{PC_i}$ use the **output** function to reconstruct their **phash**, and pass the **phash** to each other use the Hamming distance and $\mathtt{D'}$ to further judge whether the two files are similar. The process is as follows.

1. C uses **output** function to regenerate $\mathbf{ph}'_{\mathtt{c}}$

$$\mathbf{ph}'_{\mathtt{c}} = \mathtt{OutPut}(\mathtt{n}', \mathbf{ph}_{\mathtt{c}}).$$

2. C encrypts $\mathbf{ph}'_{\mathtt{c}}$ with $\mathbf{pk}_{\mathtt{p_{c_i}}}$ and sends $\mathtt{Enc}_{\mathbf{pk}_{\mathtt{p_{c_i}}}}(\mathbf{ph}'_{\mathtt{c}})$ to $\mathtt{PC_i}$.
3. $\mathtt{PC_i}$ uses **output** function to regenerate $\mathbf{ph}'_{\mathtt{c_i}}$

$$\mathbf{ph}'_{\mathtt{c_i}} = \mathtt{OutPut}(\mathtt{n}', \mathbf{ph}_{\mathtt{c_i}}).$$

4. $\mathtt{PC_i}$ encrypts $\mathbf{ph}'_{\mathtt{c_i}}$ with $\mathbf{pk}_{\mathtt{c}}$ and sends $\mathtt{Enc}_{\mathbf{pk}_{\mathtt{c}}}(\mathbf{ph}_{\mathtt{c_i}}')$ to C.
5. C and $\mathtt{PC_i}$ calculate the Hamming distance $\mathtt{d}(*)$ between $\mathbf{ph}'_{\mathtt{c_i}}$ and $\mathbf{ph}'_{\mathtt{c}}$, and judge whether the two files are similar, as shown in Algorithm 1.

Algorithm 1. Algorithm for Judging File Similarity (First Round)

$\mathtt{d_1} = \mathtt{d}(\mathbf{ph}'_{\mathtt{c}}, \mathbf{ph}'_{\mathtt{c_i}})$
if $\mathtt{d_1} > \mathtt{D'}$ **then**
  | Execute First Upload;
else
  $\mathbf{ph}''_{\mathtt{c}} = \mathtt{OutPut}(\mathtt{n}, \mathbf{ph}_{\mathtt{c}})$
  $\mathtt{Enc}_{\mathbf{pk}_{\mathtt{p_{c_i}}}}(\mathbf{ph}''_{\mathtt{c}})$.
end

We emphasize the following 2 points:

- To avoid the collusion attack of CS and C (or $\mathtt{PC_i}$), the length of the **phash** constructed in this round should be less than **n**. If the length of the current round of **phash** reaches **n**, CS can obtain the complete **phash** of the image and use the dictionary attack to obtain the clear text information of the image.
- The precondition for CS to perform the First Upload operation is that the feedbacks from $\mathtt{PC_i}$ and C to CS are both Execute First Upload. If the feedback from P and C is inconsistent, CS is confident to suspect that there exists a malicious adversary.

Step 3: This Communication Will Finally Determine Whether the Image of $\mathtt{C}$ has a Similar Image in $\mathtt{CS}$

$\mathtt{C}$ and $\mathtt{PC_i}$ continue to exchange phash and then calculate the Hamming distance, respectively. If the Hamming distance is lower than the threshold, we can think that $\mathtt{C}$ and $\mathtt{PC_i}$ have similar or identical files. The process is as follows.

1. $\mathtt{C}$ uses *output* function to regenerate $\mathtt{ph}''_{\mathtt{c}}$

$$\mathtt{ph}''_{\mathtt{c}} = \mathtt{OutPut}(\mathtt{n}, \mathtt{ph_c}).$$

2. $\mathtt{C}$ encrypts $\mathtt{ph}''_{\mathtt{c}}$ with $\mathtt{pk_{Pc_i}}$ and sends $\mathtt{Enc}_{\mathtt{pk_{Pc_i}}}(\mathtt{ph}''_{\mathtt{c}})$ to $\mathtt{PC_i}$.
3. $\mathtt{PC_i}$ uses *output* function to regenerate $\mathtt{ph}''_{\mathtt{c_i}}$

$$\mathtt{ph}''_{\mathtt{c_i}} = \mathtt{OutPut}(\mathtt{n}, \mathtt{ph_{c_i}}).$$

4. $\mathtt{PC_i}$ encrypts $\mathtt{ph}''_{\mathtt{c_i}}$ with $\mathtt{pk_c}$ and sends $\mathtt{Enc}_{\mathtt{pk_c}}(\mathtt{ph}''_{\mathtt{c_i}})$ to $\mathtt{C}$.
5. $\mathtt{C}$ and $\mathtt{PC_i}$ calculate the Hamming distance $\mathtt{d}(*)$ between $\mathtt{ph}''_{\mathtt{c_i}}$ and $\mathtt{ph}''_{\mathtt{c}}$, and judge whether the two files are simila, as shown in Algorithm 2.

Algorithm 2. Algorithm for Judging File Similarity (Second Round)

$\mathtt{d_1}' = \mathtt{d}(\mathtt{ph_c}'', \mathtt{ph}''_{\mathtt{c_i}})$
if $\mathtt{d_1}' > \mathtt{D}$ **then**
| `Execute First Upload;`
else
| `Execute Deduplication.`
end

---

1. If $\mathtt{CS}$ executes Deduplication, adds $\mathtt{C}$ into $\mathtt{PC_i}$.
2. $\mathtt{C}$ and $\mathtt{PC_i}$ have passed the mutual authentication, and $\mathtt{PC_i}$ will encrypt the $\mathtt{k_c}$ and $\mathtt{URL}$ of the decrypted image with $\mathtt{pk_c}$ and send it to $\mathtt{C}$.

We emphasize the following two points:

- The length of **phash** used for comparison here should be **n**. The longer the length of the **phash**, the more accurate the comparison and the higher the deduplication rate.
- $\mathtt{CS}$ performs a deduplication operation on the image of $\mathtt{C}$, which means that $\mathtt{S}$ and $\mathtt{PC_i}$ have similar or identical images. $\mathtt{C}$ will join $\mathtt{PC_i}$ and play a role in assisting certification in the deduplication work of $\mathtt{CS}$ in the future.

4.4 Download

Only client $\mathtt{C}$ has previously stored an image in $\mathtt{CS}$ can enter the download phase, and$\mathtt{C}$ has saved $(\mathtt{k_c}, \mathtt{url_i})$. Therefore, $\mathtt{C}$ can directly find the image storage location through $\mathtt{URL}$ and use $\mathtt{k_c}$ to decrypt the image. At this point, the whole download phase completes. The process is described as follows.

1. $\mathtt{C}$ finds the information $\mathtt{k_c}, \mathtt{url}$ related to the restored image $\mathtt{img}$.
2. $\mathtt{C}$ finds the storage address through $\mathtt{url}$, and decrypts the $\mathtt{img}$ through $\mathtt{k_c}$. The decryption formula is: $\mathtt{img} = \mathtt{De}_{\mathtt{k_c}}(\mathtt{E}_{\mathtt{k_c}}(\mathtt{img}))$.

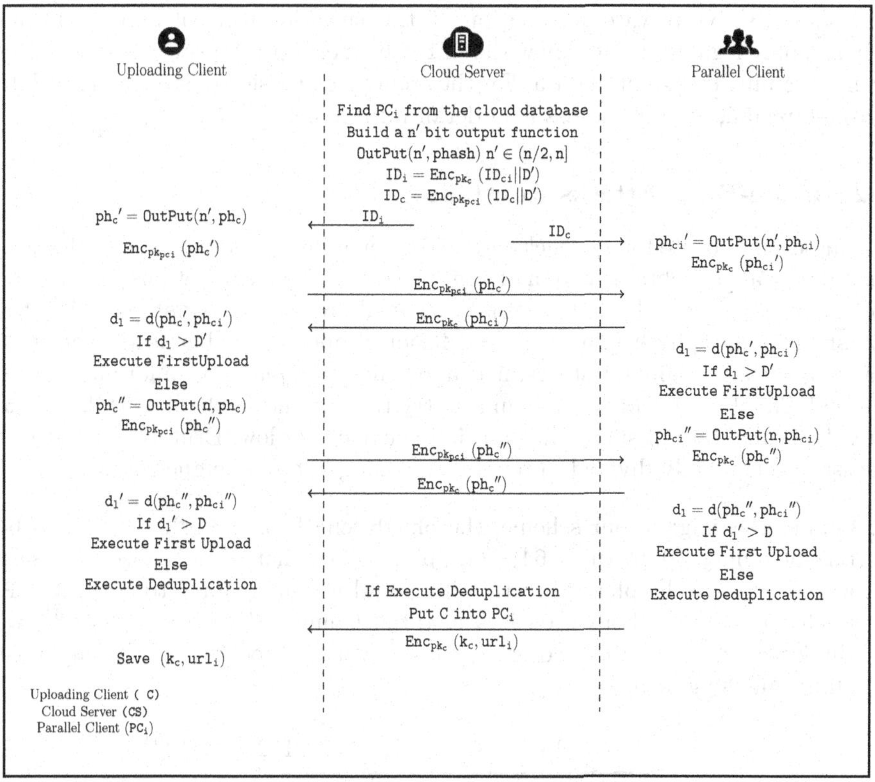

Fig. 6. Deduplication

5 Security Analysis

In this section, we extend the description to data confidentiality, collusion resistance, brute-force attack resistance, label consistency, etc., and make a detailed analysis of the security peoperties of our scheme.

5.1 Data Confidentiality

In our single server-based deduplication scheme, we particularly emphasize security. Data outsourced to the cloud server for C cannot be known by CS and PC_i, which do not own similar files. Obviously, in our scheme, CS stores the $\{ID_i$, $Enc_{pk_c}, phash_i\}$ from C, and CS does not have the key to decrypt img, so it does not have the conditions to decrypt img. Our encryption method is public key encryption, and the pk_c and sk_c designed in this method are mathematically related. We have disclosed pk_c to the public, but relying on pk_c alone cannot deduce sk_c (or we cannot crack sk_c in polynomial time). The only thing that can leak $sk_{p_{c_i}}$ in the whole scheme is PC_i, but once PC_i leaks the $sk_{p_{c_i}}$, it is equivalent to leaking its own private information, so this situation will not happen. In our scheme, only legal users can know the url, which effectively prevents adversaries from obtaining confidential data. For the security discussion of stealing user data through phash, we will discuss it in detail in Sect. 5.4.

5.2 Brute-Force Attacks Resistance

In our scheme, brute force attacks are mainly manifested in two aspects: First, a brute force attack obtains phash of img. Once the adversary obtains the original phash, it may pose a threat to C or PC_i. CS would record the $phash_i$ of C, but the $phash_i$ is a short hash (with strong collision properties). Therefore, even if CS has img with all plaintext states, it cannot guess the plaintext information of C through $phash_i$. The adversary can also try to construct a phash with length n, but the probability of successful collision is extremely low. Brute-Force Attacks Resistance is mainly divided into offline guessing and online guessing.

1. Offline guessing: In our scheme, the phash length of the original data is 64 bits of binary $\{0, 1\}^n (n = 64)$. The probability that a malicious adversary wants to guess the phase directly offline and use brute force to crack it is P. Each bit has two choices, 64 bits in total. Combined with $P = (1/2)^{64}$, we think that the probability of successful guessing is too low, so we can resist offline guessing attacks.

$$P = \underbrace{1/2 * 1/2 * 1/2 * ... * 1/2 * 1/2 * 1/2}_{(64)\ bit} = (1/2)^{64}$$

2. Online guessing: The adversary guesses during the mutual verification process between PC and C. The $phash_{i'}$ in the verification process is 26 bits longer than the $phash_i$ stored in the CS, so the probability of correct guessing is U. In particular, the number of communications between PC and C is limited, so the adversary cannot always guess. Combined with U, we believe that the probability of successful online guessing is extremely low, so it can resist online guessing attacks.

$$U = \underbrace{1/2 * 1/2 * 1/2 * ... * 1/2 * 1/2 * 1/2}_{(26)\ bit} = (1/2)^{26}$$

To sum up, our scheme can resist Brute-Force Attacks. In addition, brute force to obtain the decrypted key has been discussed in Sect. 5.1.

5.3 Resistance to Replay Attacks

Replay attacks refer to an attacker sending a packet that has been received by a destination host to deceive the system to obtain other users' private information. In our scheme, assume that the adversary obtains $phash_i$ in phase First Upload. The adversary can use $phash_i$ and CS to communicate and enter the Deduplication stage smoothly, but in the Deduplication stage, $\mathtt{PC_i}$ and the adversary will perform mutual verification and calculate the Hamming distance $\mathtt{d(hash_i,\ hash_{c_i})}$. In this process, the length of $\mathtt{phash_i}$ satisfies $(\mathtt{n}' > \mathtt{n}/2)$. There is no doubt that $(\mathtt{d} > \mathtt{D})$, so $\mathtt{PC_i}$ will not pass the verification of the opponent.

5.4 Collusion Resistance

As shown in Fig. 3, we assume that any two of the three entities can collude, even if collusion affects the entity's reputation. Collusion can be divided into the following cases.

1. CS and C conspire to defraud $\mathtt{PC_i}$ of private information. CS and C conspire means going directly to the Deduplication stage. At this stage, the $\mathtt{PC_i}$ will use its own $\mathtt{ph_{c_i}}$ and the $\mathtt{phash_c}$ of C to calculate the Hamming distance. C does not have the ability to provide $\mathtt{phash'_c}$ after changing the length, so the check will not pass. We also limit the number of online communications of each entity to more effectively prevent information disclosure.
2. CS and $\mathtt{PC_i}$ conspire to obtain the information of C. When CS deliberately lets C enter the Deduplication stage so that $\mathtt{PC_i}$ has the opportunity to steal $\mathtt{phash_C}$, then decrypt the img of C through the dictionary. In our scheme, C and CS are verified simultaneously for the first time. $\mathtt{PC_i}$ does not provide the correct $\mathtt{phash_{c_i}}$. C executes the Hamming distance calculation, and through $(\mathtt{d} > \mathtt{D})$, it will directly cancel the next communication with $\mathtt{PC_i}$, record the ID of $\mathtt{PC_i}$, and regard this $\mathtt{PC_i}$ as a malicious client.
3. C and $\mathtt{PC_i}$ conspire. CS will perform label consistency verification on C in the Upload Preparation phase. To pass the verification, C can only use the data of the accomplice $\mathtt{PC_i}$, which means that $\mathtt{PC_i}$ leaks its data to C. Therefore, we analyze that there will be no collusion between C and $\mathtt{PC_i}$.

5.5 Tag Consistency

In our scheme, there are two places where tags can be verified as follows.

1. The first verification method is shown in Fig. 2. During this process, C proves the consistency of img and phash to CS and also avoids the leakage of his own information. This method of verifying label consistency in advance makes up for the defect of post-verification (the loss is irreversible).
2. The second is in the mutual verification between C and PC. If the feedback results from C and PC to CS are inconsistent, it means that there is a problem with one party. At this time, CS only needs to check C and another $\mathtt{PC'_i}$, and according to the result of the second check, it can be determined who has a problem with C or $\mathtt{PC_i}$ (locating the adversary). CS checks for messages $\mathtt{M_1}$ from C, messages $\mathtt{M_2}$ from $\mathtt{PC_i}$ and messages $\mathtt{M_3}$ from $\mathtt{PC'_i}$, judgment criteria are as follows.

```
if (M1 == M3) PCi lied
    Else C lied
```

6 Experiment and Performance Analysis

6.1 Simulation Settings

We implement public-key encryption RSA [11,19] to encrypt image fingerprints and symmetric encryption AES to encrypt media data in our simulation. RSA security depends on the difficulty of factorization of large integers. Our system is implemented on Windows 10 with a 2.30 GH i5-8300H and 8 G RAM. The programming language we use is Python 3.90. Using the dataset Microsoft Common Objects in Context(MS COCO) dataset.

The effective deletion of approximate duplicate data directly determines the future development of our system. We selected 21844 non-repetitive images in the MS COCO dataset. These images vary in pixel size and spatial size. In addition, to calculate the deduplication rate ϱ_{p} as shown in Eq. (7). We add noise to these 21844 images, and the image is used as an approximate image atfer adding noise.

$$\varrho_{\mathrm{p}} = 1 - \varsigma/\tau \tag{7}$$

Here, ς is the simulated data that was blocked from being uploaded during the experiment, and τ is the total number of uploaded files. During the experiment, we extracted the phash length of 64 bits from img.

6.2 Simulation Results

Time Spent on Image Feature Extraction by Perceptual Hash (ahash, phash, dhash) [1,5]. Effect of Different Perceptual Hash Feature Value Extraction Methods on Similarity

We selected an image $\mathtt{img}_1$ with 219 KB and 640 × 480 pixels, then the image was modified by parameters: Brightening $\mathtt{img}_2$, Enlarge $\mathtt{img}_3$, Add contrast $\mathtt{img}_4$, Sharpen $\mathtt{img}_5$, Add colour $\mathtt{img}_6$, and Rotate 45 °C $\mathtt{img}_7$. We used ahash – phash – dhash to extract the feature values of these images and recorded the time. The result is shown in Fig. 7(a). We use (ahash, phash, dhash) methods to extract the eigenvalues of ($\mathtt{img}_1 - \mathtt{img}_7$), respectively. Compare the similarity between the feature values of the modified image and the original image (Threshold $\mathtt{D} \leq 5$). The result is shown in Fig. 7(b).

Figure 7, shows that although phash takes longer to extract feature values than ahash dhash, the similarity detection of phash is better than ahash dhash. The time spent by phash does not exceed 0.03 s, which is acceptable to the

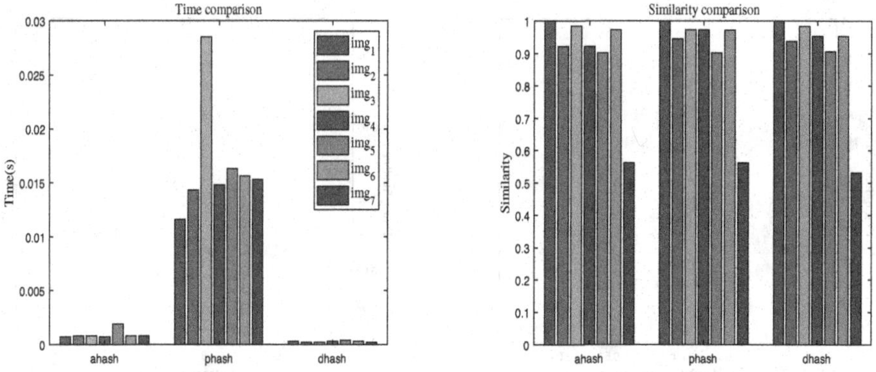

(a) Time cost (b) Similarity comparison

Fig. 7. Comparison of **ahash, phash and dhash**

client, so we use phash to extract feature values later in the deduplication rate comparison.

Effects of Various Distortions on Data Deduplication

There is no denying that any data may lose some messages during transmission. These distorted data often do not affect the use but cause data redundancy. Considering this situation, we tested the effects of salt and pepper noise, Gaussian noise, Poisson noise, and Motion blur on data deduplication in simulation experiments. We sampled 21844 images on the MS COCO dataset for testing and recorded the deduplication rate. Figures 8 and 9 records the impact of Salt and pepper noise, Gaussian noise, Poisson noise and Motion blur on the deduplication rate ϱ_{p}.

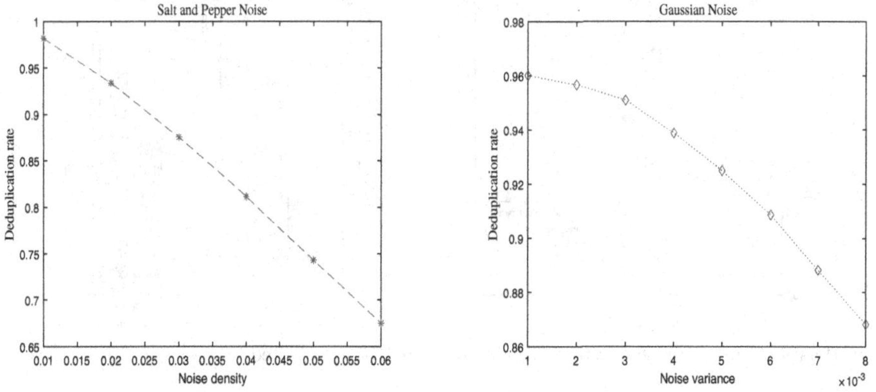

(a) Salt and pepper noise (b) Gaussian noise

Fig. 8. Salt and pepper noise and Gaussian noise compared with the original image

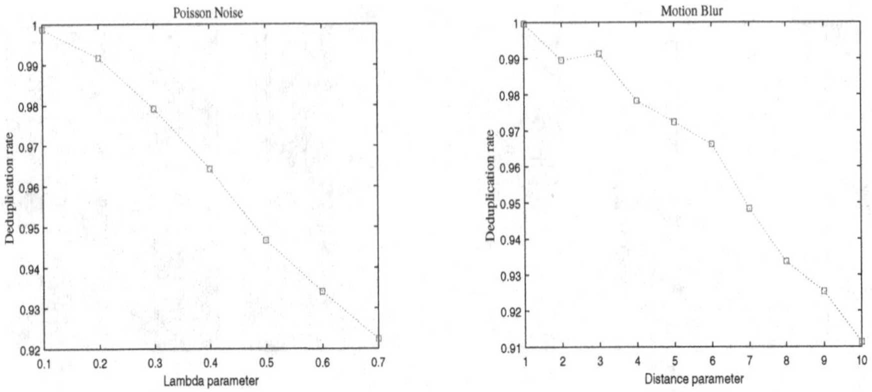

(c) Poisson noise (d) Motion blur

Fig. 9. Poisson noise and Motion blur compared with the original image

Relationship of Thresholds to Deduplication Rate

In this simulation experiment, we modify the pixels of the whole image with various noises to generate a series of redundant copies so as to explore an appropriate threshold value. We set various thresholds ($\mathtt{D} \in [1, 6]$) and designed the original **phash** as 64 bits. From Fig. 10 (a) that as the threshold increases, the deduplication rate continues to rise. When D = 5, the redundant copy with noise can achieve a deletion effect of more than 95%.

Compared with the Fuzzy Deduplication Scheme of Jiang *et al.*'s [6]

Both we and Jiang *et al.*'s [6] used the threshold value ($\mathtt{D} = 1, \mathtt{D} = 2, \mathtt{D} = 3$) as variables to compare the deduplication rate ϱ_p. We used 21844 images in the MS COCO dataset, and Jiang took 22317 images modified by 1.5% in the

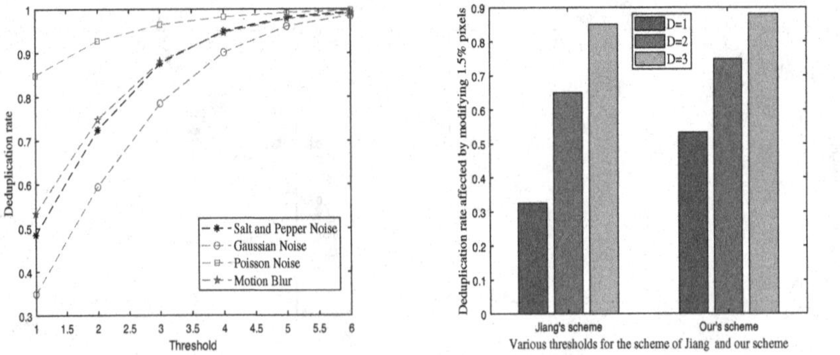

(a) Relationship of thresholds to deduplication rate (b) ϱ_p affected by modifying 1.5% pixels

Fig. 10. Influence of threshold selection and interference factor on deduplication ratio (ϱ_p)

CC_WEB_VIDEO dataset. We use motion blur (distance = 4) to modify the image by 1.5%. With a similar number of datasets and equal thresholds on both sides, our deduplication rate is significantly higher than that of Jiang *et al.'s* [6]. The experimental results are shown in Fig. 10(b).

7 Conclusion and Discussion

This paper designs a fuzzy deduplication system for similar multimedia data without any additional servers. The brute-force guessing attacks and collusion attacks are considered in this work. In addition, we propose a notion of pre-verification to realize the pre-judgment of label consistency and therefore it eliminates the irreparable loss of post-verification. In the upload preparation stage, the client constructs the phash of the original data into a short hash of n/2 length and then performs the first data deduplication judgment. Therefore it reduces the range of fuzzy data comparison and preliminarily determining whether the cloud platform retains similar copies. In the deduplication phase, the upload client and the parallel client check for each other. The verification passes the parallel client, and the uploading client shares the file decryption key.

We have made a systematic analysis of the security of the scheme and designed several experiments to show the deduplication effect of our scheme in real application scenarios. The result shows that the scheme can effectively guarantee the confidentiality of data and complete the deletion of redundant data. On the other hand, how to select a short hash with appropriate length is a challenge. If the length is too short, the deduplication rate will decrease, but if the length is too long, it is difficult to resist the guessing attack. We will leave the exploitation of these open problems in our future work.

Acknowledgement. This work was sponsored by Natural Science Foundation of Sichuan, China (2023NSFSC1400) and Chengdu Science and Technology Program (2021-YF08-00151-GX).

References

1. Arefkhani, M., Soryani, M.: Malware clustering using image processing hashes. In: 2015 9th Iranian Conference on Machine Vision and Image Processing (MVIP), pp. 214–218. IEEE (2015)
2. Bellare, M., Keelveedhi, S., Ristenpart, T.: Message-locked encryption and secure deduplication. In: Johansson, T., Nguyen, P.Q. (eds.) EUROCRYPT 2013. LNCS, vol. 7881, pp. 296–312. Springer, Heidelberg (2013). https://doi.org/10.1007/978-3-642-38348-9_18
3. Chen, L., Xiang, F., Sun, Z.: Image deduplication based on hashing and clustering in cloud storage. KSII Trans. Internet Inf. Syst. **15**(4) (2021)
4. Douceur, J.R., Adya, A., Bolosky, W.J., Simon, P., Theimer, M.: Reclaiming space from duplicate files in a serverless distributed file system. In: Proceedings 22nd International Conference on Distributed Computing Systems, pp. 617–624. IEEE (2002)

5. Fei, M., Zhaojie, J., Zhen, X., Li, J.: Real-time visual tracking based on improved perceptual hashing. Multim. Tools Appl. **76**, 4617–4634 (2017)
6. Jiang, T., et al.: Fuzzydedup: secure fuzzy deduplication for cloud storage. IEEE Trans. Depend. Secure Comput. (2022)
7. Li, X., Li, J., Huang, F.: A secure cloud storage system supporting privacy-preserving fuzzy deduplication. Soft. Comput. **20**, 1437–1448 (2016)
8. Li, Y., Wang, D., Wang, J.: Perceptual image hash function via associative memory-based self-correcting. Electron. Lett. **54**(4), 208–210 (2018)
9. Liu, J., Asokan, N., Pinkas, B.: Secure deduplication of encrypted data without additional independent servers. In: Proceedings of the 22nd ACM SIGSAC Conference on Computer and Communications Security, pp. 874–885 (2015)
10. Pönitz, T., Stöttinger, J.: Efficient and robust near-duplicate detection in large and growing image data-sets. In: Proceedings of the 18th ACM International Conference on Multimedia, pp. 1517–1518 (2010)
11. Sachdeva, A.: A study of encryption algorithms AES, DES and RSA for security. Global J. Comp. Sci. Technol. **13**(E15), 32–40 (2013)
12. Schnitzer, D., Flexer, A., Widmer, G.: A fast audio similarity retrieval method for millions of music tracks. Multim. Tools Appl. **58**, 23–40 (2012)
13. Takeshita, J., Karl, R., Jung, T.: Secure single-server nearly-identical image deduplication. In: 2020 29th International Conference on Computer Communications and Networks (ICCCN), pp. 1–6. IEEE (2020)
14. Wu, X., Hauptmann, A.G., Ngo, C.-W.: Practical elimination of near-duplicates from web video search. In: Proceedings of the 15th ACM international conference on Multimedia, pp. 218–227 (2007)
15. Yang, X., Rongxing, L., Choo, K.K.R., Yin, F., Tang, X.: Achieving efficient and privacy-preserving cross-domain big data deduplication in cloud. IEEE Trans. Big Data **8**(1), 73–84 (2017)
16. Yang, X., Lu, R., Shao, J., Tang, X., Ghorbani, A.A.: Achieving efficient secure deduplication with user-defined access control in cloud. IEEE Trans. Depend. Secure Comput. **19**(1), 591–606 (2020)
17. Zauner, C.: Implementation and benchmarking of perceptual image hash functions (2010)
18. Zhang, Y., Chunxiang, X., Li, H., Yang, K., Zhou, J., Lin, X.: Healthdep: an efficient and secure deduplication scheme for cloud-assisted ehealth systems. IEEE Trans. Indust. Inf. **14**(9), 4101–4112 (2018)
19. Zhou, X., Tang, X.: Research and implementation of RSA algorithm for encryption and decryption. In: Proceedings of 2011 6th International Forum on Strategic Technology, vol. 2, pp. 1118–1121. IEEE (2011)
20. Zikopoulos, P., Eaton, C.: Understanding Big Data: Analytics for Enterprise Class Hadoop and Streaming Data. McGraw-Hill Osborne Media (2011)

A Privacy-Preserving Takeaway Delivery Service Scheme

Lang Xu, Jiqiang Li, Hao Zhang(✉), and Hua Shen(✉)

Hubei University of Technology, Wuhan 430068, Hubei, China
1187573742@qq.com, nancy78733@126.com

Abstract. More and more applications based on location services continue to make our lives rich and convenient. However, location information may also quietly expose our privacy, such as work location, eating habits, etc. In this article, we have designed a solution to the problem of invisibly leaking our takeaway order information. In our scheme, users only need to submit a service request. The edge server is responsible for the service response and completes most calculations. The service platform generates orders based on the calculation results, sends them to the merchants and returns them, and selects suitable delivery men for the users. The proposed scheme uses non-interactive key exchange and secure Manhattan distance calculation to protect the location privacy of mobile users. Security analysis shows the proposed scheme is privacy-protected under our defined threat model. In addition, our program experiment proved to be feasible.

Keywords: location privacy · non-interactive key exchange · Manhattan distance · takeaway service

1 Introduction

The rapid advancement of mobile Internet technology in recent years has greatly facilitated peoples' daily lives [1,2]. Among these, location-based services (LBS) technology [3] has a wide range of uses, particularly in the logistics sector. The rise of Internet shopping has brought great convenience to the majority of users and has also greatly enriched people's daily lives. Although the logistics and distribution service is convenient and fast, the user's personal information is also invisibly exposed in the order, which also leaves a chance for malicious attackers to commit crimes. The existing service order usually contains the user's contact information, recipient address, and product information. Attackers can easily obtain the user's privacy or infer it from the information they collect from the order. For example, an attacker can infer the user's food preferences from a user's takeaway order and infer the user's home address, hobbies, etc. From the

M. Zhang et al. (Eds.): ProvSec 2023, LNCS 14217, pp. 385–403, 2023.
https://doi.org/10.1007/978-3-031-45513-1_21

receiving address, which will pose a huge potential threat to the personal and property safety of the majority of users [4]. Therefore, researching privacy issues in logistics and distribution services and developing the corresponding privacy-preserving application systems has considerable application value.

Takeaway delivery services are a kind of logistics and distribution service and are widely and frequently used by users. Takeout orders frequently contain a lot of personal information about users, including their name, phone number, address, and dietary preferences. Obviously, users' personal and property safety will be at risk if such sensitive information is illegally used. In this article, for these privacy issues in takeaway delivery services, we propose a privacy-preserving takeaway delivery service scheme. The main contributions are as follows:

- We propose a privacy-preserving takeaway delivery service (PP-TDS) scheme. PP-TDS splits user order information according to actual needs and sends different information to different entities. Specifically, PP-TDS determines whether to generate an order for a user and send it to a merchant according to whether the user is currently within the merchant's set physical area without knowing the user's location information. Moreover, in PP-TDS, when a merchant receives an order, it only knows the corresponding user's nickname, phone number, and the ordered goods information. Furthermore, PP-TDS selects a delivery man for an order in which the goods ordered are ready by securely calculating the minimum Manhattan distance [5] between the merchant and delivery men. The selected delivery man only knows the user's receiving address and phone number.
- We have improved a point and polygon position method for determining whether users are in merchants' set areas or not, which is more convenient and efficient to use.
- We evaluate the performance of the proposed algorithm theoretically and experimentally. Theoretical analysis and experimental results show that our scheme is feasible.

2 Related Work

Among the traditional methods for judging points and polygons, the current main methods are: calculating the position of the point; the angle method; the area method; and the ray method. Zhu et al. [6] judged whether a user was within the specified polygon by calculating the position of the point. During the judgment process, each side of the point and the polygon needs to participate in the calculation, and the calculation results are compared. Sun et al. [7] mapped a plane into a three-dimensional space and used the $sign(x)$ function and the ray method to determine whether a point is within the polygon range. This method needs to map the point and each edge of the polygon to the $sign(x)$ function and calculate the number of intersections between the horizontal ray and the polygon at a given point. Ma et al. [8] proposed an improved cross-product discrimination method that needs to calculate the result of the cross-product of a point and each side of the polygon and then make a judgment based on the result of the cross-product. In [9], the solution of the angle sum method is converted to the summation of closed vectors. However, the included angle method needs to traverse all the vertices of the polygon, and each vertex of the polygon needs to participate in the calculation. Liu et al. [11] used the area method to solve the judgment of the position relationship between points and polygons. Dong et al. [12] took a given point as a starting point to make a horizontal ray and judged whether the point was inside the polygon by the number of intersections with the polygon. However, this method can only solve the position judgment of a point and a simple polygon and cannot solve special situations such as the coincidence of the edges and vertices of the point and the polygon. [10,13] improved the ray method, which mainly solved the singular problems related to the point on the edge of the polygon and the point itself being a vertex of the polygon. Now more and more application scenarios use location-based services, such as social contact [6], daily work [14,15], Internet of Things [16] and so on. People are more and more concerned about the privacy threats in LBS applications, and many methods [17–21] have been proposed to solve the existing security problems.

3 Preliminaries

3.1 Homomorphic Encryption

In this section, we briefly describe the Paillier homomorphic encryption scheme [22]. The Paillier's homomorphic cryptographic system mainly consists of three algorithms:

Key Generation: Given a secure parameter κ, choose two κ-bit prime numbers p' and q'. Let $N = p'q'$, $\lambda = lcm(p' - 1, q' - 1)$, define a function $L(\mu) = (\mu - 1) / N$, randomly select a generator $g \in Z^*_{N^2}$, and $\mu = (L(g^\lambda \bmod N^2) - 1)$ can be calculated. Set the public key as $PK = (N, g)$ and the private as $SK = (\lambda, \mu)$.

Encryption: Pick a number $r \in Z^*_N$ and encrypt a message $m' \in Z^*_N$ with the public key PK: $C = g^{m'} \cdot r^N \bmod N^2$

Decryption: Consider the ciphertext $C = g^{m'} \cdot r^N \bmod N^2$, and recover the corresponding message with the private key SK: $m' = L(c^\lambda) / L(g^\lambda) \bmod N$.

Therefore, the Paillier cryptosystem has the following homomorphic properties: $E(m'_1) * E(m'_2) = E(m'_1 + m'_2)$ and $E(m'_1)^{m'_2} = E(m'_1 \cdot m'_2)$.

3.2 Non-interactive Key Exchange

The non-interactive key exchange protocol [23] can be roughly divided into three different parts: parameter setting, key generation and distribution, and shared key calculation.

Parameter Setting: The trusted center selects a prime number q and two q-order groups G_1 and G_2, where G_1 is the additive group and G_2 is the multiplicative group. Define an effectively calculated bilinear pair e and a cryptographic hash function H. The former satisfies e: $G_1 \times G_1 \rightarrow G_2$; the latter satisfies H: $\{0,1\}^* \rightarrow G_1$. All parameters are public.

Key Generation and Distribution: The trusted center randomly selects a master key $x \in Z_q^*$. When a user newly registers or logs in to the service platform, the Trusted Center will generate a public key $pk = H(ID) \in G_1$ and a private key $sk = xH(ID) \in G_1$ according to the user's identity id (for example, mobile phone number). And return the user's private key to the user through a secure channel.

Shared Key Calculation: Assume that users u_1 and u_2 want to send a private message, u_1 calculates u_2's public key $pk_{u_2} = H(ID_{u_2}) \in G_1$ and shared key $k_{u_1} = e(xH(ID_{u_1}), H(ID_{u_2}))$. At the same time, u_2 calculates u_1's public key $pk_{u_1} = H(ID_{u_1}) \in G_1$ and shared key $k_{u_2} = e(xH(ID_{u_2}), H(ID_{u_1}))$. According to the nature of the bilinear pair e, it is easy to see that $k_{u_1} = k_{u_2}$. Therefore, u_1 can use k_{u_1} to encrypt the message, and u_2 uses k_{u_2} to decrypt the message.

3.3 Identity-Based Elgamal Signature

The identity-based Elgamal signature scheme [26] includes four different parts: parameter setting, key extraction, signature generation, and signature verification.

Parameter Setting: The trusted center selects a prime number q and two q-order groups G_1 and G_2, where G_1 is the additive group and G_2 is the multiplicative group. Define an effectively calculated bilinear pair e: $G_1 \times G_1 \rightarrow G_2$. Define two secure hash functions: H_1: $\{0,1\}^* \rightarrow G_1$, H_2: $G_1 \rightarrow Z_q^*$. Randomly select $s \in Z_q^*$ as the global private key and compute $P_{pub} = sP$ as the global public key.

Key Extracting: According to the user's identity ID, the trusted center calculates the user's public key $Q_{ID} = H_1(ID)$ and his private key $d_{ID} = s \cdot Q_{ID}$.

Signature Generation: For a message m, randomly choose $k \in Z_q^*$, compute $r = H_2(kP)$ and $S = k^{-1}(mP - r \cdot d_{ID})$, the signature is $\sigma = (kP, S)$.

Signature Verification: According to the signature σ and the public key P_{pub}, verify whether the equation $e(S, kP)e(Q_{ID}, P_{pub})^r = e(P, P)^m$ holds or not.

3.4 Manhattan Distance

Manhattan distance [5] is generally used to calculate the sum of the absolute wheelbases of two points in the standard coordinate system. Given two vertices, $A(x_1, y_1)$ and $B(x_2, y_2)$, the Manhattan distance between A and B can be calculated as follows: $dis(A, B) = |x_1 - x_2| + |y_1 - y_2|$. According to the definition of the formula, the Manhattan distance must be a non-negative number. The smallest distance is when the two points overlap and the distance is 0.

3.5 Improved Point Location Judgment

In Fig. 1, assuming that the polygon L numbers the vertices in counterclockwise order as $P_0(x_0, y_0)$, $\cdots$, $P_1(x_1, y_1)$, $\cdots$, $P_{n-1}(x_{n-1}, y_{n-1})$, and find the normal vector $\boldsymbol{n}_1$ within the polygon range. Find the top vertex of polygon L as $P_0(x_0, y_0)$, the bottom vertex as $P_d(x_d, y_d)$, the leftmost vertex as $P_l(x_l, y_l)$, and the rightmost vertex as $P_r(x_r, y_r)$. If the position of the given point $P(x_p, y_p)$ is satisfied $x_l \leq x_p \leq x_r$ and $y_d \leq y_p \leq y_0$. Choose the two vertices $P_i(x_i, y_i)$, $P_{i+1}(x_{i+1}, y_{i+1})(0 \leq i \leq n-1)$ of the polygon closest to the given point P. Find the normal vector $\boldsymbol{n}_2$ of the triangular area surrounded by $\overrightarrow{P_iP_{i+1}}$and $\overrightarrow{P_{i+1}P}$. If k is a real number and $k \geq 0$, it means that the point $P(x_p, y_p)$ is within the range of the polygon. Otherwise, it means that the point is outside the range of the polygon.

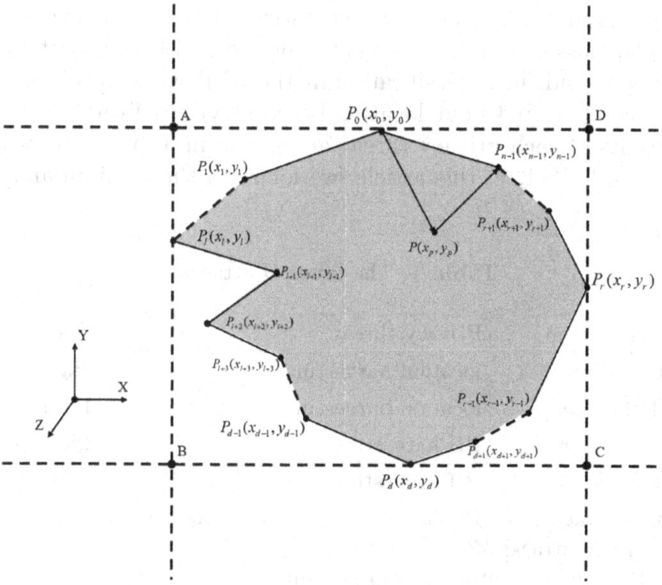

Fig. 1. Improved point and polygon judgment diagram

4 Scheme Design

4.1 The Description of System

As shown in Fig. 2, the service delivery system is mainly composed of ordinary users (User), merchants (TM), delivery men (DS), edge servers (ES), and service platforms (SP). Among them, ESs are only responsible for calculation and temporary storage. Edge servers can be the location servers of the map providers. Users place orders through the service platform. The merchants prepare the merchandise. The delivery men deliver the merchandise from merchants to users. The service platform guarantees the authenticity of the three and selects a delivery man closest to a given user and a given merchant without revealing both the users' and delivery men's locations. The locations of users and delivery men can be abstracted as points. In this article, we use the minimum Manhattan distance as the judgment standard for this selection problem. Merchants set their own order range (which can be abstracted as polygons) according to their own location. Only users within a merchant's order range can successfully launch order requests of the merchant. Once receiving such order requests, the service platform generates the corresponding orders and sends them to the merchant.

4.2 Privacy Threat Model

In this system, we suppose that service platforms, merchants, and delivery personnel are semi-honest and curious and want to know more while completing their own tasks. This assumption is reasonable. To protect users' information, if any entity has malicious behavior, the entire service process cannot proceed. Shen et al. [24] classified privacy threats in online taxi-hailing systems based on location services, and their classification method follows the OWASP risk rating method. We compare it to our location-based service delivery system, and the risk level results of each privacy threat are shown in Table 1. According to the enumeration in Table 1, in this article, we focus on the medium and high score risk issues.

Table 1. The types of attacks

Description	Privacy threat	Risk
SP→User/DS	location harvesting	High
TM→User	location harvesting	High
DS→User	PII harvesting	Medium
User→DS	PII harvesting	Low
OutAttack→SP	PII harvesting and ride data breach	High

$X \rightarrow Y$: X attacks Y

PII: Personally identifiable information

For the service platform, in the traditional store pickup mode, the user leaves after buying the item without revealing any information, while in the online order service, the user needs to fill in his own receiving address to facilitate the home delivery, but the service platform itself does not complete the delivery. According to the address filled in by the user, the platform can easily infer the user's home address, company address, and others. In addition, it is not uncommon for outsiders to attack commercial companies, especially platforms that provide location services. This type of platform holds the sensitive data of many users. Once the platform data is leaked, attackers can easily collect or infer other private information, such as the user's eating habits and home address. Thereby potentially increasing the user's safety hazards. It is important to note for merchants that many do not offer delivery services directly; instead, relevant delivery activities depend on delivery men, and merchants are not required to know the concrete whereabouts of their customers. As a result, it is important to avoid merchants having users' receiving addresses. The distribution men's responsibility is to safely deliver the goods from the merchants to the users. As for what the product is, as long as the content of the distribution meets the requirements of the platform, they should not know what it is.

The proposed scheme PP-TDS aims to achieve the following security properties:

Data Confidentiality: Data that is transferred and stored on the server is encrypted to guarantee data confidentiality.

Authentication: Ensure that the orders come from system users.

Privacy Preservation: Merchants can obtain the user order content information but not the user's delivery address information. On the premise that the service platform can meet the requirements of user services, store user data information as little as possible. The delivery men take as little users' personal information as possible.

4.3 The PP-TDS Protocol

In this section, we describe in detail the location privacy protection scheme in our delivery service. Figure 2 is a picture description of our solution. The design of the PP-TDS is as follows:

Step1: Merchants set the order scope according to their own capabilities and upload their catering list to the service platform. At the same time, the merchant uploads its location to the edge server.

Step2: After the delivery men go online, they upload their location to the edge server regularly so that the system can allocate orders for them.

Step3: The user views the merchant's information and logs in to the platform to complete the order operation. After the user selects the product information, the selected product is encrypted using the ID-based non-interactive key agreement protocol to calculate the key and upload the information.

Step4: The service platform verifies whether the user is within the range set by the merchant and, if so, generates an order for it and sends it to the merchant.

Step5: The merchant calculates key verification and decryption through a non-interactive key agreement protocol, determines whether to accept the order, and returns the result.

Step6: If the merchant receives the order successfully, the service platform calculates the minimum Manhattan distance to select the delivery personnel closest to the user and the merchant and selects the delivery men with the smallest result as the delivery personnel of the current order, and returns the contact information of each other to both parties, respectively.

Step7: The user and the delivery man establish secure communication by using an ID-based non-interactive key agreement protocol, and the user sends his recipient's address information to the delivery men.

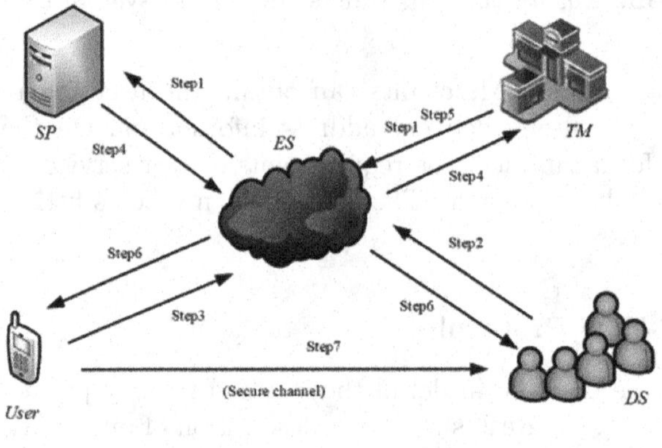

Fig. 2. Framework of PP-TDS

For this scheme, we use BGN encryption [25] and Paillier encryption, respectively, to implement. In the implementation of BGN, users, merchants, and delivery personnel need to calculate several of the following components:

$$E_i(a) =< a_{i1}|a_{i2}...|a_{i6} >=< E(x_i^2)|E(T-2x_i)|E(1)|E(T-2y_i)|E(y_i^2)|E(1) >$$
$$E_i(b) =< b_{i1}|b_{i2}...|b_{i6} >=< E(1)|E(x_i)|E(x_i^2)|E(y_i)|E(1)|E(y_i^2) >$$

Where, $E()$ is the encryption using the BGN scheme, which is then handed over to the edge server for calculation. Therefore, it can be easily verified.

$$E_i(a) \cdot E_j(b) = E(x_i^2 + x_j(T - 2x_i) + x_j^2 + y_i^2 + y_j(T - 2y_i) + y_j^2) = E(d_{ij}^2 modT)$$

Where T is chosen such that $\forall\ i, j \in \{1, \cdots, N\}$, $d_{ij}^2 < T$, $i \neq j$. Table 2 shows the description of some symbols based on Paillier in this section. The detailed process of the PP-TDS protocol is described below.

Table 2. Main Notations

Notation	Description
x	the master key (the non-interactive key exchange)
s, P_{pub}	the global private and public keys (the IDE-based Elgamal signature)
ID_u, ID_{tm}, ID_{ds}	represent the identities of users, merchants, deliver men
r, r_1, r_2	random number
$(pk_u,\ sk_u)$	public-private key pairs of Users (the non-interactive key exchange)
$(pk_{tm},\ sk_{tm})$	public-private key pairs of MTs (the non-interactive key exchange)
$(pk_{ds},\ sk_{ds})$	public-private key pairs of DSs (the non-interactive key exchange)
$(pk_{sp},\ sk_{sp})$	public-private key pair of the SP (the Paillier encryption)
$(pk_{es},\ sk_{es})$	public-private key pairs of ESs (the RSA encryption)
d_{ID_u}	Users' signature private key (the IDE-based Elgamal signature)
(x, y)	coordinate

System Initialization: Suppose there is a Trusted Center (TC), which is in charge of creating relevant system parameters, and generating public and private keys for every entity when it responds to registration requests from the entities.

The trusted center randomly selects a large prime number q of length κ_1 according to the security parameters κ_1, and generates two cyclic groups G_1 and G_2 of order q, and constructs a bilinear pair mapping e: $G_1 \times G_1 \rightarrow G_2$. Choose three secure hash functions: $H : \{0, 1\}^* \rightarrow G_1$, $H_1 : \{0, 1\}^* \rightarrow G_1$, H_2: $G_1 \rightarrow Z_q^*$. Randomly select x, $s \in Z_q^*$ as the master key and the global private key, respectively, and save them securely. Compute the corresponding global public key P_{pub}. The public parameters are $\{G_1, G_2, e, H, H_1, H_2\}$.

The trusted center calculates the public key $N = p' \cdot q'$ and private key (λ, μ) of the Paillier encryption algorithm according to the security parameter κ_2, where p', q' are large prime numbers selected according to the security parameters, and g is a generator of $Z_{N^2}^*$. Note that (N, g) and (λ, μ) are used as the service platform's public key pk_{sp} and private key sk_{sp}, respectively.

At this stage, the trusted center completes registration for all entities in the system. It uses a non-interactive key exchange protocol to generate private and public keys for users (pk_u, sk_u), merchants (pk_{tm}, sk_{tm}), and delivery men (pk_{ds}, sk_{ds}). Moreover, the trusted center also generates public-private key pairs (by using RSA encryption) for edge servers (pk_{es}, sk_{es}). The trusted center sends the private keys to the corresponding entities through secure channels.

Business Information Generation and Processing: Merchants publish product information on the service platform, such as the type of catering. And according to its own business needs, set up the service range of goods ordered on the service platform. The ordering range is abstracted as a polygon, and the polygon is represented by a vertex sequence of (x_0, y_0), (x_1, y_1), $\cdots$, (x_{n-1}, y_{n-1}). When a user logs in to the service platform to purchase merchant goods through the service platform, the service platform returns the sequence of polygon vertices to the user.

The location of the merchant is represented as $P_{tm}(x_{tm}, y_{tm})$. The merchant encrypts P_{tm} by using the public key of the corresponding edge server.

$$C'_{x_{tm}} = Enc_{pk_{es}}(x_{tm}), \quad C'_{y_{tm}} = Enc_{pk_{es}}(y_{tm}).$$

User Submits Information: According to the polygon area returned by the service platform, the user uses the method in Sect. 3.4 to locally judge whether his current location is within the delivery range of the merchant. Take the user's current real position $P_u(x_u, y_u)$ as the center, select a suitable radius to draw a circle, and randomly select position information $P(x_p, y_p)$ in the circular area. The method of judging the position relationship between repeated points and polygons ensures that the selected position information and the user's current real position are either both within the area or not both within the area. Use $P(x_p, y_p)$ to replace the user's real location P_u.

The user encrypts his location information (x_p, y_p) by using the public key pk_{sp} of the service platform.

$$C_{-x_p} = g^{(N-x_p)} \cdot {r_x}^N \bmod N^2, \quad C_{-y_p} = g^{(N-y_p)} \cdot {r_y}^N \bmod N^2.$$

The user encrypts the number of the vertex (of the given polygon) that is closest to $P(x_p, y_p)$, suppose the number is i, by using the public key pk_{es} of the corresponding edge server to obtain the ciphertext C_i. Therefore, the location-related ciphertext generated by the user is $C_p = C_{-x_p} \mid\mid C_{-y_p} \mid\mid C_i$.

The user calculates the shared key $k_{utm} = e(sk_u, pk_{tm})$ according to his private key $sk_u = xH(ID_u)$ and the merchant public key $pk_{tm} = H(ID_{tm})$. The user uses k_{utm} to encrypt his order content message m to obtain the ciphertext C_m, and calculate the corresponding signature σ by using its signature private key d_{ID_u}.

The user sends $C_p \parallel C_m \parallel \sigma$ to the corresponding edge server.

Server Processing: After receiving $C_p \parallel C_m \parallel \sigma$ from an user, the corresponding edge server decrypts C_i by using its private key sk_{es} to obtain the value of i. According to i, it finds the two vertexes $P_i(x_i, y_i)$ and $P_{i+1}(x_{i+1}, y_{i+1})$ and computes:

$$C_{x'} = (C_{-x_p} \cdot C_{x_{i+1}})^{r_1} = g^{(x_{i+1}-x_p)\cdot r_1} \cdot ((r_x \cdot r')^{r_1})^N \bmod N^2,$$
$$C_{y'} = (C_{-y_p} \cdot C_{y_{i+1}})^{r_2} = g^{(y_{i+1}-y_p)\cdot r_2} \cdot ((r_y \cdot r'')^{r_2})^N \bmod N^2,$$
$$C_{x''} = C_{(x_i - x_{i+1})/r_1}, \quad C_{y''} = C_{(y_i - y_{i+1})/r_2},$$
$$C = C_{x'} || C_{x''} || C_{y'} || C_{y''},$$

where r_1 and r_2 are random numbers generated by the edge server. The edge server sends $C \parallel C_m \parallel \sigma$ to the service platform.

The service platform uses its private key sk_{sp} to decrypt C and calculates the vector $\boldsymbol{n_2} = (x_i - x_{i+1})(y_{i+1} - y_p) + (x_{i+1} - x_p)(y_{i+1} - y_i)$. Check the user whether is in the given range or not by using the method mentioned in Sect. 3.5. If the user is actually within the given range, the service platform generates a service order for the user that includes some information such as the user's name, contact information, order number, pickup number, and ciphertext C_m. Then, the service platform sends the order to the corresponding merchant.

Merchants Accept User Orders: After receiving a new order, the merchant uses the global public key P_{pub} to verify the signature σ. If σ is valid, the merchant utilizes its own private key sk_{tm} and the user public key pk_u to calculate the shared key $k_{utm} = e(xH(ID_{tm}), H(ID_u))$ to decrypt C_m to obtain the user's order content m. According to m, the merchant decides whether to accept the order or not and reports the decision result to the service platform.

In particular, during the merchant's stocking up with goods, the order receipt on the packaging of the product is not allowed to print any information about the product,and the relevant number is used instead.

Order Distribution: After receiving feedback from the merchant confirming the order, the service platform should choose a delivery man to deliver the goods. According to the platform service strategy, the delivery men should upload their current locations (x_{ds}, y_{ds}) in the following ciphertext form to edge servers regularly (for example, every 5 min).

$$C_{x_{ds}^2} = g^{x_{ds}^2} \cdot (r_{x_{ds}^2})^N \bmod N^2, \quad C_{y_{ds}^2} = g^{y_{ds}^2} \cdot (r_{y_{ds}^2})^N \bmod N^2,$$
$$C_{-x_{ds}} = g^{(N-x_{ds})x_{tm}} \cdot (r_{-x_{ds}})^N \bmod N^2, \quad C_{-y_{ds}} = g^{(N-y_{ds})y_{tm}} \cdot (r_{-x_{ds}})^N \bmod N^2,$$
$$C_{ds} = C_{x_{ds}^2} || C_{y_{ds}^2} || C_{-x_{ds}} || C_{-y_{ds}}.$$

Edge servers should help the service platform choose the most suitable delivery man for the current order. Here we take the delivery man whose current location has the minimum Manhattan distance with the merchant as the most suitable one. Because that the edge server has the merchant's location $P_{tm}(x_{tm}, y_{tm})$ by decrypting the ciphertexts $C'_{x_{tm}}$ and $C'_{y_{tm}}$ using its private key sk_{es}. In order to facilitate the edge server's calculation of the Manhattan distance between the merchant and delivery men under the situation that it has the merchant's location and the ciphertexts of the delivery men's locations, we adopt the following transformation of the Manhattan distance:

$$|x_1 - x_2| = \sqrt{(x_1 - x_2)^2} = \sqrt{(x_1^2 - 2x_1x_2 + x_2^2}$$
$$|x_1 - x_2|^2 = x_1^2 - 2x_1x_2 + x_2^2$$
$$D = |x_{ds} - x_{tm}|^2 + |y_{ds} - y_{tm}|^2$$

The edge server first computes the ciphertexts of x_{tm}^2 and y_{tm}^2 by using the service platform's public key pk_{sp} to obtain $C_{x_{tm}^2}$ and $C_{y_{tm}^2}$. Then it calculates the Manhattan distance by computing

$$L(DS) = (C_{x_{ds}{}^2} \cdot (C_{N-x_{ds}})^{2x_{tm}} \cdot C_{x_{tm}^2}) \cdot (C_{N-y_{ds}})^{2y_{tm}} \cdot C_{y_{tm}^2}).$$

Assuming that there are t delivery men in the given range, the edge server should compute t Manhattan distances $L(DS_1)$, $L(DS_2)$, $\cdots$, $L(DS_t)$. After that, the edge server sends these t ciphertexts to the service platform.

After receiving $L(DS_1)$, $L(DS_2)$, $\cdots$, $L(DS_t)$, the service platform decrypts them by using its private key sk_{sp} to obtain t Manhattan distances. It chooses a delivery man who has the shortest Manhattan distance from the merchant to undertake the delivery task. Following this, the service platform communicates the delivery-related order information, including the order number, nickname, and pick-up number, to the delivery man. The service platform also informs the user of the current order outcome, i.e., who will accomplish the delivery service, at the same time.

Order Delivery: The user calculates the temporary session key k_{uds} according to his own private key sk_u and the delivery man's public key pk_{ds}. At the same time, the delivery man calculates k_{uds} according to his own private key sk_{ds} and the user's public key pk_u and establishes a secure channel with the user through the session key. Using the session key, the user communicates the delivery man's delivery address covertly. The delivery man then picks up goods from the merchant in accordance with the pick-up number of the order and delivers them in accordance with the delivery address.

5 Security Analysis

5.1 Privacy Analysis

For the service platform, when the user submits data to the server, the user's location coordinate information is not the real location. Secondly, the user's location information is not directly uploaded to the service platform. It is sent to the service platform after being processed by the edge server or location server. Even after the service platform is decrypted, the location coordinates of the user or delivery personnel cannot be restored. In the process of generating an order for the user, the user's selected product information is encrypted, and the platform cannot decrypt it. Finally, after the service platform selects the delivery personnel for the order, the user sends the receiving address directly to the delivery personnel, and the service platform is not visible.

In addition, the verification vector and order and delivery distance of the user's order are stored in the service platform. The goods in the order are encrypted. If the master key is not leaked, the ciphertext is safe. The verification vector is just an actual number and has no practical meaning. The delivery distance is just abstract distance data. Assuming that the attacker makes inferences based on the location of the business, he can only determine the user's range but cannot find an actual location. More importantly, the service platform may only have a phone number used to represent the user's identity and may also be encrypted data.

For merchants, in the current delivery system, even if the merchant does not provide delivery services, the merchant still knows the user's receiving address and those interested can collect the user's personal information through the merchant. In our solution, we split the merchant service from the distribution service and only send the product information ordered by the user to the merchant. Therefore, the merchant does not know the user's receiving address, which is the same as the traditional store purchase method.

For the delivery man in the current delivery system, the delivery man can know the general information of the product through the order posted on the product. In our solution, the delivery man picks up and delivers the goods from the merchant through the pick-up code generated by the system. No signs that reveal the content of the goods are allowed on the shipment, which is also the same as the traditional way of sending letters.

5.2 Manhattan Distance

Assuming two vertices $A(x_1, y_1)$ and $B(x_2, y_2)$ are given, the Manhattan distance between A and B can be calculated as $dis(A, B) = |x_1 - x_2| + |y_1 - y_2|$. The absolute value removal can be transformed into the following form, where t_1, t_2, t_3, t_4 are any real numbers:

$$\begin{cases} x_1 - x_2 + y_1 - y_2 = t_1 \\ x_1 - x_2 - y_1 + y_2 = t_2 \\ -x_1 + x_2 + y_1 - y_2 = t_3 \\ -x_1 + x_2 - y_1 + y_2 = t_4 \end{cases}$$

$$\begin{pmatrix} 1 & -1 & 1 & -1 \\ 0 & 0 & -2 & 2 \\ 0 & 0 & 0 & 0 \\ 0 & 0 & 0 & 0 \end{pmatrix} \begin{pmatrix} x_1 \\ x_2 \\ y_1 \\ y_2 \end{pmatrix} = \begin{pmatrix} t_1 \\ t_2 - t_1 \\ t_2 + t_3 \\ t_1 + t_4 \end{pmatrix}.$$

Then, we set

$$C = \begin{pmatrix} 1 & -1 & 1 & -1 \\ 0 & 0 & -2 & 2 \\ 0 & 0 & 0 & 0 \\ 0 & 0 & 0 & 0 \end{pmatrix}, D = \begin{pmatrix} x_1 \\ x_2 \\ y_1 \\ y_2 \end{pmatrix}.$$

According to the knowledge of linear algebra, the rank of matrix C is $r(C) = 2 < 4$, so the specific value of B cannot be obtained. Therefore, the edge server cannot obtain specific data without the key in this scheme. With the key, the service platform cannot calculate the coordinate information even if it obtains t_1, t_2, t_3, and t_4.

6 Performance Evaluation

In this section, according to our scheme, we use BGN and Paillier, respectively, and compare their performance based on experimental results. In the PP-TDS process, assume that only one user, n delivery personnel, and one merchant only communicates with the edge server. Below, we provide a detailed analysis of computational cost and communication overhead.

6.1 Computational Cost

As shown in Table 3, the use of BGN and Paillier solutions depends on the performance of the solutions themselves. For ease of understanding, we use EXP to mean a power operation, MUL means a multiplication operation on ciphertexts, AES, RSA means an AES, RSA encryption or decryption operation.

At merchants, in addition to uploading their product information, they also need to upload their location information. It takes at least $4EXP$ for the merchant to calculate the ciphertext of its location information. AES is required for decryption when the user order is received. When users place an order on the platform, they need to calculate and encrypt their order content, and at the same time, their position must be encrypted and uploaded. This process requires $6EXP + 1AES + 1RSA$. It is worth mentioning that RSA can be replaced with AES in actual use. The edge server needs to calculate the result for the service platform and send the calculated result to the service platform. When generating an order, it needs $2EXP + MUL + 2RSA$, and RSA can be replaced with AES. In addition, the edge server also needs to calculate the distance of the delivery staff for the user, which costs $(6n + 5)MUL$. When verifying user conditions, the service platform needs to decrypt the message from the edge server, which requires $2EXP + 2RSA$. In addition, the service platform also needs to spend $nEXP$ to select the nearest delivery man for the user.

Table 3. A Summary of Computational Costs

	Phases	BGN	Paillier
User	Initialization	–	–
	Generate orders	$6EXP + 1AES + 1RSA$	$6EXP + 1AES + 1RSA$
	Select delivery	$1AES$	$1AES$
TM	Initialization	$6EXP$	$4EXP$
	Generate orders	$1AES$	$1AES$
	Select delivery	–	–
DS	Initialization	$6EXP$	–
	Generate orders	–	$4EXP$
	Select delivery	$1AES$	$1AES$
ES	Initialization	–	–
	Generate orders	$2EXP + 2MUL + 2RSA$	$2EXP + 2MUL + 2RSA$
	Select delivery	$(6n + 5)MUL$	$(6n + 5)MUL$
SP	Initialization	–	–
	Generate orders	$2EXP + 2RSA$	$2EXP + 2RSA$
	Select delivery	$nEXP$	$nEXP$

6.2 Communication Overhead

Mobile devices often need to be more resource-constrained. Therefore, we hope every user communicates with the corresponding edge server as little as possible. In this analysis, we use M to indicate the length of the BGN ciphertext, N to indicate the length of each Paillier ciphertext, and D to indicate the bit length of the random value. As shown in Table 4, the gap between the implementation of BGN and the implementation of Paillier mainly depends on M and N. The most considerable communication overhead in the scheme is the ciphertext containing the user's location information. It will cost $6N + D$ for users to upload their location information orders. Merchants and delivery men need to upload $6N$. Finally, the edge server sends the intermediate result calculated, which requires $N + D$ and nN when selecting the delivery man.

Table 4. A Summary of Communication overhead

	Phases	BGN	Paillier
User	Initialization	–	–
	Generate orders	$6M + D$	$6M + D$
	Select delivery	D	D
TM	Initialization	$6M$	$4N$
	Generate orders	D	D
	Select delivery	–	–
DS	Initialization	$6M$	–
	Generate orders	–	–
	Select delivery	D	$4N + D$
ES	Initialization	–	–
	Generate orders	$M + D$	$2N + D$
	Select delivery	nM	nN
SP	Initialization	–	–
	Generate orders	D	D
	Select delivery	D	D

6.3 Experiment Evaluation

The experimental equipment is a Lenovo computer configured with Intel(R) Core(TM) $i7 - 6500U$@2.50 GHz and 8 GB RAM, an Android phone with a model of meizu16th. In the experiment, we acquiesced that the merchant would accept the order after receiving the information successfully. We use the JPBC library to perform bilinear pairing operations. The lengths of the keys of BGN are set to 160 and 256, respectively, the security parameter of Paillier is set to 512, and the key length of the RSA algorithm is 1024. Take the user's mobile phone number as their identity, and use it to generate keys and public keys. The average time users spend using Paillier encryption is 200ms, which is acceptable in our regular use.

It can be seen from Fig. 3(a) that as the number of sides of the convex polygon increases, the time required for the addition calculation also increases. The growth rate of our program is less than other programs, and the time required is also less than other programs. When the number of sides of a convex polygon reaches 2000, the calculation time is about 2ms, which is very efficient.

In our solution, the process in which the server selects delivery man for the user by calculating the Manhattan distance requires a large number of computing resources. In this process, the server must perform multiplication and many decryption operations on large numbers. To verify the scheme's performance, we give five-coordinate sets of different sizes, namely 20, 40, 60, 80, and 100. Each coordinate represents a delivery man. The detailed results are shown in Fig. 3(b) and Fig. 3(c).

Comparing Fig. 3(b) and Fig. 3(c), it is evident that as the number of delivery man increases, the time required for the service platform to select delivery man for users also increases. Overall, the increasing time-consuming has a linear relationship with the increasing number of delivery man. However, it can be seen from the figure that there is a big difference between the BGN-based implementation and the Paillier-based implementation of this solution. The time overhead required for BGN is much more significant than Paillier's. When the delivery staff reaches 100, Paillier calculates that the time required is only about 1000ms, while BGN is much larger than it.

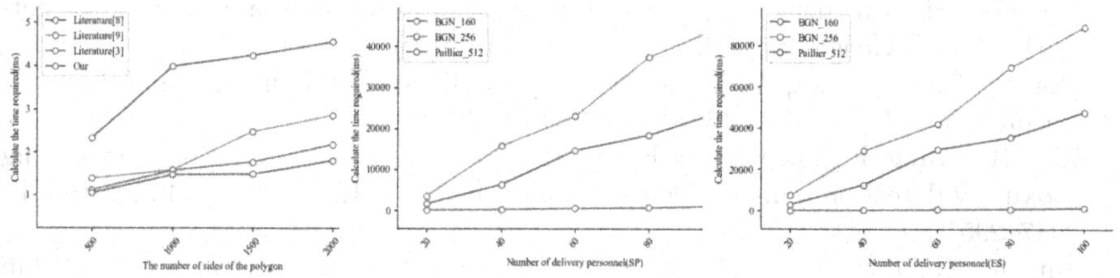

(a) Point and polygon (b) SP (c) ES

Fig. 3. Computational overhead

7 Conclusion

In this article, we propose a new solution to the privacy disclosure problem of takeaway order information in daily life. The core of our solution is to separate the user's receiving address from the product information and use a non-interactive key exchange protocol for key agreement. In the complete delivery service, the system decides whether to generate an order for the user and send it to the merchant based on whether the user is within the scope of the merchant's order. The merchant only knows the user's product information; the system selects the delivery personnel for the current order based on the Manhattan distance and delivers. The delivery man only knows the user's receiving address, the service platform only knows the Manhattan distance, and the Manhattan distance is only an abstract distance without actual physical meaning. However, this article's basic non-interactive key exchange protocol cannot resist man-in-the-middle attacks. In addition, the data submitted by ordinary users require relatively large calculation and communication costs. Our future research direction is how to reduce the user's calculation expenses and find more secure privacy protection methods.

Acknowledgements. This work is supported in part by the National Natural Science Foundation of China (61702168) and in part by the Green Industry Technology Leading Program of Hubei University of Technology (XJ2021000901).

References

1. Shen, H., Li, J., Wu, G., Zhang, M.: Data release for machine learning via correlated differential privacy. Inf. Process. Manag. **60**(3), 103349 (2023)
2. Shen, H., Zhang, M., Shen, J.: Efficient privacy-preserving cube-data aggregation aggregation scheme for smart grids. IEEE Trans. Inf. Forensics Secur. **12**(6), 1369–1381 (2017)
3. Shen, H., Zhang, M., Wang, H., Guo, F., Susilo, W.: A lightweight privacy-preserving fair meeting location determination scheme. IEEE Internet Things J. **7**(4), 3038–3093 (2020)
4. Alrayes, F., Abdelmoty, A.I., El-Geresy, W.B., Theodorakopoulos, G.: Modelling perceived risks to personal privacy from location disclosure on online social networks. Int. J. Geogr. Inf. Sci. **34**(1), 150–176 (2020)
5. Dou, J., Ge, X., Wang, Y.: Secure Manhattan distance computation and its application. Chin. J. Comput. **43**(2), 352–365 (2020)
6. Zhu, H., Wang, F., Lu, R., Liu, F., Fu, G., Li, H.: Efficient and privacy-preserving proximity detection schemes for social applications. IEEE Internet Things J. **5**(4), 2947–2957 (2018)
7. Sun, A., Zhao, G., Zhao, M., et al.: A sign(x) point in-out polygon test algorithm based on sign function and its application. Comput. Eng. Sci. **39**(4), 785–790 (2017)
8. Ma, C., Zhang, Y.: An improved method for judging relationship between point and polygon based on cross product. Sci. Surv. Mapp. **38**(1), 125–127 (2013)
9. Shen, C.: Q algorithm of point-in-polygon analysis. J. Yangzhou Univ. Nat. Sci. Ed. **4**, 24–26 (1999)
10. Zhai, Y., Xu, W., Zhang, Q.: Judgment of topological relation between point and polygon or polyhedron. Comput. Eng. Des. **4**, 972–976 (2015)
11. Liu, L.: An optimized algorithm to detemine topo-relation between point and polygon and clockwise or anti-clockwise in polygon. Geomat. Spatial Inf. Technol. **30**(1), 84–86 (2007)
12. Dong, X., Liu, R.: New algorithm for determining position relation between simple polygon and point. Comput. Eng. Appl. **45**(2), 185–186 (2009)
13. Zhang, L., He, F., Li, H.: A method for detecting points in polygons based on singular ray method, vol. 37. no. S2, pp. 133–135 (2020)
14. Shen, H., Zhang, M., Wang, H., Guo, F., Susilo, W.: A lightweight privacy-preserving fair meeting location determination scheme. IEEE Internet Things J. **7**(4), 3083–3093 (2020)
15. Sun, G., Song, L., Liao, D., Yu, H., Chang, V.: Towards privacy preservation for 'check-in' services in location-based social networks. Inf. Sci. **481**, 616–634 (2019)
16. Wang, N., Fu, J., Li, J., Bhargava, B.K.: Source-location privacy protection based on anonymity cloud in wireless sensor networks. IEEE Trans. Inf. Forensics Secur. **15**, 100–114 (2020)
17. Huang, K.L., Kanhere, S.S., Hu, W.: Preserving privacy in participatory sensing systems. Comput. Commun. **33**(11), 1266–1280 (2010)
18. Tian, S., Cai, Y., Zheng, Q.: A hybrid approach for privacy-preserving processing of knn queries in mobile database systems. In: 22nd ACM International Conference on Information and Knowledge Management, CIKM 2013, San Francisco, CA, USA, 27 October–1 November 2013, pp. 1161–1164 (2013)
19. Zhu, X., Chi, H., Niu, B., Zhang, W., Li, Z., Li, H.: MobiCache: when k-anonymity meets cache. In: 2013 IEEE Global Communications Conference, GLOBECOM 2013, Atlanta, GA, USA, 9–13 December 2013, pp. 820–825 (2013)

20. Andrés, M.E., Bordenabe, N.E., Chatzikokolakis, K., Palamidessi, C.: Geo-indistinguishability: differential privacy for location-based systems. In: 2013 ACM SIGSAC Conference on Computer and Communications Security, CCS 2013, Berlin, Germany, 4–8 November 2013, pp. 901–914 (2013)
21. Yi, X., Paulet, R., Bertino, E., Varadharajan, V.: Practical approximate k nearest neighbor queries with location and query privacy. IEEE Trans. Knowl. Data Eng. **28**(6), 1546–1559 (2016)
22. Shen, H., Wu, G., Xia, Z., Susilo, W., Zhang, M.: A privacy-preserving and Verifiable statistical analysis scheme for an E-Commerce platform. IEEE Trans. Inf. Forensics Secur. **18**, 2637–2652 (2023)
23. Sakai, R., Kasahara, M.: ID based cryptosystems with pairing on elliptic curve. IACR Cryptol. ePrint Arch., p. 54 (2003)
24. Shen, X., Wang, L., Pei, Q., Liu, Y., Li, M.: Location privacy-preserving in online taxi-hailing services. Peer-to-Peer Netw. Appl. **14**(1), 69–81 (2021)
25. Bilogrevic, I., Jadliwala, M., Joneja, V., Kalkan, K., Hubaux, J.-P., Aad, I.: Privacy-preserving optimal meeting location determination on mobile devices. IEEE Trans. Inf. Forensics Secur. **9**(7), 1141–1156 (2014)
26. Kalkan, S., Kaya, K., Selcuk, A.A.: Generalized ID-based ElGamal signatures. In: 22nd International Symposium on Computer and Information Sciences, Ankara, Turkey, 7–9 November 2007, pp. 1–6 (2007)

Blockchain Security

CDRF: A Detection Method of Smart Contract Vulnerability Based on Random Forest

Meng Huang, Jia Yang(✉), and Cong Liu

Hubei University of Technology, Wuhan 430068, China
{102111088,jia_yang,202211227}@hbut.edu.cn

Abstract. With the widespread applications of smart contract, a large number of smart contracts with virtual coins have been deployed on Ethereum. However, smart contracts may have vulnerabilities that cause huge losses. Therefore, it is a critical issue to effectively and time-savingly detect potential vulnerabilities in contracts. Oyente and Mythril are both contract analysis tools based on symbolic execution, which rely on control flow graph to detect vulnerabilities and are time-consuming. In this work, we propose CDRF to detect vulnerabilities in smart contracts with machine learning. First, we summarize four kinds of opcode fragments containing key vulnerability instructions. The opcode fragments are processed by word2vec and PCA to obtain one-dimensional binary features. Second, we use five machine learning algorithms to build the model. This method uses the 53651 real-world smart contracts on Ethereum for evaluation. When we use CDRF as the training model, the highest predictive value of F1-socre is 98.03%, and the rest are above 93%; the highest predictive value of AUC is 99.56%, and the rest are above 94%. Meanwhile, the average detection time for each smart contract is 3 s. The experimental results show that the method is effective and time-saving.

Keywords: Vulnerability Detection · Machine Learning · Random Forest · Smart Contract · Blockchain

1 Introduction

In 1994, computer scientist and cryptographer Nick Szabo first proposed the concept of smart contract [1], which is defined as "smart contract is a set of commitments defined in digital form, including agreements that parties can implement these commitments". However, due to the lack of relevant contract writing language technology in the early days, smart contracts were not used at that time. Until 2008, the first cryptocurrency Bitcoin appeared and modern blockchain technology [2] was introduced, which solved the above problem. Blockchain technology provided a secure and reliable environment for smart contracts. However, various blockchain forks had prevented smart contracts from being integrated into the Bitcoin blocknetwork.

In 2013, Vitalik Buterin released the first white paper of Ethereum, developed Ethereum [3] and formally introduced smart contracts into the blockchain.

M. Zhang et al. (Eds.): ProvSec 2023, LNCS 14217, pp. 407–428, 2023.
https://doi.org/10.1007/978-3-031-45513-1_22

Ethereum offers Solidity language for smart contract, which is an open source public blockchain platform supporting smart contracts. It provides a decentralized Ethereum virtual machine (EVM) that enables developers to deploy applications (DApps) based on smart contract on the blockchain. Smart contracts have the characteristics of certainty, real-time, verifiability and decentralization, which can be widely used in many scenarios, such as digital identity [4], digital record [5], securities [6–9], financial trade [10], Internet of Things [11], supply chain [12], insurance [13] and distributed computing [14].

With the widespread expansion of blockchain and the convenience of smart contract, smart contracts are vulnerable to intensive attacks since they are entrusted by users to process and transfer a large number of valuable digital assets. For example, US hackers took advantage of the DAO [16] contract's reentrant vulnerability to steal about 60 million worth of ether coins in June 2016; nearly 300 million worth of Ether was frozen due to the Delegatecall breach in Parity's multi-signature wallet [17] in July 2017. On the blockchain, smart contracts have the property of being immutable once deployed, so it is necessary to detect and analyze potential vulnerabilities [15] in smart contracts before contract deployment. Traditional smart contract vulnerability detection methods include feature code matching, formal verification, symbolic execution, static analysis, stain analysis and fuzzy testing. The symbolic execution representative methods are Oyente [39], Mythril [42] and Securify [40]. These tools need to find all executable paths in the contract or analyze the control flow graph of the contract for vulnerability detection. Therefore, they are complicated and time-consuming.

The smart contract vulnerability events not only cause significant financial losses, but also destroy the trust foundation of smart contract and blockchain for everyone. Therefore, the vulnerability detection of smart contract has become a key problem to be solved urgently. However, due to the lack of understanding of the semantic characteristics of the vulnerability code, the traditional vulnerability detection tools are not effective. In order to solve the above problems, this paper proposes CDRF to detect vulnerabilities in smart contracts with machine learning, which mainly extracts semantic features according to the opcodes of vulnerability codes. First, we summarize four kinds of opcode [41] fragments containing key vulnerability instructions. The opcode fragments are processed by word2vec and PCA to obtain one-dimensional binary features. Second, we use five machine learning algorithms, namely Random Forest (RF) [24], Light Gradient Boosting Machine (LightGBM) [25] extreme gradient boosting (XGBoost) [26], adaptive boosting (AdaBoost) [27] and support vector machine (SVM) [28] to build the model.

The contributions of this paper are as follows:

- We propose CDRF to detect vulnerabilities in smart contracts with machine learning, which can automatically detect vulnerabilities for smart contracts. Unlike the work that mainly relies on symbol execution, this method learns the pattern of the vulnerability code for detection.
- To more effectively characterize smart contracts, we collect 53651 smart contracts from the official website of Ethereum [29]. We analyze the principles and

key vulnerability statements of four smart contract vulnerabilities, and summarize four kinds of opcode fragments containing key vulnerability instructions, which are used to obtain code features through word2vec and PCA.
- Four vulnerabilities of smart contracts can be detected quickly and effectively with this method. When running on real-world contracts, the highest prediction value of F1-socre predicted is 98.03%, and the rest are above 93%; the highest predictive value of AUC is 99.56%, and the rest are above 94%. Meanwhile, the average detection time of each smart contract is 3 s.

The rest of this article is arranged as follows. Section 2 presents a summary of the related work. Section 3 mainly focuses on Ethereum, smart contract bytecode and opcode. Section 4 mainly describes our new vulnerability detection method. The experimental results are presented in Sect. 5. Section 6 consists of discussion and analysis. Section 7 is the conclusion of this paper.

2 Related Work

At present, the traditional methods of smart contract vulnerability detection include feature code matching, formal assay method, symbol execution method, static analysis method, blot analysis method and fuzzy test method [30]. However, three mainstream vulnerability detection methods have emerged in recent years, which are feature code matching, formal verification, automated audit methods based on symbolic execution and abstract constraints.

The feature code matching is used to extract features from source code of smart contracts containing vulnerabilities, such as DC-Hunter [31], SolidityCheck [32] and Hunting method [33]. Each type of vulnerability code is abstracted into a set of vulnerability semantic matching templates, and vulnerability identification only requires that there are fragments matching the vulnerability code in the contract. However, most of the smart contracts on Ethereum only provide bytecodes. Before vulnerability detection, the bytecode needs to be reverse analyzed and converted to source code. The huge amount of preparatory work has limited the development of this method.

The audit tools based on formal verification support few types of smart contract vulnerabilities, and most of these methods use strict mathematical theorem proving and complex mechanisms for vulnerability verification. VaaS [18], ZEUS [38], and F*framework [35] barely support contract vulnerability detection at the EVM execution layer. KEVM [36] and lsabelle/HOL [37] propose formal validation methods, but they are not suitable for actual smart contract vulnerability detection. Therefore, it is not easy to analyze and detect contract vulnerabilities by using formal validation methods.

Most detection tools based on symbolic execution can support more types of contract vulnerability detection. Symbolic execution mainly collects path constraints and finds security issues by symblolizing variables in the source code, then interpreting the instructions in the execution program line by line and updating the execution status. The current representative tools are Oyente [39],

Mythril [42] and Securify [40], but the collection of all executable paths is not comprehensive and takes a long time.

Through the analysis of the existing research methods, the detection effect is not good. Due to the lack of understanding of semantic features of vulnerability codes, some methods do not consider general methods in vulnerability detection. In this work, we propose a detection method of smart contract vulnerability based on Random Forest called CDRF, which can learn vulnerability features from training samples to detect vulnerabilities.

3 Preliminaries

In this chapter, we briefly introduce Ethereum, smart contract bytecode and opcode. In addition, we introduce reentrancy vulnerability, tx.origin vulnerability, timestamp dependency vulnerability, integer overflow vulnerability. Smart contracts are only discussed in Ethereum, the language of the contract source code is only Solidity.

3.1 Ethereum

As a publicly available blockchain platform, Ethereum [34] is a decentralized public ledger for verifying and recording transactions. It provides a decentralized Ethereum Virtual Machine (EVM), enabling users to deploy applications (DApps) based on smart contract on the blockchain. But at the meantime, it needs to address the problem of ensuring the consistency and correctness of ledger data in the unreliable asynchronous network. Ethereum presently uses a consensus protocol called proof-of-work (PoW) [19] to solve this problem. This consensus mechanism allows Ethereum network nodes to agree on the status of all information recorded on the blockchain, and prevents some attacks with economic impact.

3.2 Smart Contract Bytecode and Opcode

On Ethereum, contracts are mainly deployed through the following three steps: (1) The smart contract is written by the developer in Solidity. (2) The compiler compiles the source code into bytecode. A bytecode is an array of bytes encoded with a string of hexadecimal digits. (3) The EVM reads the bytecode in hexadecimal digits. The bytecode is analyzed in units of one byte, and each byte stands for one EVM instruction or one opcode. Currently, EVM provides 140 opcode instructions. 135 opcode instructions are defined in the Ethereum Yellow Paper [34], including the invalid operation, compare and bit-by-bit logic operations, stop and arithmetic operations, SHA3 (KECCAK256) operation, environment information operation, stack operation, memory operation, storage and flow operations, stack operation, copy operation, replacement operation, log operation, system operation and other operations.

3.3 Vulnerability Introduction.

Reentrancy Vulnerability In 2016, hackers managed to steal around 60 million dollars by reentrant vulnerabilities. The vulnerability is caused by the unique fallback mechanism [22] of smart contracts. When a smart contract performs cross-contract transfer operation, the callback function (fallbcak) in the receiver contract will be triggered. If a malicious attacker adds malicious code to the callback function, the transfer function of the victim contract is recursively called to steal the ether until the gas run out.

Tx.origin Vulnerability. Tx.origin is a global variable in the smart contract. It iterates through the call stack and returns the address of the contract that originally made the call. If smart contract uses tx.origin for user authentication or authorization, an attacker can make use of the vulnerability to attack the smart contract. Since tx.origin makes exceptions undetectable, the attacker can steal Ether.

Timestamp Dependency Vulnerability. Smart contracts usually use block timestamps confirmed by miners to achieve time constraints. The contract can retrieve the block timestamp, and all transactions in the block share the same timestamp, which ensures the consistency of the contract execution state. However, the miner can adjust the value of the timestamp within the error range at about 900 s, attackers can use this vulnerability to generate timestamps to attacks.

Integer Overflow Vulnerability. In smart contracts, integer overflow includes addition overflow, subtraction overflow and multiplication overflow. For integers, the Ethereum Virtual Machine (EVM) assigns fixed size data types, and solidity supports uint8 to uint256. For variables of type uint8, uint8 enables the storage of numbers in the range [0,255], if 256 is stored to uint8, it will cause an integer overflow error. For example, the integer overflow vulnerability of the USChain BEC contract [23] caused serious losses in 2018.

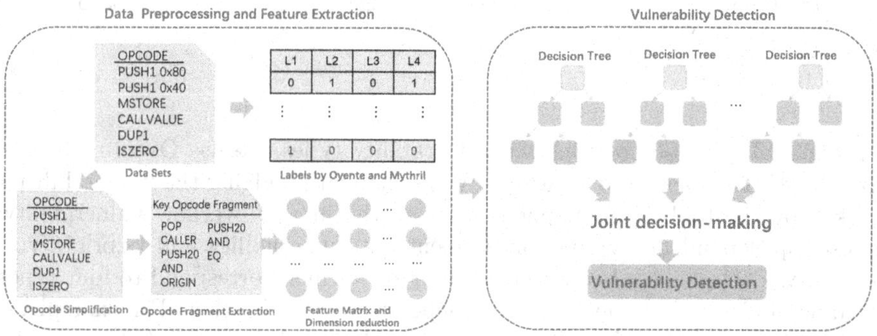

Fig. 1. *The Process of Training Models.*

4 Detection Models

As shown in Fig. 1, we build the CDRF model in three steps, which includes data preprocessing, feature extraction and vulnerability detection. Data preprocessing main includes data sets, labels and opcode simplification. Feature extraction main includes opcode fragment extraction, feature matrix and dimension reduction. Data Preprocessing: it mainly collects smart contracts, marks them as four types of vulnerabilities and decompiles them into opcodes, which are simplified by removing operands. Opcode fragment extraction: we summarize four kinds of opcode fragments containing key vulnerability instructions. Feature matrix and dimension reduction: the opcode fragment is processed by word2vec [20] and PCA [21] to obtain one-dimensional binary features. Vulnerability detection: we use five machine learning algorithms, namely Random Forest (RF) [24], Light Gradient Boosting Machine(LightGBM) [25] extreme gradient boosting (XGBoost) [26], adaptive boosting (AdaBoost) [27] and support vector machine (SVM) [28] to detect and test whether there are vulnerabilities in smart contracts.

4.1 Data Preprocessing

Data Sets. We collect 53651 smart contracts from the Ethereum official website, which have been verified before June 2022. It is obvious that data is authoritative and reliable. As shown in Table 1, the data sets which contain contracts with four kinds of vulnerabilities are described as follows.

Table 1. The Number of Data Set.

Classifier	This Type(Vulnerable)	The Rest(InVulnerabel)	Total
Integer overflow	10209	43442	53651
Timestamp	3720	49931	53651
Reentrancy	1710	51941	53651
Tx.origin	987	52664	53651

Labels. For the issue of contract vulnerability types, we use Oyente [39] and Mythril [42] to label smart contracts, while manually judging the vulnerabilities marked by the tools. This paper focuses on the integer overflow vulnerability, timestamp dependency vulnerability, reentrant vulnerability and tx.origin vulnerability. Each detected contract has four tags which correspond to four types of vulnerabilities, and the tags are independent of each other. For example, a contract is detected with a label vector of [1 0 1 0], indicating that it has the first and third vulnerabilities, namely the integer overflow vulnerability and the reentrant vulnerability. We assume that the types of vulnerabilities detected by the tool are all correct.

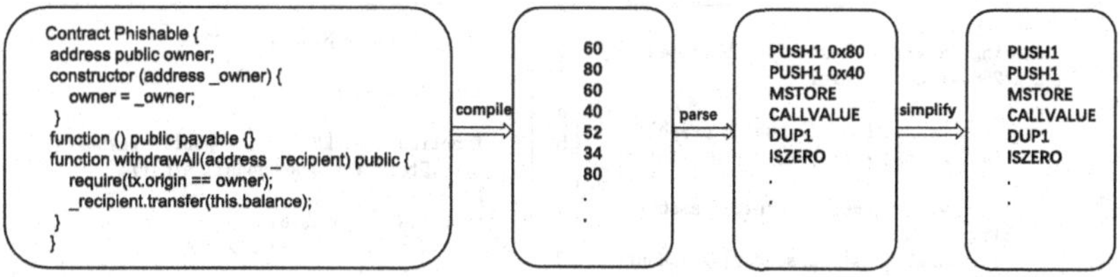

Fig. 2. The relationship between source code, bytecode, opcode, and simplified opcode.

Opcode Simplification. The data sets of smart contracts are compiled into bytecodes, the vandal tool is used to decompile the bytecodes into opcodes [43]. We take the approach of removing operands to simplify the opcode fragment, since one opcode is followed by one operand where operand does not affect the semantic relationships between source code contexts, as shown in Fig. 2.

4.2 Feature Extraction

Feature extraction is divided into three steps, which mainly includes opcode fragment extraction, feature vector and dimension reduction.

- Opcode fragment extraction: We analyze the principles and key vulnerability statements of the four vulnerabilities, and extract the opcode fragments containing key vulnerability instructions. The specific method is shown in the next section (Opcode Fragment Extraction).
- Feature matrix: When the opcode fragment is input into word2vec, word2vec will generate a feature vector matrix, where each row represents the feature vector of one opcode and includes 10 features. The 10 features of the opcode are summed to represent the feature vector of the opcode, and the word vector of each opcode is combined into an array to represent the opcode fragment feature.
- Dimension reduction: The length of the word vector is different due to the different length of the opcode fragment. Therefore, we take the length of the longest word vector as the standard. If the length of the word vector is less than this standard, the word vector is filled with 0. Next, PCA is used to reduce the dimensionality of the filled word vector.

4.3 Opcode Fragment Extraction

We analyze the principles and key vulnerability statements of the four vulnerabilities, and summarize four kinds of opcode fragments containing key vulnerability instructions.

Reentrant Vulnerability. As shown in Fig. 3, we can see that the MyStore contract has the normal function of deposit and withdrawal, but there is a reentrant vulnerability. Attackers can use the carefully constructed AttackMyStore

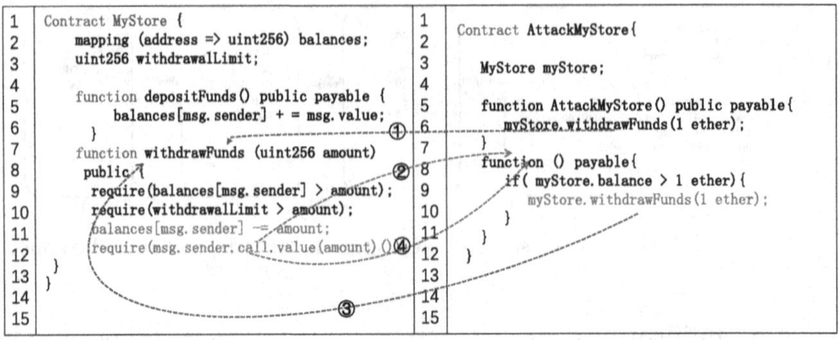

Fig. 3. MyStore Contract and Attack Contract.

contract to attack. The program first performs the transfer operation in lines 11 (red mark) of MyStore contract, resulting in the failure to execute the account balance update operation in lines 12 (red mark) of the MyStore contract. Therefore, the attacker exploits the vulnerability of unfinished function logic to attack the contract. The attack process of Fig. 3 is as follows:

- Step 1: The attacker calls the AttackMyStore function in line 5 of AttackMyStore contract, the program will call the withdrawFunds function of MyStore;
- Step 2: When the program runs to line 11 of MyStore (marked in red), it automatically runs the AttackMyStore fallback function since the contract performs cross contract transfer ether;
- Step 3: Then, the program calls the withdrawFunds function of MyStore contract;
- Step 4: Finally, it performs the AttackMyStore fallback function again.

Key vulnerability statements: *require(msg.sender.call.value (amount)()); balances[msg.sender]-= amount.*

Vulnerability opcode fragment: We look for reentrant vulnerability opcode fragments through contracts without reentrant vulnerabilities. If the account balance is updated before the transfer operation, the reentrant vulnerability can be prevented by exchanging the order of the above key vulnerability statements. Figure 4 shows the EVM instructions representing two key vulnerability statements after the exchange. The four key instructions are KECCAK256 (SHA3), SLOAD, SSTORE and CALL (marked in red). KECCAK256 (SHA3), SLOAD and SSTORE are three key instructions, which are mainly used to update the account balance, and the CALL instruction is mainly used to transfer money.

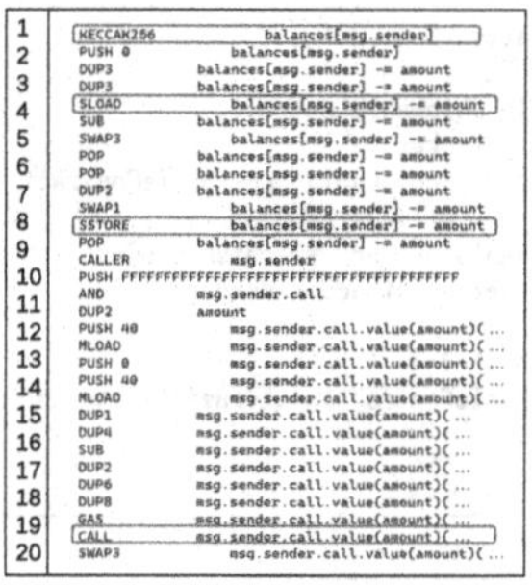

Fig. 4. The EVM of None Reentrant Contract.

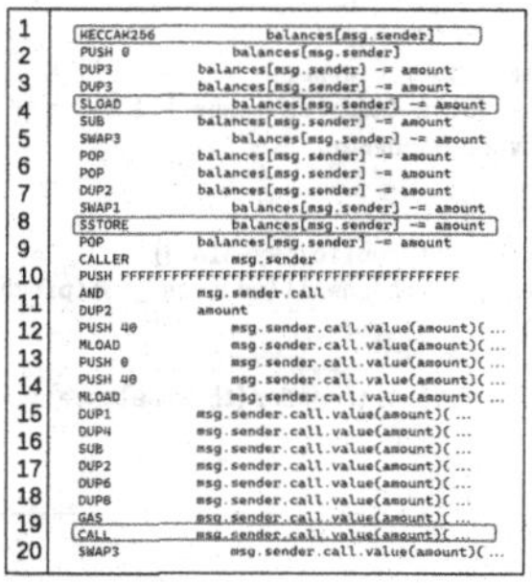

Fig. 5. The EVM of Phishable Contract.

In summary, If there are no KECCAK256 (SHA3), SLOAD, and SSTORE instructions in the opcode fragment where the CALL instruction resides, it indicates that the account balance has not been updated before the CALL transfer money operation, and the contract has the reentrant vulnerability. The opcode fragment of reentrant vulnerability is an opcode fragment containing the CALL instruction, but not the KECCAK256 (SHA3), SLOAD, and SSTORE instructions.

Tx.origin Vulnerability. As shown in Fig. 6 , we can see that the Phishable contract has a tx.origin vulnerability. The attacker can use the AttackContract to attack. Since tx.origin is a global variable in Solidity, it can iterate through the call stack and return the address of the contract that originally sent the call. The initial caller of the transaction is the contract address of Phishable contract, so tx.origin equals the owner. Therefore, the require statement (red mark) of the Phishable contract does not work, and all funds are transferred to the attacker's address. The attack process of Fig. 6 is as follows:

- Step 1: The victim calls the Phishable contract to send a transaction to the AttackContract, it will trigger the fallback function in line 9;
- Step 2: The program runs to line 9 code (red mark) of Phishable contract and the authentication is passed, then the money is transferred to the address of AttackContract, which causes all funds to be withdrawn to the attacker's address.

Key vulnerability statements: *require(tx.origin== owner).*

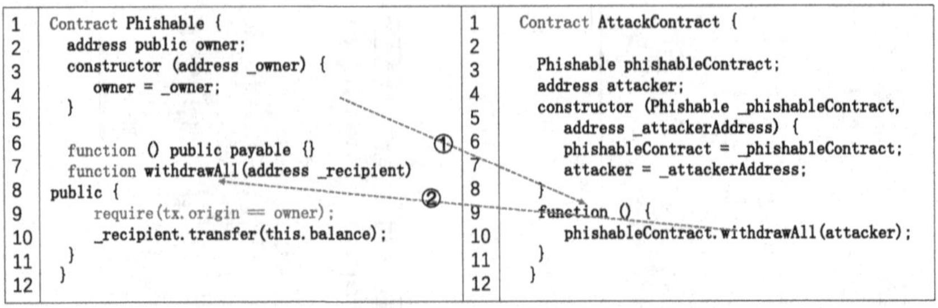

Fig. 6. Phishable Contract and Attack Contract.

Vulnerability opcode fragments: As shown in Fig. 5 , we can see that the EVM instructions of key vulnerability statements, among which the three key instructions are ORIGIN, EQ and ISZERO (red mark). The two key instructions ORIGIN and EQ are mainly to determine whether the original caller tx.origin is the same as the contract owner, and the ISZERO instruction determines the result of the EQ comparison operation.

In summary, if there are ORIGIN, EQ and ISZERO commands in the opcode fragment, it means that tx.origin is used in the smart contract to verify the identity, and the contract has the tx.origin vulnerability. The opcode fragment of tx.origin vulnerability is an opcode fragment containing ORIGIN, EQ and ISZERO instructions.

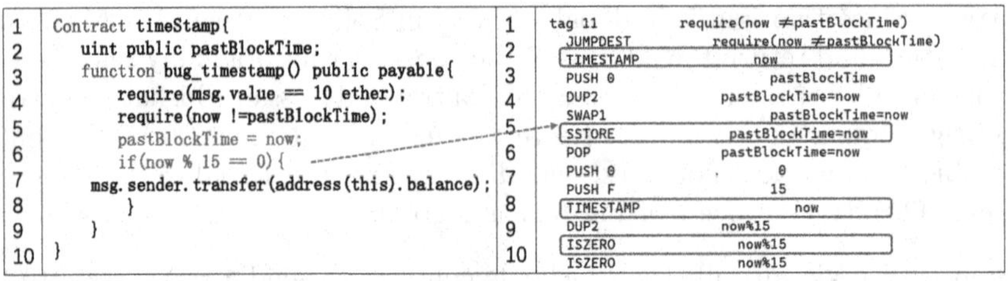
Contract timeStamp{
uint public pastBlockTime;
function bug_timestamp() public payable{
require(msg.value == 10 ether);
require(now !=pastBlockTime);
pastBlockTime = now;
if(now % 15 == 0){
msg.sender.transfer(address(this).balance);
}
}
}
tag 11 require(now ≠pastBlockTime)
JUMPDEST require(now ≠pastBlockTime)
TIMESTAMP now
PUSH 0 pastBlockTime
DUP2 pastBlockTime=now
SWAP1 pastBlockTime=now
SSTORE pastBlockTime=now
POP pastBlockTime=now
PUSH 0 0
PUSH F 15
TIMESTAMP now
DUP2 now%15
ISZERO now%15
ISZERO now%15

Fig. 7. Timestamp Dependency Contract and The EVM of Timestamp Dependency Contract.

Timestamp Dependency Vulnerability. The timestamp dependency vulnerability contract is shown in Fig. 7. During the 900 s, miners can adjust the timestamp as needed. If there are enough ether coins in the contract of Fig. 7, the miner who calculates a block will be motivated to adjust his own timestamp that is divisible by 15 (marked in red) and be the first to transfer 10 ether to the contract, then the miner will get all the ethers that were previously transferred to that contract.

Key vulnerability statements: *pastBlockTime = now;if(now % 15==0).*

Vulnerability opcode fragments: The EVM instructions of the key vulnerability statements are shown in Fig. 7. According to EVM instructions, the opcode of now is TIMESTAMP. The three key instructions are TIMESTAMP, SSTORE and ISZERO (red mark). The first TIMESTAMP and SSTORE instructions are mainly used to change the timestamp of the previous block to the timestamp of the current block. The second TIMESTAMP and ISZERO instructions are used to get the timestamp of the current block and determine whether the timestamp is divisible by the integer 15.

In summary, if the timestamp is divisible by 15 and the miner is the first to transfer 10 Ether tokens to the contract, it creates a timestamp dependency vulnerability. If there are TIMESTAMP, SSTORE and ISZERO instructions in the opcode fragment, it indicates that the contract has the timestamp dependency vulnerability. The opcode fragment of timestamp dependency vulnerability is an opcode fragment containing TIMESTAMP, SSTORE and ISZERO instructions.

Integer Overflow Vulnerability. Figure 8 shows the integer overflow contract and none integer overflow contract. If programmer does not check the user's input in calculating, the value of variable may be out of the valid range. The main reason for the vulnerability is that there is no overflow judgment on the operation results of add, sub and mul. Integer overflow vulnerability can be avoided by using the SafeMath library of add, sub, multi, and div functions for calculation and overflow judgment results.

```
Contract POC{
    function add_overflow() returns(uint256
_overflow){
        uint256 max = 2**256 - 1;
        return max+1;
    }
    function sub_underflow() returns(uint256
_underflow){
        uint256 min = 0;
        return min-1;
    }
    function mul_overflow() returns(uint256
_underflow){
        uint256 mul = 2**255;
        return mul*2 ;
    }
}
```

```
Contract Using SafeMath POC{
    using SafeMath for uint256;
  function add_overflow() returns(uint256
_overflow){
        uint256 max = 2**256 - 1;
        return max.add(1);}
  function sub_underflow() returns(uint256
_underflow){
        uint256 min = 0;
        return min.sub(1);}
  function mul_overflow() returns(uint256
_underflow){
        uint256 mul = 2**255;
        return mul.mul(2);}
}
```

Fig. 8. Integer Overflow Contract and None Integer Overflow Contract.

Key vulnerability statements: _return max + 1; return min −1; return mul * 2._

Vulnerability opcode fragments: We extract vulnerability opcode fragments through the none integer overflow contract of Fig. 8. Figure 9 shows the EVM of add, multi, sub functions in none integer overflow contract. (1) shows the key instructions are ADD, LT, ISZREO (red mark) which are mainly used to sum the parameters a and b and perform overflow judgment. (2) shows the key instructions are MUL, EQ (red mark) which are mainly used for multiplication and overflow judgment of parameters a and b. (3) shows the key instructions are GT and ISZERO (red mark) which are mainly used for subtraction and overflow judgment of parameters a and b.

In summary, if there are no LT, ISZREO, and EQ instructions in the opcode fragment where the ADD or GT or MUL instruction resides, it indicates that there is no overflow judgment on the operation of add, sub and mul and the contract has the integer overflow vulnerability. The opcode fragment of integer overflow vulnerability is an opcode fragment containing ADD or GT or MUL instructions but does not contain LT, ISZREO, and EQ instructions.

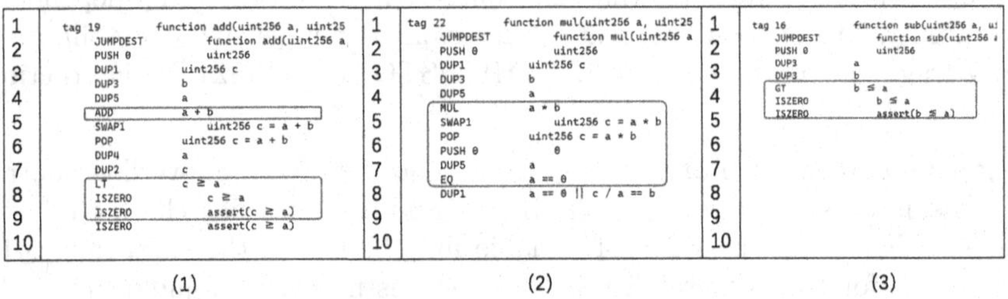

Fig. 9. The EVM of Add, Multi, Sub Functions in None Integer Overflow Contract.

4.4 Training Sets, Classification Algorithms and Model Selection

Training Sets and Classification Algorithms. In this work, we divide the dataset into training set and validation set according to the ratio of 8:2. We perform the binary classification task by ensemble learning algorithms, which perform the learning task by combining multiple base learners. The method can produce better prediction performance than a single model. There are two types of ensemble learning algorithms: Bagging and Boosting. Bagging is a parallel method and the base classifier is trained independently. Boosting is a serial method and its training depends on the previous model. In terms of variance and bias, Bagging aims to reduce variance, which can be significantly reduced since each learner is independent from each other. Boosting aims to reduce the bias, which minimizes the loss function sequentially, and the bias will naturally decrease gradually.

Based on the training set of two-dimensional feature vectors and labels, we use four kinds of ensemble learning algorithms which are RF, LightGBM, XGBoost, AdaBoost, and a simple supervised classification algorithm SVM to detect smart contracts vulnerabilities.

- *Random Forest (RF)*: The random forest is divided into 3 steps:
  1. Random sampling: randomly select n samples from the sample set through bagging.

2. Feature randomization: randomly select k features (k < d) from all features d, and then select the best segmentation feature from the k features as a node to build a CART decision tree.
3. Repeat (1) (3) two steps m times to build m CART decision trees, m CART decision trees form random forest.

- *Light Gradient Boosting Machine (LightGBM)* : LightGBM is an improved model based on GBDT, the decision trees use leaf-wise strategy to control the complexity of the model. As shown in Equation (1), the objective function is improved to a second-order Taylor expansion, and a regularization term is added.

$$L_n = \sum_{i=1}^{n} l(y^i, y^i_{n-1} + f_n(x^i)) + \Upsilon T + \frac{1}{2}\lambda \sum_{j=1}^{T} \omega_j^2 \tag{1}$$

x^i represents the ith sample, y^i represents its label. l represents the original objective function, L_n represents the objective function of the nth iteration after adding the regularization item, and f_n is the model of the nth iteration, Υ and λ are parameters, T is the number of leaf nodes, ω_j is the output value of the jth leaf node.

- *eXtreme Gradient Boosting (XGBoost)*: XGBoost is a boosting algorithm to improve speed and efficiency, and adds a regular term to the objective function to control the complexity of the model and prevent over-fitting. The objective function is defined in Equation (2), n is the number of samples.

$$f_{obj} = \sum_{i=1}^{n} l(y_i, y_i^{'}) + \sum_{t=1}^{k} \Omega(f_t) \tag{2}$$

l is the loss of a single sample, y_i represents the label of the sample, $y_i^{'}$ is the predicted value of the model for the training sample. Ω represents the regular term of the model, f_k is the k-th base model.

- *Adaptive Boosting (AdaBoost)*: AdaBoost is divided into 5 steps:
  1. Initialize the weight of the original dataset.
  2. Use weighted data sets to train weak learners.
  3. Calculate the weight of the weak learner according to the error of the weak learner.
  4. Increase the weight of the samples with incorrect classification, and relatively reduce the weight of the samples with correct classification.
  5. Repeat steps 2-4 K-1 times, and combine the results of K-1 weak learners with weights.
- *Support Vector Machine (SVM)*: SVM is a supervised classification algorithm. The purpose of SVM algorithm is to find a partition hyperplane that divides the samples into positive samples or negative samples, and choose the partition hyperplane with the best generalization ability, which can maximize the interval between positive samples and negative samples.

Model Selection. For the same learning algorithm, the classification results change with hyper parameters. Hyper parameters are parameter values that are set before starting the learning process, rather than parameter data obtained through training. Therefore, it is necessary to optimize the hyperparameters and adjust the hyperparameters of the algorithm in the model selection. The model is trained with pre-defined hyperparameters, and the best hyperparameters on the validation dataset are obtained by adjusting the parameters.

5 Experiment

We perform comprehensive experiments on the test sets in this section, and use Accuracy, Precision, Recall, F1-score, and AUC values to evaluate the performance of the different classifiers. In the end, we analyze the experimental results in detail.

5.1 Experiment Setup

Due to the large data set of this experiment, there are high demands on the memory size, hard disk capacity, and CPU performance of the experimental equipment. Table 2 describes our experimental environment.

Table 2. Experiment Setup.

Software and Hardware	Configuration
Sever Model	LAPTOP-MJME8I89
Memory Size	474 GB
CPU	11th Gen Intel(R) Core(TM) i5-11320H
Disk Capacity	1.2 TB
Operating System	Ubuntu 20.04.2 LTS

5.2 Test Sets and the Comparison of Classifiers

We publish all the experiments on our project website (https://github.com/0929hua/RFVunDetection). In the experiments, we divide the dataset into training set and test set according to the ratio of 8:2. On four test sets, we use five classifiers which are RF, LightGBM, XGBoost, AdaBoost and SVM classifiers. True positive (TP) is the number of samples correctly classified as positive. True negative (TN) is the number of correctly classified negative samples. False positive (FP) refers to the number of negative samples wrongly classified as positive samples. False negative (FN) refers to the number of positive samples wrongly classified as negative samples. Accuracy, Precision, Recall, F1-score and AUC are used to measure the performance of the classifier. Accuracy indicates the proportion of correctly predicted samples in the total samples. Precision represents the proportion of positive samples among all predicted positive samples. Recall rate represents the proportion of predicted positive samples in all actual positive samples. F1-score is a measure used to evaluate binary classifiers, it is defined as the weighted harmonic average of Recall and Precision. AUC represents the area under the ROC curve of the model.

Table 3. Accuracy Comparison of five classifiers.

Classifier	Integer overflow	Timestamp	Reentrancy	TX.origin
RF	**0.9924**	**0.9976**	**0.9954**	**0.9882**
LightGBM	0.9910	0.9972	0.9930	0.9848
XGBoost	0.9872	0.9900	0.9902	0.9720
AdaBoost	0.9850	0.9844	0.9888	0.9490
SVM	0.9774	0.9502	0.9622	0.9306

In Tables 3, 4, 5, 6, 7, it can be seen that in binary classification tasks, RF classifier produces higher scores of Accuracy, Precision, Recall, F1-score and AUC than LightGBM classifier, XGBoost classifier, AdaBoost classifier and SVM classifier. For the Accuracy index, as shown in Table III, the highest predicted value of RF classifier is 99.76%, and the rest are over 98%. For the Precision index, as shown in Table IV, the highest predicted value of RF classifier is

Table 4. Precision Comparison of five classifiers.

Classifier	Integer overflow	Timestamp	Reentrancy	TX.origin
RF	**0.9367**	**0.9675**	**0.9894**	**0.9827**
LightGBM	0.9153	0.9704	0.9926	0.9795
XGBoost	0.8642	0.9310	0.9922	0.9784
AdaBoost	0.8462	0.9512	1.000	0.9899
SVM	0.7950	0.8806	0.9912	1.000

Table 5. Recall Comparison of five classifiers.

Classifier	Integer overflow	Timestamp	Reentrancy	TX.origin
RF	**0.9367**	**0.9933**	**0.9333**	**0.8844**
LightGBM	0.9367	0.9833	0.8900	0.8489
XGBoost	0.9333	0.9000	0.8433	0.7044
AdaBoost	0.9167	0.7800	0.8133	0.4378
SVM	0.8400	0.1967	0.3733	0.2289

98.94%, and the rest are all above 93%. For the Recall index, as shown in Table V, the highest predicted value of RF classifier is 99.33%, and the rest are all over 88%. For the F1-score index, as shown in Table VI, the highest predicted value of RF classifier is 98.03%, and the rest are above 93%. For the AUC index, as shown in Table VII, the highest predicted value of RF classifier is 99.56%, and the rest are over 94%.

Table 6. F1-score Comparison of five classifiers.

Classifier	Integer overflow	Timestamp	Reentrancy	TX.origin
RF	**0.9367**	**0.9803**	**0.9605**	**0.9310**
LightGBM	0.9259	0.9768	0.9385	0.9095
XGBoost	0.8974	0.9153	0.9117	0.8191
AdaBoost	0.8800	0.8571	0.8971	0.6071
SVM	0.8169	0.3215	0.5424	0.3725

In this classification task, we can see that the performance of ensemble learning classifiers is better than that of SVM classifier. For the five kinds of data that measure the performance of the classifier, it can be clearly seen that the five index values of RF classifier are the highest. Therefore, RF classifier is selected in this model.

Table 7. AUC Comparison of five classifiers.

Classifier	Integer overflow	Timestamp	Reentrancy	TX.origin
RF	**0.9663**	**0.9956**	**0.9663**	**0.9415**
LightGBM	0.9656	0.9907	0.9448	0.9236
XGBoost	0.9620	0.9479	0.9215	0.8515
AdaBoost	0.9530	0.8887	0.9067	0.7187
SVM	0.9131	0.5975	0.6866	0.6144

5.3 Model Analysis

TPR, FNR, TNR and FPR. TPR represents the probability that correct prediction of positive class among all positive classes. FNR represents the probability of error prediction of positive classes among all positive classes. TNR represents the probability that correct prediction of negative class among all negative classes. FPR represents the probability of error prediction of negative classes among all negative classes. As shown in Fig. 10, for each type of vulnerability, TPR as high as 99.3%, and the highest TNR is 99.9%. Higher TPRs and TNRs prove the efficiency of RF classifier.

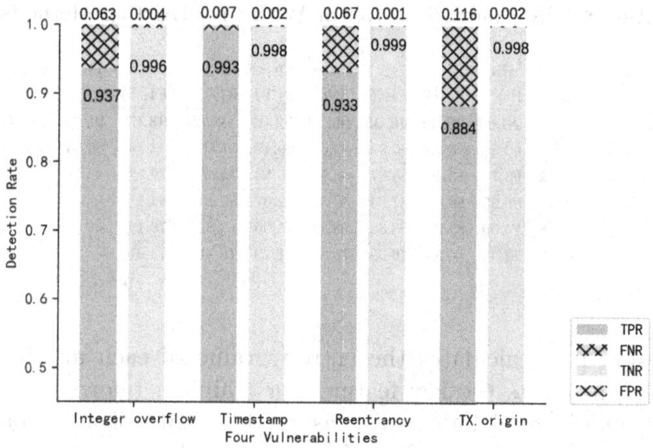

Fig. 10. TPRs, FNRs,TNRs,FPRs of RF classifier.

Comparison with Previous Studies. In order to demonstrate the advantages of CDRF model performance, we choose the models proposed in previous studies for comparison. In the same experimental environment, we select CBGRU model proposed by Lejun Zhang et al. [44], DeeSCVHunter model presented by Yu X et al. [45], AME model presented by Liu Z et al. [46], and TMP and DR-GCN models presented by Zhang et al. [47]. We choose three kinds of smart contract vulnerabilities for comparison, and the comparison results are shown in Table 8.

As shown in Table 8, we can see from the comparison results that CDRF model is superior to other models in three vulnerability detection tasks. CBGRU model is the best performing model in the comparison. CBGRU model extracts features by BiGRU model and CNN model. CDRF is composed of multiple decision trees, which can randomly select samples and features each time, and select the best feature from the features. Compared with CBGRU model, for reentrant vulnerability, the accuracy rate of CDRF model increases by 6.24% and the F1-score increases by 5.13%. For integer overflow vulnerability, the accuracy of CDRF model increases by 6.22% and the F1-score increases by 0.38%. For the timestamp dependency vulnerability, the accuracy rate of CDRF model increases by 13.22% and the F1-score increases by 11.6%. It can be concluded that CDRF adequately extracts the typical characteristics of the vulnerability.

Table 8. The Comparison Result With Five Existing Methods.

CDRF vs. Other Methods	Reentrant				Integer Overflow				Timestamp Dependency			
	A(%)	P(%)	R(%)	F1(%)	A(%)	P(%)	R(%)	F1(%)	A(%)	P(%)	R(%)	F1(%)
CDRF	**99.54**	**98.94**	**93.33**	**96.05**	**99.24**	**93.67**	**93.67**	**93.67**	**99.76**	**96.75**	**99.33**	**98.03**
CBGRU	93.3	96.3	85.95	90.92	93.02	89.47	97.45	93.29	86.54	87.23	85.66	86.43
DeeSCVHunter	93.02	90.7	83.46	86.87	80.5	85.53	74.86	79.93	-	-	-	-
AME	90.19	86.25	89.69	87.94	86.52	82.07	86.23	84.1	-	-	-	-
TMP	84.48	74.06	82.63	83.82	83.42	75.05	83.82	79.19	-	-	-	-
DR-GCN	81.47	72.36	80.89	76.39	78.68	71.29	78.91	74.91	-	-	-	-

The decision tree calculates the entropy value of each attribute, such as CART, and then selects the key features for training. Information Entropy is the most commonly used index to measure the purity of a sample set. Let's assume that the proportion of class K samples in the current sample set D is $p_k(k = 1, 2, ..., m)$, the information entropy of d is defined in equation (3). The smaller the Entropy(D), the higher the purity of D, which means that the data in D is very concentrated.

$$Entropy(D) = -\sum_{k=1}^{m} p_k \log_2 p_k \tag{3}$$

By calculating the information gain of a feature, which is the reduction in information entropy, when the information gain is greater, it means that the reduction in information entropy is greater when the sample is classified by feature, indicating that the feature is more effective. The RF is an ensemble algorithm, which is composed of multiple decision trees. RF randomly selects samples and features each time, and then selects the best feature from the features to establish a CART decision tree, which ensures that each tree is random and optimizes the over-fitting disadvantage of the decision tree. Therefore, the accuracy of RF is usually higher than that of a single decision tree. By comparing the experiments, we can see that the RF model gives the best experimental results.

Comparison of Detection Time. In the experiment, CDRF model detects 5000 real smart contracts. The model is designed to detect vulnerabilities in three steps. The first step takes 1.97 s to decompile the source code into opcode, the second step takes 0.22 s for feature extraction, and the third step takes 0.30 s for vulnerability detection. CDRF model needs about 3 s to detect a contract, Securify requires about 18 s, and Oyente needs about 29 s, which is much faster than Securify and Oyente.

Table 9. The Comparison of Detection Time (Seconds).

Detection Tool	Securify	Oyente	**CDRF**
Times	18.40	29.60	**3.0**

6 Analysis and Discussion

We analyze the vulnerability principles and key vulnerability statements of four smart contracts, and summarize four kinds of opcode fragments containing key vulnerability instructions. We use the opcode fragments as the input of word2vec and PCA to generate a one-dimensional binary features. According to the context word matrix, we can get the word vector with context co-occurrence features. Word2vec has fewer dimensions than previous embedding methods. In addition, there is a one-to-one relationship between words and vectors, the types of opcode instructions are not repeated, so there is no need to consider the problem of polysemy. PCA is used for reducing the dimensionality of high-dimensional data, retain the information of the original data to the greatest extent. As a result, word2vec and PCA can validly represent the static feature of a smart contract.

In this paper, the detection method of smart contract vulnerability based on Random Forest is very efficient and reliable. Firstly, in the feature extraction stage, we summarize four opcode fragments containing key vulnerability instructions. The opcode fragments are processed by word2vec and PCA to obtain one-dimensional binary features. Therefore, the input data of this method is simplified and dimensionality is reduced. Secondly, supervised learning has input and output variables, and its goal is to use algorithms to learn the functional mapping from input to output, and to predict the output variables when new variables are input. In the training stage, this method obtains the best model by constantly iterating and updating the parameters of the mapping function. In the prediction stage, this method can use the model obtained in the training stage to directly predict whether there is a vulnerability in the new sample. The accuracy of this method in detecting vulnerabilities depends on the authenticity of the tags generated by Oyente and Mythril. Since the proposed method is based on existing vulnerabilities, it can not be used to identify unknown vulnerabilities or undefined new vulnerabilities.

7 Conclusion

Based on the purpose of protecting the Ethereum smart contracts and purifying the trading blockchain environment, detection method of smart contract vulnerability based on Random Forest is proposed in this paper, which successfully detects four types of smart contract vulnerabilities. First, we analyze the vulnerability principles and key vulnerability statements of four smart contracts, and summarize four kinds of opcode fragments containing key vulnerability instructions. The opcode fragment is processed by word2vec and PCA to obtain a one-dimensional binary feature which represents the static feature of the contract.

The feature extraction method can effectively describe the features of static smart contracts. Second, the vulnerability detection method of Ethereum smart contracts based on Random forest is reliable and time-saving. The predicted Accuracy is up to 99.76%, and the rest are above 99%. The highest Precision prediction value is 98.94%, and the rest are above 93%. The highest predictive value of Recall is 99.33%, and the rest are more than 88%. The highest predictive value of F1-socre is 98.03%, and the rest are more than 93%. The highest predictive value of AUC is 96.63%, and the rest are above 94%. Meanwhile, each smart contract takes about 3 s on average. Third, we select three smart contract vulnerabilities for comparison. The results demonstrate that the RF model presented in this paper has superior classification capability and accuracy.

Acknowledgements. The work is supported in part by the National Natural Science Foundation of China under grants 62202146, 62072134 and U2001205, the Natural Science Foundation of Hubei Province under grants 2022CFB914 and 2021BEA163.

References

1. Szabo, N.: Smart contracts: building blocks for digital markets, extropy. J. Transhumanist Thought **16**(18), 2–20 (1996)
2. Nakamoto, S.: Bitcoin: a peer-to-peer electronic cash system, p. 21260 (2008)
3. Buterin, v., et al.,: A next-generation smart contract and decentralized application platform. White Pap. **3**(37), 2–1 (2014)
4. Yasin, A., Liu, L.: An online identity and smart contract management system. In: 2016 IEEE 40th Annual Computer Software and Applications Conference (COMPSAC), vol. 2, pp. 192–198. IEEE (2016)
5. Nugent, T., Upton, D., Cimpoesu, M.: Improving data transparency in clinical trials using blockchain smart contracts. F1000Research **5** (2016)
6. Wall, E., Malm, G.: Using blockchain technology and smart contracts to create a distributed securities depository (2016)
7. Zhang, M., Huang, S., Shen, G., Wang, Y.: PPNNP: a privacy-preserving neural network prediction with separated data providers using multi-client inner-product encryption. Comput. Stan. Interfaces **84**, 103678 (2023)
8. Zhang, M., Chen, Y., Susilo, W.: Decision tree evaluation on sensitive datasets for secure e-healthcare systems. IEEE Trans. Dependable Secure Comput. (2022)
9. Zhang, M., Yang, M., Shen, G.: SSBAS-FA: a secure sealed-bid e-auction scheme with fair arbitration based on time-released blockchain. J. Syst. Archit. **129**, 102619 (2022)
10. Wan, Z., Guan, Z., Cheng, X.: PRIDE: a private and decentralized usage-based insurance using blockchain. In: 2018 IEEE International Conference on Internet of Things (iThings) and IEEE Green Computing and Communications (GreenCom) and IEEE Cyber, Physical and Social Computing (CPSCom) and IEEE Smart Data (SmartData), pp. 1349–1354. IEEE (2018)
11. Christidis, K., Devetsikiotis, M.: Blockchains and smart contracts for the internet of things. IEEE Access **4**, 2292–2303 (2016)
12. Chang, S.E., Chen, Y.-C., Lu, M.-F.: Supply chain re-engineering using blockchain technology: a case of smart contract based tracking process. Technol. Forecast. Soc. Chang. **144**, 1–11 (2019)

13. Bader, L., Bürger, J. C., Matzutt, R., Wehrle, K.: Smart contract-based car insurance policies. In: 2018 IEEE Globecom workshops (GC wkshps), pp. 1–7. IEEE (2018)
14. Mavridou, A., Laszka, A.: Designing secure ethereum smart contracts: a finite state machine based approach. In: Meiklejohn, S., Sako, K. (eds.) FC 2018. LNCS, vol. 10957, pp. 523–540. Springer, Heidelberg (2018). https://doi.org/10.1007/978-3-662-58387-6_28
15. Atzei, N., Bartoletti, M., Cimoli, T.: A survey of attacks on ethereum smart contracts (SoK). In: Maffei, M., Ryan, M. (eds.) POST 2017. LNCS, vol. 10204, pp. 164–186. Springer, Heidelberg (2017). https://doi.org/10.1007/978-3-662-54455-6_8
16. "The dao" (2016) https://blog.ethereum.org/2016/06/17/critical-update-re-dao-vulnerability
17. "The parity multisig bug" (2017). https://blog.openzeppelin.com/on-the-parity-wallet-multisig-hack-405a8c12e8f7/
18. "Vaas.automated formal verification platform for smart contract" (2019). https://www.lianantech.com/
19. Bach, L.M., Mihaljevic, B., Zagar, M.: Comparative analysis of blockchain consensus algorithms. In: 2018 41st International Convention on Information and Communication Technology, Electronics and Microelectronics (MIPRO), pp. 1545–1550. IEEE (2018)
20. Mikolov, T., Chen, K., Corrado, G., Dean, J.: Efficient estimation of word representations in vector space. arXiv preprint arXiv:1301.3781 (2013)
21. Yang, J., Zhang, D., Frangi, A.F., Yang, J.-Y.: Two-dimensional PCA: a new approach to appearance-based face representation and recognition. IEEE Trans. Pattern Anal. Mach. Intell. **26**(1), 131–137 (2004)
22. Grossman, S., et al.: Online detection of effectively callback free objects with applications to smart contracts. Proc. ACM Program. Lang. **2**(POPL), 1–28 (2018)
23. Sam, H.: "Batch overflow bug on ethereum erc20 token contracts and safemath[eb/ol]," 2022–5-25, https://blog.matryx.ai/ batch-overflow-bug-on-ethereum-erc20-token-contracts-and-safemath-f9ebcc137434
24. Breiman, L.: Random Forest. Mach. Learn. **45**(1), 5–32 (2001). https://doi.org/10.1023/A:1010933404324
25. Ke, G., et al.: Lightgbm: a highly efficient gradient boosting decision tree. Adv. neural inf. proc. syst. **30** (2017)
26. Chen T., Guestrin, C.: XGBoost: a scalable tree boosting system. In: Proceedings of the 22nd ACM Sigkdd International Conference on Knowledge Discovery and Data Mining, pp. 785–794 (2016)
27. Freund, Y., Schapire, R.E.: A decision-theoretic generalization of on-line learning and an application to boosting. J. Comput. Syst. Sci. **55**(1), 119–139 (1997)
28. Suykens, J.A.K., Vandewalle, J.: Least squares support vector machine classifiers. Neural Process. Lett. **9**(3), 293–300 (1999). https://doi.org/10.1023/A:1018628609742
29. "The official website of ethereum," (2019). https://etherscan.io/
30. Qian, P., Liu, Z., He, Q., Huang, B., Tian, D., Wang, X.: Smart contract vulnerability detection technique: a survey. arXiv preprint arXiv:2209.05872 (2022)
31. Han, S.M., Liang, B., Huang, J.J., Shi, W.: Dc-hunter: detecting dangerous smart contracts via bytecode matching. J. Cyber Security **5**(3), 100–112 (2020)
32. Zhang, P., Xiao, F., Luo, X.: Soliditycheck: Quickly detecting smart contract problems through regular expressions. arXiv preprint arXiv:1911.09425 (2019)

33. Huang, J., et al.: Hunting vulnerable smart contracts via graph embedding based bytecode matching. IEEE Trans. Inf. Forensics Secur. **16**, 2144–2156 (2021)
34. Wood, G., et al.: Ethereum: a secure decentralised generalised transaction ledger. Ethereum Project Yellow Paper **151**, 1–32 (2014)
35. Grishchenko, I., Maffei, M., Schneidewind, C.: A semantic framework for the security analysis of ethereum smart contracts. In: Bauer, L., Küsters, R. (eds.) Principles of Security and Trust, pp. 243–269. Springer, Cham (2018). https://doi.org/10.1007/978-3-319-89722-6_10
36. Hildenbrandt, E., et al.: Kevm: A complete formal semantics of the ethereum virtual machine. In: 2018 IEEE 31st Computer Security Foundations Symposium (CSF). IEEE, 2018, pp. 204–217 (2018)
37. SAmani, S., Bégel, M., Bortin, M. and Staples, M.: Towards verifying ethereum smart contract bytecode in isabelle/hol. In: Proceedings of the 7th ACM SIGPLAN International Conference on Certified Programs and Proofs, 2018, 66–77 (2018)
38. Kalra, S., Goel, S., Dhawan, M., Sharma, S.: Zeus: analyzing safety of smart contracts. In: Ndss, pp. 1–12 (2018)
39. Luu, L., Chu, D.H., Olickel, H., Saxena, P., Hobor, A.: Making smart contracts smarter. In: Proceedings of the 2016 ACM SIGSAC Conference on Computer and Communications Security, pp. 254–269 (2016)
40. Tsankov, P., Dan, A., Drachsler-Cohen, D., Gervais, A., Buenzli, F., Vechev, M.: Securify: Practical security analysis of smart contracts. In: Proceedings of the 2018 ACM SIGSAC Conference on Computer and Communications Security, pp. 67–82 (2018)
41. Ethereum virtual machine operation codes (2019). https://ethervm.io/
42. Mueller, B.: A framework for bug hunting on the ethereum blockchain (2017)
43. Brent, L., et al.: Vandal: A scalable security analysis framework for smart contracts. arXiv preprint arXiv:1809.03981 (2018)
44. Zhang, L., et al.: CBGRU: a detection method of smart contract vulnerability based on a hybrid model. Sensors **22**(9), 3577 (2022). https://doi.org/10.3390/s22093577
45. Yu, X., Zhao, H., Hou, B., Ying, Z., Wu, B.: Deescvhunter: A deep learning-based framework for smart contract vulnerability detection. In: 2021 International Joint Conference on Neural Networks (IJCNN), pp. 1–8 (2021)
46. Liu, Z., Qian, P., Wang, X., Zhu, L., He, Q., Ji, S.: Smart contract vulnerability detection: From pure neural network to interpretable graph feature and expert pattern fusion. 08 2021, pp. 2751–2759 (2021)
47. Zhuang, Y., Liu, Z., Qian, P., Liu, Q., Wang, X., He, Q.: Smart contract vulnerability detection using graph neural network. In: Proceedings of the Twenty-Ninth International Joint Conference on Artificial Intelligence, IJCAI-20, C. Bessiere, Ed. International Joint Conferences on Artificial Intelligence Organization, 7 2020, pp. 3283–3290, main track. [Online]. Available: https://doi.org/10.24963/ijcai.2020/454

simuBits: Pool Security Verification of Novel Mining Attacks

Zunlong Zhou, Wen Chen(✉), Linrui Li, and Yilin Zhang

School of Cyber Science and Engineering, Sichuan University, Chengdu 610065, China
wenchen@scu.edu.cn

Abstract. Bitcoin pool attacks, including withholding block attacks, pose a significant threat to the Bitcoin ecosystem. However, current research on pool attacks is limited to theoretical analysis due to the lack of experimental platforms. This paper presents simuBits, a specialized experimental system designed to analyze the feasibility of mining pool attacks and propose countermeasures. The system simulates a mining pool using a group of miner processes. A new combined attack model of BWH and man-in-the-middle attack is proposed, which is more profitable and stealthy than traditional single attack patterns. A new countermeasure is also proposed that dynamically adjusts the power weight of suspected attackers through putting them into a small sub-pool. Both the combined attacks and the defense strategies were tested in simuBits, and the results confirm that the proposed countermeasure is a feasible way to defend against pool attacks, significantly reducing attackers' revenues compared to honest mining.

Keywords: Bitcoin security · Block withholding attack · Eclipse attack · Pool mining · Distributed systems

1 Introduction

Currently, most of the Bitcoin miners join mining pools to obtain stable revenues. Each miner in the pool is required to carry out two types of workload proofs [1], one is full PoW (FPoW), which is utilized by the Bitcoin system for the mining of new valid blocks, the other one is partial proof of work (PPoW), which is designed to test miners' arithmetic power contribution to the pool. After all miners submitted both proofs of work to the pool's manager, it broadcasts the received FPoW to get Bitcoin revenues, and in turn distributes the revenue to each pool member based on PPoW.

However, due to vulnerabilities in the pool protocols, pools are vulnerable to various security threats such as selfish mining [2], BWH attacks [4], Eclipse attacks [6], and PAW attacks [10]. Selfish mining [2] attackers reserve their newly found blocks in a private chain until it grows longer than the public chain. Then the attackers release the private chain, causing branch conflicts with the public chain. The selfish mining attackers wasted the mining efforts of the honest miners on the public chain, which increased their relative arithmetic power proportion in the network to get excessive revenues.

M. Zhang et al. (Eds.): ProvSec 2023, LNCS 14217, pp. 429–447, 2023.
https://doi.org/10.1007/978-3-031-45513-1_23

It is important to note that several BWH attacks have been found in reality [4, 16], causing losses to honest miners. Some new attack patterns have been proposed based on BWH attacks such as FAW [9], PAW [10], etc. A BWH attacker allocates part of its power to a puppet miner, who pretends to be an honest miner to join a victim pool. The puppet does not submit newly found valid blocks (FPoW) to the pool. However, it regularly submits PPoW and shares the pool's revenues with other pool members. It has been demonstrated [5, 7] that with a reasonable allocation of arithmetic power, the attacker can obtain more gains than honest mining.

However, limited by the lack of experimental platforms, current pool security researches mainly focus on theoretical analysis of pool attacks. In the paper, we designed simuBits (simulation of Bitcoin system, which can be download here[1]), which is an experimental platform for Bitcoin pool attacks. The platform simulates the miner's behaviour using mining process: each process implements a SHA256-based mining task and follows FPoW and PPoW. The data transmissions between miners are realized using socket communications between processes, and the distributed ledgers are stored in processes' local files. Furthermore, multiple processes can form a mining group to simulate mining together in a pool.

simuBits is used to test the gain of BWH, BWD, and Eclipse attackers [6], and the feasibility of the proposed defence strategy. We also proposed a new attack, which combined BWH (or BWD) with man-in-the-middle attack, such as Eclipse attack. The attacker controls the puppets through Eclipse attack [6] to launch BWH attacks on victim pools, and its remaining arithmetic power is for normal mining. The puppet miners cause arithmetic power loss to the victim pools, while the attacker can gain excessive gains because of the increasing of its relative power proportion in the network. Furthermore, we analysed the conditions of excessive gains of attackers using the platform simuBits. Finally, we found that the pool manager can dynamically adjust the pool's arithmetic power to break the profitable condition of attackers. We validated the theory analysis on the platform simuBits, and the results demonstrated that dynamic pool adjustment is an effective way to against pool attacks.

1.1 Related Work

Dishonest miners may exploit vulnerabilities in the pools' revenue distribution protocol to obtain super-revenue and frustrate honest miners. For example, in the BWH attack proposed by Meni Rosenfeld [4], an attacker pretends to be one honest miner to join a victim pool, it just submit PPoW while abandon FPoW. The attacker does not contribute to the pool but still share the pool rewards, which ultimately hurts the revenue of honest members in the pool.

Loi Luu [7] proved that BWH attackers are well-incentivized with super-gains. Fujita [8] analyzed the revenues of mining pools suffering BWH attacks and showed that pools can attract more miners by launching BWH attacks on other pools. Yujin Kwon [9] proposed Fork After Withholding (FAW) attack by combining BWH attack and selfish mining attack to increase the feasibility of successful attack. Shang Gao [10] combined BWH attack and selfish mining to increase excessive revenues. Wang [11] proposed to

[1] https://gitee.com/zunlongzhou/bwh.git.

use reinforcement learning to dynamically switch between BWH, FAW, and PAW to choose the best attacking strategy to obtain more revenues; Ke [12] proposed Intermittent Block Withholding Attack (IBWH) attack, and the attacker raised the reward rate by adjusting reward cycle time. Liu [13] et al. proposed BWD attack, which increases the difficulty of detecting BWH attacks by dynamically delaying the block submissions. Li [14] et al. proposed a Hidden Markov Decision Process based semi self-private mining to reduce the probability of forking the block chain and prevent the attack from being detected. Ethan Heilman [6] et al. put forward Eclipse attack, which realized full control of nodes by polluting the incoming and outgoing connections of block nodes; Ruben Recabarren [17] proposed a man-in-the-middle attack named BiteCoin against the communication protocol Stratum in the pool to hijack the work certificates submitted by miners and their revenues; Muoi Tran [18] proposed the EREBUS attack, which splits the Bitcoin network without routing operations, making the attack more difficult to detect.

However, the current studies cannot test these attacks in the real Bitcoin network, thus the attack patterns and defense strategies are mainly analyzed through theoretical deduction. Therefore, we built platform simuBits to validate BWH, BWD, P2P network attacks, and the newly proposed combination attack model BWH/BWD plus Eclipse along with our countermeasures in this paper.

The rest of this paper is organized as follows. In Sect. 2, we analyzed the principles and profitability of BWH attack, BWD attack, and Eclipse attack. In Sect. 3, the attacking strategy and condition of excessive profit are analyzed. In Sect. 4, the detail of simuBits is introduced. In Sect. 5, experiments are carried out to test the combined attacks, and the experimental results are analyzed. In Sect. 6, we discussed the countermeasures of pool attacks.

1.2 Contribution

The contributions of this paper include the followings.

(1) We designed the experimental platform simuBits, which simulates the miner's behaviour using mining process, and most of the components of current Bitcoin network including FPoW, PPoW, inter-miner communication protocols, distributed ledgers, pool management protocols and etc. are realized in simuBits. Therefore, all kinds of well-known pool attacks and defense strategies can be tested in the platform.
(2) A new combination attack BWD (or BWH) plus Eclipse is proposed to achieve a stealthy attack pattern and maintain stable excessive revenues. Extensive simulations were carried out in simuBits to compare attacker's revenue with the theoretical analysis results.
(3) We also proposed a new defense strategy, which dynamically divides the pool into sub-pools. The basic idea is to break the condition of the attackers' excessive revenue, which causes the attacker much loss compared with honest mining. The strategy can be more feasible, since it does not require the modification of basic principle of the Bitcoin networks.

Other important notations are summarized in Table 1.

Table 1. Symbol Description

Name	Description	
α	The percentage of computing power of the attackers in a pool	
γ	Ratio of computing power of the attacker to launch Eclipse attack	
p1,p2,p3	The normal mining power of three mining pool in our example	
UTL	The value of arithmetic power loss per unit time of pool	
Node Profile Properties		
Type	Attribute	Description
Info	Ip, port	Connected IP and port
	Account	Miner account
Status	BWH	Initiating a BWH attack flag
	BWD	Initiating a BWD attack flag
	Eclipse_loss	Arithmetic power loss of Eclipse attack
System	nPow	The ratio of miners' arithmetic power in a mining pool
	tUnit	Mining pools' arithmetic power

2 Preliminary

In this section, we will briefly introduce three widely studied pool attacks: BWH [5], BWD [13] and Eclipse [6].

2.1 BWH Attack

Suppose there are two mining pools P1 and P2 in the Bitcoin network, and an attacker P3 who devotes part of its computing power (as a miner M) to join pool P1. As shown in Fig. 1, the computing power of P1, P2, and attacker P3 are p_1, p_2, and p_3, respectively, and the power of M pm satisfies pm = p1 · α. Under the command of P3, M launches BWH attacks on P1 in a way that it does not contribute to P1 (drops all FPoW) but still share the revenues from the pool through regular submissions of PPoW.

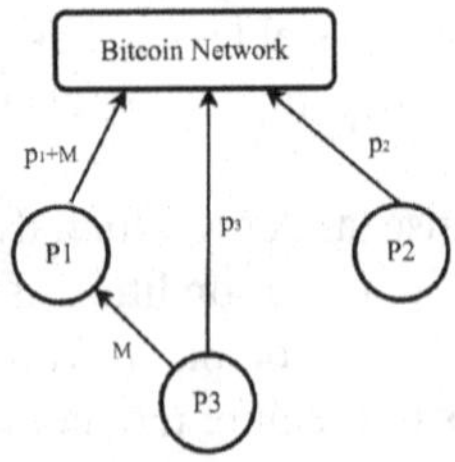

Fig. 1. Schematic diagram of BWH attack

When P3 mines honestly, it gain is $G_0 = p_3 + p_1\alpha$, and if P3 launched BWH attacks on P1, its revenues include: the gain from honestly mining $G_1 = p_3/(1 - p_1\alpha)$, and the reward from P1 $G_2 = \alpha p_1(1-\alpha)/(1-p_1\alpha)$. . Therefore P3 obtains excessive reward if G1 + G2 > G0, and the condition of excessive profit is: $p_3 > \alpha(1-p_1)$. From the condition, we can see that when the attacker's arithmetic power p_3 is fixed, BWH attackers incline to attack large mining pools to obtain more stable gains.

2.2 BWD Attack

Suppose the system has the same power distribution as in Sect. 2.1, but the miner M is controlled by P3 to launch BWD attacks on P1. M temporarily withholds the newly mined valid blocks until: 1) the mining cycle is end with probability 1- Pw; 2) other pools have found valid blocks and broadcast the FPoW with probability Pw [13]. The strategy of BWD attacker is shown in Fig. 2, in which the nodes represent the state of the mining pool at different stages. The horizontal axis represents the number of blocks in the block chain, and the vertical axis is UTL (Unit Time power Loss), which indicates the power loss per unit time of P1. Each state has two possible subsequent status, one is UTL decreased (on the black lines) which means one honest miner in P1 found a valid block or M finally help P1 earn reward with probability (1- Pw); the other direction is UTL increased, which is caused by the delayed submission of M with probability Pw.

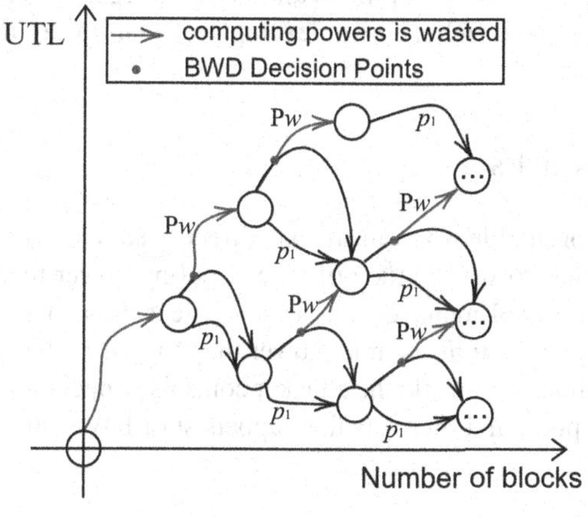

Fig. 2. BWD attack strategy

The gain of P3 also consists of two parts as shown in Eq. (1), where G1 is the gains from honest mining and G2 is the rewards from P1.

$$G = G_1 + G_2 = \frac{p_3}{1-P_w p_1\alpha} + \frac{p_1\alpha(1-P_w\alpha)}{1-P_w p_1\alpha} = \frac{p_3+p_1\alpha-P_w p_1\alpha^2}{1-P_w p_1\alpha} \tag{1}$$

Obviously, P3 can earn more revenues than hones mining if $G > p_3 + p_1\alpha$, from Eq. (1) we can get the condition of excessive profit: $p_3 > \alpha(1-p_1)$, which is the same as BWH, so BWD attackers also tend to attack large mining pools to obtain super gain more easily.

2.3 Man-in-the-Middle Attack

Man-in-the-middle attackers try to control the victim miner's communications in the Bitcoin's P2P network [6]. Usually, the miners update their address table of candidate peers using ADDR messages, containing up to 1000 IP address and their timestamps. Suppose P3 launches Eclipse attack, which is a typical man-in-the-middle attack, on honest miner M in P1. It will pollute M's address tables using many customized ADDR messages. The messages only contain the attacker's addresses and many "trash" IP addresses that are not part of the Bitcoin network. The eclipse attack continues until the victim node restarts and establishes all the outgoing connections to attacker's addresses, since the victim node cannot connect to the "trash IP".

Finally, the attacker P3 controls the incoming and outgoing connections of the victim miner M. As all the information that M can receive or send are under the control of P3, which can easily start man-in-the-middle attacks on M and P1.

For the man-in-the-middle attack on the internal communication of the mine pool, Ruben Recabarren proposed BiteCoin attacks, which hijacked the miners' computing resources and revenues. Meanwhile, BiteCoin attackers secretly modify the miners' TCP packets without disconnecting or resetting the P2P communications. In the hacker conference in 2021, Xin Liu [19] proposed a new type of man-in-the-middle attack based on "set_externance", in which "set_externance" is a function of resetting miners' subscriptions in the mining pool communication protocol Stratum. The attackers hijacked the TCP communications between miners and pool manager to achieve full control of miners' resources. We take Eclipse as an example of man-in-the-middle attack in the paper.

3 Combined Attacks

However, it is not so profitable when an attacker directly launches BWD or BWH attacks. On the one hand, it has to waste much of its computing power to join the target pool; on the other hand, the pool manager may easily detect the attacker. Since the cost of controlling P2P communications is much lower than that of BWH or BWD attacks, we proposed a new combination attack: the attacker controls puppet miners through network attacks in the target pool, and then lets the puppets start BWH attacks to get excessive revenues.

3.1 BWH with Man-in-the-Middle

As shown in Fig. 3, assume an attacker P3 using part of its computing power to join the target pool, and then launches man-in-the-middle attack network attack on target P1 suing Eclipse. After it controlled the communications of M, P3 dropped all the FPoW of M, but still forwarded PPoW to the pool manager.

Suppose P3 used γ proportion of its arithmetic power to launch Eclipse attack on M and let the remaining 1-γ arithmetic power to mine honestly, and the proportion of M's arithmetic power in P1 is α, then the gain that P3 can obtain is

$$G_1 = \frac{p_3(1-\gamma)}{1-\alpha p_1} \tag{2}$$

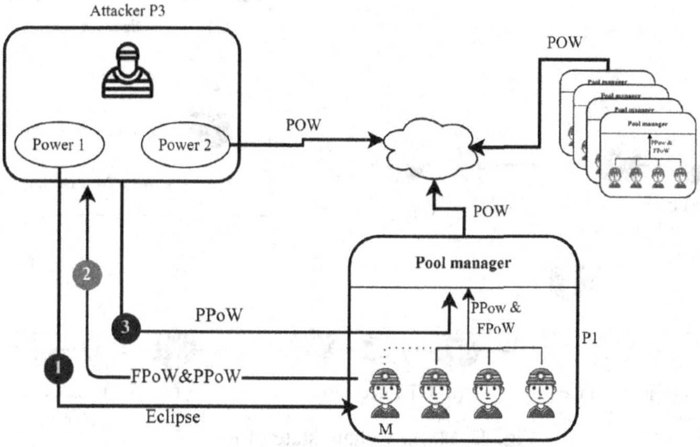

Fig. 3. BWH combined with Eclipse attack flow

Therefore, the condition of excess gain is $\frac{p_3(1-\gamma)}{1-\alpha p_1} > p_3$, which can be simplified as

$$p_1 > \frac{\gamma}{\alpha} \tag{3}$$

From this condition, we can see that regardless of the attacker's arithmetic power, P3 can gain excessive gain G_Δ by controlling the puppet miners in the target pool through a lower arithmetic cost, and $G_\Delta = G_1 - p_3 = \frac{p_3(\alpha p_1 - \gamma)}{1-\alpha p_1}$. Therefore, for a certain p_3 and γ, the attacker prefers to attack large pools and control as many puppet nodes as possible to get higher G_Δ.

Unlike the traditional BWH attack, the combination attack is able to achieve stable benefit, even if the Bitcoin system dynamically adjusted the FPoW difficulty. Because the cost of arithmetic power to control puppet M is much lower than that of P3 directly launches BWH, and P3's share of the network-wide arithmetic power also increased as M dropped its blocks. P1 and M actually get loss, while P2 indirectly gets benefit from the attack.

3.2 BWD with Man-in-the-Middle

Note that, BWD could be combined with man-in-the-middle attacks too. The only difference is that, according to the principle of BWD, P3 will forward M's FPoW works to the pool manager if no others broadcast FPoW at the end of a mining cycle.

As shown in Fig. 4, the stages of the combination attack are shown with a Markov chain, in which UTL (Unit time loss) indicates the loss per unit time in the attacked pool.

After the attacker P3 controlled miner M's communications, it will intentionally delay the forwarding of M's FPoW to the manager. As shown in Fig. 4a, in the initial stage, the UTL is zero and the attack has not cause any loss to the mining pool yet. Then, if an honest miner finds a block, all the miners will continue mining after the new block, and the UTL decreases (Fig. 4b).

When Puppet M mined a valid block (FPoW), all the messages it broadcasted are held by P3 (Fig. 4c). P3 delays the reporting of the block to P1 until at the end of the

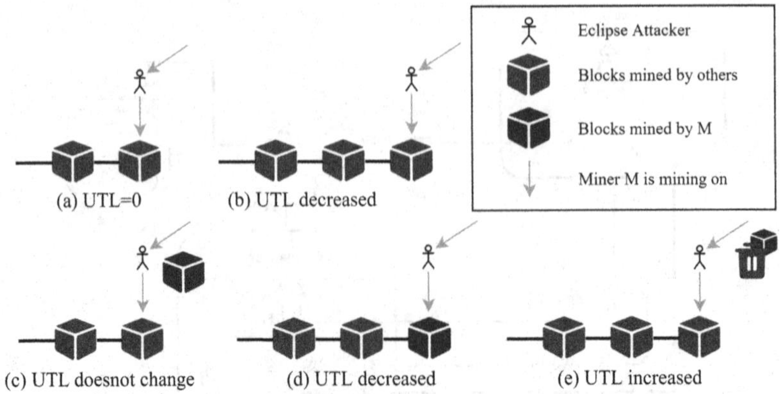

Fig. 4. Markov chain state of mining

mining cycle (Fig. 4d), in this case the UTL decreased. However, if any other miner broadcasted its valid block during the delay time, then P3 will forward the block to P1 immediately, but the pool manager of P1 still has to discard the block because of the dealy and the UTL will increase (Fig. 4e).

Obviously, the revenue of P3 is $\frac{p_3(1-\gamma)}{1-\alpha p_1}$, and the condition of its excessive gain is $p_1 > \frac{\gamma}{p_w \alpha}$, where p_w is the probability that the block is discarded.

4 Simulation System

In order to test the profit of the aforementioned attacks, we built simuBits to simulate BWH, BWD, Eclipse attacks and combined attack patterns, as well as defense methods.

The modules of simuBits are shown in Fig. 5. Miners obey the pool protocol and corporate with each other to complete the hash tasks assigned by the pool manager. The pool manager is responsible for the evaluations of miners' computing power, assigning mining tasks, validation of PPoW/FPoW, storage of ledger, distribution of the revenues to pool members, and communications with other pools.

simuBits consists of multiple miner processes, and each one responsible for a hash SHA256 based proof-of-work task. Some miner processes that adhere to a private pool protocol constitute a mining pool. One of the processes in the pool is randomly chosen to be the pool manger to collect transaction records from the system and dispatch PPoW tasks to each pool member. It is also responsible for the evaluations of each member's power contributions and revenues.

In order to facilitate the simulations, the difficulty of FPoW is reduced and far less than the real difficulty of Bitcoin system. Meanwhile, each miner process also needs to complete PPoW with difficulty factor n (N > > n). The local ledger array Share is stored in each miner's local area as the basis for the miners to share the pool revenues, as shown in Eq. (4)

$$G^i_{share} = \frac{Share[i]}{\sum_{k=1}^{p} Share[k]} \tag{4}$$

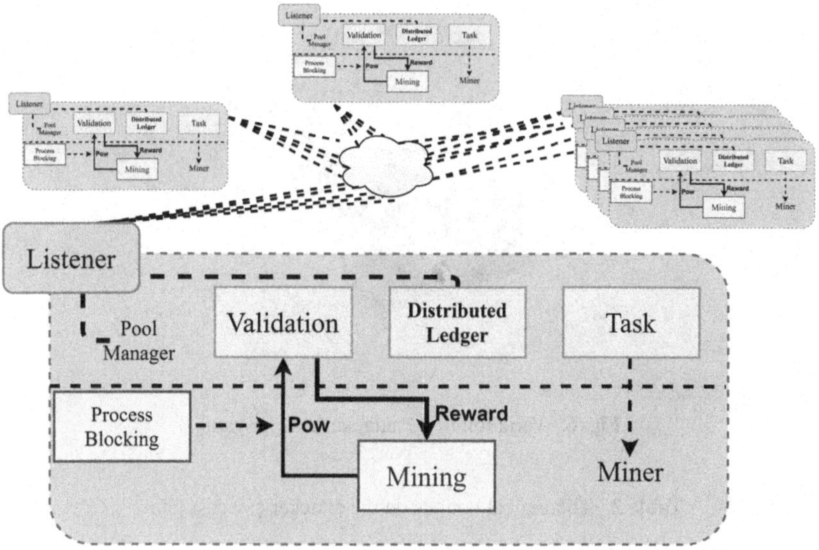

Fig. 5. System architecture diagram

The pool management process verifies the FPoW blocks submitted by miners and forwards the mined blocks to other pools in simuBits.

5 Pool Attacks in simuBits

Currently, most of the arithmetic power of Bitcoin network is held by some big pools, such that the total arithmetic power of the top ten mining pools exceeds 85% of the total arithmetic power of the network. SimuBits has five mining pools, namely attacker, P1, P2, P3, and P4, whose arithmetic power is 100, 125, 90, 95, and 90, respectively.

There are two key parameters in simuBits: the proportion of arithmetic power γ of the attacker to launch network attacks, and the proportion of arithmetic power α occupied by M in the target mining pool.

Suppose the arithmetic power of the victim pool P1 is p1, the attacker's excessive gain G returned by simuBits is shown in Fig. 6. It can be seen that the attacker needs to carefully select p_1 and α to ensure profitable gains. Otherwise, the revenues may be less than honest mining's profit. This result is consistent with the theoretical analysis in Sect. 3.1.

Attackers need to carefully analyze the least number of puppet miners to launch combined attacks on different pools when their resources are limited. According to the analysis of the conditions of excessive revenue in literatures [5, 6], the revenue's boundary parameters are shown in Table 2. It can be observed that the computing power of the victim pool p1 is inversely proportional to the ratio of miners to be controlled α. In addition, for the victim pool whose computing power is 25% of the whole network, as long as the attackers can control more than 20% of the pool member, they can obtain excess revenue from the pool.

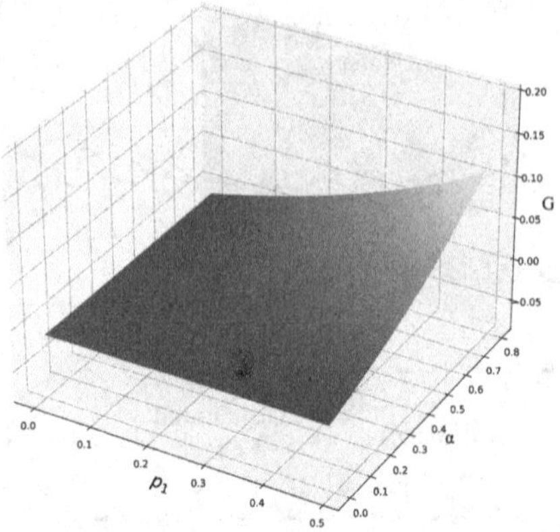

Fig. 6. Variation of the attacker's super gain

Table 2. Theoretical bounds on the attacker's excess gain

Attacker power	γ	p_1	α
0.2	0.05	0.1	0.501
		0.15	0.334
		0.2	0.251
		0.25	0.201
		0.3	0.167
		0.35	0.143

In the experiment, simuBits is utilized to test whether the profitability and feasibility of BWH combined with Eclipse attack conform to the theoretical analysis results in Table 2.

It can be seen from Fig. 7 that under the condition of reasonable choice of attack targets, attackers can obtain more excessive income by launching a combined attack of BWH and Eclipse. Since the attacker does not directly launch BWH attacks, it is more difficult for the pool manager to detect real attackers. From Fig. 8, we can see that BWH combined with Eclipse attacks are more stable than single BWH attack in terms of revenue, and less affected by fluctuations in mine pool revenue.

Similarly, the combined attacks of BWD and Eclipse are simulated and analyzed in simuBits to obtain a comparison between the attacker's super revenue and the victim's damaged revenue, as shown in Fig. 9.

We can find that the combined attack mode of BWD and Eclipse can also make the attacker obtain higher excessive profits. However, because the miner may face the decision state of BWD: the attack reached the end of mining cycle, which makes miner M has no choice but reporting the FPoW. The profits brought by BWD and Eclipse to the attacker are lower than those brought by BWH and Eclipse attack. However, the combination attack of BWH and Eclipse could be detected: the puppet M finds that

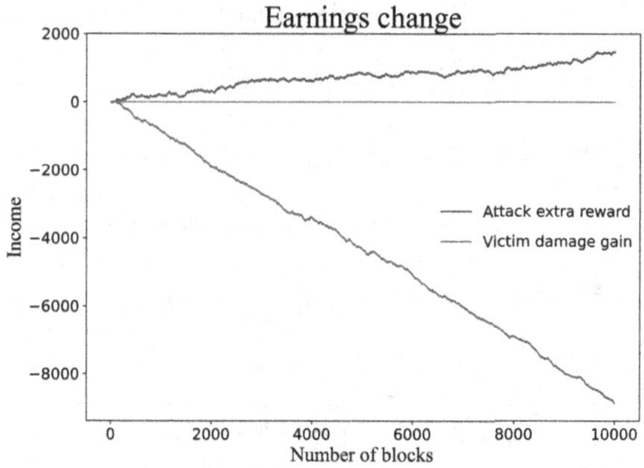

Fig. 7. Attacker's super gain and victim's damaged gain

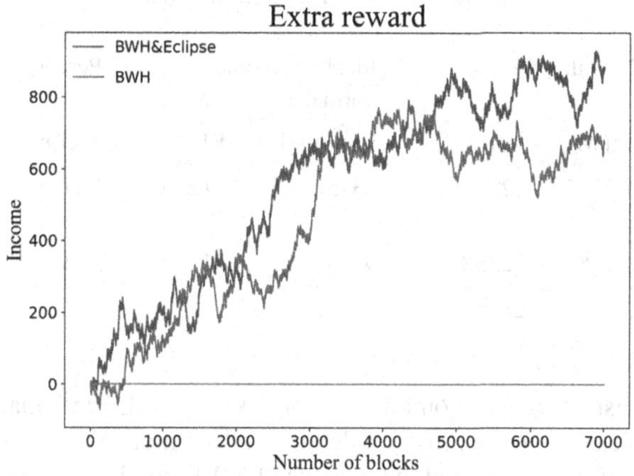

Fig. 8. Comparison of attack gains

his income has been greatly reduced and the pool administrator can percept the attack through statistical analysis of the blocks submitted by M. The combination attack of BWD and Eclipse not only reduces the probability of being detected by delaying the submission of FPoW, but also makes it difficult for Miner M to find Eclipse attacks because of the slowly change in revenue.

Table 3 shows the change of miners' M income from simuBits.

Profitability Comparison. Since the cost of controlling puppet miners is far less than directly launching BWH attacks, the combination attack effectively raised the benefits of attackers. At the same time, the traditional BWH attack mode also has the miners' dilemma: if an honest pool is and attacked by other pools, the benefits of the honest one will be reduced; If all pools launch BWH attacks against each other, the benefits of all pools will be less than those of honest mining. Therefore, many experts believe that BWH attacks are actually difficult to occur [15].

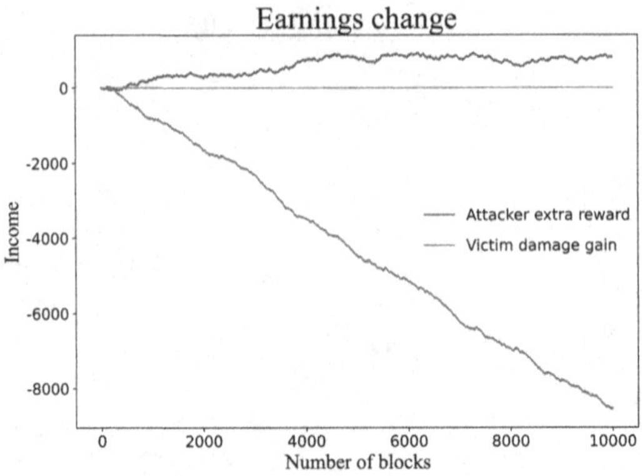

Fig. 9. Attacker's super gain and victim's damaged gain

Table 3. Miner M revenue variation

	Real earnings (BTC)		Ideal return under normal circumstances		Percentage of damage	
Role	Victim M	P1	Victim M	P1	Victim M	P1
BWD + Eclipse	6877.2525	22725	9375	31250	26.64%	27.28%
BWH + Eclipse	6754.035	22387.5	9375	31250	27.96%	28.36%

However, considering the combination of BWH attacks and man-in-the-middle attacks, attackers can avoid the miners' dilemma and are more willing to launch attacks. As shown in Fig. 10, we compared the benefits of BWH combined with Eclipse attacks with the theoretical benefits of single BWH attack, and finally we found that in most cases, attackers would gain higher and stable revenues using the combined attacks. It is not cost-effective to launch an Eclipse attack only when the attacker's own computing power is extremely low. This is because the attackers themselves can only control a limited number of nodes through Eclipse attacks, and the super profits they can obtain cannot compensate the cost of Eclipse attacks. However, if the traditional BWH attackers unreasonably allocated their computing power or selected inappropriate targets, they will also suffer a great loss.

Effect of Key Parameters With the change of various parameters, the income of combined BWH and Eclipse attackers is more stable than that of single BWH attack. In order to maximize the benefits, attackers carefully adjust the power splitting ratio γ to change the number of controlled puppet nodes, which will bring different amount of super revenues.

In the proposed new combined attack, the attacker has a variety of decision-making states. With the dynamic adjustment of the mining pool computing power, the

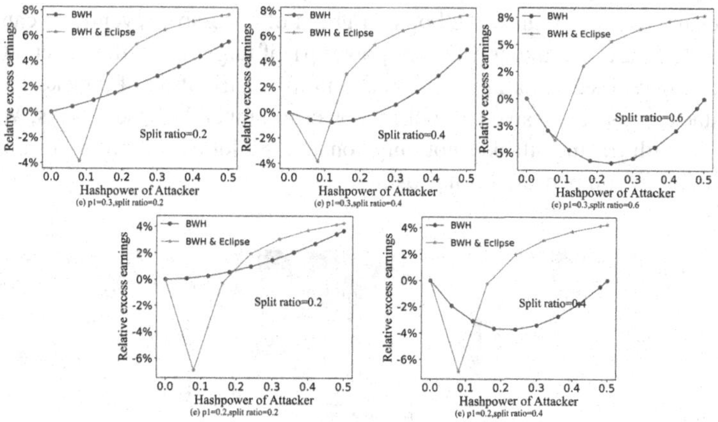

Fig. 10. Comparison of BWH, BWH & Eclipse gains

attacker's super income will change constantly, and his decision-making state will evolve dynamically. The attackers will have the following common strategies.

P-Status: launch BWHs attack with a new parameter γ setting.

N-Status: adjust parameter γ and then launch Eclipse.

T-Status: continue the attack strategy from the previous moment.

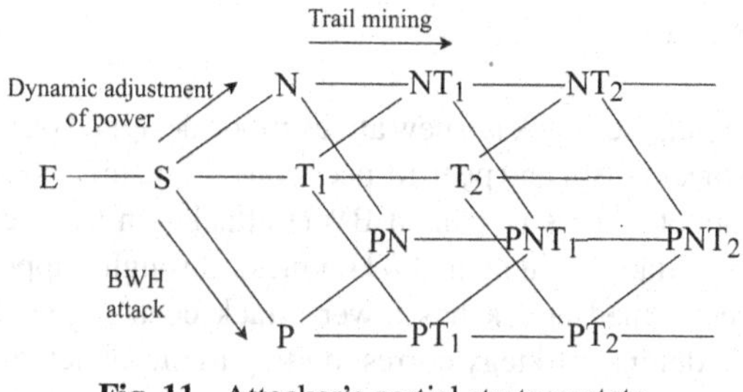

Fig. 11. Attacker's partial strategy state

These three decision combinations represent heuristic attack strategies that attackers can use individually or in combination in order to obtain higher revenues. Figure 12 shows part of the decision combination, where each side follows one of the three arrows, and for one leading to the policy state T1, we can think that T1 is the superposition of the previous state, indicating that the attacker will continue to attack the current state. If T state accompanied by P state, then T1 means the attacker continues to launch Eclipse attacks, so T1 state is more durable. Attackers may dynamically adjust their decisions through continuous observation of attack gains. For example, attackers first launch BWH attacks on the pool to reach P state, and continue to attack to get state PTn through continuous attacks, and then the attacker's strategy may reach PTn and NTn through dynamic adjustment of parameter γ. At this time, the attacker may stop the attack or continue to adjust the attack power before attacking again.

The results in Fig. 11 show the hot spot graph of excessive revenue. It can be seen that, from the figure that under different power p1 of target pool, the different choices of parameter γ will lead to a large difference in the distribution of attackers' benefits. Even if attackers use excessive computing power to launch Eclipse attacks, When γ is not matched with p1, the attacker not only consumes a lot of computing resources, but also is difficult to compensate for its cost.

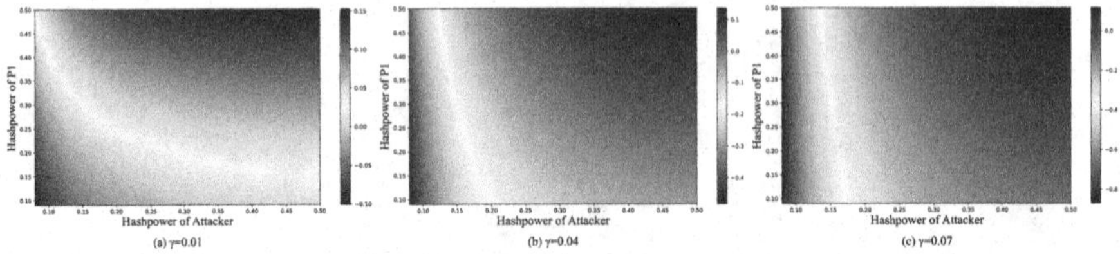

Fig. 12. Impact of the change in attacker arithmetic, γ and P1 arithmetic on attacker gains

The test results of simuBits show that BWH combined with Eclipse attack can enable attackers to obtain higher super benefits under the premise of reasonable selection of attack objects. In the next section, we will discuss the defense strategy for combination attack.

6 Countermeasures

BWH combined with Eclipse attack is a new attack mode designed based on the mine pool revenue distribution mechanism and peer-to-peer connection mechanism vulnerabilities. Attackers control puppet miners to launch BWH attacks on the victim pools through Eclipse attacks. Since attackers launch BWH attacks through puppets, compared with BWH attacks, this combined attack has lower attack cost, higher benefits and more security. If there is no defense strategy corresponding to this attack mode, the combined attack may be widely spread, which is very harmful to the pools and may lead to a crisis of trust.

For the defense of combined attacks, we proposed to prevent combination attacks by dynamically adjusting the computing power of the mining pool. The basic idea is to break the attacker's profit conditions. When the attacker's profit is less than that of honest mining, it will prevent the attacker from launching combined attacks. From the discussion in Sects. 3.1 and 3.2, we can see that attackers are easier to obtain super profits in bigger pools with high computing power. Therefore, as shown in Fig. 13a, we propose the basic process of the pool management mode as follows.

1. The pool adds a power allocation layer, and initially all the miners access the power allocation layer.
2. The power allocation layer allocates the connected miners to two abstract sub-pools of different sizes. In each sub-pool, miners share the revenues according to their power share (PPoW) in the sub-pool.

3. When the pool manager detects that the income of a certain miner's FPoW does not meet the PPoW, it will let the dividing layer dynamically allocate the suspicious miner to the small sub pool to change its proportion of computing power in the sub pool, and break the conditions for excess income.

The transfer process will break the attacker's excessive gain condition, and the attacker's super gain will gradually decrease until even failed to compensate the attack cost. It is important to note that although the total income of small pool is smaller than that of big pool, the proportion of computing power occupied by miners in small pool has also increased. Therefore, the transfer process does not damage the revenue of honest miners in the sub-pool.

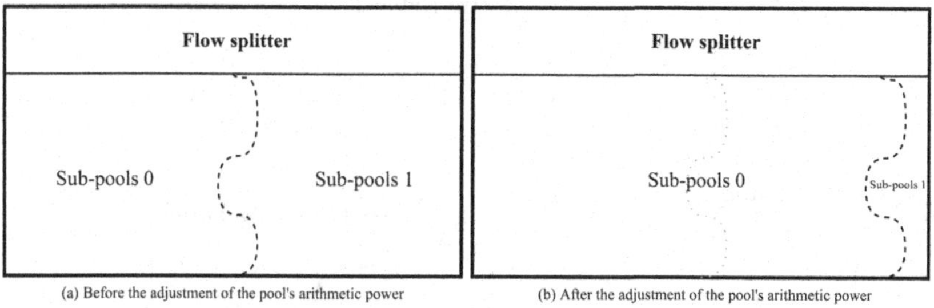

Fig. 13. Demonstration of the dynamic allocation of mining pool arithmetic power

The mining pool manager periodically performs miner behaviour detection: collects recent mining log information and analyzes whether the behaviour of individual miners is normal from the logs. First, a coarse sieve is performed to analyze the recent mining log information, and miners who have had normal FPoW submission behaviour are classified as T_{normal}. Based on the submission probability, this step can quickly filter miners who are in a normal state and quickly adjust the pool's arithmetic.

After careful inspection, most of the remaining miners are those who have made fewer contributions in recent times, and quantitative analysis of their respective submission records is required. When the difference between FPoW and PPoW submitted by a suspicious miner is greater than the threshold value, it would be put into the smaller pool, as shown in Fig. 13b.

6.1 BWH Attack Defense Verification

Suppose there are two mining pools P1 and P2 in the Bitcoin system, and an attacker P3. P1 contains a puppet miner M controlled by P3. The arithmetic power of mining pools P1, P2, and attacker P3 are p_1, p_2, and p_3, respectively, where the power share of miner M in mining pool P1 is α. The attacker controls M to launch a BWH attack on P1.

As shown in Sect. 2.1, P3's gain from the BWH attack is

$$G = G_1 + G_2 = \frac{p_1\alpha(1-\alpha)+p_3}{1-p_1\alpha} \tag{5}$$

When mining honestly, P3's gain is $G_h = p_3 + \alpha p_1$, so the excessive gain relative to G_h is

$$\Delta G = \frac{G}{G_h} - 1 = \frac{p_1\alpha(p_3+p_1\alpha-\alpha)}{1-p_1\alpha} \tag{6}$$

Obviously, the condition of ΔG is positive is $p_3 + p_1\alpha - \alpha > 0$, i.e., $p_3 > \alpha(1 - p_1)$.

Therefore, when P1's pool manager detects the difference between FPoW and PPoW submitted by M, it will put M into small sub-pool P_1'. As the overall arithmetic power of P_1' accounts for a lower proportion of the whole network, while the M 's power share in P_1' is increased from α to $\alpha' = p_1\alpha/p_1'$, which possibly breaks the excessive profit condition $p_3 > \alpha'\left(1 - p_1'\right)$ and prevents the attacker from launching BWH attacks.

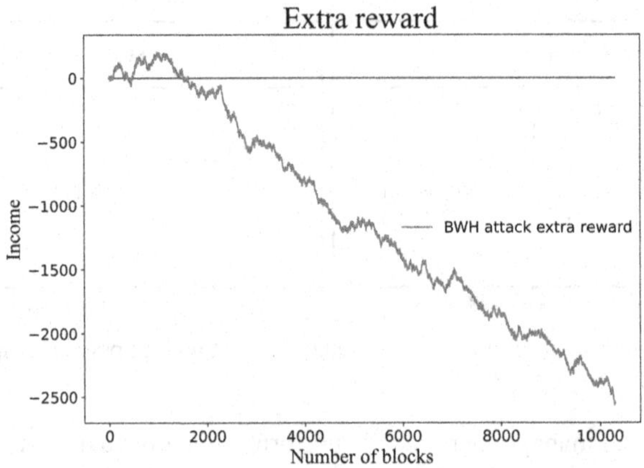

Fig. 14. The super gain of BWH attackers under the dynamic adjustment of the mining pool's arithmetic power method

From Fig. 14, we can see that the attacker can obtain super gain at the beginning of the BWH attack, but when the mining pool dynamically adjusts the arithmetic power, the attacker's attack gain decreased sharply compared to honest mining. As shown in Table 4, after the attacker sets the optimal parameters to launch the attack, the super gain of the attacker decreased to a negative because of the dynamically adjusting of the sub-pools.

Table 4. Change in attacker ΔG after arithmetic adjustment

p_1	α	Theoretical optimal β	ΔG^s_{bwh}	Adjusted p_1	ΔG^s_{bwh}
0.08	0.1	0.0401	0.2%	0.02	−0.4%
0.1	0.1	0.0501	0.25%	0.02	−0.76%
0.15	0.1	0.0752	0.38%	0.03	−1.14%
0.2	0.1	0.1005	0.51%	0.03	−2.39%

6.2 Combined Attack Defense Verification

In the combined attack model proposed in this paper, suppose the attacker P3 consumes γ proportion of arithmetic power to control the puppet miner M in the target pool P1. Then M launches a BWH or BWD attack on P1, while the attacker uses its left 1-γ proportion of arithmetic power to mine normally, according to the analysis in Sect. 3.

P3 launches a BWH + Eclipse combination attack to obtain a super gain under the condition that $p_1 > \frac{\gamma}{\alpha}$. At this point, the attacker's super gain is $G_\Delta = \frac{p_3(\alpha p_1 - \gamma)}{1 - \alpha p_1}$.

The super gain obtained by P3 launching BWD + Eclipse combination attack is $\frac{p_3(1-\gamma)}{1-\alpha p_1}$, and the condition for obtaining the super gain is $p_1 > \frac{\gamma}{p_w \alpha}$.

From this condition, it can be seen that the attacker's gain is proportional to the arithmetic power share α of the puppet miners in the target pool P1 and inversely proportional to the arithmetic power ratio γ to control puppet miners. The attacker needs to control as many puppet miners as possible in P1 with as little arithmetic power as possible to ensure a higher super gain.

For the defense case of the combination attack, the same can be done by dynamically adjusting the arithmetic power size of the mining pool so that the combination attack cannot satisfy the condition $p_1 > \frac{\gamma}{\alpha}$ (Eclipse + BWH), or $p_1 > \frac{\gamma}{p_w \alpha}$ (Eclipse + BWD), which turns the attacker's super gain into a negative value to prevent attackers from launching combination attacks.

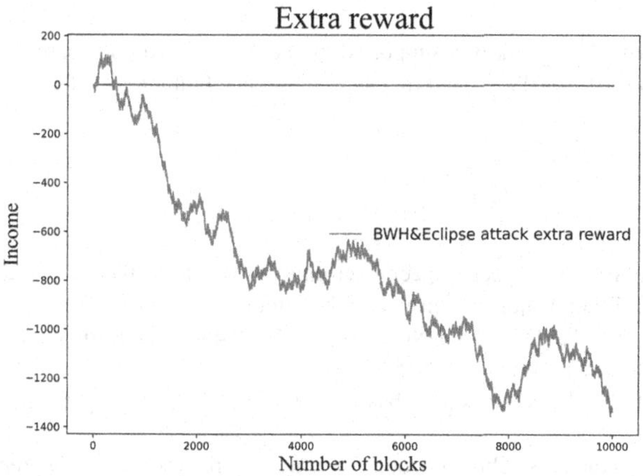

Fig. 15. Impact of combined attack attacker super gain under the dynamic adjustment of the pool's arithmetic approach

Using the same approach as in Sect. 6.1, the pool manager detect suspicious miners by comparing the deviation between their test arithmetic PPoW and the number of blocks they submit FPoW. And then move the suspicious ones into a small sub-pool P_1' with a lower arithmetic power. As shown in Fig. 15, the attacker achieves some excessive gain at the beginning of the attack, but after the subsequent dynamic adjustment of the pool's arithmetic power, the puppet miners are put into sub-pool P_1', after which the attacker's super gain will be drastically reduced to a negative number. With γ and p_w unchanged, the arithmetic share of the puppet miner W in p'_1 increased from α to $\alpha' = p_1\alpha/p'_1$, breaking the attacker's excessive-benefit condition $p'_1 > \frac{\gamma}{\alpha'}$ or $p'_1 > \frac{\gamma}{p_w\alpha'}$, making the attacker's excessive revenue negative and the overall gain lower than that of honest mining, thus preventing the combination attack from launching.

7 Conclusion

In this paper, in order to analyze pool attacks, including BWH, BWD, Eclipse attacks and their combinations, we built a pool experimental system simuBits, which can simulate all types of pool attacks and the countermeasures. It is also highly scalable and can support private protocols of pool management. SimuBits is utilized to simulate BWH, BWD, Eclipse, and combination attacks to validate the theoretical analysis of attackers' excessive revenues. We also discussed a new kind of countermeasures based on dynamic partitioning of mining power, such that the pool managers assign suspicious miners to sub-pools to break the conditions of extra-gains and frustrate attackers. Note that, the countermeasure does not require changes to the existing Bitcoin public protocols. Therefore, it is practical to prevent selfish mining attacks. We also note that some secure communication mechanism have been incorporated in pools to defend against Eclipse attacks on P2P communications between pool members. In the next step of our research, we will investigate the combination attack patterns and countermeasures for more pool attacks, such as stubborn BWH and other man-in-the-middle attack methods.

Acknowledgement. This work was supported by the National Key Research and Development Program of China (2019QY0800), and the Natural Science Foundation of China (61872255).

References

1. Nakamoto, S.: Bitcoin: a peer-to-peer electronic cash system. Tech. Rep. (2008)
2. Eyal, I., Sirer, E.G.: Majority is not enough: Bitcoin mining is vulnerable. In: Christin, N., Safavi-Naini, R. (eds.) FC 2014. LNCS, vol. 8437, pp. 436–454. Springer, Heidelberg (2014). https://doi.org/10.1007/978-3-662-45472-5_28
3. Rosenfeld, M.: Analysis of hashrate-based double spending. arXiv preprint arXiv:1402.2009 (2014)
4. Rosenfeld, M.: Analysis of bitcoin pooled mining reward systems. arXiv preprint arXiv:1112.4980 (2011)
5. Bag, S., Ruj, S., Sakurai, K.: Bitcoin block withholding attack: analysis and mitigation. IEEE Trans. Inf. Forensics Secur. **12**(8), 1967–1978 (2016)
6. Heilman, E., Kendler, A., Zohar, A., et al.: Eclipse Attacks on {Bitcoin's}{Peer-to-Peer} Network. In: 24th USENIX Security Symposium (USENIX Security 15), pp. 129–144 (2015)
7. Luu, L., Saha, R., Parameshwaran, I., et al.: On power splitting games in distributed computation: the case of bitcoin pooled mining. In: 2015 IEEE 28th Computer Security Foundations Symposium. IEEE, pp. 397–411 (2015)
8. Fujita, K., Zhang, Y., Sasabe, M., et al.: Mining pool selection under block withholding attack. Appl. Sci. **11**(4), 1617 (2021)

9. Kwon, Y., Kim, D., Son, Y., et al.: Be selfish and avoid dilemmas: fork after withholding (faw) attacks on bitcoin. In: Proceedings of the. ACM SIGSAC Conference on Computer and Communications Security, vol. 2017, pp. 195–209 (2017)
10. Gao, S., Li, Z., Peng, Z., et al.: Power adjusting and bribery racing: Novel mining attacks in the bitcoin system. In: Proceedings of the. ACM SIGSAC Conference on Computer and Communications Security, vol. 2019, pp. 833–850 (2019)
11. Wang, Y., Yang, G., Li, T., et al.: Optimal mixed block withholding attacks based on reinforcement learning. Int. J. Intell. Syst. **35**(12), 2032–2048 (2020)
12. Ke, J., Szalachowski, P., Zhou, J., Xu, Q., Yang, Z.: Ibwh: an intermittent block withholding attack with optimal mining reward rate. In: Lin, Z., Papamanthou, C., Polychronakis, M. (eds.) ISC 2019. LNCS, vol. 11723, pp. 3–24. Springer, Cham (2019). https://doi.org/10.1007/978-3-030-30215-3_1
13. Liu, L., Chen, W., Zhang, L., et al.: A type of block withholding delay attack and the countermeasure based on type-2 fuzzy inference. Math. Biosci. Eng. **17**(1), 309–327 (2020)
14. Li, T., Wang, Z., Yang, G., et al.: Semi-selfish mining based on hidden Markov decision process. Int. J. Intell. Syst. **36**(7), 3596–3612 (2021)
15. Eyal, I.: The miner's dilemma. In: 2015 IEEE Symposium on Security and Privacy. IEEE, pp. 89–103 (2015)
16. "Eligius", https://bitcointalk.org/?topic=441465.msg728267
17. Recabarren, R., Carbunar, B.: Hardening stratum, the bitcoin pool mining protocol. arXiv preprint arXiv:1703.06545, 2017
18. Tran, M., Choi, I., Moon, G.J, et al.: A stealthier partitioning attack against bitcoin peer-to-peer network. In: 2020 IEEE Symposium on Security and Privacy (SP). IEEE, pp. 894–909 (2020)
19. Liu, X.: Disappeared Coins: Steal Hashrate in Stratum Secretly. https://www.blackhat.com/asia-21/briefings/schedule/#disappeared-coins-steal-hashrate-in-stratum-secretly-22266 (2021)

Author Index

M. Zhang et al. (Eds.): ProvSec 2023, LNCS 14217, pp. 449–450, 2023.
https://doi.org/10.1007/978-3-031-45513-1

Printed in the United States
by Baker & Taylor Publisher Services

Printed in the United States
by Baker & Taylor Publisher Services